When Aseneth Met Joseph

When Aseneth Met Joseph

A Late Antique Tale of the Biblical Patriarch and His Egyptian Wife, Reconsidered

ROSS SHEPARD KRAEMER

New York   Oxford
OXFORD UNIVERSITY PRESS
1998

Oxford University Press

Oxford   New York
Athens   Auckland   Bangkok   Bogota   Bombay
Buenos Aires   Calcutta   Cape Town   Dar es Salaam
Delhi   Florence   Hong Kong   Istanbul   Karachi
Kuala Lumpur   Madras   Madrid   Melbourne
Mexico City   Nairobi   Paris   Singapore
Taipei   Tokyo   Toronto   Warsaw

and associated companies in
Berlin   Ibadan

Published by Oxford University Press, Inc.
198 Madison Avenue, New York, New York 10016

Oxford is a registered trademark of Oxford University Press

Library of Congress Cataloging-in-Publication Data
Kraemer, Ross Shepard, 1948–
    When Aseneth met Joseph : a late antique tale of the biblical
patriarch and his Egyptian wife, reconsidered / Ross Shepard
Kraemer.
        p.   cm.
    Includes bibliographical references and index.
    ISBN 0-19-511475-2
    1. Joseph and Aseneth—Criticism, interpretation, etc.   I. Title.
BS1830.J62K75   1997
221′.911—dc21   97–20389

9 8 7 6 5 4 3 2 1

Printed in the United States of America
on acid-free paper

For John, διδάσκαλος
and for Bob, ὡς διδάσκαλος

Preface

Sometimes scholarship is serendipitous. Several years ago, I agreed, somewhat cavalierly, to write a relatively brief commentary on an anonymous ancient work conventionally titled *Joseph and Aseneth* for an anthology of feminist commentaries on ancient Jewish and Christian writings, including traditional canonical scripture.[1] Composed in Greek, *Aseneth* (as I currently prefer to call it) narrates the transformation of the daughter of an Egyptian priest into an acceptable spouse for the biblical Joseph. Although virtually unknown outside scholarly circles, this story is remarkable not the least for its focus on a female character and its apparent relative absence of any overt misogyny. Over a number of years, I had worked on it in a rather piecemeal fashion. But when, in the summer of 1993, I finally sat down to write the commentary in earnest, two seemingly fortuitous experiences transformed my life, at least my life as a scholar.

A colleague at the University of Pennsylvania happened to have on his desk a copy of James Kugel's *In Potiphar's House: The Interpretive Life of Biblical Texts.*[2] It had long been on my list of books to read sooner or later, and its focus on the traditions of the biblical Joseph in the house of his Egyptian master Potiphar suddenly moved it to the top. I therefore quickly borrowed it. In this ingenious and lovely book that reads like an intellectual detective story, Kugel demonstrates the process by which early Jewish "midrashic" traditions were constructed out of anomalies and perplexing questions perceived by ancient Jewish rabbinic exegetes to exist in Jewish scripture. Reading Kugel, I suddenly realized that much of the story of Aseneth might well have been constructed in an analogous manner. Chapter 2 of this book is primarily devoted to working out the implications of that realization. An appendix considers rabbinic traditions about the marriage of Joseph and Aseneth, traditions that I am convinced are antithetical to the Greek *Aseneth* and were probably unknown to our authors (although perhaps not vice versa).

Soon thereafter, engaged in the kind of minute-scale scholarship that commentaries require, I found myself one day working on references to honey, a substance that an angelic being gives Aseneth to eat, effecting her transformation. For some reason, I remembered a passage about honey in an obscure Jewish compilation known as *Sepher ha-Razim* (The book of the mysteries), whose constituent elements were probably composed sometime in the Greco-Roman period. *Sepher ha-Razim* purports to describe the seven firmaments, the angels who dwell in them, and the favors they will do for humans if properly coerced.

Skimming rather quickly, I came almost immediately upon a passage concerning the fourth firmament that describes the angels who pull the chariot of the Sun by day and by night. Here I read the formulas by which one adjures the Sun to come down and accurately foretell one's future, including a substantial prayer in Greek transliterated into Hebrew, addressed to Holy Helios (the Greek name for the sun and the Sun God). Almost instantly, I saw that Aseneth's experience with the angelic being was in many ways similar, if not identical, to the prescriptions in this text. Chapter 4 endeavors to set this central portion of *Aseneth* within the context of ancient adjurations of divine beings, for both similar and different purposes.

Collectively, these two early insights compelled me to begin rethinking my earlier judgments about *Aseneth*, a tale with a complex textual and cultural history. Revisiting the questions of when, where, and by what sort of author *Aseneth* might have originally been composed and which of the two major textual reconstructions is likely to be earlier, I found myself more and more persuaded that much of the previous scholarship on this text is seriously flawed. Chapter 1 summarizes my current thinking on these questions and briefly considers the specific problem of the so-called shorter and longer texts. Chapter 3 compares the two reconstructions in considerable detail. Chapters 5 and 6 expand the work of chapter 4 to pursue further the range of ancient cultural and religious contexts for *Aseneth*, from the mystical themes and cosmology of Jewish *hekhalot* traditions to late antique veneration of Helios and the possible relationship with Neoplatonic beliefs and theurgic practice. Chapters 8, 9, and 10 revisit questions of date, authorial religious identity and self-understanding, and geographic provenance. A final chapter pursues the ramifications of my strong sense that *Aseneth* is a later antique work, composed initially in the late third or early fourth century C.E. and subsequently revised, probably several times, by authors whose ethnic, religious, and cultural identity continues to elude us.

As is by now apparent, what was to have been a relatively short feminist commentary on *Aseneth* quickly took on a life of its own. The first draft of the commentary was over 100 pages long. I reluctantly edited it down to a length the editors agreed to publish and devoted more than two additional years to the book it has become. Although I hope the sensitivity to issues of gender that led me to undertake the commentary in the first place pervade the entire book, only in chapter 7 do I finally turn explicitly to questions of gender.

On a great many issues, this book challenges the prevailing scholarly consensus on *Aseneth*. As my work on this book progressed, I found myself increasingly convinced that previous scholarship has been wrong not only on questions of date, provenance, identity, geographic origin, and textual relationships but also on many matters of interpretation. Eventually, I found it unproductive to engage in the kinds of traditional scholarly dialogue with most of the earlier literature. Readers interested in the comprehensive history of scholarship on *Aseneth* will need to turn elsewhere,[3] although inevitably discussion of date, origins, and textual issues do engage that scholarship selectively. Further, while I disagree with both of them on many points, I am particularly dependent on the important work of Marc Philonenko and Christoph Burchard in reconstructing Greek texts of *Aseneth* and bringing immense erudition to their discussions and notes to their respective, divergent texts.

Although readers should have no difficulty determining the nature of my disagreements, I should signal here the central theses of this book, particularly those that oppose both prior scholarship and what may be called the current scholarly consensus.

1. In general, the shorter text reconstructed by Philonenko antedates the longer text, represented by Burchard's reconstruction.

2. The changes are usually intentional and reflect the concerns of one or more redactors.

3. The current scholarly consensus as to the date, provenience, and identity of the text(s) is largely untenable and based on interlocking assumptions that are, for the most part, without foundation. *Aseneth* is not early (i.e., composed before 117 C.E.); rather, the shorter text is not likely to have been composed prior to the third century C.E., and the longer reconstruction is likely to date within a century of the shorter (although this is harder to ascertain). *Aseneth* might have been but by no means needs to have been composed in Egypt. It could easily have been composed almost anywhere Greek was written during the Roman period, and there are some intriguing reasons for thinking that it might have been composed in Syria and/or its environs. The arguments for its Jewishness are largely without foundation. Although it could be Jewish, the totality of the evidence is not definitive, and several other identifications of the author(s) of both the shorter and longer versions are plausible. In particular, a strong case can be made for Christian composition and redaction.

4. Both the shorter and longer texts interweave ancient adjuration of powerful divine beings with mystical interpretations of such experiences, overlaid on a narrative frame generated out of the Joseph story (known to us now in Genesis) and fleshed out with "traditional" elements known to us from biblical and related traditional Jewish (although also Christian) sources. Although both versions may be constructed in this manner, the longer version shows more interest in and more detailed similarities with ancient portraits of mystical encounters with angels.

5. Aseneth's gender is significant and not coincidental to the story of Joseph, and it requires explication within the context of late antique constructs of and concerns about gender.

Pursuing the implications of these findings has evoked more than once the remembrance of a comment made by a friend and colleague, Michael Stone, professor of Armenian studies at the Hebrew University in Jerusalem, during a Pseudepigrapha session at the 1990 annual meeting of the Society of Biblical Literature. What, he asked, do we do if we conclude that a particular text might in fact have been written much later than our original assessments, so much so as to remove it from our particular scholarly purview? Do we define ourselves as scholars with particular chronological, geographic, and cultural parameters and reshelve the text, or do we follow it where it leads? Although my own sense of Aseneth does not place it entirely outside the boundaries of my training and expertise, it has certainly taken me regularly to the borders and occasionally on incursions into territory that was quite unfamiliar, though it is now a little less so. In part, I have relied on the expertise of others, both in their published work and in personal exchanges, but inevitably, in delving into everything from the mysticism of Jewish *hekhalot* materials to the possibility of a Samaritan context for *Aseneth,* I have stretched the limits of my own knowledge and have made mistakes both large and small. They are for others to correct (with charity, I hope), although I do not believe that they will alter too drastically the persuasiveness of the case I have made here.

Writing this book leaves me deeply in the debt of many. The Center for Judaic Studies of the University of Pennsylvania graciously awarded me a fellowship to write a different book, on Jewish women in the Greco-Roman world, and no one there flinched when I confessed that I had become preoccupied with *Aseneth* and would devote my entire year to this study instead. Even more graciously, the center provided me a home for a second year to continue work on the book. I am thankful to the center's director, David Ruderman, for hosting me the second year; to David Goldenberg for inviting me the first year; and to everyone else at the center, particularly the wonderful and accommodating librarians, Aviva Astrinsky, Judith Leifer, Ruth Ronen, Penina bar-Kana, Kathleen Brannon, and Sol Cohen, and to Etty Lassman, the fellows' patient and accommodating secretary.

My greatest debt to an individual is to the colleague whose copy of Kugel I borrowed (and finally returned when I bought my own), Robert A. Kraft. A renowned scholar of pseudepigrapha (with which *Aseneth* is currently classed), Bob allowed me to co-opt his senior graduate seminar at Penn during 1988–89, devoting a semester to *Aseneth.* The following year we co-chaired the Philadelphia Seminar on Christian Origins on *Aseneth.* Since this project actively began to consume my work, he has served as a sounding board for countless conjectures and hypotheses and as a resource for numerous esoteric queries. I could have written this book without him, but it would have been much harder.

For their careful reading of all or portions of the manuscript, I am particularly grateful to Devorah Dimant, Robert Doran, John Gager, Maxine Grossman, Kim Haines-Eitzen, Pieter W. van der Horst, Helmut Koester, Gordon Lathrop, Shira Lander, Rebecca Lesses, and Richard Pervo. Susan Ashbrook Harvey and Kathleen McVey guided me through Syriac sources. Faculty and students at Brandeis University, Boston University, and the University of Missouri offered me opportunities to present this work as it progressed and provided constructive responses and suggestions, as have my colleagues in the Philadelphia Seminar on Christian Origins. Members of the Ioudaios electronic discussion group responded with helpful answers to various arcane questions. Maxine Grossman input the Greek text of Burchard into electronic format and produced a parallel electronic text. Debra Bucher, Jill Gorman, Kim Haines-Eitzen, Shira Lander, Susan Marks, Beth Pollard, and Sarah Schwartz patiently and painstakingly proofread.

As always, my husband Michael and my daughter Jordan have been supportive, loving, and humorous, patiently enduring what are surely too many one-sided conversations about yet another obscure late antique figure. They continue to be a large portion of my share of blessings.

Philadelphia, Pennsylvania   R. S. K.
November 1997

NOTES

1. Ross S. Kraemer, "The Book of Aseneth," in Elisabeth Schüssler Fiorenza, ed., *Searching the Scriptures: A Feminist Commentary on Scripture* (New York: Crossroad, 1994), 859–88.

2. James Kugel, *In Potiphar's House: The Interpretive Life of Biblical Texts* (San Francisco: Harper Collins: 1990; reprint, Cambridge, MA: Harvard University Press, 1994).

3. See the fine survey in Randall D. Chesnutt, *From Death to Life: Conversion in "Joseph and Aseneth,"* Journal for the Study of the Pseudepigrapha Supplement Series 16 (Sheffield: Sheffield Academic Press, 1995), 20–93.

Contents

Abbreviations

AAndrew	*The Acts of Andrew*
ABD	*Anchor Bible Dictionary.* Ed. David Noel Freedman. New York: Doubleday, 1992.
AddEst	Additions (in Greek) to Esther
AJAH	*American Journal of Ancient History*
Alleg. Int.	Philo, *Allegorical Interpretation*
ANRW	*Aufsteig und Niedergang der Römischen Welt. Geschichte und Kultur Roms im Spiegel der neueren Forschung.* Ed. H. Temporini. Berlin: de Gruyter, 1972–.
Elliott, *ANT*	J. K. Elliott, *The Apocryphal New Testament: A Collection of Apocryphal Christian Literature in an English Translation based on M. R. James.* Oxford: Clarendon Press, 1993.
AOT	*The Apocryphal Old Testament.* Ed. H. F. D. Sparks. Oxford: Clarendon Press, 1984.
Apoc. Abr.	*Apocalypse of Abraham*
Apoc. Ezra	*Apocalypse of Ezra*
Apoc. Zech.	*Apocalypse of Zechariah*
Apoc. Zeph.	*Apocalypse of Zephaniah*
Arist.	*Letter of Aristeas*
Arm.	Armenian
Asc. Is.	*Ascension of Isaiah*
AThom.	*Acts of Thomas*
BAGD	Walter Bauer, *A Greek-English Lexicon of the New Testament and Other Early Christian Literature.* 2d ed., revised and augmented by F. W. Gingrich and Frederick Danker. Chicago: University of Chicago Press, 1979.

BAR	*Biblical Archaeology Review*
BASOR	*Bulletin of the American Schools of Oriental Research*
b. Ber.	Tractate *Berakot* of the Babylonian Talmud
BCH	*Bulletin de Correspondence Hellénique*
BE	*Bulletin Epigraphique*
BHG	*Bibliotheca Hagiographica Graeca.* Ed. F. Halkin. Brussels: Société des Bollandistes, 1969.
b. Kidd.	Tractate *Kiddushin* of the Babylonian Talmud
b. Meg.	Tractate *Megillot* of the Babylonian Talmud
b. Ned.	Tractate *Nedarim* of the Babylonian Talmud
b. Sanh.	Tractate *Sanhedrin* of the Babylonian Talmud
b. Sot.	Tractate *Sotah* of the Babylonian Talmud
CBQ	*Catholic Biblical Quarterly*
CETEDOC	Centre de Traitement Electroniques des Documents, Louvain-le-Neuf
CIG	*Corpus inscriptionum graecarum*
CIJ	*Corpus inscriptionum judaicarum*
CIL	*Corpus inscriptionum latinarum*
CIRB	*Corpus inscriptionum regni Bosporani*
CPJ	*Corpus Papyrorum Judaicarum*
CRINT	*Compendia rerum Iudaicarum ad Novum Testamentum.* Assen: Van Gorcum; Philadelphia: Fortress Press.
CSCO	Corpus scriptorum Christianorum Orientalium
Dial. Try.	Justin Martyr, *Dialogue with Trypho*
EC Arm.	Ephrem, *Commentaire de l'évangile concordant, version arménienne.* Ed. L. Leloir.
EEC	*Encyclopedia of the Early Church.* Ed. Angelo Di Berardino. New York: Oxford University Press, 1992.
EHR	*Etudes d'histoires des religions.* Paris: P. Geuthner.
EJ	*Encyclopedia Judaica*
EPRO	*Etudes préliminaires aux religions orientales dans l'Empire romain.* Leiden: E. J. Brill.
ER	*Encyclopedia of Religion.* Ed. Mircea Eliade. New York: Macmillan, 1987.
FC	*Fathers of the Church.* Washington, D.C.: Catholic University of America Press.
GCS	Griechischen christlichen Schriftsteller
Gen. R.	*Genesis Rabbah*
H.E.	*Historia Ecclesiastica*
H.-R.	Edwin Hatch and Henry A. Redpath, *Concordance to the Septuagint and the Other Greek Versions of the Old Testament (Including the Apocryphal Books).* Oxford: Clarendon Press, 1897–1906.
HTR	*Harvard Theological Review*
HUCA	*Hebrew Union College Annual*
IG	*Inscriptiones graecae*
JAC	*Jahrbuch für Antike und Christentum*
JBL	*Journal of Biblical Literature*

JECS	*Journal of Early Christian Studies*
JJS	*Journal of Jewish Studies*
JRS	*Journal of Roman Studies*
JSHRZ	*Jüdische Schriften aus hellenistisch-römischer Zeit.* Gütersloh: G. Mohn, 1973–.
JSJ	*Journal for the Study of Judaism*
JSNT	*Journal for the Study of the New Testament*
JSOT	*Journal for the Study of the Old Testament*
JSP	*Journal for the Study of the Pseudepigrapha*
JTS	*Journal of Theological Studies*
LCL	Loeb Classical Library
LSJ	*A Greek-English Lexicon.* Compiled by Henry George Liddell and Robert Scott; revised and augmented by Sir Henry Stuart Jones. Oxford: Clarendon Press, 1925–40.
LXX	Septuagint
LXX/OG	Septuagint/Old Greek
m. Avod. Zar.	Tractate *Avodah Zarah* of the Mishnah
m. Ket.	Tractate *Ketubbot* of the Mishnah
m. Sot.	Tractate *Sutah* of the Mishnah
NedTTs	*Nederlands Teologische Tijdschrift*
NewDocs	*New Documents Illustrating Early Christianity.* The Ancient History Documentary Research Centre, Macquarie University.
NRSV	*New Revised Standard Version* of the Bible.
NTA	*New Testament Apocrypha.* Ed. Edgar Hennecke, Wilhelm Schneemelcher, and R. Mcl. Wilson; revised English edition. Louisville: Westminster Press, 1991–92.
Num. R.	*Numbers Rabbah*
OCD	*The Oxford Classical Dictionary.* Ed. N. G. L. Hammond and H. H. Scullard; second edition. Oxford: Clarendon Press, 1970.
OCLC	Ohio Combined Library Catalogue
OG	Old Greek
1Q Gen Ap	*The Genesis Aprocryphon* (from Qumran Cave 1)
OTP	*Old Testament Pseudepigrapha.* Ed. James A. Charlesworth. Garden City: Doubleday, 1983–85.
Paed.	Clement of Alexandria, *Paedogogus*
PG	J.-P. Migne, *Patrologia Graeca*
PGM	*Papyri graecae magicae: die griechischen Zauberpapyri.* Ed. Karl Preisendanz. Leipzig: B. G. Teubner, 1928–31.
PL	J.-P. Migne, *Patrologia Latina*
PRE	*Pirķê de Rabbi Eliezer*
PSI	*Papiri greci e latini* (Pubblicazioni della società italiana)
PW	Wilhelm Kroll and Georg Wissowa, eds., *Paulys Real-Encyclopaedie der Classischen Altertumswissenschaft.* Stuttgart: J. B. Metzler, 1913.
RAC	*Rivista di archeologia cristiana*
REJ	*Revue des études juives*
SBL	Society of Biblical Literature

SC	*Sources chrétiennes.* Paris: Editions du Cerf.
SPCK	Society for the Promotion of Christian Knowledge
T. Abr.	*Testament of Abraham*
TAPA	Transactions of the American Philological Association
t. Hul.	*Tractate Hulin* of the Tosefta
T. Job	*Testament of Job*
T. Levi	*Testament of Levi*
TLG	*Thesaurus Linguae Graecae*
T. Onq.	*Targum Onqelos*
TQ	*Theologische Quartalschrift*
t. Sot.	Tractate *Sotah* of the Tosefta
Vat. Ebr.	Vaticanus Ebraicus
Vat. Gr.	Vaticanus Graecus
WUNT	*Wissenschaftliche Untersuchungen zum Neuen Testamentum.* Tübingen: J. C. B. Mohr.
ZNW	*Zeitschrift für die neutestamentliche Wissenschaft*

When Aseneth Met Joseph

CHAPTER ONE

Introduction

> Pharaoh said to his servants, "Can we find anyone else like this—one in whom is the spirit of God?" So Pharaoh said to Joseph, "since God has shown you all this, there is no one so discerning and wise as you. You shall be over my house, and all my people shall order themselves as you command: only with regard to the throne will I be greater than you." And Pharaoh said to Joseph, "See, I have set you over all the land of Egypt," Removing his signet ring from his hand, Pharaoh put it on Joseph's hand; he arrayed him in garments of fine linen, and put a gold chain around his neck. He had him ride in the chariot of his second-in-command; and they cried out in front of him, "Bow the knee." Thus he set him over all the land of Egypt. Moreover Pharaoh said to Joseph, "I am Pharaoh, and without your consent, no one shall lift up hand or foot in all the land of Egypt." Pharaoh gave Joseph the name Zaphenath-paneah; and he gave him Asenath daughter of Potiphera, priest of On, as his wife. Thus Joseph gained authority over the land of Egypt. (Gen 41.37–45)

> Before the years of famine came, Joseph had two sons, whom Asenath, daughter of Potiphera, priest of On, bore to him. Joseph named the firstborn Manasseh...The second he named Ephraim. (Gen 41.50–52)

> To Joseph in the land of Egypt were born Manasseh and Ephraim, whom Asenath daughter of Potiphera, priest of On, bore to him. (Gen 46.20)

These few verses comprise all that the Bible has to say about the marriage between Joseph, the son of Jacob, and Aseneth, the daughter of an Egyptian priest. Although prohibitions against intermarriage occur in numerous biblical passages,[1] it would appear that for the authors and editors of the Bible, this story was unremarkable.

While subsequent Jewish (and Christian) sources have somewhat more to say about this alliance,[2] the fullest account of how this marriage came about occurs in a set of Greek texts, whose date and origins, as we shall see, are very difficult to establish. These texts often contain such significantly different readings that we may profitably speak of a shorter version and one or more longer versions. The earliest preserved version of the story[3] identifies it simply as the *Book of Aseneth*, while actual manuscripts give the story varying titles, such as *The Prayer of Aseneth, The Confession and Prayer of Aseneth,* and so forth.[4] Modern scholars have taken to using the title *Joseph and Aseneth*, following the model of ancient Greco-Roman novels named for their hero and heroine. In my own previously published translation,[5] I titled the tale *The Conversion and Marriage of Aseneth*: in this study, I have preferred simply to call it *Aseneth*.

The Greek story is set at the beginning of the seven years of plenty, as Joseph travels throughout Egypt collecting grain against the forthcoming famine. The synopsis presented here is taken from the shorter version unless otherwise noted. On his travels, Joseph comes to Heliopolis, the City of the Sun, where Aseneth lives with her father, Pentephres (an Egyptian priest), her mother, and their large household of servants. A virtuous and extraordinarily beautiful virgin, Aseneth has had no contact with any males outside her family and has spent all of her eighteen years in the family compound, residing in a sumptuously appointed high tower. Aseneth's only flaw seems to be her worship of Egyptian idols.

When Pentephres learns that Joseph is coming to his household seeking rest and refreshment, he calls his dutiful daughter and proposes that she marry Joseph. But Aseneth refuses, recounting local gossip that Joseph is an abandoned son who, sold into slavery, had sex with his master's wife—and who is therefore obviously an unsuitable husband. This is clearly an allusion to the story found in Genesis 37–39, particularly 39.6–20, where the unnamed wife of Potiphar, Joseph's owner, attempts unsuccessfully to seduce Joseph and accuses him of attempted rape when she fails, resulting in Joseph's imprisonment. Aseneth's response here contradicts the biblical text, according to which Joseph was innocent of any sexual misconduct.[6]

When Aseneth first sees Joseph, she is thunderstruck by his glorious appearance and by the power of God that emanates from him. Joseph enters the courtyard of Pentephres riding a gold chariot drawn by four snow-white horses with gold bridles. Over his white tunic, he wears a robe of purple linen embroidered in gold. On his head is a gold crown with twelve precious stones, and he holds a royal scepter in one hand. Watching Joseph's arrival from her tower window, Aseneth herself describes him as Helios (the Sun) come out of heaven in his very chariot.

When Joseph greets Pentephres, he notices Aseneth standing at her window and asks Pentephres to send her away, fearing (the narrative voices claim) that she, like all the Egyptian women, will be overcome by desire for him, another allusion to (and exaggeration of) the story in Genesis. Pentephres, informing Joseph that Aseneth is his daughter and, like Joseph himself, a pure virgin (who detests all men), invites Joseph to greet Aseneth as a sister. Joseph consents, and Aseneth's mother is sent to bring Aseneth to meet Joseph. But when Aseneth, under her father's orders, comes forward to kiss Joseph chastely, he holds her off with his hand against her chest and utters a long speech, decrying the unsuitability of physical contact between those who revere (his) God and those who revere idols. Poor Aseneth breaks into tears at this rejection, whereupon Joseph takes pity on her and prays to God that Aseneth may receive life and blessing. At this, Aseneth flees to her rooms, where, perceiving the ignorance of her judgment and the error of her idolatry, she renounces her worship of Egyptian gods, throwing all her idols out the window. She discards her extravagant jewelry and clothing, engraved and embroidered with idolatrous images, and spends the next seven days in ashes and sackcloth, fasting, weeping, and repenting. At the end of this period of self-mortification, she confesses her sins of idolatry, ignorance, and impiety to the God of Joseph and prays for forgiveness and acceptance, ending with the plea that she be delivered to Joseph as a slave to serve him for the rest of her days.

At the conclusion of her prayer, the morning star rises in the east, which Aseneth takes as a sign of her forgiveness. Miraculously, the heavens split apart, and a luminous angelic being, with the form and face of Joseph, descends to Aseneth's chamber.

Admonishing Aseneth not to be afraid, the angelic figure instructs her to rise up from the floor, to wash her face, and to put on new clothing. When she does so, he informs her that the Lord has heard her confession and that the words of Joseph's earlier prayer for her will be fulfilled: she will be made anew, formed anew, and revived and will eat the bread of life, drink the cup of immortality, and be anointed with the oil of incorruptibility. Aseneth receives a new name, City of Refuge, indicating her future role as the refuge and protection of all those who devote themselves to God in repentance, a role already played by Aseneth's heavenly double, the divine Metanoia (Repentance), the daughter of God.

The angelic figure then informs Aseneth of her future as Joseph's bride and instructs her to change her clothing yet again into appropriate bridal finery. Overjoyed, Aseneth responds by throwing herself at the angel's feet and offering to prepare him a table of bread and wine. The angel requests that she also bring a honeycomb, which she finds, miraculously, in an inside chamber. When Aseneth proposes that the honeycomb has come from the angel's own mouth, he blesses her and confirms that the honey of the comb is angelic food, which confers immortality on all who consume it.

The angel then shows Aseneth an astonishing mystery, in which snow-white bees with purple wings and gold diadems on their heads rise up from the honeycomb, entwining Aseneth from head to toe. At the angel's commands, they all fall down dead and then rise up and fly away to the courtyard of her tower. Shortly thereafter, the angel ascends back to heaven in a fiery chariot. In a wedding celebration given by Pharaoh, and with the blessings of her family, Aseneth marries Joseph, her preordained spouse, and soon conceives and gives birth to Manasseh and Ephraim.

Although the story could end here naturally, both the shorter and longer versions contain an appendix of sorts, chronicling the events of the seven years of famine. When Joseph departs to distribute grain, Pharaoh's son, who had previously sought to marry Aseneth, attempts to abduct her with the aid of Joseph's brothers Dan and Gad. Their treachery is attributed to their being Jacob's sons by Bilhah and Zilpah, the slaves of Jacob's legitimate wives, Leah and Rachel. In good romantic form, the plot is foiled by the virtuous brothers of Joseph and the miraculous intervention of God, invoked by Aseneth. Since Pharaoh's son is killed in the action, Joseph becomes heir to the throne of Egypt and rules for forty-eight years before ceding the throne to Pharaoh's grandson.

Although *Aseneth* has received considerably less attention than many comparable texts, a scholarly consensus of sorts has emerged about its origins, date, provenience, and central concerns.[7] Most recent scholarly reference works describe *Aseneth* as a Jewish text written sometime between about 100 B.C.E. and 135 C.E., probably in Alexandria or perhaps elsewhere in Egypt, whose central concern is conversion and missionizing.[8]

Under close scrutiny, much of this consensus emerges as either unsubstantiated, improbable, or simply wrong. There is no compelling evidence (such as internal references, ancient attestation or quotation, or manuscripts, fragmentary or complete) for dating *Aseneth* any earlier than the fourth century C.E. Nor, as we shall see, does anything compel its identification as a work composed, at least initially, by a self-consciously Jewish, non-Christian author. All our extant manuscripts of *Aseneth* are manifestly Christian (the earliest being seventh-century Syriac Christian), and we have no evidence that *Aseneth* was ever transmitted by Jews or circulated among Jews, let alone composed by Jews. Although the story is clearly set in "biblical" Egypt, it could easily have been composed in any number of ancient geographic locations, the feasibility of which is clearly linked to judgments about its date and authorial identity. Whether the context of the tale is proselytism and conversion to Judaism is similarly problematic and, once again, linked to those judgments.

Although it is customary to begin a study of this sort with a detailed examination of such questions, I have chosen to postpone discussion of date, authorial identity, and provenience to the end of the book, after I have analyzed *Aseneth* from a variety of perspectives. I have made this decision partly because some of my arguments about these questions are supported by my analysis of numerous passages within the texts and should be more comprehensible to readers once they have read the text-focused chapters.

Consequently, chapters 2 through 7 neither assume nor preclude a date of the third century C.E. or later for *Aseneth*, nor do they assume or preclude a particular identity of authorship. Rather, they consider a great deal of material attested primarily in the third and fourth centuries C.E., on the assumption that only by considering *Aseneth*'s affinities with later material will we be in a better position to assess the probabilities of date, provenance, and so forth. Although these chapters may appear to give priority to a Jewish context, in that they explore the affinities between *Aseneth* and known Jewish traditions and sources, the use of Jewish materials to illuminate aspects of the text does not constitute and is not intended as affirmation of the thesis that some putative earliest form of *Aseneth* was composed by a person whom we would designate as simply Jewish. In chapter 9 ("The Authorial Identity of *Aseneth* Reconsidered"), I will explore this issue in depth, but here it is sufficient to observe that many persons in antiquity, from Christians to Samaritans to curious Gentiles, had access to traditions circulating among among Jews in antiquity, and the extensive use of this material does not automatically allow us to identify the self-understanding of authors who use such material. Thus chapters 2 through 7 also remain flexible on the question of the religious and cultural identity of the author or authors of *Aseneth*. Those readers who come to this text with no particular opinion on these matters may find it sufficient to read the book in its present order, whereas readers already conversant with these questions may perhaps wish to read the later chapters first.

Because they have a more immediate and direct bearing on the chapters in the first section, however, two introductory matters are addressed in this introduction, namely, textual dilemmas, particularly the relationship of the so-called shorter and longer texts, and the question of *Aseneth's* genre.

Textual Dilemmas

Although other recent scholars have generally been in accord about the origins, date, and provenance of *Aseneth*, there has been considerable discussion about the precise nature of the "original" text. The Greek manuscripts we now have contain significantly different readings, as do the various versions in different languages. Scholars generally concur that all of the extant manuscripts reflect some degree of alteration from earlier forms of the story. While some scholars favor the textual reconstruction of Marc Philonenko, who has argued for the priority of a "shorter" version of the text (which he published in 1968),[9] an increasing majority have accepted the arguments of Christoph Burchard in favor of a "longer" version of the "original," which he first set forth in 1965.[10]

Both Burchard's and Philonenko's arguments are largely grounded in traditional text-critical concerns. Both have set forth extensive and detailed arguments for their positions, which have been subsequently well summarized by, among others, Randall Chesnutt and Burchard himself in the introduction to his English translation of *Aseneth*. Rather than recapitulate the details here, I refer interested readers to the original discussions as well as to the several competent summaries.[11]

Although he published a few responses to Burchard's arguments and concerns, Philonenko eventually dropped out of the debate, publishing his last contribution to the discussion in 1975.[12] Burchard continued his efforts to identify for the extant manuscripts a textual archetype that differed significantly from the shorter text proffered by Philonenko, which Burchard believed to be an intentional abridgement of a longer, earlier work. In 1985, he published an English translation of a provisionally reconstructed Greek text.[13] Although his printed Greek text contained no variants, Burchard's English translation was accompanied by a lengthy introduction and copious textual notes, although not a formal and complete apparatus.[14] A minor critical edition was promised in the not-too-distant future.

While the majority of scholars who have since published on *Aseneth* have tended to accept Burchard's arguments, Burchard himself has expressed deepening reservations about his earlier work. In 1987, he published a brief essay in an anthology with considerably less circulation than the volume in which his English translation appeared, in which he modifies much of his earlier position, although not particularly in favor of Philonenko.[15] Regrettably, few scholars appear to have read this article and so continue to assert a position about which Burchard himself now appears much more tentative, namely, that the textual difficulties of *Aseneth* are largely resolved.

In his last published statement, Burchard affirmed his sense that the search for a common archetype (ω) of all the extant *Aseneth* manuscripts should begin with the longer β family:

> An editor in search of ω . . . will have to constitute an eclectic text on the base of β, never reconstructed in itself so far . . . I had a stab at it, not too wholeheartedly, by establishing a preliminary text because I needed one to translate for *JSHRZ* and *OTP* [his German and English translations, respectively], and Batiffol or Philonenko would not do.[16]

He goes on to express his increasing doubts about the viability of this enterprise:

> The trouble with this text is that in piecing it together I have come to realize that the existence of β is far from being proven. [Manuscript family] **b** is a very variegated group in which several subgroups are discernible. My conclusion that they form a family with a common ancestor may have been precipitated by the discovery that they do not belong to either **a, c,** or **d**, but that is not enough. Further research into **b** is in order and of course, if **b** happens to disintegrate in the process, into the relationship of the ancestors of such new groups as may appear, and the established ones, $\alpha\delta$, and ζ.[17]

After recommending additional research into the Syriac, Armenian, and Latin versions, Burchard expresses serious reservations about our ability to reconstruct the original Greek should these versions turn out to constitute better witnesses than any of the extant Greek manuscripts. More optimistically, though, he assures us that "[f]ortunately, many of these problems will not affect a translation."[18] But such difficulties weaken the feasibility of a major critical edition, and Burchard now expresses only the hope that he might be able to prepare a minor edition in the distant future.

Burchard, thus, also considers a dilemma few scholars have taken seriously enough: the problematic relationship between the hypothetical archetype and any "original" text of *Aseneth*. Recalling that *Aseneth* is often transmitted with the *Life of Joseph,* which is attributed to the fourth-century Syrian Ephrem, Burchard acknowledges that even ω may not be older than the fourth century C.E., and that we know nothing of the textual history of *Aseneth* between its apparent composition in the first or second century C.E., and its appearance in the fourth century or even a little later.[19] Although Burchard does not here challenge the thesis that some form of *Aseneth* was composed prior to the early second century C.E., he comes fairly close to the position that the texts as we have them are later compositions whose relationship to any earlier forms is virtually inaccessible. He cites with interest the recent thesis of Jacques Schwartz that "[t]he extant forms of [*Aseneth*] . . . are the outcome of a complicated process of rewriting most of which occurred in early Byzantine times in the context of Christian hagiography, with no such thing as an archetype discernible."[20] From this position to my proposal that no evidence for any such earlier form exists and that the texts are much more likely to have originated in the later period is not a very great leap.

Several years ago, *Aseneth* was the topic for both the Philadelphia Seminar on Christian Origins[21] and a graduate seminar at the University of Pennsylvania.[22] We focused our work not only on text-critical issues but also on the content differences of the various reconstructions and began to find ourselves generally siding with Philonenko's thesis that the shorter version represented by **d** had been expanded into the longer version reconstructed by Burchard, rather than vice versa. After we wrote to Burchard, sharing some of our concerns and seeking his most recent thoughts on the matter, he graciously acknowledged his own reservations about the limits of a strictly text-critical approach:

> Generally, I feel that I have worked too narrowly along the orthodox lines of textual criticism and failed to do, except here and there, what you propose now, most sensibly to my mind, i.e. "to identify motivations for various textual modifications and to locate them in relation to known Jewish and Christian interest."[23]

It is thus clear to me that scholars who consider the text-critical questions largely resolved base their position on an acceptance of Burchard's earlier analysis, which he always considered much more tentative and preliminary than his readers and about which he himself has now expressed possible reservations.

In the end, I have chosen to work with the reconstructions published by Philonenko and Burchard, respectively, and to treat them as reasonable approximations of the texts that ancient readers would have encountered, though probably not before the third or fourth centuries C.E. at the earliest. Rather than pursue an elusive "ur-text" of *Aseneth*, I have chosen to focus on these two particular versions (with occasional consideration of other readings). After painstaking comparison of the content of the differing reconstructions, I have come to conclusions that contradict the prevailing scholarly consensus favoring Burchard's initial position. In general, I am convinced that Philonenko's text represents an earlier form of the story and that Burchard's text represents intentional subsequent revision of that earlier form. I think it highly likely that Burchard's text may reflect several layers of revision and that occasionally it may preserve material that was deleted from the shorter text, but this is normally not the case. Rather than present detailed arguments in support of this position here, I will endeavor to demonstrate its viability throughout the book itself. But I should add a note of caution that even if the shorter version is an intentional abridgement, a position I find difficult to accept, it would not alter my basic thesis that all the extant *Aseneth* materials are late and must be analyzed within a late antique context.

The absence of a definitive original text makes it difficult to write about *Aseneth* without some ambiguity of language. To what, after all, does the title *Aseneth* (or any other title we attribute) refer? To the putative archetype? To a specific manuscript? To the collectivity of apparently related texts about Joseph and Aseneth? To minimize this awkward situation, I will generally refer to the shorter version or reconstruction, by which I mean Philonenko's printed text (or a close approximation thereof), and to the longer version or reconstruction, by which I mean Burchard's printed text (or a close approximation thereof). Philonenko's so-called "first long recension" is quite close to Burchard's text.[24] The text printed by Batiffol represents a somewhat different longer reconstruction, from a different textual family, which Philonenko designated the third longer recension.[25] Sometimes I will use the moniker *Aseneth* when the precise textual form is irrelevant or when I wish to refer to the total collectivity of texts. Since it is similarly awkward to know how to refer to those individuals responsible for *Aseneth*, I have chosen to use a variety of terms, as the context appears to warrant. If I were more certain that a single ur-text of *Aseneth* were accessible and represented the work of a single, individual author, I would be more confident using such terms as "the author" or "the writer," and occasionally the dictates of style and convenience impel me to such terminology. I wish to be clear, however, that I do not think we know whether one or more individuals were responsible for any particular version of *Aseneth* we might reconstruct and that the reconstructions with which, of necessity, I work in this book reflect the authorial activity of a number of ancient persons of unknown identity.

Genre

Questions of genre are particularly germane for their effect on our expectations as readers. Our assessment of the literary genre of a work determines to a significant degree not only the formal characteristics we expect it to display, but also the ways in which we respond to the text and the authority we cede to the claims it makes to describe reality. Not only do we expect novels, biographies, poems, legal documents, scholarly monographs, and now even e-mail to differ in their structure, language, form, and content but we also assess their claims to describe reality by criteria that are integrally related to our perception of their form. So, too, we expect ancient decrees of the Roman Senate to have different structures, forms, and language from ancient tax decrees, ancient magical formulas, or ancient personal correspondence, and we read those texts very differently depending, in part, on the genres by which we classify them.

In the case of *Aseneth*, our assessment of its genre may determine, or at least affect, our understanding of its structure, form, and sometimes content. Virtually all scholars place it within the broad category of a Greco-Roman romance or novel,[26] whose specific concern is the conversion of Aseneth to Judaism and her subsequent marriage to Joseph. Most consider it a thinly veiled projection of Hellenistic Jewish beliefs (and possibly also practices) onto the biblical narrative of Genesis. Behind *Aseneth*, various scholars claim to have detected the influence of everything from Egyptian myths and folktales to gnostic allegorical dramas.

In support of the classification of *Aseneth* as an ancient romance, Philonenko pointed to what he saw as the classical elements of ancient novels: the love story (between Joseph and Aseneth), the adventure story (the unsuccessful abduction and rape by the son of Pharaoh, aided by Joseph's unscrupulous brothers), the presentation of the exotic (the setting in Egypt), and the essential religious underpinnings.[27] He catalogued such stereotypical features as the exceptional beauty of the heroine and hero; love at first sight; lovesickness; the kiss; separation; the unscrupulous rival; and the chastity of heroine and hero.[28] More recently, Larry Wills has described *Aseneth* as "[t]he Jewish novella that is most similar to Greek novels"[29] and argues that it is "a 'free' narrative, which actually has more in common with motifs from Greek novels."[30]

The burgeoning study of ancient Greek novels in the last few years offers both additional support for classifying *Aseneth* as antique romance and some cautions about the limited utility of such categorization. We now recognize that the general features of these novels include folktale, myth, allegory, and intertextuality—including a penchant for literary imitation and engagement of classical subtexts.[31]

Beyond these generalities, Brigitte Egger has recently illuminated the centrality of licit marriage in ancient novels, arguing that in the so-called classical Greek novels[32] marriage is at the core of these narratives and drives the composition of the stories, all of which culminate in a wedding (or reunion of married lovers).[33] Even threats of rape envision marriage, and would-be seducers have legal "marriage" in mind. The paradigm of the couple is that of married lovers, a paradigm on the rise in the first few centuries of the era.[34]

Aseneth thus displays not only the similarities to ancient novels that Philonenko and others have recognized but additional ones as well. It, too, is a tale in which licit marriage figures prominently; in which even the antagonists have married love in mind. Egger points out that the setting of these novels in an idealized past that is intentionally not the Roman period is a typical feature of second-century C.E. Second Sophistic literature,[35] a feature that may also be true of *Aseneth*. Further, she notes that the heroines of these tales are all brotherless, as is our Aseneth.[36]

Yet *Aseneth* differs in significant details from the pattern Egger identifies. Whereas the protagonists in ancient novels usually fall in love at first sight, Aseneth's immediate response to Joseph isn't precisely romantic love, although it turns out to be, and

Joseph clearly doesn't fall in love with Aseneth immediately, at least not in any way that is explicit. Romantic heroes typically win their heroines through feats of masculine endurance and skill, but Joseph performs no such deeds, and when Aseneth is in peril of her chastity, Joseph himself plays no part in her rescue.[37]

Egger observes that in these novels, the marriage of daughters is almost always at the discretion of fathers: mothers are not involved, and the daughter's consent is unnecessary. Although some romance fathers oppose the union of the protagonists, it usually turns out that the "good romance father" marries his daughter to the right husband.[38] *Aseneth* conforms to this model only in certain respects. Certainly, Pentephres' choice of a husband for Aseneth turns out to be the "right" one. Initially, however, he does seek his daughter's assent, and when she fails to give it, he does not insist.[39] Ironically, perhaps, in *Aseneth*, it is precisely Pentephres who proposes the marriage and Joseph who declares his immediate opposition to marriage with an idolator.

The narratives of Greek novels depend for much of their plot elaboration on an extended separation of the lovers, but in *Aseneth,* Aseneth's separation from Joseph lasts only one week, and the drama of that week is entirely an interior one. During that extended separation, the heroine is subjected to repeated threats to her chastity, and sometimes the hero is to his own as well. Clearly the theme of threatened chastity occurs in *Aseneth*, but in significantly different form. While Aseneth herself is initially presented as a threat to Joseph's chastity, only in the second part of the narrative is Aseneth herself endangered, after she and Joseph are married and after Manasseh and Ephraim are born.

Pared down to its basic structural elements, the story of Aseneth and Joseph does exhibit the main features common to ancient Greek novels, though not with precision. In chapter 7, I will consider further the utility of these similarities in analyzing of the role of gender in *Aseneth*. In addition, *Aseneth* contains some elements of ancient "quest" tales, as Elizabeth Hog Doty considers in her dissertation.[40] The story also displays features common in certain respects to ancient narratives of mystical initiation into cults such as those of Isis, Mithra, and others.[41] Unquestionably, then, *Aseneth* draws heavily on the common cultural currency of the later Greco-Roman world, including its literary genres.

Yet I think the emphasis on these similarities has minimized some of the dissimilarities and the degree to which many of these seemingly common elements are easily derived from compositional and interpretive techniques like those illuminated by Kugel. Further, it has obscured the central paradigm of angelic adjuration and transformation, which I now believe lies at the core of the text.

In the chapters that follow, I shall attempt to demonstrate these claims in considerable detail. But here, I need to conclude this introduction with a few technical matters. First, I have chosen to cite the texts of *Aseneth* primarily in English translation in order to make the book accessible not only to scholars but also to others interested in the material who may know little if any Greek. Since in my experience, the use of foreign fonts often deters students and other interested general readers, I normally provide transliterations of ancient languages within the main text, while the notes utilize Greek and Hebrew fonts.

Second, to facilitate analysis of the relationship between the shorter and longer reconstructions, I frequently provide a combined citation whose format is designed to allow the reader to see where the texts are essentially in agreement and where they differ. In these combined citations, text printed in roman typeface is essentially identical in both texts. (Text in parenthesis in roman typeface is found only in the shorter text.) **Text in boldface is found only in the longer text.** [Square brackets contain editorial and explanatory material as necessary, regardless of typeface.] **(Boldface text in parentheses denotes Burchard's additions, usually to improve the sense in English.)** Versification in roman typeface (e.g., 8.3–4) is either common to both texts or that of Philonenko. **Versification in boldface (e.g., 8.4–5) is that of Burchard's text, following his system of notation in his English translation.**[42] Translation of the shorter text is my own; translation of the longer is based on Burchard's, modified as necessary to show consistencies in the underlying Greek or for clarification, felicity of English, and so forth.

Finally, throughout this study, I use the phrase Septuagint/Old Greek (abbreviated LXX/OG) to designate the collection of Jewish scriptures in Greek as available now in the edition by A. Rahlfs, in the Göttinger *Septuagint,* and in the Cambridge *Septuagint.* [43] I use this hybrid to emphasize that the ancient translations of Jewish scripture into Greek that we now possess are not homogeneous.[44] Those occasional references to Septuagint (LXX) alone designate only the translation of the Torah (Pentateuch).

NOTES

1. E.g., Gen 34.8–25 (the story of Dinah); Exod 34.13–16; Num 25; Deut 7.3; 1 Kgs 11.1; Neh 13.23–27. Within the narrative structure of Torah, though, all of these prohibitions "postdate" Joseph. Prohibitions occur also in *T. Levi* 14.5–8; *T. Job* 45.4; *Jub.* 30.11–17; Philo, *Spec. Leg.* 3.29; Josephus, *Ant.* 8.191–93. See also Shaye J. D. Cohen, "The Prohibition of Intermarriage from the Bible to the Talmud," *Hebrew Annual Review* 7 (1983): 23–29.

2. See the appendix. Rabbinic Jewish traditions about Aseneth are collected and discussed in detail in V. Aptowitzer, "Asenath, the Wife of Joseph: A Haggadic Literary-Historical Study," *Hebrew Union College Annual* 1 (1924): 239–306, although I disagree with his interpretation of the relationship between those traditions and our *Aseneth.*

3. See chapter 8.

4. On the various manuscript titles, see P. Batiffol, "Le Livre de la Prière d'Aseneth," in *Studia patristica: Etudes d'ancienne littérature chrétienne* (Paris: Leroux, 1889–90), 1/2: 6–7. The title "Life and Confession of Aseneth" seems fairly common but not necessarily original; the title Batiffol prints for his Greek text is *ΠΡΟΣΕΥΞΗ ΑΣΕΝΕΦ*; for the Latin, *Liber de Aseneth.*

5. Ross S. Kraemer, ed. *Maenads, Martyrs, Matrons, Monastics: A Sourcebook of Women's Religions in the Greco-Roman World* (Philadelphia: Fortress Press, 1988) no. 113, 263–79.

6. Joseph's encounter with the unnamed wife of Potiphar was the subject of extensive rabbinic midrash, which is the focal point of Kugel, *In Potiphar's House.* On the theme of Joseph's possible acquiescence, see ibid., chapter 4, "Joseph's Change of Heart."

7. This is represented in such major studies of *Aseneth* as Christoph Burchard, "Joseph and Aseneth: A New Translation and Introduction," in James H. Charlesworth, ed., *The Old Testament Pseudepigrapha,* Vol. 2 (Garden City, NY: Doubleday, 1985), 177–247; Christoph Burchard, *Untersuchungen zu "Joseph und Aseneth," Uberlieferung—Urtsbestimmung,* WUNT 8

(Tübingen: Gutersloh, 1965); Randall D. Chesnutt, *"Conversion in 'Joseph and Aseneth': Its Nature, Function, and Relation to Contemporaneous Paradigms of Conversion and Initiation"* (Ph.D. dissertation, Duke University, 1986), revised and published as Chesnutt, *From Death to Life;* Randell D. Chesnutt, "The Social Setting and Purpose of 'Joseph and Aseneth,'" *JSP* 2 (1988): 21–48; Marc Philonenko, *"Joseph et Aséneth." Introduction, texte critique, traduction et notes,* Studia Post-biblica (Leiden: E. J. Brill, 1968); Dietrich Sänger, *Antikes Judentum und die Mysterien: Religionsgeschichtliche Untersuchungen zu "Joseph und Aseneth,"* WUNT 2, no. 5 (Tübingen: Mohr, 1980); Angela Standhartinger, *Das Frauenbild im Judentum der hellenistischen Zeit: Ein Beitrag anhand von "Joseph & Aseneth"* Arbeiten zur beschichte des antiken Judentums und Urchristemtus 26 (Leiden: E. J. Brill, 1995). An excellent survey of the treatment of Aseneth by scholars, with consideration of current views of origins, date, textual priorities, and so forth, may be found in Chesnutt, *From Death to Life*, 20–64, 65–93.

8. Chesnutt, *From Death to Life*, 41–46, conveniently summarizes some of this consensus, which he himself affirms, as does Gideon Bohak in his recent review of the published version of Chesnutt in *Ioudaios Review* 5.008, May 1995. Handbook treatments include the introduction by Sparks to Cook's translation in *AOT* 465–70; Burchard, "Joseph and Aseneth," (187 on date); Chesnutt in *ABD* 3:969–71. Emile Puech, *La croyance des Esseniens en la vie future: Immortalité, résurrection, vie éternelle? Histoire d'une croyance dans le judaïsme ancien,* Études bibliques n.s. 21–22 (Paris: Librairie Lecoffre, 1993), 1:169, n. 150, contains a useful summary of the conclusions of other scholars on the subject of date. See also Chesnutt, *From Death to Life*, 40–41. Apart from a recent dissertation by Gideon Bohak at Princeton University (*"Joseph and Aseneth" and the Jewish Temple in Heliopolis*, Early Judaism and Its Literature 10 [Atlanta: Scholars Press, 1996]), who argues for a date in the mid-second century B.C.E., no one has recently argued for a date outside these parameters.

9. Philonenko, *Joseph et Aséneth.*

10. Burchard, *Untersuchungen,* and "Zum Text von 'Joseph und Aseneth,'" *JSJ* 1, no. 3, (1970): 3–34. See also above, note 7. Burchard has recently collected his studies in *Aseneth: Gesammelte Studien zu Joseph and Aseneth,* Studia in Veteris Testamenti Pseudepigrapha 13 (Leiden: E. J. Brill, 1996).

11. See also several other dissertations on *Aseneth*: Edgar W. Smith, *"'Joseph and Asenath' and Early Christian Literature: A Contribution to the Corpus Hellenisticum Novi Testamenti"* (Ph.D. dissertation, Claremont Graduate School, 1974); Susan Elizabeth Hog Doty, *"From Ivory Tower to City of Refuge: The Role and Function of the Protagonist in 'Joseph and Aseneth' and Related Narratives"* (Ph.D. dissertation, Iliff School of Theology and University of Denver, 1989). See also the recently published 1991 McGill University dissertation of Edith M. Humphrey, *The Ladies and the Cities: Transformation and Apocalyptic Identity in "Joseph and Aseneth," 4 Ezra, The Apocalypse, and "The Shepherd"* (Sheffield: Sheffield Academic Press, 1995).

12. Marc Philonenko, "Un mystère juif?" in *Mystères et syncrétismes, Etudes d'histoire des religions* 2, (Paris: Guethner, 1975), 65–70. These surveys do not take into account the work of Angela Standhartinger, *Das Frauenbild.* Her comparison of the representation of Aseneth in the longer and shorter reconstructions has led her to conclusions closer to mine regarding the relationship between the two. Standhartinger argues that the shorter text cannot be an abridgement of the longer text(s), and that any process of revision must have been carefully thought out and intentional (see her discussion on 219–25, esp. 220–21). With both of these I clearly agree. But Standhartinger shies away from concluding that the present longer text(s) constitute an intentional revision of the present shorter reconstruction. Instead, she maintains that each represents a different version of the same story, a conclusion I find difficult to share. However, I wholeheartedly agree with her insistence that both versions of the

story deserve serious consideration, on which point see my further discussion in chapter 3. Finally, while Standhartinger has commendably rethought the issue of textual relationships, she continues to accept the consensus that both the shorter and longer reconstructions of Aseneth are the product of Jewish authorship, most likely in the first century C.E.

13. Now printed in Albert-Marie Denis, *Concordance grecque des pseudépigraphes d'Ancien testament: Concordance, corpus des textes, indices,* avec la collaboration d'Yvonne Janssens et le concours du CETEDOC (Louvain-la-Neuve: Université Catholique de Louvain, 1987), 852–59. Published also in German in 1983 as *Joseph und Aseneth.*

14. See also his *Untersuchungen zu Joseph und Aseneth.*

15. "The Present State of Research on Joseph and Aseneth," in J. Neusner, Peder Borgen, Esnest S. Frerichs, and Richard Horsley, eds., *Religion, Literature, and Society in Ancient Israel, Formative Christianity and Judaism: Ancient Israel and Christianity,* New Perspectives on Judaism 2 (Lanham, MD: University Press of America, 1987), 31–52.

16. Burchard, "Present State," 34.

17. Burchard, "Present State," 34.

18. Burchard, "Present State," 34.

19. Burchard, "Present State," 34–35.

20. Burchard, "Present State," 35, referring to the thesis of Jacques Schwartz, "Recherches sur l'évolution du roman de Joseph et Asenath," *REJ* 143 (1984): 273–85, that the earliest Aseneth story was formulated prior to 117 C.E. and consisted only of a bare-bones romance, and perhaps the plot of Pharaoh's son's revenge. The extant forms "are the outcome of a complicated process of rewriting most of which occurred in early Byzantine times in the context of Christian hagiography, with no such thing as an archetype discernible (an idea also suggested by Philonenko, but his textual reconstruction runs counter to it)" (Burchard, "Present State," 35). Much of Schwartz's argument has to do with the relationship between *Aseneth* and two Christian hagiographic works entitled the *Martyrdom of Saint Irene* and the *Martyrdom of Saint Christine* (on which, see chapters 8 and 9). He concludes that we no longer have the "original" story, which he appears to find detectable in *Irene,* an original that would have been composed prior to 117 C.E. To this original would have been added a proselytism element drawing on the stories of Rahab and Ruth. Schwartz sees a link with Nisibis, the locale of the story of Irene, not before the end of the fourth century. He does not, however, take a strong stand on the question of which of the current texts is "earlier" nor on the relationships between them (274, n. 6).

21. Chaired by myself and Robert A. Kraft.

22. Taught by Robert A. Kraft.

23. From a letter dated 24 June 1991 to Robert A. Kraft, cited with permission.

24. Philonenko designated the Greek manuscripts D, E, and F, from family β, as the first long recension. Burchard based his eclectic text on these three, supplemented with numerous other readings as he thought appropriate.

25. He designated the Greek manuscript H as the second longer recension.

26. The secondary literature on Greco-Roman romance has burgeoned in the last few years, aided by the publication of B. P. Reardon, ed., *Collected Ancient Greek Novels* (Berkeley: University of California Press, 1989), with its English translations of the five "classic" Greek romances and other less well-known fragments. See, e.g., Shadi Bartsch, *Decoding the Ancient Novel: The Reader and the Role of Description in Heliodorus and Achilles Tatius* (Princeton, NJ: Princeton University Press, 1989); James Tatum, ed., *The Search for the Ancient Novel* (Baltimore: Johns Hopkins University Press, 1994); Judith Perkins, *The Suffering Self: Pain and Narrative Representation in the Early Christian Era* (London: Routledge, 1995); Kate Cooper, *The Virgin and the Bride* (Cambridge, MA: Harvard University Press, 1996); Margaret Anne Doody, *The True Story of the Novel* (New Brunswick, NJ: Rutgers University Press,

1996); Gareth Schmeling, ed., *The Novel in the Ancient World*, Mnemosyne, Bibliotheca Classica Batava Supplement 159 (Leiden: E. J. Brill, 1996).

27. Philonenko, *Joseph et Aséneth*, 43–47.

28. Philonenko, *Joseph et Aséneth*, 43.

29. Lawrence M. Wills, "The Jewish Novellas," in John Morgan and Richard Stoneman, eds., *Greek Fiction: The Greek Novel in Context* (London: Routledge, 1994), 233. See also Lawrence M. Wills, *The Jewish Novel in the Ancient World* (Ithaca: Cornell University Press, 1995); Richard I. Pervo, "Aseneth and Her Sisters: Women in Jewish Narrative and in the Greek Novels," in Amy-Jill Levine, ed., *"Women Like This": New Perspectives on Jewish Women in the Greco-Roman Period*, Early Judaism and Its Literature 1 (Atlanta: Scholars Press, 1991), 145–60; and "The Ancient Novel Becomes Christian," in Gareth Schmeling, ed., *The Novel in the Ancient World*, Mnemosyne, Bibliotheca Classica Batava Supplement 159 (Leiden: E. J. Brill, 1996), 685–712.

30. Wills, *Jewish Novel*, 175. Wills actually offers here an intriguing theory that *Aseneth* consists of two layers—a national hero romance (including the tale of Pharaoh's son and the misguided brothers) overlaid by a conversion narrative (179–84). Although Wills classifies *Aseneth* as a Jewish novel, it is noteworthy that whereas all the heroines of his other Jewish novellas (Judith, Sarah in Tobit, Susanna, and Esther), and perhaps Ruth as well, can be seen to symbolize the circumstances of Israel in the diaspora, Aseneth as character cannot. At best, she can represent the experience of the idolater who comes to join Israel. This distinction, while hardly dispositive, seems consistent with my perception that *Aseneth* does not, in fact, fit within Wills's classification as a Jewish novel of the early Roman period.

31. Brigitte Egger, "Women and Marriage in the Greek Novels: The Boundaries of Romance," in Tatum, *Search for the Ancient Novel*, 265.

32. Namely, Chariton, *Chareas and Callirhoe* (probably second century C.E., perhaps associated with Aphrodisias); Achilles Tatius, *Leucippe and Cleitophon* (also probably second century C.E.); Heliodorus, *Aethiopica* (interestingly, the author identifies himself as a native of Emesa in Syria, "son of Theodosius, of the race of the Sun,"—in other words, a devotee of Helios; the work is usually dated to the third century C.E.); Longus, *Daphnis and Chloe* (date uncertain); and Xenophon of Ephesus, *Ephesiaca*, or *Anthia and Habracomes* (second to third century C.E.). But it should be noted that dating these stories is complicated.

33. Egger, "Women and Marriage," 262.

34. Egger, "Women and Marriage," 260.

35. Egger, "Women and Marriage," 266.

36. Egger, "Women and Marriage," 268: "All heroines of romance, in fact, seem to be *epikleroi* by classical standards, since they have no brothers."

37. Egger, "Women and Marriage," 265, points out that Chareas in Chariton's *Chareas and Callirhoe* gains Callirhoe not so much by valiant deeds as by other, more passive means but that, subsequently, he does display more heroism.

38. Egger, "Women and Marriage," 268–69.

39. Interestingly, Egger "Women and Marriage," 268–69, notes that in Heliodorus, the father is unable to insist on his choice of a husband.

40. Doty, "From Ivory Tower." But recent feminist analysis of ancient romances makes me think that Doty's view of *Aseneth* as a tale of self-realization may be overly "optimistic." See chapter 7.

41. See, e.g. Sänger, *Antikes Judentum*, who argues that these features are superficial and that *Aseneth* is not, in fact, a novel of initiation ("[Joseph and Aseneth] ist kein Mysterienroman" [190].) See also Chesnutt, *From Death to Life*, 217–53, who reaches similar conclusions. For comparative purposes, the key text is usually Apuleius, *Metamorphoses* 11, describing the

initiation of the protagonist, Lucius, into the mysteries of Isis and Osiris, a text thought by many scholars to be semi-autobiographical. The date cannot be earlier than the mid-second century C.E.

42. "Joseph and Aseneth." There, Burchard used the letter "x" to designate additional verses. In the version of the text printed in Denis, *Concordance,* the letters B and following are used for such material (e.g., *Aseneth* 15:12x in "Joseph and Aseneth" corresponds to 15:12B in Denis, *Concordance*).

43. A. Rahlfs, *Septuaginta, id est Vetus Testamentum Graece iuxta LXX interpretes* (Stuggart: Deutsche Bibelgesellschaft, 1935; reprint, 1979); *Septuaginta Vetus Testamentum Graecum* (Göttingen: Auctoriate Academiae Scientiarum Göttingenesis editum, 1931–); A. E. Brooke, N. McLean, and H. St. J. Thackeray, eds., *The Old Testament in Greek according to the Text of Codex Vaticanus Supplemented from Other Uncial Manuscripts* (Cambridge: Cambridge University Press, 1906–40).

44. See R. A. Kraft, "Septuagint: B. Earliest Greek Versions ('Old Greek')," in *The Interpreter's Dictionary of the Bible,* Supplementary Volume (Nashville: Abingdon Press, 1976) 811–15. See also Melvin K. H. Peters, "Septuagint, in *ABD* 5:1093–1104.

PART I

Reinterpreting *Aseneth*

CHAPTER TWO

Composing *Aseneth*

The Construction of Aseneth *out of Traditional Elements and Techniques*

Ancient readers of Jewish scripture often found themselves confronted by textual anomalies, which they attempted to resolve.[1] The means by which at least one circle of Jewish readers frequently did so is brilliantly illuminated in Kugel's study of midrashic rabbinic traditions about Joseph and the wife of Potiphar, where he demonstrates their formulation and development as logical responses to textual and contextual anomalies and questions.[2]

For early Jewish exegetes, the verses in Genesis that recount the marriage of Joseph and Aseneth and the birth of their sons Manasseh and Ephraim appeared to contain no anomalies, and they took these verses at face value. Aseneth the daughter of Potiphera married Joseph; their sons are the eponymous ancestors of the half-tribes Manasseh and Ephraim.[3] Demonstrably early Greek Jewish authors such as Philo and Josephus and the authors of "rewritten" Bible, such as Pseudo-Philo, evince no explicit interest whatsoever in Joseph's marriage to Aseneth.[4]

The trigger for the relatively modest early traditions about Aseneth that we find in the *Book of Jubilees* (34.11, 40.10) and the early Aramaic targumim of *Onqelos* and *Neofiti 1* (to Gen 41.45, 41.50, 46.20) seems to have been the identification of Joseph's owner, Potiphar, with Joseph's father-in-law, Potiphera. Both men have the same name, Petefres, in early Greek translation of Genesis. Ultimately, although it is hard to say precisely when, the transfer of Potiphar's characterization as a eunuch to Potiphera creates exegetical difficulties that various rabbinic Aseneth stories appear to address and resolve in differing ways, such as the question of how a eunuch could have had a daughter. Yet the earlier rabbinic traditions consistently identify Aseneth as the biological daughter at least of her mother, Potiphar/Potiphera's wife, and usually of Potiphar/Potiphera himself.[5]

Significantly, our Aseneth stories appear grounded in different concerns, which they, too, endeavor to address. The identification of Joseph's master with his father-in-law is either irrelevant or intentionally (but implicitly) refuted in our stories, which instead focus on the transformation of Aseneth, the daughter of an Egyptian priest, into an appropriate wife for Joseph, the son of a Hebrew and the second-in-command of all Egypt.

While previous scholars have recognized the presence of biblical motifs and parallels in both the shorter and longer reconstructions of *Aseneth*, none has considered the degree to which such materials may constitute the principal building blocks of the stories.[6] Yet it now seems to me that both the skeletal structure of the Greek Aseneth story and many (although by no means all) of its specific elements of dialogue and narrative detail could have initially been formulated by a process comparable to the one Kugel illuminates for tales of Joseph and Potiphar's wife. The basic framework of the text may be derived from the constraints of the three specific verses currently in Genesis, together with the larger biblical story of Joseph.[7]

Although early exegetes may have found nothing problematic in the marriage of Joseph and Aseneth, how such a marriage came about could easily have perplexed ancient readers. At the very least, the circumstances under which such a marriage was arranged might have prompted speculation.[8] The primary initial problems are fairly obvious. First, how did Joseph, an Israelite, marry an Egyptian woman, who was the daughter of an Egyptian priest, particularly in light of numerous biblical prohibitions against such marriages?[9] Second, why did Pharaoh make the marriage, rather than the family members of Joseph and Aseneth, as one would generally expect both from biblical descriptions of Israelite marriage arrangements[10] and possibly from "customary practice" as the author(s) knew it, although this is less crucial.

While the traditions preserved in rabbinic sources resolve the first problem by claiming that Aseneth was really the daughter of Dinah, Joseph's half-sister making Aseneth his niece and kin,[11] the Greek stories of Joseph and Aseneth offer the answer that Aseneth underwent a transformation. Most scholars have easily adopted the terminology of "conversion" for her experience, but since the texts themselves do not use such language, I will generally avoid it in favor of the language of "transformation." Following Kugel's analysis of the ways in which speculation about anomalies in biblical texts could generate whole stories, we may easily envision authors who generated virtually the entire Aseneth story (particularly as reconstructed by Philonenko) out of questions about this process.

For example, claiming that Aseneth renounced her idolatry and was transformed into an acceptable daughter of the Hebrews immediately generates questions about when, where, why, and how she did so. To answer the question of when, the author or authors draw on two elements: the story as we presently have it in Genesis itself and the desire to transform Aseneth prior to her marriage to Joseph, a desire that is itself driven by the tradition that Aseneth will be the mother of two Israelite (half) tribes, Manasseh and Ephraim; her premarital transformation assures their legitimacy. Other issues might conceivably be present here, such as concerns about actual proselyte marriages, but they need not be. The answer the text offers to these questions is relatively straightforward: it locates Aseneth's transformation before the marriage, before the conception of Manasseh and Ephraim, and within the parameters of the Genesis tale itself, when Joseph was collecting grain during the seven years of plenty.[12]

That same detail from Genesis allows the author(s) to address another crucial question: what was the catalyst for Aseneth's transformation? Several answers are possible. The story at hand claims that it was the appearance of Joseph himself. This immediately drives the composition of the narrative, requiring answers to questions such as how they met, what happened when they met, and so forth. It is easy to see how the narrative now in Genesis also affords certain answers: Joseph and Aseneth met when Joseph was traveling around Egypt, collecting grain, and came to Pentephres' house. Why did he come? He was in need of rest and refreshment. Where would such a high official as Joseph stay? In the best house he could find, in this case, the home of Pentephres, the high priest of Heliopolis.

Similarly, in the seven chapters (10.2–17.6) that describe the process of Aseneth's transformation from Strange/Foreign Woman to the consummate woman who reveres God (*theosebēs gynē*), much of the narrative can be seen as an attempt to answer questions about such an experience. How did Aseneth become acceptable? She repented and accepted Joseph's God. What was the catalyst for her repentance? The appearance of Joseph. What exactly did she do and say during her repentance? Read on. How did Aseneth know that her repentance had been accepted? God sent an angelic being, a dead ringer for Joseph, to announce her transformation. What happened between Aseneth and the angelic being? Read on again.

While it is not always possible to see precisely the question that drives the composition of the narrative, it is occasionally possible in the case of the shorter text and somewhat more frequently possible in the longer text. For instance, the initial confrontation between Aseneth and her father provides at least a partial answer to the question of why Pharaoh rather than the respective fathers of the couple arranged the marriage by claiming that Pentephres attempted to marry Aseneth to Joseph but she (stubbornly and in ignorance) refused to agree. Much later (20.6–7), the text will offer an explanation for why Jacob was not a party to the wedding arrangements.

Several conceptual frameworks contribute to the choices the author or authors make for both the narrative structure and the details of the story. The author of the shorter text sees the marriage of Joseph and Aseneth as far more than just the marriage of an Israelite patriarch and the daughter of an Egyptian priest. Rather, the marriage of Aseneth and Joseph is simultaneously the union of Wisdom personified as female and the Wise Man, which permeates not only Proverbs but many other Jewish texts, and that of the lovers in Song of Songs. Further (and perhaps obviously) these unions are themselves understood as the divine union of Israel and God, exemplified particularly in the relationship between the suffering and penitent sinner and the forgiving God in many Psalms. Most intriguingly, as the text itself makes clear, the marriage of Joseph and Aseneth enacts the divine union of the son and daughter of God—who, again, may or may not be Wisdom and the Wise Man. Less obvious, but also present underneath the longer text and perhaps also the shorter, is the paradigm afforded by the primordial couple in Genesis, particularly 1.26–27. Aseneth herself represents the soul's quest for and attainment of restoration to primordial angelic identity, which is itself derived from interpretations of the tradition in Genesis 1. Finally, although the angel does not explicitly inform Aseneth of the coming conception and birth of her two sons, Manasseh and Ephraim, the story also draws on at least one ancient annunciation tale (Judg 13) and may draw on others as well.

Thus, as we shall see, the choices by the author(s) of both narrative and detail draw repeatedly from these paradigms and from the biblical traditions that express them. As numerous examples in this chapter will demonstrate, *Aseneth* is awash in imagery, language, motifs, and metaphors known to us now especially, though not exclusively, from Greek Jewish scripture, particularly Genesis, Proverbs, Psalms, and Song of Songs, as well as Isaiah and Ezekiel.

In this chapter, then, I will endeavor to demonstrate the many points at which the story common to both the shorter and longer reconstructions of *Aseneth* is constructed out of this traditional material. In the following chapter, I will compare the readings of these two reconstructions at various points and demonstrate that just as the shorter reconstruction draws on traditional materials for the composition of *Aseneth,* so the longer reconstruction itself exegetes and develops the shorter text, answering questions implicit in the shorter narrative, resolving apparent anomalies or inconsistencies, and expanding biblical imagery or making more explicit the biblical allusions of the shorter. The consistent pattern of these differences between the shorter text and the longer makes it highly unlikely that they are the product of editorial deletion rather than editorial expansion and substantiates my hypothesis that the shorter text precedes the longer.

The Figure of Aseneth Herself

At the very outset of the story, Aseneth is described for us as an unsurpassingly beautiful virgin of eighteen (1.6), attended by seven similarly beautiful virgins (2.10–11), living in a large apartment in a high tower within the compound of her father, Pentephres (2.1). So great is the reputation of her beauty that numerous aristocratic young men seek her as a bride, including the son of Pharaoh (1.9–11). Beautiful virgins who live in high towers and young men who desire them are stock items in folktales, and similar motifs are easily discernible in ancient Greco-Roman romantic novels.[13]

Despite the common nature of such motifs, both the description of Aseneth and a considerable portion of her encounter with Joseph and with his heavenly double draw heavily upon the association of Aseneth with an assortment of traditional figures, virtually all of them female: Wisdom and/or the Wise Woman and her antithesis, the Strange or Foreign Woman; Daughter figures, including Daughter of the King, Daughter Zion, Daughter of Jerusalem, and Jerusalem itself; the soul (feminine in Greek) in search of angelic transformation; the female lover and bride in Song of Songs; and the penitent sinner. Each of these identities implies a corresponding role for Joseph. As Aseneth is Wisdom, so Joseph is the man who loves Wisdom; as Aseneth is the soul, so Joseph is psychopomp and God's messenger, if not God himself; as Aseneth is the female lover, so Joseph is her beloved; as Aseneth is the divine bride, so Joseph is her groom; as Aseneth is penitent, so Joseph is again the messenger of God, if not the forgiving God himself.

Aseneth as Wisdom and/or Her Antithesis, the Strange Woman

The tradition of Wisdom personified as female and her antithesis, the Strange or Foreign Woman, looms large in the tale of *Aseneth,*[14] which is in some ways a tale of the transformation of the latter into the former.[15] The opening verses of the story reflect a tension between these two representations. The daughter of an Egyptian priest, Aseneth is by definition foreign in relation to Joseph, yet the narrator claims that she was in no way like (the daughters of) the Egyptians.[16] Further, Aseneth's dress and demeanor will momentarily contradict this claim, for what good Israelite daughter venerates foreign gods (2.5) and clothes herself in their images (3.10)?

Not only Aseneth's initial garments but also her possessions, as described in the opening chapters (her gold and silver, her jewelry and linens) conform to this dual association. Her storerooms filled with costly goods are just such riches as Proverbs 24.3 assigns to Woman Wisdom: "By Wisdom a house is built: by knowledge the rooms are filled with all precious and pleasant riches." But if her rooms allude to Wisdom's house, they initially contain the representations of Aseneth's Egyptian gods and, like Aseneth herself, require transformation. While the presence of such idols is consistent with Aseneth's identity as the daughter of an Egyptian priest and fulfills an important need for the narrative, it also accords with the presentation, particularly in Proverbs, of the Foreign or Strange Woman, who is the antithesis of Woman Wisdom. As the Strange Woman's house is filled with the dead (Prov 9.18), so Aseneth's gods are also ultimately shown to be dead, and deaf and dumb as well (8.5, 12.6).[17]

As with her rooms, Aseneth's garments encode this dual association of the Strange Woman and Woman Wisdom. The garments that Aseneth wears, both at the beginning and the end of the story, accord well with traditions about Woman Wisdom. At the outset of the dramatic action, learning that her parents have returned from their ancestral estate, Aseneth adorns herself in clothing and jewelry that has multiple referents (3.7–11). She wears a linen robe the color of hyacinth, woven with gold, and trousers of gold cloth; over these she wears a gold girdle. Her bracelets and necklace are made of precious stones. A tiara rests on her head, a diadem around her temples. A veil on her head completes the arrangement. In this respect, her clothing resembles that of the virtuous woman in Proverbs 31, who wears fine linen and purple (*byssos* and *porphyra*, the same terms that occur in *Aseneth*). In Sirach, Wisdom wears an ornament of gold, and her bonds are a purple (*hyakinthos*) cord. The wise man "will wear her like a robe of glory and put her on like a crown of gladness" (Sir 6.30–31).[18] But in one crucial detail, Aseneth's initial ensemble points to her foreignness, for her bracelets and necklace are made of precious stones that bear engraved on them the images and names of the gods of Egypt.

After her initial encounter with Joseph, Aseneth strips off all this fine, idolatrous clothing and dons, instead, the black robe of mourning she had worn at the death of her brother. This act thus symbolizes the "death" of the Foreign Woman and the beginning of Aseneth's transformation into Wisdom. In 18.3, after her repentance and transformation, Aseneth again adorns herself in clothing and jewelry that are described almost identically to her initial garments, except that, unsurprisingly, they contain no images or names of Egyptian gods.

Aseneth's representation as the Strange Woman is heightened in the initial scene with her parents (4.1–16). It is not surprising that, greeting her father and mother in clothing that also signifies her identity as a bride, a motif to which we will return, Aseneth immediately finds herself in a discussion with her father on the subject of marriage.

Pentephres proposes to marry Aseneth to Joseph, whom he describes as "a man who reveres God" (*theosebēs anēr*) and who is temperate and a virgin like Aseneth herself. Aseneth responds with horrified anger. Recounting a version of the story found in Genesis 39, in which, contrary to the biblical text, Joseph did, indeed, sleep with Potiphar's wife, she accuses her father of wishing to enslave her to a foreigner and counters that rather than marry Joseph, she will instead marry the firstborn son of Pharaoh.[19] The narrator's voice informs us that Pentephres was ashamed to speak any further with his brazen daughter. By her response, the as yet untransformed Aseneth is here an exemplar of the Foreign/Strange Woman and of the person devoid of Wisdom. As in Proverbs 9.13, the Strange Woman is foolish (*aphrōn*), arrogant (*thraseia*), and without proper understanding, so Aseneth is ignorant (of the truth about Joseph, as demonstrated by the false rumors she accepts), foolish, arrogant, and lacking in filial piety.

This portrait of Aseneth as the paradigm of the Strange Woman is further reinforced in subsequent scenes. On the heels of Aseneth's rejection of her father's suggestion that she marry Joseph, a courtier announces Joseph's imminent arrival, whereupon Aseneth flees back to her upper chambers. At the sight of the glorious Joseph, whose appearance I will consider later, Aseneth realizes instantly the error of her prior judgments. The language she uses is identical to that of Proverbs 8.5: "*aphrōn kai thraseia.*"[20]

As Aseneth has seen Joseph, so, too, Joseph has seen Aseneth at her window. In lovely ironic reciprocity, Joseph initially makes the same erroneous assumptions about Aseneth that she previously made about him. Imagining Aseneth to be a foreign woman, who, like other Egyptian women, desires to seduce him, Joseph asks Pentephres to send her away. The narrator informs us that many Egyptian women, including all the wives and daughters of Egyptian officials, were overcome by sexual desire for Joseph, so great was his beauty. Joseph, it turns out, was able to resist the advances of these women by remembering the commandments of his father Jacob to stay away from intercourse with foreign women, which is "perdition and corruption" (7.6). Although absent in the biblical text, Jacob's "commandments" are found in some rabbinic sources and in *Jubilees* 39.6–8, where the commandment is, however, to stay away not from strange women but from the wives of other men.[21] The message here is clear: Joseph initially perceives Aseneth as a foreign woman, with whom intercourse (*koinōnia*) is death.

Aseneth's representation as Strange or Foreign Woman is most apparent in a scene that transpires shortly thereafter. In response to Joseph's characterization of his daughter, Pentephres responds that Aseneth is in fact not a foreigner but his daughter and a virgin who detests men. He offers to have Joseph meet Aseneth, whom he designates as Joseph's sister (7.8). Rejoicing that Aseneth is a virgin who detests men, Joseph agrees. After her mother brings Aseneth down to meet Joseph, Pentephres suggests that Aseneth kiss Joseph, whom he calls "your brother." But when Aseneth attempts to comply, Joseph balks. Putting his right hand on Aseneth's chest, he utters a long speech, asserting that "a man who reveres God" (*theosebēs anēr*), blesses God with his mouth, eats blessed bread, drinks a blessed cup, and is anointed with blessed oil cannot possibly "kiss a foreign woman, who blesses dead and deaf idols with her mouth, eats the bread of strangling from their table, and drinks the cup of ambush from their libations and is anointed with the ointment of perdition." Pentephres' assertions aside, Aseneth remains a foreign woman, and Joseph will not have any physical contact with her that might be construed as "*koinōnia*." (This prohibition, though, apparently does not prevent him from placing his hand against her chest!)

Still, within this same scene, Aseneth's identity as Strange Woman and as Wisdom are intermingled. First, there are the contradictory assessments in the mouths, respectively, of Pentephres and Joseph. Second, Aseneth has already demonstrated the beginnings of her transformation to Wisdom when, on first seeing Joseph, she correctly perceives both his true identity and the error of her earlier ignorance. Third, in her compliant obedience to her father and mother, she has resumed the role of dutiful daughter, consonant with the idea of filial piety as an aspect of wisdom.

In addition, a small element in these same scenes also points to Aseneth's beginning transformation into Wisdom. When Pentephres introduces the now dutiful Aseneth to Joseph, he remarks upon the affinity between the two: "Greet your brother, for he is a virgin as you are today, and detests all foreign [or: strange] women as you detest all foreign men" (8.1). Only three verses earlier, Aseneth was said to detest men in general, but now her animosity is directed specifically or else particularly at foreign men. At least in the shorter version, which, unlike the longer, does not subsequently catalogue misandry as one of Aseneth's sins, this precision may mitigate her hatred of men, transforming it from misandry to a virtue and an analogy to the wise son's rejection of strange women.

In addition, the designation of Aseneth as Joseph's sister points to the underlying framework of the traditions in Proverbs.[22] Consider, for example, Proverbs 7.4–5:

> My son, keep my words and store up my commandments with you;
> Keep my commandments and live . . .
> Say to Wisdom, you are my sister
> and call insight your intimate friend,
> that they may keep you from the strange woman
> from the adulteress with her smooth words.[23]

Of particular interest is the translation of the Old Greek, which seems to speak only of one woman, the "strange and wicked one," rather than two, the Strange Woman and the adulteress. In fact, the Old Greek reading makes sense of *Aseneth* 7.6, where Jacob taught his sons to guard themselves from foreign women, whereas *Jubilees* 39.6, perhaps drawing on the Hebrew, has Joseph remember Jacob's teachings to guard himself from any woman who belongs to another man.[24]

Early sections of the story thus cast Aseneth primarily as the Strange Woman, with hints of her true or ultimate identity as Wisdom intermingled. Many of Aseneth's characteristics are equally those of Wisdom, from such general traits as her beauty to more idiosyncratic details such as her height.[25] In classic praises of Wisdom found in Wisdom of Solomon 6–11, for instance, or Sirach 24, Wisdom is beautiful, radiant, pure. Once Aseneth's transformation begins, the depiction of her as Wisdom intensifies.

For instance, immediately after Joseph refuses to let Aseneth kiss him, he prays for her transformation. In *Aseneth* 8.11, he says, "And may she drink the cup of your blessing, she whom you chose before she was conceived." The notion that Aseneth was chosen by God before her birth clearly puts her into an elite class that includes only male figures, including Samuel, Jeremiah, Isaac, and Samson, and may reflect

biblical traditions of the pre-existence of Wisdom, as explicitly expressed in Proverbs
8.22; Psalm 139.16,[26] Sirach 24.9; Wisdom of Solomon 9.9, and so forth.

Aseneth's relationship to her seven virgin companions also appears to draw from
an association with Wisdom. That the companions specifically number seven accords
with Proverbs 9.1: "Wisdom has built her house; she has hewn her seven pillars." This
association is at best implicit in the shorter text, but it is much clearer in the longer
version, where in **17.6** the angelic figure blesses the seven virgins and explicitly calls
them "the seven pillars of the City of Refuge." Not only the seven pillars but also the
City of Refuge calls to mind the figure of Woman Wisdom in the book of Proverbs
(e.g., 9.1, etc.).[27]

The association of Wisdom with the word of God may undergird the strange scene
in *Aseneth* 16.6–7, where Aseneth speculates that the newly materialized honeycomb
has come forth from the angel's mouth, and he appears to assent, saying, "Blessed are
you, Aseneth, that the secrets of God have been revealed to you." In Sirach, Wisdom
is said to come forth from the mouth of the Most High. Similar imagery occurs in
Proverbs 2.6: "For the Lord gives wisdom; from his mouth come knowledge and
understanding." Honey and honeycombs are also closely associated with Wisdom, as
in Sirach 24.19, where Wisdom herself says, "Come to me, you who desire me, and
eat your fill of my fruits. For the memory of me is sweeter than honey, and the possession of me sweeter than the honeycomb."[28] These passages suggest a complex
relationship between Aseneth and Wisdom, one in which not only is the honeycomb
from the angelic figure's mouth Wisdom, but the consumption of that Wisdom transforms Aseneth not merely into a wise person but into Wisdom herself.

Yet another detail associating Aseneth with Wisdom may be seen in 10.12–13,
where the repentant Aseneth throws her rich clothing and her gold and silver idols out
the window to the poor. That she divests herself of these tangible signs of her former
identity needs no particular explanation, but that she throws them to the poor is more
intriguing. While I will shortly argue that such concern for the poor is associated with
true repentance in Isaiah 58, it is also the case that concern for the poor characterizes
the Virtuous Woman (the human version of Woman Wisdom) in Proverbs 31.20.

The characteristics of Wisdom especially undergird the description of Aseneth's
heavenly counterpart, Metanoia, whose identity is revealed to her by the angelic figure after her transformation.

15.7–8
For Metanoia (Repentance) is a daughter of the Most High, and she appeals to the Most
High on your behalf every hour, and on behalf of all those who repent, because he is the
father of Metanoia and she is the mother of virgins, and at every hour she appeals to him
for those who repent, for she has prepared a heavenly bridal chamber for those who love
her, and she will serve them for eternal time. And Metanoia is a very beautiful virgin,
pure and holy and gentle, and God the Most High loves her, and all the angels stand in
awe of her.

As far as I know, this description of Metanoia, and indeed the entire personification of Metanoia, is unique to the texts of *Aseneth*, and I will return to it in subsequent
chapters. In both versions, Metanoia's attributes are those of Woman Wisdom, particularly in her various virtues, such as beauty, purity, holiness,[29] her intercessory

functions, and God's love for her and those who love her. "I [Wisdom] love those who love me, and those who seek me diligently find me" (Prov 8.17); "The Lord loves those who love her" (Sir 4.14); "The Lord of all loves [Wisdom]" (Wis Sol 8.3); "Wisdom is radiant and unfading, and she is easily discerned by those who love her" (Wis Sol 6.12). Metanoia's hourly petitioning of God on behalf of the repentant resembles Wisdom's daily petitioning of God: "I was daily his delight; rejoicing before him always" (Prov 8.30). To the extent that Metanoia is Aseneth's divine double, Metanoia's traits are also those of Aseneth. As we shall see, these attributes are expanded and given more explicit expression in the longer text.[30]

Aseneth as Daughter

That daughter imagery plays a significant role in the Aseneth story may be signaled by Aseneth's initial appearance in the text in 1.6–8: "And the daughter of Pentephres was a virgin . . . in no ways like the daughters of the Egyptians." The ancient repertoire of daughter imagery pervades the depiction of Aseneth, triggered perhaps by, or at least consistent with, her designation in Genesis as the daughter of Potiphera.

For instance, the portrayal of Aseneth within her secure compound, attended by virgin companions, coheres nicely with the imagery in OG/LXX Psalm 44:

> The daughter of the king, all her glory (is) within
> In many-colored garments, fringed with gold, is she clothed.
> She is led to the king; (the) virgins (following) behind her.[31]

Although some particular difficulties are associated with the translation and interpretation of this verse, it contains some of the central elements of Aseneth's attributes, including her seclusion and her virgin companions. If it is not the impetus for her description in *Aseneth,* it at the very least affirms the appropriateness of the details.

Aseneth as Daughter of Zion

Traditional descriptions of the daughters of Zion as a metaphor for Israel feminized in relation to God may contribute to the depiction of Aseneth, particularly the description of her repentance and the initial divine response. Although much of what Aseneth does conforms to a pattern of ritualized death and funerary practices, it is also strikingly consonant with biblical paradigms.

Consider in particular Isaiah 3.16–26, a prophecy of the fate of the proud daughters of Zion. These verses assert that because the daughters of Zion are haughty, God will afflict them by taking away all their fine clothing and jewelry. Isaiah 3.18–23 contains a long list of the specific items, among which are bracelets, headdresses, sashes, rings, festal robes, mantles, cloaks, linen garments, and veils.

> Instead of perfume, there will be a stench,
> and instead of a sash, a rope;
> and instead of well-set hair, baldness;

and instead of a rich robe, a binding of sackcloth;
instead of beauty, shame . . .
her gates shall lament and mourn;
ravaged, she shall sit upon the ground.

Aseneth's penitence incorporates many of the details here. The text explicitly has her remove her royal robes, her golden girdle, her tiara, her diadem, and her bracelets. If we assume that she removes all of the garments she initially wore in *Aseneth* 3.9–11, we may add to this the details of linen and hyacinth, her necklace, and her headcovering. In their place, she wears a black mourning robe, tied with a rope (10.9–11). In 10.16, she ties a sack about her hips and undoes her carefully braided hair, covering herself with the ashes she procured in 10.3–4 (by sneaking down to the gate past the sleeping gatekeeper) and falling onto the ground.

In the midst of her all-consuming repentance, it is interesting to see that Aseneth discards the trappings of her wealth in a manner that benefits the poor (10.12–14). This is perfectly consonant, however, with an author who consistently appears to consider biblical traditions an authoritative source of descriptive details. In numerous biblical passages, fasting is an integral part of repentance. Isaiah 58 provides a particularly relevant configuration of elements.[32] An acceptable fast is described as one in which the penitent person shares bread with the hungry and covers the naked. For the one who has done so

Then shall your light break forth like the dawn
and your healing shall spring up quickly;
your vindicator [or vindication] shall go before you,
the glory of the Lord shall be your rear guard;
then shall you call, and the Lord will answer;
you shall cry for help, and he will say, Here I am.
. . .Then your light shall rise in the darkness
and your gloom be like the noonday.
The Lord will guide you continually,
and satisfy your needs in parched places,
and make your bones strong;
and you shall be like a watered garden,
like a spring of water,
whose waters never fail.
Your ancient ruins shall be rebuilt
you shall raise up the foundations of many generations;
You shall be called the repairer of the breach,
the restorer of streets to live in.
. . .Then you shall take delight in the Lord,
and I will make you ride upon the heights of the earth;
I will feed you with the heritage of your ancestor Jacob,
for the mouth of the Lord has spoken.

Many of the motifs of this passage are echoed in Aseneth's story. When Aseneth completes her repentance, which began with concern for the poor,[33] the light that breaks forth is precisely the dawn: "And as Aseneth finished confessing to the Lord, behold, the morning star rose in the heaven to the east" (14.1). As Aseneth has cried out for help to God, so now she is answered.

Although the correspondences are by no means identical, both the Isaiah passage and *Aseneth* draw on the identification of the redeemed one with the city. In Isaiah, the city is clearly Jerusalem rebuilt. In *Aseneth*, it would be astonishing if the reference to Jerusalem were explicit, but it is fascinating that Aseneth transformed is called City of Refuge, in whom many nations take refuge. Both Aseneth and the penitent in Isaiah receive new names consonant with their restorative powers.

As in Isaiah, the reward for the righteous person includes food from God, so the angelic figure feeds Aseneth. It may be noteworthy that just as Isaiah identifies that food as "the heritage of your ancestor Jacob," so the angel who feeds Aseneth appears in the form of Joseph, himself the heritage of Jacob. Additionally, of course, not only does Aseneth receive this food from the angelic double of Joseph, but also she ultimately receives Joseph himself.

Aseneth as (Daughter) Jerusalem

Another biblical passage whose imagery may underlie the portrait of Aseneth may be found in Ezekiel 16. There, Jerusalem is depicted as a beautiful woman beloved of God and chosen as his bride, who nevertheless lusts after other men. Although God punishes her for her infidelity, in the end he remembers his covenant with her, forgives her, and enters into an everlasting covenant with her. The correspondence with the tale of *Aseneth* is hardly perfect. As opposed to Jerusalem, Aseneth is always chaste, both in her premarital virginity and in her marital fidelity. But in Ezekiel (and many other biblical traditions), adultery is a favorite metaphor for Israelite idolatry, and Aseneth is clearly an idolater.

Like Jerusalem in Ezekiel 16.3, Aseneth is a foreigner, the daughter of foreigners. After a graphic depiction of the abandonment of the infant Jerusalem in an open field in 16.4–5, the speaker (God) recounts Jerusalem's childhood and maturing: You grew up and became tall . . .[34] your breasts were formed, and your hair had grown; yet you were naked and bare; . . . you were at the age for love. I spread the edge of my cloak over you, and covered your nakedness: I pledged myself to you and entered into a covenant with you." While this passage is by no means identical with the description of Aseneth, it is interesting that Aseneth, too, is described as tall, mature (literally, ripe), and beautiful.

In Ezekiel 16.9–13, God bathes Jerusalem in water, washing off her blood and anointing her with oil. He clothes Jerusalem in embroidered cloth and fine sandals; in fine linen *(byssos)* and hyacinth cloth. So, too, in *Aseneth* 3.9–11, she dresses in a *stolē* of fine linen *(byssos)* and in cloth of hyacinth and gold. God adorns Jerusalem with ornaments: bracelets, a necklace, a nose ring, earrings, and a beautiful crown on her head. Aseneth, too, dons bracelets (head and foot), gold trousers, a necklace, a tiara, a diadem, and a veil. Aseneth wears no crown here, although when she dresses for Joseph in *Aseneth* 18.4, she does indeed don a gold crown. Jerusalem is adorned with silver and gold; if there is an analogue here, it may be in the gold and silver of

Aseneth's idols. Jerusalem becomes exceedingly beautiful, fit to be a queen, and her fame spreads among the nations because of her beauty. So, too, Aseneth is exceedingly beautiful *(Aseneth* 1.6), and the fame of her beauty spreads throughout the land, even to its borders (1.9). Although Aseneth's sins are not precisely those of Jerusalem, as I noted above, they have a comparable effect: both daughters become sick at heart (Ezek 16.30).

It is probably also worth remarking that all this is temple imagery—Jerusalem is the temple as well as Israel, and her sins are partly the idolatrous acts the Israelites commit in the temple itself (Ezek 16.16–22). Both the description of Jerusalem and the description of Aseneth rely on what is almost certainly shared bridal imagery, if not actual practice.

Aseneth as the Female Lover and Divine Bride

While Aseneth's portrayal as the female lover is hardly remarkable in a story that climaxes in marriage, her representation as divine bride is somewhat more significant. That she is such a figure is signaled early in the text. Although the garments and adornments she first puts on at 3.9–11 have multiple associations, their bridal connotation is announced immediately, at 4.2: "And Pentephres and his wife rejoiced in their daughter Aseneth with great gladness, for her parents beheld her adorned as a bride of [G]od." The meaning of "bride of [G]od" *(nymphē theou)* is, however, far from obvious. Convinced that *Aseneth* draws heavily on Egyptian imagery, Philonenko considered this description an allusion to the possible marriage between Aseneth and the son of Pharaoh, since ancient Egyptians believed Pharaoh to be the divine incarnation, and the son of Pharaoh would presumably one day become that incarnation himself. But if so, the allusion is ironic, for Aseneth will become the bride not of an Egyptian god's son but of the true God's son, Joseph. However, the image of divine bride also reflects the numerous images of sacred marriage *(hieros gamos)* within the story, including the unions of Wisdom and the Wise Man, the lovers in Song of Songs, Selene (Moon) and Helios (Sun), God and Israel, and perhaps others.

Consistent with these notions, portions of the text draw particularly on images in Song of Songs. Aseneth's walled residence with its garden and abundant sources of water resonates strongly with passages such as Song of Songs 4.12: "A garden locked is my sister, my bride; a garden locked, a fountain sealed."

The use of imagery from Song of Songs and/or related erotic traditions may also account for the use of sibling terminology to characterize the relationship of Joseph and Aseneth. In the first encounter between the pair, Pentephres characterizes Aseneth as Joseph's sister and Joseph as Aseneth's brother (Song 7.8–8.3).[35] The future bride is called "my sister, my bride" several times in Song of Songs (4.9–10, 4.12, 5.1). Sibling language for the marital relationship also occurs in the Book of Tobit. After the wedding of Sarah and Tobias, Raguel, Sarah's father, tells his new son-in-law that Sarah is now Tobias's sister and that she is his brother.[36] Yet another reference to sibling terminology for spouses appears in the *Genesis Apocryphon* where the wife of Lamech, called Bathenosh, calls her husband "my brother, my lord."[37]

Biblical and "Parabiblical" Components in the Construction of Aseneth's Encounter with the Heavenly Figure (14.1–17.6)

In many ways, the section from 14.1 to 17.6 constitutes the central and critical portion of the story. After Aseneth has abased herself for seven days, culminating in her exculpatory prayer to God, Aseneth sees the morning star rising in the east, which she takes as a sign that God has heard her. Consonant with many ancient narratives, this relatively unremarkable event is immediately followed by an extraordinary one: the heaven splits apart near the morning star, and an indescribable light appears.[38] While Aseneth prostrates herself, a human figure appears out of heaven in Aseneth's chamber, who is clearly an emissary of the divine, if not an actual manifestation of God.

The Greek here is *anthrōpos*, frequently translated as "man." It is usually taken as a generic, signifying not gender but humanity,[39] and occurs in the Old Greek Genesis for the primordial being who is not yet differentiated into male and female.[40] Here, as in Daniel and 1 Enoch, the use of *anthrōpos* apparently signals that this being has the form, although not the identity, of a human. In my earlier translation of *Aseneth*, attempting to avoid an unnecessarily gendered translation, I rendered *anthrōpos* as a "human figure" or a "figure."[41] Here I employ a range of English expressions, all of which translate the same *anthrōpos*, including "figure," "human figure," "angelic figure," and sometimes even "angel."

Seeing the morning star, Aseneth interprets it as evidence of her redemption, saying, " [T]his star is an *angelos*." Construed narrowly, the identification of the star as an *angelos* could mean nothing more than the star's function as a messenger of God, a connotation both of *angelos* itself and of the Hebrew *malach* that *angelos* frequently translates.

Nevertheless, in the construction of this scene, an ancient author steeped in biblical and related "parabiblical" traditions could easily have concluded that repentance is followed by tangible evidence of God's acceptance, which takes the form of an angelic visit. The appearance of the morning star is reminiscent of Isaiah 58.8, considered previously, which connects the breaking forth of the dawn with God's acceptance of the proper fast. Many early Jewish sources, particularly though not exclusively from Greek-speaking communities, evince well-developed beliefs about angels as immortal beings closely associated with God and suggest an identification of angels with stars.[42] From this perspective, Aseneth's perception of the star as *angelos* should be taken as a more direct claim that the star is a divine being, who brings the word of God.

As we shall see in later chapters, many of the specific details of Aseneth's encounter with the angelic double of Joseph are drawn from a wide variety of ancient traditions concerning angels. Nevertheless, two narratives now present in biblical works, one from the Greek additions to the book of Esther and one from Judges, appear to me as strong candidates for the underlying narrative framework.

The so-called Greek additions to the Hebrew book of Esther, the scenes where Esther prepares to plead her people's cause before her husband, the king, and subsequently does so, appear to have strong similarities with Aseneth's encounter with the divine being. If the author(s) of *Aseneth* did not draw directly on this material, some relationship between the two tales seems obvious.

The consonance between Esther and Aseneth extends back to Aseneth's repentance. According to the Hebrew version of Esther, when Esther learns through Mordecai that Haman plans the destruction of the Jews of Susa, she sends word to Mordecai to gather all the Jews to fast on her behalf for three days and three nights. She and her attendants will also fast. "After that," Esther says, "I will go to the king, though it is against the law [to appear before the king unsummoned] and if I perish, I perish."[43] On the third day, Esther puts on her royal clothing and stands in the inner court, where the king can see her. Without any narrative elaboration, he holds out his scepter to her, granting her permission to approach and present her petition, and promises her whatever she wishes, even to half his kingdom. Esther replies with the proper formality: "This is my petition and request: If I have won the king's favor, and if it pleases the king to grant my petition and fulfill my request, let the king and Haman come tomorrow to the banquet that I will prepare for them."[44] Esther's preparation for her audience before the king bears structural resemblance to Aseneth's repentance that prefaces her petition to God. So far, though, the similarities might simply reflect pervasive ancient patterns of preparation for petitioning kings and gods alike in ancient societies.

The writer of the Greek Esther (which contains significant additional passages) concurs with the Hebrew of Esther 4.15–17, but then the Greek narrative diverges. First Mordecai offers a lengthy prayer to God, which again conforms fairly well to ancient patterns of personal prose prayer.[45] Hearing Mordecai's prayer, Esther responds as follows:

> Then Queen Esther, seized with deadly anxiety, fled to the Lord. She took off her splendid apparel and put on the garments of distress and mourning, and instead of costly perfumes she covered her head with ashes and dung, and she utterly humbled her body; every part that she loved to adorn she covered with her tangled hair.[46]

Aseneth, too, does just these things, although in far greater detail, and for a full seven days. Esther then utters a prayer to God that reflects many of the concerns of the writer of the Greek editions, raised by the apparent peculiarities of the Hebrew. These concerns include Esther's seemingly nonchalant wearing of pagan royal clothing, which the author may have assumed contained representations of pagan deities, like Aseneth's robes (or perhaps the crown?); her apparent consumption of unkosher food; and her participation in sexual intercourse within the context of an (illicit) intermarriage.

> Save us by your hand, and help me, who am alone and have no helper but you, O Lord. You have knowledge of all things, and you know that I hate the splendor of the wicked and abhor the bed of the uncircumcised and of any alien. You know my necessity—that I abhor the sign of my proud position, which is upon my head on days when I appear in public. I abhor it like a filthy rag, and I do not wear it on the days when I am at leisure. And your servant has not eaten at Haman's table, and I have not honored the king's feast or drunk the wine of libation.[47]

Still on the third day, having completed her prayer, Esther again arrays herself in glorious garments,[48] as Aseneth will shortly do at the direction of the angel. Although she is terrified, she looks radiant and happy, as though beloved.[49] Accompanied by two maids, she stands before the king, who is himself "seated on his royal throne, clothed in the full array of his majesty, all covered with gold and precious stones."[50] At the sight of this awesome and angry figure, Esther faints, a response similar to the prostration of Aseneth before the awesome figure of the angel. When Esther does this, her husband is moved (by God) to kindness and comforts her in his arms. Both his words and their implicit assocations are strikingly similar to those spoken by the angel to Aseneth: "What is it, Esther?" he says. "I am your brother [*adelphos*]; take courage [*tharsei*]; You shall not die."[51] Although the text does not say so explicitly, it is obvious that the king also does what angels generally do in such situations, namely he raises the queen to her feet (particularly since she will shortly faint and fall a second time and so must somehow have regained her standing position in the interim).

Esther's own words make explicit the angelic association. Once the king has touched her with his scepter, granting her permission to speak, she says to him: "I saw you, my lord, like an angel of God and my heart was shaken with fear at your glory."[52] So, too, does Aseneth view not only the appearance of an actual angel who looks just like Joseph, her "brother" and eventual husband, but also the initial appearance of the human Joseph, who looks just like a king and the god Helios.

The second pertinent biblical narrative is Judges 13, whose relationship to *Aseneth* is even more obvious than the Esther account. Judges 13 relates two encounters between an angel of the Lord and the future parents of Samson, a man named Manoah and his unnamed wife. In the first visitation, the angel appears only to the wife and announces to her that although she has been childless, she will now conceive and bear a son who will deliver Israel from the Philistines. He instructs her to abstain from alcohol and unclean food.[53]

The wife then reports her experience to her husband, saying, "A man of God [*'ish ha-'elohim*] came to me, and his appearance was like that of an angel of God [*malach ha-'elohim*], most awe-inspiring; I did not ask him where he came from and he did not tell me his name."[54] Manoah then prays for God to send the angel a second time. Again the angel appears to the wife and again the husband is not present, but this time, she runs and brings the husband, and the remainder of the encounter involves all three.

After the angel repeats all he had said to the woman the first time, Manoah invites the angel to stay for a meal of cooked goat. The angel declines, saying that he will not eat their food, but proposes that they offer a burnt offering to God instead. While the wife of Manoah explicitly had not asked the angel his name, her husband now does so, ostensibly to honor him when his prediction of the birth of Samson comes true. But the angel replies, "Why do you ask my name? It is too wonderful." Manoah then offers the goat and grain on a rock altar, and the angel ascends to heaven in the sacrificial flames as Manoah and his wife watch. Terrified, they fall to the ground. Perceiving the true identity of the angel, Manoah fears that he and his wife will now die, having seen God, but his wife wisely points out that God would not have accepted their offering or sent the angel to announce the future birth of their son if he had intended for them to die. And indeed, they do not die, and they do have a son, Samson.

Aseneth's encounter with the angelic figure sufficiently resembles Judges 13 (and to a lesser extent, the appearance of an angel to Gideon in Judg 6) that it seems reasonable to propose that this portion of *Aseneth* is modeled after the Judges narrative. Further, as I will argue in the next chapter, the revisions of the longer version bring the story into even closer conformity with Judges 13, suggesting that the writer(s) of the longer *Aseneth* took Judges 13 to be the subtext of the narrative.

Already in the shorter version, though, the similarities are considerable. Both recount the appearance of an angel[55] to a woman, who brings similar tidings to each: the announcement of Samson's conception, birth, and destiny to his mother; the announcement of her marriage to Joseph and destiny to Aseneth. Both figures are suitably awesome, although the description in Judges is minimal and that in *Aseneth* extensive. As the future mother of Samson does not ask the angel where he comes from, nor does he tell her his name, so Aseneth does not ask the figure where he comes from, nor does he tell her his name (*Aseneth* 14.5–7). Interestingly, Aseneth does ask the figure who he is, but she carefully refrains from asking his actual name. His answer is similarly careful; he identifies himself as "commander of the house of the Lord, and commander of all the army of the Most High" but does not tell her his name (14.7).

As Manoah offers the angel a meal, following the angel's announcement, so, too, Aseneth offers to prepare food for her visitor, although interestingly, while Manoah offers cooked goat, Aseneth proposes a table of bread and good wine (15.14). In *Aseneth,* this offer triggers the scene with the honeycomb and the bees, which has, of course, no analogue in Judges. At the conclusion, though, of the honeycomb episode and the drama of the bees, the angelic figure "touched the honeycomb, and fire rose up from the table and consumed the comb. The burning honeycomb exuded a sweet odor" (17.3). Shortly thereafter, the angel instructs Aseneth to remove the table. As she does so, the angel disappears, and "Aseneth saw something like a fiery chariot being taken up in the heaven to the east" (17.6). In Judges, the disappearance of the angel occurs in similar fashion: when Manoah offers the goat as a sacrifice, the angel ascends in the flame of the altar and disappears. In the remainder of the story, unsurprisingly, the angel's predictions come true, as do those of Aseneth's angelic visitor.

Many other elements of Aseneth's encounter with this angelic figure display affinities to biblical and parabiblical traditions. The opening dialogue between Aseneth and the enigmatic figure follows the language of biblical encounters between key male figures (particularly Abraham and Moses) and the divine[56]: "[O]ut of heaven a human figure came toward her. And he stood at her head and called her Aseneth. . . . And the figure called to her a second time and said, 'Aseneth, Aseneth'" (14.4, 14.6). This dialogue is virtually identical to that between Aseneth and her father in *Aseneth* 4.5: "And Pentephres said to his daughter, 'Child,' and she said, 'Here I am, Lord.'"[57]

When Aseneth looks up to see the speaker, she beholds a being who resembles Joseph in every way but who clearly is not the human Joseph. Rather, the figure's primary characteristic seems to be light: his face is like lightning, his eyes like the light of the sun, his hair like a burning flame, and his feet like iron from the forge. Descriptions of angels as beings of light occur in numerous ancient sources, as I will explore further in chapter 4; here I am particularly interested in biblical paradigms. In the opening chapter of Ezekiel, the visionary describes "the appearance of the likeness of the glory of the Lord."[58]

> [S]eated above the likeness of a throne was something that seemed like a human form. Upward from what appeared like the loins I saw something like gleaming amber, something that looked like fire all around; and downward from what looked like the loins I saw something that looked like fire, and there was a splendor all around.[59]

Daniel 10.2–6 contains a vision of a being similar to the figure in *Aseneth,* which the visionary records seeing under the following circumstances:

> At that time, I, Daniel, had been mourning for three weeks. I had eaten no rich food, no meat or wine had entered my mouth, and I had not anointed myself at all, for three full weeks. On the twenty-fourth day of the first month, as I was standing on the bank of the great river (that is, the Tigris), I looked up and saw a man clothed in linen, with a belt of gold from Uphaz around his waist. His body was like beryl, his face like lightning, his eyes like flaming torches, his arms and legs like the gleam of burnished bronze.[60]

Aseneth's initial response to this vision is to throw herself back down on the floor in fear and trembling. In many biblical texts (Hagar in Gen 16.13, Gideon in Judg 6, the parents of Samson in Judg 13), humans who have seen such manifestations express the fear that anyone who sees the divine risks death (although, ironically, none of them ever actually dies from this!). In Exodus 33.20, God tells Moses that no one can see the face of God and live. In narratives that describe encounters between humans and angels, terror and prostrating oneself are typical responses on the part of the human (Dan 8.17–19, 10.9; Judg 13, etc.).[61] Aseneth's responses here appear closely patterned on the biblical narratives.

The angel's response is also fairly typical of these narratives: he admonishes her not to be afraid and tells her to stand up. This, by the way, is also precisely what Ahasueras does for Esther, reminding us that these actions have their analogue in the protocols of royal palaces.

When Aseneth stands up, the figure instructs her to remove the black garment of mourning and exchange it for a brand-new garment and the double girdle of her virginity and to shake off the ashes and to wash her face in living (probably meaning running) water. Change of clothing is a typical feature in rituals of transformation. But it is also consonant with texts such as LXX/OG Psalm 29.12–13 ("You have turned my mourning into dancing; you have taken off my sackcloth and clothed me with joy")[62] and the fascinating vision of the high priest Joshua in Zechariah 3.1–5. There, an angel shows the prophet a vision of the high priest Joshua dressed in filthy clothes, standing before the angel of the Lord, with the Adversary ready to accuse the priest.

> The angel said to those who were standing before him, "Take off his filthy clothes." And to him he said, "See, I have taken your guilt away from you, and I will clothe you with festal apparel." And I said, "Let them put a clean turban on his head." So they put a clean turban on his head and clothed him with the apparel; and the angel of the Lord was standing by.[63]

Aseneth's Name Inscribed in the Book of Life (15.2b–3)

In *Aseneth* 15.3, after Aseneth has followed the angel's directions to wash her face and change her clothing, and after the angel has three times exhorted her to take courage, he now informs Aseneth that her name is inscribed forever in the Book of Life.[64] The author may here draw on the tradition of a primordial book recording allotted lifespans, which we find in numerous texts, such as Psalm 138.16:[65] "In your [God's] book were written all the days that were formed for me, when none of them as yet existed."[66] Particularly interesting is a reference in Isaiah 4.3 that refers to "everyone who has been recorded for life in Jerusalem." Not only does this passage come close on the heels of the description of the fallen daughters of Zion, whose actions, I have suggested, provide a pattern for Aseneth's repentance,[67] but additional verses suggest at least a general consonance with what follows that repentance.

> Seven women shall take hold of one man in that day, saying, "We will eat our own bread and wear our own clothes: just let us be called by your name: take away our disgrace. On that day the branch of the Lord shall be beautiful and glorious, and the fruit of the land shall be the pride and glory of the survivors of Israel. Whoever is left in Zion and remains in Jerusalem will be called holy, everyone who has been recorded for life in Jerusalem, once the Lord has washed aware the filth of the daughters of Zion and cleansed the blood-stains of Jerusalem from its midst by spirit of judgment and by a spirit of burning. Then the Lord will create over the whole site of Mount Zion and over its places of assembly a cloud by day and smoke and the shining of a flaming fire by night. It will serve as a pavillion, a shade by day from the heat, and a refuge and a shelter from the storm and rain.

While Exodus imagery appears to undergird this description and thus perhaps to be internally anachronistic for *Aseneth*, the points of resonance with our *Aseneth* are intriguing. The seven companions whom the angel blesses at Aseneth's behest may allude to the seven women. As the cleansing of the paradigmatic daughter of Zion entails a "spirit of judgment" and a "spirit of burning," so, too, Aseneth's repentance and cleansing involve judgment (conveyed by the angelic figure) and the burning of the honeycomb. As all who remain in Jerusalem will be called holy and recorded for life, so, too, Aseneth is for the first time called holy in *Aseneth* 19.2, by Joseph when they are reunited, and so, too, is her name inscribed in the Book of Life. And, finally, as the canopy that God now provides for Zion will be a refuge and a shelter (*skepē*), so Aseneth as City of Refuge will provide refuge for many nations and shelter (*skepazō*) for many peoples.

Aseneth's Name Change (15.6)

After announcing her forthcoming marriage to Joseph, the figure informs Aseneth that she will no longer be called by that name but rather City of Refuge (*polis katafygēs*). This is clearly an allusion to the six biblical cities of refuge designated as safe havens for those who unintentionally commit homicide.[68]

Many biblical texts associate God with tower and fortress imagery, such as Proverbs 18.10–11, "The name of the Lord is a strong tower." If the designation of Aseneth as City of Refuge has some basis in the constellation of biblical sources and imagery from which the author(s) drew so frequently, it may perhaps be seen particularly in Psalm 91:

> You who live in the shelter of the Most High,
> who abide in the shadow of the Almighty,
> will say to the Lord, "My refuge and my fortress,
> My God in whom I trust."
> . . . Because you have made the Lord your refuge,

the Most High your dwelling place,
no evil shall befall you,
no scourge come near your tent.
For he will command his angels concerning you
to guard you in all your ways.
On their hands they will bear you up,
so that you will not dash your foot against a stone.
You will tread on the lion and the adder,
the young lion and the serpent
you will trample underfoot.[69]
Those who love me, I will deliver;
I will protect those who know my name.
When they call to me, I will answer them;
I will be with them in trouble,
I will rescue them and honor them.
With long life I will satisfy them,
and show them my salvation.
(Ps. 91.1–3, 9–16)

These verses may also contribute to the construction of the final portion of the story (chaps. 22–29), which does indeed demonstrate God's deliverance of Aseneth, who knows his name and calls upon God when she is in trouble: God rescues Aseneth, satisfies her with long life, and, in the earlier scene with the bees, shows her visually his salvation.[70]

The Mystery of the Honeycomb and the Bees (15.14–17.7)

After she blesses God, Aseneth asks (somewhat rhetorically) to speak and invites the angelic figure to eat and drink before he leaves. As I have already indicated, this scene has particularly close affinities with the narratives of Judges 6 and 13, as well as with that of the Greek Esther and perhaps also with the less detailed traditions about Wisdom's table (such as those in Prov 9.1–6).

The Mystery of the Honeycomb (16.1–9)

In response to Aseneth's offer to prepare him a meal, the angelic figure tells Aseneth to bring him a honeycomb as well, an element that is clearly absent from the narratives in Judges 6, Judges 13, Esther, and others that we have so far considered. Aseneth replies that she will send to the family estate for a honeycomb, but the angel tells her that she will find one in her chamber. And, indeed, on the table she discovers a snow-white honeycomb, whose fragrance is like the scent of life.

The ensuing dialogue between Aseneth and the angel is frustratingly esoteric. The angel asks Aseneth, "Why did you say 'There is no honeycomb in my house,' and behold, you bring this to me?" Aseneth speculates that the honeycomb might have come from the angel's own mouth, "since its fragrance is like the fragrance of perfume."

The angel's response confirms Aseneth's wisdom, putting his hand on her head, the angel says:

16.7

Blessed are you, Aseneth, that the secrets of God have been revealed to you; and blessed are those who devote themselves to God in repentance, for they shall eat from this comb. For this honey the bees of the paradise of delight have made, and the angels of God eat of it, and all who eat of it shall not die for eternity.

And after eating some of the honey himself, the angel places it in Aseneth's mouth as well. Aseneth's consumption of angelic food must signify her transformation (or perhaps initiation) into the angelic ranks and guarantees her ultimate immortality.

Both honey and honeycombs are featured predominantly in ancient Wisdom traditions, where honey is the food of the righteous, although without any explicit mystical associations. "My son, eat honey, for it is good, and the drippings of the honeycomb are sweet to your taste. Know that wisdom is such to your soul; if you find it, you will find a future, and your hope will not be cut off."[71] In fact, this particular passage has interesting affinities with the scene in *Aseneth,* whom the angel compels to *find* the honeycomb, who tastes the sweet extrusion of the honeycomb, and whose discovery brings her precisely what Proverbs promises: a secure future, both in this life and after death.[72]

The Mystery of the Bees (16.10–17.3)

After Aseneth eats from the honeycomb, the angelic figure calls forth bees from the honeycomb, which encircle Aseneth. The passage begins with a strange reference that led some earlier scholars to identify the text as Christian. The heavenly figure traces a path on the honeycomb that can be read as crosslike, leaving a bloodlike trace. The significance of this symbol, and indeed of the entire following scene, is not explained in either the shorter or the longer text.

Bees then come forth out of the hive of the honeycomb, attired in garments and adornments that echo particularly the appearance of Joseph. As he wears a white chiton, so the bees' bodies are white. As he wears a purple chiton of fine linen woven with gold, so the bees have purple wings, the color of hyacinth and as golden thread. As he wears a golden crown, so the bees have gold diadems and sharp stingers.[73] These bees swarm around Aseneth, while "other bees, as large as queen bees, attach themselves to her lips." The figure commands them to go away to their own place (*topos*), whereupon the bees leave Aseneth and fall down dead. He then commands them to arise and go back to their place, whereupon they fly to the courtyard. When the figure asks Aseneth whether she has seen ("perceived"?) what was said, Aseneth replies in the affirmative. The figure replies, "So shall be the words I have spoken to you."

The entire scene with the bees has evoked little persuasive analysis. Philonenko points, for instance, to the association of bees with Neith, while Burchard considers, with little enthusiasm, a range of interpretive options: the appearance of the bees, understood as angels, demonstrates that the honey truly is angelic.[74] The clothing of the bees is clearly significant and associates them with Joseph and with Aseneth, with royal garb, with priestly clothing, and presumably with angels as well.

Unlike many elements in *Aseneth*, the scene with the bees has no obvious and necessary connection to biblical and other traditional motifs and imagery. In chapter 6, I will argue that the key to understanding the mystery of the bees may be found in Neoplatonic symbolism of the bee as the righteous soul awaiting (re)incarnation. Nevertheless, it is worth observing an intriguing possible association with Psalm 117.10.[75]

> All the nations surrounded me
> In the name of the Lord I cut them off
> They surrounded me, surrounded me on every side
> In the name of the Lord, I cut them off
> They surrounded me like bees
> They were extinguished.[76]
> In the name of the Lord I cut them off.

At the conclusion of this scene, the figure touches the honeycomb, and it is consumed by fire that rises up from the table, exuding a sweet odor as it burns. This is clearly an allusion to sacrifice, particularly as described in Judges 6 and 13.

The Ascent of the Angelic Figure (17.6–7)

In the shorter text, the figure now instructs Aseneth to remove the table. As she turns to do so, the figure disappears, and Aseneth glimpses something like a fiery chariot being taken up to heaven in the east. While this description recalls the disappearance of the angelic being in both Judges 6 and 13, it also draws on the ascension of Elijah into heaven in 2 Kings 2.11: "As they [Elisha and Elijah] continued walking and talking, a chariot of fire and horses of fire separated the two of them, and Elijah ascended into heaven in a whirlwind." This entire description once again recalls Joseph's entrance in *Aseneth* 5.5.

Aseneth's Angelic Transfiguration

A few verses later, anticipating Joseph's arrival, Aseneth instructs a young female attendant to bring "pure water from the spring," presumably the spring that runs through the courtyard in 2.20 and alludes to the rivers that watered the Garden of Eden. Looking into her reflection in this water, Aseneth is transfigured: her face is "like the sun," and her eyes are "like the rising morning star" (18.7). This constellation of images appears in Song of Songs 6.10: "[W]ho is this that looks forth like the dawn, fair as the moon, bright as the sun?"

Taken together with her garment of light, this scene affirms Aseneth's angelic transformation. It may also allude to the transformation of Moses in Exodus 34.29–34, which recounts that when Moses came down from Sinai, he did not know that his face shone because he had been talking to God. After this experience, Moses veils his face before the Israelites except when he goes to speak with God. Such an association lends the veiling of Aseneth an alternative interpretation. In subsequent Jewish mystical traditions, Moses' face was believed to shine with the reflection of God's glory. Aseneth's veiling may be analogous to that of Moses: just as Moses spoke with God face to face and beheld an aspect of God, so Aseneth has conversed with God or at least with God's manifestation in the form of the angel. Therefore, like Moses, her face shines and requires a veil to protect others from the brilliance of her face.

Part Two: The Plot against Aseneth and Joseph in the Seven Lean Years (22–29)

Scholars are much divided on the nature and origins of chapters 22 through 29. The tale they tell is in no way central to the story of the marriage nor of Aseneth's transformation, and there seems to be no inherent reason why *Aseneth* could not have ended with the birth of Manasseh and Ephraim in 21.8. Some scholars have thus suggested that the second portion constitutes a supplement to the first, while others have argued for its integral connection. Burchard, for instance, argues that "Part II is so close to I in both style and thought content that it is not likely to have come from a different hand."[77] His judgment here, as at numerous points, is affected by his belief that the longer text precedes the shorter, since it is in fact true that chapters 22–29 of the longer version display considerable similarities of style and detail with the previous chapters, similarities that may have more to do with the redactor than with the underlying text(s). Philonenko, who recognized that the disparity between the two parts is less apparent in the longer text, took a more or less agnostic stance on this question.[78] It seems to me not inconceivable that chapters 1–21 were composed separately from chapters 22–29, but if so, the redactors of the longer version had both portions before them, since many of the revisions in 22–29 are consistent with revisions in chapters 1–21.[79]

That chapters 22–29 are also grounded in traditional elements seems clear. The story is now set in the seven lean years and may draw on elements of Genesis 48, which tells how Jacob and his sons come to Egypt, and on Genesis 49 in its presentation of Joseph's brothers.[80] It functions, among other things, to explain how Joseph ruled Egypt instead of Pharaoh's son (a tradition not found in the biblical narrative but found, inter alia, in Artapanus[81] and in the relatively late rabbinic anthology of *Pirkê de Rabbi Eliezer*)[82] by killing off Pharaoh's proper heir, his firstborn son, and having Pharaoh designate Joseph as his heir (Joseph was, after all, described in the text as Pharaoh's son). The last paragraph also accounts for the fact that Joseph's descendants do not continue to rule in Egypt, when Joseph cedes the throne to Pharoah's younger son. This last, by the way, constitutes an explanation of the title of Joseph in Genesis as "*'av l' Pharaoh*" (father to Pharaoh), and, interestingly, here and only here, both the shorter and longer texts say that "Joseph was *like* a father to him in Egypt." It is not inconceivable that chapters 22–29 also have their basis in Genesis 50:15, whose repeated emphasis on the crime of Joseph's brothers and the wrong they did to Joseph might have resulted in the composition of an additional story of such wrong, beyond the biblical narrative of their selling him into slavery. Finally, it is worth pointing out that for those scholars who emphasize the similarity between *Aseneth* and Greco-Roman novels, chapters 22–29 are seen to provide the elements of adventure, threatening the chastity of the heroine that typifies such novels, although usually prior to the marriage, not subsequently.

Miscellaneous Instances

Finally, a small number of other details in the text may have their origins in biblical and parabiblical traditions. The description of the courtyard, the fruit trees, and the river and spring that water it are strongly reminiscent of both the description of the Garden of Eden in Genesis 2.8–14 and the descriptions of paradise in numerous Jewish and Christian texts. One version of 2 Enoch 8 offers a fine example of the description of Paradise in the third heaven:

> [T]hat place is inconceivably pleasant. . . . I saw the trees in full flower. And their fruits were ripe and pleasant-smelling, with every food in yield and giving off profusely a pleasant fragrance. And in the midst (of them was) the tree of life, . . . indescribable for pleasantness and fine fragrance, and more beautiful than any (other) created thing that exists. . . . [I]t covers the whole of Paradise. And it has something of every orchard tree and of every fruit. . . . And paradise is in between the corruptible and the incorruptible. And two streams come forth, one a source of honey and milk, and source which produces oil and wine. And it is divided into 4 parts, and they go around with a quiet movement. And they come out into the paradise of Edem.[83]

Each of the four gates of Pentephres' courtyard was guarded by eighteen armed strong young men.[84] Although nothing more of significance is said of these guards, they are reminiscent of the angels who guard the entrances to the various heavens as well as of the cherubim and sword that God placed at the entrance to the Garden of Eden after the expulsion of Adam.[85]

The description of Aseneth's idols as silver and gold (2.4, 10.13) and dead and mute (12.6) echoes material that occurs both in Psalms 115.4–8 and 135.15–18:[86]

> The idols of the nations are silver and gold,
> the work of human hands.
> They have mouths, but do not speak;
> They have eyes, but they do not see;
> and there is no breath in their mouths.[87]

Interestingly, few other passages explicitly describe idols as silver and gold.[88] No other biblical passages combine in one place these various attributes of idols. Thus it seems possible, though clearly not certain, that *Aseneth* draws precisely on the constellation in the Psalms.[89]

One other small but interesting detail in the description of Aseneth's repentance may have its origins in an interpretive process. The text claims that the robe Aseneth dons for her repentance is the one she wore when her brother died. This detail has been seen as evidence of a rabbinic mentality behind the text. It has been thought to resolve concern over how Aseneth as a woman could inherit from her parents, in demonstrating that her parents' male heir, her brother, had previously died, allowing her to inherit in accordance with rabbinic law.[90] But we can also easily envision an author who needed to show readers how an eighteen year-old unmarried, wealthy young woman was in possession of appropriate penitent garb and who answered the question with the story of a deceased brother. Surely, such a story reflects the reality of the ancient world, where even among the elite, many children died before they reached maturity.[91] But conceivably the author found the language of Psalm 34.13–14[92] a useful resource:

> I wore sackcloth
> I afflicted myself with fasting . . .
> as though I grieved for a friend or a brother
> I went about as one who laments for a mother
> bowed down, and in mourning.[93]

Conclusion

Throughout this chapter, we have seen evidence that the basic framework of *Aseneth* and many of its narrative details are consistent with traditional elements and paradigms and are likely to draw heavily on those materials, if not to have originated with them. Further indication of the "biblical" associations of these materials is evidenced precisely by their treatment in the longer narrative, where textual allusions are frequently made explicit, expanded, and elaborated upon.

The next chapter, then, compares readings from the shorter and longer reconstructions of the text. In doing so, I intend to develop my thesis that the shorter text precedes the longer and that the longer text expands upon the shorter in a consistent manner, identifying and addressing or resolving anomalies and rendering biblical imagery much more explicit, with closer conformity to biblical texts.

Yet it is important to recognize that many elements of the stories have no precise analogue in biblical and parabiblical traditions and that the work of these two chapters still leaves many details "unexplained." In chapters 4, 5, and 6, I hope to demonstrate that beyond these traditional frameworks, the author(s) and redactor(s) of *Aseneth* drew heavily on a rich and diverse assortment of ancient paradigms of encounters with divine beings, for both the narrative and the details of the story.

NOTES

1. In the preliminary version of this study (Kraemer, "Aseneth"), I utilized the category of "midrash" to analyze the composition of *Aseneth* out of certain kinds of questions and use of traditional materials, particularly those transmitted in Jewish scripture. On further reflection, I have chosen to avoid such language, primarily for two reasons. First, the terminology of midrash is closely associated with particular Jewish circles and traditions, especially those rabbis and rabbinical schools associated with the formulation and transmission of the Mishnah, Tosefta, and both Talmudim, whose actual connections with *Aseneth* are tenuous at best. Second, to call the process of *Aseneth*'s composition midrashic may, for some readers, suggest that

Aseneth is definitively the work of self-conscious Jewish production, a position I by no means intend (see chapter 9). In fact, whether Christians engage in the kinds of interpretive techniques that might be categorized as "midrash" is a complex issue. Clearly, Christians do compose narratives out of biblical (and other traditional) material, as the gospels amply demonstrate. For some useful discussion about possible differences in Christian and Jewish interpretive techniques and concerns, see James L. Kugel and Rowan A. Greer, *Early Biblical Interpretation* (Philadelphia: Westminster Press, 1986).

2. Kugel, *In Potiphar's House.*

3. This is the stance also of the *Testament of Joseph.* But whether the *Testament of Joseph* can be classed as demonstrably early and Jewish is, as with *Aseneth*, highly problematic. As de Jonge writes, in their present form, the *Testaments of the Twelve Patriarchs* are demonstrably Christian and date to the latter half of the second century C.E. Although many scholars have argued that the present form represents Christian redaction of earlier Jewish work (dated by various scholars as early as the mid-second century B.C.E. , on which, see e.g., Howard C. Kee's discussion in *OTP* 1:777–78), de Jonge cautions that "Christian passages cannot be removed without damaging the fabric of large sections of the work" and concludes that "[i]t is, in fact, uncertain whether one should speak of a Christian redaction of an existing Jewish *T.12 P.* or of a Christian composition" (Marinus de Jonge, "Patriarchs, Testaments of the Twelve," ABD 5:183; see also Marinus de Jonge, *The Testaments of the Twelve Patriarchs: A Study of their Text, Composition and Origin* [Leiden: E. J. Brill, 1953], and the discussion in Sparks, *AOT* 508–12).

4. See, however, the discussion of Ps. Philo's treatment of Joseph in chapter 7. Ps. Philo is usually dated to the late first century C.E., based in part on arguments that it relies on a "Palestinian" biblical text type that was probably suppressed after 100 C.E., and on the fact that it shows no clear awareness of the destruction of the temple in 70 C.E. (see D. J. Harrington, *OTP* 2:299).

5. See the appendix.

6. Burchard, *"Joseph and Aseneth,"* 184, identifies some of the obvious biblical "sources," including Genesis and Judg 13, and writes that "[t]he prayers . . . meditations . . . and eulogies . . . could hardly have been composed without knowledge of traditional forms of such devotional texts" (185). Philonenko's notes to the text are replete with instances of similar and parallel phrases in various ancient sources, biblical and otherwise, but he does not expand on the significance of such similarities for the composition of the text. Aptowitzer, "Asenath," 239–306) notes many parallels to biblical materials, but his assumption that the original text was Hebrew and within a rabbinic stream makes many of his identifications tenuous. However, he correctly notes the extensive use of Song of Songs (294) and the relationship between Aseneth and Esther. He also offers the interesting suggestion that the author was influenced by Is 19.18–25, a prophecy that reads in part, "On that day the Egyptians will be like women. . . . On that day there will be five cities in the land of Egypt that speak the language of Canaan and swear allegiance to the Lord of hosts. One of these will be called the City of the Sun [Heliopolis]. On that day, there will be an altar to the Lord in the center of the land of Egypt and a pillar to the Lord at its border. It will be a sign and a witness to the Lord of hosts in the land of Egypt; when they cry to the Lord because of oppressors, he will send them a savior, and will defend and deliver them. The Lord will make himself known to the Egyptians, and the Egyptians will know the Lord on that day, and will worship with sacrifice and burnt offering, and they will make vows to the Lord and perform them." Although the consonance between this prophecy and *Aseneth* is not exact, numerous elements in the plot of *Aseneth* are consistent with this passage, including the location of Heliopolis, the female Egyptian protagonist, the sending of a savior in response to Egypt (Aseneth's) cry, the Lord made known to Egypt (Aseneth), and the Egyptians' (Aseneth's) vows to God. Aseneth's offer to prepare a meal for

the angel and the disappearance of the honeycomb in fire might also be seen as a reflection of the worship and sacrifices envisioned here, although the correspondence is not exact.

7. In arguing thus, it is not my intention to engage in discussion about how the author or authors knew this material, nor to what extent they considered it "scripture." That is, I am not (at least for the shorter text) claiming that the use of such material by the author(s) demonstrates or requires their access to biblical books, known to them as such. I will argue, though, that the author(s) of the longer text does know the material in biblical texts and intentionally revises the shorter to conform more closely to that material. On the question of whether the author(s) of the longer text knew biblical materials as "scripture," I cannot say definitively.

8. One possibility is that the marriage poses problems after the formulation of the matrilineal principle of descent, for then Manasseh and Ephraim are potentially reckoned as Egyptians rather than "Jews" and the lineage and identity of both tribes are tainted. Nevertheless, no rabbinic sources raise this problem. On the origins of the matrilineal principle in the rabbinic period, see Shaye J. D. Cohen, "The Origins of the Matrilineal Principle in Rabbinic Law," *Association of Jewish Studies Review* 10 (1985): 19–53. But another possibility is somewhat different: that interest in Aseneth as a type of "proselyte" (the word itself isn't used in the texts at all) compels its composition.

9. For some examples, see chapter 1, no. 1; see also Victor P. Hamilton, "Marriage (OT and ANE)," *ABD* 4: 564–65, on biblical prohibitions against marriage with Gentiles. The problem might be more complex, in that the actual prohibitions against intermarriage all "postdate" Joseph in the internal chronology of Jewish scripture. The story of Joseph's sister, Dinah, told in Gen 34, appears to suggest that Israelite women may marry outsiders who are first circumcised. In the narrative reality of Genesis, though, this proves to be false, since the circumcision of Hamor and his men is a ruse by Jacob's sons to avenge the rape of their sister. In any case, this passage does not address the question of Israelite men marrying foreign women.

10. See Hamilton, "Marriage," 562–63, on parentally arranged and self-initiated marriages. Pharaoh's arrangement of the marriage between Joseph and Aseneth fits into neither category, and the problem is addressed somewhat explicitly in *Aseneth* 20, when Pentephres proposes to make the marriage feast of the couple and Joseph responds that Pharaoh must give him Aseneth, "because he is my father" (20.7). For a discussion of the different treatment of this scene and this phrase in the shorter and longer reconstructions, see chapter 3.

11. See the appendix; see also Aptowitzer, "Asenath."

12. In this formulation, it may seem that I am arguing for an author or authors who were familiar with a text of Genesis itself, and they may well have been. Although this is certainly possible, if not probable, it may not be necessary—it may only be necessary for them to know the tale that we now have in Genesis. The later the composition of *Aseneth,* of course, the more likely it becomes that the author or authors did indeed know such a text.

13. See, for example, Chariton, *Chaereas and Callirhoe,* 1.1.1, conveniently available in Reardon, *Collected Ancient Greek Novels.*

14. On Woman Wisdom in early traditions, see Claudia Camp, *Wisdom and the Feminine in the Book of Proverbs,* Bible and Literature 11 (Sheffield: Almond Press, 1985).

15. Interestingly, although other scholars are well aware of the predominance of Wisdom motifs in the texts, they may have tended to focus on Joseph as Wisdom or at least on Joseph as sage (see, e.g., Karl-Gustav Sandelin, "A Wisdom Meal in the Romance 'Joseph and Aseneth,'" in *Wisdom as Nourisher: A Study of the Old Testament Theme, Its Development within Early Judaism, and Its Impact on Early Christianity* [Abo, Sweden: Abo Akademi, 1986], 151–57.

16. The textual traditions here are quite complicated. Philonenko's (*Joseph et Aséneth*) reconstruction of verse 7 ("And she was in no way like the daughters of the Egyptians but was in all ways like the daughters of the Hebrews") is actually a pastiche of readings from the

shorter and longer manuscripts. The reading common to all appears to be, "[A]nd she was in no way like the Egyptians." The words "daughters of" are found in one of the shorter manuscripts, B, but not in D; the phrase "but was in all ways like the daughters of the Hebrews" is taken from one of the longer manuscripts, A (the basis of the text printed by Batiffol); a variant occurs in another long manuscript, H. See Philonenko's textual note to 1.7, *Joseph et Aséneth,* p. 130.

17. Philonenko, *Joseph et Aséneth,* cites Habakkuk 2.18 and *Clementine Homilies* 11.14; also pertinent is material that occurs in slightly different form in Pss 115.4–8 (LXX 113.12–16) and 135.15–18 (LXX 134.15–18). In the former it reads, "The idols of the nations are silver and gold, the work of human hands. They have mouths, but do not speak; they have eyes, but do not see; they have ears, but do not hear; they have noses, but do not smell; they have hands, but do not feel; they have feet, but do not walk; they make no sounds in their throats. Those who make them are like them, and all those who trust in them." This verse is quoted explicitly in the *Martyrdom of Saint Barbara* (in Agnes Smith Lewis, *Select Narratives of Holy Women from the Syro-Antiochene or Sinai Palimpsest, as Written above the Old Syriac Gospels by John the Stylite, of Beth-Mari-Qanun in A. D. 778* [London: C. J. Clay and Sons, 1900] fol. 95a, p. 80. A similar passage in *Irene* (fol. 11b, p. 103) is also identified by Lewis as a quotation of this verse, but it is, in fact, from the version in Ps 135.16b–17 ("[T]hey have eyes, but they see not; they have ears, but they hear not, and there is no breath in their mouth"). The translation here is from Lewis (ibid.). For further discussion of *Barbara* and *Irene,* see chapters 8 and 9.

18. LXX: Hebrew is slightly different.

19. For the most part, as Kugel discusses, rabbinic (and other) traditions concur that Joseph was blameless and did not have sex with Potiphar's wife. However, he also surveys a number of traditions in which Joseph is suspected of varying degrees of complicity (*In Potiphar's House,* 94–98).

20. *Aseneth* 6.6. In 6.7 she repeats the designation ἄφρων. Elsewhere, although in different language (12.7 and 13.10), she confesses to insolence, arrogance, and ignorance of Joseph's true identity.

21. This material is treated extensively in Kugel, *In Potiphar's House,* 106–112.

22. It points also to imagery from Song of Songs that I will consider below.

23. Trans. NRSV from the Hebrew, adapted slightly.

24. Interestingly, though, Prov 6:24 asserts that the teachings of parents (both father and mother [6.20]) protect the wise son from the woman who belongs to another man and from the smooth words of the strange woman.

25. At *Aseneth* 1.8, Aseneth is tall (μεγάλη) like Rebecca; in Sir 24.13–14, Wisdom grows tall like various trees; however, the Greek is not the same (it is verbal: ἀνυψώθην).

26. LXX/OG 138.

27. See also Philonenko, *Joseph et Aséneth,* 187.

28. In the Christian *Odes of Solomon* 30.4–5, a similar description occurs for the water of the living spring of the Lord: "Its waters are far pleasanter than honey, and the honeycomb of bees is not to be compared with it. Because it comes out from the lips of the Lord, and from the heart of the Lord is its name." For extensive discussion of the significance of the *Odes of Solomon* for *Aseneth,* see chapter 9.

29. Wis Sol 7.22 (Wisdom as ἅγιον); 7.24 (Wisdom as most pure).

30. Particularly noteworthy is a general consonance between the experience of the speaker in Wis Sol 7–8, and the experience of Joseph in *Aseneth,* particularly in the longer version. The portrait of Wisdom in these chapters is consonant (though not identical) with Aseneth and with Metanoia. As Aseneth is portrayed as light, so Wisdom is described in similar imagery, "more beautiful than the sun, excelling the constellation of stars" (Wis Sol 7.29). She is initiate in the

knowledge of God, and, like Aseneth, of noble birth. Wis Sol 8 is also, at least generally, reflective of the narrative of Joseph, particularly verses 10–18, which describe the benefits of Wisdom to the man who loves and desires her. Such a one has glory among the multitudes and honor in the presence of elders, though he is young. He is keen in judgment, admired in the sight of rulers, governing peoples, with nations subject to him and monarchs afraid, capable and courageous in war (this last is a little less like Joseph!). Life with Aseneth brings Joseph rest, gladness and joy, and immortality (at least in the form of their children if not also in the immortality conferred in the scene with the angel).

31. LXX/OG Ps 44.14–15. This translation is my literal one, from the Greek. In Hebrew, the Psalm is 45.13b–13. The alternate translation of the Hebrew, in the NRSV, reads: "All glorious is the princess [the daughter of the king] within, gold embroidery is her clothing; in many-colored robes she is led to the king; behind her the virgins, her companions, follow."

32. Is 58.5 critiques the traditional fast of sackcloth and ashes, insisting that true repentance requires something more. "Is such the fast that I choose, a day to humble oneself? Is it to bow down the head like a bulrush, and to lie in sackcloth and ashes? Will you call this a fast, a day acceptable to the Lord?"

33. It is significant, though, that Aseneth does not fulfill the requirement to feed the hungry, doubtless because her food, consecrated to idols, is unacceptable food. It may or may not suggest something about the author's religious self-identification that the real problem with Aseneth's food is its idolatrous consecration. While we know this was a serious issue for Christians in late antiquity, Jews would have been no less repulsed by such meat. Further, the story of Aseneth takes place prior to the divine regulation of meat, so the absence of any allusion to *kashrut* specifically is not necessarily significant.

34. I have deliberately omitted a portion of the verse here that is somewhat problematic. The Hebrew reads literally: "ornament of ornament"; the editors of the NRSV correct this to "[you] arrived at full womanhood." Interestingly, the LXX/OG reads "city of cities," apparently misreading "ir"(עִיר) for "or (אוֹר)." What connection this might have with designation of the transformed Aseneth as a city, specifically, City of Refuge, is hard to say, but certainly interesting. Of course, the association of daughter Aseneth with daughter Jerusalem could be sufficient to make such a connection seem obvious.

35. In the longer version only, sibling terminology is also employed for the relationship between their divine counterparts, Metanoia and the angelic figure with the form of Joseph; see chapter 3.

36. Tob 7.11. Aptowitzer, "Asenath," 264–68, saw the designation of Aseneth as Joseph's sister as yet another allusion to the Dinah tradition, interpreting "sister" as a term of general kinship, but this is wholly unnecessary, even apart from the other problems with the Dinah traditions in *Aseneth*. Philonenko, *Joseph et Aséneth,* agrees that the author of *Aseneth* knew the Dinah legend but appears to disagree with Aptowitzer that her designation as "sister" is further proof. On the contrary, he suggests that by omitting the detail that Aseneth was Dinah's daughter, the author intentionally refutes such an interpretation (37). Whether or not the author was from Egypt (see chapter 10), it may be noteworthy that ancient Egyptian rulers frequently were married to their sisters and that the marriage of the goddess Isis to her brother Osiris afforded a divine paradigm for such practices. We even have evidence for actual brother-sister marriages in Egypt in the Roman period (*CPJ* 442, discussed in *CPJ* 2:227). In gnostic texts, too, the syzygies are also siblings.

37. 1Q *Gen Ap* Col. 2.9. In his notes to *Aseneth* 7.11, Philonenko remarks that sibling terminology is part of the romantic vocabulary of Hellenistic novels and attributes its presence particularly to the heritage of ancient Egyptian poetry (*Joseph et Aséneth,* 153). For detailed discussion of the use of sibling terminology for ancient sexual and marital relationships, see John Boswell, *Same-Sex Unions in Pre-modern Europe* (New York: Villard Books, 1994), 41; 67–71.

38. For the affinity of this scene with Is 58:8, see earlier discussion.

39. Although Dorothy Sly argues that for Philo both ἀνήρ and ἄνθρωπος are gendered and that the latter is not then generic, she says that "Philo's perception of woman is of a being other than man" (*Philo's Perceptions of Women,* Brown Judaic Studies 209 [Atlanta: Scholars Press, 1990], 59–70, quotation on 216).

40. See Phyllis Trible, *God and the Rhetoric of Sexuality,* Overtures to Biblical Theology (Philadelphia: Fortress Press, 1978), 12–23.

41. Other translators (including Burchard, Philonenko, and Cook) have used the more problematic "man" or its French and German equivalents.

42. See chapter 6.

43. Est 4.16.

44. Est 5.7–8.

45. LXX/OG Est 4.17a–j = AddEst 13.9–17. On ancient prose prayer, see Moshe Greenberg, *Biblical Prose Prayer as a Window to the Popular Religion of Ancient Israel* (Berkeley: University of California Press, 1983).

46. AddEst 14.1–2; LXX/OG 4.17k. The language of AddEst here recalls Is 3.24, discussed earlier. While both *Aseneth* and AddEst could draw independently on Isaiah or related traditions for this description of penitence and preparation, the additional similarities between Esther and Ahasueros and Aseneth and the angelic double of Joseph suggest a more complex interrelationship.

47. AddEst 14.15–17; LXX/OG 4.17w–x.

48. The NRSV translation, "splendid attire" here and above "splendid apparel," masks the use of δόξα, which I think intentionally links royal garments to concepts of divine imagery and reflection (see chapters 5 and 6).

49. AddEst 15.5; LXX/OG 5.1b. Literally, "her face [or: countenance] was happy, as though beloved [or: in love (προσφιλές)], but her heart was contracted [ἀπεστενωμένη] with fear."

50. AddEst 15.6; LXX/OG 5.1c.

51. This translation differs slightly from the NRSV, which translates ἀδελφός as "husband." Although it clearly means that as well, it is the use of the term ἀδελφός for "husband" that is of interest to us, just as Joseph is presented to Aseneth as her "brother."

52. AddEst 15.15; LXX/OG 5.2a.

53. Judg 13.3–5.

54. Judg 13.6.

55. In both Alexandrinus and Vaticanus, the angel is called ἄνθρωπος (A has τοῦ θεοῦ; Vat has θεοῦ), the same term for the figure in *Aseneth.*

56. Abraham in Gen 22.1: ὁ θεὸς . . . εἶπεν πρὸς αὐτόν Αβρααμ, Αβρααμ· ὁ δὲ εἶπεν ἰδοὺ ἐγώ. Abraham again in Gen 22.11: καὶ ἐκάλεσεν αὐτόν ἄγγελος κυρίου ἐκ τοῦ οὐρανοῦ καὶ εἶπεν αὐτῷ, Αβρααμ, Αβρααμ. Moses in Exod 3.4b: ἐκάλεσεν αὐτὸν κύριος ἐκ τοῦ βάτου λέγων, Μωυσῆ, Μωυσῆ. ὁ δὲ εἶπεν τί ἐστιν; Note, though, that in Exod 3.4b, the Greek reads τί ἐστιν for Moses' response, whereas in Hebrew, Moses' response is identical to that of Abraham: וַיֹּאמֶר הִנֵּנִי. *Aseneth* 14.6 reads: καὶ ἐκάλεσεν αὐτὴν ὁ ἄνθρωπος ἐκ δευτέρου καὶ εἶπεν Ἀσενὲθ, Ἀσενὲθ. Καὶ εἶπεν ἰδοὺ ἐγώ.

57. It is also the language between Eli and Samuel in 1 Sam 3.16: "Eli called Samuel and said, 'Samuel, my son.' He said, 'Here I am.'" In inverted form, it occurs when Isaac calls Abraham in Gen 22.7.

58. Ezek 1.28.

59. Ezek 1.26–27.

60. Some other examples include Matt 17.2; Rev 1.14, 1.16, 19.12, 9.17, 11.15; also 3 Enoch 15; 2 Enoch 1.5.

61. In the Enoch traditions on which later chapters focus, this is also the response of Enoch to the sight of the angels, the cherubim, etc. (2 Enoch 1.7; 3 Enoch); see Martha Himmelfarb, *Ascent to Heaven in Jewish and Christian Apocalypses* (New York: Oxford University Press, 1992), 39.

62. NRSV Ps 30.11–12.

63. Zech 3.4–5.

64. Philonenko, *Joseph et Aséneth,* 169, note to 12.5, points out that this has associations with the Yom Kippur liturgy.

65. LXX/OG; NRSV Ps 139.16.

66. Others include Ps 69.28 (NRSV), "the book of the living"; Exod 32.32, where God says to Moses, "whoever has sinned against me, I will blot out of my book"; Dan 12.1. For additional references and bibliography, see Philonenko, *Joseph et Aséneth,* 182, note to 15.3.

67. Earlier, this chapter.

68. Num 35.6–13; Deut 4.41–43, 19.1–13; Josh 20. Philo offers a fascinating allegorical interpretation of the cities of refuge in which the mother city (metropolis) is none other than the Logos and the other five cities are colonies. Each of these is represented, according to Philo, by some aspect of the temple furnishings (*de Fuga,* 85–118). Philonenko, *Joseph et Aséneth,* 183, argues that the portrait of Aseneth, the City of Refuge, and the seven pillars is an intentional effort to dissociate Aseneth from Logos and associate her instead with Wisdom.

69. In the longer text, Aseneth explicitly hears the old lion, the father of the Egyptian gods, and his children, the lions (see chapter 3).

70. Some scholars have seen in this an allusion or at least a parallel to the rabbinic notion that the feminine Shekinah sheltered proselytes under her wings. For references, see Philonenko, *Joseph et Aséneth,* 183. This imagery, of course, is already present in Ps 91.4, with respect to God: "[U]nder his wings you will find refuge." Various scholars note that proselytes frequently took a new name when they became Jews. While there are numerous precedents for biblical characters receiving new names that are actually phrases related to their experiences (Hagar, Joseph himself, Gideon, etc.), the few actual examples of this practice suggest that the new names of proselytes, while significant, were still "ordinary" names. The best example is *CIJ* 523, the inscription of an eighty-six-year-old woman named Veturia Paulla (or perhaps Paucla), who, according to the inscription, converted to Judaism at age seventy, and took the name of Sarah. For another possible example, see the discussion of *CIJ* 462 in David Noy, *Jewish Inscriptions from Western Europe vol. 2: The City of Rome* (Cambridge: Cambridge University Press, 1995), 55.

71. Prov 24:13; see also 16:24.

72. Honey is also associated with the lovers in Song 4.11, 5.1, and is generally holy food. For much more extensive exploration of honey and of bees, see chapter 6.

73. As Burchard notes, anthropomorphic insects occur also in Rev 9.7–10.

74. Burchard, "Joseph and Aseneth," 230, n. 16h2.

75. LXX/OG; NRSV 118.

76. Hebrew. The NRSV prefers the reading of the Greek here: "[T]hey blazed like a fire of thorns."

77. Burchard, "Joseph and Aseneth," 182.

78. Philonenko, *Joseph et Aséneth,* 27.

79. See chapter 3. For the view that the division into these two parts is misleading and inaccurate, see Wills, *Jewish Novel.*

80. If Aptowitzer is correct in his belief that *Aseneth* draws on the prophecy of Is 19.16–22, it is possible that chapters 22–29 elaborate on 19.17 and 19.22, but this is not transparently obvious.

81. In Eusebius, *Preparatio Evangelica,* 9.27.4.

82. *PRE,* 11.

83. Translation of the longer recension, designated J, by F. I. Andersen in *OTP* 1:102–213. I will return to these Enoch traditions in chapter 5. Here it is worth remarking that Andersen considers *2 Enoch* "in every respect . . . an enigma" (96). After a judicious discussion (94–96), he admits to favoring for at least some nucleus of the work a relatively early date (perhaps late first century C.E.) and a Jewish community as context, but he acknowledges the real possibility that *2 Enoch* would also make sense for a community of what he terms "gentile converts to moral monotheism" *(*96).

84. This must be what the text means, since 18 is indivisible by 4, and 18 x 4 produces 72 guards, a plausible figure.

85. See also Ezek 28.14–16 on a guardian cherub in Eden.

86. LXX/OG 113 and 134, respectively. There are some differences in the two versions: Ps 115 contains additional description of the idols, and the final lines (115.8, 135.18) are inverted.

87. In Ps 113, this line reads, "they make no sound in their throats."

88. In Deut 29.16, Moses reminds the Israelites of the idols in Egypt, "of wood and stone, of silver and gold." Hab 2.19 may utilize a similar tradition: "See, [the idol] is gold and silver plated, and there is no breath in it at all." Hos 8.4 speaks of idols of silver and gold, but in a passage that is unlikely to constitute a backdrop for our authors, given its extensive critique of the house of Ephraim and northern Israelite calf worship.

89. Interestingly, this same material occurs explicitly in *Barbara* and unacknowledged in *Irene,* as noted above, n. 17.

90. Philonenko, *(Joseph et Aséneth,* 163, note to 10.10) saw it as an allusion to underlying Egyptian myths, arguing that the phrase ὁ ἀδελφὸς αὐτῆς ὁ πρωτότοκος (her brother, the firstborn) alluded to the title of Osiris as firstborn and therefore relied here on an identification of Aseneth and Isis. Burchard was generally unimpressed with Philonenko's hypothesis (*"Joseph and Aseneth,"* 216, nn. s and t), particularly since he preferred the reading νεώτερος ("younger" rather than "firstborn") of manuscripts E, F, and G (also Syriac, Armenian, L1). If, however, the reading he prefers represents an intentional revision, it could be seen as a deliberate attempt to take away from the brother the title of Joseph as πρωτότοκος. As in many other instances, these diverse interpretations demonstrate the influence of the reader on the reading!

91. The protagonists of Greek novels are also routinely only children; see chapter 7.

92. LXX/OG 34; NRSV 35.

93. Another significant passage here may be Zech 3.1–5, on the garments of the high priest Joshua before God and the Satan; see earlier discussion, this chapter.

CHAPTER THREE

Recasting *Aseneth*

The Enhancement of Traditional Elements in the Longer Reconstruction

While previous scholarship has endeavored to resolve the relationship of the shorter and longer versions of *Aseneth* primarily through traditional text-critical approaches,[1] I have focused on the content of the different readings, a focus that has produced significantly different results. As I hope to demonstrate in this chapter, a comparative reading of the shorter and longer reconstructions of the text reveals a plethora of instances in which the longer text appears to expand upon the shorter in a consistent manner, resolving anomalies, clarifying ambiguities, and rendering biblical and related imagery much more explicit, bringing the longer text into closer conformity with biblical texts. In many cases, these changes are effected through the subtle addition of only a few words, consistently added at appropriate points. All of this strongly suggests to me that, in general, the longer text as reconstructed by Burchard represents an intentional and careful reworking of a shorter text and that it makes far more sense to account for the numerous divergent readings as expansions from the shorter rather than deletions from the longer. While not attempting to be absolutely comprehensive, in this chapter I will consider a number of examples that I think demonstrate my thesis. Subsequent chapters also contain additional evidence for this thesis, particularly chapter 7, where I devote further consideration to the differing stances of the shorter and longer texts with regard to gender construction.

The First Encounter between Joseph and Aseneth (7.2–9.1)

Joseph first glimpses Aseneth at the window of her upper rooms, where she has fled following her altercation with her father over his proposal that she marry Joseph. Concerned lest Aseneth be one of those Egyptian women who lust after him, Joseph is quickly reassured by Pentephres that Aseneth is, like Joseph himself, a virgin and that she hates foreign men, a slight distinction from 2.1, which we considered in the previous chapter. After Aseneth comes back down, Pentephres instructs her to come forward and kiss Joseph, but as she does so, Joseph balks.

8.3–4/**8.4–5**
And Pentephres said to Aseneth, "Come forward and kiss your brother." And as she came forward to kiss Joseph, (he) **Joseph** stretched out his right hand, and placed it on her chest [*to stēthos*], **between her two breasts, and her breasts were already standing up like ripe apples.**

Compared with Joseph's relatively straightforward actions in the shorter text, one effect of the longer reading is to sexualize the scene and depict Aseneth as another of the Egyptian women physically aroused by Joseph, thus expanding on Joseph's earlier concerns at 7.3–7 about precisely such women. Although this may initially seem gratuitous and inexplicable, it may be one example of the tendency of the longer text to make biblical allusions more explicit, here drawing further on the characterization of Aseneth as the female lover or beloved. Song of Songs exalts the beauty of the woman's breasts several times,[2] most suggestively in the following verse:

Oh, may your breasts be like clusters of the vine,
and the scent of your breath like apples.[3]

Though one hardly needs Song of Songs to associate breasts with apples, other imagery from Song of Songs is sufficiently present in the longer text, as we shall see, to suggest that the particular choice of simile may have a textual basis.[4]

The concluding lines of this section take quite different forms in the shorter and longer reconstructions:

8.10/**8.11**
And may she drink the cup of your blessing, (she whom you chose before she was conceived) **and number her among your people, that you have chosen before all (things) came into being** and may she enter into your rest,[5] which you have prepared for your chosen ones **and live in your eternal life for ever and ever.**

The notion that Aseneth was chosen by God before her birth raises some difficult problems. As I considered in the previous chapter, it is consonant with the identification of Aseneth with Wisdom. Numerous male biblical figures (Jeremiah, Samuel, Isaac, Samson) are also chosen by God before their birth, and Aseneth's general association with such figures may have already been signaled in the words with which Aseneth responded to her father's greeting. The reading of the longer text suggests some discomfort at the association of Aseneth with preexistent Wisdom and with exalted male figures. The longer version retains the general notion of divine choice prior to Creation but claims that it was not Aseneth but the People of Israel whom God had chosen.

Aseneth's Repentance

A small but telling example of the differing readings occurs in the description of Aseneth's actions as she embarks on her repentance. As we have seen earlier, she begins by throwing out the window all of the physical emblems of her Egyptian self: her idols, her idolatrous clothing, and her food and wine (sacrificed to false gods).

10.4/**10.13**

And Aseneth took her royal dinner—the fatted meats and fish and dressed meat—and all the sacrifices to her gods and the vessels of wine for their libations, and threw all of it out the window **looking north and gave everything to** (for) the **strange** dogs (to eat). **For Aseneth said to herself, "By no means must my dogs eat from my dinner and from the sacrifice of the idols, but let the strange dogs eat those."**

Not only does the shorter version contain no concern that the idolatrous food might be consumed by her dogs, but the same relatively small difference is carefully picked up again in Aseneth's recapitulation of her acts of penance in her prayer at 13.7/**13.8**:

Behold, Lord, my royal dinner (and fatted meats) **and the cereals,** I have given to the **strange** dogs.

This same passage back in chapter 10 provides an example of the longer text's tendency to clarify potential ambiguities. When Aseneth discards all her goods, the shorter text narrates only that she does so out the window. But the longer text repeatedly specifies that the window was the north window (which we know from 2.13 to be the one that faces out to the street—the longer text also specifies "where people passed by"—and not inward to Pentephres' compound). Thus the longer text removes any possible ambiguity that Aseneth threw her contaminated property into the courtyard of her own home. This small detail is repeated in the longer text each time Aseneth throws something out the window (**10.11, 10.12,** and **10.13**).[6]

A Spatial Dislocation

At 9.1, both reconstructions have Aseneth retire to her rooms and collapse on her bed. At 10.9/**10.8**, Aseneth goes into the second room, where she takes out the black mourning clothing and where, in the shorter version, the remainder of the drama appears to take place. But then, at 14.15, the angel sends her for a new robe, and she goes into the room where her treasure chests are. According to 2.6, this room is the second chamber, although the shorter text does not here identify it as such. There appears thus to be a problem with the shorter text's location of the action.

The readings of the longer reconstruction appear designed to remedy this difficulty.

10.9–10/**10.10**

And Aseneth rose and opened the door quietly and went into her second chamber where her chests [*thēkai*] of ornaments were, and opened her coffer [*kibōtion*] and took out a black and somber tunic. And this was her tunic of mourning that she wore when her (first-born) **younger** brother died. **In this Aseneth had dressed and mourned for her brother. And she took her black tunic and carried it into her chamber and closed the door again firmly and slipped the bolt across.**

Thus, in the longer reconstruction, Aseneth has once again returned to the first chamber, in which the drama takes place, a detail allowing her, in chapter 14, to go once again into the room where her clothing is kept to obtain yet another change of garments. In the shorter version (at 14.13), the angelic figure merely tells Aseneth to change out of her mourning clothing, into new garments. At 14.15, the text reports that "Aseneth went into the room where her chests of ornaments were and opened her *kibōtion*" and took out the requisite garments. But in the longer text, at **14.12** and again at **14.14**, the room where these garments are stored is explicitly designated "the second."

Aseneth's Confession (12.1–13.12)

On the eighth day of her repentance, unable to move her limbs, Aseneth offers up an eloquent confession to God. Aseneth's actual prayer, particularly in the shorter versions, shows an unsurprising similarity to both the structure and content of biblical prose prayer, which is itself consonant with other ancient prose prayers.[7] Such prayers typically have a threefold structure. The opening invocation names the deity whose favor is sought and often stresses those powers and characteristics of the deity that are particularly relevant to the petitioner's needs. The central portions of the prayer identify the petitioner in ways that seek to establish a commonality of interest between the deity and the petitioner. Finally, the prayer asks for specific favors and assistance, sometimes providing an explicit motivation for the deity to comply.

In a brief and lucid analysis of biblical prose prayers, Moshe Greenberg makes several observations that throw Aseneth's prayer into sharper relief. Petitionary prayer draws heavily on the protocol of petitionary address to kings and other persons of power and prestige.[8] That social context itself depended on ideas about mutual obligations and reciprocity between hierarchical superiors and subordinates, especially rulers and their vassals, patrons and their clients. Petitionary prayer, as all rhetoric, is designed to persuade the one petitioned that the interests of both parties coincide.[9] In biblical texts, anyone may pray to the God of Israel for assistance, as the example of the sailors in the Book of Jonah demonstrates.[10] In contrast to psalms and temple prayers, the content of prose prayers is situation specific. Various biblical examples suggest that the appropriate response to answered prayer is to bless God publicly.[11] Greenberg notes that this follows the pattern in Numbers 5.7, where confession of sin is followed by expiatory sacrifice.[12]

Consistent with the structure of prose prayers, Aseneth begins by invoking the "Lord, God of the ages, **Who established and gave life to everything**, Who gives to all **your whole creation** the breath of life" (12.2/**12.1**). After a fuller statement of God's creation of the cosmos, Aseneth catalogues her sins before God: lawlessness, impiety, profane speech. She has worshiped dead idols rather than the living God. At 12.7–8, Aseneth endeavors to create this sense of reciprocity: she is the persecuted one who flees to God as a child to its father and mother; God is the loving father who stretches out his hand to his child.

The longer and shorter reconstructions display particularly interesting differences in the composition of these prayers. The longer text expands the shorter at numerous points, providing fuller details of speech and various minor clarifications. Whereas the shorter text, for instance, begins by identifying Aseneth's primal opponent as a lion, at 12.9, and then proceeds to identify this figure as the devil in the same verse and "like" a wolf at 12.10, the longer text consistently refers to a lion (at **12.10** and **12.11**).[13]

Most obviously, the longer text contains two lengthy silent monologues (**11.3–19**), absent in the shorter version, whose motifs are also largely absent in the shorter text, including a great concern for the significance of the name of God, a greatly expanded emphasis on Aseneth's rejection by all those around her, and an enhanced interest in father imagery.

The narrative section introducing the first of these soliloquies claims that Aseneth was so completely devastated by her seven days of abasement that she is unable to speak and so utters this first confession "**in her heart**" only. At the conclusion of this internal speech, Aseneth regains enough strength to sit up on her knees, but she is still terrified to name the name of God aloud and so silently recites a second soliloquy expressing her fears about opening her mouth to God and speaking the divine name aloud. These verses may be seen, inter alia, as a device intended to smooth the insertion of these prayers into the briefer narrative of the shorter text, where the exhausted Aseneth simply speaks.[14]

Much of the second silent speech concerns itself precisely with endowing Aseneth with sufficient courage to open her mouth to God, a mouth that was previously defiled by sacrifices to idols. While Aseneth has already spoken in this story, her prior speech has always either been in private to herself (3.8) or in response to speech initiated by her hierarchical superior (her father or Joseph). All of the silent prayers could be generated on the basis of the spoken prayer, which contains the seemingly anomalous claim at 12.6 that "I am not worthy to open my mouth before you." Chapter 11 in the longer text could have been composed as an answer to the question, "How could Aseneth have spoken aloud to God if she was indeed unworthy?" Answer: first she prayed silently, not only confessing her sins but also praying to God for the courage to speak aloud. A passage such as LXX/OG Psalm 29.12–13[15] might well have provided the skeletal framework for this section: "You have turned my mourning into dancing; you have taken off my sackcloth and clothed me with joy, so that my soul[16] may praise you and not be silent."

In a fascinating study of silent prayer in antiquity, Pieter van der Horst documents a general ancient distrust of silent prayer as suspicious and nefarious.[17] He argues that the prayer of Hannah, the mother of Samuel, was particularly instrumental in a gradual Jewish (and Christian) acceptance of silent prayer. In 1 Samuel 1, the childless Hannah, distraught over the taunts of her fertile co-wife, Peninah, prays inaudibly to God, pouring out her sorrow and vowing to dedicate to God any child that he might grant her. Hannah's lips move, but no sound is heard, leading the priest Eli to mistake her for a drunk.

The revisions of the longer text may be influenced by the Hannah narrative. First, the author(s) may intend to suggest that a woman who prays must (or might) do so in silence. The language of the longer *Aseneth* here echoes the Greek biblical text closely: both Hannah and Aseneth speak *en tē kardia autēs* (in her heart).[18] This consonance may further suggest that the author intends an association of the two women.

The theme of the first silent speech is essentially Aseneth's unworthiness, contrasted with God's compassion and mercy toward the (presumably repentant) afflicted. The portrait of the persecuted penitent is rife in the texts, on whose themes both versions of *Aseneth* draw.[19] Aseneth describes herself as a desolate orphan, abandoned and hated by everyone, especially her parents, who are particularly angry with her for her destruction of their gods. The claim that Aseneth's parents have disowned her on account of her destruction of their gods occurs in a milder form in the shorter text at 12.11 and may reflect the idea in a passage such as Psalm 45.10–11: "Hear, O Daughter, and incline your ear; forget your people and your father's house, and the king will desire your beauty."[20] As I considered in the previous chapter, the subsequent verses of this psalm may undergird the opening description of Aseneth. But the narrative has given us no indication that Aseneth's parents have rejected her for any reason, and at the conclusion of the story Aseneth will be welcomed by her parents.

The use of biblical materials to expand and develop Aseneth's experience is particularly discernible in the construction of chapters 11 and 12. Immediately following **11.7–9**, where Aseneth's words expand upon her unworthiness to speak to God because of her prior defilement from her idolatrous worship and sacrifices, Aseneth says:

> **But I have heard many saying**
> **that the God of the Hebrews is a true God,**
> **and a living God, and a merciful God,**
> **and compassionate and long-suffering and pitiful and gentle,**
> **and does not count the sin of a humble person,**
> **nor expose the lawless deeds of an afflicted person at the time of his affliction.**
> **Therefore I will take courage too and turn to him,**
> **and take refuge with him,**
> **and confess all my sins to him,**
> **and pour out my supplication before him.**
> **Who knows, (maybe) he will see my humiliation**
> **and have mercy on me.**
> **Perhaps he will see this desolation of mine**
> **and have compassion on me,**
> **or see my orphanhood**
> **and protect me.**

At this point, the text then agrees with the reading of the shorter narrative at 12.11, except that the shorter uses the second person:[21]

> [B]ecause he is the father of the orphans
> and a protector of the persecuted
> and the helper of the (oppressed) **afflicted**.

Chapter **11.10** thus constitutes one of the few places where the text actually employs the language of biblical texts almost verbatim.[22] Aseneth's description of the God of the Hebrews as "*theos eleēmōn kai oiktirmōn kai makrothymos kai polyeleos kai epieikēs*" is extremely close to Exodus 34.6 and Psalms 85.15, 102.8, and 144.8:[23] "*Kyrios ho theos oiktirmōn kai eleēmōn, makrothymos kai polyeleos kai alēthinos*" (the Lord God, gracious and merciful, long-suffering and full of compassion and truthful).

The construction of the silent prayers in chapters 11 and 12 in the longer version (virtually all of which is absent in the shorter text) seems to incorporate precisely the motifs and language of the Psalms in which the phrase found in Exodus recurs,[24] as well as the continuation of the passage in Exodus. There, God's qualities of mercy, truth, and enduring compassion are manifest in divine forgiveness of lawlessness and unrighteousness and sin (*aphairōn anomias kai aidikias kai hamartias*). So, too, Aseneth's words in **11.11–12** make this same connection and express Aseneth's hope that God will have mercy on her (*eleēsei*) and be merciful (*oikteirēsei*) to her.

LXX/OG Psalm 85 begins with the words "Incline, Lord, your ear, and attend to me, for I am poor (*ptōxos*) and needy (*penēs*)" and continues to expand on this theme in ways that are quite consonant with Aseneth's experience. In 85.2, the penitent psalmist cries to God all day long and calls up God in his day of trouble, for God answers (85.6–7). In 85.9, the psalmist prophesies that all nations shall glorify God's name, and in 85.12, the psalmist will do so forever. Only once in the shorter text does the name of God ever appear, at 15.13. There, having heard the angel's pronouncements of her forgiveness, transformation, and forthcoming marriage to Joseph, Aseneth says: "Blessed is the Lord God who sent you to me to deliver me from the darkness and to lead me into the light, and blessed is his name forever."[25]

In LXX/OG Psalm 144, where the phrase in Exodus occurs at verse 8, the motif of blessing God's name dominates the entire psalm from beginning to end. It begins, "I will magnify you, O my God, O my king, and bless your name forever and ever," and ends, "My mouth will speak the praise of the Lord, and all flesh will praise his holy name forever and ever." Psalm 102 also combines the Exodus phrase with an emphasis on blessing the holy name of God. The longer text thus displays considerably more interest in the name of God. Interest in the divine name may point to the religious sensibilities of the redactors (as I shall argue in chapters 4, 5, and 6), but here it seems not insignificant that the motif of glorifying God's name appears in two of the three psalms that contain the language of the longer version of *Aseneth* at **11.10**.

Psalm 144 also envisions God's graciousness as accessible to all, a concept quite appropriate for the tale of a repentant Egyptian daughter. God's mercy toward all who call on him is elaborated in imagery that yet again generally describes the Aseneth narrative:

> The Lord is faithful in all his words,
> and gracious in all his deeds.
> The Lord upholds all who are falling
> and raises up all who are bowed down.
> The eyes of all look to you,
> and you give them their food in due season.
> You open your hand,
> satisfying the desire of every living thing.
> . . . .
> The Lord is near to all who call on him,
> to all who call on him in truth.
> He fulfills the desire of all who fear him [*tōn phoboumenōn*];
> he also hears their cry, and saves them.[26]

So, in *Aseneth,* God (or his angelic deputy) raises up the prostrate, fallen Aseneth, who raises her eyes to him; he gives her (angelic) food by his own hand; he hears Aseneth's cry and saves her. Further, though both versions of *Aseneth* prefer the terminology of *theosebeia* to expressions for "fearing" God, derived from *phobeō,* the theme of the righteous who fear God is apparent both in *Aseneth* and in this psalm.

All three psalms, 85, 102, and 144, may have provided the redactor(s) of the longer version with additional imagery. The image of God as compassionate father is much stronger in the longer text than in the shorter:

12.7–8
Deliver me **before I am caught** from my persecutors,
for unto you I have fled for refuge,
as a **little** child **who is afraid flees** to its father (and mother).
and the father, stretching out his hands, snatches him off the ground,
and puts his arms around him by his breast,
and the child clasps his hands around his father's neck,
and regains his breath after his fear,
and rests at his father's breast,
the father, however, smiles at the confusion of his childish mind,
likewise
And you, Lord, stretch forth your hands to me,
as a father who loves his child and is affectionate,

12.11/**12.11–15**
Save me, Lord, the desolate one,
because my father and my mother disowned me, **and said, "Aseneth is not our**
   daughter,"
because I destroyed and broke their gods **and have come to hate them,**
and now I am desolate and orphaned,
And there is no hope for me, Lord, if not with you,
and no other refuge except your mercy, Lord
For you are the father of the orphans,
And the protector of the persecuted,
And the helper of the oppressed.
Have mercy upon me, Lord,
and guard me, a virgin abandoned and an orphan,
because you, Lord, are a sweet and good and gentle father.
What father is as sweet as you, Lord,
and who (is) as quick in mercy as you, Lord,
and who (is) as long-suffering toward our sins as you, Lord?
For behold, all the (worldly goods) **gifts** of my father, Pentephres,
which he gave me as an inheritance, are transient and ephemeral;
but the gifts of your inheritance, Lord, are incorruptible and eternal.

It may be noteworthy that this image occurs explicitly in Psalm 102.13 (LXX/OG), linked with theme of fearing God. "As a father has compassion [*oiktirei*] for [his] sons, so the Lord has compassion [*oiktirēsen*] for those who fear him [*phoboumenous auton*]."

The description of God as "quick in mercy" and "long-suffering [*makrothymos*] toward sins" recalls **11.12**, with its more precise use of the language of Exodus 34.6: "The Lord God, gracious and merciful, long-suffering [*makrothymos*] and full of compassion and truthful."[27]

It may be significant that it is only in the longer text that Aseneth mentions those who hate her (**11.6**) in addition to her parents, bringing this presentation of Aseneth into closer conformity with the underlying biblical paradigm. Nowhere in the shorter text is Aseneth said to be hated by anyone other than her parents.

Interestingly, the longer reconstruction omits the reference to the mother and contains instead a lengthy image of a terrified child finding sanctuary in the arms of a comforting father. Unable to find precedent for the imagery of both parents in biblical traditions, the redactor(s) may be attempting to bring the text into closer conformity with the traditions we do have, particularly Psalms 102.13,[28] quoted above, which combines the ideas of the compassionate father, and those who fear God. In **12.9–11**, this imagery is developed further: Aseneth presents herself as the orphan whose parents have abandoned her because she destroyed their idols, and God is the father of orphans and the protector of the persecuted.

Psalm 85 appears to have influenced the redaction of the longer version elsewhere in the text as well. In the shorter version, after the angel departs in 17.7, Aseneth says only: "[B]e merciful, Lord, to your slave, because I spoke evil[29] in ignorance before you." In between these two clauses, the longer text inserts the line "*kai pheisai tēs paidiskēs sou*" (and spare your serving girl), perhaps to bring the passage in closer conformity with Psalm 85.16 "*dos to kratos sou tō paidi sou kai sōson ton huion tēs paidiskēs sou*" (Give strength to your slave/child, and save the son of your serving girl). The deletion of the words "son of" are obviously required, given the narrative, as is perhaps the use of the gender-specific *doulē* instead of the neuter *pais*. The other small change in the longer text also suggests intentional revision designed to conform with an earlier revision. Unlike the shorter text, Aseneth here speaks "in herself," consistent with her silent soliloquies in chapters 11 and 12.[30]

In chapter 13, Aseneth recapitulates in hymnic form the prior narrative of her abasement. The juxtaposing of a poetic version of the story with a prose version may itself be an artificial device intended to evoke biblical forms, such as the duplicative telling of the story of Deborah, Barak, Jael, and Sisera in Judges 4 and 5 or the deliverance of the Israelites and the celebratory songs of Moses and of Miriam in Exodus 15. In all three instances, the poetic form follows the prose narrative. The longer and shorter texts are relatively close here, with some predictable differences: as I noted earlier, the shorter text reiterates that Aseneth threw her dinner to the dogs, while, consistent with the earlier difference, the longer identifies the dogs as foreign or strange. The longer text also contains the detail, inconsistent with the prior narrative, that the smashed gold and silver idols were snatched up by thieves. Both texts have Aseneth reiterate that she sinned against God out of ignorance and spoke blasphemy against Joseph. Woven into 12.7–13.2 are Aseneth's specific petitions to God: to deliver her from her persecutors (12.7); to stretch forth his hands to her and snatch her out of the hands of the enemy (12.8); to deliver her from the devil (*ho diabolos*, 12.9); to save her (12.11); to pardon her sin of speaking in ignorance about Joseph (13.9); and finally, in 13.12, to guard Joseph within the wisdom of God's graciousness and to deliver Aseneth to Joseph as a servant.

Aseneth's Initial Words to the Angel

In the shorter and longer descriptions of the initial exchange between Aseneth and the angelic figure, a very subtle difference occurs that may possibly suggest that the author of the shorter text either knows the Hebrew texts or knows a Greek translation that is closer to the Hebrew than the Septuagint/Old Greek.

The angel's call to Aseneth and her response closely follow the formula present in several biblical narratives, including God's call to Abraham in Genesis 22.1, the call of the angel of the Lord to Abraham in Genesis 22.11, God's call to Moses in Exodus 3.4, and God's call to Samuel in 1 Kings 3.4 and 3.6. In the shorter version, at 14.4, the angel calls Aseneth's name, and she wonders who is calling her. At 14.6, he calls her name twice, "Aseneth, Aseneth," and she replies, "Here I am."[31]

Curiously, that the angel seems to call Aseneth once at 14.4 and twice at 14.6 also characterizes the narrative of the Hebrew Genesis 22. At 22.1, God calls Abraham's name just once; when the angel calls Abraham in Genesis 22.11, he repeats the name twice. But in the LXX of Genesis 22.1, God calls Abraham's name twice. However, in the longer text, at 14.6 and at 14.4, the angel calls Aseneth's name twice. Something similar is also true for the Greek of 1 Kings 3.4 and 3.6. Whereas the Hebrew has God call Samuel by name twice in 3.4 and once in 3.6, the Septuagint/Old Greek has God call Samuel twice in both verses. This may suggest that the revision of the longer text is a deliberate attempt to bring the Aseneth call into closer conformity with the readings of the Septuagint/Old Greek, a tendency that appears to characterize the concerns of the redactor(s).

The Angel Foretells Aseneth's Future:
Aseneth's Name Inscribed in the Book of Life (15.2b–3)

At the end of chapter 14, the angelic figure instructs Aseneth to remove her mourning garments, wash her face in living water, and clothe herself in new garments. When she complies, he says the following:

15.2–5/**15.4–6**
Behold, (the Lord has) **I have** heard **all the words of** your confession **and your prayer**.
Behold, I have also seen the humiliation and the affliction of the seven days of your want (of food).
Behold, from your tears and these ashes, plenty of mud has formed before your face.
Take courage, Aseneth, **holy virgin**.
For behold, your name was written in the book of (Life) **the Living in (the) heaven, in the beginning of the book; your name was written first of all, by my finger** and it shall not be erased for all time.[32]
Behold, from today, you will be renewed
and formed anew
and revived,
and you will eat **blessed** bread of life,
and drink a **blessed** cup of immortality

and be anointed with **blessed** ointment of incorruptibility.

Take courage, Aseneth, **holy virgin**.

Behold, **I** have given you **today** to Joseph for a bride, and he **himself** will be your bride-groom **forever and ever**.

The differences between the two versions, while sometimes subtle, are quite significant. The consistent additions of the phrase "holy virgin" to describe Aseneth and of the word "today" for the various actions effected may demonstrate consistent redactional repetition of the immediately prior pronouncement of the angelic figure at 15.1: *today* you are a *holy* virgin (*ei parthenos hagnē sēmeron*). The careful description in the longer reconstruction of the bread, cup, and ointment as *blessed* may reflect redactional desire to be consistent with Joseph's speech at 8.5, where these three things are all described as "blessed."

In the shorter text, the figure informs Aseneth that the Lord has heard her confession and has given her to Joseph. In the longer, it is the figure himself who performs these deeds, and he speaks throughout in the first person.[33] When he then tells Aseneth that he has heard her confession *and her prayer*, we may have yet another instance of self-conscious redactional acknowledgment of the appending of the silent prayers to the voiced confession of the shorter text.

The longer reconstruction modifies and supplements the statement that Aseneth's name is written in the Book of Life, changing this to the Book of the Living in heaven and specifying that her name was written by the speaker's finger. The tradition of a divine list of names occurs in Exodus 32.32–33, and *Jubilees* 30.22 (and 36.10) specifically mentions a "book of life."[34] Imputing the writing of the book to "the finger" of the angelic being may relate to Exodus 31.18, where the tablets of stone are written by the finger of God. This motif recurs shortly, at **15.12x**, in the longer text only, as I will consider later.

After announcing her forthcoming marriage to Joseph, the figure informs Aseneth that she will no longer be called by that name, but rather City of Refuge (*polis katafygēs*), as discussed in the previous chapter (and also chapter 9). In the subsequent narrative, not surprisingly, Aseneth goes right back to being called by her ordinary name.

15.6/**15.7**

And no longer shall you **your name** be called Aseneth, but your name shall be City of Refuge, because in you many nations shall take refuge **with the Lord God the Most High** and under your wings many peoples **trusting in the Lord God** shall take shelter and in your fortress/walls those who devote themselves to **the Most High** God through Repentance shall be protected.

Although the longer and shorter texts are reasonably close here, the longer text will reintroduce the name change when Joseph and Aseneth are finally united, almost as though the redactor has noticed this inconsistency and seeks to rectify it. Further, the longer text consistently inserts the name of God into this passage, twice using the adjectival *Hypsistos* (Most High). The impetus for these changes may in fact be the last phrase of 15.6 (to God through Repentance) and the continuation of the description of Repentance in the shorter text at 15.7 as daughter of the Most High.

The Figure of Metanoia (Repentance) in the Shorter and Longer Versions

The differences between the shorter and longer depictions of Metanoia, or Repentance, who appears to be Aseneth's heavenly double just as the angelic figure is Joseph's double, are consistent with the different treatments of the angel's statements immediately preceding this pronouncement.

15.7–8

For Metanoia (Repentance) is **in the heavens, an exceedingly beautiful and good** a daughter of the Most High, and she appeals to the Most High on your behalf every hour, and on behalf of all those who repent **in the name of the Most High God**, because he is the father of Metanoia and she is the (mother) **guardian** of virgins, and **loves you very much and** at every hour she appeals to (him) **the most High** for those who repent, for she has prepared (a heavenly bridal chamber for those who love her) **for all those who repent a place of rest in the heavens and she will renew all those who repent** and she will serve them for eternal time.

And Metanoia is a very beautiful virgin, pure **and laughing always** and holy and gentle, and God the Most High **Father** loves her and all the angels stand in awe of her. **And I, too, love her exceedingly, because she is also my sister. And because she loves you virgins, I love you, too**.

Consistent with the additions to the previous verse, the longer text specifies God as the object of repentance, and emphasizes his fatherhood. Metanoia is explicitly located in the heavens, in line with the tendency of the longer version to specify spatial and other details.

Rather than the mother of virgins, Metanoia is here said to be the guardian, or overseer (*episkopos*),[35] of virgins. Rather than a bridal chamber, the Metanoia of the longer text prepares a place of rest for the repentant. These two changes are probably linked together, altering the more gender-specific imagery of Metanoia as the mother who prepares her daughter's bridal chamber to a more inclusive image of the overseer who prepares a place of rest.[36] The Metanoia of the longer text is not only beautiful, pure, virgin, and meek, but always laughing. In the previous chapter, I suggested that Metanoia's hourly petitioning of God on behalf of the repentant resembles Wisdom's daily petitioning of God in Proverbs 8.30a: "I was daily his delight." The seemingly small detail of her perpetual laughter in some versions of the longer text may derive from the second half of that verse: "rejoicing before him always."[37]

It also appears that the longer text revises the portrait of Metanoia to conform to Wisdom traditions more closely in other ways. When the longer text has Metanoia prepare a place of rest rather than a bridal chamber, this is consistent with traditions that with Wisdom, the Wise Man finds rest (Wis Sol 8.16), and she rescues from their troubles all who serve her (Wis Sol 10.9).

In the shorter text, Wisdom's residence in the heavens may be implicit in her proximity to God and in her hourly appeals on behalf of the repentant. In the longer text at 15.7, it is explicit: "For Metanoia is in the heavens, a beautiful and exceedingly good [*agathe*] daughter of the Most High." In the same section of Wisdom of Solomon, Wisdom resides in the heavens, by the throne of God's glory (Wis Sol 8.10).[38]

In the shorter version, Metanoia's qualities are juxtaposed with God's love for her and the angelic respect she commands. In the longer version, the narrator's voice asserts a causal relationship between her attributes and divine response. In the prior verses of the longer version, the heavenly figure claimed responsibility for actions that the narrator of the shorter version attributes directly to God. At this point, the figure distinguishes himself from God, claiming that Metanoia is his sister, whom he loves exceedingly. In subsequent chapters, I will consider the probability thatthis, too, strengthens the identification of the figure in the longer text as the divine co-regent.

The last additional line of this section is quite puzzling, for it appears to be addressed to a plural audience whose presence is not justified by the narrative. "**And because she [Metanoia] loves you [plural] virgins, I love you, too.**" It would be tempting to suggest that this phrase points to the audience of the revised version.[39]

The Mystery of the Figure's Name (Longer Text Only) 15.11–12x

Both reconstructions concur that at the conclusion of the figure's speech, Aseneth throws herself on the ground yet again and blesses the God who sent the angelic figure. The phrasing in the longer text is, as usual, much more expansive. It inserts the otherwise missing title "Most High" and expands the description of Aseneth's obeisance to the figure to conform to her earlier actions at 14.10 (and to general protocols for such response). Most significantly, it contains an important additional interchange between Aseneth and the figure.

> 15.12–13/**15.11–12x**
>
> And as the figure finished speaking **these words** (to) Aseneth, (she) was **exceedingly** joyously happy **about all these words** and threw herself before his feet **and prostrated herself face down to the ground before him** and said to him: "Blessed is the Lord **your** God **the Most High** who sent you to me to deliver me from the darkness and to lead me (into the light) **up from the foundations of the abyss,** and blessed (is his) **be your** name forever."[40] **What is your name, Lord; tell me in order that I may praise and glorify you for ever (and) ever. And the man said to her: "Why do you seek this, my name, Aseneth? My name is in the heavens in the book of the Most High, written by the finger of God in the beginning of the book before all (the others), because I am chief of the house of the Most High. And all names written in the book of the Most High are unspeakable, and man is not allowed to pronounce nor hear them in this world, because those names are exceedingly great and wonderful and laudable."**

In the shorter text, Aseneth concludes by blessing the name of God forever. Such behavior accords well with the notion underlying biblical protocols for prayer that fulfilled prayer required a public response. But in the longer reconstruction, she then blesses not the name of God but the name of the figure. But of course, within the narrative framework of the text she doesn't know the figure's name; all she knows is the figure's identity as angelic commander. So she asks the figure: "**What is your name, Lord; tell me in order that I may praise and glorify you for ever (and) ever.**" The figure refuses to divulge his name but does say that his "name" is written in the heavens in the Book of the Most High, by the finger of God in the beginning of the book, before all other names. This response creates a careful analogue between the name of the angel and Aseneth's name: her name is the first name in the Book of the Living, written by the finger of the angelic figure; his name is the first name in the Book of the Most High, written by the finger of God. But the names that are written in the Book of the Most High may not be pronounced or heard by humans in this world, whereas the names in the book of the living may presumably be safely pronounced.

It is only in the longer text that Aseneth asks the angel his name and only in the longer text that the angel refuses to divulge this. In chapters 5 and 6, I will explore the implications of these differing versions further. But here we may note that part of the changes in the longer version are quite consistent with the pattern of certain additions, whose function (if not also intention) appears to be to bring the text into closer conformity with an underlying biblical paradigm. Assuming the narrative of Judges 13 to be the framework of the story, as I have argued in the previous chapter, the redactor of the longer version notices that a key scene from Judges 13 is missing (v. 17, where Manoah asks the angel his name) and so creates such a scene, with a similar answer. The interrelation between Judges 13 and *Aseneth* **15.12x** is easier to see when one compares the Greek:

Judges 13.17–18 (Alexandrinus) [A]
Ti onoma soi, hina, hotan elthē to rhēma sou, doxasōmen se: kai eipen auto ho angelos kyriou Hina ti touto erōtas to onoma mou: kai autō estin thaumaston.
"What is your name, so that when your words come to pass, we will glorify you," and the angel of the Lord said to him, "Why do you ask my name: it is too wonderful."[41]
(Vaticanus) [B]
Ti to onoma soi; hoti elthoi to rhēma sou, kai doxasomen se. Kai eipen autō ho angelos kyriou Eis ti touto erōtas to onoma mou kai auto estin thaumaston.
Aseneth **15.12x**
Ti esti to onoma sou kyrie anaggelon moi hina hymnēsō kai doxasō se eis ton aiōna chronon.
What is your name, Lord, tell me, that I may sing hymns and glorify you for eternal time?

The angel's lengthy response to Aseneth concludes in accord with the Judges 13.18 in its emphasis on the wondrous quality (*thaumaston*) of his name.[42] Furthermore, the insertion of the phrases "these words" (*ta rhēmata tauta*) and "all these [Burchard: literally his] words" (*pasi tois rhēmasin autou*) at **15.11** may also be attributed to the language of Judges 13.17: "What is your name, so that when *your words* come to pass, we may glorify you?" It is also likely that concern for consistency accounts for the repeated presence of the phrase *ta rhēmata mou* (translated by Burchard as "what I have to say") in the longer reading at **14. 8**, **14.11**, and **14.13**.

Also relevant for the construction of this scene is Genesis 32.27–29, the story of Jacob wrestling with an angel. When Jacob prevails, the angel gives Jacob his new name, Israel, but when Jacob then asks the angel's name, he responds by saying, "[W]hy do you ask my name?" and then blesses Jacob, without ever revealing his name.[43]

The longer text may thus be seen to manifest a serious interest in the name of the angel as well as in the name of God, not only here but also particularly in the pre-confession soliloquies (**11.17–18**), which is absent in the shorter version.

The Angel and the Honeycomb

In both versions, after Aseneth blesses God, she offers to prepare a meal of bread and wine, an offer that continues the paradigm of Judges 13. But in a response absent from Judges, the angel asks her to bring a honeycomb as well. Once again, the shorter and longer texts are predictably somewhat different, but in both, Aseneth finds a honeycomb in her storeroom and brings it to the angel.

16.4–8/**16.8–14**

And Aseneth went into her chamber and found a honeycomb lying on the table, and the comb was **big and** as white as snow and full of honey. **And that honey was like dew from heaven** and its breath was like the (scent) **breath** of life. **And Aseneth wondered and said in herself, Did then this comb come out of the man's mouth, because its breath is like the breath of this man's mouth?** And Aseneth took the comb and brought (it) to him, **and put it on the table which she had prepared before him** and the figure said to her, "Why did you say 'There is no honeycomb in my (house) **storeroom**,' and behold you bring (it) **a wonderful honeycomb** (to me)?"

And Aseneth **was afraid and** said, "I did not have, lord, any honeycomb in my (house) **storeroom, at any time**, but as you said, it has happened.[44] Might it not have come from your mouth, since its breath is like the breath (of perfume) **of your mouth**?"

And the figure **smiled at Aseneth's understanding, and called her to himself and** stretched forth his **right** hand and took hold of her head **and shook her head with his right hand. And Aseneth was afraid of the figure's hand, because sparks shot forth from his hand as from bubbling (melted) iron. And Aseneth looked, gazing with her eyes at the figure's hand. And the figure saw it and smiled** and said, "Blessed are you Aseneth, that the unspeakable (things) **mysteries**[45] of (God) **the Most High** have been revealed to you; and blessed are those who devote themselves to **the Lord** God in repentance, for they shall eat from this comb. **For this comb is the spirit of Life**.

For this (honey) the bees of the paradise of delight have made **from the dew of the roses of life that are in the paradise of God**, and **all** the angels of God eat of it, **and all the chosen of God and all the sons of the Most High, because this is a comb of life** and all who eat of it shall not die for eternity.

Once again, the longer version repeatedly uses the qualifier *Hypsistos* (Most High). Only in the longer text is the honey explicitly identified, twice, with dew. The heavenly honey is food not only for the angels of God but also for all the chosen (or the elect) of God and all the sons of God. This is consistent with the longer version's emphasis on Aseneth as only one of God's chosen or elect. It is not immediately apparent to whom the terms "chosen of God" and "sons of the Most High" apply and whether they make distinctions among the inhabitants of the heavenly realms.[46] Aseneth's silent reflection on the nature of the honeycomb repeats the form (though not the content) of her earlier silent prayers that occur only in the longer reconstruction.

In the longer version, Aseneth responds to the angel's touch with fear because hot sparks emanate from his hand. Significantly, this small detail is also present in the description of the angelic figure when he first appears to Aseneth, at **14.10**, where only the longer text specifies that "sparks shot forth from his hands and feet." This scene is reminiscent of Isaiah 6.6, through which the redactor may also have refracted the scene where the angel touches the honey to Aseneth's mouth:

> Then one of the seraphs flew to me, holding a live coal that had been taken from the altar with a pair of tongs. The seraph touched my mouth with it, and said, "Now that this has touched your lips, your guilt has departed and your sin is blotted out."

Interestingly, this same imagery occurs in the writings of the fourth-century C.E. Syrian Christian Ephrem, who identifies the Coal of Fire in Isaiah 6.6 with Christ and gives the following description of the Encounter of Christ with Anna in the temple:

> The prophetess Anna embraced Him
> and put her mouth to His lips.
> The Spirit rested on her lips, as on Isaiah's
> his mouth was silent, but the Coal of Fire
> opened up his mouth by touching his lips.[47]

Anna then sings a hymn to Christ. In Ephrem's interpretation, Christians are able to consume the Coal of Fire, whereas even the seraph in Isaiah, let alone Isaiah, could not.[48] Whether or not Ephrem's work has some bearing on the use of this tradition in which the longer version,[49] at the very least, the redactor may rely on a tradition in which forgiveness of sins requires such an act.

Next, in the shorter version (16.9), the angel simply breaks off a piece of the comb, eats it, and puts some honey into Aseneth's mouth with his hand. In the longer version, he first instructs her, saying, "[E]at."

16.9/**16.15–16x**
And the figure stretched out his right hand and broke off (a piece) from the comb and ate, and **what was left he** put (a piece) of the comb into Aseneth's mouth with his hand **and said to her, "Eat." And she ate. And the figure said to Aseneth, "Behold you have eaten bread of life and drunk a cup of immortality and been anointed with ointment of incorruptibility. Behold, from today your flesh (will) flourish like flowers of life from the ground[50] of the Most High, and your bones will grow strong like the cedars of the paradise of delight of God, and untiring powers will embrace you, and your youth will not see old age,[51] and your beauty will not fail forever. And you shall be like a walled mother-city of all who take refuge with the name of the Lord God, the king of the ages." And the figure stretched out his right hand and touched the comb where he had broken off (a portion) and it was restored and filled up, and at once it became whole as it was in the beginning.**

The seemingly small addition of the angel's injunction to Aseneth to eat allows the story to be read now as an inversion of Genesis 2–3. There, of course, a woman eats the fruit of mortality and shares it with her husband. Here a masculine figure (a double of Aseneth's future husband, Joseph) eats the food of immortality and then gives some to the woman. Not only does the angel give this transformative food to Aseneth, but he explicitly tells her to eat it. In Genesis 3.12, Adam says only that Eve gave him the fruit and he ate it. But in Genesis 3.17, God says to Adam, "[Y]ou have listened to the voice of your wife," implying that Eve actually spoke to Adam. Thus this small detail reverses the biblical account with careful precision.[52]

Immediately after, the angel makes a statement that is significantly absent from the shorter text, equating the consumption of the honey with the triple acts of eating the bread of life, drinking the cup of immortality, and being anointed with the oil of incorruptibility. Although some scholars have seen this as evidence for an actual ritual that represented this triad,[53] it may instead point to a redactor who noticed the absence of explicit fulfillment of the triple blessing promised to Aseneth by Joseph, and who solved the problem by equating the three with the one.[54]

The remainder of **16.16–16x** contains additional allusions to the restoration of paradise, all of which is, again, absent in the shorter text. The introductory phrase, "Behold, from today," echoes the language of the shorter version at 15.4, found also in the longer reconstruction at **15.5**.[55] Particularly interesting here is the phrase "your bones will grow strong [*ta osta sou pianthēsontai*] like the cedars of the paradise of delight of God." The reference to bones growing strong also occurs in verse 11 of Isaiah 58 (*ta osta sou hos botanē anatelei kai pianthēsetai*), whose possible role in the construction of this narrative I considered in the previous chapter. The comparison to the cedars of the paradise of delight (a phrase used in the Septuagint/Old Greek to describe the garden of Eden) calls to mind Sirach 24.13, where Wisdom, recounting her flourishing in the temple of God in Jerusalem, says, "I grew tall like the cedars in Lebanon." Similar imagery also occurs in Psalm 91.13–15 (Heb 92.13–14): "The righteous one . . . grows like a cedar in Lebanon" (*Dikaios . . . hosei kedros hē en tō Libanō plethynthēsetai*). Yet again, the longer tradition appears to know and enhance the traditional language and imagery implicit in the shorter text.

In the longer text here, as at a number of other points, the alterations may contribute to the enhanced presentation of Aseneth as Wisdom. In the shorter text, when Aseneth correctly identifies the source of the honeycomb, the angel pronounces her blessed because the unspoken things of God (*ta apporēta tou theou*) have been revealed to her (16.7). In the longer text **(16.14)**, she is the recipient of *ta apporēta mysteria tou hypsistou*—the unspeakable mysteries of the Most High, perhaps consonant with the tradition in Wisdom of Solomon 8.4 that Wisdom is an initiate (*mystos*) in his knowledge (Wis Sol 8.4).

The longer narrative of this section concludes with the angel's restoration of the honeycomb to its original whole condition. This may or may not be intended as a symbol of the restoration of paradise that Aseneth's deeds have effected, but the language of the verse certainly allows that reading: "[A]t once it became whole as it was in the beginning [*en archē*]," precisely the words with which the Greek Genesis opens.

The Drama of the Bees

In the subsequent scene, the angelic figure shows Aseneth a most puzzling drama of the bees. Once again, significant and consistent differences distinguish the shorter and longer reconstructions.

16.10–17.2/**16.17–17.2**
And **again** the figure stretched forth his **right** hand and put his finger on the edge of the comb facing east, **and drew it over the edge looking west** and the path of his finger

became like blood. And he stretched forth his hand a second time and put his finger on the edge of the comb facing north, **and drew it over to the edge looking south** and the path of his finger became like blood.

And Aseneth stood to the left and observed everything the figure did.

And the figure said to the comb, "Come." And bees came up out of the hive **cells** of the comb, **and the cells were innumerable, ten thousand (times) ten thousand and thousands upon thousands**[56] and they were white as snow, and their wings were purple and the color of hyacinth and **like scarlet stuff and** as golden thread, and there were gold diadems on their heads and sharp stingers **and they would not injure anyone.**

And all the bees entwined around Aseneth from [her] feet to [her] head, and other bees **were** (as) large **and chosen like their** (as) queens [bees], **and they rose (from the damaged part of)**[57] **the comb and** attached themselves to Aseneth's **mouth and made upon her mouth and lips**(.) **a comb similar to the comb which was lying before the figure. And all those bees ate of the comb which was on Aseneth's mouth.**

And the figure said to the bees, "Go then away to your own place." (And they all left Aseneth) and all **the bees rose and flew and went away into heaven. And those who wanted to injure Aseneth** fell down to the ground and died. And the figure **stretched out his staff over the dead bees and** said **to them** "Arise **you, too** and go (back) **away** to your place." And (they) **the bees who had died** rose up and went away, (all of them), to the courtyard adjacent to Aseneth(.)**'s house and sought shelter on the fruit-bearing trees**.

And the figure said to Aseneth, "Have you perceived what was said [*eorakas to rhema touto*]?" And she said, "(Behold), lord, I have perceived all this [*(idou egō) nai*, kyrie, eoraka tauta panta]." And the figure said, "So shall be the words I have spoken to you **today** [*houtos estai ta rhēmata ha elalēsa pros se sēmeron*]."

Some of the changes in the longer reconstruction are consistent with redactional efforts to be precise and consistent (specifying the right hand,[58] qualifying the words spoken "today," and perhaps also clarifying the motions of the figure's hand). The description of the bees as "chosen like their queens" may echo the reference to the "chosen of God" in **16.8**. It is also interesting that only in the longer text, at **12.7** and **28.14**, is Aseneth described as "queen," an identification that may then allow the longer text to be read as intentionally associating the queen bees with Aseneth the queen.[59]

Not inconceivably, some of the other additions of the longer text are grounded in the terse allusion to two sets of bees in the shorter text ("all the bees," and the "other bees" at 16.14) and represent an effort to account for the second set of bees and their actions.

Although I will explore the possible interpretations of this passage at length in subsequent chapters, it may be that the longer text wishes to make some statement either about good and bad angels or about good and bad souls, or both. What was, in the shorter text, a general scenario of death and resurrection takes on a moral quality directly related to Aseneth: those who wish to harm her die and are resurrected, assuming their place in the courtyard, while the good bees do not appear to experience death in the first place but rather go directly to heaven.[60] But the phrase governing the bees in the longer text (**16.21**), "*kai anestēsan pasai hai melissai,*" does employ the same verb used in Christian texts to designate resurrection from the dead. It seems obvious that the longer version of this scene lends itself to a different allegorical interpretation, but scholars have been singularly unsuccessful in their attempts to decode it.[61]

At the conclusion of this scene in the shorter text, the figure touches the honey-comb, and it is consumed by fire that rises up from the table, exuding a sweet odor as it burns. This is clearly an allusion to sacrifice, particularly as described in Judges 6 and 13. The longer text specifies that the figure touches the damaged part of the comb, which is odd, since in 16.16x the honeycomb has been restored to its original state. It also mentions that the table was not consumed by the fire, perhaps in response to the obvious concern that it might have been!

The Blessing of the Seven Virgins 17.4–17.5

Aseneth then asks the angelic figure to bless her seven virgin companions as he has blessed her, to which he assents.

17.4–5/**17.4–6**

And Aseneth said to the figure, "There are, lord, seven virgins with me serving me, raised with me since my childhood, born on the same night with me, and I love them **as my sisters**. I will call them and you will bless them as you have blessed me."

And the figure said, "Call **them.**" And Aseneth called (them) **the seven virgins and stood them before the figure**, and the figure blessed them and said, "God, The Most High, will bless you **and you shall be seven pillars of the City of Refuge, and all the fellow inhabitants of the chosen of that city will rest upon you** for eternal time."

Not only do the seven pillars and the City of Refuge call to mind the figure of Woman Wisdom in the Book of Proverbs,[62] but this insertion reinforces the imagery of Metanoia at **14.7**, as does the designation of the virgins as Aseneth's sisters, imagery that is also present only in the longer reconstruction.

In the shorter text, the figure now instructs Aseneth to remove the table. As she turns to do so, the figure disappears, and Aseneth glimpses something like a fiery chariot being taken up to heaven in the east.

17.6/**17.7–8**

And the figure said to Aseneth, "Remove this table." And Aseneth turned to move the table, and the figure disappeared from her sight, and Aseneth saw something like a (fiery) chariot **of four horses** being taken up into the heaven to the east. **And the chariot was like a flame of fire, and the horses like lightning. And the man was standing on that chariot.**

This description not only recalls the disappearance of the angelic being in both Judges 6 and 13 but also appears to draw on the ascension of Elijah into heaven in 2 Kings 2.11: "As they [Elisha and Elijah] continued walking and talking, a chariot of fire and horses of fire separated the two of them, and Elijah ascended into heaven in a whirlwind." Consonant with its preference for additional, often biblicized details, the longer text specifies that the heavenly figure stood on the chariot, which had four horses like lightning.

Observing the figure's disappearance, Aseneth responds as follows:

17.7/**17.9–10**

And Aseneth said, "**Foolish and bold am I**, because I have spoken with audacity and said that a man came into my chamber from heaven; and I did not know that God [or: a god] came to me. And behold, now he is traveling (back) into heaven to his

place. And she said in herself, "Be merciful, lord, to your slave **and spare your maid-servant**, because I spoke (evil) **boldly all my words** in ignorance (before you)."

Here again, the longer text not only clarifies what it is that Aseneth said in ignorance but also appears to expand the underlying imagery of this scene, drawing, as I have suggested earlier, on LXX/OG Psalm 85.16 to supply the additional language. That Aseneth once again speaks "in herself" appears to be a characteristic feature of the longer version and here serves as an inclusio. Just as Aseneth's formal plea to God begins with a silent prayer at 11.2 followed by vocalized prayer beginning at 11.19, so, too, the conclusion of her transformation and associated pleas to God are ended with vocalized speech, followed by a silent prayer.

Joseph's Arrival Imminent (18.1–2)

As Joseph's angelic double ascends into heaven, a servant of the earthly Joseph appears to announce his imminent arrival. Aseneth responds by instructing the steward of her house to prepare a fine dinner. This terse scene encapsulates Aseneth's transformation, with its suggestion that now Aseneth's table will be acceptable to Joseph.

In the shorter text, Aseneth then goes to her chamber and dresses herself in anticipation of Joseph's imminent arrival. The longer text here interjects a scene between Aseneth and a male servant called a *tropheus* (literally, one who provides nourishment, translated by Burchard as "foster-father"), who appears now for the first time. This episode is wholly without precedent in the shorter version.

The *tropheus* immediately notices the terrible shape Aseneth is apparently still in, as a result of her weeklong ordeal, and expresses his great concern, weeping himself, and kissing her hand. Aseneth conceals the truth of her experience from him, offering him a variant of the excuse she first gave to the seven virgins. She attributes her appearance to a headache and the subsequent lack of sleep. While the detail of the headache may come from the earlier scene, common to both reconstructions, it is possible to see some of the elements of this scene as drawn from traditions such as Psalm 31.11–13:[63]

> I am the scorn of all my adversaries
> a horror to my neighbors,
> an object of dread to my acquaintances;
> those who see me in the street
> flee from me.

But as I shall shortly discuss, the story of the *tropheus* ultimately functions to minimize the impact of Aseneth's transformation into an angel in the chapters to come.

Aseneth's Final Physical Transformation

18.3–6/**18.5–6**
And Aseneth remembered the man and his commandment and she hurried and went into her **second** chamber **where the chests (containing) her ornaments were** and

opened her **big** chest and took out her first robe, **(the one) of wedding**, which had the appearance of lightning, and put it on. And she girded herself with a brilliant, royal girdle. This girdle was the one with precious stones. And she put gold bracelets around her hands, and gold trousers[64] about her feet, and a precious ornament about her neck **in which innumerable and costly precious stones were fastened**, and she placed a gold crown on her head; and on this crown in front **on her brow was a big sapphire stone and around the big stone** there were **six** very expensive stones. And she covered her head with a veil, **like a bride and she took a scepter in her hand**.

In both versions, Aseneth's completed costume is virtually identical to the one she wore when she first expected to meet Joseph, with the notable absence of the stones bearing the images and names of the gods of Egypt and the presence, in the longer reconstruction, of a scepter.

In the shorter version, thirty terse verses separate the figure's instructions in 15.10 to dress in wedding clothes and prepare to meet Joseph from Aseneth's performance of them in 18.3. But in the longer version, partly because of the insertion of the scene with the *tropheus*, the interval is considerably greater, which may account for the insertion of the phrase, "And Aseneth remembered the figure and his commandment" (**18:5b**), implicitly explaining why it has taken her so long to carry out his earlier command.

In both texts, Aseneth takes out a robe called "first," which has the appearance of lightning. Clearly evoking the clothing of gods and angels, it may also allude to the primal garments of Adam and Eve. The tradition that the primal couple were originally clothed not in garments of skin (Gen 3.21) but in garments of light or a robe of glory occurs in a number of early Christian and somewhat later Jewish sources.[65] It is particularly significant in Ephrem, for whom the purpose of Christ's incarnation is to restore this lost robe of glory to Adam—to return Adam (and Eve) to Eden in the garment of light.[66]

In the longer version, Aseneth's robe, called "first," is explicitly said to be a wedding gown, and when she covers her head with a veil, she is said to do so "as a bride." It seems quite conceivable that the redactor here has noticed that although, at 15.10 (in both versions), the angelic figure instructed Aseneth to put on a wedding gown (*stolēn gamou*) and dress as a bride,[67] in the shorter version of 18.3, there is nothing explicitly bridal about Aseneth's attire.

Immediately after Aseneth changes her garments and ornaments, she asks an attendant for water.

18.7/18.7–9.

And she said to her (young female attendant) **foster-sister**,[68] "Bring me pure water from the spring **and I will wash my face." And she brought her pure water from the spring and poured it into the basin.** And Aseneth bent down **to wash her face and saw her face** in(to) the water (in the bowl on the conch shell). And (her face) **it** was like the sun, and her eyes like (the) **a rising** morning star **and her cheeks like the fields of the Most High, and on her cheeks red like a son of man's blood, and her lips like a rose of life coming out of its foliage, and her teeth like fighting men lined up for a fight, and the hair of her head like a vine in the paradise of God prospering in its fruits, and her neck like an all-variegated cypress, and her breasts like the mountains of the Most High God.**

In the shorter text, Aseneth gives no reason for requesting the spring water. Philonenko saw in this a clear allusion to the ancient practice of divination by inspecting a bowl of water.[69] The use of a silver cup for divination is explicitly attributed to Joseph in Genesis 44.5. Burchard disputes this claim, arguing that "the text neither says that Aseneth had anything but washing in mind, nor that she was transformed because she looked into the water."[70] His second objection seems reasonable enough, since the water appears to serve more as a mirror than anything else.[71] But his first objection is too influenced, I think, by his preference for the reading of the longer text, which does attribute to Aseneth the desire to wash her face in the spring water.

However, this is highly problematic. For one thing, in both reconstructions, Aseneth has already washed her face (at 15.17/**15.14**), although the longer text has her wash her hands as well. Burchard himself suggests that "[i]n a more hellenized environment she would doubtless have ordered a bath."[72] But since she is already fully clothed, I do not think she washes only her face out of modesty at all.

Although it is precisely the longer text that expands the entire section with the angel, the longer text here appears to minimize, if not contradict, the interpretation of Aseneth's appearance as angelic. This passage may well be the key to the insertion of the story about the *tropheus*.[73] In the longer version, after she dresses, Aseneth remembers the *tropheus*'s observations about her dire appearance, and she worries that Joseph will see her and despise her. Despite the assurance of the angel that Joseph is her divinely ordained spouse forever, Aseneth is now depicted as worrying that Joseph won't want her because she looks a mess! In the longer reconstruction, it is out of such concern that Aseneth asks for the spring water and, as leans over to wash, sees her reflection and is amazed.

The response of the *tropheus* to Aseneth's new appearance is itself quite interesting. His reaction to her spectacular beauty follows precisely the pattern of Aseneth's own response to the angelic figure: he is alarmed, speechless, and frightened, and he ultimately falls at her feet. But when he finally speaks, he recognizes her not as an angelic being but as the chosen bride of God's firstborn son, Joseph, an amazing phrase in itself.[74]

It seems quite possible, then, that the entire episode of the *tropheus* and his concern for Aseneth's appearance may have been inserted in order to downplay the angelic implications of this scene and to emphasize Aseneth's transformation into a bride, even a somewhat heavenly bride at that.[75] Interestingly, Burchard reads this passage as evidence that Aseneth "comes close" to being an angelic being, but he seems to deny her actual transformation, and cites the interesting parallel of 2 Corinthians 3.7–8.

The actual description of the transformed Aseneth is far more expansive in the longer text and is strikingly similar to the description of the beloved woman in Song of Songs:

How beautiful you are, my love,
how very beautiful!
Your eyes are doves behind your veil,[76]
Your hair is like a flock of goats,
moving down the slopes of Gilead.

Your teeth are like a flock of shorn ewes
that have come up from the washing
all of which bear twins,[77]
and not one among them is bereaved.
Your lips are like a crimson thread,
and your mouth is lovely.
Your cheeks are like halves of a pomegranate
behind your veil.
Your neck is like the tower of David,
built in courses;
on it hang a thousand bucklers,
all of them shields of warriors.
Your two breasts are like two fawns,
twins of a gazelle,
that feed among the lilies. (4.1–5)

Several of these verses are repeated in Song of Songs 6.[78] The order is different, as are the actual similes, but the features described are virtually identical: Aseneth's eyes, hair, teeth, lips, cheeks, neck, and breasts. We have already seen that the phrasing of 18.7 in the shorter version, "And her face was like the sun, and her eyes like the rising morning star," shares the imagery of Song of Songs 6.10: "Who is this that looks forth like the dawn, fair as the moon, bright as the sun." Once again, then, the redactor of the longer version fleshes out the text with additional details drawn from the biblical texts that appear already to undergird the shorter version. Perhaps this constitutes an intentional further recasting of Aseneth in the person of the beloved bride, thereby muting the mystical angelic motifs, even for an author for whom Song of Songs was indeed the description of God's bride. This would be in concert with a redactor who also included the scenes about the name but ironically did not have Aseneth learn the name of the angel! But it also seems possible that the bride/lover in Song of Songs was interpreted in mystical traditions as a description of the feminine aspect of God.

The longer text appears to intensify the association of Aseneth with Wisdom. In Wisdom of Solomon 7.26, Wisdom is associated with light (the primordial light of creation) "[S]he is a reflection of eternal light; a spotless mirror of the working of God, and an image [eikōn]of his goodness." Such imagery is reminiscent of the scene in the shorter version at 18.7. But in the longer text, this association is made stronger at **20.6**: "[A]nd [her parents] saw Aseneth like the appearance of light [*eidos phōtos*], and her beauty was like heavenly beauty."[79]

Taken together with her garment of light, this scene in the shorter version affirms Aseneth's angelic transformation. It may also allude to the transformation of Moses in Exodus 34.29–34, which says that when Moses came down from Sinai, he did not know that his face shone because he had been talking to God. After this experience, Moses veils his face before the Israelites except when he goes to speak with God. This lends the veiling of Aseneth an interpretation alternative to the view that it reflects her status as a respectable woman. In subsequent Jewish mystical traditions, Moses' face was believed to shine with the reflection of God's glory. Aseneth's veiling may be analogous to that of Moses: just as Moses spoke with God face to face and beheld an aspect of God, so Aseneth has conversed with God, or at least God's manifestation in the form of the angel. Therefore, like Moses, her face shines and requires a veil to protect others from the brilliance of her face. If so, the reading of the longer text, which makes her veil unambiguously that of a bride, effectively, and perhaps intentionally, mutes the association of Aseneth with Moses.[80]

Joseph and Aseneth Are "Reunited" (19.1–20.4)

In the shorter text, immediately following Aseneth's transformation, a servant then announces Joseph's arrival "before the doors of the courtyard." Aseneth and the seven virgins go down to greet him.

19.2–3/**19.4–20.1**

And (when) Joseph saw her, **(he) was amazed at her beauty and** he said to her, "**Who are you? Quickly tell me.**" And she said to him, "**I am your maidservant, Aseneth, and all the idols I have thrown away from me and they were destroyed. And a man came to me from heaven today, and gave me bread of life, and I ate, and a cup of blessing, and I drank. And he said to me 'I have given you for a bride to Joseph today, and he himself will be your bridegroom for ever (and) ever.' And he said to me, 'Your name will no longer be called Aseneth, but your name will be called City of Refuge and the Lord God will reign over many nations for ever, because in you many nations will take refuge with the Lord God, the Most High.' And the man said to me, 'I will also go to Joseph and speak into his ears concerning you what I have to say.' And now, you know, my Lord, whether that man has come to you and spoken to you concerning me.**" And Joseph said to Aseneth, "**Blessed are you by the Most High God, and blessed (is) your name forever, because the Lord God founded your walls in the highest, and your walls (are) adamantine walls of life, because the sons of the living God will dwell in your City of Refuge and the Lord God will reign as king over them for ever and ever. For this man came to me today and spoke to me words such as these concerning you. And now.** Come here to me, holy virgin, (because I have good news concerning you from heaven, which has told me everything about you) **and why do you stand far away from me.**" And Joseph stretched out his hands and **called Aseneth by a wink of his eyes. And Aseneth also stretched out her hands and ran up to Joseph and fell on his breast. And Joseph** took Aseneth in his arms, and she him, and they embraced for a long time, and their spirits were rekindled. **And Joseph kissed Aseneth and gave her spirit of life, and he kissed her the second time and gave her spirit of wisdom, and he kissed her the third time and gave her spirit of truth. And they embraced each other for a long time and interlocked their hands like bonds.**

This scene thus revisits their initial meeting, but whereas then Joseph refused to touch Aseneth, now he embraces her gladly, signifying her transformation into an acceptable spouse for him. The Joseph of the shorter text has learned the wonderful announcement of Aseneth's repentance and transformation and wastes no time taking her in his arms. But in the longer reconstruction, Joseph (like the *tropheus* at 18.11) is astonished by Aseneth's appearance (which goes unremarked in the shorter text) and feigns ignorance of her identity. In response to his inquiry, Aseneth summarizes the plot and her encounter with the angelic figure.

Aseneth's retelling recapitulates much of the language of the longer reconstruction of chapter 15, although it contains some puzzling details. She claims that the figure gave her the bread of life, which she ate, and the cup of blessing, which she drank, when in the narrative, all Aseneth actually ate was the honey, of which she makes no reference here. The text thus has Aseneth accept the equation of that honey with the bread, wine, and oil. But it is interesting that she omits any reference to anointing with the oil of incorruptibility. If such anointment is associated with sexuality and marriage, its absence here would make sense, since Joseph and Aseneth have not yet engaged in marital intercourse.

Retelling the angel's words at **15.6**, Aseneth now inserts the phrase "and the Lord will reign as king over many nations for ever," language that is similar to but not identical with LXX/OG Psalm 9.37.[81] Joseph's responsive blessing to Aseneth not only repeats this but expands on Aseneth's role as City of Refuge. Finally, he concedes that the angelic figure has visited him with this news, thus acknowledging the somewhat artificial nature of his opening question to her.

In the longer reconstruction, at this point, Joseph and Aseneth not only embrace but they kiss for a long time. Joseph is said to kiss Aseneth three times: the first kiss confers a spirit of life, the second a spirit of wisdom, the third, a spirit of truth. While Burchard suggests that similar ideas and rituals are widespread in ancient sources,[82] the three kisses may also be drawn from Song of Songs 1.2–3, where the three final clauses may be construed to represent the number of kisses:

> Let him kiss me with the kisses of his mouth:
> For your love is better than wine,
> your anointing oils are fragrant,
> your name is perfume poured out.

Given the transparent use of Song of Songs only a few verses earlier at **18.9**, such a suggestion appears particularly feasible.

By contrast, in the shorter text, whether Aseneth and Joseph kiss before their wedding is, at best, ambiguous. At 20.4, Joseph takes Aseneth's hand and kisses either her or her hand (the Greek has only the feminine direct object, so we cannot say, although Philonenko reads it as her hand); in return Aseneth kisses Joseph's head. But in any case, this action takes place only after an additional scene inside the house, as follows.

After Joseph and Aseneth embrace, Aseneth invites Joseph into the house:

20.1/**20.1–2a**
And Aseneth said to (him) **Joseph**, "Come here, **my** lord, come into (my) **our**[83] house **because I have prepared our house and made a great dinner**." And she took his right hand and led him into her house.

It seems quite feasible that the redactor here continues to construct the longer version on the basis of Song of Songs 8.3, having seen in 19.3 of the shorter text (and Aseneth "led him into her house") another allusion to that book. In the biblical verse, we find precisely the connection between the uniting of the lovers and the kiss on which this passage may depend, together with the sibling/lover imagery employed earlier in both versions.

> Oh, that you were like a brother to me,
> who nursed at my mother's breast,
> If I met you outside, I would kiss you

and no one would despise me.
I would lead you and bring you into the house of my mother,
and into the chamber of the one who bore me.

In support of this thesis, we may note another small but significant difference in the reading of the longer text against the shorter. At 19.1, in the latter, we read only that Joseph is before the courtyard doors and that "Aseneth went down with the seven virgins to meet him." But in the longer reconstruction, much more specific spatial relationship is provided. Aseneth comes down and stands in the entrance of the house, while Joseph enters the courtyard. While he is still there, Aseneth goes out of the entrance to meet him. In part, this may reflect redactional concern to explain why, at 20.1, Aseneth invites Joseph into the house, by clarifying that at the time of their initial embrace, he was outside the house. But it also then provides the more detailed consonance with Song of Songs ("if I met you *outside*").

The use of this text may also explain another subtle difference in the two versions. The Aseneth of the shorter text calls the house "hers," while the longer text appears to designate it "ours." Although, as Burchard notes, the textual situation here is quite varied, such a change would be consonant with the implicit reading of Song of Songs, since the house is now not simply hers but her mother's as well.

In both versions, once Joseph is seated on Pentephres' throne, he and Aseneth engage in a small dispute over Aseneth's intention to wash Joseph's feet. Joseph proposes that Aseneth let one of the seven virgins do this, since such activity is presumably the responsibility of servants.[84] Footwashing in antiquity was a mark of deference and associated with ancient hospitality.

20.2– 4/**20.2b–5**

And (Joseph sat down) [**she**] **seated him** upon the throne of Pentephres, her father, and she brought water to wash his feet. And Joseph said (to her), "Let one of the virgins come and wash my feet." And Aseneth said to him, "No, lord, **because you are my lord from now on, and I (am) your maidservant. And why do you say this (that) another virgin (is) to wash your feet?** for my hands are your hands, and your feet are my feet, **and your soul my soul** and no other may wash your feet." And she constrained him and washed his feet. **And Joseph looked at her hands, and they were like hands of life, and her fingers like (the) fingers of a fast-writing scribe.** And **after this** Joseph took her **right** hand and kissed it [or her], and Aseneth kissed his head **and sat at his right (hand).**

In the longer text, Aseneth first grounds her response in her identity as Joseph's servant and then identifies her feet and hands with Joseph's. She also claims that their souls are identical. Burchard views this as "a poetic expression of loving someone like yourself," while Philonenko reads it as an illustration of the mystical union of the two, an interpretation to which Burchard objected.[85] But it may be that again Burchard's view is influenced by his textual choices, for certainly Aseneth's claim that she is Joseph's servant emphasizes her subordination to him and mutes the view of the two as one being. It also seems plausible to me that Philonenko's text has in mind the primordial human being in Genesis 1.26–27 as the dominant paradigm of marital love, whereas Burchard's text here subtly brings in the subordination of Eve to Adam in Genesis 2–3, as it appears to have done earlier in the scene with the eating of the honey.

Still following the longer text, Joseph then observes that Aseneth's hands are like "hands of life" and her fingers like those of a fast-writing scribe. Then he takes her right hand and kisses it. It is conceivable that this insertion is designed to answer the question prompted by a reading of the shorter text: what prompted Joseph to kiss Aseneth's hand (and which hand did he kiss)?

Aseneth Reconciled to Her Family

In a scene that is relatively brief in both reconstructions, Aseneth's parents return from their estate to find the now-united couple.

> 20.5/**20.6–8**
> And (her parents) **her father and mother and his whole family** came from the family estate and saw Aseneth **like (the) appearance of light and her beauty was like heavenly beauty. And they saw her** sitting with Joseph and wearing a wedding robe **And they were amazed at her beauty** and they rejoiced and glorified God **who gives life to the dead** and ate and drank **and celebrated**.

The details of the longer version accord with its earlier passages. Aseneth resembles light, and her beauty has a heavenly quality: it amazes them, just as it amazed Joseph at 19.4. Interestingly, in the shorter text, the first person to be amazed at Aseneth's beauty is Pharaoh, a few verses later, at 21.3. The amazement of Joseph, Aseneth's parents, and even the implicit amazement of the *tropheus* may point to a redactor who found it odd that only Pharaoh appeared amazed at Aseneth's beauty and retrojected that amazement on all who saw Aseneth, not just Pharaoh.[86]

Aseneth's parents' actions are fascinating, for they suggest that her parents, too, have become devotees of Joseph's God, although no elaborate transformation experience is attributed to them. The longer text qualifies the mention of God with the descriptive phrase, "who gives life to the dead."[87] To the claim of the shorter text that her family ate and drank, the longer text also adds that "they celebrated." Citing several biblical and parabiblical examples, Burchard points out that "'to eat, drink and celebrate' is a traditional threesome."[88] This seemingly minor addition may be yet another of the many instances in which the redaction of the longer reconstruction seeks to bring the shorter text into closer conformity with such traditional language, whereas its intentional deletion would be harder to explain.

Pentephres Offers to Make the Wedding

This scene, which is also relatively brief in both texts, addresses an obvious question of the biblical narrative itself, namely, why it was Pharaoh who married Aseneth to Joseph, when presumably that was the normal prerogative of fathers.[89]

> 20.6–7/**20.8–10**
> And Pentephres said to Joseph, "Tomorrow I will call the magnates and satraps of **the whole land of** Egypt and make a wedding for you, and you shall take **my daughter** Aseneth as your wife." And Joseph said, "First, I (must report) **will go** to Pharaoh **the king** (concerning Aseneth), because he is **like a** (my) father **to me, and appointed me**

chief of the whole land of Egypt and I will speak about Aseneth into his ears, and he will give Aseneth to me as a wife." **And Pentephres said to him, "Go in peace."**

While Pentephres offers to make the wedding, Joseph insists that Pharaoh must do so. In the shorter text, this is because Pharaoh is Joseph's father, and he will give Joseph Aseneth for a wife, whereas in the longer text, it is partly because Pharaoh is *like* Joseph's father. Virtually the identical difference occurs at chapter 22.3, when in the shorter version, Aseneth says to Joseph, "I will go and see your father, because your father Israel is my father." In the longer version, Aseneth says, "I will go and see your father, because your father Israel is **like** a father to me **and [g]od**." A similar situation also occurs at 24.13, where the speaker is now Pharaoh's unnamed son. One of the shorter manuscripts[90] reads, "Pharaoh my father is father to Joseph," while the longer texts and another of the shorter manuscripts[91] read, "Pharaoh my father is **like (a)** father to Joseph."

Though it may seem initially (and may partly be true) that the longer text here displays discomfort with an obvious narrative flaw (that Pharaoh, rather than Jacob, is Joseph's father), these passages may reflect an ancient interpretation of Genesis 45.8, where Joseph tells his brothers that Pharaoh has made him "*'av l'Pharaoh*" (father to Pharaoh), apparently an old title of viziers.[92] It would seem initially to reflect some puzzlement or denial of that phrase, since it clearly calls Pharaoh father to Joseph rather than the other way around.[93] But in the end of the tale, the title "Father to Pharaoh" is given a somewhat different explanation. At 29.11/29.9, we read:

> And Joseph was king in Egypt for forty-eight years. And after this Joseph gave the crown to Pharaoh's (grandson) **younger offspring, who was at the breast when Pharaoh died**; and Joseph was like a father to (him) **Pharaoh's younger son** in the land of Egypt **all the days of his life**.

Thus the Pharaoh to whom Joseph is "father" is not the Pharaoh of the Joseph saga in Genesis but a subsequent Pharaoh absent from the biblical narrative. It is not inconceivable that the explanation of the shorter text at 29.12 plays a part in the revision of the longer text back at **20.9, 22.3**, and **24.13**. Further, the claim that the new Pharaoh is the older Pharaoh's younger son, who had been an infant when his father died, may have its origins in the narrative of the shorter version in the verses immediately preceding:

29.8
On the third day, Pharaoh's son died from the wound of Benjamin's stone. And Pharaoh mourned for his eldest son.

When the shorter text then has Joseph turn over his crown to Pharaoh's grandson, it raises several problems that the longer text may be seen to resolve. An astute reader might wonder about the introduction of an otherwise unmentioned grandson and wonder further about whose son this child was and what implications, if any, that might have had for lines of succession. One might also conclude from the explicit designation of the dead son as "eldest" that there must have been a younger one. The longer text thus eliminates the problematic grandson altogether and replaces him, instead, with a younger son, whose existence is implicit in the earlier text and whose apparent absence from the prior narrative is explained by the fact that he was a mere infant when his father, Pharaoh, died.

We may make one further observation about the differences at **20.8–9**, which expand the reading "Egypt" to "the whole land of Egypt" at **20.8** and insert a second reference, to Joseph as ruler over "all the land of Egypt" at **20.9**. This change brings the text once again into closer conformity with biblical formulations, this time of Genesis 41.41, "and Pharaoh said to Joseph, 'See, I have set you over all the land of Egypt,'" a phrase subsequently repeated numerous times.[94]

Shorter and Longer Readings in the Second Part

Aseneth and Jacob

In chapter 22, Jacob and his family settle in Goshen (Genesis 47.27–28), and Aseneth and Joseph go to see him. As we have just seen, the longer version alters Aseneth's words to Joseph in a manner consistent with previous changes. As usual, the initial meeting between Joseph and Aseneth and Jacob is relatively terse, while the longer reading contains several significant differences that accord with earlier passages.

In the shorter text, no description of Jacob is provided, nor does Jacob say anything upon meeting his daughter-in-law. The longer reconstruction supplies a description of Jacob reminiscent of the longer text's readings in chapters 18 and 21, where, as we have seen, various characters are "amazed" at Aseneth's beauty. Here, at **22.7–8**, Aseneth herself is amazed at Jacob's beauty. Not only does the longer text describe Jacob as a beautiful angel with extraordinary physical features, it also contains a scene between Aseneth and Jacob that echoes earlier encounters between humans and angelic figures, whether Joseph himself, his heavenly double, or Aseneth transformed.

22.5–6/**22.6–10**
And they came to Jacob. **And Israel was sitting on his bed, and he was an old man in comfortable old age. And Aseneth saw him and was amazed at his beauty, because Jacob was exceedingly beautiful to look at, and his old age (was) like the youth of a handsome (young) man, and his head was all white as snow, and the hairs of his head were all exceedingly close and thick like (those) of an Ethiopian, and his beard (was) white reaching down to his breast, and his eyes (were) flashing and darting (flashes) of lightning, and his sinews and his shoulders and his arms were like (those) of an angel, and his thighs and his calves and his feet (like) those of a giant. And Jacob was like a man who had wrestled with God.**[95] **And Aseneth saw him and was amazed, and prostrated herself before him face down to the ground. And Jacob said to Joseph, "Is this my daughter-in-law, your wife? Blessed she will be by the Most High God." And Jacob called her to himself and** (he) blessed (them) **her and** kissed (them) **her** and Aseneth **stretched out her hands and grasped Jacob's neck and** hung upon the neck of (his) **her** father (Jacob) **just like someone hangs onto his father's neck when he returns from fighting into his house**, and kissed him.

Interestingly, this angelic description of Jacob is reminiscent of the Prayer of Joseph known to Origen in the third century C.E., whose significance for *Aseneth* I will consider in further detail in subsequent chapters.

Both the shorter and longer texts appear to depend on the tradition occurring in Genesis 46.29 that when Joseph and Jacob were finally reunited in Goshen,[96] Joseph "fell upon (his father's) neck and wept," together with the description of Joseph's reunion with Benjamin in Genesis 45.14–15, where Joseph also "hangs on (his brother's) neck" and weeps and kisses him. In the shorter text, when Aseneth meets Jacob, he blesses and kisses both her and Joseph,[97] and she responds by hanging on his neck and kissing him. In the longer text, Aseneth responds to the more angelic Jacob with predictable response. Amazed yet a second time at the sight of him, she prostrates herself on the ground. As in the shorter text, she then also hangs on his neck, but the longer text inserts additional father imagery here, as it did also in Aseneth's prayer at **12.8**.

Aseneth and Levi

In the shorter text, Joseph and Aseneth return to their own home escorted by Joseph's brothers, Simeon and Levi. The longer text specifies that Simeon and Levi are the sons of Leah and continues: "[B]ut the sons of Zilpah and Bilhah, Leah's and Rachel's maidservants did not escort them, because they envied (them) and were hostile against them."[98] In this passage, too, consistent patterns of alteration are apparent.

22.8–9/**22.13**

And Aseneth took Levi's hand. **And Aseneth loved Levi exceedingly beyond all of Joseph's brothers,** because (she loved him as) **he was one who attached himself to the Lord and was** a **prudent** man (who) **and** was a prophet **of the Most High and sharp-sighted in his eyes**, and (revered God and feared the Lord.)[99] (A)nd he used to see letters written in the heaven **by the finger of God, and he knew the unspeakable things of the Most High God** and (he) would (read them and) interpret them for Aseneth privately **because he, himself, Levi, would love Aseneth very much**, and Levi saw her place of rest in the highest (realms) **and her walls like adamantine eternal walls, and her foundations founded upon a rock of the seventh heaven.**[100]

That Aseneth loves Levi "exceedingly" is a small example of the longer text's preference for this modifier.[101] To the claim that Levi saw letters written in the heavens, the longer text inserts "by the finger of God,"consistent with **15.12x**.[102] Levi knows the "unspeakable (things) of the Most High God," just as at **15.12x**, the angel tells Aseneth that "all names written in the book of the Most High are unspeakable." As in the longer version of **15.7–8**, the angel loves Aseneth's heavenly double Metanoia exceedingly, who prepares a place of rest for those who repent, so in the longer version of **22.13**, Levi loves Aseneth very much[103] and sees her place of rest. Finally, as in the longer version of **19.8**, where Joseph refers to Aseneth's "adamantine walls," so here in **22.13**, Levi sees Aseneth's walls like "adamantine eternal walls." Taken together, these readings suggest that for the longer text, Levi is also an angelic figure analogous to Joseph, whose attributes and actions are revised from the shorter version to emphasize their similarity.

Although the shorter and longer texts are generally fairly close in the remainder of the story that follows, the subtle but consistent pattern of changes may be detected there as well. At both **22.13** and **22.8**, the redactor of the longer version includes the detail that the prophetic Levi was "sharp-sighted with his eyes," a phrase missing from the shorter text, whose insertion may explain how Levi could read the heavenly "grammata." The longer text fleshes out part of the encounter between Pharaoh's son and Levi in such a way as to heighten the suggestion in the shorter text that Levi is a superior or divine being before whom Pharaoh's son must be subordinate.

23.14–16/23.15–17

And Pharaoh's son saw their drawn swords **and was exceedingly** afraid and trembled **over his whole body, because their swords were flashing forth like a flame of fire, and the eyes of Pharaoh's son darkened,** and he fell on his face on the ground beneath their feet. And Levi stretched out his **right** hand and lifted him up/**grasped him,** and said **to him, Rise and** do not be afraid: only be careful you say nothing against our brother **Joseph.**

Conclusion

Throughout this chapter, I have compared a considerable portion of the shorter and longer readings and observed consistent patterns of difference. At numerous points, the longer reconstruction contains details that bring the text into closer conformity with probable underlying biblical and parabiblical paradigms. At other times, the different readings of the longer text appear to clarify ambiguities or to resolve anomalies or difficulties that may be perceived in the shorter reconstruction. In its descriptions of Jacob and of Levi, the longer reconstruction heightens their presentation as angelic figures. While it also appears to do this with regard to Aseneth's transformation, at the same time the longer text appears concerned to subordinate a reading of Aseneth as angelic to her role as Joseph's pre-ordained wife.

Despite the length at which I have pursued some of these differences, I have not exhausted every instance in which the differing readings support these findings. Rather, I think it sufficient to argue here that the nature of these changes is such that it is far easier to account for them as the product of deliberate and careful editorial expansion than to account for them as the result of equally careful editorial abridgement. While it is often, although not always, easy to see what may motivate the change if the movement is from the shorter to the longer, it becomes almost impossible to explain what might have motivated a redactor to excise precisely the bits and pieces that consistently enhance allusions to biblical paradigms, resolve anomalies, and effect the various other changes I have documented here. For these reasons, I think it much more probable that the longer readings generally expand upon the shorter text as reconstructed by Philonenko, and for the remainder of this study, I will assume precisely such a relationship. Nevertheless, in doing so, I will intentionally not follow the path of prior scholarship that, having allegedly determined the "original" or "earliest" reading of the text, abandons the revisions as subsequently uninteresting or insignificant. Rather, for my purposes, both reconstructions of the text are highly significant and of great interest in locating the tale of Aseneth within its late antique context(s).

NOTES

1. However, Philonenko *Joseph et Aséneth,* 8–11, looks cursorily and selectively at some of the issues I consider here.

2. Song 4.5, 7.3. See also breast imagery in Song 8.1, 8.8–10, and Prov 5.12–20: "[R]ejoice in the wife of your youth . . . may her breasts satisfy you at all times."

3. Song 7.8. Another instance of an angel touching a woman's breast occurs in the *Life of*

Adam and Eve 21, in a scene which is essentially a birth annunciation: "And behold, twelve angels and two excellencies came and stood to the right and to the left of Eve. And Michael stood to the right and touched her from her face to her breast and said to Eve, 'Blessed are you, Eve, because of Adam . . . ,'" and Eve commences the delivery of Cain. Translation here from M. D. Johnson, in *OTP* 2.

4. Of potential interest may be Prov 5.19b–20. The English, translated from the Hebrew, reads: "May the breasts [of the wife of your youth] satisfy you at all times; may be you be intoxicated always by her love; Why should you be intoxicated, my son, by another woman, and embrace the bosom of an adulteress?" In the longer text, what Joseph refuses to do is embrace the breasts of a strange woman. But since the LXX/OG does not retain the breast imagery, it may or may not be relevant.

5. Interestingly, later on the longer text will substitute the notion of rest for that of the bridal chamber, in chapter 15 and insert Aseneth's place of rest in the scene with Levi, in chapter 22.

6. The north window does not occur in the recapitulation narrative, but this is probably not surprising, since the shorter version does not mention the window at all, removing the need for the redactor to specify which window.

7. See Greenberg, *Biblical Prose Prayer.*

8. Greenberg, *Biblical Prose Prayer,* 20–21.

9. Greenberg, *Biblical Prose Prayer,* 14.

10. Greenberg, *Biblical Prose Prayer,* 17.

11. Greenberg, *Biblical Prose Prayer,* 30–31.

12. Greenberg, *Biblical Prose Prayer,* 29s–30.

13. 12.2–12/**12.1–15**

    Lord, God of all the ages

    Who established and brought everything to life,

    Who gave to all **your whole creation** the breath of life,

    Who brought into the light that which was unseen

    Who made everything, and made manifest that which was without manifestation

        [the texts differ somewhat here, but the sense is similar],

    Who raised the heaven **and established it upon a firmament upon the back of**

        the winds (and) **who** established the earth upon the waters,

    Who fastened great stones on the abyss of the water, (which) **and the stones** shall

        not be immersed,

    but they are like oak leaves (floating) on top of the water,

    and they are living stones

    and hear your voice, Lord,

    and keep your commandments which you have commanded to them,

    and never transgress your ordinances

    But which, to the end, do your will.

    For you, Lord, spoke and they were brought to life,

    because your word, Lord, is life for all your creatures,

    With you I take refuge, Lord

    Lord, (my God), to you I will cry,

    to you, I will pour out (Hear) **my supplication,**

    (And) to you, I will confess my sins,

    And before you, I will reveal my lawlessness.

    (I have sinned) **Spare me**, Lord, **because** I have sinned **much before you**,

    I have been lawless, and impious, and have spoken evil **and unspeakable (things)**

        before you.

    My mouth has been polluted by sacrifices to idols,

and by the table of the gods of the Egyptians.

I have sinned, Lord, before you,

I have sinned **much in ignorance** (and have been impious), revering dead and
   mute idols,

And I am not worthy to open my mouth before you, **Lord**,

(I, the wretched one.

I have sinned, Lord, before you.)

I, **Aseneth**, the daughter of Pentephres, the priest, **the virgin and queen, who was
   once** insolent and arrogant **and prospering in my riches beyond all people
and now an orphan and desolate and abandoned by all people.**

I bring my prayer before you, Lord, and cry unto you,

Deliver me **before I am caught** from my persecutors,

for unto you I have fled for refuge,

as a **little** child **who is afraid flees** to its father (and mother).

and the father, stretching out his hands, snatches him off the ground,

and puts his arms around him by his breast,

and the child clasps his hands around his father's neck,

and regains his breath after his fear,

and rests at his father's breast,

the father, however, smiles at the confusion of his childish mind,

likewise

And you, Lord, stretch forth your hands to me,

as a father who loves his child and is affectionate,

And snatch me (out of the hand of the enemy) **off the earth**.

For behold, the ancient savage lion pursues me,

because he is father of

(And) the gods of the Egyptians (are) **and** his offspring **are the gods of the idol
   maniacs**.

And I have come to hate them, because they are the lion's children,

Whom I cast away from myself, and destroy them,

And their father, the (devil) **lion**, (attempts to consume me) **furiously persecutes
   me**.

But you, Lord, deliver me from his hands,

And pull me out of his mouth,

Lest me snatch me up like a wolf (**lion**), and tear me apart,

And throw me into the abyss (**flame**) of fire,

and the fire will throw me into the hurricane,

and the hurricane (will) wrap me up in darkness and throw me

(And) into the (tempest) **deep** of the sea,

And (let not) the great whale **who exists since eternity will** consume me **and I
   will be destroyed forever and ever.**

Rescue me, Lord, before all this comes upon me.

Save me, Lord, the desolate one,

because my father and my mother disowned me, **and said, "Aseneth is not our
   daughter,"**

because I destroyed and broke their gods **and have come to hate them,**

and now I am desolate and orphaned,

And there is no hope for me, Lord, if not with you,

and no other refuge except your mercy, Lord

For you are the father of the orphans,

And the protector of the persecuted,
And the helper of the oppressed.
Have mercy upon me, Lord,
and guard me, a virgin abandoned and an orphan,
because you, Lord, are a sweet and good and gentle father.
What father is as sweet as you, Lord,
and who (is) as quick in mercy as you, Lord,
and who (is) as long–suffering toward our sins as you, Lord?
For behold, all the (worldly good) **gifts** of my father, Pentephres,
which he gave me as an inheritance, are transient and ephemeral;
but the gifts of your inheritance, Lord, are incorruptible and eternal.

Burchard, "Joseph and Aseneth" observes that the reading εἰδωλομάνες (idol maniacs) is somewhat problematic, with numerous variants. One of his concerns is that it is first attested in the late second century C.E. (221, n. 12e2). But, of course, alternatively, one could take its usage here to suggest a later date for the text (see chapter 8).

14. Particularly interesting here is Philonenko's (*Joseph et Aséneth*, 7) stinging assessment of the redactive nature of these prayers.

15. NRSV Ps 30.11–12.

16. "My soul" is the NSRV translation. In Hebrew (כבוד) and Greek (δόξα) another more common translation, would be "glory." On this semantic field of considerable interest, chapter 6.

17. Pieter W. van der Horst, "Silent Prayer in Antiquity," *Numen* 41 (1994): 1–25. Among other things, silent prayer was taken as evidence that one wished to conceal one's prayers from one's enemies, lest they counteract them; as evidence of embarassment over the request, usually due to the sexual nature of the prayer; or as evidence of magical practices.

18. 1 Sam 1.13; *Aseneth* **11.3**. The LXX/OG closely approximates the Hebrew text, which also says literally that "Hannah was speaking in her heart."

19. Biblical examples of persecuted penitents include Pss 30.11–12; 31.11–24 (NRSV; LXX/OG 29 and 30).

20. NRSV; LXX/OG 44.

21. This same reading occurs again in the longer **12.13**.

22. Beyond a few words that, while present in the biblical text, could conceivably reflect common idioms of speech, such as the phrase ἄφρων καὶ θρασεῖα (Prov 9.13) or ἐν τῇ καρδίᾳ (see earlier discussion, on Hannah). At 12.7, ῥῦσαι με ἀπὸ τῶν διωκόντον με, Philonenko (*Joseph et Aséneth*) notes the close similarity to Ps 141.7 (Heb/Eng 142.6b): ῥῦσαι με ἐκ τῶν καταδιωκόντον με.

23. All versification here is LXX/OG. Burchard's notes identify the parallel with Exod 34.6 and with Ps 85.15.

24. In using this language, I in no way intend to imply that Exodus is consciously being quoted in the Psalms—for my purposes, the historical relationship of that material is irrelevant.

25. Philonenko, *Joseph et Aséneth*, here cites as a parallel Ps 71.17.

26. LXX/OG Ps 144.13a–19.

27. Κύριος ὁ θεὸς οἰκτίρμων καὶ ἐλεήμων, μακρόθυμος καὶ πολυέλεος καὶ ἀληθινός.

28. NRSV 103.

29. So D sl F; B reads τὸ ῥήμα τοῦτο (these things, or: words).

30. In addition, one might explore the possible usages of LXX/OG Ps 36.18, which connects inheritance (κληρονομία) with refuge, and LXX/OG Ps 46.5, where "our inheritance" is the pride of Jacob, whom God loves. Of particular interest for the construction of Aseneth's prayer

in chapter 12 may be LXX/OG Ps 60 (NRSV 61). A relatively short psalm, it could be taken in its entirety to describe the general outline of *Aseneth*. Particularly interesting are the consonance of vocabulary with Aseneth's prayer and the general consonance of language and theme.

Hear my cry, O God; listen to my prayer [τῆς δεήσεώς μου, πρόσχες τῇ
   προσευχῇ μου; cf. *Aseneth* 12.4/**12.5**]
From the end of the earth I call to you, [ἐκέκραξα; cf. the same verse]
when my heart is faint.
Lead me to the rock that is higher than I,
for you are my hope [Hebrew: refuge], a strong tower against the enemy.
Let me abide in your tent forever,
Let me be sheltered [σκεπασθήσομαι] under the shelter [σκέπη] of your wings.
For you, O God, have heard my vows,
you have given me the heritage of those who fear your name [κληρονομίαν τοῖς
   φοβουμένοις τὸ ὄνομά σου].

We might also consider LXX/OG Ps 110 (NRSV 111), which partially "quotes" the phrase at hand: ἐλεήμων καὶ οἰκτίρμων ὁ κύριος (the Lord is merciful and gracious). In its description of God as one who gives food (τροφή) to those who fear (φοβουμένοις) him (110.4–5), it could be taken to describe what the angel does with Aseneth. This psalm, too, emphasizes the importance of "fearing" God: the fear of the Lord is the beginning of Wisdom (v. 10).

31. καὶ ἐκάλεσεν αὐτὴν ὁ ἄνθρωπος εκ δευτέρου καὶ εἶπεν, Ἀσενέθ, Ἀσενέθ. Καὶ εἶπεν ἰδοὺ ἐγώ. ἰδοὺ ἐγώ appears to be a fairly standard translation for הנני. Note, though, that in Exod 3.4b, the LXX reads τί ἐστιν for Moses' response, whereas in Hebrew, Moses' response is identical to that of Abraham: ויאמר הנני.

32. Translation mine, from Burchard "Joseph and Aseneth," 15.4. The Greek is actually somewhat more awkward than this, but this seems to be its sense.

33. Biblical narratives of encounters between humans and the divine often display a similar blurring of the distinction between divine messengers and God, but later I argue that this is not so much "slippage" as an intentional portrait of the figure as the divine co-regent.

34. Burchard's ("Joseph and Aseneth") other references include 1 QM 12.1.f; Luke 10.20; Rev 20.12, 15. Philonenko's list (*Joseph et Aséneth*) is more extensive: Is 4.3; Dan 12.1; 1 *Enoch* 47.3, 104.1, 108.3; Coptic *Apocalypse of Sophonia* 4; Rev 3.5; 13.8, 17.8, 20.12, 20.15, 21.27. See H. Odeberg, *3 Enoch* (Cambridge: Cambridge University Press, 1928; reprint, New York: KTAV, 1973), 63, n. 24.

35. The term also occurs in the longer version at **21.11**, where it describes Pentephres as ἐπίσποκος πάντων.

36. For examples of mothers who prepare their daughters' bridal chambers, see, e.g., the figure of Anna in Tobit or the mother of Seila in Ps. Philo's retelling of the story of Jephthah's daughter.

37. In addition, at least in some respects, Metanoia closely resembles the portraits of Sophia and other feminine manifestations of the divine in gnostic texts. Burchard's text may here demonstrate traces of Christian redaction, which interweaves the visible figures of Aseneth and Metanoia, the invisible figures of the Virgin Mary, and consecrated Christian virgins. At the very least, later Christians readers are likely to have read the text in precisely this way. If *Aseneth* were the early Jewish text that most scholars now take it to be, these passages would constitute evidence for a Jewish constellation of ideas about virginity, repentance, and the feminine divine that become visible in subsequent Christian formulations about Mary, the mother of Jesus, but as will become clearer in chapter 9, I think this unlikely.

38. This is implicit in the speaker's request for God to send Wisdom forth from the holy heavens and from the throne of God's glory.

39. See chapter 9. Not inconceivably, this verse refers to the seven virgin companions and could, I suppose, be out of place.

40. For the general language of this passage, Philonenko, *Joseph et Aséneth,* points to Ps 71.17: ἔστω τὸ ὄνομα αὐτοῦ εὐλογημένον εἰς τοὺς αἰῶνος.

41. If not for the thrust of the passage and the meaning of καὶ (which here seems clearly oppositional rather than conjunctive), one could translate this as "It [my name] is 'thaumaston.'"

42. μεγάλα ἐστί τὰ ὀνόματα ἐκεῖνα καὶ θαυμαστὰ καὶ ἐπαινετὰ σφόδρα.

43. LXX 32.28–30: εἶπεν δὲ αὐτῷ Τί τὸ ὄνομά σου ἐστιν; ὁ δὲ εἶπεν Ιακωβ. εἶπεν δὲ αὐτῷ Οὐ κληθήσεται ἔτι τὸ ὄνομά σου Ιακωβ, ἀλλὰ Ισραηλ ἔσται τὸ ὄνομά σου, ὅτι ἐνίσχυσας μετὰ θεοῦ καὶ μετὰ ἀνθρώπων δυνατός. ἠρώτησεν δὲ Ιακωβ καὶ εἶπεν Ἀνάγγειλόν μοι τὸ ὄνομά σου. καὶ εἶπεν Ἵνα τί τοῦτο ἐρωτᾷς τὸ ὄνομά μου καὶ ηὐλόγησεν αὐτὸν ἐκεῖ. (He said to him, "What is your name"; he said, "Jacob." He said to him; No longer will your name be called Jacob, but Israel will be your name, because you have striven/contended with God and with powerful 'men.'" [the translation of ἄνθρωπος seems to me quite ambiguous]. Jacob answered and said, "Tell me your name." But he said, "Why do you ask my name," and he blessed him.)

Note also that the angel's naming of Aseneth (at 15.6) is fairly close to this verse: καὶ οὐκέτι κληθήσει Ἀσενέθ, ἀλλ, ἐσται τὸ ὄνομά σου πόλις καταφυγῆς.

44. Burchard, "Joseph and Aseneth," translates here: "but you spoke and it came into being"; this may be a better translation, though Burchard's own notes confirm the possibility of translating as I have.

45. For the numerous variants here, see the notes to Philonenko, (*Joseph et Aséneth*) and to Burchard ("Joseph and Aseneth" 229, n. 16m), who insists that the term μυστηρια "should be retained" despite the divergent readings.

46. Burchard suggests, for example, that the chosen (or elect) may be the dead. ("Joseph and Aseneth," n. 16o). Sons of God could refer to the heavenly beings in Genesis 6, in which case a gender-specific translation is appropriate, since that passage deals with the sexual relationships and consequent offspring of the sons of God with the daughters of humans.

47. Ephrem, *Hymns on Nativity* 6.13–14, here translated from Sebastian P. Brock, *The Luminous Eye: The Spiritual World Vision of Saint Ephrem,* Cistercian Studies Series 124 (Kalamazoo: Cistercian Publications, 1992), 103.

48. Ephrem, *Hymns on Faith* 10.10, here translated from Brock, *Luminous Eye,* 104.

49. See chapter 9.

50. τῆς γῆς, which Burchard translates as "ground." But he notes that several manuscripts read πηγῆς (spring), a reading that, as he notes, provides just as good a parallel with paradise and that I suspect may be the better reading, tying in with the spring in the courtyard in 2.12 and with the water from the spring in 18.9. Nevertheless, I have left it here, as this quotation reproduces his translation in entirety, except for the translation of ἄνθρωπος as "figure."

51. In the longer description of Jacob at **22.7**, his old age is described as "like the youth of a handsome man" (καὶ τὸ γῆρας αὐτοῦ ὥσπερ νεότης ἀνδρὸς ὡραίου). His powers are still apparent, and he is still beautiful.

52. See also chapter 7.

53. See Chesnutt, *From Death to Life,* 128–35, also 250–52, for a survey and critique of this position. Some of Chesnutt's concern here is with the claim that a ritual of bread, cup, and ointment intentionally presents entrance into Judaism as comparable to initiation in Isiac and perhaps other Hellenistic mystery religions, with comparable benefits.

54. Sandelin, "Wisdom Meal," 154–55, appears to concur with my judgment here, although he does not consider the kind of process I suggest.

55. ἰδοὺ (δὴ) ἀπὸ τῆς σήμερον. The longer version consistently introduces the emphatic particle δη.

56. As possible parallels to this, Burchard notes Dan 7.10; *Apoc. Zech.* 4.4, 13.1; *1 Enoch* 40.1, 60.1, 71.8; Rev 5.11; *1 Clem* 34.6, and wonders about Deut 33.17: "the myriads of Ephraim and the thousands of Manasseh" ("Joseph and Aseneth," 230 n. 16a2.)

57. Burchard notes that this reading is somewhat dubious, as well as inconsistent with 16.16x, where the comb has been restored, although 17.3 also assumes that the comb is still damaged ("Joseph and Aseneth," 230 n. 16e2.)

58. See chapter 6.

59. Burchard points out that in antiquity, hives were assumed to be ruled by kings, not queens, rendering this particular image particularly puzzling, although he notes that there is a "queen of the bees" in Epictetus's *Diss.* 3.22.99 (Burchard, "Joseph and Aseneth," 230, n. 16d2). On bees in antiquity, see esp. chapter 6.

60. This passage bears a curious affinity, by no means exact, to the scenario in Rev 20.4-6, where the martyred dead rise first and reign with Christ for 1,000 years; the remainder of the dead are not resurrected until afterward.

61. See chapter 6. In his recently published doctoral dissertation at Princeton University, Gideon Bohak, *Joseph and Aseneth,* has offered an imaginative interpretation that I nevertheless find unpersuasive.

62. E.g., Prov 9.1, etc. See also Philonenko, *Joseph et Aséneth,* 187.

63. LXX/OG Ps 30.

64. I find this reading odd, since all the objects described here are jewelry and other "accessories." Something like ankle bracelets would seem more appropriate, especially since they go "on her feet," but "trousers" is the only meaning LSJ provides for ἀναξυρίδες, which it describes as Persian in origin.

65. *Gen. R.* 20.12 (to Genesis 3.21), which claims that R. Meir's text read this way (אור [light] instead of עור [skin]). *PRE* 14 says that Adam was first covered by a skin of nail and a cloud of glory; see also *Targum Yerushalmi* to Genesis 3.7 and 3.21. Note that all of these are relatively late, at least in the form in which we now have them. The tradition also occurs in somewhat earlier Christian writers, including Irenaeus (*Against Heresies* 3.23.5) and Tertullian (*On Chastity* 9; *On Resurrection* 7). For additional references to this motif in later Jewish sources, see Louis Ginsberg, *Legends of the Jews,* trans. Henrietta Szold; vol. 3, trans. Paul Radin (Philadelphia: Jewish Publication Society, 1909–38), 5:103–4, n. 93.

66. Ephrem, *Hymns on Nativity* 1.43, quoted in Brock, *Luminous Eye,* 87–88.

67. Note, however, that even in chap. 15, the longer text expands on the bridal imagery, calling Aseneth's ornaments bridal as well and exhorting her to dress not merely as a bride, as in the shorter text, but as a good bride (νύμφη ἀγαθή). Interestingly, though, στολὴν τοῦ, γάμου is absent in A (Batiffol, "Livre") and in the Syriac at 15.10, and this entire episode is absent in L1; according to Burchard, "Joseph and Aseneth," it is present in L2.

68. Other readings include "one of the virgins, her companions" (Syr); "the virgins." See Burchard "Joseph and Aseneth," 232, n. 18l.

69. Philonenko, *Joseph et Aséneth,* 193.

70. Burchard, "Joseph and Aseneth," 232m n. 18o.

71. In chapter 6, I will discuss the affinities of this allusion with Neoplatonic imagery.

72. Burchard, "Joseph and Aseneth," 232 n. 18 m.

73. This may suggest another level of redaction and indicate that this isn't part of either the early text or an initial revision.

74. Burchard ("Joseph and Aseneth," 233, n. 18b2) points out that "[t]he reading 'his firstborn son, Joseph' is a reconstruction from 'his firstborn son' F Syr. L2; 'his son Joseph' A; 'Joseph' PQ Arm.; 'the most beautiful Joseph' G." Joseph is, however, called Son of God elsewhere in the texts, at 6.2, ὁ υἱὸς τοῦ θεοῦ, 6.6 Ιωσηφ υἱὸς τοῦ θεοῦ ἐστὶ; 13.10 (twice); and πρωτότοκος at 21.3/**21.4**.

75. That the story of the *tropheus* is an insertion, and a somewhat awkward one at that, may be further supported by the fact that it appears to contradict the claim that no man had seen Aseneth, prior to Joseph's arrival, because the *tropheus* has obviously seen Aseneth in the past. At the same time, one could argue that in ancient understandings of female seclusion, male members of the woman's household, as well as male slaves and servants, are implicitly excluded from such claims.

76. τῆς σιωπήσεώς σου.

77. Aseneth doesn't bear twins: but she does have two sons, both of whom live.

78. Song 4.1b–2 = 6:5b–6; 4.3b = 6.7.

79. In Wis Sol 7.26, Wisdom is the image (εἰκὼν) of God's goodness (ἀγαθότητος).

80. Whether this is intentional is difficult to say. It seems possible that some of the effects of the redaction are unintentional byproducts. In this case, for example, wishing to elaborate on the bridal imagery of 15.10 could produce inconsistent or conflicting "messages." But they may also be intentional on the part of the redactors.

81. Heb 10.16. See also LXX/OG Ps 145.10; Wis Sol 3.8.

82. Burchard, "Joseph and Aseneth," 233, n. 19m.

83. As Burchard indicates, the pronouns differ considerably in various manuscripts; for the details, see Burchard, "Joseph and Aseneth," 234, nn. 20.b, c, d.

84. Aptowitzer, "Asenath," 290, saw this scene as a reflection of 1 Sam 25.41, where Abigail tells emissaries from David, "Your servant is a slave to wash the feet of the servants of my lord." He also saw it as an allusion to the obligations of Jewish wives to wash the face, hands, and feet of their husbands, and to prepare their beds, citing *m. Ket.* 5.5 (although this does not specify footwashing but only bread baking, wool working, bed making and the like). Ibid. 290.

85. Burchard, "Joseph and Aseneth," 234, n. 20g.

86. See Philonenko, *Joseph et Aséneth*, 8, whose view is essentially the same.

87. **20.7**: τῷ θεῷ τῷ ζωοποιοῦντι τοὺς νεκρούς. Burchard ("Joseph and Aseneth," 234, n. 20p) claims that this phrase has become a Jewish definition of God. Comparable language occurs in the 18 benedictions; in *Num. R.* 15.13; in R. Nehuniah ben ha Qanah (see David J. Halperin, *The Faces of the Chariot: Early Jewish Responses to Ezekiel's Vision* [Tübingen: J. C. B. Mohr (Paul Siebeck), 1988], 378). But there are numerous Christian instances of this language and of the verb ζωοποιέω s.v. *BAGD*, 341. Ἀναζωοποιέω occurs in Aseneth at 8.11 and 15.4; it also occurs in *Testament of Abraham* 18 and the *Acts of Xanthippe* 41 (s.v. G. W. H. Lampe, *A Patristic Greek Lexicon* [Oxford: Clarendon Press, 1961–68]).

88. Burchard, "Joseph and Aseneth," 230, n. 20q.

89. Or at least not routinely the prerogative of rulers to arrange the marriages of their subjects.

90. Manuscript D.

91. Manuscript B.

92. E. A. Speiser, *Genesis: A New Translation with Introduction and Commentary,* Anchor Bible (Garden City: Doubleday, 1964), 316–17.

93. On Joseph as father to Pharaoh, see Origen, *Fragments on Genesis PG* 12.129, 136, 140; see also Chrysostom, *Homilies on Genesis PG* 54.546, 557.

94. At Genesis 41.44; slightly abridged in 41.45 ("Thus Joseph gained authority over the land of Egypt"), 41.55, etc.

95. Gen 32.24–32.

96. In *Aseneth*, the place is called Gesem, but in the LXX Gen 46.28–29, it is called Ἡρώων πόλις. This raises some interesting issues that are beyond the scope of this study.

97. In Genesis 48.15, Jacob blesses Joseph.

98. Burchard ("Joseph and Aseneth," 239, n. 22m) observes that this tradition of enmity between the brothers has no firm biblical base and suggests that it derives from ancient Jewish tradition, citing Aptowitzer, "Asenath," 284–85.

99. The Greek of the shorter reconstruction reads: ὡς ἄνδρα προφήτην καὶ θεοσεβῆ καὶ θοβούμενον τὸν κύριον.

100. The reading of this last insertion is taken from Syriac and Armenian translations; see Burchard "Joseph and Aseneth," 239, n. 22s.

101. E.g., 27.2/**27.1**, 28.1. Although σφόδρα occurs twelve times in the shorter text, its (frequent) addition in the longer text appears to be another example of the tendency of the longer text to "biblicize" the language of the shorter. Numerous instances of φοβέω in the LXX/OG are modified by σφόδρα, particularly, although by no means exclusively, in Jdt, 1 Macc, 1 Sam.

102. See earlier discussion, this chapter.

103. πάνυ rather than σφόδρα.

CHAPTER FOUR

Aseneth and the Adjuration of Angels

In the later antique Mediterranean world, belief in the possibility, if not the probability, of encounters between humans and divine beings was widespread. These beliefs testify to a cosmology in which the heavens are populated with numerous lesser divine beings who limit human access to the highest divinity. Such cosmology corresponds closely to the political realities of the period, in which increasingly complex government bureaucracies, both local and Roman, distanced virtually everyone from kings and emperors. Whether our sources are formulas for compelling the appearance of suprahuman beings or narratives of such experiences, encounters with lesser divine beings are typical whereas encounters with the highest God are rarer and require considerable effort and expense, analogous again to the political realities.

Contemporary scholarly classifications of the sources prescribing and describing such encounters not infrequently propose a distinction between "magical" materials on the one hand and "mystical" materials on the other.[1] Thus, the various manuals of formulas for adjuring suprahuman beings, originating in Greco-Roman Egypt, are titled by modern editors *The Greek Magical Papyri,*[2] while a highly similar assemblage of Hebrew materials from the Cairo Geniza, thought to be roughly contemporaneous with those papyri, is published under the title *Sepher ha-Razim* (The book of the mysteries),[3] and the many Roman-period Jewish materials prescribing and describing encounters with various angels are uniformly classed as "mystical." This is not to say that within this amalgam of materials, no useful distinctions may be made. Certainly, people in antiquity themselves utilized a category expressed by such language as *magos*, *mageia*, *goēteia*, and a range of semantically linked terms, although what they intended by such language is undoubtedly different from our indiscriminate "magic," even while it shares some of same polemical connotations.[4]

Depictions of encounters between humans and divine beings are clearly present in the Jewish scriptural traditions from which *Aseneth* drew. The vast majority of biblical references to encounters between humans and heavenly beings envision such experiences as the descent of the divine into the earthly human realm. Angels visit Abraham at the oak of Mamre, confront Hagar fleeing to Egypt, and call upon the future parents of Samson out in their fields. In the Christian Gospel of Luke, an angel appears to the priestly father of John the Baptist in the temple itself and to the mother of Jesus in the town where she lives. But many early Jewish (and some Christian) texts portray human beings as ascending to the heavens. Paul, for example, alludes to "a person" he knows in Christ who ascended to the third heaven and heard things that no mortal is permitted to disclose (2 Cor 12.2–4).[5] Most of these experiences are attributed to biblical characters, such as Enoch, Noah, Abraham, Moses, or to (past) rabbinic masters, such as Ishmael in *3 Enoch* or Akiba in *Merkabah Rabbah*.[6] Other ancient traditions, including biblical works such as Isaiah and Ezekiel, the Revelation of John, or the late first-century C.E. book known as 4 Ezra portray such experiences somewhat differently, as taking place in a visionary state, although the distinction between such visions and heavenly ascent is not always firm.[7]

In biblical narratives, such encounters are never initiated by humans: the intrusion of the divine into the earthly or extrusion of the earthly into the divine is always initiated by divine agency. Indeed, some fascinating biblical passages, such as the story of Saul's consultation of the dead seer Samuel through the agency of a female medium, convey the stance of biblical writers that human attempts to initiate contact with the divine for the purpose of securing knowledge of the future and power for themselves were illicit and dangerous.

By contrast, in ancient adjuration materials, as well as in certain narratives of mystical encounters, humans have the means to initiate, indeed to compel, such encounters, whether the descent of the divine or the ascent of the human. In this chapter, while intentionally distancing myself from the terminology of magic, I wish to focus on those ancient practices and traditions that envision the ability of human beings to adjure (that is, compel) divine beings to appear and to perform the bidding of the adjurer, whose requests encompassed everything from questions about the future to assistance in matters of love, finance, and intrigue. I will demonstrate that many of the specific elements in the Aseneth narratives, particularly the details of Aseneth's repentance and encounter with the angelic double of Joseph, are best accounted for within such contexts. In the succeeding chapters, I will offer evidence that further light is shed on the composition and interpretation of *Aseneth* from a detailed comparison of our narratives with so-called mystical traditions from late antique sources, both Jewish and non-Jewish. Further, because much of the material treated in these three chapters emanates from the third and fourth centuries and because some of it appears to be unique to those centuries or to have originated in those centuries, these chapters will greatly strengthen my claim that *Aseneth* itself is most likely composed in those same centuries.[8]

The perception of *Aseneth* as fundamentally a tale of conversion has so dazzled earlier scholars,[9] including myself at one point, that we have largely failed to see the encounter between Aseneth and the angelic figure for what it is: a tale of the adjuration of an angel by a woman. This is not to say, of course, that the Aseneth stories do not in fact recount a transformative experience that we might well consider "conversion." But the assumption that the Greek stories are primarily a narrative of religious conversion (dated, moreover, to the early second-century C.E. at the latest) has obscured our ability to recognize paradigms and elements that ancient readers, I suggest, would instantly have perceived.[10]

In all fairness to my predecessors, Philonenko did recognize some of this: his discussion of the shared meal of Aseneth and the angel incorporates parallels from the Berlin papyrus *(PGM* 1),[11] where he writes: "The scene described in *Joseph and Aseneth* shows nothing more than the romantic transposition of a magical practice."[12] Apropos of the use of honey in Mithraic mysteries, he cites Porphyry, *On the Cave of the Nymphs*, a text to which I will return in chapter 6.[13] But Philonenko did not sufficiently recognize or develop the significance of so-called magical materials, and he clearly was unable to pursue the connections with third- and fourth-century traditions and symbols, given his belief that the text was composed several centuries earlier. Further, his focus on what he believed to be the earliest accessible version of the text and his concomitant disinterest in later versions of the text prevented him from exploring the further consonance between Burchard's readings and the Berlin papyrus. On the other hand, Burchard flatly denies any relation of *Aseneth* to adjurative materials, but his assertions here are without support.[14] Philonenko, too, was put off from a more thorough discussion of the adjurative elements by his belief that the rituals enacted by Aseneth and the angel reflect actual rites of conversion and initiation performed among Jews,[15] and he concludes that the rite of entrance into the Jewish community was a mystery initiation, along the lines proposed by E. R. Goodenough.[16]

As I have described in the preface, my own realization that the story of Aseneth and Joseph is grounded in ancient practices and beliefs of Jews and non-Jews alike about the adjuration of divine beings came more or less fortuitously, when, pursuing ancient references to honey in the hopes of illuminating Aseneth's consumption of angelic honey, I remembered a passage about storehouses of honey in *Sepher ha-Razim.* Dating this reconstructed work is difficult, although an internal reference to the Roman system of dating by the fifteen year cycle of indictions supports the suggestion that it is no earlier than the fourth century C.E.[17] Virtually all scholars are agreed that the incantations within the text and the rituals prescribed have widespread analogies within Greco-Roman praxis and thus may be much earlier, perhaps by centuries. Some of the prayers prescribed are actually Hebrew transliterations of Greek, suggesting a Greco-Roman milieu for at least some of the material, consonant with the late Roman dating.

According to *Sepher ha-Razim*, the fourth firmament contains the "lovely bridal chamber of the sun" and the two sets of angels who lead the sun during the day and at night. Central to this section are the two rituals to be performed by one who wishes to see the sun either by day or by night:

> If you wish to view the sun during the day, seated in his chariot and ascending; guard yourself, take care, and keep pure for seven days from all food, from all drink, and from every unclean thing.[18] Then on the seventh day stand facing (the sun) when he rises and burn incense of spices weighing three shekels before him, and invoke seven times the names of the angels that lead him during the day. Then if you are not answered after these seven times, go and invoke them in reverse order seven times, and say:

I adjure you, angels that lead the sun in the power of your strength on the heavenly paths to illuminate the world, by the One whose voice shakes the earth, who moves mountains in his anger, who calms the sea with His power, who shakes the pillars of the world with His glance, who sustains everything with His arm, who is hidden from the eyes of all the living, who sits upon the throne of greatness of the kingdom of the glory of his holiness, and who moves through the entire world; I repeat (your names) and adjure you by His great, fearful, powerful, majestic, forceful, mighty, holy, strong, wondrous, secret, exalted and glorious name; that you will do my will and desire at this time and season, and will remove the radiance of the sun so I may see him face to face as he is in his bridal chamber. Let me not catch fire from your fire and give me permission to do my will.

At the completion of your adjuration, you will see him in his bridal chamber and you can ask him (to foretell questions) of death or life, good or evil.[19] And if you wish to release him, repeat the adjuration and say:

I adjure you that you return the radiance of the sun to its place as in the beginning.
Then the sun will go on his way.[20]

Following this are directions for seeing the sun at night, which requires a longer purification period, and the repetition of the night angels' names twenty-one times, followed by a different adjuration, including the request that he

speak with me as a man speaks with his friend and tell me the secret of the depths, and make known to me hidden things, and let no evil thing happen to me.

When you finish speaking, you will hear a peal of thunder from the north and you will see something like lightning come forth and light up the earth before you. And after you see him, you will assuredly bow down to the ground and fall upon your face to the earth and pray this prayer:

Holy Helios who rises in the east, good mariner, trustworthy leader of the sun's rays, reliable (witness), who of old didst establish the mighty wheel (of the heavens), holy orderer, ruler of the axis (of the heaven), Lord, Brilliant Leader, King, Soldier. I, N son of N [the petitioner fills in his name and typically his mother's name], *present my supplication before you, that you will appear to me without (causing me) fear, and you will be revealed to me without causing me terror, and you will conceal nothing from me and will tell me truthfully all that I desire.*[21]

Then stand up and you will see (the sun) in the north proceeding to the east. After this, put your hands behind you, and bow your head low, and ask whatever you desire. And after you have questioned him, lift your eyes toward heaven and say [a final adjuration to return the sun to his course].[22]

It seemed to me immediately apparent that the sum and substance of what Aseneth does is precisely an adjuration of the Sun, which brings her true knowledge of hidden things, life and death, her own identity and future. As we have already seen, the association of Aseneth's mysterious visitor with the Sun and with Joseph is quite explicit in the text, although they have received insufficient attention by scholars. Viewed from this perspective, many seemingly arbitrary details of the story of Aseneth were suddenly thrown into sharp relief.

Rituals for summoning the Sun occur also in ancient Greek "magical" papyri preserved in the dry climate of Egypt, most of which papyri are dated approximately to the fourth century C.E.[23] The following excerpts come from a lengthy text that appears to be titled *The Sacred, Hidden Book of Moses called Eighth, or Holy* and that describes itself as "the ritual using the name that encompasses all things."[24] It also has directions for a meeting with the god "in which you will succeed if you leave out nothing [of what is prescribed]."

After a forty-one-day purification, complex sacrificial preparations, and many long adjurations, the petitioner says:

> Come to me, lord, faultless, who pollute no place, joyful, unflawed, for I call on you, King of Kings, Tyrant of tyrants, most glorious of the glorious, daimon of daimons, most warlike of the warlike, most holy of the holy. Come to me, willing, joyful, unflawed.
>
> An angel will come in, and you say to the angel: "Greetings, lord. Both initiate me by these rites I am performing and present me [to the god], and let the fate determined by my birth be revealed to me." And if he says anything bad, say, "Wash off from me the evils of fate. Do not hold back, but reveal to me everything, by night and day and in every hour of the month, to me, NN, son of NN. Let your auspicious form be revealed to me, for under your [order] I serve [your] angel. . . .
>
> I call on you, lord, holy, much hymned, greatly honored, ruler of the cosmos. . . . Protect me from all my own astrological destiny, destroy my foul fate; apportion good things for me in my horoscope; increase my life; and [may I enjoy] many good things, for I am your slave and petitioner and have hymned your valid and holy name, lord, glorious one, ruler of the cosmos, of ten thousand names [?], greatest, nourisher, apportioner [[Sarapis]].
>
> Having drawn in spirit with all your senses, say the first name in one breath to the east, the second to the south, the third to the north, the fourth to the west.[25]

The petitioner should be dressed in clean linens, be crowned with an olive wreath, and have ready a tablet on which to write what the angel says, a knife with which to sacrifice, and a libation to pour. Among other things, cinnamon is prescribed as pleasing to the god. The text then says:

> Accordingly, as I said before, when you have purified yourself in advance [through the last][26] seven days while the moon is waning, at the dark of the moon begin sleeping on the ground. Rising at dawn, greet the sun [Helios] through seven days, each day saying first the [names of the] gods of the houses, then those set over the weeks . . . doing so until the eighth day.[27]

On the eighth day, in the middle of the night, the petitioner must have assembled two roosters; two lamps, lighted; a mixing bowl of milk from a black cow; and wine not mixed with seawater. After dipping a magical stele into the bowl, before drinking its contents, the petitioner must lie down, holding the tablet and stele, and recite an account of creation.

> Now when the god comes in do not stare at his face, but look at his feet while beseeching him, as written above, and giving thanks that he did not treat you contemptuously, but you were thought worthy of the things about to be said to you for correction of your life. You ask then, "Master, what is fated for me?" And he will tell you even about your star, and what kind of daimon you have, and your horoscope and where you may live and where you will die. And if you hear something bad, do not cry out or weep, but ask that he may wash it off or circumvent it, for this god can do everything. Therefore, when you begin questioning, thank him for having heard you and not overlooked you. Always sacrifice to this [god] in this way and offer your pious devotions, for thus he will hear you.[28]

Several other examples from the papyri illustrate the importance of these materials for a more complete analysis of the Aseneth texts. The first is a long spell for the procurement of a divine assistant found in a famous Paris papyrus. I quote only a small portion of it here, since I will return to it at length below:

> [A]ttach yourself to Helios in this manner: At whatever sunrise you want (provided it is the third day of the month) go up to the highest part of the house and spread a pure linen garment on the floor. Do this with a mystagogue. But as for you, crown yourself with dark ivy while the sun is in mid-heaven, at the fifth hour, and while looking upward lie down naked on the linen and order your eyes to be completely covered with a black band. And wrap yourself like a corpse, close your eyes and, keeping your direction toward the sun, begin these words.[29]

Another is apparently a generic spell for inducing a revelation of which, again, I quote only portions:

> Keep yourself pure for 7 days before the moon becomes full by abstaining from meat and uncooked food, by leaving behind during the prescribed days exactly half of your food in a turquoise vessel, over which you are also to eat, and by abstaining from wine. When the moon is full, go by yourself to the eastern section of your city, village or house and throw out on the ground the leftover morsels. Then return very quickly to your quarters and shut yourself in before he can get there, because he will shut you out if he gets there before you. [The petitioner must then suspend a beetle over a brand-new lighted earthenware lamp.] . . . Stay calm after you have thrown out the morsels, gone to your quarters, and shut yourself in; for the one you have summoned will stand there and, by threatening you with weapons, will try to force you to release the beetle. But remain calm, and do not release it until he gives you a response, then release it right away.[30]

Two other formulas for the adjuration of Helios are also worth reproducing:

> Say toward the east, "I am he on the two cherubim, between the two natures, heaven and earth, sun and moon, light and darkness, night and day, rivers and sea. Appear to me, O archangel of those subject to the cosmos, ruler Helios, set in authority by the One and Only Himself. The Eternal and Only orders you." Say the Name. And if he appears glowering, say "Give me a day, give an hour; give a month; give a year, lord of life." Say the Name.[31]
>
> "I am he on the two cherubim, between the two natures, heaven and earth, sun and moon, light and darkness, night and day, rivers and sea. Appear to me, O archangel of those subject to the cosmos, ruler Helios, set in authority by the One and Only Himself." With this spell perform acts of thanksgiving to Helios, attain goals, win victories and in short, everything.[32]

Aseneth's Adjuration and Encounter with the Angel

A plethora of ancient sources, from formulas for the adjuration of angels preserved on papyri such as those I have just surveyed to lengthy literary depictions of encounters between angels and humans (much already discussed), constitute evidence for a basic pattern of such encounters that illuminates many elements of the Aseneth stories. This pattern includes necessary preparation by the human being specific acts to draw down the heavenly being or enable the human to ascend to the heavens, appropriate human responses to the divine being(s) and vice versa, the conferral of benefits on the human being, and the ultimate return of the parties to their proper spheres/loci. Such encounters exhibit the phases of ritual elucidated and analyzed by Victor Turner,[33] namely, separation, liminality, transformation, and reintegration.

Typically, the phase of separation requires the individual to abstain from ordinary human actions and intercourse, including food, drink, sex, and sleep. Often the individual is required to remove all signs of cultural identity, such as clothing and other adornment, consonant with Turner's liminal phase. Symbolically and socially, the individual may be characterized as dead. In some sources, the changes wrought appear to have the intention of transforming the human body into a heavenly body that is then able to interact with other angelic beings.

Drawing down the divine or ascending to heaven is accomplished in a variety of ways: by performing certain acts, including the utterance of powerful commands, or by prayer, among others. Once the human and the angelic or divine beings are together, it is common for the human to experience fear and to lie prostrate. The angelic being typically responds by admonishing the human not to be afraid and by having the human stand up. At this point, the human being sometimes receives new clothing and a new name, reflective of the transformation. In the ensuing encounter, the divine being confers some benefit on the human, whether a revelation of the future, a vision of the highest deity, or even temporary transformation into the divine company. Frequently, the human reciprocates to some extent by offering the divine being a sacrifice, whether in the form of a meal or other offerings. At the conclusion of the encounter, the divine being ascends back to the heavens, or the human being descends back to earth and is reintegrated into ordinary human social relations. As we shall see, this paradigm is closely related to ancient protocols for encounters between kings and their subjects, if not also superiors and their subordinates, in ancient social hierarchies.

Preparation/Separation

Aseneth's preparation for her adjuration of the angelic being, who bears striking resemblance to Helios, consists of a series of actions, each of which has counterparts in numerous ancient prescriptions for the adjuration of angels and other divine beings, both Jewish and otherwise.

In both reconstructions of the text, Aseneth begins her adjuration and transformation by withdrawing to her upper chambers (9.1), weeping, and repenting of idols—this last action is a specifically Jewish (or Christian) concern. Withdrawal to a solitary space is prescribed in *PGM* 4:52–73; *PGM* 3:616 instructs the petitioner to "[g]o at the sixth hour of the day . . . to a deserted place [*en erēmo topō*]"; *PGM* 3.693 contains a similar, more fragmentary reference (*topon erēmon*)[34] Another papyrus specifies a place from which the Nile has recently receded, where no one has yet stepped.[35] Aseneth then engages in a number of activities with clear parallels to mourning rituals in ancient cultures: she fills the leather curtain outside the door of the gate with ashes and lays the curtain on the floor of her room. The curtain has certain mystical implications, which I will discuss in the next chapter, but here we may note the similarity of these acts to another Helios incantation:

"At whatever sunrise you want (provided it is the third day of the month) go up to the highest part of the house and spread a pure linen garment on the floor. . . . [W]hile looking upward lie down naked on the linen and order your eyes to be completely covered with a black band. And wrap yourself like a corpse, close your eyes."[36]

The requirement that the petitioner go to the highest part of the house may reflect the idea that one facilitates the descent of the divine (or one's own ascent) by beginning at the closest point to the heavens one can reasonably manage.

Change of Clothing

Aseneth's encounter with the angelic being involves three changes of clothing. After some initial mourning behavior (weeping, collecting the ashes, and refusing food), Aseneth exchanges her magnificent but idolatrous multivalent clothing for a simple black *chiton,* which the text explicitly describes as the one she wore when her brother died. We have already seen one possible basis for this initial change of clothing in biblical imagery and recognized the utility of mourning garments as a symbol of Aseneth's ritual death. But preparatory changes of clothing are a routine feature of ancient texts and formulas describing the adjuration of divine beings, including those for the adjuration of Helios. The rite for acquiring a divine assistant who will do the petitioner's bidding requires one to "go [up] onto a lofty roof after you have clothed yourself in a pure garment."[37] A spell to enable one to gain control of one's shadow requires the practitioner to go "to a deserted place, girt about with a [new] dark-colored palmfiber basket, and on your head a scarlet cord as headband."[38] One of the many formulas for the adjuration of Helios requires the adept to wear "pure clothing."[39]

When Aseneth ultimately adjures Helios (the angelic being), she again undergoes a change of clothing at the angel's command, into garments that more closely resemble those prescribed in the magical texts and that appear to replicate angelic garments themselves. Typically, these garments are new, clean, pure, often of linen, and sometimes white. I will return to this second change of clothing in the discussion of Aseneth's transformation.

Abstinence from Food and Drink

Even before she collects the ashes and changes into her mourning garments, Aseneth is said to refrain from eating and drinking. Subsequently, she continues this abstinence for the entire seven days of her self-abasement (10.20).[40] In addition, she rids herself of the rich meal that apparently awaited her in her chambers, throwing out for the dogs "the fatted meats and fish and dressed meat," as well as the vessels of wine for libations to her gods.

Ancient prescriptions for contact with the divine often prescribe some sort of food restrictions as preparation. Several examples from *Sepher ha-Razim* are particularly apt. The formula for the adjuration of Helios in the Fourth Firmament is particularly close to *Aseneth* here, prescribing seven days of abstinence from all food and drink to see Helios by day, in his chariot and ascending. To see Helios at night requires three weeks of abstinence from food and drink.[41] To ask anything of those who stand on the steps of the Second Firmament requires a three-week abstinence from all fruit of the palm, all animal meats, fish, and wine. A love charm requires more general abstinence from wine and meat.[42]

One of the most interesting parallels to *Aseneth* comes from the generic formula I quoted at the beginning of this chapter.[43] Prescribing a seven-day partial fast involving abstention from meat and uncooked food, as well as wine, it requires the adept to dispose of leftovers in the following manner:

> When the moon is full, go by yourself to the eastern section of your city, village or house and throw out on the ground the leftover morsels. Then go very quickly to your quarters and shut yourself in before he [the being invoked] can get there, because he will shut you out if he gets there before you.

These instructions bear some fascinating resemblances to Aseneth's disposal of her own dinner, which she throws out the windows facing the street. According to 2.13, these windows would have faced north, but the entire section of Aseneth's tower would seem to be in the easternmost portion of the building, since it has windows facing north, east, and south, but not west.[44] In our texts, Aseneth's treatment of her food is probably related both to the impurity of the meats and to their representation of her past idolatry. Her food is impure at the very least because of its associations with her gods, if not for its implicit violation of the "future" kosher laws; her wine is similarly defiled because of its use in libations to those same gods. Yet the prescription in the papyri suggests that throwing out certain foods, in specific locations, from specific directions was also understood to be efficacious.

Abstinence from Sexual Behavior

Although they are absent from the passages with which I began this discussion, admonitions to abstain from sexual contact are not unusual in the prescriptions for adjuring divine beings and may well be implicit in many of the general prescriptions that the adept "keep pure" for a specified period of time prior to the adjuration. A lamp divination for Apollo specifies abstinence not only from all unclean things (*apo pantōn mysarōn pragmatōn*) and from all fish but also from all sexual intercourse (*pasēs synoysias*), "so that you may bring the god into the greatest desire toward you."[45]

Interestingly, while the formulas from the Greek papyri are often gender-neutral in the actual rites they prescribe, some of the formulas contained in *Sepher ha-Razim* clearly envision male performers, particularly those found under the heading "The Second Firmament."[46]

> If you wish to ask something of any who stand on the steps of the second firmament, cleanse yourself for three weeks from all fruit of the palm, from all kinds of animals, small and large, from wine, from (all) types of fish and from all (animals) that yield blood (when slaughtered); and do not approach a woman in her impurity, and do not touch anything which has died, and do not come near a leper or one afflicted by venereal discharge,

even accidental, and guard your mouth from every evil word and from every sin; and
sanctify yourself from every sin.[47]

If you wish to rescue your friend from a bad judgment or from any difficulty, purify yourself from all impurity, and do not cohabit with a woman for three days.[48]

If you wish to restore to office one who has fallen from his place . . . purify yourself from
all impurity, and do not eat [meat from an animal which has died from natural causes] and
do not touch a woman's bed for seven days.[49]

If you wish to know in which month you will be taken from the world . . . before you perform [the] rite, purify yourself from all impurity for three weeks of days, and guard yourself from all (meat of) small animals and from all that yields blood (when slaughtered)
even fish, and do not drink wine, and do not come near a woman, and do not touch a
grave, be wary of nocturnal pollution, and walk in humility and prayer, and make your
prayers and supplications long, and devote your heart to the fear of heaven, and you will
succeed.[50]

Viewed against the backdrop of these associations of adjuration with sexual abstinence, the emphasis on Aseneth's virginity takes on additional meaning. Not only is
Aseneth virgin for the reasons we explored in the previous chapter, but her sexual
purity is consonant with the requirements for the adjuration of angels in various
sources and probably facilitates her ability to adjure Helios/Joseph.

Abstinence from All Forms of Social Intercourse

Numerous papyri as well as prescriptions in *Sepher ha-Razim* and the *hekhalot* materials appear to presume that the petitioner must abstain from all forms of social intercourse with other humans and perform rites of adjuration alone. (In fact, Fritz Graf
proposes that it is just this isolated, private aspect of these rituals that distinguishes
them from other forms of religious behavior).[51] A formula for securing an oracular
dream prescribes going to sleep without speaking to anyone.[52] At least one papyrus,
though, specifically prescribes the presence of a ritual specialist, a mystagogue.[53] The
various instructions we have do assume that practitioners must consult professionals
in order to know what to do, but they still seem to assume that the actual practice of
adjuration takes place in private (with or without the presence of a ritual specialist).

Aseneth clearly performs her acts of repentance and adjuration in private. When
the virgin whom Aseneth loved most hears her weeping in sorrow, she wakes the rest
of the virgins and asks Aseneth what makes her sad, entreating her to open her locked
door. But Aseneth refuses the company and the consolation of the seven virgins with
a white lie: she feigns a headache and tells them to go back to their own rooms.

Transformation of the Place into an Acceptable Dwelling
(Temple) for the Divine

Aseneth's abstinence from food, drink, and sexuality, as well as her change of clothing, all function to transform her own body and prepare her for the encounter with the

divine. But it is also clear that drawing down the divine requires preparation of her chambers themselves. The idea that divine beings will only appear in appropriate places may also underlie the preference for solitary or deserted space noted in numerous examples above.

In fact, what Aseneth appears to do is transform her rooms into an appropriate house for a divine being: a pure temple. I will develop the imagery of Aseneth's rooms as temple further in the following chapter, but here we may note that one of Aseneth's rooms explicitly functions as a temple to her Egyptian gods (2.3–5). By throwing out the gold and silver statues of gods, together with her ornaments engraved with the names of the gods,[54] as well as the sacrifices and libations for the gods, Aseneth purifies not only herself but also her rooms. The removal of all these impurities transforms this space into an appropriate house for the divinity whom she will subsequently call down.

Prayer as Adjuration

Numerous ancient sources show us that prayer was one well-accepted means of adjuring a divine being. The papyri are full of prescribed prayers whose utterance brings down the desired deity. As we have seen in the previous chapter, Aseneth's central prayer is similar in structure, theme, and content to biblical prose prayers. It invokes God and describes God as the creator of all; it presents Aseneth's confession of sin and her self-deprecation; it identifies God as the guardian of the oppressed and the orphaned and seeks God's favor and protection for Aseneth precisely because she is orphaned and oppressed or, more accurately, because she presents herself as such. But in these regards, Aseneth's prayer (and indeed, biblical prose prayer) is strikingly consonant with other ancient personal prose prayers, which both have the same general structure of invocation, self-description, and petition and the same general function of establishing a bond between the petitioner and the deity in order to procure the desired result.

The prayer addressed to Typhon in *PGM* 4:154–285 provides an excellent example. The prayer (here called *logos*) begins with an invocation to powerful/mighty Typhon, whose many epithets delineate the great extent of his powers.[55] The central section identifies the petitioner as one whose interests closely coincide with the god:

> I am he who searched with you the whole world and
> Found great Osiris, whom I brought you chained. . . . As your soldier
> I have been conquered by the gods, I have
> Been thrown face down because of empty wrath.[56]

The prayer concludes with petitions to raise up the petitioner, who is the god's friend, and to grant the petitioner the ability to compel the gods to come by means of powerful phrases (*vox magicae*).

Interestingly, though, the prayers in *Sepher ha-Razim*, to Helios, for example, accord with the structure of petitionary prayers in some respects but not in others. The prayer to Helios in the Fourth Firmament invokes Helios and identifies him by epithets appropriate, generally, to the task. But by way of his own credentials, the petitioner appears to present only his own name and the name of his mother. Conceivably, each individual petitioner is expected to insert his (or her?) own unique qualifications, although the prayer to Typhon provides these. Further, the final section of the prayer is phrased not so much as a petition as the expected consequences of the petitioner's supplication: "I, so and so, present my supplication before you, that you will appear before me without causing me fear, and you will be revealed to me without causing me terror, and you will conceal nothing from me and will tell me truthfully all that I desire." [57]

This truncated pattern of invocation and petition also appears to characterize many of the formal adjurations contained in *Sepher ha-Razim*. These adjurations are generally addressed to intermediary figures, whose assistance is sometimes invoked in the name of God (although in other instances, the angels of the various firmaments are petitioned directly):

> I bring my petition before you, O Moon, who travel[s] by day and by night with chariots of light and angels of mercy before and behind you, I adjure you by the King who causes you to rise and set. [58]

> I adjure you angels that lead the sun, by the One whose voice shakes the earth. [59]

This raises some interesting questions about whether the adjurations' form is related to petitions addressed to intermediate functionaries in ancient courts or even, conversely, the commands that such intermediaries themselves issued in the name of the king, which seems more appropriate, in which case the adjuration may be an inversion of such commands.

Some of the differences between the longer and shorter version of Aseneth's prayer, together with the two preliminary speeches found only in the longer reconstruction, have already been considered. The element of silence in those preliminary speeches receives additional illumination from the adjuration sources. As van der Horst points out, silent prayer in antiquity was frequently associated with malevolent activities and with magical practices. [60] One passage he cites, from Apuleius's *Metamorphoses*, associates silent prayer with the invocation of Helios. The story concerns an Egyptian prophet who attempts to resurrect a dead person. After placing herbs on the corpse and on himself, "he turned himself to the East and made silently certain prayers to the proud and rising sun, which caused all the people to marvel greatly at the sight of this solemn act and to look for the strange miracle that should happen." [61] *PGM* 77:1–5 calls for silent recitation of the requisite incantation. [62]

Descent of the Divine (the Angelic Being)

As we have already considered in the previous chapter, an angel appears out of the heavens at the conclusion of Aseneth's prayers. From an external textual vantage, the relationship between the two, Aseneth's prayers and the angel's appearance, is not automatic. Our further analysis in this chapter suggests a different reading, in which the angel's appearance is compelled by the power of Aseneth's prayers. Consider once more the formulas for the adjuration of Helios in *Sepher ha-Razim*. After reciting the appropriate adjurations, the one who wishes to see the sun during the day will indeed see him in his bridal chamber. The one who wishes to see the sun at night "will hear a peal of thunder from the north, and . . . will see something like lightning come forth and light up the earth before you."[63]

Although the analysis of the previous chapter suggested that the specific imagery of the morning star and the splitting heavens is modeled on biblical traditions, a rite for acquiring a divine assistant contains the following strikingly similar motif: "At once there will be a sign for you like this: [A blazing star] will descend and come to a stop in the middle of the housetop, and when the star [has dissolved] before your eyes, you will behold the angel whom you have have summoned and who has been sent to you."[64]

The same papyrus contains a spell to Selene (the Moon) that reads: "Having said this [the spell], you will see some star gradually free itself from [heaven] and become a god."[65]

Encounter between the Human and the Heavenly Being

Aseneth's encounter with the angel adheres to patterns present not only in biblical texts such as Judges 6 and 13 and the Greek Esther, which we have already considered, but also in the many ancient sources that envision such encounters. These patterns are themselves closely related to ancient protocols for encounters between kings and subjects. Typically, at the sight of the divine, or in the presence of the divine, the human falls down prostrate, experiencing fear and trembling. Such a response is precisely the obeisance rendered to ancient royalty. The divine being raises up the human being, exhorting her or him to be courageous and not to be afraid. Often, the human being inquires about the identity of the divine, although the divine being always knows the identity of the human.

These same protocols are present in the adjuration materials. At the splitting of the heavens and the appearance of the indescribable light, Aseneth falls prostrate before she actually looks up and sees the angelic figure himself in 14.8. She then prostrates herself a second time, immediately after she sees the angel. This is essentially the response prescribed in *Sepher ha-Razim* once Helios appears at night: "And after you see him, you will assuredly bow down to the ground and fall upon your face to the earth."[66]

When Aseneth falls on her face for the second time, at 14.10, the text adds that she did so "in great fear and trembling." That not only obeisance but fear is an appropriate response to the appearance of divine beings, angelic or otherwise, is implicit in the prayer prescribed in *Sepher ha-Razim*, once the petitioner is prostrate: "[A]ppear to me without (causing me) fear and . . . be revealed to me without causing me terror."[67] Such fear and terror may, in fact, be a typical human response in such situations, but as we have seen, it also has a close analogy in the response of humans prostrate before powerful superiors, including kings, who had the power of life and death over their subjects, as in this passage from the biblical Esther: "All the king's servants and the people of the king's provinces know that if any man or woman goes to the king inside the inner court without being called, there is but one law—all alike are put to death. Only if the king holds out the golden scepter to someone, may that person live."[68]

The angel's response to Aseneth's prostrations is typical of angelic responses in numerous sources. The first time, he tells her rise to her feet, after which he will speak with her. When she looks up and sees an angelic double of Joseph and throws herself back down at his feet, he exhorts her to take courage and not to fear and urges her again to stand, which she finally does.[69] Similar words of encouragement occur in numerous ancient texts that narrate encounters between humans and angels,[70] as do instructions to rise to one's feet.[71] *Sepher ha-Razim* directs the one who sees Helios at night to "stand up. . . . After this, put your hands behind you, and bow your head low, and ask whatever you desire."

Following these patterned exchanges, angelic figures typically grant human requests, as kings sometimes granted the requests of their subjects. Even before she has looked at him directly, Aseneth asks the angel who he is, to which he replies only that he is "the commander of the house of the Lord, and the commander of all the army of the Most High."[72] Subsequently, without her asking, he promises to tell her everything he has been sent to announce and proceeds to describe her future. The angel's accurate prediction of Aseneth's future here is particularly consonant with the Helios adjuration in *Sepher ha-Razim* and with other formulas for the adjuration of Helios in the Greek papyri.[73]

Prior to revealing the details of her future to Aseneth, the angel instructs her to wash her face and to change out of the black mourning garb into new, fresh clothing. Numerous papyri require the adept to wear similarly new, clean clothing. A passage from *Sepher ha-Razim* concerning the angels of the first firmament advises one who wishes to enter the presence of a king, or other exalted figure, to wash first in living water.[74] Several papyri prescribe ritual bathing or purification by water together with new or fresh clothing.

> [J]ump into the river. Immerse yourself in the clothes you have on, walk backwards out of the water, and after changing into fresh garments, depart without turning round.[75]

> After you have said this three times, there will be this sign of divine encounter. . . . But as for you, rise up and clothe yourself with white garments.[76]

> Say the formula seven times and you will see something wonderful. Then go away without turning back or giving an answer to anyone, and when you have washed and immersed yourself, go up to your own [room] and rest and use [only] vegetable food.[77]

> [G]o to an ever-flowing river . . . bathe, and go in pure garments.[78]

After Aseneth changes her clothes and washes her face, the angel proceeds to pronounce her future (15.3–11). Her name is now inscribed in the Book of Life and will never be erased. She will eat the bread of life, drink the cup of immortality, and receive the ointment of incorruptibility. She will be Joseph's bride and he will be her bridegroom. She will henceforth be called City of Refuge.

After these pronouncements, Aseneth offers to prepare the angel a meal of bread and fine wine. We saw in the previous chapter that this offer conforms to the pattern of angelic-human encounters in biblical passages such as Judges 13. Aseneth's offer of a meal is not simply hospitality and good manners but an offer of sacrificial thanksgiving. The table she proposes to set before the angel is analogous to the numerous food offerings for divine beings prescribed in a wide range of Greco-Roman sources.

> If you wish to speak with the moon or with the stars about any matter, take a white cock and fine flour, then slaughter the cock (so that its blood is caught) in "living water." Knead the flour with the water and blood and make three cakes and place them in the sun, and write on them with the blood the name(s) of (the angels of) the fifth encampment and the name of its overseer and put the three of them on a table of myrtle wood, stand facing the moon or facing the stars and say [the following].[79]

Particularly telling is the continuation of the rite for acquiring a divine assistant from which I have already drawn several times. After the angel (or god; the text uses both terms interchangeably) appears as a star and after learning the decisions of the gods about the future, the human party is advised as follows: "[T]ake the god by the hand and leap down, [and] after bringing him [into] the narrow room where you reside [sit him] down. After first preparing the house in a fitting manner and providing all types of foods and Mendesian wine, set these before the god."[80]

The spell to Selene from the same papyrus contains similar prescriptions for setting a table before the adjured:

> [S]ay to him: "What is your divine name? Reveal it to me ungrudgingly, so that I may call upon it." . . . If he tells you his name, take him by the hand, descend and have him recline as I have said above, setting before him part of the foods and drinks which you partake of. And when you release him, sacrifice to him after his departure what is prescribed and pour a wine offering, and in this way you will be a friend of the mighty angel.[81]

This spell is particularly intriguing for several reasons. In it, the adept is to have the angel recline, as is customary for honored guests at banquets. The offering of a gracious meal and of a sacrifice appears contingent on the angel revealing his name to the petitioner. Neither of these elements occurs in the shorter version of *Aseneth*, but both occur in the longer reconstruction. In the shorter version, after the angel informs Aseneth of her future, she blesses God, who sent the angel, and God's name and makes her offer of a table set with bread and wine (15.13–14). But in the longer version, Aseneth blesses God and the angel's name and proceeds to ask the angel his name in order that she might glorify him forever and ever.[82] Although he refuses to divulge his name, she still invites him to a banquet, prefacing her invitation thus:

> **And Aseneth stretched out her right hand and put it on his knees and** said to him, "I beg you, Lord, sit down a little on this *klinē*, **because this *klinē* is pure and undefiled, and a man or woman never sat on it.** And I will set a table before you, and bring you bread and you will eat, and bring you **from my storeroom old and** good wine . . . and you will drink from it."[83]

I have here deliberately left *klinē* untranslated. Burchard gives the translation as bed, following his interpretation of this piece of furniture in Aseneth's chamber as the bed on which she sleeps. But *klinē* also signifies a dining couch, and here, at the very least, a kind of double-entendre may be intended. The use of *klinē* reinforces the idea that Aseneth invites the angel to a banquet.[84] These differences suggest something we have already seen: that the longer version makes more explicit the associations of the shorter—here, not only the biblical but also the adjurative.[85]

Ascent of the Divine: Separation of the Human and the Divine

According to the shorter version, at the conclusion of their encounter, the angel tells Aseneth to remove the table she had set for him. As she turns to obey, the angel disappears from her sight, and she sees something "like a fiery chariot being taken up into the heaven to the east" (17.6). The longer text is characteristically more explicit and precise: Aseneth sees something "like a chariot of four horses traveling into heaven toward (the) east. And the chariot was like a flame and the horses like lightning. And the man was standing on that chariot" (17.8).

The ascent of the angel back into heaven is, as we have already considered, consistent with the narrative of Judges 13 and with other biblical imagery of a divine chariot. In the Berlin papyrus formula for acquiring an assistant, the god automatically gets up to leave after three hours, at which point the adjurer says, "Go, lord, blessed god, where you live eternally, as you will." The god then vanishes.[86]

But if the imagery of the shorter text generally resembles biblical materials and is consonant with the general idea in ancient formulas that adjured angels vanish as ethereally as they appear, the imagery of the longer text creates a much more precise visual image of Helios in his quadriga: the four-horsed chariot that draws the sun through the heavens and whose representation we know particularly from the mosaic floors of several Jewish synagogues in the land of Israel, dating from the fourth to the sixth centuries C.E. As with many elements discussed in this chapter, we will pursue the significance of Helios further in the next chapter. Here, however, it is important to remember how many of the spells and formulas we have considered are specifically prescribed to adjure Helios, both in *Sepher ha-Razim* and in the papyri.[87]

With the return of Helios or the angel to the heavens, elements of adjuration subside into the background of the text, which devotes itself to fulfilling the prophecies of the heavenly being and effecting the marriage of Joseph and Aseneth. But we may note the presence of a few additional features of the story that accord well with the paradigms of adjuration.

First, seven virgins occur in a context that is quite intriguing: *PGM* 4:662–73. After invoking and greeting Helios, the initiate sees doors thrown open "and seven virgins coming from deep within, dressed in linen garments, and with the faces of asps. They are called the Fates of Heaven." They are the companions of Minimirrophor and the most holy guardians of the four pillars.

Second, after the angel feeds himself and Aseneth the angelic honey but before he calls forth the bees from the hive, the angel traces designs on the comb with his finger, first from west to east, then from south to north. This apparent tracing out of a cross has led (probably misled) some interpreters to detect evidence of Christian symbolism.[88] Equally if not more feasible is an association between these acts and various rituals performed in the commerce with angels. *The Sacred, Hidden Book of Moses called the Eighth, or Holy*, preserved on papyrus, contains the following instructions:

"Having drawn in spirit with all your senses, say the first name in one breath to the east, the second to the south, the third to the north, the fourth to the west, and having knelt to the left [on] your right knee once, say to the earth once and to the moon once, to water once and to sky once [36 letters]." [89]

Another set of instructions from the same papyrus calls for the petitioner to recite the seven vowels in order, first *alpha* facing east, then *epsilon* north, *eta* west, *iota* south, *omicron* looking down to the earth, *upsilon* into the air, and *omega* up to the sky.[90] These actions (and others) suggest that the angel's actions must be viewed similarly, although perhaps not identically.[91]

Finally, Aseneth's transformation into an immortal angel herself, attested both in her consummation of angelic honey and in her physical transformation in 18.7, has precedent in the papyri. A text called "The Prayer of Jacob"[92] begins with an address to the "Father of the patriarchs, Father of the All . . . Creator of angels and archangels" and summons that deity, whom the same text shortly calls "god of gods." It concludes with the following prayer: "Strengthen me, Master; fill my heart with good, Master, as a terrestrial angel, as one who has become immortal, as one who has received the gift from you, Amen, amen."

Conclusion

In this chapter, we have seen striking similarities between Aseneth's encounter with the angelic double of Joseph and the materials associated with the adjuration of angelic beings, known to have circulated among Jews and non-Jews alike.[93] Particularly obvious is the invocation of Helios, the deity of the Sun. It is my contention that these similarities are not the result of mere coincidence but point in the direction of an author or authors who knowingly and intentionally drew upon the imagery of such paradigms for the construction of *Aseneth* experience and that the readers of *Aseneth* would have recognized these scenes for what they were.

NOTES

1. A valuable discussion of the problem may be found in John Gager's introduction to *Curse Tablets and Binding Spells from the Ancient World* (New York: Oxford University Press, 1992), where he rejects the utility of the category of magic altogether: "[M]agic, as a definable and consistent category of human experience, simply does not exist" (24). Particularly concerned with an artifical and pejorative distinction between magic and religion, Gager quotes the critique of O. Petersson: "'Magic' became—and still becomes—a refuse heap for the elements which are not sufficiently 'valuable' to get a place within 'religion,' (Petersson,"Magic—Religion: Some Marginal Notes to an Old Problem," *Ethnos* 3/4 (1957): 119). See also C. R. Phillips III, "*Nullum Crimen Sine Lege*: Socioreligious Sanctions on Magic," in Chris Faraone and Dirk Obbink, eds., *Magika Hiera: Ancient Greek Magic and Religion* (New York: Oxford University Press, 1991); 260–76. For a somewhat different view, see Hans D. Betz, "Magic and Mystery in the Greek Magical Papyri," in Faraone and Obbink, *Magika Hiera*, 244–59. For additional bibliography, see Gager, *Curse Tablets*, 39, n. 114.

2. E.g., K. Preisendanz, ed., *Papyri Graecae Magicae: Die Griechischen Zauberpapyri*, 2

vols. 2d ed. (Stuttgart: Teubner, 1973–74); Hans Dieter Betz, ed., *The Greek Magical Papyri in Translation, Including the Demotic Spells* (Chicago: University of Chicago Press, 1986).

3. Hebrew text in Mordecai Margolioth, *"Sepher ha-Razim": A Newly Discovered Book of Magic from the Talmudic Period* (Jerusalem, 1966; in Hebrew); English translation in Michael Morgan, *"Sepher ha-Razim": The Book of the Mysteries* (Chico, CA: Scholars Press, 1983).

4. See Phillips, *Nullum Crimen*.

5. Most scholars take this statement to be autobiographical. Whether it should be classified as Jewish or Christian, though, is more complex. On Paul's mysticism, see especially Alan Segal's chapter, "Paul's Ecstasy," in his *Paul the Convert: The Apostolate and Apostasy of Saul the Pharisee* (New Haven: Yale University Press, 1990), 34–71.

6. P. Schäfer, *Synopse zur Hekhalot-Literatur in Zusammenarbeit mit Margarete Schlüter und Hans Georg von Mutius: Herausgegeben von Peter Schäfer*, Texte und Studien zum Antiken Judentum 2 (Tübingen: J. C. B. Mohr, 1981), §685–86, where Ishmael describes Akiba's experience before the Merkabah.

7. In the Christian *Ascension of Isaiah*, the visionary experiences ascent, but those who are present apparently think that Isaiah has been with them the entire time. See, e.g., 6.10–16, which claims, inter alia, "His eyes were indeed open, but his mouth was silent, and the mind in his body was taken up from him."

8. Gershom Scholem thought that the *hekhalot* materials, while edited fairly late, had their origins in second-century Palestine (see, e.g., his *Major Trends in Jewish Mysticism*, 3d ed. (New York: Schocken Books, 1954; reprint, 1960, 45). More recent scholarship has argued strongly for later dates. See, e.g., Halperin, *Faces of the Chariot;* chap 7, sec. 2c, who prefers Babylonian Jewish communities in the fourth century, while admitting that some materials look as though they might be fourth-century Caesarean; P. Schäfer, *The Hidden and Manifest God: Some Major Themes in Early Jewish Mysticism*, trans. Aubrey Pomerance (Albany: SUNY Press, 1992), 8, for a dating ranging from late Talmudic to Geonic periods. Michael Swartz argues for dates from the third to eighth centuries C.E. and both Palestinian and Babylonian provenance ("Book and Tradition in Hekhalot and Magical Literatures," *Jewish Thought and Philosophy* 3 [1994]: 190; see also Michael Swartz, *Mystical Prayer in Ancient Judaism* [Tübingen: J. C. B. Mohr (Paul Siebeck), 1992], 216–20).

9. See, e.g., Chesnutt, *From Death to Life*, 145–49, 256–65.

10. Burchard vacillates on this point throughout his discussion in "Joseph and Aseneth."

11. Philonenko, *Joseph et Aséneth*, 96–97.

12. Philonenko, *Joseph et Aséneth*, 97.

13. Philonenko, *Joseph et Aséneth*, 98.

14. "This narrative does not represent a magic rite to entice a *daimon parhedros* (against Philonenko, *Joseph et Aséneth*, 97)" (Burchard, *Joseph and Aseneth*, 228, n. 17f2).

15. "The communion of honey could well have been an actual ritual of initiation. It is after this 'first communion' that converts would have been admitted to the sacred meal and would have received the bread, the cup, and the ointment" (Philonenko, *Joseph et Aséneth*, 98).

16. Philonenko, *Joseph et Aséneth*, 98.

17. 1.27–28. The fifteen-year indiction cycle began in 312 C.E.; Alexander observes that it was initially used only for taxation and only gradually for other datings, so its mention here suggests a date well into the fourth century (see "Incantations and Books of Magic," in Emil Schürer, *The History of the Jews in the Age of Jesus Christ,* G. Vermes, F. Millar, and M. Goodman [Edinburgh: T & T Clark, 1986], 47–50). See also Ithamar Gruenwald, "Sefer ha-Razim," in his *Apocalyptic and Merkavah Mysticism* (Leiden: E. J. Brill, 1980), 225–34, where he critiques the edition of Margolioth and argues for a later dating of 6th or 7th century C.E. Morgan (*Sepher ha-Razim*, 8, n. 1) defends Margolioth's textual skills and notes that Gruenwald is virtually alone in his dating. However, since my own arguments in this study similarly take a con-

trary, indeed lone, stance, I am wary of dismissing voices contrary to consensus on that basis alone! For my purposes, whether the reconstructed collection dates to the fourth century or several centuries later is not crucial.

18. Morgan's (*Sepher ha-Razim*) English translation reads "from all (impure) food, from all (impure) drink." But the Hebrew text in Margolioth's (*Sepher ha-Razim* 4.26) edition is unqualified, and I am less confident than Morgan that the formula calls for such a modified abstention.

19. More literally: "[Y]ou can ask him if death; if life, if good, if evil (אם למות אם לחיים אם לטוב אם לרע). The translation here, from Morgan, *Sepher ha-Razim* 4.39–40, and his insertion of the phrase "to foretell questions" may misconstrue the text and obscure a probable allusion to Deut 30.15, an allusion that appears to be closer to the known Greek texts. While the Hebrew Deut reads: (I set before you today) "את־החיים ואת־הטוב ואת־המות ואת־הרע (life and good, death and evil), the LXX reads τὴν ζωὴν καὶ τὸν θάνατον τὸ ἀγαθὸν καὶ τὸ κακόν. Nevertheless, it seems that the petitioner here asks Helios which of the alternatives in Deuteronomy awaits. In addition, there may be a second allusion to Moses in this material. This particular spell removes the radiance of the sun so that he can be seen "face to face" (פנים בפנים; 4.37–38). This is not precisely the language of Num 12.8, which claims that God spoke with Moses "mouth to mouth" (פה אל־פה; στόμα κατὰ στόμα). Ironically, "face to face" is the standard English translation. But the idea is clearly quite similar.

20. *Sepher ha-Razim* 4.25–43, italics original.

21. This prayer is Greek transliterated in Hebrew.

22. *PGM* 4:55–70. All *PGM* translations are from Betz, *Greek Magical Papyri*.

23. See Betz, *Greek Magical Papyri*, xxiii-xxviii, for dates and charts.

24. *PGM* 13:343–734.

25. *PGM* 13:604–45 excerpts.

26. This editorial addition addresses the discrepancy between 7 and 41 days.

27. *PGM* 13:671–79.

28. *PGM* 13:705–17.

29. *PGM* 4:170–179.

30. *PGM* 4:52–73.

31. *PGM* 13:255–62.

32. *PGM* 13:335–41.

33. Victor Turner, *The Ritual Process: Structure and Anti-Structure* (New York: Cornell University Press, 1969; reprint, 1977).

34. Differences in English translation are the result of different translators for different papyri, without editorial uniformity, so one translator renders ἐν ἐρήμῳ τόπῳ as "in a deserted place," while another translates τόπον ἔρημον as "solitary place." But the Greek is essentially identical.

35. *PGM* 4:27–28. This also suggests a ritual performed in the late fall, when the Nile recedes, although the exact time of year would depend on the precise location of the petitioner, among other things. Most scholars have taken the calendrical references in *Aseneth* 1.1 and 4.1 ("in the second month, on the fifteenth day," and "in the fourth month, on the eighteenth day") to set the central encounter of Joseph and Aseneth at the time of the summer solstice (see Philonenko, *Joseph et Aséneth*, 128, nn. 1,2). Yet there are some reasons to think that *Aseneth* is set in the fall. The specific fruits that Aseneth's parents bring back from their country estate (dates, figs, pomegranates, and grapes) are all associated with the fall harvest season, not only in ancient Egypt, but throughout the eastern Mediterranean. Such fruits are represented as typical of the fall harvest in the zodiac mosaics of several ancient synagogues. At Beth Alpha (sixth century C.E.), Autumn is accompanied by fruits that Sukenik identified as pomegranate, fig, apple, and grapes. The pomegranate and grapes are most clearly apparent, while the identification of the fig

seems plausible and the apple conceivable (E. L. Sukenik, *The Ancient Synagogue of Beth Alpha* [Jerusalem, 1932], 39). Another zodiac mosaic recently excavated at ancient Sepphoris, dated to the early fifth century C.E., portrays Autumn accompanied by pomegranates, other fruit shapes, and probably also grapes (Ze'ev Weiss and Ehud Netzer, *Promise and Redemption: A Synagogue Mosaic from Sepphoris* [Jerusalem: The Israel Museum, 1996], 28 (English and Hebrew); drawing on 26 and color photograph on 27; unfortunately, enlarged detailed photographs are not given for Fall [Tishri]).

36. *PGM* 4:154–285, here 170–79.

37. *PGM* 1:56.

38. *PGM* 3:615–18.

39. *PGM* 3:692, 701.

40. In characteristic fashion, the shorter text says that she did not taste anything, while the longer specifies that she neither ate nor drank.

41. *Sepher ha-Razim* 4:25–26.

42. *Sepher ha-Razim* 2:36–37.

43. *PGM* 4:52–85.

44. If the tower is square, there is no eastern portion per se.

45. *PGM* 1:290.

46. In many of the *hekhalot* texts, sexual abstinence in preparation for conjuring the angel who gives instantaneous knowledge of Torah is explicitly linked with the purifications prescribed in Exod 19:15 as preparation for the revelation at Sinai (see chapter 5).

47. *Sepher ha-Razim* 2:6–11.

48. *Sepher ha-Razim* 2:144–46.

49. *Sepher ha-Razim* 2:160–63.

50. *Sepher ha-Razim* 5:19–37.

51. Fritz Graf, "Prayer in Magical and Religious Ritual," in Faraone and Obbink, *Magika Hiera*, 196.

52. *PGM* 22b:32–35.

53. *PGM* 4:171.

54. Actually, the text is not absolutely explicit on this point. Aseneth breaks the statues and throws them out to the poor; she also throws out her robe, all of it, which I take to include the engraved stones. Given the general tenor of the text, it is impossible to imagine that the author(s) thought she retained those emblems of idolatry.

55. *PGM* 4:180–84.

56. *PGM* 4:186–94.

57. *Sepher ha-Razim* 4:64–65.

58. *Sepher ha-Razim* 2:166–68.

59. *Sepher ha-Razim* 4:30–31.

60. Van der Horst, "Silent Prayer," 7–9.

61. Apuleius, *Metamorphoses* 2:28. A new translation may be found in P. G. Walsh, *Apuleius: The Golden Ass* (Oxford: Clarendon Press, 1994).

62. See also *PGM* 4:744–46, cited in van der Horst, "Silent Prayer," 9.

63. *Sepher ha-Razim* 4:58–59.

64. *PGM* 1:74–77.

65. *PGM* 1:154–55.

66. *Sepher ha-Razim* 4.59–60.

67. *Sepher ha-Razim* 4.64–65.

68. Est 4.11.

69. *Aseneth* 14.1–12 in both versions.

70. E.g., *1 Enoch* 9.15, 9.3; *Apocalypse of Zephaniah* 3.1, 6; *Apocalypse of Paul* 14;

2 *Enoch* 21.3; 22.5. Martha Himmelfarb, *(Ascent,* 39) suggests that the exhortations in *1 Enoch,* Zephaniah, and Paul are based on God's words to Joshua in Josh 1.7 ("be strong and very courageous"). The LXX/OG reads ἴσχυε οὖν καὶ ἀνδρίζου, which does not correspond to the language in *Aseneth,* which is θαρσε. Although Himmelfarb may be right that the texts she considers draw on the language of Joshua, I think the general admonition not to fear is part of the broader pattern of divine angelic encounters.

71. E.g., 2 *Enoch* 21.3.

72. On the precise identity of the figure, see chapter 5; see also chapter 10.

73. E.g., *PGM* 77.1–24.

74. *Sepher ha-Razim* 1.132–33.

75. *PGM* 4:42–44.

76. *PGM* 4:209–14.

77. *PGM* 7:439–43.

78. *PGM* 3:691–92. This particular formula is associated with Helios and with a goddess, inter alia.

79. *Sepher ha-Razim* 1:161–65.

80. *PGM* 1:82–86.

81. *PGM* 1:160–72.

82. *Aseneth* **15.12x.**

83. *Aseneth* **15.14**.

84. Interestingly, as I remarked earlier (n. 14), Burchard, "Joseph and Aseneth," denies that this constitutes "a magic rite to entice a *daimon parhedros.*"

85. Burchard argues that the relevant parallels here are Judg 13 ("Joseph and Aseneth," 184–85) and Gen 18.1–5, concerning Abraham and Sarah at the oaks of Mamre, where they prepare cakes for the angel, a kid (ibid., 228, n. 15f2). But although I agree that Judg 13 is a framework for the narrative, the Genesis story is less clearly relevant (except in Abraham's statement to the angel, "If I have found favor with you"). This, however, seems to be what subordinates say to their superiors; it is similarly what Esther says to Ahasueras. All these materials reflect very old customs about encounters between superiors and subordinates, especially royalty and subjects.

86. *PGM* 1:93–95.

87. E.g., *PGM* 4:88–93, 5:1–47, 36:211–30. *PGM* 4:475–829 (the so-called Mithras Liturgy) declares at the beginning that the rites about to be set forth were revealed by the great god Helios Mithras through his archangel. It is also worth remarking that this particular, lengthy treatise appears intended for a daughter.

88. Philonenko, *Joseph et Aséneth,* 189, concedes the possibility but points to the use of crosses in Mithraic rituals, inter alia.

89. *PGM* 13:641–45.

90. *PGM* 13:824–34.

91. In chapter 6, I will offer another interpretation of these actions, one that is different but not incompatible with the suggestions I offer here.

92. *PGM* 22b:1–26.

93. However, the issue of Christians and the adjuration of angels is more complex.

CHAPTER FIVE

Aseneth and Mystical Transformation in the *Hekhalot* Traditions

Within the traditions that envision intercourse between the human and the divine, encounters with suprahuman beings often exhibit a strong mystical dimension. They focus, that is, on the extraordinary and the spiritual, on the fate of souls and the cosmos. Sometimes they impute cosmic significance to seemingly ordinary or earthly events. They may be contrasted, perhaps, with narratives such as those in Judges 6 and Judges 13 that focus on events in this world, on the ordinary, and on the bodily, although the distinction may often be a subtle one of emphasis and degree rather than kind. Already within the biblical tradition, the visions of Daniel afford an excellent example of such mystical encounters, where the "human figure" whom Daniel sees comes to "help you understand what is to happen to your people at the end of days."[1] Within the wider circle of Greco-Roman religious traditions, encounters with the divine in the mysteries of Isis, Mithras, Cybele, Demeter, and Dionysos similarly had significance for the fate of the soul, particularly after death.

Of particular significance[2] for the analysis of *Aseneth* are a group of texts, extant mostly in Hebrew, which are commonly called *hekhalot,* from the Hebrew word for palaces (*hekhal*), a frequent term for the heavens to which adepts traveled or from which angels descended. By all reasonable criteria, these materials are clearly Jewish, although there is considerable debate about the actual social and historical matrix from which they emerged.[3] Key features of the *hekhalot* traditions shed light on some of the specific details of the *Aseneth* narratives, as well as on the cosmology, or view of the universe, that undergirds the texts.

A demonstration of the strong affinity of *Aseneth* with the peculiarly Jewish *hekhalot* traditions may seem a tacit concession that *Aseneth* is the product of Jewish authorship. But I should make clear that I do not intend it as such, any more than I intend my exploration of the affinities between *Aseneth* and Syrian Christian literature[4] to be a tacit concession of Christian authorship. The significant similarities between the two need only be evidence of contact, direct or otherwise, between the author or authors of *Aseneth* and the traditions in the *hekhalot* materials.[5] It may also well be that both *Aseneth* and the *hekhalot* materials themselves draw on broad religious sensibilities of the late ancient Mediterranean, which they then express in the precise forms appropriate to the concerns of the authors and their communities.

The *hekhalot* materials defy easy description. To borrow the language of Michael Swartz, "Hekhalot literature consists less of books with well-defined beginning and endings than of clusters of pericopae which vary significantly in wording and order between manuscripts."[6] Until very recently, the *hehkalot* texts were available only to a very few scholars with access to the actual manuscripts.[7] Although now more widely available, both in their original languages and in modern translations, they continue to pose particularly vexing problems for contemporary scholars.[8]

Peter Schäfer, who has collected and edited *hekhalot* texts and written several major studies on them, has proposed that the *hekhalot* materials fall loosely into three categories. In one set, the "descent" or heavenly journey tradition, we find accounts of "righteous" men, usually identified as rabbis of one sort or another, who ascended[9] to the heavens, discoursed with angels, observed (and sometimes participated in) the angelic liturgies, saw God enthroned amid the heavenly hosts, were transformed themselves into angels, received revelations about the past and the future, and so forth. Such experiences are typically described as "descent to the chariot" (a reference to the chariot visions of Ezekiel), and the adept is usually called the *yored merkabah* (the one who descends to the *merkabah*).[10]

In Schäfer's second category are those narratives in which the adept adjures an angel, compelling the divine being to descend from the heavens and to appear and do the adept's bidding. Into this category, Schäfer places those materials that are usually called the *Sar ha-Torah* (the Prince of the Torah) traditions, in which the adept adjures this prince in order to obtain command of the Torah.[11] In the paradigmatic formulation of this material, according to Schäfer, Israel takes possession of Torah against the opposition of angels, through artful means rather than through traditional rabbinic learning, and thereby guarantees power on heaven and earth.[12] In Schäfer's view, the purpose of the adjuration traditions is always the same: command of Torah (procured through the assistance of the Prince of the Torah) and protecting oneself from forgetting that knowledge.[13] His third category consists of those traditions that combine the two, descent and adjuration.[14]

Aseneth and the Enoch Traditions

Aseneth's similarities with the *hekhalot* traditions are particularly illuminated through a comparison with two texts associated with the biblical figure of Enoch that contain scenes of encounters with angels and mystical transformations. In Genesis 5.24, the fate of Enoch, the sixth direct male descendant of Adam through his third son, Seth, is described with uncharacteristic, ambiguous language: "Enoch walked with God; then he was no more, because God took him." Numerous ancient traditions understood

Enoch to have escaped the fate of ordinary mortals and to have been translated into the presence of God without first dying and offered extensive accounts of the precise nature of Enoch's experience.[15]

A lengthy account of Enoch's ascent to the heavens is contained in a work known as *2 Enoch,* which is preserved only in Slavonic and about which there is great debate and little consensus.[16] Interestingly, *2 Enoch* shares some of the difficulties we encounter with *Aseneth.* It exists in both longer (A) and shorter (J) recensions, whose relationship to one another is difficult to determine.[17] Despite the highly misleading assignment of a late first-century C.E. date printed on the introductory page in *OTP,* there is great uncertainty about date.[18] Of particular interest are Anderson's observation that the text contains nothing distinctively Christian, his belief that there is no clear evidence that the book is Jewish, and his suggestion that the text be associated with "God-fearers."[19]

The book begins at the end of Enoch's 365 years (Gen 5.23). Asleep on his bed, Enoch experiences great inexplicable distress and weeps in his sleep. Then, two enormous men appear in his bedroom, described thus:

> Their faces were like the shining sun;
> their eyes were like burning lamps;
> from their mouths fire was coming forth;
> their clothing was various singing;
> their wings were more glistering than gold;
> their hands were whiter than snow.[20]

Standing at the head of Enoch's bed, these men call him by name. Enoch awakes and finds that they are truly there, whereupon he bows, terrified. True to the pattern of such encounters we have seen in previous chapters, the men exhort Enoch not to be afraid and announce that God has sent them to bring Enoch up to heaven with them. At their instigation, Enoch issues instructions to his sons on how they are to conduct themselves in his absence, admonishing them to keep God's commandments, avoid idolatry, and "bless the Lord with the firstborn of [their] herds and the firstborn of [their] children." Enoch then ascends, receiving a guided tour of the various heavens and their occupants, including Paradise in the third heaven, the gates through which the sun enters and departs, the movements of the sun and the moon, and numerous angels and archangels who preside over everything from the sun to human affairs.

In the tenth heaven, Enoch beholds the face of the Lord, at the sight of which he again falls down prostrate in obeisance. True to form, the Lord exhorts Enoch to be brave and to stand up forever in front of the divine face (J 22.6; also A). Michael lifts Enoch up and brings him before the face of the Lord, who instructs Michael to extract Enoch from his earthly clothing, anoint him with extraordinary oil, and clothe him with divine glory, all of which Michael does. Enoch perceives himself to have "become like one of God's glorious ones, and there was no observable difference" (J 22.10; also A).

So transformed, Enoch now receives instruction from an archangel on the nature of the world, including the coming flood, which he commits to writing. God then commands Enoch to return to earth with this knowledge and these books, in order to transmit this knowledge to his sons. Enoch does so, recapitulating much of his experience and visions in the heavens and concluding with lengthy moral exhortation before he is taken again into the heavens.

Yet another work associated with Enoch is a Hebrew text known as *3 Enoch,* which represents itself as the visions and ascent of one Rabbi Ishmael. It, too, has proved difficult to date with any certainty, although Alexander argues that a final redaction in the fifth to sixth centuries C.E. seems reasonable.[21] During his heavenly journey, Ishmael encounters the angel Metatron, who reveals to Ishmael that he was originally the human being Enoch, whom God took up into heaven and transformed into Metatron. This figure recounts his transformation and experiences to Ishmael in great detail.

Ishmael's initial encounter with Metatron follows the pattern of human encounter with a divine being, with some interesting modifications. Having ascended through six palaces (*hekhalot*), Ishmael arrives at the door of the seventh palace, where he prays that the merit of Aaron may protect him from the rage of angels who seek to cast him back down. God immediately sends him Metatron, who brings him safely before the throne of glory to gaze at the chariot. Neither the sight of Metatron nor proximity to the divine throne evokes fear in Ishmael, but when the princes of the chariot and the seraphim turn their gazes on him, he is overcome by their radiance and falls down trembling. At this, God himself rebukes them and commands them to avert their eyes. Metatron then revives him and lifts him up, although it takes Ishmael another hour to recover sufficiently to sing praises before God.

Metatron then proceeds to recount for Ishmael his own transformation from the human Enoch to his present angelic state. The Holy One had sent an angel bearing his own name, Prince Anapi'el YHWH, to bring Enoch to heaven in a fiery chariot with fiery horses, similar to the description of the ascension of Elijah in 2 Kings 2.11. There God grants Enoch a long list of "excellent, praiseworthy qualities more than all the denizens of the heights" (8.2). Enoch then expands in size until he matches the world in length and breadth and acquires extraordinary light. God places him on a throne comparable to the divine throne and appoints him ruler of "the denizens of the heights" (10.3).

The robe and crown that God fashions for Metatron are particularly noteworthy. In Metatron's robe are all kinds of luminaries: in his cloak are "brightness, brilliance, splendor, and luster of every kind." His crown is a royal one, with forty-nine stones, each like the sun. Setting it upon Metatron's head, God calls him "the lesser YHWH" (12.1–5). At the sight of the crowned Metatron, all the heavenly princes fall prostrate, unable to bear the magnificence of the crown.

Enoch's transformation into Metatron includes a transformation of his physical body: "[A]t once my flesh turned to flame, my sinews to blazing fire, my bones to juniper coals, my eyelashes to lightning flashes, my eyeballs to fiery torches, the hairs of my head to hot flames, all my limbs to wings of burning fire, and the substance of my body to blazing fire" (15.1).

This description is not really unique to Metatron, though, since many of the heavenly princes are subsequently described in essentially the same terminology, as brilliant, fiery beings whose light is virtually unbearable.[22]

After recounting his own transformation, Metatron shows Ishmael the wonders of the heavens, including such things as the letters by which various phenomena were created, the souls of the wicked, the souls of the angels, and much else. At one point, he shows Ishmael both those souls that have already been created and that have now returned and those souls still awaiting creation (or embodiment, apparently).[23] Consequently, Ishmael realizes that this scene is the explication of a biblical verse.[24] Soon thereafter, Metatron shows Ishmael the curtain of the Holy One, on which are spread all the generations of the world and all their deeds, past and present.[25]

As we shall see, these elements and others from the Enoch traditions bear significant resemblance to aspects of Aseneth's encounter with the angelic being.

Paradigms of Mystical Transformation

Drawing both on the *hekhalot* traditions and other ancient Jewish sources, Christopher Morray-Jones has recently sketched a useful working model of early Jewish mysticism.[26] In what he calls "visionary–mystical traditions," there are numerous accounts of an individual adept, whom Morray-Jones elsewhere describes as "an exceptionally righteous man," cultivating the ability to ascend into the heavens, ultimately to reach the seventh heaven or palace (*hekhal*), where the adept beholds "the appearance of God as a vast and overpoweringly glorious form of fire or light enthroned."[27] This appearance of God is often called "glory" (Hebrew, *kabod;* Greek, *doxa*); "great glory" (*hakkabod hagadol*); or "Power" (*haggeburah;* Greek, *dynamis*).[28] The identification of the "glory" of God with the "Name" of God and with the creating word, or Logos, of God occurs in multiple ancient sources, some of them quite early, such as Philo and *Jubilees.*[29] Particularly striking is a passage in the second-century Christian apologist Justin Martyr that God has begotten a power from himself that is also called "Glory of the Lord," Son, Wisdom, Angel, God, Lord, and Word.[30] This power is also called by Justin *anēr* or *anthrōpos*[31] (this last the precise term for the heavenly figure in *Aseneth,* as I shall explore further later on). Many sources also testify to beliefs in a secondary divine figure who bears the Name of God and embodies the divine Glory. Such figures, of whom Metatron in *3 Enoch* may be considered an exemplar, frequently play a role in the mystical encounter, guiding the visionary and revealing and interpreting heavenly secrets,[32] sometimes by announcing the decrees of heavenly books of deeds or life.[33]

In addition to beholding the enthroned divine Glory, the righteous adept is "transformed into an angelic being and enthroned as celestial vice-regent, thereby becoming identified with the Name-bearing angel who either is or is closely associated with the *kabod* itself and functions as a second, intermediary power in heaven."[34] The transformation of the adept frequently involves anointing with special oils and robing in garments with royal or divine associations (themselves hardly mutually exclusive).[35] Robing, crowning, anointing, enthronement, and metamorphosis into fire and light are thus all typical elements of the transformation experience.[36] Not infrequently, the transformative experience is initiated or induced through the recitation of "grandeloquent, rhythmical and apparently ecstatic or ecstasy-inducing hymns and prayers."[37]

Although the alert reader will by now have already seen many similarities between these ascent traditions and our *Aseneth* texts, a detailed consideration of both the similarities and differences is warranted. We may begin with a discussion of the similarities.

Use of Prayers and Other Preparatory Activities

In the previous chapter, we saw that in the numerous adjurative sources, prayer was one of the means by which ancient practitioners prepared themselves to draw down the divine or ascend to the heavens themselves. So, too, the mystical sources often contain lengthy prayers either as part of the narrative of mystical experiences or as part of the instructive prescriptions for initiating such encounters.[38] Morray-Jones suggests (as have others) that the lengthy repetition of such prayers and incantations could themselves have brought about the physiological perception of precisely the light and fire described in these texts. As we have already seen, prayers form a crucial part of Aseneth's performance prior to her encounter with the angelic double of Joseph, particularly in the longer reconstruction.

In prior chapters, I have noted that Aseneth's prayers follow the general patterns of ancient prose prayer, known from both biblical and nonbiblical sources, Jewish and otherwise. Here it is instructive to compare Aseneth's prayers to those of the *hekhalot* traditions.[39]

Swartz identifies a sixfold pattern of Jewish mystical prayers: (1) blessing and address to God; (2) description of God's establishment and creation of the heavens and earth; (3) focus on the heavenly beings and their continual praise; (4) correspondence of angelic and human praise; (5) declaration of the recitation of God's Glory or Name; and (6) liturgical blessing.[40] Against the suggestion that these prayers were primarily trance-inducing devices whose content and structure were relatively insignificant, Swartz argues that the prayers are "saturated with literary convention,"[41] although he agrees that they functioned both to initiate visions and to protect the practitioner.[42]

Though both *hekhalot* prayers and Aseneth's prayers more generally resemble ancient prose prayer in numerous ways, Aseneth's prefatory prayers, whether in the shorter or longer reconstructions, lack the distinctive mystical elements of the *hekhalot* prayers, such as the focus on heavenly beings and their praise of God, the correspondence of angelic and human praise, recitation of God's Name, and liturgical blessing. But significantly, these elements are introduced into the text with the angel's pronouncements to Aseneth, which articulate a correspondence between the human and the angelic (Joseph and the heavenly figure; Aseneth and the heavenly Metanoia). In the shorter version, Aseneth blesses the name of God, while in the longer version, as we have seen, she blesses the unknown name of the angelic figure, triggering the angel's complex response. Although Aseneth's prefatory prayer is clearly not identical to what we find in *hekhalot* traditions, it does function in much the same way, as the immediate antecedent to her visionary encounter, and may well be not merely the antecedent to that encounter but a significant causal factor.

As they do in the adjurative materials, Aseneth's other prefatory actions have close analogies in the mystical traditions as well. In 9.1–2, Aseneth begins what will be the process of her transformation by retiring to her bed, weeping, and grieving. In *2 Enoch,* Enoch weeps in distress before his mysterious angelic visitors appear in his bedchamber. In *4 Ezra* 3.1–3, the visionary lies on his bed in distress and agitation.[43] Her preliminary fasting[44] and mourning have their counterparts in numerous texts.[45]

Numerous elements of Aseneth's preparation are common to the prefatory acts for various religious encounters in antiquity. Fasting, mourning, weeping, removal of status-indicative clothing, sexual abstinence, withdrawal to sacred spaces, abstention from ordinary activities, all separate the individual from ordinary social definitions and both establish and affirm the individual's liminal status. In addition, though, both Aseneth's preparations and those of the *hekhalot* texts appear to have a particular focus that scholars have generally not identified or emphasized, namely, the transformation of the human body into an angelic body. Depriving the body of all those elements that transform the natural body into the social body (food, clothing, sexual and social contact with other humans) appears to make the adept's body as close to that of an angel as is humanly possible. Such preparation rests on ancient notions of angelic bodies as essentially spiritual rather than material. Angelic bodies were composed of light and fire, requiring neither the physical sustenance of food and drink nor the physical acts of love to produce angelic children. And thus, interestingly, another crucial component of angelic transformation is not only abstinence from sexuality but also a concomitant repudiation of gender.

Descent of the Heavenly Being

Aseneth's preparatory actions, including her mourning, fasting, prayer and confession, rejection of idols, and purification of her chambers (these last elements unsurprisingly absent from the narratives about already pious Jews) lead predictably to her encounter with the angelic being and ultimately to her transformation. But whereas in the Enoch texts and some other *hekhalot* traditions the result of preparations is the ascent of the adept into the heavens, in *Aseneth* it is the angelic figure who emerges out of the heavens and descends directly into Aseneth's chamber.

The significance of this difference is not immediately apparent. First, although ascent may be typical of the *hekhalot* narratives, it is by no means universal, as Schäfer's own cataloguing of the materials, noted at the outset of this chapter, demonstrates. In this particular regard, Aseneth's experience is similar to that of the visionary in 4 Ezra, whose multiple encounters with an angel usually take place in his bedchamber, although his final visions take place in a field, after he has eaten nothing but flowers.[46]

Further, despite the obvious descent of the angelic being into Aseneth's chambers, numerous elements in *Aseneth* suggest that the space in which the entire sequence occurs is not ordinary space at all but rather, at the very least, a temple and an analogue of the heavens themselves. Thus, while the angel may be said to descend to Aseneth, it may also be possible that Aseneth herself has ascended to meet the angel in a sacred location. Interestingly, in this regard, the paradigm of their encounter seems not unlike Moses' encounter with God on Sinai, where Moses ascends and God descends.[47] To consider this suggestion requires a brief digression.

The Heavens, Paradise, and Aseneth's Palace

While in chapter 2 I suggested that some of the description of Aseneth's rooms could have been constructed out of traditions about Wisdom's house, here I would like to explore further the possibility that the entire complex may be viewed as a kind of mystical cosmic map, with the courtyard representing Paradise, the seven rooms of

the seven virgins representing the seven heavens, and Aseneth's three-room apartment representing a three-chambered temple. Not inconceivably, the location of the
ten rooms on the top of a tower could be taken to signal the towers' representation of
a mountain, analogous not only to Sinai in Exodus 24 but also to the mountains in
texts such as *1 Enoch*.[48]

THE COURTYARD AS PARADISE

Many ancient Near Eastern traditions envision a divine garden typified by the
unmediated presence of the deity; the council of divine beings; the issuing of decrees;
the source of subterranean life-giving waters; fertility; and the supernatural, extraordinarily beautiful trees.[49] In some sources, the divine garden is also the site of divine
sexual unions.[50]

Several features of Pentephres' courtyard suggest it is an analogue of such gardens,
probably the Garden of Eden (identified with Paradise).[51] According to *Aseneth* 2.17,
Pentephres' house is surrounded by the courtyard, itself walled with large, rectangu-
lar stones. The courtyard contains "all sorts of mature, fruit-bearing trees" (2.19).
According to Genesis 2.9, the Garden of Eden contains "every tree that is pleasant to
the sight and good for food." In *Aseneth* 2.20, we learn that the courtyard is abun-
dantly supplied with water: a river passes through the courtyard and waters all the
trees. So, too, in Genesis 2.10, a river flows out of Eden and waters the garden. The
courtyard's four gates are guarded by eighteen young men (each), reminiscent of the
angels who guard the entrances to the various heavens as well as of the cherubim and
sword that God placed at the entrance to the Garden of Eden after the expulsion of
Adam (see also Ezek 28.13–16).[52] In the longer version of *2 Enoch* 30, God explicitly says, "And I laid out the paradise as a garden, and I enclosed it; and I placed
armed guards."

The identification of the courtyard as Paradise is strengthened in chapter 16, when
the angel shows Aseneth the mystery of the bees. Blessing the honey he is about to
give her to eat, the angel says, "[T]his honey the bees of the paradise of delight have
made" (16.8). This phrase, *"ho paradeisos tēs trufēs"* (the garden of luxuries or
delights), occurs several times in the LXX/OG Genesis as the translation for *Gan
Eden*.[53] In the next scene, in the shorter reconstruction,[54] after the angel calls forth the
bees from the honeycomb and they entwine themselves around Aseneth, he instructs
them first to go away to their own place, whereupon they all die. He instructs them a
second time to go back to their place, whereupon they are resurrected and fly to the
courtyard. If these are the bees of the paradise of delight and the courtyard is indeed
their true place, the courtyard must be equated with that same Paradise.[55]

A passage from *2 Enoch*[56] cited earlier offers a description of Paradise in the third
heaven that combines features now found in biblical descriptions (Gen 2.8–10; Ezek
28.13–14) with some of the elements in Aseneth, including the ripeness of the fruits
and the presence of guardians (cherubim in Genesis and Ezekiel; angels in *2 Enoch;*
"strong men" in *Aseneth*).

Similarly, in pseudepigraphic narratives about Adam and Eve (the closely related
Greek *Apocalypse of Moses* and the Latin *Life of Adam and Eve*), we find further
descriptions of Paradise that resemble the courtyard in *Aseneth*. These texts envision

two different Paradises, a heavenly one, located, as in *2 Enoch,* in the third heaven (*Apoc. Mos.* 40.1), and an earthly one.[57] Like Pentephres' courtyard, the earthly heaven is surrounded by a wall (*Apoc. Mos.* 17.1) with gates (19.1; *Vita* 40.1, 31.1–3).

THE SEVEN ROOMS OF THE SEVEN VIRGINS AS SEVEN HEAVENS

The number seven is an extremely significant number in both Jewish and non-Jewish symbolic systems in the ancient world.[58] Numbers in general and seven specifically were of particular importance in post-Platonic schemata of the cosmos, including the works of Philo of Alexandria.[59]

Most interestingly, perhaps, Philo explicitly associated seven with virginity, although he acknowledges that the association is not his own. In his treatise on the Decalogue, he calls seven "virgin [*parthenos*] among the numbers, and motherless in essence."[60] Elsewhere he writes that "the number seven neither produces any of the numbers within the decade nor is produced by any. By reason of this the Pythagoreans, indulging in myth, liken seven to the motherless and ever-virgin Maiden, because neither was she born of the womb nor shall she ever bear."[61] Philo also observes that seven is a fitting symbol of the original Ruler and Sovereign.[62]

Seven is of particular significance in the *Songs of the Sabbath Sacrifice,* found at Qumran, which envisions a sevenfold division of angelic priests, seven holy areas (or seven sanctuaries in the holy temple), seven chief princes, and seven deputy princes.[63] Carol Newsom, who edited these Qumran texts, commented that "[t]he entire composition seems at times to be a rhapsody on the sacred number seven."[64]

One of the most compelling ancient associations of the number seven, though, is with the heavens. This may be found already in Sumerian and Babylonian sources and characterizes Mithraic cosmology.[65] Philo, too, attributes to general knowledge the understanding that heaven is encircled by seven regions.[66] Although seven obviously has strong angelic and heavenly associations in the Sabbath songs from Qumran, Newsom points out that the seven heavenly sanctuaries there are not synonymous with heavens.[67] Explicit mention of seven heavens occurs in *2 Enoch,*[68] *3 Enoch* 1, 17.1–3, 18.1–2, the *Ascension of Isaiah* 6–11, and the *Apocalypse of Abraham* 19. According to Irenaeus, Valentinian gnostics attributed the creation of seven heavens to the demiurge.[69] *Sepher ha-Razim* envisions a sevenfold division of the heavenly realms. Burchard also thinks that *Aseneth* itself contains a reference to seven heavens, but this reading is not without difficulty, as he himself acknowledges.[70]

Numerous *hekhalot* texts, apart from *2* and *3 Enoch,* envision seven heavens and/or seven palaces, often arranged concentrically.[71] A wall mural from the third-century C.E. synagogue at Dura Europos appears to offer graphic testimony to beliefs in a similar cosmology.[72] There, an enigmatic painting of a closed temple is superimposed on a background of seven colored walls. The pillars on the side of the temple themselves number seven.[73] Also, *3 Enoch* actually combines a scheme of seven palaces in the seventh heaven, which Alexander sees as "the confluence of two originally independent streams of tradition."[74]

Given the numerous cosmological schemes that coexisted in the Greco-Roman world, it seems obvious that the seven rooms of the seven virgins in *Aseneth* would easily have lent themselves to cosmological interpretation, with or without their proximity to the courtyard and to Aseneth's tri-chambered apartment. Philonenko was seduced (in his own words) by the interpretation that the seven virgins are the seven stars of the constellation Ursa Major,[75] a reading he based in part on the description of the seven virgins' beauty as like that of the stars. From my perspective, though, it is precisely this astral language that lends additional support to the idea that the rooms of the seven virgins are heavens of some sort. As I have observed earlier, a plethora of ancient sources identify stars and angels.[76] If the seven rooms are heavens, and the seven virgins are stars, each heaven may also have its own angelic occupant.[77]

ASENETH'S THREE CHAMBERS AS TEMPLE

That Aseneth's three rooms constitute a kind of temple is essentially explicit in the texts themselves, since the first room contains gold and silver idols (2.4–5).[78] Ancient temples were above all else houses of the gods, evidenced by the presence of a statue of the deity. Aseneth worships these idols and offers them sacrifices, presumably in these very rooms. The precise number of rooms, three, corresponds to the three chambers of both the first and second Temples in Jerusalem.[79] Beyond the fact that the first room contains statues of Aseneth's gods, additional details point to the identification of her apartment as a temple.

The other two rooms serve as storehouses for Aseneth's treasures. One contains all her jewelry and luxurious clothing, while the other contains "all the good things of the earth," presumably foodstuffs. In addition to their role as divine houses, ancient temples functioned as treasuries and storehouses, stockpiling and protecting not only the wealth of the temple but also that of private individuals. In other words, a complex of three rooms—one that contained gold and silver statues of gods; a second that contained gold, silver, jewels, and expensive cloth; and a third that contained abundant stores of food—is entirely consonant with ancient descriptions of temples, although it clearly also has elements in common with royal palaces, particularly in the description of the second and third rooms.[80]

The identification of these three rooms with a temple may also be signaled by Joseph's appearance at the house (identifying Joseph with the divinity entering his temple) and intensified in subsequent chapters, when it is to this very place that the angelic being descends to Aseneth.[81]

One other detail in the description of Aseneth's quarters may possibly be related to the presentation of Aseneth's chambers as a temple. Before Aseneth begins her seven-day period of abasement, she goes down from her apartment to the gate and takes down the leather curtain (*katapetasma*), which she then fills with ashes.

In Greek translations of the Hebrew Bible, *katapetasma* signifies the curtain that hung before the ark of the covenant and in the Jerusalem temple, shielding the holy of holies from view.[82] In *3 Enoch* 45, a curtain (*pargod*) shields the angels from the glare of God's glory and contains on it a depiction of all of human history.[83] Elsewhere in the same text (*3 Enoch* 17), the name of the first heaven is *Wilod*: Alexander comments that this is derived from the Latin *velum* (veil) and means, in ordinary rabbinic usage, "a door curtain."[84] In some other texts with mystic connotations, a cosmic curtain separates the first heaven from the nonheavenly realm.[85]

It is thus tempting to suggest that the *katapetasma* has symbolic value, alluding perhaps to the complex as Temple, perhaps to the complex as map of the heavens, and perhaps even to both at the same time. Such an interpretation may in part be dependent on the precise location of this curtain, which is not absolutely clear in the texts. To get there, in the shorter version, Aseneth descends (*katelthe*) from her tower to the gatehouse (gateway), where she finds the gatekeeper (a woman) asleep with her children. In the longer version she descends the stairs of her tower and goes to the gatehouse. While these different readings may intend to represent identical actions, the shorter may be taken to mean that the gatehouse in question lay by the tower itself, while the longer text could mean that this gatehouse is the gatehouse for the entire complex. The former location seems more consistent with a reading of the curtain as symbolic (demarcating Aseneth's ten-room tower).[86]

However, the fabric of the curtain and Aseneth's actions seem inconsistent with other descriptions of holy curtains, earthly or heavenly. In Exodus 26.31–28.43 (LXX), the *katapetasma* must be made out of those exalted materials, *hyakinthos, porphyra, kokkinos* (crimson), *byssos*—the same ones used for priestly garments. But Aseneth's *katapetasma* is leather (skins),[87] and she unceremoniously removes it from the doorway and fills it with ashes, both of which actions seem to me to weaken any interpretation of the curtain as having symbolic significance.

Finally, the spatial arrangement of Pentephres' compound is strikingly consonant with Philo's numerical schema of the divine. For Philo (according to Goodenough's perceptive presentation), God, who is One, is nonetheless manifest to those below as a group of three, with yet a second group of three below that. God then can be expressed as one, as three, and as seven. This is precisely the arrangement of space in Aseneth: one courtyard, three rooms for Aseneth, seven rooms for the seven virgins.[88] Goodenough also points out that for Philo, the decade (10) was also the equivalent of One:[89] yet another way to describe the configuration of the compound would be as one courtyard and the ten rooms of Aseneth.

Although we cannot be certain of the precise signification, for either the author(s) or the audience of *Aseneth,* of Pentephres' compound, including its numerical and spatial arrangements, it does seem clear that the correspondence between the compound and ancient cosmological systems is not coincidental and that the readings I have offered here are highly consistent with the texts as a whole.

To return, then, to our discussion of *Aseneth's* conformity with ancient mystical paradigms, the fact that the angel descends to Aseneth, rather than Aseneth ascending to heaven, does not constitute a meaningful departure from ancient patterns of such encounters, although I will argue below that it is not without further significance.

The Identity and Appearance of the Heavenly Being

The being who descends to Aseneth at the conclusion of her repentance is a highly enigmatic figure. His form is that of an *anthropos,* which several English translations render by the technically accurate but insufficient term "man."[90] More precisely, his form is that of the human Joseph, whose own beauty and splendor are already extraordinary[91]—except that the angelic figure displays the typical hallmarks of a divine being in ancient literature:

14.9
His face was like lightning, and his eyes like the light of the sun, and the hair on his head was like a burning flame, and his hands and his feet were like iron from the fire **and sparks shot forth from his hands and feet.**

Here we may recall again the description of Enoch's night visitors in *2 Enoch* 1.5:

Their faces were like the shining sun;
their eyes were like burning lamps;
from their mouths fire was coming forth.

In chapter 3, I identified many of the salient differences between the portrait of the angelic figure in the shorter and longer reconstructions. Here I wish to explore those differences further, particularly in light of comparable figures in the *hekhalot* and related traditions.

In the shorter version of *Aseneth,* we learn little more about the figure's identity than we can deduce from this description. At 14.6, hearing him call her name, Aseneth asks the figure who he is and how he has managed to enter her chamber, whose tower is high and whose doors are shut. In response, using the technical formula of divine pronouncement (*egō eimi*),[92] he identifies himself as "the commander of the house of the Lord and the commander of all the army of the Most High." In the shorter version, Aseneth is content with this response and asks nothing further. As we have initially seen in chapter 3, the longer version, though, diverges significantly in its presentation of the figure and in the details of these scenes.

The first significant difference occurs at 15.3/**15.4:**

Take courage, Aseneth, **holy virgin.** For behold, your name was written in the book of (Life) **the Living in (the) heaven, in the beginning of the book; your name was written first of all, by my finger** and it shall not be erased for all time.[93]

In both versions, the figure then announces to Aseneth the fulfillment of Joseph's prayer for her that she be made new, formed anew and revived, and eat the bread of life, drink the cup of immortality, and be anointed with the ointment of incorruptibility. He pronounces her name change to City of Refuge and compares her new status to that of the heavenly Metanoia (Repentance). Finally, he instructs her to dress herself as a bride and prepare for Joseph's arrival.

In the shorter version, Aseneth then blesses the God who sent the figure and asks to prepare him a table and bread; his answer initiates the scene with the honeycomb. But in the longer version, Aseneth blesses not only "the Lord, your God" but also the name of the angel. Then, seeming to realize that she does not know it, she asks him his name in order to "sing hymns and glorify you for all time."[94] The angel replies by asking her why she seeks his name although she has just told him her intention and refuses her request.

15.12/**15.11–12x**
And as the figure finished speaking **these words** (to) Aseneth, (she) was **exceedingly** joyously happy **about all these words** and threw herself before his feet **and prostrated herself face down to the ground before him** and said to him: "Blessed is the Lord **your** God **the Most High** who sent you to me to deliver me from the darkness and to lead me

(into the light) up from the foundations of the abyss, and blessed (is his) be your name forever." What is your name, Lord; tell me in order that I may praise and glorify you for ever (and) ever. And the man said to her: "Why do you seek this, my name, Aseneth? My name is in the heavens in the book of the Most High, written by the finger of God in the beginning of the book before all (the others), because I am chief of the house of the Most High. And all names written in the book of the Most High are unspeakable, and man is not allowed to pronounce nor hear them in this world, because those names are exceedingly great and wonderful and laudable."

This scene is extraordinarily important. In chapter 3, I suggested that the difference between the two scenes could be partially accounted for by the hypothesis that the longer text seeks to bring the shorter into conformity with the underlying narrative framework of Judges 13. There, indeed, Manoah does ask the angel his name, in order to be able to "glorify" (*doxasōmen*) the angel when his prophecy proves true, and there, too, the angel similarly declines to provide it, claiming that his name is "too wonderful." But although I think it highly possible that the redactors of the longer version are influenced by the narrative of Judges 13, the changes here go far beyond Judges 13, suggesting additional concerns of the revisionists.

Aseneth wishes not only to glorify the figure, language that might be imported from Judges 13, but *to sing hymns.* Further, she wishes to do so not, as in the case of Manoah, as a finite gesture in recognition of the angel's correct prophecy but eternally. This perpetual glorification and singing of hymns is precisely the activity envisioned for the angels in heaven in so many *hekhalot* and mystical–visionary texts.[95] Taken together with other passages, particularly in the longer version, it points to Aseneth's own desire not only to become like the angels in heaven but also to do so in accordance with a particular understanding of angelic identity and activity.

In these scenes, we see another significant difference between the longer and shorter version in the language of the angel when he addresses Aseneth that points further to his identity and to the circles from which these scenes might emanate. In the shorter version, all of the angel's speech preserves a distinction between himself and God. As in the longer version, he identifies himself initially as the commander of the house of the Lord and of the army of the Most High. At 14.13–14, he instructs her to change into new clothing, after which he will tell her "the things I was sent to say to you."[96] At 15.2, he assures her that the Lord has heard her confession and at 15.5 that the Lord has given her to Joseph. At 15.9 he promises to go see Joseph on Aseneth's behalf, a gesture consonant, I suspect, with the role of a messenger, heavenly or otherwise.

But in the longer version, this distinction breaks down. At **14.8, 14.11,** and **14.13,** the angel repeats his intention to tell Aseneth "what I have to say."[97] The angel's words are here not those he has been sent to say but his own speech (*ta rhēmata mou*). In the scene that follows, it is now not God but the figure himself who has heard Aseneth's confession, seen her humiliation and affliction (**15.3**), and now gives her to Joseph as a bride (**15.6**).

In the longer description of Metanoia, the angel speaks of God in the third person. Metanoia entreats God the Most High, who himself loves his daughter, Metanoia. But then the angel draws an analogy between himself and God, while at the same time distinguishing himself from "all the angels" who also love Metanoia.

15.8
And Metanoia is a very beautiful virgin, pure **and laughing always** and holy and gentle, and **therefore** God the Most High **Father** loves her and all the angels stand in awe of her. **And I, too, love her exceedingly, because she is also my sister. And because she loves you virgins, I love you, too.**

The relatedness of the angel and God is suggested in several other passages in the longer version. One may be inferred, as I have already noted, from Aseneth's own blessing not only of God (as in the shorter version) but of the name of the angel as well. Another comes at the time of the angel's departure:

17.6–7
And the figure said to Aseneth, "Remove this table." And Aseneth turned to move the table, and the figure disappeared from her sight, and Aseneth saw something like a (fiery) chariot **of four horses** being taken up into the heaven to the east. **And the chariot was like a flame of fire, and the horses like lightning. And the man was standing on that chariot**.

As I observed in chapter 3, the shorter version follows the imagery of Judges 6 and 13, while the imagery of the longer version utilizes details found in other biblical traditions of heavenly ascent and divine chariots.[98] This imagery is particularly common in the literary iconography of the Name-Bearing Angel (and, as we shall also see, closely resembles ancient representations of Helios). Finally, as the angel ascends, Aseneth remarks in the longer version:

17.6/17.9–10
Senseless and audacious am I, because I have spoken with boldness[99] and said that an *anthrōpos* **came into my chamber out of heaven, and did not know that [G]od came to me. And behold now he is traveling back to heaven to his place. And she said in herself,**[100] Be gracious, Lord, to **your slave, and spare** your maidservant, because I spoke (evil) **audaciously** before you, in ignorance **(was) all my speech.**[101]

For Aseneth, at least, the identity of the being the authors of both versions call *anthrōpos* is in fact incorrect: his true identity, in the longer version, is as *theos,* as God. Here, the redactor of the longer version may be playing with the multivalence of *anthrōpos.*

Indeed, the designation of the divine being by the term *anthrōpos* is in itself likely to be intentional and significant.[102] Morray-Jones identifies numerous ancient texts that point to an association of the primordial *Anthrōpos* in Genesis 1.26–27 with the divine Glory. These range from Philo, who differentiates the man of clay in Genesis 2–3 from the heavenly *anthrōpos,* who is not only in the divine image but may also be the divine Logos[103] to the *Testament of Abraham* 11, where the patriarch sees "the first-formed Adam [that is, the *Anthrōpos*] on a throne at the entrance to Paradise."[104] The designation of the angelic double of Joseph as *Anthrōpos* may point, then, to his association with the primal Adam, who is himself the Image of the Divine and thus probably closely associated, if not to be identified, with the Name-Bearing Angel.[105]

At the very least then, the differences between the longer and shorter versions point to significantly different interpretations of the identity of the heavenly being who appears in Aseneth's chamber. In the shorter version, he appears as a heavenly messenger, in the guise of the earthly Joseph, although no one, not even Aseneth herself, is in the least bit fooled by his seeming resemblance to Joseph. In this regard, he is a figure well known in numerous biblical accounts, including the narratives of Judges 6 and 13. Even more so than some biblical narratives, the shorter version is careful to preserve a distinction between the figure and God at virtually all times.

But in the longer version, the portrait of the figure is far more complex. As we have seen, speeches and actions assigned to God in the shorter version are here arrogated to the figure, who himself has heard Aseneth's confession and himself gives her to Joseph as a bride. It seems possible to suggest that in these scenes, the speech of the angel and the speech of God are one and the same, which may in turn support an interpretation of the figure as the speech, or the Logos, of God.[106] In the scene describing Metanoia, the figure distinguishes himself from God, on the one hand, and from all the rest of the angels, on the other, consistent perhaps with his self-identification as the *archon* of the house of the Most High. This scene provides yet another clue to his identity, in that he claims to be the brother of Metanoia, who is herself the daughter of God, thus implying that he is the Son of God. This identification is also supported by the titles assigned to Joseph in the text, whose double the figure is and who is called Son of God, Powerful One (*dunatos*) of God, and so forth.[107]

The angel's claim, in the longer version, that his name is written first in the book of the Most High, written before all the others, points to an identification of the figure with the Logos, with Wisdom, and with the primordial *Anthrōpos* of Genesis 1.26–27, all of which are said, in various traditions, to have been either the first of God's creation or antecedent to God's creation.[108] It is also possible that a similar identification undergirds the angel's action in a scene that occurs only in the longer version at **16.16x,** where the angel restores the honeycomb to its original whole condition, as it was in the beginning. This phrase by itself alludes to creation in Genesis, and if the honeycomb here symbolizes creation, the angel has just performed an act of the creator, restoring creation to its original perfection.

Yet another detail of the scene with the honeycomb may allude to the identification of the angel as the Logos of God (and therefore the divine vice-regent). In chapter 3, I suggested that the longer version of the angel feeding honey to Aseneth alludes to the story of Adam and Eve in Genesis 2–3, an allusion that is much harder to see in the shorter version. If this reading is correct, it suggests an analogue between the angel and Adam that further strengthens the interpretation that this figure is the primordial *Anthropos,* whose full identity can only be explicated by a close analysis of the traditions associated with the Name of God, the Glory, the Name-Bearing Angel, and so forth.

Although the angel never tells Aseneth his name, both Philonenko and Burchard declare that the figure must be the archangel Michael, who is called at 14.7/**14:8** *stratiarchēs* and in some manuscripts *archistrategos,* which is a conventional title of Michael in several of the ancient sources we have been considering for their other resemblances to *Aseneth.*[109] In all of those cases, though, the texts explicitly name Michael. If the figure is indeed to be understood as Michael, the absence of his name in *Aseneth* may be related to the underlying narrative framework of Judges 13, as well as, at least in the longer reconstruction, to concerns about the worship of angels. Yet whether or not either the authors or the early audiences of *Aseneth* would have recognized this figure as Michael, calling him by this name is insufficient exploration of what is almost certainly a far more complex identity that differs considerably in the shorter and longer versions of the story. Furthermore, by identifying him as Michael, Philonenko and Burchard impute to the angelic figure a fixed identity that obscures the fluidity of traditions about angels in the ancient sources.[110]

A careful examination of the attributes of the angelic double of Joseph demonstrates his affinity with numerous ancient angelic figures, particularly, although by no means exclusively, that of Metatron,[111] a complex figure known from orthodox rabbinic sources[112] as well as from various *hekhalot* texts. According to Morray-Jones, Metatron has two major characteristics: he is the "Angel of the Lord" or the "Prince of the Presence" and he is also the celestial transformation of the human patriarch Enoch.[113] In his capacity as primary angel, Metatron

> functions as the celestial vice-regent who ministers before the Throne, supervises the celestial liturgy and officiates over the heavenly hosts. He sits on a throne which is a replica of the Throne of Glory and wears a glorious robe like that of God. He functions as the agent of God in creation, acts as intermediary between the heavenly and lower worlds, is the guide of the ascending visionary, and reveals the celestial secrets to mankind. He is, by delegated divine authority, the ruler and judge of the world. He is thus a Logos figure and an embodiment of the divine Glory.[114]

As Alexander notes, Metatron shares many attributes with Michael, which may suggest that Michael and Metatron were originally understood to be the same angel— Michael being the exoteric name and Metatron the esoteric.[115]

Although the correspondence is by no means perfect, the enigmatic angel in *Aseneth* performs a significant number of these functions and appears to share key characteristics of Metatron. He mediates between heaven and earth and serves as a kind of divine marriage broker for Aseneth and Joseph. He serves as Aseneth's psychopomp, showing her mysteries and ensuring that she understands them. His physical appearance closely resembles the description of Metatron in some sources, such as *3 Enoch,* and he ascends to heaven in a divine chariot. Although his participation in creation is not a focus of *Aseneth,* I have suggested earlier that it may be implicit in several scenes in the texts, particularly in the longer version. By his own admission, the angel is the head of God's army and God's household.

Metatron receives particular articulation in *3 Enoch,* the text that details the transformation of the earthly Enoch into the celestial Metatron. Morray-Jones contends that *3 Enoch* represents a relatively late development of the Enoch traditions that reinterprets earlier Metatron traditions in light of his identification with the biblical patriarch.[116]

Although the figure in *Aseneth* and Metatron in *3 Enoch* share numerous similarities that may be explained by their common angelic nature, two scenes in *3 Enoch* exhibit more than passing similiarity to scenes in *Aseneth*. In *3 Enoch* 46, Metatron proposes to show the visionary Ishmael "the spirits of the stars—which stand like fiery sparks around the chariot of the Omnipresent One," whereupon he shows Ishmael a scene quite similar to the scene in *Aseneth* 16, where the angel instructs the bees to fly to their places:

> What did Metatron do? At once he clapped his hands and chased them all from their places. Immediately they flew up on wings of flame and fled to the four sides of the throne

of the chariot, and he told me the name of each of them, as it is written, He counts the number of the stars and gives each of them a name. [Ps 147.4]

The second scene is *3 Enoch* 43, which depicts the souls of the righteous that have returned to the presence of God and those that have not yet been created, to which I will return later.

Whether the angelic figure in *Aseneth* may reasonably be identified as Michael or Metatron (or both, or neither),[117] there is one final consideration for the thesis that the figure must be understood in the tradition of the divine co-regent or the Great Angel, namely, the paradigm of Pharaoh and Joseph. The verse in Genesis 41 that first informs us of Joseph's marriage to Aseneth comes at the conclusion of Pharaoh's speeches and actions in Genesis 41.38–45, where he responds to Joseph's interpretation of his dreams and to Joseph's recommendations to protect the Egyptians against the forthcoming famine.

> Pharaoh said to his servants, "Can we find anyone else like this—one in whom is the spirit of God?" So Pharaoh said to Joseph, "Since God has shown you all this, there is no one so discerning and wise as you. You shall be over all my house, and all my people shall order themselves as you command; only with regard to the throne will I be greater than you." Removing his signet ring from his hand, Pharaoh put it on Joseph's hand; he arrayed him in garments of fine linen, and put a gold chain around his neck. He had him ride in the chariot of his second-in-command; and they cried out in front of him, "Bow the knee."[118] Thus he set him over all the land of Egypt. [Gen 41.38–44]

In an earlier, if not initial, context, this scene describes the investiture of a grand vizier. However, by now, it is easy to see how the language of this passage could have been particularly fraught with significance when interpreted through mystical lenses. Pharaoh himself serves as an analogue of God, while Joseph becomes a particularly suitable image of the divine co-regent.[119] Joseph becomes the commander of Pharaoh's house, as his angelic double in *Aseneth* is the commander of the house of the Lord (14.7). The human Joseph in *Aseneth* indeed rides in the chariot of Pharaoh's "second-in-command," while his angelic double ascends back to heaven in a fiery celestial chariot. Both the earthly and the heavenly Joseph wear "garments of fine linen," although those of the angel are distinguished by their fiery light.

The language of Genesis 41.40 ("only with regard to the throne will I be greater than you") could clearly have been read to signal the distinction between God (Pharaoh) and his vice-regent (Joseph) and would have accorded well with throne imagery. And Genesis 41.43 could be the most pregnant verse of all, for there the heralds preceding Joseph are instructed to shout out, "Bow the knee," a phrase that could easily be construed to command worship of the divine angel.[120]

The analogy here required between God and Pharaoh is virtually explicit in the shorter text of *Aseneth*. In 6.2 and 6.6, Aseneth, seeing Joseph in the courtyard, calls him the Son of God, while in 21.3, Pharaoh himself declares Joseph to be the "first-born son of God." Only a few verses earlier (20.7), Joseph tells Pentephres that he cannot accept his offer to make the wedding until he first goes to Pharaoh, "because he [Pharaoh] is my father." Taken together, these verses equate God and Pharaoh, both of whom are represented as Joseph's father.

In the longer version, the force of this equation is muted by a slight change: instead of calling Pharaoh his father, Joseph now calls him "like my father."[121] This alteration clearly weakens the identification of Pharaoh as God (apparently intentionally), but the general paradigm of Pharaoh and Joseph as the analogue of God and his vice-regent remains clearly visible in the text.

Conclusions: The Identity of the Angelic Being

In both versions of *Aseneth,* the relationship between Pharaoh and Joseph lends itself easily to interpretation as the paradigm of God and his divine vice-regent. But it is particularly in the longer text that the angelic figure is more closely aligned with the figure developed in other sources as the Name-Bearing Angel—the virtual double of God, the Son of God, the Logos of God, and so forth. Yet, interestingly, the longer text exhibits some concern over the problem of angel worship and takes the stance that many scholars have identified with Jewish sources: that this figure is not to be confused with God, despite his enormous resemblances to God, at least to the extent that he may not be worshiped.[122] Aseneth may call him God, and she may essentially be correct in her perception, but she may not worship him. The angel refuses to tell her his name and so prevents her from singing hymns, presumably to him, and from glorifying him. She thus may not (and does not) do for this being what the angels in heaven do for the true God—sing continual hymns and glorify him.[123]

Precisely what this means for the setting of *Aseneth* continues to puzzle me. On the one hand, the angel's refusal to accept Aseneth's worship would seem to align the text more with those who opposed angelic worship. But in many other respects, the longer version in particular, and the shorter version to a lesser extent, appears to emanate from a context both similar to and closely aligned with the mystical–visionary traditions, particularly though by no means exclusively the *hekhalot* traditions. But there is more to be said about this when the entire text has been analyzed, particularly in its other differences with *hekhalot* materials.

Aseneth's Transformation

As I noted earlier, Morray-Jones identifies the basic common elements of angelic transformation as robing, crowning, anointing, enthronement, and metamorphosis into a being of fire and light, all of which are apparent in the Enoch traditions.[124] Consider again *2 Enoch* 22.8–10 and *3 Enoch* 12:

2 Enoch 22.8–10 (J)[125]
And the LORD said to Michael, "Go, and extract Enoch from [his] earthly clothing. And anoint him with my delightful oil, and put him into the clothes of my glory." And so Michael did, just as the LORD had said to him. He anointed me and he clothed me. . . . And I looked at myself, and I had become like one of his glorious ones, and there was no observable difference.

3 Enoch 12
R. Ishmael said: Metatron, Prince of the Divine Presence, said to me: Out of the love which he had for me, more than for all the denizens of the heights, the Holy One, blessed be he, fashioned for me a majestic robe, in which all kinds of luminaries were set, and he clothed me in it. He fashioned for me a glorious cloak in which brightness, brilliance,

splendor, and luster of every kind were fixed, and he wrapped me in it. He fashioned for me a kingly crown in which 49 refulgent stones were placed, each like the sun's orb, and its brilliance shone into the four quarters of the heaven of 'Arabot, into the seven heavens, and into the four quarters of the world. He set it upon my head and he called me, "The lesser YHWH," in the presence of his whole household in the height, as it is written, "My name is in him."

The key elements of transformation narratives such as these are found within the *Aseneth* narratives as well.

Although the angel never explicitly anoints Aseneth, he announces to her (15.4/**15.5**) that from this day on, she will "eat the bread of life and drink the cup of immortality and be anointed with the ointment of incorruptibility." In the longer text only, at **16.6,** after she has eaten from the honeycomb, the angel announces that Aseneth has now "eaten bread of life, and drunk a cup of immortality and been anointed with ointment of incorruptibility."[126] Both passages envision Aseneth's transformation as involving anointing with a substance that presumably renders Aseneth's body impervious to the corruption that mortal bodies suffer after death and that appears to confer on her body the same immunity to corruption that angelic bodies by their very nature have. Why the texts then contain no scene in which the angel actually anoints Aseneth is impossible to determine, although one possibility has to do with sensitivity to ancient norms of propriety. Despite her angelic transformation, Aseneth is still a woman and will shortly become the bride of Joseph, and it may simply have been too indelicate to have the angel physically anoint Aseneth.[127]

Perhaps for the same reasons, although perhaps not, the angel does not himself dress Aseneth in new clothing. But there is no question that both versions of the story have Aseneth dress in glorious new clothing, not once, but twice. Immediately after the angel appears in her bedroom, he instructs Aseneth to remove her garments of mourning, to wash her face with living water, and to put on a brand-new robe, together with the "double girdle of her virginity," all of which she does.[128] After the angel departs, Aseneth changes her clothing a second time:

18.3–6/18.5–6
And Aseneth **remembered the man and his commandment and she hurried and** went into her **second** chamber **where the chests (containing) her ornaments were** and opened her **big** chest and took out her first robe, **(the one) of wedding,** which had the appearance of lightning, and put it on. And she girded herself with a brilliant, royal girdle. This girdle was the one with precious stones. And she put gold bracelets around her hands, and gold trousers[129] about her feet, and a precious ornament about her neck **in which innumerable and costly precious stones were fastened,** and she placed a gold crown on her head; and on this crown in front **on her brow was a big sapphire stone and around the big stone** there were **six** very expensive stones. And she covered her head with a veil, **like a bride and she took a scepter in her hand.**

As I observed in chapter 3, the changes in the longer text may partly be attributable to redactional desire to clarify the bridal imagery of the shorter text at 15.10. But as a whole, they have the curious effect of muting the imagery of divine transformation.

This scene clearly resembles the robing and crowning of Ishmael and Enoch. Also of interest in this regard is a scene in chapter 21, where Pharaoh crowns the nuptial pair.

21.4/21.5–6
And Pharaoh took golden crowns and placed them on their heads **which had been in his house from the beginning and of old. And Pharaoh set Aseneth at Joseph's right side and put his hands on their heads, and his right hand was on Aseneth's head. And Pharaoh** said, **(May)** God the Most High (will) bless you **and multiply you and magnify and glorify you forever.**

In the shorter version, in particular, the elements of robing and crowning are admittedly not unambiguous indicators of Aseneth's angelic transformation, although Pharaoh's words to Joseph and Aseneth (**"may God . . . magnify and glorify you forever"**) could be construed to reflect their exalted status. But such a scene follows immediately in chapter 18.

18.7/18.8–9
And she said to her (young female attendant) **foster-sister,**[130] "Bring me pure water from the spring **and I will wash my face." And she brought her pure water from the spring and poured it into the basin.** And Aseneth bent down **to wash her face and saw her face** in(to) the water (in the bowl on the conch shell). And (her face) **it** was like the sun, and her eyes like (the) **a rising** morning star **and her cheeks like the fields of the Most High, and on her cheeks red like a son of man's blood, and her lips like a rose of life coming out of its foliage, and her teeth like fighting men lined up for a fight, and the hair of her head like a vine in the paradise of God prospering in its fruits, and her neck like an all-variegated cypress, and her breasts like the mountains of the Most High God.**

As usual in the shorter version, the scene is terse. Although the language of this scene is difficult, it appears that Aseneth peers into the water, which has now been poured into a bowl. With "her face . . . like the sun, and her eyes like the morning star" (18.7),[131] Aseneth's angelic transformation is complete.

As with its treatment of her clothing, the longer text again appears to attempt to mute the significance of Aseneth's experience. Now, Aseneth's intention in requesting the water is explicitly to wash her face.[132] Still, when she looks into the water to wash her face,[133] she sees her own face transfigured, in a passage that, as we have seen, draws on expanded imagery in Song of Songs to detail her features.[134] Once again, the text interprets itself in terms of bridal imagery, as Aseneth's foster-father (a character present only in the longer text) concludes that Aseneth's changed appearance is a great beauty indicative of her worthiness to marry Joseph: "At last the Lord God of heaven has chosen you as a bride for his firstborn son, Joseph" (**18.11**).

Interestingly, similar language occurs in the *Sar ha-Torah* myth, at the conclusion of a long list of things God knows the "Israelites want." The full passage, which is quite interesting, reads:

You want much Torah, vast learning [*talmud*], multitudes of traditions. You look forward to investigating *halakhah*. You yearn for the multitude of my secrets, to pile up testimony like mountains, wondrous wisdom like hills [?], to make learning great in the streets and dialectic in the lanes, to multiply *halakhot* like the sands of the sea and [make them?] as many as the dust of the earth. [You want] to establish academies at the entrances of tents, there to distinguish the forbidden from the permitted, to decide what is impure and what is pure, and to tell menstruating women what they must do. [You want] to bind garlands on your heads, royal crowns on your children's heads. [You want] to force kings to bow to you, princes to fall down before you. [You want] to spread your name beneath the sky, your reputation in the seacoast towns. [You want] your faces to shine like daybreak, [the place?] between your eyes like the planet Venus.[135]

Another use of Song of Songs occurs in *Hekhalot Zutarti,* where the petitioner is instructed to repeat: "Great, mighty, terrible, powerful, exalted, strong God. *My beloved is white and ruddy,* and so forth, hosts. *His head is pure gold,* and so forth, hosts," and on through all of Song of Songs 5.10–16.[136] These verses are closely related to those that appear to be the basis of the longer reading of *Aseneth* **18.9,** namely, Song of Songs 4.1–5.

Aseneth's transformation has a second dimension. Not only does she become an angelic immortal, but she also becomes the City of Refuge.

15.6/**15.7**

And no longer shall (you) **your name** be called Aseneth, but your name shall be City of Refuge, because in you many nations shall take refuge **with the Lord God the Most High** and under your wings many peoples **trusting in the Lord God** shall take shelter and in your walls those who devote themselves to **the Most High** God through Repentance shall be protected.[137]

As the angel is the celestial double of Joseph, so Aseneth also has a celestial double named Metanoia (Repentance). That Aseneth and Metanoia are to be identified with one another is apparent in both versions, although it is stronger in the longer reconstruction. In the shorter text, this identification may be inferred from the fact that both Metanoia and Aseneth are called by the title "daughter of the Most High,"[138] as well as from their analogous functions. On earth, Aseneth will henceforth shelter those who "devote themselves to God through repentance [*metanoia*]," while in heaven, Metanoia herself continually petitions God on behalf of all those who repent.

In the longer text, the analogy between Aseneth and Metanoia is subtly altered, though still present; both are still designated daughter of God. As City of Refuge, Aseneth will shelter and guard **"those who attach themselves to God the Most High *in the name of* Repentance."** This alteration renders more explicit the invocation of the heavenly Metanoia and portrays the relationship between the angel and Metanoia as analogous to that of Joseph and Aseneth: they are brother and sister.[139]

In chapter 3, I considered how we might account for the significant divergences in the presentation of Metanoia in the shorter and longer versions of *Aseneth.* Here, I would like to suggest that the differences in the longer text are also consonant with that version's differing and more explicit mystical cosmology and angelology, particularly in the explicit identification of Metanoia not only as the daughter of the Most High but also as the beloved sister of the angel.

As I also indicated in chapter 3, the figure of Metanoia is extremely enigmatic, far more so, in fact, than that of the unnamed angel. No ancient Jewish source that I know of, *hekhalot* and otherwise, envisions an explicitly female angel in the heavenly cosmology. Angels may be portrayed as without sexuality, but they are clearly and uniformly imaged as masculine. Although Jewish and Christian sources exploit the feminine imagery of Wisdom, and Jewish sources envision the presence of God as the feminine Shekinah, only in gnostic sources do we find heavenly beings assigned both male and female gender and attributes.[140]

Philonenko thought the identity of Metanoia simple enough, based on her title of "daughter of the Most High." She represents another aspect of Wisdom, whom Aseneth personifies. Philonenko relies here, as often, on Philo, in this case on Philo's description of Wisdom as the daughter of God.[141]

Yet the figure of Metanoia deserves far more elucidation than this, particularly from the mystical vantage point from which we have been considering *Aseneth.* To the best of my knowledge, the presentation of Metanoia as the divine daughter of God who resides in heaven and perpetually beseeches God on behalf of those who repent is unique to the Aseneth stories, despite its obvious resemblance not only to Wisdom traditions[142] but also to Christian notions of the intercessory functions of Mary the mother of Jesus.[143] One possibility, of course, is that Metanoia is a creation of this story, rendering any investigation of her identity a fairly futile enterprise.

Intriguingly, there are some significant resemblances between Metanoia and the figure of Metatron, but the explanation for those resemblances remains elusive. Although its significance may only be that of coincidence, the similarity of their names is immediately apparent. More significantly, they share certain attributes. Both are intercessory figures, mediating between the human and the divine. Both are described as exceedingly beautiful.[144] One of Metatron's names is Yofi'el, which Halperin interprets as a variant of Yefefiah, "Beautiful."[145] Just as Metanoia is beloved by God in heaven (and in the longer version, by the angel as well), so also Metatron is said in some texts to be much loved in heaven.[146]

One of the most interesting suggestions about the figure of Metatron is Halperin's suggestion of a complex association of Metatron with Moses. At the conclusion of a *hekhalot* cluster he dubs "the Moses/Metatron text,"[147] Halperin writes:

> As Metatron is a "lesser" Yahweh, so he is a "greater" Moses. More exactly, he is Moses gone a step farther.
>
> Moses ascends to heaven; Metatron becomes ruler of heaven. Moses defeats the angels; Metatron dominates them. Moses grasps God's throne; Metatron sits on a throne identical to it. When Metatron grants revelation to Moses, he is giving a helping hand to his junior alter ego. When the author of the passage on the "prince" tells us that this being "was given" to Moses, what he is saying is that the ascending and conquering Moses shared in the essence of the exalted being whom most *Hekhalot* writers call Metatron.[148]

Though as is Moses, Metatron is frequently called *'ebed,* the servant of God, and they share other titles.

If, in some circles, Metatron and Moses were associated, if not identified, and if the angelic figure in *Aseneth* may also be associated with Metatron, then an intriguing possibility emerges that in the longer text the figure of Metanoia, there the sister of the angelic figure, is a divine analogue of Miriam, the sister of Moses.

Although the evidence for such a hypothesis is admittedly exceedingly thin, the following snippets of texts and allusions are intriguing. In *3 Enoch* 45.4, Miriam is the only woman mentioned in the long list of the humans whose generations are engraved on the heavenly *pargod* (the curtain [*katapetasma*]).[149] Josephus calls Moses *stratēgos* and Miriam *adelphē tou stratēgou.*[150] In his treatise on the contemplative Therapeutics,

Philo describes their double choir, the women led by a female conductor who symbolized Miriam at the Reed Sea, and the men led by a male conductor who symbolized Moses.[151] If Philo's description here accurately reflects ancient practice, the figure of Miriam played a significant function in the ritual and theological life of the
Therapeutics, closely linked with that of her brother, Moses. Finally, Louis Ginzberg
makes mention of a Jewish legend according to which in the messianic age, Elijah will
reveal three things hidden at the destruction of the Temple: three jars of manna, water
from Miriam's well, and holy oil. These three are associated with the triad of Moses,
Miriam, and Aaron, and they are, interestingly, quite close to the triad of bread, drink,
and oil associated with Aseneth's transformation.[152]

In the attempt to further illuminate the identity of Metanoia, one other text may be
particularly significant, although its discussion within this chapter may seem odd, and
I shall return to it again in chapter 9, on the discussion of authorial identity. It is a
Coptic text titled "The Installation of the Archangel Michael," in which the attributes
of Michael have striking affinities not only with the angelic figure who appears in
Aseneth but, more interestingly, with Metanoia herself.[153]

In this text, which is explicitly Christian, resonances with the cosmology of *Sepher
ha-Razim* and with many *hekhalot* materials are apparent. Michael is located in the
seven aeon, and the angels have their specific tasks: "those over the day and over the
night, those over the dew and those over the air and those over the wind and those
over the fruits." Christ sets Michael over all these. The text explicitly envisions consonance between heavenly deeds of angels and earthly (ritual) deeds of humans: "As
they gather together in the heavens, so they gather together on the earth. Moreover
the rite [Hall notes: literally, pattern] which is performed on the earth is performed
also in the heavens among the heavenly beings of the light, those whose thrones are
in the kingdom of the perfect divinity."[154]

Most fascinating, though, are the attributes of Michael himself. He is called "greatest of all the angels in heaven," "great," and "mighty." He is "guardian of Life,"
"good," and "gentle." While the first two are associated with the angelic figure in
Aseneth, Metanoia is called "gentle" and "guardian." Like the angelic figure, who is
depicted as the image of Helios, Michael is associated with the sun, which rises over
the earth because of him. And like Metanoia, Michael here has no other job than continual intercession for the souls of human beings, and like her, he prostrates himself
and prays (and weeps) on behalf of sinning human beings.

Although it is impossible to say precisely how this text might be related to the
materials we have been considering, it seems quite plausible that it bears some relationship to the depiction of Metanoia and that her representation draws on traditions
of a male intercessory figure here identified as Michael.

"Fearing God" and Mystical Transformation

One of the most puzzling aspects of the *Aseneth* texts is their fondness for the term
theosebēs, present almost equally in the shorter and longer texts (twelve and fourteen
times, respectively). The ordinary semantics of the word are not difficult—it is a
compound derived from *theos* ([G]od) and *sebō, sebomai, sebizō,* meaning, respectively, to worship or honor; to be religious, to feel awe or fear, shame or dread; to

honor with pious awe, to worship or venerate, to worship, honor, or devote oneself. What has engaged contemporary scholarship in considerable debate has been the usage of the term in the Roman period, particularly when applied to persons apparently associated with Jews and Judaism.[155] Many believe that the term is normally a technical one designating persons not born Jewish who adopt various elements of Jewish practice and belief yet who do not undertake something that can be called formal conversion to Judaism.[156]

In many biblical passages, the concept of "fearing" God—usually translated in the LXX/OG as *phobomenos ton theon* or much less frequently as *sebomenos ton theon*—is standard language for the appropriate stance of the wise person toward the divine.[157] Interestingly, the adjectival *theosebēs* and the substantive *theosebeia* occur relatively rarely in the Greek Jewish scriptures.[158] Some scholars would argue that *theosebes* has precisely such a sense in *Aseneth,* where it is primarily an attribute of Joseph and other righteous Israelite men and secondarily an attribute of the transformed Aseneth. But in its frequent usage of "theosebic" language, *Aseneth* is virtually unique among the texts classed as pseudepigrapha,[159] suggesting that further investigation into the significance of this terminology is warranted.

At the very least, it is clear that the motif of "fearing" plays a central role in the several versions of our Aseneth tale. Various forms of the verb *phobeō* express the responses of numerous characters to diverse situations. Aseneth fears (*phobeō*) the gods of the Egyptians at 2.5,[160] is frightened (*phobeō*) at Joseph's appearance at 6.1,[161] and is terrified (*phobeō*) at the sight of the angelic being at 14.10/**14.11.** Predictably, the longer text contains several additional instances of her fear.[162] Joseph fears (*phobeō*) that Aseneth will attempt to seduce him.[163] In the second part of the tales, Pharaoh's son is frightened at the sight of the swords of the righteous brothers,[164] and the scheming sons of Bilhah and Zilpah are afraid when God answers Aseneth's prayer for help and turns their swords to ashes.[165]

Significantly, in virtually all of these instances, the characters' fears are ultimately unfounded: no harm comes to Aseneth from the Egyptian gods, from Joseph, from the angel, or even from Pharaoh's son and his cohorts who seek to molest her. Aseneth does not seduce Joseph into illicit sex, and the sons of Bilhah and Zilpah are ultimately forgiven by their brothers and by Aseneth herself.[166] In many of these scenes, the person who experiences fear is exhorted by another, often more powerful person to take courage and not fear.[167]

Both the longer and shorter versions seem to consider fear of anything other than God (expressed by the verb *phobeō* and the noun *phobos*) generally unwarranted. The only appropriate fear is fear of God, usually expressed by the term *theosebēs,* although Joseph is once said to fear (*phobeō*) the Lord,[168] as also Benjamin,[169] and, obviously, no harm comes to those who do so.

In chapter 9, on the provenance of *Aseneth,* I will return to the possibility that *theosebēs* does carry the meaning imputed to it by many recent studies, namely, the connotation of devotion to Jews and Judaism without full conversion according to normative rabbinic models. Without excluding the possibility that such a context underlies the frequency of *theosebēs* in *Aseneth,* here I would like to consider some of the associations of "fearing" God in mystical sources and traditions.

In a *Sar ha-Torah* passage in the *hekhalot* materials usually designated *Merkabah*

Rabbah,[170] we find an esoteric version of the tradition in *Pirke Avot* concerning the transmission of oral Torah. According to the opening lines of *Pirke Avot,* Moses received Torah at Sinai and transmitted it to Joshua, who transmitted it to the elders, who transmitted it to the prophets, who transmitted it to the hasidim, who transmitted it to the men of the great synagogue. But according to *Merkabah Rabbah,* that which Moses received and transmitted was "mysteries and inner mysteries," "secrets and inner secrets." The list of tradents corresponds to that in *Avot,* with two significant additions. In between the hasidim and the men of the great synagogue are those called "God-fearers,"[171] and the chain of transmission stops not with the men of the great synagogue but with all Israel.

A second reference to fearing God in mystical traditions is noted by Morray-Jones. Commenting on the phrase "The Lord of Hosts, he is the King of Glory," *Midrash Tanḥuma* reads, "(This means that) He apportions some of His glory to those who fear Him."[172] Slotki's edition[173] reads as follows:

> What is the implication of the text, *The Lord of hosts; He is the King of glory. Selah?* It signifies that He gives a share of His own glory to those who fear Him. How do you prove this? He is called God, and He called Moses a god; *See, I have set thee as a god to Pharaoh* (Ex vii, i). He quickens the dead, and He gave a share of His glory to Elijah so that he also revived the dead. . . . As for the king, the Messiah, He will clothe him in His own robes; for it says, *Honour and majesty wilt Thou lay upon him* (Ps. xxi, 6).

Morray-Jones adduces this passage as part of his exploration of rabbinic opposition to traditions about the Name-Bearing Angel as a second God. The passage just cited could be construed to mean that others bear the glory of God and that, in particular, a second divine being does so. The very next portion of *Numbers Rabbah* (15.14) is explicit about the dangers of worshiping two deities and appears to suggest that those who did so adduced passages like "My son, fear thou the Lord and the king," in support of their position, inter alia.

Noteworthy in the passage from *Numbers Rabbah* is the language of vivification of the dead.[174] In the longer version of *Aseneth,* when Aseneth's parents first see her again after her transformation, they "glorify" God "who gives life to the dead." The insertion of this qualification is unique to the longer version and consistent with the stronger presence of other elements shared with mystical Jewish sources. The same language also occurs in a *hekhalot* text, the so-called *Chapter of R. Nehuniah b. ha-Qanah,* where R. Ishmael discusses how to make use of the adjuration of Metatron and concludes one section with the words: "Blessed be you, Lord, who brings the dead to life."[175]

Additional evidence for the association of fearing God with mystical ascent and glorious transformation comes from *2 Enoch:*

43.3 (J)
Even though these sayings are heard on every side, nevertheless there is no one better than he who fears God. He will be the most glorious in that age.

43.3 (A)
(But there is) no one better than he who fears the Lord; for those who fear the Lord will be glorious forever.[176]

Still another relevant passage may be found in *3 Enoch* 46, discussed above for its description of the stars surrounding the chariot of God, whose behavior at the instigation of Metatron bears tantalizing resemblance to the activity of the bees at the instigation of the angelic figure. At the beginning of this section, Metatron tells R. Ishmael that these stars "stand night by night in fear of the Maqom."[177]

On the basis of these passages, it seems quite possible that the terminology of fearing God in *Aseneth* bears some specialized mystical connotations or at the very least that it acquires them in the longer version, which appears, on the whole, to clothe the shorter version in more mystical garments. Such an interpretation has, of course, interesting implications for the interpretation of *theosebeis* terminology elsewhere, but this is outside the scope of my concerns here.

Contrasting *Aseneth* with (Jewish) Mystical Paradigms

Despite these many important similarities, which almost certainly point to common cultural contexts, significant differences between *Aseneth* and the paradigm of mystical experience and transformation are observable in the *hekhalot* and associated traditions. Paramount among these differences is that of gender. Although biblical narratives of angels descending to converse with humans do not appear to discriminate on the grounds of gender (Hagar, Manoah's unnamed wife, and Mary the mother of Jesus [among others] all receive angelic visitors),[178] in all the *hekhalot* and related traditions, individual adepts are exclusively male, and some of the preparatory rites prescribed assume that contact with women inhibits contact with the angels, frequently drawing on the narrative of the revelation at Sinai (Exod 19.15) as proof.[179]

In those texts whose Jewish identity is feasible, excluding for the moment *Aseneth* itself, I know of only two that purport to describe any such experience on the part of a woman. One is a brief passage in *The Life of Adam and Eve* (the Greek *Apocalypse of Moses*), which ascribes to Eve a vision of the heavens and of Adam being received into the angelic company after his death.[180] The other occurs at the end of *The Testament of Job,* when Job gives his three daughters a spiritual inheritance of mystical bands that transform them "so that [they] no longer [think] about earthly things" and that enable them to chant hymns to God in the language of the angels, hymns that they subsequently write down and collect in works called "the Hymns of Kassia" and "the Prayers of Amaltheias-Keras."[181] Although this last work is particularly interesting for its final scene, where the soul of Job is taken up by an angel, who then ascends to heaven in a chariot, both examples are relatively brief, and neither expands on the experience of women. While it is impossible to be certain, Aseneth's gender may be partly responsible for the failure of other scholars to perceive the consonance between *Aseneth* and other ancient narratives of mystical transformation.[182]

Beyond this significant difference, *Aseneth* may be distinguished from the mystical paradigm elaborated here both in terms of elements present in the paradigm that are missing or different in *Aseneth* and in terms of elements present in *Aseneth* yet absent in the paradigm.

Elements of the Mystical Paradigm Missing or Different in Aseneth

As I noted earlier, in *Aseneth* the divine being descends to Aseneth after, as I have argued, she performs a series of acts recognizable as adjuration, whereas in most of the *hekhalot* and related materials, the adept ascends to the heavens. As Schäfer points out, though, the extant texts reflect a diversity of traditions about who may engage in these practices, both adjuration and ascent (couched in the language of "descent"), and what they obtain.[183] Schäfer suggests that ascent ("descent") traditions tend to limit eligible practitioners, while the widest scope is attributed to the adjuration tradition.[184]

Yet even this, as Schäfer acknowledges, is not absolute. One of the most interesting passages in this regard occurs in *Hekhalot Rabbati,* which specifies that "'anyone' who is free from idolatry, lewdness, bloodshed, slander, false oath, profanation of the (divine) name, impudence and baseless animosity, and who observes all the command and prohibitions, can erect a ladder in his house and 'descend' to the Merkavah."[185]

With the notable exceptions of lewdness, bloodshed, and false oath, these faults correspond closely to Aseneth's deeds prior to Joseph's arrival and constitute the sins of which she confesses and repents and of which she is perforce now innocent: idolatry, slander (of Joseph), profanation of the name, impudence, and baseless animosity. A passage in *Hekhalot Zutarti* has Akiba report the words of God as follows: "I will attend even to someone who has just this moment converted to Judaism, as long as his body is pure of idol-worship and bloodshed and illicit sex. I will attach my servant Metatron to his footsteps, for much learning of Torah."[186]

Aseneth probably qualifies as someone who has just "converted" and who is clearly free of idol-worship, bloodshed, and illicit sex (indeed she is free of licit sex as well, at least for the moment). As we have considered, there are fascinating resemblances between Aseneth's unnamed angelic visitor and Metatron, although whether what Aseneth learns can be construed as Torah is considerably less apparent. And if Schäfer is correct that the most open tradition is that of adjuration, it may be no accident that Aseneth, a foreigner, "proselyte," and female, partakes of an adjuration experience and not an ascent. Finally, I have also proposed above that even this last element is complex, since Aseneth ascends to the upper rooms, where her transformation occurs, and those rooms are themselves described in imagery suggestive of the heavens.

Whatever the actual relationships between *Aseneth* and the *hekhalot* traditions, the texts envision differing effects and objectives for mystical encounters. As Schäfer emphasizes, the *hekhalot* adjuration narratives are explicitly preoccupied with knowledge of Torah. This theme appears altogether absent in *Aseneth,* where mystical experience leads not only to angelic transformation and knowledge of cosmic mysteries, as is also true in the *hekhalot* materials, but also to ordinary, earthly marriage, love, and children. While one might argue that this difference is largely a function of careful pseudepigraphy, since the story of Joseph and Aseneth is set prior to Moses' receipt of Torah at Sinai, the same is true of the Enoch story, which precedes Joseph by many chapters in the book of Genesis and thus cannot be an explanation. Rather, at the very least, we must suspect some differences of community and cosmology behind divergent interpretations of mystical transformation.

Still, Morray-Jones's interpretation of the functions of transformation for the community of the adept illuminates a significant similarity between the *hekhalot* materials and *Aseneth* that a focus on differences may otherwise obscure. He argues that mystical angelic transformation renders the individual able to accomplish for the community what the priest in the Temple in Jerusalem previously effected: namely, mediation between heaven and earth, serving as the conduit for the transfer of power from the divine to the human.

> The traditions examined above suggest that a variety of mythical and historical figures were credited with having achieved such a transformation on what might be called a "cosmic" scale and with having become veritable incarnations of the Name or Power of God. . . . [S]uch a transformation was also considered possible, if only temporarily, for exceptionally holy individuals in this life. Such men were gifted with supernatural power and knowledge, and became intercessors between the divine and human worlds, because they had become conformed to the divine Image or *kabod,* and, like the High Priest in the Temple sanctuary, had been vested with the Name of God.[187]

The designation of Aseneth as City of Refuge and as the earthly counterpart of the heavenly Metanoia both point toward an analogous function for the transformed Aseneth, who is thus presented as a particularly efficacious intermediary between God and those who repent, whether that constitutes a more general designation or refers specifically to those who choose to affiliate themselves with the community of those who worship the God of Israel. Again, what is particularly distinctive here is the designation of a woman in such a role.[188]

In many of the *hekhalot* narratives, the adept ultimately attains a vision of the enthroned Glory, a vision that is muted, if not altogether absent, in *Aseneth.* There is clearly no explicit throne vision in the *Aseneth* tales. Instead, Aseneth sees the mystery of the bees, a scene similar to several shown to Ishmael in *3 Enoch,* including the spirits of the stars in chapter 46 and perhaps also the souls of the righteous already created, and those still awaiting creation, in chapter 43.[189] But she also sees Joseph's heavenly double, who may constitute a vision of the Divine–and who is, at the very least, the Powerful One of God, the Son of God, and, as I have argued, *Aseneth*'s version of the Name-Bearing Angel, the Image and Glory of God.

In addition to these differences, *Aseneth* contains several elements absent from the paradigm distilled by Morray-Jones (and others). First, Aseneth's transformation is accomplished through an act of eating, an act that appears to be absent in the *hekhalot* narratives, with their strong emphasis on abstinence from such definitively mortal characteristics as eating, drinking, sexual intercourse, and so forth. It is eating angelic food, specifically the honey made by the bees of the Paradise of delight, that conveys angelic essence and immortality on Aseneth. Although I do not presently know the significance of this distinction, I have argued in chapters 2 and 3 that these scenes are constructed with significant resonances of Genesis 1–3.[190]

Second, unlike the *hekhalot* narratives, even *2* and *3 Enoch,* this particular tale of transformation is located in a specific historical context. It is set at a particular point in "historical" time, although in the past, during the first of the seven years of plenty, and in a particular place, the city of Heliopolis in Egypt. While some of the revelation given to Aseneth concerns the fate of souls, including her own, and shows her cosmic mysteries, the rest of the angel's disclosure concerns Aseneth's earthly experience as Joseph's wife and the mother of Manasseh and Ephraim. The second part of the story also takes place "in history" and narrates the deeds of "historical" persons: Pharaoh's son and his retinue, Joseph's brothers, and his father.

While the significance of this difference is also elusive, given our virtual ignorance about the authors, date, and provenance of the texts under discussion,[191] it may well reflect a fundamentally different stance toward history and ordinary human experience. Several scholars of the *hekhalot* traditions and early Jewish mysticism have argued that these sources are symptomatic of authors and audiences who feel powerless in the face of history, particularly in the absence of the Temple, and who believe that the sphere of God's redemptive activity has been transferred from an earthly venue to a heavenly one.[192] If they are correct, the differing setting of *Aseneth* may point to an alternate perspective, in which the earthly and the divine are considerably less alien to one another and in which human beings, while aware of their true angelic identity, may yet lead ordinary and fruitful lives, ruling wisely, loving faithfully, bearing children, acting righteously, and revering the true God. If *Aseneth* is Jewish, this alternate voice may constitute a deliberate counterpart to the *hekhalot* traditions; if it is not, it still articulates a meaningfully different understanding of the nature of human existence.

NOTES

1. Dan 10.14.

2. Virtually no one has devoted serious consideration to the significance of the *hekhalot* traditions for *Aseneth* (or vice versa). Howard C. Kee, in "The Socio-Cultural Setting of 'Joseph and Aseneth,'" *New Testament Studies* 29 (1983): 394–413, and "The Socio-Religious Setting and Aims of 'Joseph and Asenath,'" *SBL Seminar Papers* 15 (Missoula, MT: Scholars Press, 1976), 183–92, does suggest that the *hekhalot* traditions are significant for locating the context of *Aseneth*, but his arguments differ from mine in various ways. Like most recent scholarship, Kee's work relies on Burchard's text, which, as we shall see, contains far more material consonant with *hekhalot* traditions and assumes that *Aseneth* is both early and unequivocally of Jewish origin. Kee was motivated by a desire to find a Jewish exemplar for the paradigm he perceives in *Aseneth*, in which a revelatory experience is followed by a time of trial and testing, and argues that such a paradigm may be observed in the Merkabah traditions, whose roots are themselves located in the chariot traditions associated with the biblical experiences of Isaiah and Ezekiel ("Socio-Cultural Setting," 406–7). Kee was also particularly intrigued by the chariot motif that *Aseneth* shares with Merkabah writings (ibid., 409). Since he accepts an early dating for *Aseneth*, Kee was content to conclude that *Aseneth* might have had its origins in the same circles out of which later Merkabah materials developed.

Chesnutt, however, disputes any meaningful similarities between *Aseneth* and Merkabah traditions and between *Aseneth* and gnostic traditions as well (*From Death to Life*, 202–15) and argues that "[w]hen the net of comparison is cast beyond the similarities noted by Kee to include . . . broader questions, the case for close kinship between *Joseph and Aseneth* and Merkabah mysticism is greatly diluted" (ibid., 209). Chesnutt is correct that Kee's arguments, as presented in these essays, are not particularly detailed or compelling, yet as I hope to demonstrate in this chapter, comparison of *Aseneth* and *hekhalot* traditions is much more productive than either Kee or Chesnutt realized. Both Kee and Chesnutt are particularly affected by their assumptions about the date of the text and the priority of Burchard's reconstruction, so that neither analyzed the details I will consider here nor contemplated the possibility that the two (*Aseneth* and *hekhalot*) might emanate not indirectly over centuries from related cultural contexts but in fact be located much closer in time, space, and community. Kee's essays in particular evince the peculiar dilemmas that assuming an early date for *Aseneth* creates: he finds it difficult to reconcile his observations about the text (including the centrality of Helios imagery, the chariot, mystical experience, and other elements) with what he thinks he knows about first-century Judaism(s) and endeavors valiantly, although in my mind largely unsuccessfully, to propose a plausible location for *Aseneth* within the parameters of consensus scholarship. That the elements he perceives as crucial might be better accounted for in other contexts did not occur to Kee.

3. Although the *hekhalot* traditions clearly seem to emanate from a cultural context closely associated with rabbinic Jewish circles and *Aseneth,* as we have seen, seems in many ways alien to rabbinic perspectives, it is also the case that the *hekhalot* traditions stand in considerable tension to "orthodox" rabbinic stances, and it is not at all inconceivable that the authors and editors of *Aseneth* were acquainted with the paradigms of angelic encounters present in the *hekhalot* traditions and that both the similarities and the differences are not coincidental.

4. See chapter 9.

5. Accounting for both the similarities and the differences between *Aseneth* and the *hekhalot* traditions is a complex endeavor, and whether there is any direct relationship between the two is almost impossible to establish. The differences of language are significant, although not insurmountable. Few Greek-speaking Jews in the Greco-Roman period seem likely, after the first century C.E. or so, to have known Hebrew well, although obviously some did, such as those who produced new translations of Hebrew scripture into Greek and those Jews from whom Christian scholars learned Hebrew. It is not inconceivable that enough people, Jews and Christians alike, were sufficiently facile in Greek and in semitic languages such as Hebrew and Aramaic for traditions in one language to have been accessible to those formulated in another.

6. Swartz, "Book and Tradition," 195.

7. Schäfer, *Synopse,* provides texts in parallel columns. References without other identication utilize Schäfer's numbering. Translations of some of the *hekhalot* materials may be found in Schäfer's various studies; in Halperin, *Faces of the Chariot;* and elsewhere. I am grateful to Rebecca Lesses for sharing her own translations of some of these passages.

8. See esp. Halperin, *Faces of the Chariot;* Himmelfarb, *Ascent;* Peter Schäfer, *Hekhalot-Studien,* Texte und Studien zum Antiken Judentum 19 (Tübingen, J. C. B. Mohr [Paul Siebeck]), 1988, Schäfer, *Hidden and Manifest God;* Swartz, *Mystical Prayer.* On the difficulties of distinguishing "texts," see in particular Schäfer's "Tradition and Redaction in Hekhalot Literature," in his *Hekhalot-Studien,* 8–16.

9. The language of travel is often of "descent." Alan Segal suggests, against Gruenwald, that the imagery of descent comes from the practice of the mystic putting his head between his knees, as described in the ninth-century work of Hai Gaon—the posture of Elijah praying for rain in 1 Kgs 18.42 (Segal, "Paul and the Beginning of Jewish Mysticism," in John J. Collins and Michael Fishbane, eds., *Death, Ecstasy, and Other Worldly Journeys: Essays in Memory of Joan P. Culianu* (Saratoga Springs: SUNY Press), 97–98, 115, n. 2.

10. Despite the language of descent, one particular narrative serves as sufficient demonstration that ascent to the heavens is to be understood: "As I [Akiba] was being dismissed from before the throne of glory, to *go down* and be with humanity, he said to me, 'Akiba, *go down* and bear witness to people of this method [of encounter with the divine].' So R. Akiba *went down* and taught people this method" (emphasis added). Schäfer, *Synopse,* §686, translated in Halperin, *Faces of the Chariot,* 382.

11. Schäfer, *Hidden and Manifest God,* 144. These traditions are sometimes also called *Sar ha-Panim* (literally "Prince of the Face," usually translated as "Prince of the [Divine] Presence." Alan Segal, "Paul and the Beginning of Jewish Mysticism," 105, suggests that the meaning of the phrase *Sar ha-Panim* may be found in *2 Enoch* 22.7, where God commands that Enoch should stand in front of God's face forever. According to Schäfer, however, there is at least one adjuration of the *Sar ha-Panim* that is different from the adjuration of the *Sar ha-Torah,* usually transmitted as part of *Hekhalot Rabbati,* "Tradition and Redaction," 12. *Sar ha-Panim* materials are collected in Schäfer, *Synopse,* §623–39. For another edition of §623–39, with translation and discussion, see Schäfer, "Die Beschwörung des sar ha-panim," in his *Hekhalot-Studien,* 118–53. On this material, see also Rebecca Lesses, "The Adjuration of the The Prince of the Presence: Performative Utterance in a Jewish Ritual," in Marvin Meyer and Paul Mirecki, eds., *Ancient Magic and Ritual Power,* Religions in the Greco-Roman World 129 (Leiden: E. J. Brill, 1995), 185–206.

12. An English translation of virtually the complete section (Schäfer, *Synopse,* §281–306) is provided by Halperin, *Faces of the Chariot,* 430–34.

13. Schäfer, *Hidden and Manifest God,* 144. For a very different view of the purpose of heavenly journeys, see Halperin, *Faces of the Chariot,* esp. 439–46, for his provocative theory that these stories reflect the challenges of the *am ha'aretz* to the authority and power of the rabbinic intelligentsia and are ultimately rooted in adolescent fantasies and conflicts of power between male adolescents and their elders.

14. See Halperin, *Faces of the Chariot,* 372, for evidence that the linkage of these two traditions is purposeful and points to the functions and motivations of the heavenly journey.

15. J. Collins notes that the phrase "Enoch walked with *elohim*" (actually *ha-elohim*) may signify an ascent experience prior to Enoch's final taking by God (John J. Collins, "A Throne in the Heavens: Apotheosis in Pre-Christian Judaism," in Collins and Fishbane, *Death, Ecstasy, and Other Worldly Journeys,* 45).

16. For basic bibliography, see the introduction by F. I. Andersen, *OTP* 1:91–100; see also the introduction in Sparks, *AOT,* 321–28. All references to *2 Enoch* are taken from Andersen's parallel translation of two representatives of the longer and shorter recensions. The English translation in Sparks, *AOT,* is based on a different manuscript; as a result, the versifications differ.

17. See Andersen, *OTP* 1:93. Andersen provides parallel translations of two manuscripts, J representing the longer recension and A representing the shorter.

18. Andersen, *OTP* 1:94–95, who notes, among other issues, the fact that the earliest manuscripts are fourteenth century, and no reliable attestation of the work in ancient sources can be adduced.

19. Andersen, *OTP* 1:96.

20. *2 Enoch* 1.5 (J), from the translation in Andersen, *OTP* 1, who notes parallels to 4 Ezra 7.79; Dan 10.6; and numerous places in Revelation.

21. Alexander, *OTP* 1:229, with discussion of various arguments for dating pp. 225–29. More recently, Collins "Throne in the Heavens," 49, posits a date no earlier than the sixth century C.E.

22. See, e.g., the description of Kerubi'el, prince of the cherubim: "His body is full of burning coals, it is as high as the seven heavens, as broad as the seven heavens, as wide as the seven heavens. The opening of his mouth blazes like a fiery torch, and his tongue is a consuming fire. His eyelashes are as the splendor of lightning, his eyes like brilliant sparks, and his face looks like a blazing fire. . . . [O]n his right hand a flame blazes; on his left hand fire burns; coals blaze from his body and firebrands shoot from him; lightnings flash from his face" (22.3–5, 9). See also the descriptions of Serapi'el (26.2–7), the description of the angels in 35, and numerous other instances.

23. On the significance of this passage for the scene with the bees, see later discussion.

24. *3 Enoch* 43. The verse is identified by scholars as Is 57.16, though its exegesis here requires a different meaning than either the Hebrew or the LXX/OG.

25. *3 Enoch* 45.

26. Morray-Jones, "Transformational Mysticism in the Apocalyptic-Merkabah Tradition," *JJS* 43, no. 1 (1992): 1–31. In addition, Thomas J. Sappington, *Revelation and Redemption at Colossae,* JSNT Supplement Series 53 (Sheffield: JSOT Press, 1991), catalogues the practices associated with divine revelation, including fasting, confession, mourning and the contemplation of God's judgment, and meditation (65–67). He concludes (69) that no precise sequence consistently leads to revelation. See also Segal, *Paul the Convert,* 34–71; Segal, "Heavenly Ascent," *ANRW* II.23.2, 1333–94; Martha Himmelfarb, "Heavenly Ascent and the Relationship of the Apocalypses and the *Hekhalot* Literature," *HUCA* 59 (1988): 73–100.

27. Morray-Jones, "Transformational Mysticism," 2.

28. Morray-Jones,"Transformational Mysticism," 3, notes that the root כבד means "to be heavy" and hence to take on a materialized form that God does "in human form and/or as light." On the semantic fields of "glory," see particularly the detailed discussion in Carey Newman, *Paul's Glory-Christology: Tradition and Rhetoric* (Leiden: E. J. Brill, 1992).

29. Morray-Jones, "Transformational Mysticism," 3–4. Supporting evidence here consists of numerous secondary studies, including the enormously detailed work by Jarl Fossum, *The Name of God and the Angel of the Lord: Samaritan and Jewish Concepts of Intermediation and the Origins of Gnosticism* (Tübingen: Mohr Siebeck, 1985).

30. *Dialogue with Trypho* 61.1; from Fossum, *Name of God,* 181.

31. *Dialogue with Trypho* 128.2; cited also in E. R. Goodenough, *Jewish Symbols in the Greco-Roman Period,* Bollingen Series 37, 13 vols. (New York: Pantheon, 1953–68)*,* 1:49, who also gives references to *Trypho* 46, 67.7.

32. Here Morray-Jones, "Transformational Mysticism," 8–9, writes: "The tradition of the Name-bearing angel and celestial vice-regent is apparently ancient and widespread. He appears in both apocalyptic and Hekhalot literature under a variety of names and titles. In some circles, Michael seems to have retained this function, while . . . other groups assigned this supreme role to Gabriel." For an excellent introduction to this figure, often described as the Great Angel, see Segal, "Paul and the Beginning of Jewish Mysticism," 98–101. See also Margaret Barker, *The Great Angel: A Study of Israel's Second God* (Louisville, KY: Westminster/John Knox Press, 1992), whose particular interest is the significance of these traditions for early Christian understanding of Jesus and who clearly identifies the figure in (the longer) *Aseneth* as this Great Angel (77).

33. Morray-Jones does not include discussion of the heavenly books, but I note them here since they are relevant to the longer version of *Aseneth*. Their occurrence in revelation traditions is catalogued and discussed in Sappington, *Revelation and Redemption,* 102, n. 1, including *1 Enoch* 47.3, 104.1, 108.3; *Jub* 36.10; Rev 2:12, *Apoc. Zeph.* 9.2 (in Akhmimic).

34. Morray-Jones, "Transformational Mysticism," 10–11.

35. Morray-Jones, "Transformational Mysticism," 12–13, also notes that the adept is sometimes clothed in the Name of God or puts on garments of divinity, with numerous examples.

36. Morray-Jones, "Transformational Mysticism," 22–23. For the presence of this element in early Syrian Christian traditions, particularly the *Odes of Solomon,* see chapter 9.

37. Morray-Jones, "Transformational Mysticism," 25–26.

38. See Swartz, *Mystical Prayer.* Other examples include 4 Ezra 3.3–36, 5.21–30. At 6.31, the angel advises "Ezra" to pray again and fast for seven days, which he does (6.35–59); see also 9.23–28. In *2 Baruch,* the angel Ramael appears to "Baruch" after lengthy prayer (54.1–55.3, 56.1, 76.1). Also, in *3 Baruch* weeping and praying results in the appearance of an angel who discloses "the mysteries of God" (1.1–8, Greek). This is hardly an exhaustive list.

39. Chesnutt suggests, in his arguments against Kee (see earlier discussion, n. 2), that such a comparison is fruitless. Chesnutt claims that in the *hekhalot* materials, hymns and prayers

serve a theurgical function that they "obviously" do not serve in *Aseneth* (210). He writes, "There is no hint that [Aseneth's] prayers represent a tradition wherein ecstasy is induced or a mystical or revelatory experience is sought or enhanced by means of prayer" (210). But as I intend to show here, I disagree that Aseneth's prayers serve no adjurative function.

40. Swartz, *Mystical Prayer,* 15; see also 171–89 for a more detailed discussion.

41. Swartz, *Mystical Prayer,* 17; see also his comments on 6–7.

42. Swartz, *Mystical Prayer,* 24.

43. Lucius's restoration to his human form in Apuleius's *Metamorphoses* begins with a nocturnal experience of fear (11.1).

44. For a wonderful discussion of fasting in antiquity, see Aline Rousselle's chapter, "From Abstinence to Impotence," in her *Porneia: On Desire and the Body in Antiquity,* trans. Felicia Pheasant (London: Basil Blackwell, 1987), 160–78.

45. E.g., Dan 10.2–3; 4 Ezra 9.23–28, 12.51; *2 Bar* 9.2, 12.5, 20.5–6, 21.1–2, 43.3, 47.2; *Apoc. Abr.* 12.1–2; Schäfer, *Synopse,* §313–14, 424, 560, 565, 623. Lucius's several initiations all require abstinence from "profane and unlawful foods" (11.23); later passages (11.23, 11.30) specify his abstinence from animal flesh and wine.

46. 4 Ezra 9.1–14.27.

47. Exod 24.9–18. Below, I will suggest that the figure of Moses might loom larger in *Aseneth* than one might immediately suspect, particularly for a text allegedly set before the time of Moses.

48. E.g., *1 Enoch* 24–32, 52, 77.

49. Howard N. Wallace, "Eden, Garden of," *ABD* 2:282.

50. Wallace, "Eden," 906.

51. Adela Yarbro Collins, "The Seven Heavens in Jewish and Christian Apocalypses," in Collins and Fishbane, *Death, Ecstasy, and Other Worldly Journeys,* 67, points out that the designation of the Garden as "Paradise" ("from an old Persian word meaning 'park' or 'garden' with no particular religious significance") is not found in the Hebrew Bible but occurs "in the Septuagint version" of Gen 2–3. By the third century B.C.E., she writes, it must have acquired the significance of an abode of the righteous. On the etymological issue, see Wallace, "Eden," 281–82. Segal, "Paul and the Beginning of Jewish Mysticism," 120, n. 33, claims that Paradise/the Garden was often thought to be located in the heavens, citing Martha Himmelfarb, *Tours of Hell* (Philadelphia: University of Pennsylvania Press, 1983).

52. For various instances of angelic guardians of the heavenly doors or gates, see Alexander's introduction to *3 Enoch, OTP* 2:243.

53. Gen 3.23–24. Elsewhere, the LXX translates *Gan Eden* as παράδεισος, although some variant readings supply τῆς τρυφῆς (see, e.g., the critical apparatus for Gen 2.15; 2.16 in John William Weavers, *Genesis, Septuaginta: Vetus Testamentum Graecum,* vol. 1 (Göttingen: Vandenhoeck and Ruprecht, 1974). Philonenko, *Joseph et Aséneth,* gives Gen 2.15 as another instance of παράδεισος τῆς τρυφῆς, but it is found there only in some variants. See also Joel 2.3 (παράδεισος τρυφῆς); Ezek 28.13 (ἐν τῇ τρυφῇ τοῦ παραδείσου τοῦ θεοῦ); Ezek 31.9 (τοῦ παραδείσου τῆς τρυφῆς τοῦ θεοῦ).

54. For a comparison of the readings, see chapter 3.

55. Philonenko proposes the equation of the Greek τόπος with the Hebrew מקום, and thus with Paradise, but he doesn't here connect it with the imagery of the courtyard as Paradise (Philonenko, *Joseph et Aséneth,* 189, note to 16.15).

56. *2 Enoch* 8. See also *Apoc. Abr.* 21.6 for another description of Eden typified by the rivers and trees.

57. Beliefs in an earthly and a heavenly paradise may be found in various ancient sources—earthly paradise: 4 Ezra 3.6; *Jub* 3.9–35, 4.23–25, 8.18–19; heavenly paradise: *1 Enoch* 24–25, 28–32; 4 Ezra 8.52; *T. Levi* 18.1–14.

58. Notable biblical examples run the gamut from the days of creation (including the Sabbath) in Gen 1; to the seven-branched candelabra (Exod 25.31–40, 37.17–24) of the Temple (which becomes the symbol par excellence of Jews and Judaism in Greco-Roman iconography); to the seven fat and lean cows and years in Pharaoh's dream and Joseph's interpretation (Gen 41.1–36). Seven plays a major role in the symbolism of Revelation. For additional examples and discussion, see Jöran Friberg, "Numbers and Counting," *ABD* 4:1139–46. The index to E. R. Goodenough, *Jewish Symbols,* vol. 13, contains numerous instances of symbolic uses of seven. See also Collins, "Seven Heavens."

59. In his two lengthy discussions of the number seven, Philo offers a long list of natural phenomena that occur in sevens: the number of the planets, the changes of the moon, the movements of the body, the internal organs, the apertures of the face, bodily excretions, the number of days of women's menstrual periods. Vowels are seven in number, as are "modulations in pronunciation," (see *Alleg. Int.* 1.8–15; *On the Creation,* 89–128).

60. *On the Decalogue,* 102–5. Interestingly, no mention is ever made of the mothers of the seven virgins in *Aseneth.*

61. *Alleg. Int.* 1.15; see also *Creation,* 100.

62. *Creation,* 100.

63. Carol Newsom, *Songs of the Sabbath Sacrifice: A Critical Edition,* Harvard Semitic Studies 27 (Atlanta: Scholars Press, 1985), 31–51.

64. Newsom, *Songs,* 49.

65. See A. Collins, "Seven Heavens," esp. 64–66, where she argues that the use of seven heavens in Jewish traditions is not likely to be an internal development but instead probably reflects Babylonian paradigms, as is also true for the use of three heavens. In Mithraic practice, devotees ascended the heavens by means of a ladder with seven gates, each equated with a metal (Origen, *Against Celsus* 6.22; extensive notes in Henry Chadwick, *Origen, Contra Celsum* [Cambridge: Cambridge University Press, 1953; reprint, 1986], 334–35). See also later discussion. See, further, A. Collins, "Seven Heavens," 81–83, on seven in Mithraic traditions.

66. *Creation,* 112.

67. Newsom, *Songs,* 50.

68. In the shorter recension. In the longer recension, three additional heavens are mentioned; for a discussion of the differences, see Andersen, *OTP* 1:134–35, n. 20a.

69. Irenaeus, *Against Heresies* 1.5.2.

70. The passage is *Aseneth* **22.13.** "Levi . . . would . . . see [Aseneth's] walls like adamantine eternal walls, and her foundations founded upon a rock of the seventh heaven." But Burchard notes that this reading is taken from the Syriac and from an Armenian manuscript; other Armenian manuscripts read "third" or "second" heaven, and this whole clause is absent from the families *a* and *d.* In his Greek text printed in Denis, *Concordance,* this clause is marked off by pointed brackets.

71. *Re'uyot' Yehezqel* contains the tradition that R. Meir is the authority for the claim that "God created seven heavens," in which are seven chariots (Ithamar Gruenwald, "ראיית יחזקאל" [The visions of Ezekiel], in Israel Weinstock, ed., *Temirin: Texts and Studies in Kabbala and Hasidim,* vol. 1 [Jerusalem: Mossad Harav Kook, 1972; in Hebrew]; extensive discussion of *The Visions* in Halperin, *Faces of the Chariot,* 262–358). Seven *hekhalot* also occur in *Maaseh Merkabah* 6 (Schäfer, *Synopse,* §554–55); *Hekhalot Rabbati* 15–16 (§198–205) and *Masseket Hekhalot* 4 (edition A. Jellinek, *Bet ha-Midrash,* [Vienna, 1853–57; reprint, Jerusalem, 1967], 2:42).

72. According to Herodotus, the Medean fortress of Ecbatana consisted of seven concentric walls, at the center of which were the king's palace and treasuries (*History* 1:98). Each circular battlement had its own distinctive color: white, black, purple, blue, or orange. The inner two circles were silver and gold, respectively. H. P. L'Orange, *Studies on the Iconography of Cos-*

mic Kingship in the Ancient World, Instituttet for Sammenlignende Kulturforskning, Serie A: Forelesninger 23 (Oslo: H. Aschehoug [W. Nygaard], 1953), 10, comments that "[t]he seven walls rising up one with another—recalling the seven tiers of the cosmic temple towers of Babylonia and Assyria—obviously are an image of the seven cosmic spheres, in the middle of which the Sun-King is seated: the golden wall around the royal palace reflects the brilliance of the sun, the silver wall next to it apparently that of the moon." L'Orange also points to the circular design of ancient Near Eastern royal cities that, he argues, are designed as cosmic maps (10–15). For further discussion of this material and its possible significance for *hehkalot* traditions, see also Halperin, *Faces of the Chariot,* 241–45.

73. Plate in Goodenough, *Jewish Symbols,* 11:pl. 11; discussion in 10:42–73; but note that Newsom's description of seven concentric walls is difficult to derive from the flat portrayal of the painting, though it is by no means impossible. Goodenough suggests that the colors of the walls correspond to a system of metals similar to the Mithraic scheme discussed above.

74. Alexander, *OTP* 1:240.

75. Philonenko, *Joseph et Aséneth,* 74. Philo also identifies seven with Ursa Major. Philonenko was here particularly influenced by Egyptian sources, which he believed underlay *Aseneth.* His discussion, 72–74, contains some interesting additional uses of seven in antiquity.

76. Above, chapter 2. *1 Enoch* 21 provides an excellent example, though with negative connotations.

77. Irenaeus also reports that according to the Valentinians, "the seven heavens are intellectual and [they] postulate that they are angels" (*Against Heresies* 1.5.2, translated in Bentley Layton, *The Gnostic Scriptures: A New Translation* [New Haven: Yale University Press, 1987], 291). According to Origen, the Ophites taught that the seven heavens had malefic, archontic occupants (*Against Celsus* 6:24–38).

78. Here, I am in accord with Bohak, *Joseph and Aseneth* (see esp. 180–91), although not with his interpretation of this portrait as evidence for an Oniad origin. Pagination follows the dissertation rather than the published version.

79. See *EJ* 15:942–88; also Carol Meyers, "Temple, Jerusalem," *ABD* 6:350–69; 1 Kgs 6.3; Josephus, *War* 5.207–19; *m. Middot* 4.7, all noted and discussed in Himmelfarb, *Ascent,* 14. Ezek 41.15–16 also seems to envision three divisions to the heavenly pattern of the Temple: a nave, an outer vestibule, and an inner room. This threefold division is probably not unique among ancient temples, whose architecture and design could vary significantly in different areas and chronological points, but it is characteristic of the Jerusalem temple. Greek temples, for instance, characteristically had two main spaces, a *naos,* and a porch, while Egyptian temples seem to have had several rooms. For the architectural design of other ancient temples, see the entries under "Temples and Sanctuaries," *ABD* 6:369–82, with helpful bibliography; also, though less detailed, discussions in *ER* 14:383–88 on "Ancient Near Eastern and Mediterranean Temples." See also Parry, Ricks, et al., *Bibliography.* On the identification of Aseneth with a temple, see Bohak, *Joseph and Aseneth.*

80. And as we have seen earlier, the correspondence between temples and palaces is strong.

81. Aseneth's use of these rooms as her personal chambers is almost a little awkward. Her bed is said to be in the room that nurtured her virginity, yet it is not clear which of these rooms is meant.

82. E.g., Exod 26.31–35, 40.3 on the curtains of the tabernacle; on the Temple curtain, 2 Chr 3.14; see also the references to the torn curtain of the Temple in Matt 27.51; Mark 15.38; and Luke 22.45.

83. In *Songs of the Sabbath Sacrifices* (4Q405 15 ii–16), the veil (*pirochet*) is apparently worked with figures of cherubim; see Newsom, *Songs,* 287–88.

84. *OTP* 1:269, n. 17f.

85. Such an image occurs in *b. Hag.* 12b; see also *Midrash 'aseret hadibberot* (Jellinek, *Bet ha-Midrash,* 1:63ff., cited in *OTP* 1:269, n. 17f. *Hypostasis of the Archons* 94 and 95 also refer to a καταπέτασμα that separates the heavens from the lower regions: the work, given a modern title of *On the Origin of the World* 98, mentions a παραπέτασμα that separates humans and celestials.

86. Bohak, *Joseph and Aseneth,* considers the καταπέτασμα to be extremely important in his reading of Aseneth's rooms as a temple; he writes: "The Greek word used here . . . is such a rare word that we could hang our whole argument on it alone" (184, with discussion 183–87).

87. Bohak, *Joseph and Aseneth,* argues, though, that δέρρις means here not "skin" but "sheet" (184, n. 30).

88. Goodenough, *Jewish Symbols,* 9:191–92.

89. Goodenough, *Jewish Symbols,* 9:195.

90. Burchard, "Joseph and Aseneth" (and Bohak, *Joseph and Aseneth,* following him); Cook (who translated the shorter text in *AOT*) and Brooks, *Joseph and Asenath.*

91. I will analyze this in much greater depth in the subsequent section on Helios.

92. The formula ἐγώ εἰμι is associated with divine pronouncements in ancient religions ranging from the aretalogies of Isis (see, e.g., Kraemer, *Maenads,* no. 133), to the speeches of Jesus in the Gospel of John, to the speaker of the *Thunder, Perfect Mind* (Kraemer, *Maenads,* no. 134); it is also what God says to Moses in Exod 3.14, ἐγώ εἰμι ὁ ὤν.

93. Translation mine. The Greek is actually somewhat more awkward than this, but this seems to be its sense.

94. *Aseneth* **15.12x:** ἵνα ὑμνήσω καὶ δοξάσω σε εἰς τὸν αἰῶνα χρόνον. Interestingly enough, the verb δοξάζω occurs only once in the shorter text, at 20.5, where it describes the activity of Aseneth's parents. Its introduction here into the longer text constitutes yet further evidence that the longer recension is much more concerned with imposing paradigms familiar from traditional biblical and parabiblical sources. It occurs one other time in the longer version, at **21.6,** where Pharaoh prays that God will glorify Joseph and Aseneth forever. The longer text also contains one further use of δόξα in **20.7,** where Aseneth's parents are said to "give glory" to God. Δόξα does not appear at all in the shorter version. The relative absence of this terminology is interesting, particularly in light of Carey Newman's evidence that Glory is a regular part of the semantic field of visionaries: "Glory thus forms part of the characteristic field of signifiers used to denote and connote divine and semidivine beings that populate the heavens. In short, when a seer peered into the heavens, he saw Glory—be it God, a throne or an angel" (Newman, *Paul's Glory-Christology,* 103).

95. See, e.g., Rev 4.9; *2 Enoch* 17, 20; *3 Enoch* 1.12; *Asc. Is.* 9.28–10.6; *Apoc. Abr.* 17–18. See also Rachel Elior, "Mysticism, Magic, and Angelology: The Perception of Angels in Hekhalot Literature," *Jewish Studies Quarterly* 1, no. 1 (1993): 50.

96. λαλήσω σοι τὰ ῥήματα τὰ πρὸς σε ἀποσταλέντα.

97. More literally, perhaps, "I will speak my words to you" (λαλήσω σοι τὰ ῥήματά μου) (**14.13**); **14.8, 11** read, λαλήσω πρὸς σε τὰ ῥήματά μου. See also chapter 3 for these changes as deliberate expansion of traditional material.

98. See chapter 3.

99. Παρρησία is a little difficult to translate here. Burchard, "Joseph and Aseneth," gives "with frankness." According to Johannes P. Louw and Eugene A. Nida, A *Greek-English Lexicon of the New Testament Based on Semantic Domains* (New York: United Bible Societies, 1988), παρρησία has the connotation of courage and boldness in the face of "intimidating circumstances" (25.158 on 1:307). All their examples have a positive connotation. In an interesting discussion of παρρησία in relation to gender constructions in the late antique period, Kate Cooper, *Virgin and the Bride,* 133–34, also points to the connotation of παρρησία as "frank

speech," positively construed. Burchard, "Joseph and Aseneth," however, sees this as a more negative usage. The term does not occur at all in the shorter version but does occur again in the longer version, in **23.10,** where it describes the speech of Levi to the son of Pharaoh: "And Levi said to Pharaoh's son with παρρησία, his face cheerful, and there was not the least bit of anger in him, but in meekness [πραότης—the term used also of Metanoia] of heart he said to him. . . ."

100. Identifying this final speech of Aseneth's as a silent one inverts the nature of her speeches at the beginning, which were initially in herself and then aloud: these are aloud and then in herself. Whether this inversion is an intentional inclusio is an interesting possibility.

101. A smoother translation of the longer reconstruction might be: "because I spoke audaciously before you all my words/speech in ignorance."

102. It is also different in other versions: in Batiffol's ("Livre") Greek text, the figure is initially called ἄνθρωπος ἐκ τοῦ οὐρανοῦ, but then various titles, including ὁ θεῖος ἄγγελος, ὁ ἄγγελος κυριοῦ, and at first appearance, ὁ θεῖος ἀρχιστράτηγος. In the Latin text printed by Batiffol (ibid.), the figure is initially *vir de celo,* then *angelus domini,* and usually just *angelus,* though sometimes again *angelus domini.* In both reconstructions of the Greek text, ἄγγελος is never used of the figure. It occurs in 14.2, as the identification of the morning star, and the figure himself uses it in the plural to denote heavenly beings: the angels who revere Metanoia (15.8) and the angels who eat the mysterious honey (16.8). It also occurs in 23.2, 24.3, and 25.7. Burchard's ("Joseph and Aseneth") reconstruction contains one additional usage, in the passage portraying Jacob as an extraordinary being: in **22.7,** where Jacob's arms are "like (those) of an angel."

103. *On the Confusion of Tongues* 41.

104. Morray-Jones, "Transformational Mysticism," 16–17.

105. Segal, "Paul and the Beginning of Jewish Mysticism," offers a sensible analysis of the interpretative logic behind these associations. Readers of Jewish scripture noted in the first place instances of a human figure on the divine throne, whom they associated with the angel of the Lord in Exod 23, an angel who "embodied, personified or carried the name of God" (98). In the Greek translation of Ezek 1.26, the figure on the throne is identified with the *eidos* of man. Since in Platonic thought, *eidos* meant "the unchanging immortal ideal of man that survives death" (100), the figure on the divine throne came to be identified, for Jewish mystics such as Philo, with the ideal and immortal man.

106. This may be why, for instance, Aseneth can ask the angel to bless the seven virgins as he has blessed her, and he can respond by saying, "May the Lord God the Most High bless You," although in this regard, the longer text follows the shorter.

107. Joseph is called Son of God at 6.2 (ὁ υἱός τοῦ θεοῦ); 6.6 (Ἰωσὴφ υἱός τοῦ θεοῦ ἐστι); **13.10** (twice); **18.11,** where Joseph is called ὁ υἱός αὐτοῦ ὁ πρωτότοκος (but see chapter 3 for diverse textual readings of this verse); also 21.3/**21.4,** where Joseph is also called ὁ υἱός τοῦ θεοῦ ὁ πρωτότοκος; he is called δυνατός of God at 3.6, 4.8, 18.1, 18.2.

108. On the preexistence of Wisdom, see, e.g., Prov 8.22; Ps 139.16; Sir 24.9; Wis Sol 9.9. Philonenko, *Joseph et Aséneth,* argues for Joseph as Logos, using as his model Philo's understanding of Logos (86–87). In any case, read thus, Joseph = the Son of God = (masculine) Logos; Aseneth = Daughter of God = feminine Wisdom?

109. Philonenko, *Joseph et Aséneth,* 178; Burchard, "Joseph and Aseneth," 225 n. 14k, citing Philonenko, *Joseph et Aséneth.* Some instances include *T. Abr.* A, 19; *Apoc. Ezra* 4.24; *2 Enoch* 33.10; *PGM* 13:928. See also the numerous texts listed in *BHG* 2, nos. 118–23. The identification of Michael as the figure in *Aseneth* has found its way into much of the secondary literature, despite its uncertainty. Philonenko also stressed the significance of Michael in Coptic sources, which is not surprising given his insistence that Aseneth is Egyptian, but in fact, Michael is also well attested in traditions associated with Asia Minor (see chapter 10).

110. See, e.g., the listings under Michael in the index to *OTP* 2:977–78. See also the obser-

vation by Alexander in his introduction to *3 Enoch* (in *OTP* 1:242) on the absence of a uniform angelology in the *hekhalot* traditions. Alexander points out that the *hekhalot* texts mention a number of angelic offices: the offices remain constant, but the angels who fill them vary from tradition to tradition. Morray-Jones indicates that in some circles the Name-Bearing Angel is Michael but elsewhere Gabriel (including Mandean and Muslim sources) (Morray-Jones, "Transformational Mysticism," 8–9, with references in n. 42). For studies of the prevalence of angelology in late antique religion and cosmology, see, e.g., A. R. R. Sheppard, "Pagan Cults of Angels in Roman Asia Minor," *Talanta* 12–13 (1980–81): 77–101; Stephen Mitchell, *Anatolia: Land, Men, and Gods in Asia Minor,* vol. 2: *The Rise of the Church* (Oxford: Clarendon Press, 1993), 43–51; R. A. Kearsley, "Angels in Asia Minor: The Cult of Hosios and Dikaios," in *NewDocs* 6 (1992): 206–9; F. Sokolowski, "Sur le culte d'angelos dans le paganisme grec et romain," *HTR* 53 (1960): 225–29.

111. On Metatron, see the introduction to Odeberg, *3 Enoch,* esp. 79–146; M. Black, "The Origin of the Name Metatron," *Vetus Testamentum* 1, no. 3 (1951): 217–19; Saul Lieberman, "Metatron: The Meaning of His Name and His Functions," in Itamar Gruenwald, ed., *Apocalyptic and Merkavah Mysticism* (Leiden: E. J. Brill, 1980), 235–41; Gedaliahu Stroumsa, "Form(s) of God: Some Notes on Metatron and Christ," *HTR* 76, no. 3 (1983): 269–88; W. Fauth, "Tatrosjah-Totrosjah und Metatron in der jüdischen Merkabah-Mystik," *JSJ* 22, no. 1 (1991): 40–87. See also discussion in Halperin, *Faces of the Chariot,* 377–82, 417–27, 491–94, 519–21, and elsewhere.

112. E.g., *b. Avod. Zar.* 3b; *b. Hag.* 15a; *b. Sanh.* 38b.

113. Morray-Jones, "Transformational Mysticism," 8.

114. Morray-Jones, "Transformational Mysticism," 8.

115. Alexander, *OTP* 1:244–45, with references in nn. 64 and 65, where, inter alia, he cites the *Visions of Ezekiel:* "What is [the Prince's] name. . . . Mitatron, like the name of the Power." Lieberman, "Metatron," 240, suggested that Metatron was originally a title meaning *sunthronos,* which he demonstrates was a title assigned to humans, as well as to lesser divine beings, and that it ultimately became a name on its own. The modification to *metathronos* may have been intended to respond to the di-theist implications of *sunthronos.*

116. Morray-Jones, "Transformational Mysticism," 10.

117. In *3 Enoch,* Metatron is not Michael, who is clearly named by Metatron as the Great Prince, in charge of the seventh heaven at 17.3.

118. This is the NRSV translation, but it is clearly difficult. The translators here comment: "Abrek, apparently an Egyptian word similar in sound to the Hebrew world meaning 'to kneel.'" This is particularly significant if kneeling before Joseph can thus be construed as the obeisance due to God. For various interpretations of the original meaning of "Abrek," see Geza Vermes, "Bible and Midrash: Early Old Testament Exegesis," in his *Post-Biblical Jewish Studies,* Studies in Judaism in Late Antiquity 8 (Leiden: E. J. Brill, 1975), 63–64.

119. Philonenko, *Joseph et Aséneth,* 87, also argued for the identification of Pharaoh as the God of Israel. He based this on his identification of Joseph as Logos, but he does not develop the implications as fully as he might have.

120. See earlier discussion. Regardless of the meaning of the Hebrew, the Greek translations indicate that this is how the passage was read. Interestingly, *T. Onqelos* reads: "[A]nd they proclaimed before him, 'This is the father of the king'" (translation from Bernard Grossfeld, *The Targum Ongelos to Genesis,* Aramaic Bible, vol. 6 [Wilmington, DE: Michael Glazier, 1988]). *Neofiti 1* reads: "[A]nd they acclaimed before him, 'Long live the father of the king who is master in wisdom, although small in beauty and tender in years'" (translation from Martin McNamara, *Targum Neofiti 1: Genesis,* Aramaic Bible, vol. 1A [Collegeville, MN: Liturgical Press, 1992]); while Ps. Jonathan reads, "This is the father of the king, who is tender in years" (translation from Maher, *Targum Pseudo-Jonathan: Genesis,* Aramaic Bible,

vol. 1B [Collegeville, MN: Liturgical Press, 1992]). The notes in McNamara (*Targum Neofiti,* 188, n. 33) and Maher (*Targum Pseudo-Jonathan,* 137, n. 17) are particularly helpful unpacking the underlying logic of these "translations," which depend upon reading the אב of "Abrek" as אב (father).

121. See chapter 3.

122. See Larry Hurtado, *One God, One Lord: Early Christian Devotion and Ancient Jewish Monotheism* (Philadelphia: Fortress Press, 1988); Elior, "Mysticism, Magic, and Angelology," argues that Jewish opposition to the worship of angels (see, e.g., *t. Hul.* 2.18, which identifies sacrifices in the name of Michael with offerings of meat to the dead) reflects precisely such practices in other Jewish circles, as evidenced by the prescriptions in *Sepher ha-Razim* (41–42.) Particularly interesting is her assessment that "[o]pposition to angels in rabbinic literature, the diminution of their figures, and the suppression of works dealing with them were associated with a consciousness of the pagan origin of angelology, of its connection with polytheistic myth, and of the place which it occupied in popular circles" (42); also *b. Sanh* 38b; Newman, *Paul's Glory-Christology,* 98. But angel worship is also a problem for Christian communities as early as Col 2.18, and Rev 19.10 and as late as the fourth or fifth century: it is forbidden, for example, in Canon 35 of the Council of Laodicea.

123. Another example of such refusal occurs in *Asc. of Is.* 7.4. Isaiah asks the angel his name, and the angel replies: "[W]hen I . . . have shown you the vision on account of which I was sent, then you will understand who I am; but my name you will not know, for you have to return into this body."

124. They are also prevalent in the (Christian) *Odes of Solomon* (see chapter 9).

125. The two texts are quite close here.

126. For analysis of this difference as intentional redaction, see chapter 3.

127. I don't generally like explanations such as this, which seem too obvious, but it seems not impossible that concern for the purity of Aseneth's body is at issue here. It is also true that the text omits any act that may be construed as Aseneth's drinking the cup of immortality, unless her consumption of the honey is simultaneously the eating of the bread and the drinking of the cup. In the longer text, the eating of the honey appears to constitute all three acts, the bread, the cup, and the anointing.

128. 14.12–17.

129. See chapter 3 for discussion of this item.

130. Other readings include "one of the virgins, her companions" (Syr); "the virgins." See Burchard, "Joseph and Aseneth," 232, n. 18l.

131. Schäfer, *Synopse,* §287–88, translated in Halperin, *Faces of the Chariot,* 431.

132. On the akwardness of this addition, see chapter 3.

133. The phrase is repeated.

134. See chapter 3.

135. Schäfer, *Synopse,* §287–88, translated in Halperin, *Faces of the Chariot,* 431.

136. Schäfer, *Synopse,* §418–419, translated in Halperin, *Faces of the Chariot,* 372.

137. In the longer version only, at **19.5,** Aseneth repeats to Joseph the speech of the angelic figure, as follows: "**And he said to me, 'Your name will no longer be called Aseneth, but your name will be called City of Refuge and the Lord God will reign over many nations for ever, because in you many nations will take refuge with the Lord God, the Most High.'**" Note that she does not precisely repeat the words of the figure at **15.7;** here she adds the phrase "**and the Lord God will reign over many nations for ever.**"

138. Metanoia in 15.7; Aseneth in 21.3.

139. In the Latin printed by Batiffol, "Livre," Penitencia shares many features of Metanoia in the longer text (she is, e.g., *intendens super virgines*), but she is not the sister of the angel, nor does the angel proclaim his love for her. Her new name is not City of Refuge but *Multis*

refugii. This appears to be a misreading of the Greek πόλις (city) as πολύς (many). I owe this suggestion to Robert Kraft. But in Aseneth's recapitulation of this scene in 19, she tells Joseph that her new name, according to the angel, is *Civitas refugii.*

140. The relevant texts include *Thunder, Perfect Mind, Hypostatis of the Archons, Pistis Sophia,* and others. See also Karen King, ed., *Images of the Feminine in Gnosticism* (Philadelphia: Fortress, 1988).

141. Philonenko, *Joseph et Aséneth,* 85, who provides no specific references from Philo. Rather, his note is to E. Bréhier, *Les Idées philosophes et religieuses de Philo d'Alexandrie* (Paris: Librairie philosophique J. Vrin, 1925; 3d ed., 1950), 119. Brehier's discussion of the figure of Sophia, the relationship between Sophia and Logos, and the Anthropos in Philo is quite interesting, but here he bases his claim of Sophia as daughter of God in Philo on Philo's exegesis of Sarah, citing two passages in particular. In *On Drunkenness* 61, Philo understands Gen 20.12 to mean that Sarah "is declared, too, to be without a mother, and to have inherited her kinship only on the father's side and not on the mother's, and thus to have no part in female parentage. For we find it said, 'Indeed she is my sister, the daughter of my father, but not my mother.'" I imagine it is particularly the next line that provides a linkage to wisdom: "She was not born of that material substance . . . which is called mother or foster-mother or nurse of created things in whom first the young plant of wisdom grew; she is born of the Father and Cause of all things" (translation from F. H. Colson and G. H. Whittaker in *LCL*). That is, Sarah here appears to be identified with "the young plant of wisdom," although I find the text more than a little opaque at this point. In *Who is the Heir* 62, Philo again describes Sarah as motherless, "begotten of her father alone, even God the Father of all," quoting again Gen 20.12. Here Sarah is explicitly called Virtue (ἀρετή) but not Wisdom. Apart from Philo, there are some other interesting "daughter of God" traditions in Jewish sources. According to 1 Chr 4.18, a descendant of Judah named Mered married a woman named Bithiah, daughter of Pharaoh, a tradition with an interesting exegetical history that is largely outside the scope of this study. Although this Bithiah is mentioned in the lineage of Judah, she appears to become associated with the daughter of Pharaoh, who rescues and raises the baby Moses, a tradition that is doubtless helped by the fact that in 1 Chr, one of her children is named Miriam. *b. Meg.* 13a explains that Pharoah's daughter, Bit/yah is called *yehudi(a)* because her going down to bathe in the river is interpreted by R. Yochanan as evidence of her cleansing herself of idols. A similar tradition of the "conversion" of the daughter of Pharaoh occurs also in *b. Sot.* 12b, also associated with R. Jochanan but without the name Bityah. In *Leviticus Rabbah,* the passage in Chronicles is explained as follows: "R. Joshua of Siknin said in the name of R. Levi, 'The Holy One, blessed be He, said to Bithiah, the daughter of Pharaoh: "Moses were not your son, yet you called him your son; you, too, though you are not My daughter, yet I will call My daughter"'" (translation from J. Israelstam and Judah J. Slotki, *Midrash Rabbah: Leviticus,* 3d ed. [London: Soncino Press, 1983]).

142. Here, some of Bréhier's observations are interesting: "As there is a celestial logos and a terrestial Logos, there is also a divine wisdom and a terrestial wisdom which is its imitation" (*Idées,* 115). Clearly, the Anthropos, Joseph, Metanoia, and Aseneth could be taken to correspond, respectively, to the heavenly Logos, the earthly Logos, the heavenly Sophia, and the earthly Sophia. But it also important to note that in *Aseneth,* her heavenly counterpart is not explicitly Sophia but rather Metanoia, some of whose precise attributes cannot be derived from a simple identification of the two.

143. However, a passage in some versions of *Hekhalot Rabbati* (Schäfer, *Synopse,* §147–49, mss. New York 8128 and Vatican 228), quoted and discussed by Morray-Jones, "Transformational Mysticism," 20–21, contains the interesting notion that the adept has taken over the priestly function of atonement. God tells R. Ishmael, "Beloved are repentent sinners, for repentance reaches and extends across the 390 firmaments to the Throne of Glory. Repentant

sinners are greater than the ministering angels." In this material, when Israel is exiled, Metatron goes up to heaven to intercede on their behalf. The denizens of heaven protest his entrance, but God silences them, saying: "I cannot save them until their bones are healed by words of Torah, for among them are no repentant sinners who pray for compassion upon them." The passage concludes: "Therefore is it taught that repentant sinners are greater than the ministering angels." This certainly suggests yet another parallel with Metatron (whose size is enormous). Within the context of *hekhalot* traditions, Metatron's actions are the paradigm for the adept.

144. Metanoia in 15.8/**15.7.**

145. Schäfer, *Synopse*, §397 (the so-called Moses/Metatron text), cited in Halperin, *Faces of the Chariot,* 424–25. The beauty of Metatron is also explicit in *3 Enoch* 8.2.

146. *Hekhalot Zutarti* (Schäfer, *Synopse,* §685 in Halperin, *Faces of the Chariot,* 381); also *The Chapter of R. Nehunah ben Qanah,* translated in Halperin, *Faces of the Chariot,* 378; *3 Enoch* 12.1, 13.1.

147. Halperin, *Faces of the Chariot,* 417–20, "The Moses/Metatron text"; with discussion, 420–27.

148. Halperin, *Faces of the Chariot,* 426. Other titles include ‎ספרה רבה‎; see Lieberman, "Metatron," 237, n. 27.

149. The list is overwhelmingly male in its presentation, making the appearance of Miriam all the more striking. "And I saw . . . Moses and his generation, their doings and their thoughts; Aaron and Miriam, their works and their doings." One manuscript, E (printed in Jellinek, *Bet ha-Midrash,* 5:170–90), reads, "Aaron and his generation, their thoughts and their doings: Miriam and her generation, their thoughts and their doings," which is all the more striking for its presentation of Miriam as progenitor.

150. *Ant.* 3.6.1.

151. *On the Contemplative Life,* 83–88.

152. Ginsberg, *Legends of the Jews,* 6:19.

153. R. G. Hall, "The Installation of the Archangel Michael," *Coptic Church Review* 5, no. 4 (1984): 108–11.

154. Hall, "Installation," 110.

155. See, e.g., Shaye J. D. Cohen, "Crossing the Boundary," 13–33; Louis Feldman, "'Jewish Sympathisers' in Classical Literature and Inscriptions," *TAPA* 81 (1950): 200–208, "The Omnipresence of the God-fearers," *BAR* 12, no. 5 (Sept./Oct. 1986): 58–63, "Proselytes and "Sympathizers" in the Light of the New Inscriptions from Aphrodisias," *REJ* 148 (1989): 265–305; T. M. Finn, "The God-fearers Reconsidered," *CBQ* 47 (1985): 75–84; A. T. Kraabel, "The Disappearance of the 'God-fearers,'" *Numen* 28 (1981): 113–26, reprinted in A. Overman and R. MacLennan, eds., *Diaspora Judaism: Essays in Honor of, and in Dialogue with A. Thomas Kraabel,* South Florida Studies in Judaism (Atlanta: Scholars Press, 1992); Jerome Murphy O'Connor, "Lots of God-fearers? Theosebeis in the Aphrodisias Inscription," *Revue Biblique* 99 (1992): 418–24; J. A. Overman, "The Godfearers: Some Neglected Features," *JSNT* 32 (1988): 17–26; J. Reynolds and R. Tannenbaum, *Jews and Godfearers at Aphrodisias,* suppl. vol. 12 (Cambridge: Cambridge Philological Society, 1987); F. Seigert, "Gottesfürchtige und Sympathisanten," *JSJ* 4 (1973): 109–64; E. Mary Smallwood, "The Alleged Jewish Tendencies of Poppaea Sabina," *JTS* 10 (1959): 329–35; R. Tannenbaum, "Jews and God-fearers in the Holy City of Aphrodite," *BAR* 12, no. 5 (1986): 55–57; Paul R. Trebilco, "'God-worshippers' in Asia Minor," chap. 7 of *Jewish Communities in Asia Minor,* Society for New Testament Studies Monograph Series 69 (Cambridge: Cambridge University Press, 1991), 147–66; Pieter W. van der Horst, "Jews and Christians in Aphrodisias in the Light of Their Relations in Other Cities of Asia Minor," *NedTTs* 43 (1989): 106–21; M. H. Williams, " θεοσεβής γαρ ἦν,—the Jewish Tendencies of Poppaea Sabina," *JTS* 39 (1988): 97–111.

156. See chapter 10.

157. Numerous instances of φοβέω with τὸν θεον, τὸν κύριον, etc., may be found in Edwin Hatch and Henry A. Redpath, *A Concordance to the Septuagint and the Other Greek Versions of the Old Testament (Including the Apocryphal Books)*, 2 vols. (Oxford, 1897; with supplements, 1900–1906; reprint Graz, 1954) (v. φοβεῖν), or by searching the LXX on the TLG or PHI disks or any other appropriate electronic version of the Greek Jewish scriptures. There are far fewer instances of φοβεῖν with τὸν θεόν or τὸν κύριον (see Hatch and Redpath, ibid.). Such language is particularly common in the Psalms, Proverbs, and other wisdom literature, notably Sirach (as in 1.14: ἀρχὴ σοφίας φοβεῖσθαι τὸν κύριον [to fear the Lord is the beginning of wisdom]). In his marginal notes to 2 Enoch 43.3 (*OTP* 1:171), Andersen gives Sir 10.22 as a parallel, though more of Sir 10 is relevant here; 19–24 expound on the virtues of the one who fears (φοβούμενος) the Lord.

158. Θεοσέβεια translates יִרְאַת אֲדֹנָי or יִרְאַת אֱלֹהִים, in Gen 20.11; Job 28.28; Sir 1.24; Bar 5.4; 4 Macc 7.6, 7.22 (S), 15.28 (S), 17.15. Notable among these is Job 28.28, ἡ θεοσέβεια ἐστιν σοφία (fearing God is wisdom, or perhaps more interpretively, wisdom consists of fearing God). Θεοσεβής translates יְרֵא אֱלֹהִים once in Exod 18.21; once in Judith to refer to Judith herself, 11.17; three times in Job 1.1, 1.8, and 2.3; and twice in 4 Macc, 15.28 and in 16.11, where it refers to the mother of the seven martyrs.

159. According to Denis, *Concordance*, there are only two other instances: in *T. Naph.* 1.10, Abraham is Θεοσεβής (see also Gen 22.12); it is also used in the plural to describe righteous people in *Arist.* 179.3. Admittedly, the category of "pseudepigrapha" is an artificial one. For additional occurrences, see chapter 9.

160. 2.5/**2.5.**

161. 6.1 (both).

162. At **10.1**, the longer text adds to the description of Aseneth's distress that she was filled with great fear (ἐφοιβεῖτο φόβον μέγαν; literally, she was frightened with a great fear). At **11.15**, in the second additional soliloquy, Aseneth is afraid (φοβέω) to open her mouth to God. At **16.11** the longer reconstruction adds to 16.6 the phrase "and Aseneth was afraid" (φοβέω). At **16.13** Aseneth fears (φοβέω) the figure's sparking hot hand. At **18.11**, Aseneth's "fosterfather" is filled with fear (ἐφοβήθη φόβον μέγαν) at the sight of her transformation.

163. 7.3/**7.2.**

164. 24.14.

165. 28.1. The longer text adds the emphatic σφόδρα (see chapter 3).

166. 28.4/**28.7.** Aseneth's responses here parallel those of the angel to her earlier, perhaps reflecting her new angelic identity.

167. Aseneth by the angelic figure in 14.11; by Joseph in 26.2 when she expresses concern about traveling without him; the sons of Bilhah and Zilpah by Aseneth herself in 28.4/**28.7.**

168. 8.9/**8.8.**

169. 27.2/**27.1.** Here also, the longer text reads "greatly" (σφόδρα). These two additions may evidence the tendency of the longer text to "biblicize" the language of the shorter. Numerous instances of φοβέω in the LXX/OG are modified by σφόδρα, particularly though by no means exclusively in Jdt, 1 Macc, and 1 Sam. Also, at **28.7**, the longer version adds to the description of the sons of Rachel and Leah as ἄνδρες θεοσεβεῖς that they are fearing (φοβούμενοι) God and respecting every person (ἄνθρωπον). Given the use of ἄνθρωπος in this text to designate the angelic figure, one could reflect further on the accuracy of "person" as a translation. Burchard notes that this reading comes from one Greek manuscript, G, and is supported by the Syriac and by an Armenian manuscript; for additional textual notes, see Burchard, "Joseph and Aseneth," 246, n. 27e.

170. Schäfer, *Synopse*, §675–87: here §676. See Halperin, *Faces of the Chariot*, 542, n. 1, where he writes that "it seems barely possible that [this] . . . is a nod to the semi-converts men-

tioned in rabbinic and Greek sources." A different version occurs in the "Moses/Metatron text," translated in Halperin, *Faces of the Chariot,* 418, also published as *3 Enoch* 48.10 in Odeberg, *3 Enoch,* 178–79. "So [Metatron] gave [the ineffable names] to Moses, and Moses [gave them] to Joshua, Joshua to the elders, the elders to the prophets, the prophets to the men of the great synagogue, the men of the great synagogue to Ezra the Scribe, Ezra the Scribe to Hillel the elder, Hillel the Elder to R. Abbahu, R. Abbahu to R. Zera, R. Zera to the men of faith, the men of faith to the masters of faith" (Schäfer, *Synopse* §80, cited incompletely as §79 in Halperin, who notes that the Hebrew for these last two is אנשי אמונה and בעלי אמונות and comments that he doesn't know what difference, if any, exists between these two [*Faces of the Chariot,* 418, n. 58]).

171. Schäfer, *Synopse* §676. The various manuscripts have slightly different readings: MS NY has ירִיאֵ שמים; O has ירִיאֵ השם; M has ה ירִיאֵ.

172. Morray-Jones, "Transformational Mysticism," 14, *Tanḥuma,* pt. 4, p. 26a, ed. S. Buber (Vilna, 1885) (= *Num. R.* 15.13). *Num. R.* 15–23 is essentially *Midrash Tanḥuma;* see H. Strack and G. Stemberger, *Introduction to the Talmud and Midrash,* trans. Markus Bockmuehl (Minneapolis: Fortress Press, 1992), 329–33, 337–39; the date is quite late (on which, see the appendix).

173. P. 654, cited in Morray-Jones, "Transformational Mysticism."

174. See chapter 3.

175. Schäfer, *Synopse,* §312, cited in Halperin, *Faces of the Chariot,* 378.

176. Andersen himself offers some intriguing suggestions about an association of *2 Enoch* with "God-fearers." On *OTP* 1:96, he writes: "This does not mean that the work is Jewish: it lacks some of the most distinctive and definitive tenets of main-line Judaism. In fact, it knows nothing of developments between the Flood and the end of the world, so there is no place for Abraham, Moses, and the rest; there is no reference to the Torah. Instead the writings attributed to Enoch are advanced as the essential guide to life and salvation; but the vital knowledge they convey does not go any further than belief in one God as the Creator, and the practice of a simple ethical code. It would go a long way toward solving the mystery of *2 Enoch* if we could discover a religious community that venerated it on its own terms. If the work is Jewish, it must have belonged to a fringe sect. If it was ever a sacred scripture of a real group, they could have been a community of God-fearers (the highest virtue in *2 Enoch* 43:3), who were able to combine a strictly Jewish belief in one Creator-God (based on Gen, but combined with hellenistic metaphysics) and simple but strict ethical rules, with speculations about the cosmos, including a tincture of astrology. Add to this some typical sectarian concerns about such things as tying the four legs of an animal when making a sacrifice, which is documented as a deviant practice on the margins of Judaism, and a fanatical belief in the correctness of their own solar calendar (everything is regulated by astronomy, hence the week is not a unit in God's time and there is no interest in the sabbath)." These observations could, with a few alterations, apply to *Aseneth* as well (however, see Himmelfarb, *Ascent to Heaven,* 43, against the view that *2 Enoch* refers to sectarian sacrificial practices). He then continues with more interesting, if somewhat snide, remarks: "If *2 Enoch* does go back to the turn of the era, it is a source of the highest importance for the history of syncretism of selected parts of the Jewish faith with cosmological speculation. It has no intellectual strength, for there is no system, and the attempt to be philosophical is spoiled by unreflective folk notions. *2 Enoch* could derive from any region in which Jewish, Greek, Egyptian and other Near Eastern ideas mingled. . . . Egypt, or Syria–Palestine, or Asia Minor could have been the seedbed; but it is impossible to discern how early or how late such ideas were around."

177. For Odeberg's emendation in this reading, see both the Hebrew text and the English translation and notes, *3 Enoch,* 148.

178. But it does seem to be the case that "biblical" angels visit women only to announce the birth of important sons.

179. So, for example, *Hekhalot Zutarti:* "R. Akiba said: . . . If he is an adolescent, he may say [this mishnah] as long as he does not have an emission. If he is married, he must be prepared [that is, continent] three days in advance; as it is written, *Be prepared for the third day [do not come near a woman;* Exodus 19.15]" (Schäfer, *Synopse,* §424, translated in Halperin, *Faces of the Chariot,* 374).

180. *Apoc. Mos.* 32–37 has some interesting affinities with *Aseneth,* particularly Eve's prayer ("I have sinned, Oh God, I have sinned, O Father of all, I have sinned against you. . . ." [*Apoc. Mos.* 32, cf. *Aseneth* **21:11–21**]). For the identification of *The Life* as Jewish and relatively early (c. 100 B.C.E.–200 C.E.), see the introduction by M. D. Johnson in *OTP* 2:249–52. The argument that the text is both Jewish and relatively early rests heavily on the thesis that the present Greek and Latin texts translate an earlier Hebrew. Recently, however, Bertrand has pointed out the deficiences in this thesis, concluding than an original Greek composition is just as likely, if not more so; see Bertrand, *La vie grecque d'Adam et d'Eve: Introduction, texte, traduction et commentaire,* Recherches Intertestamentaires 1 (Paris: Librairie Adrien Maisonneuve, 1987), 26–28. Bertrand concurs, though, that the *Life* is undoubtedly Jewish (36) and probably no later than the mid–first century C.E. As is the case with *Aseneth,* the manuscripts are all relatively late and the work has no early attestation and no known transmission in Jewish circles.

181. *T. Job* 46–52. This is another enigmatic work in terms of date and authorial identity. It is listed in the sixth-century Gelasian decree (5.6.4) but is otherwise unattested in ancient sources. Apart from a Coptic fragment dated to the fifth century, it is known only from medieval manuscripts. Its use of Jewish scripture in Greek is uniformly recognized, but whether it should be classed as Jewish or Christian continues to evoke debate. It is interesting that both *T. Job* and *Aseneth* have been thought (by Philonenko himself for *T. Job* and Delcor for *Aseneth*) to be the work of Philo's Therapeutics, views that have gained little scholarly assent. See M. Philonenko, "Le Testament de Job et les Thérapeutes," *Semitica* 8 (1958): 41-53; M. Delcor, "Un roman d'amour d'origine Therápeute," *Bulletin de littérature écclesiastique* 63 (1962): 3–27. For recent discussion, see R. Spittler, "Job, Testament of," *ABD* 3:869–71, who concludes that the text is probably of "unclear sectarian origin within Judaism" in the period c. 100 B.C.E.–200 C.E.; his discussion in *OTP* 1:829–37 is more detailed but less judicious. See the particularly sane and agnostic discussion of Sparks, *AOT* 618–19, who also points out that if the author was Christian (something he considers feasible), a relatively late date for the text is possible. In any case, *T. Job* contains a small section (46–52) on the inheritance of Job's daughters, heavenly bands that when worn allow the three women to speak angelic and cherubic language, but the passage is not more specific about their experiences.

182. In this regard, it is quite interesting that none of the essays in Collins and Fishbane, *Death, Ecstasy, and Other Worldly Journeys,* takes note of *Aseneth.* In his book *Paul the Convert,* Alan Segal does note mystical affinities in *Aseneth* but does not develop them, and he accepts the scholarly consensus on date, provenance, and identity of the text. As I noted at the outset of this chapter, Howard Kee does recognize some potential similarities between *hekhalot* traditions and *Aseneth* but does not develop the latter's similarity to such narratives.

183. In *Hekhalot Rabbati,* it is a combination of persons but also "anyone." In *Hekhalot Zutarti,* Moses, Akiba, who bring the names to their students; in *Maaseh Merkabah,* heroes of the past but also Ishmael and "anyone"; and in *Midrash Rabbati,* all Israel, including proselytes. See Schäfer, *Hidden and Manifest God,* 147.

184. Schäfer, *Hidden and Manifest God,* 147. "It is perhaps no accident that this most comprehensive and open tradition is to be found in connection with the adjuration tradition and not the heavenly journey."

185. Schäfer, *Hidden and Manifest God,* 146, citing Schäfer, *Synopse,* §199. According to Alexander's introduction to *3 Enoch,* however (*OTP* 1:234), another passage in *Hekhalot Rabbati* (20.1 in Jellinek, *Bet ha-Midrash,* 3:98) restricts ascent to those who have mastered Bible,

Mishnah, *halachot,* and *haggadot* and who observe the whole Mosaic law. Alexander argues, however, that these texts have undergone orthodox editing, which might account for the decidedly orthodox rabbinic character of these readings.

186. Schäfer, *Synopse,* §686, translated in Halperin, *Faces of the Chariot,* 382. It may or may not be of some interest that the section immediately preceding concludes with a quotation of Exod 34.6, one of the few passages in the Bible that *Aseneth* comes close to citing, albeit allusively (see chapter 3). The same verse is cited again in the *Chapter of R. Nehuniah b. ha-Qanah,* at §310.

187. Morray-Jones, "Transformational Mysticism," 26.

188. Interestingly, something like this seems to be what the daughters of Job do: leaving aside earthly cares and characteristics, they acquire knowledge of the hymns the angels sing to God in heaven and make them available to humans in books bearing their names, thus enabling others to sing the same hymns on earth that the angels sing on heaven. And of course, the other female figure who comes to mind as efficacious intermediary between the heavenly and the divine is Mary, the mother of Jesus.

189. On the bees as souls awaiting incarnation, see chapter 6.

190. Although I cannot claim to be comprehensive in my knowledge, I do not know of any other accounts of angelic transformation accomplished through eating. It is interesting to reflect on whether the Eucharist accomplishes transformation through an act of eating.

191. See chapters 8, 9, and 10.

192. See, e.g., Elior, "Mysticism, Magic, and Angelology," with a summary on 51–53.

CHAPTER SIX

Aseneth and Late Antique Religious Sensibilities

Although the comparison of *Aseneth* with demonstrably Jewish (and, to a lesser extent, Christian) mystical traditions illuminates otherwise obscured aspects of the texts, it is still an incomplete excavation of the mystical paradigms that undergird the text. As I hope to show in this chapter, two crucial elements of the *Aseneth* tale, the identification of Joseph and his angelic double with Helios and the mystery of the bees, are best accounted for within the framework of late antique religious sensibilities, including solar henotheism and Neoplatonic cosmology and mysticism.

Many of the central images and beliefs that appear to undergird *Aseneth* were widespread in the later Roman empire among Jews, Christians, and pagans alike. Particularly relevant is the late antique trend toward a universalist theology, "a persistent effort to integrate the pantheon of paganism into a system governed by a single guiding principle or a supreme god."[1] Beliefs in a highest God and his co-regent, which we considered extensively in the prior chapter, were not limited to Jewish and Christian circles but permeate pagan religious sensibilities as well, particularly from the mid–second century C.E. on, evidenced in everything from theological treatises to oracles to burial inscriptions.[2] Such sources utilize titles for the deity familiar from *Aseneth,* such as God the Highest (*ho theos to hypsistos*), place great emphasis on the Name of God and on the Power of God (*ho dynamis tou theou*),[3] and speak frequently of angels.[4] A series of inscriptions from a sanctuary in Stratonicaea address "Zeus the Most High and the Divine Angel,"[5] "Zeus the Most High and the Divine Heavenly Angel," "the Divine Angel," and other similar combinations. In his rich study of religious sensibilities in Roman Asia Minor, Stephen Mitchell offers striking examples of pagan, Jewish, and Christian beliefs in and devotion to angels, commenting that "[a]ngels, who linked men with the gods in all three religious systems, helped to bind together the diverse strands of pagan, Jewish and Christian belief in later Roman Anatolia."[6] One of the most intriguing of these inscriptions, for our purposes, may be an altar inscription from

Andeda in Pisidia dedicated to God the Most High and Sacred Refuge (*Hagia Katafygē*), this second a figure about whom nothing seems to be known but whose name is reminiscent of the title of Aseneth as *Polis Katafygēs* (City of Refuge) and of her heavenly counterpart Metanoia.[7]

In addition to the prevailing trend toward henotheism (the belief in an overarching deity who subsumes all others), two major components of religious sensibilities in the later Roman empire prove particularly significant for the interpretation of *Aseneth*. First is the tendency to express such henotheism in solar terminology and imagery, as I will explore below. Second is the rise of Neoplatonism, a reinterpretation of Platonic cosmogony and cosmology that centered on uniting the soul with the Divine, particularly (although the practice was controversial) through theurgy—the adjuration of divine beings to compel their presence and their participation.[8] The third and fourth centuries saw the heyday of Neoplatonism and the flourishing of such Neoplatonic philosophers as Plotinus and Porphyry (in the third century) and Iamblichus (in the fourth).[9] Although Neoplatonism was ultimately identified with pagan survival and resistance to Christianity, particularly in the fifth and sixth centuries, in the third and fourth, it was quite possible for Christians to incorporate Neoplatonic ideas, and the same may well have been true for educated Jews as well.

In the two sections that follow, I will explore first the centrality of Helios imagery in the tales of *Aseneth,* specifically imagery with strong ties to the third and fourth centuries and to Neoplatonic cosmology. Second, I will argue that the critical mystery of the bees that comprises the core of the angel's revelation to Aseneth is best understood as a drama of the fate of souls drawn from Neoplatonic imagery and ideology. Finally, I will consider the possibility of further points of contact between *Aseneth* and Neoplatonism.

Helios

That Helios imagery is central to the tale of Aseneth is obvious from the outset of Joseph's actual appearance on the scene. Seeing him from her window, Aseneth herself says, "[B]ehold the sun out of heaven came toward us in his chariot and came into our house today"(6.5/**6.2**). As I will show, not only is Joseph's physical appearance highly consonant with ancient representations of Helios, but also it utilizes iconography that may securely be dated to the third and fourth centuries, further strengthening my thesis for dating the stories. Helios imagery and its attendant cosmic associations, as we know of them in the third and fourth centuries, thus provide crucial keys for the interpretation of many elements in the story.

Those of us who live in modern industrial cities where one may live a lifetime without ever seeing the dazzling brilliance of a star-filled night sky may find it difficult to comprehend the awe with which people in antiquity observed the daily rotation of the sun, the moon, and the stars, and the central significance they attached to the solar, lunar, sidereal, and seasonal cycles. Throughout the ancient Mediterranean, these heavenly bodies were venerated and often propitiated out of deeply held beliefs that human welfare was dependent upon the continued order of the heavens. Many, if not most, people believed the sun and the moon to be divine beings, while there were diverse traditions about the nature and identity of the stars.[10] The four seasons, also, were frequently personified, particularly in funerary iconography, although also in texts such as the Orphic Hymn 43 to the Seasons.[11]

There is no question that worship of the Sun (Helios) and the Moon (Selene) may be traced far back in ancient Mediterranean religions, whether in Greece, Rome, Egypt, or elsewhere. Apollo was venerated as the sun god, Artemis as the moon goddess.[12] Solar worship received solar sanction within ancient Israel itself, as the following passages illustrate:

> And he [Josiah] retired the idolatrous priests whom the kings of Judah had dedicated to burn incense at the high places in the towns of Judah and the environs of Jerusalem, those who burned incense to Baal, to the sun, to the moon and to all the Host of Heaven.[13]

> And he removed the horses which the kings of Judah had dedicated to the sun from the entrance of the House of the Lord, by the chamber of Nathan-Melech the official, within the stoas, and the chariots of the sun he burned with fire.[14]

> And he brought me into the inner court of the house of the Lord; there, at the entrance of the temple of the Lord, between the porch and the altar, were about twenty-five men, with their backs to the temple of the Lord, and their faces toward the east, prostrating themselves to the sun toward the east.[15]

Even among allegedly monotheistic Jews, there is strong evidence for similar, although not identical, beliefs and practices, such as Morton Smith's proposal that Essenes at Qumran were engaged in solar veneration.[16]

Evidence for Greco-Roman Jewish utilization of Helios imagery may be found in the writings of Philo of Alexandria. In his treatise on dreams, Philo sets forth the range of figurative meanings of Helios in Scripture.[17] Sometimes, he writes, "Sun" designates the human mind, "which is erected and set up as a city by those who under compulsion serve creation in preference to the uncreated One."[18] The second meaning of Helios is "sense perception" (*aisthēsis*), for the Sun rising awakens the five senses.[19] The third meaning is "divine Word" (*ho theios logos*), while for the fourth, Helios is applied to the Ruler of the world himself: "He [Moses] symbolically called the father of the whole Helios:[20] to whose sight all things are open, even those which are perpetrated invisibly in the recesses of the understanding."

In numerous places, as Goodenough points out, Philo employs the language of the divine charioteer for God, appropriating the imagery of Helios in his chariot driving across the heavens.[21] God is the invisible charioteer who "guides in safety the whole universe."

Although Goodenough uses Philo's imagery to explicate the Helios mosaics of late antique Jewish synagogues, which I will discuss shortly, it is clear that Philo is in no way evidence for a simplistic devotion to Helios, despite his admission that Helios in Jewish scripture sometimes does refer to God. The following passage, in which Philo catalogues the views current in various Hellenistic schools,[22] clarifies the possibility that Philo himself would have advocated such devotion, although it by no means enables us to determine the stances of other philosophically minded Jews of his time.[23]

No small error has taken hold of the majority of the human race with regard to a matter which properly should be established beyond all question in every mind to the exclusion of, or at least above, all others. For some have deified the four elements, earth and water and air and fire; others the sun and moon and the other planets and the fixed stars; still others only the heaven; and others still the entire cosmos.[24]

Yet in their treatment of the sun, the moon, the stars, the heavens, the planets, and God himself,[25] Philo's writings do demonstrate a mystical, allegorical understanding of astral beliefs among Jewish philosophical circles in first-century Alexandria.

Significantly, though, a considerable portion if not the majority of Jewish Helios material dates from the third through the sixth centuries C.E., including numerous Helios mosaics in the floors of Jewish synagogues, the Helios invocations in *Sepher ha-Razim* and other magical papyri, and some literary references.[26] Since I have already discussed the invocations of Helios at length in chapter 4, it is the Helios mosaics of Jewish synagogues, all of them in the land of Israel, that are of central concern here.[27]

As Goodenough writes, "One of the best attested designs from Jewish religious art of the late Roman Empire and the 'Byzantine' centuries is the circle of the zodiac with its twelve signs, in the center of which Helios drives his quadriga."[28] At least five[29] Jewish synagogues excavated so far in the land of Israel have yielded mosaic zodiac floors: Hammath Tiberias,[30] Beth Alpha,[31] Isfiya,[32] Na'aran,[33] and, most recently, Sepphoris.[34]

The best preserved of these is the mosaic from Beth Alpha. The synagogue there has been dated to the sixth century C.E., on the basis of an inscription referring to the Emperor Justin.[35] The mosaic floor of Beth Alpha comprised three panels, the first depicting the *Aron ha-kodesh,* the second (and largest) the Helios zodiac, and the third the sacrifice of Isaac.[36] The zodiac mosaic is contained within roughly square borders. The outer circle depicts the twelve signs of the zodiac, each labeled in Hebrew letters. In the four corners of the square the seasons are depicted as beautifully adorned female busts, accompanied by seasonal symbols and also marked in Hebrew. In the center of the zodiac at Beth Alpha, Helios rides his four-horsed chariot. Seven red rays emanate from his haloed head. A crescent moon hangs to the right, while twenty-four stars are scattered about, mostly under the chariot and beneath the hooves of the horses. Thus, the mosaic appears to represent the Sun rising, a motif popular in ancient Greek art from the fifth century B.C.E. on.[37]

The synagogue at Hammath Tiberias also contained a three-paneled mosaic floor[38] that Moshe Dothan dates to the late third or early fourth century.[39] The "top" panel contains a depiction of an ark partially covered by a tied curtain: to the right and to the left are relatively identical seven-branched menorahs on tripods, themselves centered between what appears to be a *lulav* and *ethrog* on the left and an incense shovel and *shofar* on the right. In the "bottom" panel, two lions on the right and left each face nine dedicatory inscriptions in Greek, arranged in three boxes of three.

Here, too, the central panel features a Helios zodiac. In the later fourth or perhaps fifth century C.E., however, the synagogue was rebuilt, with a wall running roughly through the center of the earlier Helios mosaic that obscures part of that design. Female busts depicting the Four Seasons occupy the corners of the square, although in distinction from those at Beth Alpha, their heads extend toward the circle rather than out to the corners. Both the Seasons and the signs of the zodiac are labeled in Hebrew. A young Helios may still be seen in the center circle, with seven red rays extending from his haloed and crowned head. His right arm is raised, while his left holds a celestial globe[40] and a whip. Dothan offers the following description of his clothing:

> Helios wears a white tunic with long sleeves (*tunica manicata*) and cuffs. Suspended from his shoulders is a purple cloak, most probably a *paludamentum,* fastened at his right shoulder by a circular clasp. He seems to wear a second tunic: both are bound by a wide, richly adorned girdle (*cingulum*). His right shoulder is covered by a square red and yellow panel, most probably a *segmentum.*[41]

The horses and the chariot itself are no longer visible, except for a few fragments.

In his discussion of the Hammath Tiberias mosaic, Dothan identifies some key differences in the representation of Helios in the third-century mosaic as compared to the sixth-century depiction at Beth Alpha. The older figure exhibits the characteristic features of Helios as emperor, including the raised hand, the celestial globe, and the crown, while the mosaic at Beth Alpha displays more stereotypic features of Helios as sun god.[42]

Dothan argues that in the third and fourth centuries, the gesture of the raised right hand signified power:[43] "Sol Invictus with raised hand and globe was one of the most prominent deities depicted on the coins of Pupienis, Gordianus, Gallienus, Postumus and Probus. . . . In replacing Jupiter, Sol aquired the attributes of *kosmokrator,* the raised right hand and the globe."[44]

According to H. P. L'Orange, not until the third century is the Sun Emperor depicted in Roman iconography by the "oriental" depiction of Sol dropping the reins and raising the right hand.[45] He further claims that the gesture of the outstretched right hand was a "primeval magical sign of power in the East," conveying both blessing and curse. "It is the expression of the irresistible power and might of the divinity and his chosen being."[46] Coins of Roman emperors beginning with Geta and including Elabagalus, Gordian III, Gallienus, Postumus, Claudius Gothicus, Aurelian, Probus, Diocletian, and others, demonstrate this gesture, which became predominant in the depiction of Constantine[47] and persisted well into the Middle Ages.[48] L'Orange first associates the gesture of the outstretched right hand as a specific sign of salvation with the Severan period (193 C.E.–235 C.E.),[49] whereas he interprets pre-Severan depictions of the emperor with outstretched hand as a sign of greeting.[50] While earlier depictions of the emperor in his triumphal chariot show him in profile, often carrying a twig,[51] from the third century he is shown frontally, with right hand raised and globe in left. L'Orange argues that the gesture of the emperor is actually a gesture of third-century C.E. "oriental" gods, transferred to the emperor.

He also insists that the gesture is above all that of Sol Invictus[52] and that Sol never appears on Roman coins in this gesture of benediction before the Severan period.[53] He interprets this gesture as the cosmocrator ruling and moving the cosmos.[54] L'Orange also notes that to stretch out the right hand to the gods (*dexiousthai theois*) simply means to pray, in Greek, and he briefly discusses the right-hand greeting (*dexiousthai*) as a gesture in which stretching out the right hand accompanies a verbal greeting and strengthens its force.

As Dothan points out, in the fourth century, the obverse of coins of Constantius II (353–61) show the emperor "with his right hand raised and his left holding a globe, for these attributes had by then become symbols of sovereignty; on the reverse, the Emperor rides in a chariot, his right hand raised and a globe in his left."[55]

Dothan also notes that once Christianity was adopted as the imperial religion, the radiating gilt crown is never worn by Christian emperors but is solely an attribute of Christ. However, the solar nimbus (halo) is reintroduced as an imperial symbol around 300 and appears on subsequent representations, such as the "Calendar of 354."[56] Dothan concludes that "the representation of Helios at Hammath Tiberias possesses all the attributes of Sol Invictus and . . . these were also attributes of the Roman Emperors of a specific period,"[57] that is, from Aurelian to Constantine I.

While the mosaic floor at Na'aran, dated by Sukenik to the fifth century C.E.[58] is not as well preserved (and appears to have been deliberately defaced, perhaps by iconoclastic Jews), it, too, contains a zodiac mosaic with a representation of Helios driving his quadriga in the center. Goodenough describes him as "rayed, if not also haloed."[59] Remains of a zodiac with Seasons were also found in the synagogue at Isfiya (sixth century C.E.), which Goodenough speculates also contained a representation of Helios at its center, although there is no identifiable trace of this now remaining.[60]

Most recently, during the 1991 excavation season, a new zodiac mosaic was uncovered at a synagogue in ancient Sepphoris.[61] Although portions of the zodiac are severely damaged, most of the central circle is easily visible. Four horses, in obvious motion, pull the solar chariot, in which rides not an anthropomorphic representation of Helios but a depiction of the solar disk, from which emanate ten rays.[62]

Even by themselves, these mosaics demonstrate that Greek-speaking Jews, particularly in synagogues in late Greco-Roman Palestine, were strongly drawn to the imagery of Helios. Discovering why this might have been so and how this may contribute to the interpretation of the figures of Joseph and the enigmatic angel in *Aseneth* requires a closer look at the history of solar devotion in the later Roman empire.

While non-Jewish devotion to the Sun also dates back centuries before the common era, the third century C.E. saw two major imperial attempts to impose worship in the Roman empire that may have a significant bearing on our attempts to locate the composition of *Aseneth* and interpret the story within its proper cultural context. The first of these occurred in the early third century C.E. under the emperor Elagabalus, who changed his name to Heliogabalus to reflect his devotion to the Sun, while the second occurred some fifty years later under Aurelian, who established the imperial cult of Sol Invictus.[63] Although both of these movements enjoyed only limited success and encountered significant resistance, solar imagery continued to play a significant role in Roman imperial religion under Constantius Chlorus and Constantine himself.[64] A century after Aurelian, the emperor Julian also promulgated Helios worship as part of his program to restore a kind of universalist polytheism as the official religion of the empire.[65] A variety of literary sources from the third century or later document this rise in solar devotion. Julian himself composed a *Hymn to King Helios* that draws heavily on his Neoplatonic education. A writer whose very name, Heliodorus, "Gift of the Sun," alludes to his religious proclivities (or those of his family)[66] composed a lengthy, typical Greco-Roman romantic novel known as *An Ethiopian Tale,* in which two lovers are seemingly doomed to be sacrificed to the Sun and the Moon.[67] Several third-century C.E. Orphic Hymns contain elements of solar imagery consistent with imperial motifs, such as the sun as charioteer.[68] As we have seen, the so-called Greek magical papyri are full of hymns and prayers to the Sun or associated with Helios.[69] In the very late fourth or early fifth century, a writer named Macrobius[70] devoted six chapters of a work titled the *Saturnalia,*[71] to demonstrating the identification and unity of the Sun with a wide range of pagan deities, from Liber to Mars to Mercury to Aesculapius to Adonis to Horus to Pan to Saturn to Jupiter himself. Particularly intriguing is his discussion of each of the signs of the zodiac as "properly related to the natural attributes of the sun."[72] Also of interest may be Macrobius's description of the status of Zeus at Syrian Heliopolis (Baalbek), a statue he claims was originally brought from the Egyptian town of Heliopolis:[73] "The statue, a figure of gold in the likeness of a beardless man, presses forward with the right hand raised and holding a whip, after the manner of a charioteer; in the left hand are a thunderbolt and ears of corn; and all these attributes symbolize the conjoined power of Jupiter and the sun."[74]

Macrobius, a Neoplatonist, also composed a commentary on the Dream of Scipio (a favorite text of the Neoplatonists), in which he presents the Sun as a "visible image of the unique Supreme God."[75]

Numerous studies of the religious climate of the third century C.E. have pointed to the increasing prominence of this "consciously universal . . . henotheist or monotheist religion."[76] That such beliefs emerge at a time of enormous political, social, and economic upheaval cannot be accidental, and several recent works have explored the complex dynamics operative here. Although the exact extent to which the third century may properly be considered a time of extreme crisis is the subject of debate, there can be no question that it was a time of significant political, economic, and concomitant social instability.[77] And there can also be no question, at least to my mind, that imperial attempts to impose a henotheistic solar theology were integrally related to imperial efforts to restore order and unify an increasingly fractious empire.

A useful description of what he himself titled "astronomical religion" is offered by Goodenough, who regrettably failed to elucidate the correlations between this phenomenon and the historical circumstances of the third and fourth centuries.

> In general, the astronomical religion of the period saw three chief values in the heavenly bodies and their changes as reflected upon earth in the seasons. The first was one of circular or cyclic determinism, the heavenly causation of all things earthly. As still in astrology, one's character and fate were considered set by the suns under which one was born. . . . Secondarily, the seasons and the cycle of the heavenly bodies suggested death from life, and life from death, that is the hope of immortality, as sunrise, the east, the seasons, and the germination of seeds still make a comforting allusion when we bury our dead. And thirdly, the mystic saw in the planets, as well as in the heavenly bodies in general, a great ladder to the world beyond. The hope, in material terms, was to be able to rise and share in the great cycle with Helios and the stars: or, in immaterial terms, to climb beyond the material universe altogether to the immaterial.[78]

In this cosmology, the Seasons played a significant role, "primarily marking the regularity and order of the universe, and of the God of the universe." Goodenough follows George Hanfmann's arguments here that "during the Empire interest steadily shifted from science and philosophy to religion, from concern for the structure and nature of reality to anxiety about the relation of the individual to the cosmos and about his fate after death."[79] The Seasons become "the bearers of annual and seasonal sacrifices, and as symbols of the passing time, of the recurrent succession of life and death, even in successive incarnations."[80] Ultimately, they become "the four horses of the solar quadriga which took the emperors to immortality."[81] Goodenough concludes: "[T]he real meaning of the Season itself was the hope inspired by the regularity of the seasons, the fertility and new life which always followed decay and death, hope that man, too, was safe in the regularity and reviving power of God or nature."[82]

In a particularly fascinating article, E. M. Staerman articulates the connections between solar theology and imperial ideology in the third and fourth centuries, demonstrating the ways in which beliefs about the sun, the moon, and the stars were part of a complex hierarchical cosmology in which the heavenly and earthly realms were intricately linked. In this cosmology[83] the stars were considered divine beings who then conferred some of their own qualities onto souls as those souls descended into bodies.[84] Those souls that became human acquired part of the spirit of the Sun. The relationship between God, stars, and souls was itself hierarchical and replicated in an earthly hierarchy. The figure of the King/Emperor, who was last in the cosmic hierarchy but first in the earthly hierarchy, served as the link between heaven and earth.[85]

In particular, Staerman proposes that imperial solar theology linked the belief in the Sun with the belief in Time as a creation of the Sun: the emperor, as the Sun, was seen as the source and distributor of Time and, therefore, Eternal—as also was the empire itself.[86] In this theology, the empire and the cosmos were one.

Furthermore, the characteristics of the Sun, particularly as portrayed in Neoplatonism, were particularly apt for the portrayal of the emperor in the third century, when the empire was in a state of severe crisis. Just as the Sun was eternal and outside the confines of Time, so too was the emperor, which implied that the empire itself was stable, eternal, and constant—divinely ordained and therefore immutable.[87]

> According to these [doctrines], the deity, being not inserted into the cosmos, but located outside its limits, was eternal, but before the creation of the world, time did not exist, because it was the movement of the Sun which created it [time]. Within this time, human affairs change, now coming into being, now perishing. The invariable portion of the world extends from the fixed sphere of the stars to that of the Moon: the changeable portion—the realm of fate and of death—from the Moon to the Earth. Souls, by falling into the sublunar sphere, receive from the Moon their submission/subjection to Change and begin to exist within Time. At the moment of Chaos, time did not exist, because it was determined by the movement of the heavens. . . . The Sun united these two worlds, that of supreme Eternity, where it reigns, and that here below, where [the Sun] created time with its divisions: century, year, seasons. As we have seen, the king occupied the same position between the divine world, that is, eternity, and the terrestrial, changing, living in time.[88]

As we have already seen, the identification of the emperor with the Sun led immediately to the iconographic representation of the emperor as Helios, including their representation in quadrigas.

For Staerman, only the despotic powers of the emperor could possibly repair the fracturing and fragmenting of social classes and economic links in the third century, and to this end, she suggests, various emperors devoted enormous energy, attempting to consolidate and unify the empire, especially through the imposition of the imperial cult. The choice of solar theology as the primary expression of that cult was dictated by numerous factors. It would not have been sufficient to utilize available and consonant philosophical ideology. Rather, it was also necessary to incorporate beliefs popular throughout the empire, and here again, solar theology was extraordinarily conducive. Associations of the Sun with Justice, particularly popular in Asia Minor and in eastern portions of the empire, afforded third-century emperors the opportunity to present themselves as the protectors of ordinary people against the powers of the elite.[89] In fact, the prevalence of solar worship in so many ancient Mediterranean traditions undoubtedly made it a particularly potent unifying force.[90] This is apparent in Macrobius's identification of the Sun with much of the known masculine pantheon, as noted earlier.[91] In fact, it is precisely the solar theology of Macrobius that Staerman cites as exemplary. In Staerman's characterization of that theology, "the Sun was a visible image of the unique Supreme God. . . . This God not only ruled the cosmos but he is near to humans, directs their lives, takes care for them, offers them all good things, inspires them to virtue, chastizes their wrongdoings and their insolence, with an eye to justice that opens (along with piety) the route to heaven."[92] Clearly, third-century emperors would have loved to have been seen in such light.

Helios, Joseph, and Aseneth

Against this background, we may now return to the description of Joseph when he first arrives at Pentephres' household in *Aseneth*.

5.4–11/**5.4–7**
And the gates of the courtyard which faced east were opened, and Joseph entered, seated on the chariot of Pharaoh's second-in-command. And four horses were yoked together, white like snow, with gold-studded bridles, and the chariot was covered **entirely** in **pure** gold. And Joseph was clothed in a special white tunic, and the robe wrapped around him was fine purple linen woven with gold. He had a gold crown upon his head, and around the crown were twelve precious stones, and above the stones twelve gold rays, and a royal scepter [*skeptron*] **wand [*rabdos*] in his left hand and** in his right hand (And) he held an olive branch, and it had much fruit on it **and in the fruit there was a great wealth of oil.** And Joseph entered the courtyard, and the gates **of the courtyard**[93] were closed. But (whether) man or (whether) woman **all** foreigners remained outside, because the guards at the gates **drew tight and** had closed the doors **and all foreigners were closed outside.** And Pentephres came, with his wife and his whole family, except their daughter Aseneth, and prostrated themselves before Joseph, with their faces upon the ground. And Joseph descended from his chariot, and gave them his right hand in greeting.[94]

The differences between the shorter and longer versions are consistent with the patterns illustrated earlier. For instance, *rabdos* is far more prevalent in the LXX/OG, particularly in the Pentateuch and the Prophets, whereas *skeptron* is considerably less frequent and not found in the Pentateuch at all. The change thus brings the longer text into closer conformity with "biblical" readings. The minor addition of the phrase "of the courtyard" brings the text into conformity with the earlier reading of "the gates of the courtyard" in 5.4. Further, the longer text appears to clarify the potential ambiguity of where Joseph held the olive branch and the *rabdos,* which is here clearly in the left hand, while the olive branch is explicitly in his right.[95]

It is important to note that the description of Joseph here is at best only partly derived from or consonant with the text of Genesis 41.41–43. There, Pharaoh gives Joseph his ring, dresses him in fine linens, places a gold chain around his neck, and puts him in the chariot of his second-in-command. Here, there is no mention of Pharaoh's ring nor of the gold chain; only the fine clothing and the "second" chariot may be found, and the clothing is perhaps the most generic element. Clearly, the source(s) or perhaps the explanation for the details of the description of Joseph must be found elsewhere,[96] as also for the description of Joseph's angelic double, who appears in 14.8–9. Although, as I have discussed earlier, Joseph's clothing bears a broad resemblance to both priestly and royal garments in numerous ancient traditions, here it is my contention that the precise description of Joseph closely resembles the iconography of Helios, particularly as Sol Invictus.

The claim that Joseph is here depicted as Helios is by no means an original observation on my part. But whereas other scholars have minimized the significance of this portrait,[97] here I will attempt to show not only that it is intentional but also that it accounts for specific details of the text and further reinforces the probability that *Aseneth* is composed in the third or fourth centuries C.E.

To begin, Pharaoh's second chariot on which Joseph rides is a quadriga, a chariot drawn by four horses, that is, the classic vehicle for Helios. In the Helios mosaic from Beth Alpha, as in *Aseneth,* the horses are white, and their reins appear to be gold.[98] Regrettably, the Hammath Tiberias mosaic does not preserve much of the horses themselves. With the association of the emperor with the Sun, emperors, too, are depicted in such chariots, a depiction that intentionally conveys the identification of the two.[99] As Dothan notes, the depiction of Helios driving a solar chariot is hardly a late antique invention,[100] but the solar associations of the quadriga are paramount. Further, the significant differences between earlier and later representations suggest that the description in *Aseneth* is unlikely to antedate the third century C.E.

The clothing that Pharaoh gives Joseph in Genesis 41.42 is simply a *stolē bussinē,* a fine linen cloak. In both the shorter and longer texts of *Aseneth,* Joseph wears a white tunic (*chitōn*) under a purple cloak of fine linen woven with gold, just as the Helios in the Hammath Tiberias mosaic wears a white (long-sleeved) tunic and a purple[101] cloak that appears to have large gold-colored sections. In the Helios mosaic from Beth Alpha, the charioteer's clothing appears to be obscured by the chariot. Furthermore, it may be of some interest that according to Herodian, a priest of Elagabal named Bassianus appeared in public "wearing a long-sleeved 'chiton' that hung to his feet and was gold and purple. His legs from the waist down to the tips of his toes were completely covered similarly with garments ornamented with gold and purple. On his head he wore a crown of precious stones glowing with different colors."[102] Millar also notes that according to Dio, the third-century emperor himself (Elagabalus) abstained from eating pork, had himself circumcised, wore the dress of Syrian priests, and sang hymns to the gods.[103]

Genesis 41 says nothing about Pharaoh crowning Joseph. But in *Aseneth,* Joseph wears a golden crown with twelve precious stones, from which twelve rays emanate. This depiction, too, strongly resembles the iconography of Helios, including the Hammath Tiberias mosaic, where Helios wears a gold crown, out of which seven rays may be seen to emanate—the remainder presumably being invisible from a frontal perspective.

Although the Helios at Beth Alpha is also depicted with seven rays emanating from his headgear, Dothan argues that these depictions are significantly different and that the Helios of Hammath Tiberias "possesses all the attributes of Sol Invictus and that these were also attributes of the Roman Emperors of a specific period."[104] In particular, Dothan points to three crucial differences—the rayed crown, the raised right hand, and the globe—as distinctive elements that locate the Hammath Tiberias mosaic as Helios–Sol iconography of the late third and early fourth centuries. Here I would like to suggest that the literary description of Joseph is significantly closer to the Hammath Tiberias mosaic than to that at Beth Alpha and for precisely the reasons that Dothan identifies, namely, its intentional utilization of Helios–Sol imagery from the period in question.

Dothan points out that the Helios of Beth Alpha (and probably also Na'aran) lacks the distinctively imperial crown of the Hammath Tiberias Helios. "Instead, rays simply emanate from the nimbus around their heads." If he is correct in this observation, the fact that Joseph wears a crown from which the gold rays emanate becomes highly significant, suggesting the Helios–Sol imperial iconography.

Furthermore, earlier representations portray Helios holding the reins of the quadriga and a whip.[105] In comparison, third- and fourth-century C.E. depictions of Helios typically depict him holding not the reins but a whip and globe in the left hand and raising the right hand in a gesture of power.[106] Dothan points out that the Beth Alpha mosaic seems to draw more closely on the older traditional iconography and lacks the raised right hand and the globe. Although the description of Joseph in *Aseneth* is not precisely consistent with either, I would like to argue that it is far closer to the second than to the first.

Recall again that in the shorter version, our Joseph holds in his right hand the royal scepter and an olive branch full of olives, while in the longer he holds the scepter in his left hand and the olives in his right. Burchard asserts that the olive branch is a sign of peace, signifying Joseph's ambassadorial function.[107] E. H. Kantorowicz, however, points out that third-century C.E. representations of Helios Oriens (Helios rising) typically depict the rising Sun as radiate, with right hand raised, and left hand usually carrying the globe or whip, although some coins show him carrying palm or laurel branches.[108] Richard Brilliant also notes that imperial triumphators were portrayed on many third-century medallions as moving to the left in chariots, carrying laurel branches that signified the triumph of their virtue.[109] That Joseph as Helios carries branches is thus still consistent with third-century C.E. depictions of the Sun rising, although the specific identification of the branches as olives appears puzzling.[110]

Helios's raised right hand, so prominent in the Hammath Tiberias mosaic, is clearly one of the definitional features of imperial solar iconography.[111] When we first see Joseph, nothing is said about the position of his right hand. But when Pentephres and his entire family except Aseneth come forward and prostrate themselves before

Joseph, he responds by descending from the chariot and gesturing with his right hand. Is this gesture the right hand of power associated particularly with imperial solar iconography in the third and fourth centuries?

Admittedly, the correspondence is not absolute. The wording of the *Aseneth* texts could be construed to have a somewhat more general meaning, reading *kai edexiōsato autous en tē dexia autou* in both versions. This could simply mean "to raise the right hand in greeting."[112] This appears to be the interpretation of other translators, such as Philonenko ("Joseph . . . les salua de la main droite") or Burchard ("Joseph . . . greeted them with his right hand"). Crook gives a slightly different twist: "Joseph . . . extended his right hand to them."[113] This translation may or may not reflect a slightly different understanding of just what Joseph does. After all, stretching forth the hand is frequently significant in *Aseneth:* it is what the angel does numerous times in the scene between himself and Aseneth.[114] The outstretched hand is, as L'Orange explores, extremely important in ancient depictions of divinity, including those of ancient Israel,[115] and its association with both Joseph and the angel clearly has such implications.

Further, this entire scene is essentially consonant with depictions from the third century and afterward of the advent of the emperor, as Brilliant demonstrates. The arrival of the emperor is depicted by the gesticulate equestrian. The king arrives on horseback, raising his right hand in a gesture of greeting and power, and his arrival is signified by the reception of subordinates.[116] Thus, taken together with the many other elements of imperial solar iconography, I think it highly likely that this gesture of Joseph's, whatever its initial origin may have been, here conveys third- and fourth-century connotations of imperial power associated specifically with Helios.

One central element of this imperial solar iconography appears to be missing from the portrait of Joseph in *Aseneth* 5, namely, the globe that Helios holds in his left hand in the Hammath Tiberias mosaic. Yet an allusion to such a globe may occur elsewhere in the Aseneth story, immediately after the angel feeds Aseneth the transforming honey:

16.10–11/16.17

And the figure stretched forth his **right** hand and put his finger on the edge of the [honey]comb facing east, **and drew it over the edge looking west** and the path of his finger became like blood. And the figure stretched forth his hand a second time on the edge of the comb facing north, **and drew it over to the edge looking south,** and the path of his finger became like blood.

Like the scene with the bees that immediately follows these verses, no one has offered a convincing explanation for this image. For scholars who have argued for the Christian identity of *Aseneth,* or at least for the Christian redaction of *Aseneth,* the angel's gesture has occasionally been seen as the drawing of a cross.[117] Particularly interesting is Philonenko's diagram of this event: he reproduces a circle divided into four equal quadrants by two perpendicular diametric lines.[118] Such an image occurs precisely in the globe that Helios holds in the Hammath Tiberias mosaic. Even the bisecting lines are red, as the lines the angel draws take on the color of blood. Dothan notes that the lines in the Helios mosaic represent the Equator and the Zodiac or the Meridian and speculates that the quadrants "showed schematic representations of stars."[119] L'Orange offers considerable evidence for ancient representations of the cosmos as a circle divided into four quadrants, representing the four quarters of the world, and of ancient circular cities that constituted earthly representations of this cosmic structure.[120] Thus, although somewhat distanced from the initial descriptions of Joseph, the image on the honeycomb may evoke the cosmic globe carried by Helios, which, in *Aseneth,* the angel is able to bring into being by the action of his finger.[121]

Finally, one other curious element connected with the description of Joseph may point to third- and fourth-century equations of Helios and the emperor, namely, the fact that the angelic figure is said to resemble Joseph in every way except for his obvious angelic attributes of light. Kantorowicz points out that in the third century C.E. and afterward, it was common to commingle the faces of emperors and God, a convention related, apparently, to the understanding of imperial ascension as not only the deification of the dead emperor but also the glorification of the new living one. He writes that facial similarities of emperor and god are "almost the rule in the jugate busts of emperors and gods which become customary in the third century."[122] The phenomenon does seem to have earlier antecedents in the second century,[123] but in view of the other consistencies in Joseph's portrayal as Helios with third- and fourth-century imagery, this, too, may be drawn from the same iconographic traditions. On balance, then, we may conclude that the iconography of Joseph in *Aseneth* 5 points strongly to a late antique context of the third and perhaps fourth centuries C.E.

The Bees: A Mystical Perspective

The scenes with the honeycomb and the bees in 16.1–17.3 are both the most enigmatic and the least well-explicated of the entire tale of *Aseneth.* Apart from a highly creative recent attempt to see the drama of the bees as a scenario of priestly conflict in the second century B.C.E. that I nevertheless find unpersuasive,[124] scholars have offered almost no interpretation of these scenes, convincing or otherwise. Philonenko, for example, appears to think that the association of bees with the Egyptian goddess Neith, whose presence he thinks lurks very close to the surface throughout the story, is sufficient to account for these scenes.[125] According to Burchard, Philonenko acknowledges traditions in which a swarm of bees descended on such notables as Plato, Pindar, and Ambrose while still in their cradles, "symbolizing their future inspiration and eloquence."[126] Burchard disagrees that the point must be that Aseneth receives "poetic or theological inspiration" but also concedes that there is, as of his writing, no satisfactory discussion of this scene or the bee imagery.[127]

Yet bees and honey played substantial roles in the intertwined religious and cultural symbols of the ancient Mediterranean world, many of which are pertinent to the imagery of *Aseneth.* In ancient Egypt, for example, an early myth relates that bees were born from the tears of the sun god Re, which fell to earth and became bees, thus establishing an early connection between bees and the solar deity.[128] Honey was generally regarded as a substance that fell from heaven, analogous to manna (which is itself associated with honey). Hélène Chouliara-Raios claims that the Pharaoh was always identified with the bee and with the sacred royalty of divine-ancestor kings.[129]

Various Egyptian goddesses, including but by no means limited to Neith, were associated with bees, including Nut, who could appear in the form of a bee.[130] Hathor ate forbidden honey at Dendur, and this substance was apparently widely used in the rites of the god Min.[131] Finally, Chouliara-Raios notes that "for the Egyptians, bees eventually became considered as the guides of the dead during their journey to the next world."[132] Though insufficient to allow us to decode the bees and the honey in our *Aseneth* story, all of these associations seem consonant with its motifs—the solar connection, the motif of Pharaonic and divine royalty, the affinity with goddesses, and even the association with death.

In Greek and Roman cultural milieux, bees had even more complex and suggestive associations. Bees were known for their wisdom and their virtues;[133] for their chastity and sexual abstinence; for their love of cleanliness and their hatred of dirt; for their abhorrence of unpleasant smells and their abstinence from meat.[134] Bees were believed to be augurs of the future, sometimes of misfortune, and the indoor flight of a bee was believed to presage the arrival of a stranger, a belief that Chouliara-Raios remarks is still held in some regions of the Mediterranean.[135] They symbolized peace[136] as well as the virtues of the proper woman: chastity, purity, and diligence.[137] These associations, too, accord with the bees in *Aseneth*. Their appearance may be construed both as a general augur of the future that the angel announces to Aseneth and as a sign specifically presaging the arrival of Joseph.[138] These symbolic values of bees are remarkably consistent with the portrait of Joseph and with that of the transformed Aseneth, who was always chaste and is now wise, virtuous, clean, and even appears to abstain from meat. In this regard, and others, bees are also like angels—asexual, pure, and perhaps immortal.

The association of bees with sexual purity, chastity, and fidelity is explored in further depth by Maurizio Bettini in a fascinating study.[139] The asexuality of bees is explicit in Virgil, who claims that bees engage in neither conjugal intercourse nor sexual love, nor do they bring forth young in labor.[140] Bettini notes that Rufinus of Aquileia cited this aspect of bees as support for his claims of the virginity of Mary. Bettini also gives instances of tales in which bees serve as the mediators between lovers and as the agents of punishment for unfaithful lovers: "As the go-between for the two lovers, the bee symbolizes the bond of purity and fidelity which should bind the one to the other."[141]

Bettini also offers the intriguing example of a German folk belief that placing oneself in front of a hive is a test of purity for girls and young brides. Whether ancient writers and readers would have interpreted Aseneth's encirclement by the bees in this manner is impossible to know, but such a reading is certainly quite consistent with the text: the failure of the bees to sting or otherwise harm Aseneth could easily be construed as proof of her chastity. Yet another reading of this scene is prompted by an observation of Chouliara-Raios regarding the association between bees and eloquence of speech.[142] Various legends recount that bees posed on the lips of such famous ancients as Pindar, Plato, Sophocles, and Hesiod to give them the gift of eloquent speech. This suggests another meaning for the bees that swarm around Aseneth, especially on her lips.

In Greek, Roman, and Egyptian contexts, bees and honey had numerous cultic associations. Bees were associated with religious oracles, including that at Delphi, and the name *melissae* was given to women who participated in the festival of the Thesmophoria to Demeter at Athens. Bettini points out that as part of these rites, the women abstained from sexual contact for three days.[143] Bees appear to have been associated with the worship of Artemis at Ephesus.[144] In Egypt, honey was offered both to deities in temples and to the spirits of the dead (mixed with the blood of sacrificed animals). In the so-called magical papyri, several deities are associated with honey, including Helios.[145] In rabbinic Jewish sources, honey is associated not only with Wisdom but also with mystical experience. In the famous passage of the four sages who entered Pardes (variously translated as Paradise, the Garden, the Grove, etc.)[146] is the portion about Ben Zoma, "who looked and went mad. Scripture says of him, 'Have you found honey?'" The passage then quotes the rest of Proverbs 25.16 ("If you have found honey, eat only enough for you, or else, having too much, you will vomit it"), thus equating honey with the mystical vision.

According to the Neoplatonist teacher Porphyry, initiates into certain Mithraic rites symbolizing the transmutation of the soul (metempsychosis) "washed the hands in honey and cleansed the tongue with the same."[147] With this observation, we may shift the discussion to a different plane, for it is precisely the association of bees with souls and souls' transformation and immortality that is most significant for decoding the scenes in *Aseneth.*

The explicit association of bees with souls, particularly the souls of the dead or the life force of the dead animal, may be found in Virgil's *Georgics,* a four-part treatise on agriculture, of which book 4 is specifically devoted to bees and beekeeping. "Some say bees partake of the divine mind and heavenly souls,"[148] he writes, claiming that all things draw their life from God and that "unto Him all beings thereafter return, and, when unmade, are restored; no place is there for death, but, still quick [living], they fly unto the ranks of the stars, and mount to the heavens aloft."[149]

The association of bees with the life of the dead animal, particularly the ox, comes from the end of the *Georgics,* where Virgil offers advice for what to do if your bees die completely and you require a wholly new swarm. He prescribes the method of *bugonia*[150] (the generation of a swarm of bees from the corpse of an ox) and relates the origins of this practice in the story of Aristaeus, son of the nymph Cyrene, who offered a sacrifice to Eurydice as expiation for indirectly causing her death and returns to find a swarm of bees erupting from the flesh of the oxen.[151] The bees generated out of the decaying flesh (from which they flee in abhorrence) are understood to constitute the now-transformed life force (*anima*) of the dead animal.

The equation of bees with souls, particularly the souls of now dead beings, accords further with the imagery of *Aseneth,* particularly in the scenario of the bees who first fall down dead and then rise and fly to the courtyard Garden. But in the writings of Porphyry, the third-century Neoplatonist, bees and honey exhibit a symbolic association that accords even more closely with the drama in *Aseneth.* Here, honey is the food of the gods that prevents putrefaction and therefore conveys immortality. Bees symbolize the soul awaiting rebirth and, even more precisely, virtuous souls that are, in Bettini's telling language, "destined to live justly and return where they came from after having done the will of the gods."[152] While some of Porphyry's associations are clearly drawn from older traditions, this last identification of bees as righteous souls awaiting incarnation occurs, to the best of my knowledge, no earlier than Porphyry.[153]

His treatise, *On the Cave of the Nymphs,* has been characterized as

a discourse of the soul's descent into the world of generation, its passage over "the sea of time and space" and its return to its native kingdom, in the form of a commentary on a passage from the Odyssey seen as a symbolic narrative, which describes Odysseus arriving at last on his native isle of Ithaca, near the Cave of the Nymphs.[154]

After an exegesis of the cave itself, and of its waters and Nymphs, Porphyry turns to the question of why the amphorae in the cave are filled with honey rather than water. The passage is sufficiently significant that I reproduce it here at length:

Theologists, also, have made honey subservient to many and different symbols, because it consists of many powers; since it is both cathartic and preservative. Hence, through honey, bodies are preserved from putrefaction. . . . [I]t is also sweet to the taste, and is collected by bees, who are ox-begotten, from flowers. When, therefore, those who are initiated in the Leontic sacred rites, pour honey instead of water on their hands; they are ordered [by the initiator] to have their hands pure from everything productive of molestation, and from every thing noxious and detestable. . . . And they likewise purify the tongue from all the defilement of evil with honey. But the Persians, when they offer honey to the guardian of fruits, consider it as the symbol of a preserving and defending power. Hence some persons have thought that the nectar and ambrosia, which the poet pours into the nostrils of the dead, for the purpose of preventing putrefaction, is honey, since honey is the food of the Gods. . . . [T]he sweetness of honey signifies, with theologists, the same thing as the pleasure arising from copulation. . . . Since, therefore, honey is assumed in purgations, and as an antidote to putrefaction, and is indicative of the pleasure which draws souls downward to generation; it is a symbol well adapted to acquatic Nymphs, on account of the unputrescent nature of the waters over which they preside, their purifying power, and their co-operation with generation. For water co-operates in the work of generation. On this account the bees are said, by the poet, to deposit their honey in bowls and amphorae; the bowls being a symbol of fountains . . . And fountains and streams are adapted to acquatic Nymphs, and still more so the Nymphs that are souls, which the ancients peculiarly called bees. . . . Hence Sophocles does not speak inappropriately when he says of souls—
   In swarms while wandering, from the dead,
   A humming sound is heard.[155]

Porphyry then continues with a discussion of bees as souls.

The priestesses of Ceres, also, as being initated into the mysteries of the terrene Goddess, were called by the ancients bees; and Proserpine herself was denominated by them [honeyed]. The moon, likewise, who presides over generation, was called by them a bee, and also a bull. . . . But bees are ox-begotten. And this appellation is also given to souls proceeding into generation. . . . To which may be added that honey is considered as a symbol of death, and on this account, it is usual to offer libations of honey to the terrestrial Gods.[156]

As I shall explore momentarily, the affinities between the associations in these passages and the scenes in *Aseneth* seem to me so striking as to compel some historical and cultural connection. But the strongest similarity comes in the next phrases, which I have already noted above:

All souls, however, proceeding into generation, are not simply called bees, but those who will live in it justly, and who, after having performed such things as are acceptable to the

Gods, will again return [to their kindred stars]. For this insect loves to return to the place from whence it first came, and is eminently just and sober.[157]

After a few other comments about bees' avoidance of beans, Porphyry concludes that "honey-combs and bees are appropriate and common symbols of the acquatic Nymphs, and of souls that are married [as it were] to [the humid and fluctuating nature of] generation."[158]

The symbolic associations in this passage from Porphyry afford us a significant resource for interpreting the drama of the bees. Just as in Porphyry, honey is the food of the gods and prevents the putrefaction of death, so in the words of Aseneth's heavenly visitor:

16.8/**16.14**
([T]his honey) the bees of the paradise of delight have made **from the dew of the roses of life that are in the paradise of God,** and **all** the angels of God eat of it, **and all the chosen of God and all the sons of the Most High, because this is a comb of life** and all who eat of it shall not die for eternity.

Interestingly, the similarities are clearer in the simpler description of the shorter text.

In Porphyry, honey is also associated with "the pleasure arising from copulation" and with "the pleasure which draws souls downward to generation." In *Aseneth,* the consumption of honey by Aseneth and the angelic double of her future husband Joseph may also point to the generative ties between them, the more so because the outcome of the tale is generation, namely, the birth of Manasseh and Ephraim.

In these same verses, Porphyry speaks of the association of honey with acquatic Nymphs, particularly Nymphs that are souls (equated with bees). The Greek word *nymphē* often means bride, and it is used of Aseneth precisely in that context.[159] He goes on to claim that the acquatic nature of Nymphs is particularly appropriate, as "water co-operates in the work of generation," and he develops the association of bees with bowls, amphorae, and fountains. Of similar interest is another passage, which appears to see a mystical association in the fact that married women (*gamoymenai*) are called *nymphae* (brides)*,* and are bathed in water taken from springs (*pegē*) and other sources of flowing water.[160] Although the precise association is difficult to identify, this constellation of related images may have something to do with the puzzling scene in 18.7/**18.8–9** where Aseneth asks for "pure water from the spring" and sees her transfigured face in the bowl on the conch shell.

Porphyry's discussion of bees as souls comes startlingly close to the scene enacted by the bees, particularly in the shorter version of *Aseneth.* Bees are another name for souls that proceed into generation (that is, into bodies) and live righteously, doing what is acceptable to God, before returning to the place from which they came—that is, God. In the shorter *Aseneth,* the bees emerge from the hive of the honeycomb, attired in garments and adornments that echo the appearance of Joseph.[161] These bees swarm around Aseneth, while "other bees, as large as queen bees, attach themselves to her lips." The figure commands them "to go away then to your own place," whereupon the bees fall to the ground and die, thus, I propose, enacting the incarnation of souls into bodies and their eventual death. The figure then speaks a second time, saying, "Arise and go back to your own place," whereupon the bees "rise" and fly to the courtyard representing heaven, the place of God.

Although, as I have discussed earlier, the differences in the longer text may have various explanations,[162] the imposition of a moral distinction among the bees may suggest that the author/redactors of the longer version were concerned with the moral dimensions of this scene, a dimension explicit in Porphyry. Bees are not simply souls proceeding to incarnation but righteous souls that will do God's bidding (like Aseneth and Joseph) and then return to their proper place with God. Perhaps, as discussed in chapter 3, for the author(s) of the longer version, who may have missed the coherence of this passage, the second group of bees must be distinguished from the first, precisely along the lines of righteousness.[163]

One other ancient association with bees may be particularly intriguing for *Aseneth,* namely, the belief that bees were unable to be defined as either masculine or feminine.[164] This, of course, has interesting implications for the angel's characterization of Aseneth at 15.1 as (temporarily?) androgynous, particularly if we read Aseneth's entire encounter as a metaphor of the experience of the soul dying and being reincarnated. As that soul, Aseneth is neither male nor female, though she ultimately regains her gendered identity.

Interestingly enough, some concern for these issues may be detected in a passage in Porphyry's letter to his wife, Marcella, the widow of a friend, whom he married later in life to assist her in raising her six children.

> So then, if we should rise above their witchcraft and guard against their seductive snare, we have enchained what has enchained us. Therefore, do not be overly concerned about whether your body is male or female; do not regard yourself as a woman, Marcella, for I did not devote myself to you as such. Flee from every effeminate element of the soul as if you are clothed in a male body. For the most blessed offspring come from the virginal soul and unmated Intelligence.[165]

Thus, the scenes in *Aseneth* with the honeycomb and the bees may be read as indicators of Neoplatonic mystic sensibilities, if not of an actual Neoplatonic context. The scene in the shorter version lends itself easily to an interpretation comparable to that in Porphyry: that the bees symbolize (or may actually be) souls, which die and are reborn and whose ultimate home is that of paradise (the garden in Aseneth's courtyard). Porphyry's own description seems quite apt here: the bees are souls destined to live justly and return whence they came after having done the divine will. In *Aseneth,* that is precisely what the bees do: they go to their proper place after having obeyed the angel. The imagery is quite similar to that in *3 Enoch* 46 of the sparks/spirits who also obey the will of Metatron.[166] These souls, like Aseneth and Joseph, are sexually chaste, righteous (*theosebeis*), and ultimately immortal.

Yet another significance of this analysis is its further support for dating *Aseneth* to the third and/or fourth centuries C.E. Cook seems to suggest that the association of bees not simply with the soul after death but also with the Nymph and unborn soul is a specifically mystic interpretation.[167] This is potentially quite significant for dating *Aseneth,* for if the specific constellation of symbols on which *Aseneth* seems to draw are not found until the third century, this would offer an important support for a later date, consonant with much of the other evidence I have amassed and to which I will return in chapter 8.

Conclusions

Several highly significant conclusions emerge from the discussions of these last two chapters. First, as I explored in chapter 5, *Aseneth* displays significant affinities with traditions about the adjuration of angels and "ascent" to the heavens as known to us from the problematic *hekhalot* and related materials. These affinities illuminate numerous elements of the *Aseneth* texts and are sometimes considerably more pronounced in the longer reconstruction.

Second, the imagery of Joseph and of the angelic figure is most consonant with imperial solar imagery of the third and fourth centuries: imagery used not only by pagans within overtly political contexts but also by Jews in synagogue mosaics from the fourth century C.E. on and ultimately also by Christians.[168] This consonance further strengthens my arguments that *Aseneth* dates no earlier than the third century C.E. and possibly as late as the fourth century C.E.[169]

Third, Neoplatonic cosmology appears to undergird this text (and indeed many of the other sources already analyzed, from the magical papyri to *Sepher ha-Razim*) and provides the most cohesive interpretation of the scene with the bees. Although the encounter between Aseneth and the unidentified Helios/Joseph figure is couched in the structure and language of adjuration of angels, the mystery that the angel shows Aseneth is fundamentally Neoplatonic, cast within the framework of a biblical episode, and suggests that the entire encounter between Aseneth and the angel may be read as such.

Yet elucidating these elements complicates as much as it clarifies. We can posit no simple relationship between our texts and these traditions and materials. The strong similarities may point to close cultural and social connections or may merely suggest that the fashioners of *Aseneth* drew easily and comfortably from the pervasive symbols and paradigms widespread in late antique culture. Here I can only pursue some of the possibilities a little further.

Given the nature of our sources, it seems impossible to know what if any actual connections might exist between *Aseneth* and the *hekhalot* traditions. But if the longer version of *Aseneth* in particular does stand in some self-conscious relationship to the *hekhalot* traditions, gender may well be a significant factor in the differences. In the *hekhalot* traditions as we have them, women are conspicuous by their total absence, except occasionally as persons to be avoided (by the presumed male practitioners) when preparing for adjuration and/or ascent. Not inconceivably, *Aseneth* might constitute a deliberate critique of the views of both heaven and earth implicit in these materials.

Much more, however, may be said about *Aseneth* and Neoplatonism. Although the suggestion that *Aseneth* displays significant affinities with Neoplatonic imagery, particularly that found in Porphyry, may strike some readers as historically and culturally jarring, it is a connection that has, in fact, a fair amount of historical and cultural feasibility. Porphyry, we should remember, was born in Syria in 232/3 C.E. and lived into the first decade of the fourth century. Among his major works was a fifteen-book attack on Christianity entitled *Against the Christians,* which, not surprisingly, survives (like Celsus's *True Doctrines*) only through quotations in Christian refutations.[170] Both the

surviving fragments and the refutations of the work confirm that Porphyry was intimately acquainted with Jewish and Christian scripture and that his critique anticipated
contemporary modern biblical criticism by many centuries. Particularly noteworthy
was his assessment, affirmed by contemporary scholarship, that the Book of Daniel
was not, as it claims, prophecy from the period of Babylonian captivity but rather was
composed in the second century B.C.E. within the context of the Seleucid–Maccabean
conflict.[171]

For my purposes, what is significant about *Against the Christians* is that it allows
us to make the reasonable inference that if Porphyry was well schooled in Jewish and
Christian scripture, the traffic in knowledge could easily have gone both ways. It
appears quite plausible that Porphyry was acquainted with the writings of Christian
exegetes,[172] if not also with Christians themselves. According to Eusebius, Porphyry
actually claimed to have known Origen in Caesarea.[173] Further, because Christian
scholars such as Origen depended on Jews, at least to some extent, for their knowledge of Hebrew and Jewish exegesis,[174] it seems not unreasonable to assume that
someone like Porphyry, too, might also have had contact with Jews. And if such contacts seem reasonable supposition, it appears similarly feasible that Jews and/or
Christians could have become acquainted with the writings and ideas of Porphyry.
This is not to suggest, by any means, that Jews (and Christians) had no other means
of knowing Neoplatonic works, symbols, and cosmology; it is rather to point out one
very concrete way in which they might have become aware of precisely the imagery
that occurs in *Aseneth.*

The claim that *Aseneth* utilizes both paradigms of adjuration and Neoplatonic
imagery inevitably invites discussion about possible connections with Neoplatonic
theurgy. Itself a complicated subject, theurgy in Neoplatonic circles essentially
involved the drawing down of the divine into statues (or into the practitioner), based
on the concept of Sympatheia, "a notion which assumes a direct correspondence
between a given deity and his or her symbolic representation in the animal, mineral
and vegetable worlds."[175] Properly fashioning the material image of the deity, according to techniques believed to have been revealed by the gods themselves, could persuade the deity to appear, usually in the form of light—an illumination that itself
aided the purification of the soul.

While Neoplatonic theurgy appears to have undergone significant development and
change, in terms of both practice and interpretation,[176] the basic components of
theurgy have much in common with the practices of adjuration and ascent described
in the previous chapters of this study.

The similarities between *Aseneth* and theurgy are of considerable interest.[177] As
Sarah Johnston points out, the ultimate goal of the theurgist was heavenly ascent, but
that ascent required precisely the same kinds of preparation discernible in the papyri,
in *hekhalot* texts, and in *Aseneth* itself. Prior to ascent, the theurgist apparently underwent some form of initiation whose purpose not only was preparatory but also provided essential protection from demons (described as "dogs") who would otherwise
inhibit the ascent. There may be some connection between these demonic canines and
the ferocious animals depicted at 12.9 as Aseneth's antagonists in her prayers. The
belief that demons appear in order to threaten and discourage initiates, theurgic and

otherwise, may also account for the mention of the diabolic father of the Egyptian gods in this same passage.

Interestingly, silence appears to have been particularly important in theurgic performance.[178] As we have seen, the longer reconstruction of *Aseneth* places particular emphasis on Aseneth's silent prayers that preface the appearance of the angelic figure. Although I have suggested a variety of possible interpretations of this emphasis, the concern for silence in theurgic ritual may further illuminate its presence and functions in the longer text.

As in *Aseneth,* the motif of immortalization plays a central role in theurgy. Johnston's observations here may be particularly helpful for understanding Aseneth's apparent immortalization. She points out that although to modern ears immortalization (*athanatismos*) has a permanent ring, in the Mithras Liturgy we find specific mention of immortalization procedures of one day's duration that can be undergone several times a year.[179] She suggests that "becoming immortal" meant "that for the duration of the ritual [the performer] was of a status equal to the gods, or perhaps simply . . . was protected from death. Surely the same is true of the immortalization that resulted from theurgic ascent."[180] And so perhaps also for Aseneth.

Most significantly, solar imagery was prevalent in theurgic ritual. Johnston argues that the theurgist was probably instructed to inhale the rays of the sun itself, an inhalation that "would give the soul of the theurgist the same qualities of the heavenly realm." Particularly intriguing is her observation that the theurgist could expect to receive some assistance from angels (*angeloi*). One fragment of the *Chaldean Oracles* "mentions that the *angeloi* lighten the soul of the theurgist with a 'warm breath,'"[181] an image evocative of Aseneth's own assessment of the honeycomb as the product of the angel's exhalation, an assessment to which he appears to assent (16.6–7). Johnston further argues that for later theurgists such as Julian, the rays of the Sun were clearly seen to be the means by which the soul ascended and that such a notion may already be present in a fragment of the Oracles.[182]

Devotion to Helios unquestionably played a significant role in much of so-called Neoplatonism from the third century on, as evidenced not only by the examples just noted but also by such works as Julian's *Hymn to King Helios,* Proclus's *Hymn to the Sun,* and Porphyry's own exegesis of Mithraic rites in the passage analyzed elsewhere in this chapter. If, in fact, the emphasis on Joseph as Helios in *Aseneth* does relate in some way to Neoplatonic interest in Helios, it may also explain an aspect of *Aseneth* that is otherwise relatively arbitrary, namely, the use of the angelophany in Judges 13 as the narrative framework of the angelophany in *Aseneth* itself.[183]

In his eponymous study of Julian's gods, Rowland Smith writes:

> The emphasis laid in the hymn [to King Helios] on the motif of Helios' cosmological centrality and "connectiveness," then, is easily and economically explained once the extent of Julian's debt to the [Chaldean] *Oracles*—or rather, to the Iamblichan interpretation of them—is appreciated. And the same holds true for the motif in its soteriological application. Like the hymn, the *Oracles* give Helios a central role in the raising of souls. Theurgic ritual aimed to effect by an invocation of solar rays an *anagogia* of the souls that would carry it up to the Father; in that process, the Sun connects souls with his higher counterpart Aion, and Aion in turns connects the Sun with the Father. And

once more, there is clear evidence that Julian had the Chaldean notion of *anagogia* as his model in the hymn.[184]

Although one might argue that the choice of Judges 13 as the model of angelophany in *Aseneth* is relatively arbitrary (i.e., any biblical angelophany would do), several aspects of this particular angelic visitation suggest otherwise. It may be of some significance that in Judges 13, the angel ultimately ascends back to heaven in the flames of the altar fire, which might be visualized as the fiery rays of the sun. In *Aseneth,* this imagery is combined with the imagery of other biblical traditions, particularly the ascending chariot, which is of course also associated with Helios and not present in Judges itself, whether in Judges 13 or in the somewhat similar angelophany to Gideon of Judges 6. In the same vein, we may note that other biblical angelophanies do not utilize these same elements and may even contain components that would have been more problematic for *Aseneth.* For instance, in Genesis 18, the angels who appear to Abraham do not subsequently ascend in sacrificial flames, and unlike the angel in *Aseneth* (and the angel in Judges 13.16 who refuses the offer of a goat dinner), they do eat the meal that Abraham prepares, including the meat. In Genesis 16, the angel of the Lord who appears to Hagar neither eats nor ascends—in fact, the text tells us nothing of how the angel departs. The enigmatic figure with whom Jacob wrestles in Genesis 32, presumably an angel, also neither ascends nor eats.[185]

My point here is that while one could, in theory, argue that the choice of Judges 13 has no initial meaning but that, once chosen, Judges 13 subsequently determines the details of the narrative (the angel who refuses the meal, the ascent in flames, and, in the longer text, the conversation about the name), one could also argue the converse—that the text of Judges 13 is particularly appealing to the author of *Aseneth* precisely for this constellation of elements. It is, in this context, of some interest that Porphyry himself wrote a treatise advocating vegetarianism, and he opposed animal sacrifice.[186] Thus, the use of Judges 13 as the narrative framework for the angelic appearance may in fact be seen as a conscious choice motivated by interest in precisely the components found there but not in other traditional angelophanies. Whether there might be an even more complex dynamic here, whereby the tradition of Judges 13 also supports the formulation of those elements as significant, lies beyond the scope of this discussion.

I want to be clear, though, that I am not arguing here that *Aseneth* is a straightforward Neoplatonic account of theurgy that could easily have been recognized as such by knowledgeable ancient readers. There are certainly significant distinctions between *Aseneth* and Neoplatonic theurgy that should not be minimized, most significantly, I think, *Aseneth's* rejection of polytheism. I am arguing, though, that the affinities between *Aseneth* and Neoplatonic images and practices are significant; that they suggest some awareness, direct or indirect, of Neoplatonism and theurgy on the part of at least some of *Aseneth's* fashioners; and that recognizing this affords us further insight into specificities of the texts themselves. I have also suggested that Porphyry himself might have been a conduit for some of this exchange, although I cannot do more than show the plausibility of such a transfer.

Reading *Aseneth* in light of Neoplatonic theurgy affords additional insights. Johnston points out that "[t]heurgy . . . offered a revelatory religion that aligned with many of the popular trends of the age and yet improved upon them."[187] Whereas prior traditions were dependent on divine ancient revelation, theurgy provided a means for the practitioner to obtain revelation at will, as it were. "[T]heurgy learned to cause [revelations]"[188] and thus transferred power from the divine to the human realm.

Concern for this distinction between divine agency and human agency permeates ancient discussions of theurgy as well as those of modern scholars. Ruth Majercik argues, for instance, that Christian sacraments "depend for [their] effect[s] on an irruption of the Divine into an otherwise natural order," whereas theurgy "depends not on any inbreaking of the Divine but, rather, on a recognition of the Divine's presence in even the basest of matter."[189] In Majercik's view (and that of others), the practices of ancient "magicians" were essentially coercive, compelling the cooperation of suprahuman beings whose participation was hardly voluntary. The crucial distinction between theurgy and ancient "magic" can be seen as one of purpose—"magic" had profane goals such as securing a lover or achieving financial success, whereas theurgy aimed at the salvation of the soul.[190]

Whether theurgy shared with *goēteia* the coercion of the latter was a matter of concern to Neoplatonists themselves. Iamblichus argued that, unlike *goēteia,* theurgy entailed "a free and willing bestowal of Divine power by which the gods purify the devout and draw them upward."[191] Johnston puts the matter succinctly: "That the gods fully approved of [theurgic invocation] is implied by the fact that they were the ones who taught the theurgist how to do it."[192] Porphyry himself seems to had some reservations about theurgy and apparently thought that theurgy only worked on the sensible cosmos and could not affect the higher souls of the gods.[193]

Although what transpires between Aseneth and the angelic being, in both versions of the tale, is not identical with theurgy, it does, in fact, display significant consonance with these ideas.

Johnston herself points to a useful distinction between theurgy and the ascent of enraptured persons in Jewish and Christian literature that may further illuminate the dynamic of *Aseneth.* The stories of figures such as Enoch

> undoubtedly served as ideological predecessors to ritualized ascent by suggesting that such journeys were possible. They could not, however, serve as practical models, for the enraptured individual seldom did anything to cause his ascent; god or god's messengers chose him and usually did all of the work. Moreover, the purpose for which the theurgist ascended was significantly different from that of the enraptured individual. The former ascended and interacted with the gods in order to derive personal spiritual benefits; the latter usually returned from his trip with important information for his society and was charged with disseminating it. Indeed as Segal, Himmelfarb and others have noted, the underlying purpose of many rapture stories was the establishment of a theodicy or new eschatological doctrine.[194]

As I have explored in chapter 3, whether or not Aseneth's experience should be characterized precisely as ascent, it seems clear to me that with regard to Johnston's valid distinctions, *Aseneth* is a hybrid, sharing some of the features of theurgic experience and some of the features of the "rapture" tradition. Although I think the active role of the practitioner may be stronger in theurgic and other adjurative traditions, I do think that Aseneth's actions are far too similar to the techniques prescribed in those traditions not to be responsible for the appearance of the angelic figure in her bed-room. To the degree that *Aseneth* mutes or obscures Aseneth's active agency, we may see a reflection of the kinds of concerns noted by Majercik and R. T. Wallis that for Christians (and probably Jews as well) contact between the human and the divine is more likely to be presented as an inbreaking of the Divine into the human realm rather than vice versa. Interestingly, it is probably not accidental, and certainly consistent with the stance of Porphyry himself on the limits of theurgic efficacy, that Aseneth effects the appearance of the angelic being but not actually that of God.

Clearer, I think, is the second point of comparison. The benefits of Aseneth's encounter with the divine are largely, if not wholly, personal rather than communal. Aseneth receives personal spiritual benefits, including angelic identity and immortal-ity, as well as personal benefits of a more ordinary sort, most notably a happy and fruitful marriage. Although one may detect hints of a communal element in the angel's prophecy at 15.6 that in Aseneth, as City of Refuge, "many nations shall take refuge and under your wings many peoples shall take shelter and in your fortress those who devote themselves to God through repentence shall be protected," nowhere in the text is Aseneth charged with the dissemination of heavenly truths or new doc-trines and nowhere do we see this prophecy of the angel's fulfilled. At least at the explicit narrative level, the tale of *Aseneth* is largely about the transformation and spiritual fulfillment of Aseneth herself.

Aseneth's apparent affinities with, if not knowledge of or even dependence on, Neoplatonic imagery, cosmology, and theurgic practice may have some bearing on the question of authorial identity, which I will consider in chapter 8. Our willingness to recognize the probable relationships between *Aseneth* and Neoplatonism may depend, in some measure, on our prior assessments of the cultural context(s). If, as I shall explore in chapter 8, *Aseneth* is the product of self-conscious Jewish composi-tion, locating it within a context that might include receptivity to Neoplatonism is not inherently problematic. Since, for instance, Philo of Alexandria was a noted Platon-ist, to argue that *Aseneth* is at once self-consciously Jewish and infused with Neopla-tonic imagery might not raise any inherent objections on the grounds of cultural implausibility. Our sources are unfortunately silent on the interest, knowledge, or par-ticipation of late antique Greek-speaking Jews in later Platonism, although we do know of at least one fifth-century Samaritan, Marinus of Neapolis, who became a noted Neoplatonic philosopher. And I have argued here that the social location of Por-phyry himself points to the possibility of real contacts between Neoplatonists and Jews in the third and fourth centuries C.E.

If, however, *Aseneth* is at least as likely to be the work of self-consciously Christ-ian composition, the argument that its imagery depends to some degree on Neopla-tonism may seem more problematic. As Porphyry himself demonstrates, some Neo-platonists were deeply hostile to Christianity, and various modern scholars have explored the severe philosophical differences that Neoplatonists perceived to exist between themselves and Christians.[195] Yet if non-Christian Neoplatonists saw Chris-tianity and Neoplatonism as mutually exclusive, the same cannot be said for many philosophically minded Christians, who sought with varying degrees of success to embrace the two.[196] Thus, by itself, the identification of Neoplatonic materials in

Aseneth sheds little if any light on whether the author(s) of *Aseneth* were self-consciously Jewish or Christian.

NOTES

1. S. Mitchell, *Anatolia,* 43.

2. Ample useful documentation can be found in Mitchell, *Anatolia,* 43–51, particularly of evidence from Asia Minor.

3. Mitchell, *Anatolia,* 45.

4. On angel worship in Asia Minor, see not only Mitchell, *Anatolia,* but also F. Sokolowski, "Sur le culte d'angelos," 225–29, and Sheppard, "Pagan Cults," 77–101; see also Kearsley, "Angels," 206–9.

5. Mitchell, *Anatolia,* 45, with references in n. 262; texts from Louis Robert, "Reliefs, votifs et cultes d'Anatolie," *Anatolia: Revue Annuelle d'Archéologie* 3 (1958): 115 = Louis Robert, *Opera Minora Selecta: Epigraphie et antiquités grecques,* 7 vols. (Amsterdam: A. M. Hakkert, 1969–90), 1:414: θεῷ ὑψίστῳ καὶ θείῳ αγγελῷ and elsewhere.

6. Mitchell, *Anatolia,* 46. It is precisely the widespread use of such language that creates some severe problems in the indentification of such materials as "pagan," Jewish, or Christian, as Mitchell himself acknowledges. Noting that Jews and pagans in Lydia and Phrygia both worshiped "a wrathful god of Justice, to be appeased not only by adhering to divine law but by songs of praise" and that they shared both religious values and religious terminology, particularly the use of εὐλογία and εὐλογέω (terms that occur twenty-four times in Philonenko's shorter text and thirty-two times in Burchard's longer reconstruction), Mitchell writes: "In such an environment contemporaries may have been as hard pressed as modern scholars to ascertain whether a dedication to the highest god was the work of a pagan or a Jew" (*Anatolia,* 37; see also 48).

7. Mitchell, *Anatolia,* 34, fig. 16: from G. E. Bean, "Notes and Inscriptions from Pisidia, II," *Anatolian Studies* 10 (1960): 70, n. 122; Robert, *BE* 1961: 750, 1965: 412. The inscription is discussed on p. 49, as part of his treatment of the cults of Theos Hypsistos; he argues that the concept of Hagia Katafyge is derived from the Jewish Psalms but offers no specifics.

8. So, once again, Goodenough: "The phenomenon of astralism . . . along with Neoplatonism was becoming the great religious reform of late paganism" (*Jewish Symbols,* 12:152).

9. In addition to various editions of ancient texts, there is an extensive scholarship on Neoplatonism. Classic studies in English include A. H. Armstrong, *Cambridge History of Later Greek and Early Medieval Philosophy* (Cambridge: Cambridge University Press, 1970); R. T. Wallis, *Neoplatonism* (London: Duckworth, 1972); and J. M. Rist, *Plotinus: The Road to Reality* (Cambridge: Cambridge University Press, 1977). More recent studies, with further bibliography, include John Peter Kenney, *Mystical Monotheism: A Study in Ancient Platonic Theology* (New Hampshire: University Press of New England, 1991); A. C. Lloyd, *The Anatomy of Neoplatonism* (Oxford: Clarendon Press, 1990); Gary M. Gurtler, *Plotinus: The Experience of Unity* (New York: Peter Lang, 1989); Robert M. Berchman, *From Philo to Origen: Middle Platonism in Transition* (Chico, CA: Scholars Press, 1984); Robert Lamberton, *Homer the Theologian: Neoplatonic Allegorical Reading* (Berkeley, CA: University of California Press, 1986); Gregory Shaw, *Theurgy and the Soul: The Neoplatonism of Iamblichus* (State College: Pennsylvania State University Press, 1995); R. T. Wallis, ed., *Neoplatonism and Gnosticism* (Albany: State University of New York Press, 1992); see also S. Lilla, "Platonism and the Fathers," *EEC* 2:689–98. Also of interest for many themes of this study is Rowland Smith, *Julian's Gods: Religion and Philosophy in the Thought and Action of Julian the Apostate* (London: Routledge, 1995).

10. Helpful summary of these stances may be found in Alan Scott, *Origen and the Life of the Stars: A History of an Idea* (Oxford: Clarendon Press, 1991); also such older works as E. R. Dodds, *Pagan and Christian in an Age of Anxiety: Some Aspects of Religious Experience from Marcus Aurelius to Constantine* (Cambridge: Cambridge University Press, 1965; reprint, New York: W. W. Norton, 1970), and Franz Cumont, *Astrology and Religion among the Greeks and Romans* (New York: G. P. Putnam's Sons, 1912; reprint, New York: Dover Publications, 1960), particularly the lectures on theology, astral mysticism, and eschatology.

11. Extensive discussion of Greco-Roman astronomical symbols in Goodenough, *Jewish Symbols,* 8:167–218, with conclusions, 219–32. The classic work on the Seasons is G. F. Hanfman, *The Seasons Sarcophagus in Dumbarton Oaks* (Cambridge, MA: Harvard University Press, 1951).

12. For detailed survey of ancient references, see Jessen, "Helios," in *PW* 8:58–96. For a summary of early Greek veneration of the sun (and the moon), see K. Rudolph, "Helios," in *ABD* 3:123–24. H. J. Rose writes that "traces of sun-cult in Greece are few and often uncertain" and his entry under Helios in the *OCD* (2d ed., 1970, 494) is disappointing.

13. 2 Kgs 23.5, translation from J. Glen Taylor, *Yahweh and the Sun: Biblical and Archaeological Evidence for Sun Worship in Ancient Israel,* JSOT Supplement Series 111 (Sheffield: JSOT Press, 1993).

14. 2 Kgs 23.11, translation from Taylor, *Yahweh,* 176. The use of horses and chariots in ancient solar cults is documented in numerous traditions, including Assyria (see Taylor, *Yahweh,* 176–82), but also in Greek sources: "The only god they worship is the sun, to which they sacrifice horses; the idea behind this is to offer to the swiftest of the gods the swiftest of mortal creatures" (Herodotus 1:216, quoted in Reardon, *Ancient Greek Novels,* (562, n. 234). Or this scene from Heliodorus' "Ethiopian Story": "[T]o the Sun they offered a team of four white horses dedicating to the swiftest of the gods, it seems, the swiftest of all mortal creatures; and to the Moon a pair of bullocks" (bk. 10.6). Doubtless, there are numerous others.

15. Ezek 8.16, translation from the NRSV.

16. Taylor, *Yahweh;* see also Morton Smith, "Helios in Palestine," *Eretz Israel* 16 (1982): 199–214, who reviews the earlier evidence and argues here for Essene worship of the Sun at Qumran on the basis of the Temple Scroll. Several first-century C.E. manumission inscriptions from Gorgippia (*CIJ* 690 = *CIRB* 1123; *CIJ* 690a = *CIRB* 1126) that may be Jewish include invocations of Zeus, Helios, and Ge, but as Lifshitz notes ("Prolegomenon," *CIJ* 1:68), such formulas were required legal language and by themselves say nothing about Jewish usage of Helios. (For discussion of whether these are Jewish, see Ross S. Kraemer, "Jewish Tuna and Christian Fish: Identifying Religious Affiliation in Epigraphic Sources," *HTR* 84, no. 2 (1991): 146–47. A doctoral dissertation on Jewish inscriptions from the Crimea was completed as this study was in press: "The Jewish Manumission Inscriptions of the Bosphoran Kingdom," by Leigh Gibson at Princeton University. Other evidence for Jewish usage of such oaths comes from Philo (*On the Special Laws* 2:5) and from rabbinic opposition (*m. Avod. Zar.* 3:3). Smith claims that oaths by the Sun were so common that rabbinic law finally permitted them ("Helios in Palestine," 206). His evidence, though, consists of a reference to Saul Lieberman, *Greek in Jewish Palestine: Studies in the Life and Manners of Jewish Palestine in the II-IV Centuries C.E.* (Philadelphia: Jewish Publication Society, 1942), 137–38, and *Hellenism in Jewish Palestine: Studies in the Literary Transmission, Beliefs, and Manners of Palestine in the I Century B.C.E.–IV Century C.E.* (New York: Jewish Theological Seminary of America, 1950), 214–15. The discussion in the latter repeats and expands on the former, but in both cases his evidence is essentially Maimonides, who says that it is all right to swear by the stars if one has the Creator in mind and that it is like swearing by the sun and having the Lord of the sun in mind. Lieberman believes that Maimonides (*Sepher ha-Mitzvot*) "probably drew from a now lost rabbinic source" (*Hellenism,* 214).

17. *On Dreams* 1:77–119.

18. *On Dreams* 1:77. Interestingly, it is in this passage that Philo mentions Aseneth: "And everyone who has accepted the citizenship of the body, and the name of such is Joseph, chooses for his father-in-law the priest and devotee of Mind. For Moses says that Pharaoh 'gave him Asenath, daughter of Potiphera, priest of Heliopolis'" (1:78). Potiphera as priest of the sun is priest of the Mind. Obviously then, for Philo, the marriage of Joseph to Aseneth poses no enormous difficulty. This exegesis may have considerably more bite to it than might appear here, though, because several sections later, Philo calls the senses "Mind's daughters" (1.88) and basically describes them as whores. As priest of Mind, then, is Potiphera associated with these daughters, and does the taint extend to his daughter as well?

19. *On Dreams* 1:79–84. The sun, upon rising, wakes the senses but plunges into sleep the virtues of justice, knowledge, wisdom, and so forth. Philo argues here that this is why persons are unclean until evening, when sense perception ceases: "[T]he mind also becomes pure because it is darkened by no object of sense" (84).

20. Translation thus far is my own; the remainder follows Colson, *LCL.*

21. E.g., *On the Decalogue,* 53, 60; *On the Cherubim,* 24; *On the Creation of the World,* 46; *On the Special Laws,* 1:14. In the same section from which this last reference comes, Philo makes clear that while some believe the sun, moon, and stars to be absolute gods, Moses believed them to be appointed as rulers (ἄρχοντες) subordinate to God (1:13–14).

22. See Scott, *Origen and the Life of the Stars,* 65; also chap. 4, "The Hellenistic Schoolroom."

23. This is itself complex. This passage comes from his treatise on the Ten Commandments and, as such, might be read as a commentary on Pentateuchal passages that treat astral idolatry (see Taylor, *Yahweh,* 107–14) rather than as a commentary on contemporaneous practice.

24. *On the Decalogue,* 53, from Colson, *LCL,* modified.

25. On Philo's interpretation of the stars, angels, and the soul, see later discussion.

26. E.g., *Pirḳê de Rabbi Eliezer* 6: "The sun has three letters of (God's) Name written upon his heart, and the angels lead him; such as lead him by day do not lead him by night, and such as lead him by night do not lead him by day. The sun rides in a chariot and rises, crowned as a bridegroom, as it is said, 'Which is as a bridegroom coming out of his chamber, and rejoiceth as a strong man to run his course' (Ps. xix. 5)" (trans. Gerald Friedlander, *Pirḳê de Rabbi Eliezer: The Chapters of Rabbi Eliezer the Great* [London, 1916; reprint, New York: Sepher-Harmon Press, 1981], 40). For the position that Helios reverence increases in late antiquity and that Roman Helios worship is not necessarily evidence for earlier practices, see Smith, "Helios in Palestine," 205. Though not definitive, this lends support to my thesis that the centrality of Helios in *Aseneth* may be an indication of its later date.

27. No iconographic representation of Helios appears to have been found for Jews in the West, though Goodenough, *Jewish Symbols,* 8:174, argues that the use of seasons in the ceiling decorations of Jewish catacombs (in the Vigna Randanini and Torlonia) make it highly likely that the same general astral symbolism was in use in the West as well. He also points to Cumont's observation that specific astral signs in the pagan West are also rare. This might suggest that an eastern locale is the more likely setting for the composition of *Aseneth,* but, as I will discuss in chapter 10, that doesn't really tell us much.

28. *Jewish Symbols,* 8:167.

29. A discussion of all the synagogues with mosaics known to Goodenough at the time may be found in *Jewish Symbols,* 1:238–64. Goodenough also discusses the probability of a Helios mosaic in a building excavated by Sukenik at Yafa, which he thinks probably was a synagogue (1:216–18).

30. Dothan, *Hammath Tiberias.*

31. E. L. Sukenik, *The Ancient Synagogue of Beth Alpha* (Jerusalem: University Press; London: Oxford University Press, 1932); see also Marilyn Chiat, *Handbook of Synagogue Architecture,* Brown Judaic Studies 29 (Chico, CA: Scholars Press, 1982), 121–27.

32. M. Avi-Yonah and N. Makhouly, "A Sixth-Century Synagogue at Isfiya," *Quarterly of the Department of Antiquities in Palestine* 3 (1933): 118–31; see also Chiat, *Handbook,* 158–61.

33. E. L. Sukenik, *Ancient Synagogues in Palestine and Greece,* Schweich Lectures of the British Academy, 1930, published for the British Academy by H. Milford (London: Oxford University Press, 1934), 28–31; for additional bibliography, see Goodenough, *Jewish Symbols,* 1:253, n. 513. See also Chiat, *Handbook,* 256–60.

34. Very recently published by Ze'ev Weiss and Ehud Netzer, *Promise and Redemption: A synagogue Mosaic from Sepphoris* (Jerusalem: Israel Museum, 1996) (English and Hebrew).

35. Justin I reigned from 518 to 527 C.E.; Justin II from 565 to 578 C.E.

36. Descriptions and plates in Sukenik, *Beth Alpha;* description and discussion in Goodenough, *Jewish Symbols,* 1:248–51; also 8:167ff.

37. Sukenik, *Beth Alpha,* 35, with additional bibliography.

38. Detailed descriptions and discussion in Dothan, *Hammath Tiberias: Early Synagogues and the Hellenistic and Roman Remains* (Jerusalem: Israel Exploration Society, 1983), 33–52.

39. Interestingly, some of Dothan's arguments for dating the mosaic come from his analysis of the Helios mosaic; see the discussion immediately following.

40. Dothan, *Hammath Tiberias,* 40.

41. Dothan, *Hammath Tiberias,* 40.

42. Dothan, *Hammath Tiberias,* 40.

43. Dothan, *Hammath Tiberias,* 41.

44. Dothan, *Hammath Tiberias,* 41.

45. H. P. L'Orange, *Studies on the Iconography of Cosmic Kingship in the Ancient World,* Instituttet for Sammenlignende Kulturforskning, serie A: Forelesninger 23 (Oslo: H. Aschehoug [W. Nygaard], 1953), 113. His chap. 16 (139–70) is titled "The Gesture of Power: Cosmocrator's Sign."

46. L'Orange, *Cosmic Kingship,* 140.

47. See, e.g., his coins in 309, when Sol becomes his protective deity, in Dothan, *Hammath Tiberias,* 41.

48. Dothan, *Hammath Tiberias,* 140–41; see also 41.

49. L'Orange, *Cosmic Kingship,* 143.

50. L'Orange, *Cosmic Kingship,* 143, n. 6.

51. Numerous examples from H. Mattingly, *Coins of the Roman Empire in the British Museum* (London: Trustees of the British Museum, 1950), 144, n. 1.

52. Citing his own "Sol Invictus Imperator: Ein Beitrag zur Apotheose," *Symbolae Osloenses* 14 (1935).

53. L'Orange, *Cosmic Kingship,* 147, esp. n. 4.

54. L'Orange, *Cosmic Kingship,* 148; see also 152–53. L'Orange argues that beginning in the third century, the fusion of Sol and the emperor is apparent iconographically. Numerous coins, for instance, depict various emperors with the radiant crown, raised right hand, and globe of the Sun. "The type of the emperor with raised right hand on the triumphal chariot shows an especially clear adaption to the chariot-driving Sun of late antiquity" (153). This obviously has important ramifications for the depiction of Joseph as Helios; see later discussion.

55. Dothan, *Hammath Tiberias,* 41.

56. Detailed references and notes in Dothan, *Hammath Tiberias,* 41–42.

57. Dothan, *Hammath Tiberias,* 42.

58. Goodenough concurs in *Jewish Symbols,* 1:256; citing Sukenik, *Synagogues,* 31.

59. Goodenough, *Jewish Symbols,* 1:255, pl. 1b in Sukenik, *Beth Alpha.*

60. Goodenough, *Jewish Symbols,* 1:257–59.

61. Weiss and Netzer, *Promise and Redemption.*

62. A full photograph of the mosaic is in Weiss and Netzer, *Promise and Redemption,* 27, in the Hebrew half of the volume; a smaller photograph may be found on p. 27 of the English version, with a description of the mosaic on pp. 26–28.

63. See, e.g., H. Seyrig, "Le culte du Soleil en Syrie à l'époque romaine," *Syria* 48 (1971): 337–73; G. H. Halsberghe, *The Cult of Sol Invictus,* EPRO 23 (Leiden: E. J. Brill, 1972); R. Turcan, "Le culte impérial au III siècle," *ANRW* II.16.2:996–1084; R. Turcan, *Héliogabale et le sacre du soleil* (Paris: Editions Albin Michel, 1985) (with extensive bibliographies of ancient sources and contemporary studies, including critique of Halsberghe); Fergus Millar, *The Roman Near East, 31 B.C.–A.D. 337* (Cambridge, MA: Harvard University Press, 1993), 300–309 (on Elagabalus, with critique of Turcan's work).

64. See Dothan, *Hammath Tiberias,* 41, and notes.

65. On Julian's solar worship, see esp. Rowland Smith, *Julian's Gods,* esp. 139–63.

66. Tcherikover points out, in his discussion of the Sambathions in *CPJ* 3:43–56, that people with theophoric names often testify more to the religious proclivities of their parents than to their own, to the extent that it is parents who give children their names. This also applies to slaves, whose owners had control over their names (and who were sometimes renamed when they changed hands). Individuals obviously could choose new names to reflect religious choices, and Heliodorus could be a pen name.

67. Translation in Reardon, *Ancient Greek Novels,* with helpful introduction on the possible relationship of this story to solar religion. Recent scholarship has focused on affinities between the Hellenistic novels, including this one, and Christian romances, such as the *Acts of (Paul and) Thecla;* see, e.g., Kate Cooper, *The Virgin and the Bride;* Perkins, *Suffering Self;* Richard I. Pervo, "The Ancient Novel Becomes Christian," in Gareth Schmeling, ed., *The Novel in the Ancient World,* Mnemosyne, Bibliotheca Classica Batava Supplement 159 (Leiden: E. J. Brill, 1996), 685–712. There are also some very general affinities with *Aseneth* in the form of the chastity of the lovers and the fame of the beauty of the heroine; see chapters 1 and 7.

68. *Hymn* 8, to the Sun; see Apostolos N. Athanassakis, *The Orphic Hymns: Text, Translation, and Notes,* Texts and Translations 12, Graeco-Roman Religion Series 4 (Missoula, MT: Scholars Press, 1977), 115, who comments that the sun as charioteer is not found in Homer, though it does appear in some Homeric Hymns (his examples are 2.63, 68, 4.69, 28.14). Other Orphic Hymns also draw on astral imagery, e.g., *Hymn* 9, to the Moon. On the third-century C.E. date for these Orphic Hymns, see Athanassakis *Hymns,* viii, who argues for the second half of the third century as a reasonable guess. Homeric Hymn 31, to Helios, may also be third century C.E. In the fifth century, the Neoplatonic philosopher Proclus also wrote a hymn to the Sun.

69. E.g., *PGM* 3:197–261, 3:494–611, 4:88–93, 4:475–829, 6:1–47, 14:856–75, 875–85, 36:211–30.

70. About Macrobius, little is known, although he is usually identified with a Macrobius cited in the Theodosian Code as vicar of Spain (399), proconsul of Africa (410), and "Grand Chamberlain" (*praepositus sacri cubiculi*) (422); see Percival Vaughan Davies's translation of the Saturnalia, *Macrobius: The Saturnalia* (New York: Columbia University Press, 1969). See also A. Cameron, "The Date and Identity of Macrobius," *JRS* 56 (1966): 25–38. If the author is this Macrobius, his last office title would apparently have compelled him to be a Christian, at least formally, but the Saturnalia itself hardly seems the work of a professing Christian, however elastic that category may have been.

71. Macrobius, *Saturnalia,* 1.17–23.

72. Macrobius, *Saturnalia,* 1.21.18; the whole presentation of the zodiac runs from 1.21.13–1.21.27.

73. Macrobius, *Saturnalia,* 1.23.10.

74. Macrobius, *Saturnalia,* 1.23.12.

75. Summary from E. M. Staerman, "Le culte impérial, le culte du Soleil et celui du

Temps," in Marie-Madeleine Mactoux and Evelyne Geny, eds., *Mélanges Pierre Leveque* 4 (Paris: Les Belles Lettres, 1990), 376, who relies extensively on Macrobius for some of her arguments.

76. Garth Fowden, *Empire to Commonwealth: Consequences of Monotheism in Late Antiquity* (Princeton, NJ: Princeton University Press, 1993), 41. See also Kenney, *Mystical Monotheism.*

77. See, e.g., Averil Cameron, *The Later Roman Empire* (Cambridge, MA: Harvard University Press, 1993), 10–11, for the view that it was not as bad as it seems.

78. Goodenough, *Jewish Symbols,* 1:250.

79. The classic expression of this view is Dodds, *Pagan and Christian.* This work has been much critiqued; see Robert Smith and John Lounibos, *Pagan and Christian Anxiety: A Response to E. R. Dodds* (Lanham, MD: University of America Press, 1984).

80. Goodenough, *Jewish Symbols,* 8:190.

81. Goodenough further notes that the Seasons were so strongly associated with immortality that early Christians used them to represent the Resurrection. Here he proffers Hanfmann's citation of Augustine, *Sermo,* 361, 10 (= PL 39, 1604), and reflects on Hanfmann's observation that the Seasons take on erotic and Dionysiac associations (*Jewish Symbols,* 8:191ff.).

82. Goodenough, *Jewish Symbols,* 8:191–92.

83. Staerman, "Le culte impérial," 371, traces this particularly to astrological components of Greco-Roman mystery religions.

84. See also discussion about astral ideas in Scott, *Origen and the Life of the Stars.* See also discussions of Jewish and Christian ideas about stars as angels and as the righteous dead in previous chapters.

85. Staerman, "Le culte impérial," 371.

86. Staerman, "Le culte impérial," 376. She also argues that this solar imperial theology drew not primarily on foreign, eastern elements but also on Greco-Roman philosophical and popular beliefs (378, also 379), but whether she is correct in this regard is irrelevant for my purposes. Here, I suspect she is combating L'Orange, *Cosmic Kingship,* and perhaps also Ernst H. Kantorowicz, "Oriens Augusti—Lever du Roi," *Dumbarton Oak Papers* 17 (1963): 119–77, who argue for the Eastern roots of solar imperial theology.

87. Staerman, "Le culte impérial," 373.

88. Staerman, "Le culte impérial," 374–75.

89. Staerman, "Le culte impérial," 371, 374, 375. Staerman notes that Helios was the symbol of justice, particularly in Asia Minor, and particularly justice for ordinary people against the power of the elite.

90. This is true, at least to a limited extent, even for Jews and for Christians to some degree, though it is complicated.

91. That this pantheon is masculine is probably not accidental and raises an interesting question. It appears that Macrobius associated all female deities with the Earth and so didn't have to identify them with the Sun in order to produce his One One.

92. Staerman, "Le culte impérial," 376, citing Macrobius, *Commentary on the Dream of Scipio* 1, 1.4–9, but the specific passage cited does not support these claims.

93. The addition here brings the phrase "the gates" into conformity with the earlier reading of "the gates of the courtyard" in 5.4, again consistent with the patterns demonstrated in chapter 3.

94. καὶ ἐδεξιώσατο αὐτοὺς ἐν τῇ δεξιᾷ αὐτοῦ. A more literal translation might be, "[H]e gave them the right hand greeting with his right hand."

95. In Batiffol's text ("Livre"), the ῥάβδος βασιλικὴ is in Joseph's right hand; the olive branch appears to be affixed to the ῥάβδος.

96. See also chapters 2 and 3.

97. See Burchard, "Joseph and Aseneth," 208 n. 5k, who claims that Joseph wears royal attire and that the description is suggested by Genesis but is actually more like Esther 8.15. There, in the LXX/OG, Mordecai wears the robes of the king, with a golden crown and a diadema of purple fine linen. While the descriptions have basic similarities, this is only true to the extent that all these descriptions of clothing have some general basis in royal garments. The portrait of Joseph is in fact different from that of Mordecai in significant ways, as discussed in the main text. Burchard does acknowledge that the twelve stones and the rays are in fact characteristic of Helios and suggests that "[t]he author may remember some statue of Helios or generalize his memory of such statues." But Burchard denies that there is much significance to this portrait: "This does not mean that Joseph is regarded as a god or that Helios is explained as a deification of Joseph. . . . Joseph is not wearing all this of his own right. He is a representative, outwardly of Pharaoh, but really of God, of whom the sun can be a symbol." Obviously, I disagree with Burchard's attempt to minimize the significance of this imagery.

98. Sukenik, *Beth Alpha,* v. frontplate.

99. For references, see Dothan, *Hammath Tiberias,* 41.

100. Dothan, *Hammath Tiberias,* 41.

101. Thus Dothan's description of the color of the cloak. The actual color of the mosaic is closer to red. But in fact, purple (*porphyra*) is often understood as a form of red in antiquity (see e.g., H. J. Rose, "Colours, Sacred," *OCD* 267. In *LSJ* 1452, the verb πορφύρω can mean "to dye something red."

102. Herodian V,3,6, from the *LCL* translation, cited in Millar, *The Roman Near East,* 307. Millar points out that the description is consonant, in general terms, with that known at Hierapolis (from Lucian and a relief sculpture in Syria, in R. A. Stucky, "Prêtres syriens II: Hierapolis," *Syria* 53 [1976]: 127).

103. Dio LXXIX, 11, 1–3. The emperor is also said to have sacrificed young boys.

104. Dothan, *Hammath Tiberias,* 42. He mentions in particular two other relevant exemplars of Helios-Sol: a Christian mosaic beneath St. Peter's (42, n. 226) and a Mithraic painting of Sol from a Mithraeum on the Aventine (42, n. 228).

105. Dothan cites a fifth-century B.C.E. representation on a black-figure *krater* in the Bibliothèque Nationale in Paris, with references from Kantorowicz, "Oriens Augusti," 120, n. 4.

106. See also the detailed discussion of Kantorowicz, "Oriens Augusti."

107. Burchard, "Joseph and Aseneth," 209, n. 5n. See also his previous note on the discrepancies about which hand holds the branch.

108. Kantorowicz, "Oriens Augusti," 123, and nn. 22, 23.

109. Brilliant, "Gesture and Rank," 177–78.

110. For the possibility that the emphasis on olives points to a Christian context, see chapter 9. It may also be possible that Joseph's olive branches signify the victory that laurel also signifies and thus communicate something about Joseph's triumph (over his enemies or over his brothers) and perhaps also his virtue, since, as Brilliant, "Gesture and Rank," points out, the emperor's triumph was associated with beliefs in his virtue.

111. See, e.g., Dothan, *Hammath Tiberias,* 41; L'Orange, *Cosmic Kingship,* chap. 16, "The Gesture of Power: Cosmocrator's Sign"; see also Brilliant, "Gesture and Rank," and Kantorowicz, "Oriens Augusti."

112. S.v. δεξιόομαι (*LSJ* 379).

113. Interestingly, Batiffol's ("Livre") text reads ἐδεξιώσατω αὐτοῦ ἐν τῇ χειρὶ αὐτοῦ, which Brooks translated as "Joseph . . . greeted them with his hand."

114. As usual, there are interesting differences between the shorter and longer versions. At **15.14,** in the longer version only, before she offers a meal to her visitor, **"Aseneth stretched out her right hand and put it on his knees."** At 16.7/**16.13,** we read: "And the figure **smiled at Aseneth's understanding, and called her to himself, and** stretched forth his **right** hand

and took hold of her head **and shook her head with his right hand** . . . and said. . . ." At 16.9/**16.15** the angelic being stretches forth his right hand and breaks off the piece of honey. At 16.10/**16.17**, he stretches out his **right** hand and traces the west to east line; in 16.11/**16.17**, he stretches out his hand a second time and traces the south to north line. In **16:16x,** he stretches out his **right** hand and touches the broken-off portion of the honey comb, and it is restored. The reading of the longer text at 17.3 is particularly interesting: "And the angelic figure **stretched out his hand for the third time and** touched **the damaged part of** the comb." In fact, in the longer version, this is the sixth time the angel has stretched out his right hand in this scene (previously at **16.13, 16.15, 16.16x,** and **16.17,** twice). Conceivably, the origins of the reading lie in the shorter text, which at 16.11/**16.17** explicitly says that the angel stretches out his hand a second time. By itself, this reading makes sense, if it refers merely to the context of the immediate scene, where the angel traces the his finger on the honeycomb. But in the longer text, the designation of the second occurrence in **17.3** as the *third* time the angel stretches out his hand appears to ignore all the occurrences prior to **16.17** and thus to depend on the reading of the shorter text. Further, at 19.3/**19.10,** when Aseneth and Joseph are reunited, they stretch out their hands to each other, apparently both hands. At 20.1, Aseneth takes Joseph's right hand and leads him into her house. At 20.4/**20.5,** Joseph takes Aseneth's **right** hand (and kisses either it or her) and she kisses his head. In **20.5** only, Aseneth then sits at his right. This careful emphasis on right hands may point to the later setting of the longer text. Brilliant ("Gesture and Rank," 163) comments that "[t]he increased potency of the Imperial hand is a symbolic attribute of the fully developed charisma of the absolute Monarch who came to rule the Late Roman Empire and govern the affairs of all civilized men." Brilliant also gives a brief discussion of the conjoined hands as symbols of marital unity.

115. He has a whole section, for instance, on "Jahve's High Hand." See L'Orange, *Cosmic Kingship,* 159–62.

116. Brilliant, "Gesture and Rank," 173–77.

117. This occurs less frequently than one might imagine. See Philonenko, *Joseph et Aséneth,* 189.

118. Philonenko, *Joseph et Aséneth,* 188.

119. Dothan, *Hammath Tiberias,* 40, citing F. Boll, *Sphaera: Neue griechische Texte und Untersuchungen zur Geschichte der Sternbilder* (Berlin, 1903), 121ff., and F. Cumont, *Fouilles de Doura Europos* (Paris 1926), 1:103, 129–32, 2:pls. 17, 50.

120. L'Orange, *Cosmic Kingship,* chap. 1, esp. 15, for a wonderful thirteenth-century Norwegian drawing of Jerusalem in a bifurcated circle. Philonenko, *Joseph et Aséneth,* notes in passing that the liturgical bread used by Mithraic rites were marked by a cross (189, n. to 16, 10–11, citing Franz Cumont, *Les religions orientales,* pl. xiii, no. 2, although I wonder if he has picked the right example for the wrong reason—that it is, in Mithraic symbolism, also a cosmic city map. In the longer version, the drawing of the symbol is preceded by a reference to Aseneth as a walled metropolis, though this duplicates the scene with Aseneth and Joseph later and is not found in the shorter version at this point.

121. It may also allude to the City that Aseneth becomes.

122. Kantorowicz, "Oriens Augusti," 128.

123. Kantorowicz, "Oriens Augusti," 128–29, gives the examples of a relief of Sol with the face of Domitian and a depiction of Caracalla as the Sun God, as well as a solar charioteer in the military garb of an emperor, perhaps Marcus Aurelius. A similar phenomenon occurs in Christian Apocryphal Acts, dated to the second and third centuries C.E., where various characters see Jesus in the form of an apostle, such as Paul in the *Acts of Thecla* 21, or Thomas in the *Acts of Thomas* 11 (here related perhaps to the idea of Thomas as the twin of Jesus).

124. Bohak, *Joseph and Aseneth.*

125. Philonenko, *Joseph et Aséneth,* 65–69.

126. Burchard's note, "Joseph and Aseneth," 230, n. 16f2, cites Philonenko, *Joseph et Aséneth,* 189, but no such discussion occurs there.

127. Burchard, "Joseph and Aseneth," 230, n. 16h2, where he refers to W. Telfer, "'Bees' in Clement of Alexandria," *JTS* 28 (1926–27): 167–78, a generally unsatisfactory discussion.

128. Hélène Chouliara-Raios, *L'abeille et le miel en Egypte d'après les papyrus grecs* (Ioannina, Greece: Universite di Jannina, 1989), 31. I am indebted to this detailed study for much of this portion of the discussion.

129. Chouliara-Raios, *L'abeille,* 33–34. She also claims that as a solar symbol, the bee was regularly associated with royalty.

130. Chouliara-Raios, *L'abeille,* denies that there was an Egyptian bee goddess but subsequently speaks of Artemis of Ephesus's association with bees and of a bee goddess at Ephesus (52–53).

131. Chouliara-Raios, *L'abeille,* 33–34.

132. Citing E. A. Wallis Budge, *The Book of the Dead,* 2d ed. (London: K. Paul, Trench, Trubner; New York: E. P. Dutton, 1923), 147, where the gods respond to Re "en empruntant aux animaux des 'cris' ou des 'bruits' dont le bourdonnement des abeilles."

133. For references, see Chouliara-Raios, *L'abeille,* 53, n. 57.

134. Chouliara-Raios, *L'abeille,* 54–55, with references in the notes.

135. Chouliara-Raios, *L'abeille,* 54, esp. n. 64.

136. Chouliara-Raios, *L'abeille,* 55.

137. Chouliara-Raios, *L'abeille,* 57.

138. Bettini even notes the association of this tradition with the arrival of a future son-in-law; see Maurizío Bettini, "The Bee, the Moth, and the Bat: Natural Symbols and Representations of the Soul," pt. 3 of *Anthropology and Roman Culture: Kinship, Time, Images of the Soul,* trans. John van Sickle, Ancient Society and History (Baltimore: Johns Hopkins University Press, 1991), 217.

139. Bettini, "The Bee, the Moth, and the Bat."

140. Virgil, *Georgics* 4:197–209. Bees do not engage in conjugal intercourse (*quod neque concubitu indulgent*) nor fruitlessly engage their bodies in sexual release (*nec corpora segnes in Venerem solvunt*); the *LCL* translation reads, "nor idly unnerve their bodies in sexual love." I confess that I don't precisely understand the implication of *segnes* here, but for our purposes, the general meaning of the passage is clear enough. Nor do they bring forth offspring in labor (*aut fetus nixibus edunt*). Rather Virgil claims that the bees (female: *ipsae*) themselves gather their children in their mouths from leaves and sweet herbs.

141. Bettini, "The Bee, the Moth, and the Bat," 201.

142. She points out that the Hebrew for Bee (*devorah*) is derived from the root meaning word or speech. Chouliara-Raios, *L'abeille,* 58.

143. Bettini, "The Bee, the Moth, and the Bat," 200, with various references on 305, n. 8. Numerous helpful references on bees in Greek traditions are collected and discussed by A. B. Cook, "The Bee in Greek Mythology," *Journal of Hellenic Studies* 15 (1895): 1–24.

144. For the various references, see Cook, "Bee," 11–14. Particularly provocative here is his suggestion that a special diet enjoined on devotees to Artemis at Orchomenos and Ephesus entailed abstinence from meat and consumption of honey (13), precisely the configuration in *Aseneth.* See also Hilda H. Ransome, *The Sacred Bee in Ancient Times and Folklore* (London: Allen and Unwin, 1937; reprint, Bridgwater, Eng., 1986).

145. *PGM* 5:6–7; also *PSI* 28, l. 57, from Ashmounein, third or fourth C.E., cited in Chouliara-Raios, *L'abeille,* 61.

146. *B. Hag.* 11b.

147. *On the Cave of the Nymphs,* 15, cited in Cook, "Bee," 22–23. Particularly interesting, à propos of Mithraism, is a red jasper cameo whose reverse depicts a bee (as the symbol of the

soul) in the mouth of a lion, surrounded by seven stars and Greek "magical" inscriptions. See Franz Cumont, *The Mysteries of Mithra,* trans. Thomas J. McCormack (New York: Dover Publications, 1956), 185, fig. 42; see also Franz Cumont, *Textes et monuments figurés relatifs aux mystères de Mithra* (Brussels: H. Lamertin, 1899), 450.

148. Or perhaps pure souls (*haustus aetherios*). This portion of the translation is my own.

149. Virgil, *Georgics,* 4:226–27. *Scilicet huc reddi deinde ac resoluta referri omnia, nec morti esse locum, sed viva volare sideris in numerum atque succedere caelo.*

150. Virgil, *Georgics,* 4:281–314.

151. Virgil, *Georgics,* 4:554–58.

152. Bettini, *Anthropology,* 199, from Porphyry, *On the Cave of the Nymphs,* 795. N. Thomas Taylor translated this passage thus: "All souls, however, proceeding into generation, are not simply called bees, but those who will live in it justly, and who, after having performed such things as are acceptable to the Gods, will again return [to their kindred stars]. For this insect loves to return to the place from whence it first came, and is eminently just and sober" (*Porphyry, On the Cave of the Nymphs,* trans. Thomas Taylor [1758–1835], with an introduction by Kathleen Raine [Grand Rapids, MI: Phanes Press, 1991], 42).

153. However, we may see hints of this in Virgil, *Aeneid* 6:703–18. There, Aeneas sees a grove and forests and the river Lethe drifting by: "About it hovered peoples and tribes unnumbered [*hunc circum innumerae gentes populique volabant*]." His (dead) father Anchises tells him that these are spirits (*animae*) to whom fate owes another incarnation (*animae, quibus altera fato corpora debentur*)—that is, these are souls awaiting reincarnation. While Virgil does not equate these souls with bees, he compares the hovering spirits to bees in meadows in cloudless summer days who light on various blossoms, so that the whole field murmurs with their humming. Bettini, "The Bee, the Moth, and the Bat," 198–99, seems to think that Virgil's use of this simile was quite intentional; he suggests that Virgil "had good reason to chose the simile he did to represent the souls on the verge of reincarnation." But the hard evidence for the confluence of associations seems to come from Porphyry, and Bettini appears to be reading Porphyry into Virgil, I think.

154. Raine, Introduction to *Porphyry,* 11–12.

155. Porphyry, *Nymphs,* 7 (38–41 in Raine's edition of Taylor's translation).

156. Porphyry, *Nymphs,* 8 (41–42 in Raine's edition of Taylor's translation).

157. Porphyry, *Nymphs,* 8 (42 in Raine's edition of Taylor's translation).

158. Porphyry, *Nymphs,* 8 (42 in Raine's edition of Taylor's translation).

159. At 4.2/**4.1,** 4.10/**4.8,** 15.5/**15.6,** 15.10, (21.3 retroverted).

160. "Hence also it is customary to call wedded wives νύμφαι, since they are united to us for purposes of child-bearing, and to bathe them with lustral water taken from wells or streams or ever-flowing fountains" (Porphyry, *Nymphs* 12, here translated by Cook, "Bees," 16).

161. See chapter 2.

162. See chapter 3; I reproduce the texts here for convenience: "And Aseneth stood to the left and observed everything the figure did. **And the figure said to the comb, 'Come.'** And bees came up out of the (hive) **cells** of the comb, **and the cells were innumerable, ten thousand (times) ten thousand and thousands upon thousands** and they were white as snow, and their wings were purple and the color of hyacinth and **like scarlet stuff and** as golden thread, and there were gold diadems on their heads and sharp stingers **and they would not injure anyone.** And all the bees entwined around Aseneth from (her) feet to (her) head, and other bees were, (as) large **and chosen like their** (as) queens (bees), **and they rose (from the damaged part of) the comb and** attached themselves to Aseneth's **mouth and made upon her mouth and lips(.) a comb similar to the comb which was lying before the figure. And all those bees ate of the comb which was on Aseneth's mouth.** And the figure said to the bees, 'Go then away to your own place.' (And they all left Aseneth) and **all the bees rose and flew and**

went away into heaven. And those who wanted to injure Aseneth (all) fell down to the ground and died. And the figure **stretched out his staff over the dead bees and** said **to them** 'Arise **you, too** and go (back) **away** to your place.' And (they) **the bees who had died** rose up and went away, (all of them), to the courtyard adjacent to Aseneth**'s house and sought shelter on the fruit-bearing trees."**

163. This second scenario may also relate to ideas about righteous and fallen angels, but this is not definitive.

164. Bettini, "The Bee, the Moth, and the Bat," 202, citing Aristotle, *Gen. a.* 759b and Augustine, *City of God* 15.27.4.

165. *Porphyry to Marcella* 33, in Kathleen Wicker, *Porphyry the Philosopher to Marcella: Text and Translation with Introduction and Notes* (Atlanta: Scholars Press, 1987).

166. "[The spirits of the stars] were standing like fiery sparks around the chariots of the Omnipresent One. What did Metatron do? At once he clapped his hands and chased them all from their places. Immediately they flew up on wings of flame and fled to the hour sides of the throne of the chariot." *3 Enoch* 43 also utilizes relevant imagery: "R. Ishmael said: Metatron said to me: 'Come and I will show you the souls of the righteous who have already been created and have returned, and the souls of the righteous who have not yet been created.'" See chapter 5.

167. Cook, "Bee," 19–20.

168. On Christian solar imagery, see particularly Kantorowicz, "Oriens Augusti," 137–52. In the *Acts of Philip* 95 (perhaps fourth century C.E.), Christ explicitly calls himself ὁ τῆς δικαοισύνης ἥλιος (the sun of righteousness).

169. The identification of Joseph/Helios with Christ might seem to presuppose Christian appropriation of the empire and of imperial imagery and thus be more suited to the mid–fourth century. I will discuss the possibility of Christian composition of *Aseneth* extensively in chapter 9.

170. See Anthony Meredith, "Porphyry and Julian against the Christians," *ANRW* II.23.2:1119–49; see also A. Smith, "Porphyrian Studies since 1913," *ANRW* II.36.2:717–73.

171. Frag. 43, from Jerome, *Commentary on Daniel.* For discussion of the originality of Porphyry's critique, see Meredith, "Porphyry and Julian," 1132–34.

172. Meredith, "Porphyry and Julian," 1133.

173. *Church History,* 6.19.3–9, citing Porphyry's third book of *Against the Christians.*

174. One might also ponder the significance of Porphyry's Syrian birth for his knowledge of Semitic languages.

175. Ruth Majercik, *The Chaldean Oracles: Text, Translation, and Commentary,* Studies in Greek and Roman Religion 5 (Leiden: E. J. Brill, 1989), 27. See also the description in Wallis, *Neoplatonism,* 107.

176. Scholars of Neoplatonic theurgy have identified significant differences between theurgic practices and interpretation as set forth in the *Chaldean Oracles* (which functioned as scripture for many Neoplatonists) on the one hand, and its subsequent expression in Porphyry, Iamblichus, Proclus, and so forth, on the other. See, e.g., Wallis, *Neoplatonism,* 100–110; Georg Luck, "Theurgy and Forms of Worship in Neoplatonism," in Jacob Neusner, Ernst Frerichs, and Paul Virgil McCracken Flesher, eds., *Religion, Science, and Magic: In Concert and in Conflict* (New York: Oxford University Press, 1989), 185–225; Sarah Iles Johnston, "Rising to the Occasion: Theurgic Ascent in Its Cultural Milieu," in Peter Schäfer and Hans G. Kippenberg, eds., *Envisioning Magic: A Princeton Seminar and Symposium* (Leiden: E. J. Brill, 1997), 165–94.

177. I consider Chesnutt's dismissal (*From Death to Life,* 210) of these affinities erroneous and unfortunate. He argues, against Howard Kee, that in the *hekhalot* traditions, hymns and prayers serve a theurgical function that they "obviously" do not in *Aseneth.* Chesnutt asserts here that "there is no hint that [Aseneth's] prayers represent a tradition wherein ecstasy is

induced or a mystical or relevatory experience is sought or enhanced by means of prayer." I totally disagree.

178. *Chaldean Oracles,* frag. 132, cited in Johnston, "Theurgic Ascent," 176; see also Johnston, 185–86, where she discusses the significance of admonitions to silence in the Mithras Liturgy, which she considers to be essentially theurgic.

179. *PGM* 4:747, cited in Johnston, "Theurgic Ascent," 179.

180. Johnston, "Theurgic Ascent," 179.

181. *Chaldean Oracles,* frag. 123, in Johnston, "Theurgic Ascent," 181; here she also cites frag. 122, where the *angeloi* help "the soul of the theurgist separate from his body by causing it to shine with fire."

182. *Chaldean Oracles,* frag. 115, in Johnston, "Theurgic Ascent," 182. For further development of solar motifs, see Johnston, "Theurgic Ascent," 181–83.

183. The Samson cycle itself appears to have solar associations, something noted by Ransome, *Sacred Bee,* 66, within the context of her discussion of Samson and the bees in 1 Sam 14.5–9. Samson's name (שִׁמְשׁוֹן) appears to mean "little sun," Manoah lives near Beth Shemesh, which may be translated as "house (or temple) of the Sun," and so forth (see also James L. Crenshaw, "Samson," in *ABD* 5:950). Such an association renders the use of the narrative in Judges 13 as the subtext for *Aseneth* particularly intriguing.

184. Smith, *Julian's Gods,* 154.

185. However, he does have a conversation with Jacob that is similar to that in *Aseneth;* see chapter 2.

186. *On Abstinence,* bk. 2; see also Wallis, *Neoplatonism,* 109.

187. Johnston, "Theurgic Ascent," 174.

188. Johnston, "Theurgic Ascent," 174.

189. Majercik, *Chaldean Oracles,* 24; see also Wallis, *Neoplatonism,* 108.

190. Majercik, *Chaldean Oracles,* 22.

191. Majercik, *Chaldean Oracles,* 22–23, citing Iamblichus, *On the Mysteries* 1:12, 14, 2:6, 11, 3:1, 10, 18, 4:2.

192. *Chaldean Oracles,* frag. 142, in Johnston, "Theurgic Ascent," 170, where Hekate "explains that, although the gods have no true form that mortals can comprehend, they graciously assume comprehensible forms when they make their epiphanies out of consideration for the theurgists."

193. Wallis, *Neoplatonism,* 109–10.

194. Johnston, "Theurgic Ascent," 175.

195. See esp. Meredith, *"Porphyry and Julian"*; Wallis, "Anti-Christian Polemic and the Problem of Theurgy" in *Neoplatonism,* 100–110; A. H. Amstrong, "Man in the Cosmos: A Study of Some Differences between Pagan Neoplatonism and Christianity," in W. den Boer et al., eds., *Romanitas et Christianitas: Studia Iano Henrico Waszink* (Amsterdam: North Holland Publishing Co., 1973), 5–14, reprinted in A. H. Armstrong, *Plotinian and Christian Studies* (London: Variorum, 1979), chap. 22.

196. See, e.g., Mary T. Clark, "The Neoplatonism of Marius Victorinus the Christian," in H. J. Blumenthal and R. A. Markus, eds., *Neoplatonism and Early Christian Thought: Essays in Honour of A. H. Amstrong* (London: Variorum, 1981), 153–59, where she writes: "These few considerations of the Trinitarian theology of Marius Victorinus indicate that he did not think that his Christian faith required him to alter in any radical way the Neoplatonism of his day" (158).

CHAPTER SEVEN

Why Is Aseneth a Woman?

The Use and Significance of Gender in the Aseneth Stories

Although the protagonist of *Aseneth* is most certainly a woman and although tales of exemplary women are hardly the norm in the corpus of Hellenistic Jewish literature,[1] until very recently studies of *Aseneth* have given little consideration to issues of gender.[2] This statement, I should note, should hardly be taken as a tacit concession that *Aseneth* is Jewish—I frame my observation in this way primarily because other scholars consider it such. Yet what significance, if any, attaches to Aseneth's gender in these tales? Or to phrase it slightly differently, when is a text about a woman a text about a woman?

Stories that appear to be about a woman, or women, may, hypothetically, be about any number of things. They may be about a real woman or real women, or they may be fictionalized accounts of real women's experiences. Alternatively, they may utilize the device of allegory, whereby female characters represent something other than real women—the soul, for instance, or the people of Israel. Or stories of women may in fact be centrally concerned with constructions of gender, particularly female gender. And, of course, many stories may be an amalgamation of two or more of these possibilities.

No study of *Aseneth* has seen it as a story of a real woman, at least if that is taken to mean a historical, biographical account of the marriage of Joseph and Aseneth in Egypt during the late second millenium B.C.E. But it might be read as a thinly disguised narrative of women's lives and experiences. From this perspective, many elements in the text can be read as a thinly veiled portrait of elite life in the author's time and social community. The portrait of the daughter raised in seclusion, of familial relationships, of clothing, of food, and of household arrangements all might reflect social realia. Perhaps most important, according to this approach, Aseneth's transformation, which, as I have remarked earlier, most scholars unreflectively label as "conversion,"[3] is best understood as a fictionalized narrative of conversion experiences and rituals undergone by actual non-Jews adopting Judaism. Indeed, in my own previous work,[4] I took essentially such a stance, analyzing *Aseneth* as a reflection of both the real experiences of female converts to Greek-speaking Jewish communities in the earliest centuries of the Common Era and attitudes toward women and women proselytes prevalent in at least some circles in those communities.

Yet many interpreters have treated ancient stories about women as essentially allegorical: while seeming to be tales of female protagonists, they are really "about" something else. Judith, for example, is seen to be fundamentally a tale about Israel: Judith (whose name may be translated simply as "Jew-ess") is simply Israel feminized, a metaphor frequently utilized in the Hebrew Bible, particularly when Israel is set in relation to a masculine God. Similarly, some scholars would read *Aseneth* as allegory: while seeming to be a tale about the transformation of Aseneth and her subsequent marriage to Joseph, it is "really" about the purification of the "soul," or about Wisdom, or, as Gideon Bohak has recently proposed, about the purification of a Jewish temple built in Egypt at Leontopolis in the second century B.C.E. by a group of dissident Jerusalem priests on the site of a former temple to the Egyptian goddess Bast.[5]

Viewed in this way, the relationship between a story about a woman and real women becomes problematic in the extreme. At one level, if the story is "merely" an allegory, then nothing it says is "really" about women, and it would be foolish for modern interpreters to attempt to read it as such. And indeed, Bohak's dissertation makes no attempt to read the story as a text about a woman or about women: Aseneth's gender in the tale is a byproduct of the feminine gender of certain ancient terms and perhaps of a tradition of the female personification of cities, temples, and so forth and may be left otherwise unanalyzed.

While it is not inherently impossible that the choice of a woman as the protagonist of *Aseneth* is primarily grounded in the (conveniently but arbitrarily?) feminine gender of the particular phenomenon the author wishes to explore (such as Wisdom or the Soul), such analysis is insufficient, particularly given the relative rarity of such texts in antiquity. On the other hand, the preceding chapters have revealed a sufficient degree of artifice in the construction of these texts to raise serious questions about the correspondence between the Aseneth of the texts and real women's experiences in the ancient world.

If neither allegory nor representation of social practice accounts for this tale of a woman, there is another option, one made clearer by recent studies on late Hellenistic and early Christian fiction, romances in which female protagonists play central roles. Stories seemingly about women may rather be particularly reflective of ancient conversations about gender, that is, meanings ascribed to the categories male and female, meanings that are neither fixed nor uniform but are themselves the products of cultural activity and therefore variable. In such stories, women characters may serve a variety of functions. They may represent their authors' ideal women (who may have little connection to real women, ordinary or otherwise). Moreover, as some recent studies have suggested, they may in fact function as stand-ins for male authors and readers, a heuristic device by which ancient men explored concerns about identity and gender.[6]

An excellent example of such an approach may be found in A.-J. Levine's reading of the Book of Tobit as a tale in which the proper subjugation and domiciling of women serves as the vehicle to express and resolve anxiety about something else—in this case the conditions of diaspora.[7] In Tobit, a young woman named Sarah is the unwilling object of affection of a demon that kills every man Sarah marries, thwarting the attempts of Sarah and her family to achieve a proper and fruitful marriage for her. In Levine's analysis, the story of Sarah and her eventual husband, Tobias, becomes the medium for discussion of the larger question of how Jews in the diaspora can reproduce and flourish. Levine argues that by exaggerating various representations of difference, boundaries, and definitions and then resolving them, Tobit symbolically restores order to a potentially disordered diaspora existence, an order that is further guaranteed by adherence to certain social practices and norms.

For Levine, central to Tobit is the substitution of geneaology for geography.

> In order to distinguish the Israelites from the Gentile, the Book of Tobit advances a program centered on endogamy. Women properly domiciled in an endogamous relationship become the means by which the threat of the diaspora is eliminated. That territorial relations are displaced onto gender relations is reinforced by the manner in which hierarchical, value-laden gender differences structure the novella.[8]

> By constraining women's roles, by using women as tokens of exchange to preserve economic and kinship ties, by depicting them as the cause as well as the locus of despair, and by removing them from direct contact with heaven, the Jewish male has brought order to his diaspora existence. In captivity, he can assert his freedom and his self-identity by depicting the other as in captivity to him. With boundaries redefined in relation to as well as upon bodies, Tobit's family is more stable than the world of the exile.[9]

While Levine does not rule out the possibility that elements of Tobit reflect actual social experience, she is clear in this article that the story of Sarah and Tobias is not primarily a story of how marriages are made. While I do not think that the marriage of Joseph and Aseneth in our texts addresses the same concerns Levine detects here,[10] her analysis does suggest some of the ways in which a story about a woman might be only indirectly about women.

What, then, is the significance of Aseneth being female? Although I am no longer confident that it points to a simple correlation with actual female experience, what we may have here is complicated interplay between social reality, ancient constructions of gender, and allegory as well, with significant, if subtle, differences between the shorter and longer versions. In this chapter, then, I would like to consider some of the ways in which constructions of gender are utilized in both the shorter and longer texts before reconsidering the degree to which *Aseneth* is likely to tell us anything about the experiences of real women in the Greco-Roman world of any religious community, geographic location, or specific time period.

Gender and Aseneth's Transformation from Dangerous Foreign Woman to *Theosebēs Gynē*

Paramount among the aspects of Aseneth's transformation is her change from a foreign (Egyptian) idolater, wholly unsuitable as a wife for a man who reveres God (a *theosebēs anēr*), to the diametric opposite: a pious woman (*theosebēs gynē*) who herself worships only the same God and renounces all her former idolatry. To phrase it slightly differently, the story of Aseneth recounts her transformation from the Other to the Self, viewed of course from the perspective of the author(s), who here clearly identifies with the household and community of Joseph.

Aseneth's otherness has many dimensions. She not only worships Egyptian gods but also embodies her otherness by wearing emblems of her idolatry on her clothing and jewelry and eating food unacceptable to "Hebrews." Nowhere in this text is this otherness more forcefully conveyed than in the scene where Joseph prevents Aseneth from kissing him (in obedience to her father's instructions) by holding her at arm's length and saying the following words:

8.5–7
It is not appropriate for a man who reveres God [a *theosebēs anēr*] who blesses the living God with his mouth and eats the blessed bread of life and drinks the blessed cup of immortality and is anointed with the blessed ointment of incorruptibility, to kiss a foreign woman, one who blesses dead and deaf idols with her mouth and eats the bread of strangling from their table and drinks the cup of ambush from their libations and is anointed with the ointment of perdition. But a man who reveres God [a *theosebēs anēr*] will kiss his mother; and his sister **by his mother and his sister** who is of his own tribe and family; and his wife, who shares his bed; those women who with their mouths bless the living God. Similarly, also it is not appropriate for a woman who reveres God [a *theosebēs gynê*] to kiss a strange man, because such is an abomination before **the Lord** God.

In this passage, the Self and the Other are clearly differentiated with respect to food, worship, and physical contact, both sexual and filial.

Aseneth's otherness has additional components. She is ignorant in her idolatry and her slandering of Joseph, insolent toward her father, and arrogant in her hatred of men. Her transformation from Other to Self incorporates all of these elements. At the conclusion of the story, Aseneth worships the living God, eats proper food, and wears pristine, primordial garments devoid of idolatrous images. She displays her newly acquired wisdom in appropriate ways: in her humility before her father (and mother) and in her subordination to her husband, Joseph, whose feet she washes and whose commands she obeys.

The significance of gender in the representation of Aseneth's transformation should not be underestimated. In the first place, it is the Other, the Egyptian, who is here represented by a woman, while the Self, the one who reveres God, is represented by a man.[11] Given the story's grounding in the tale we have now in Genesis, this assignment may seem inevitable and unremarkable. However, this begs the question of whether the foreigner is a woman because Joseph is said to have married an Egyptian or whether the story of Joseph and Aseneth receives such extensive articulation precisely (though certainly not only) because it offers the opportunity to elaborate upon the transformation of a woman. The choice of a woman as the exemplar of one transformed (or even "converted"), most familiar in the biblical story of Ruth, may reflect an idea of woman as a more natural exemplar of the Other and therefore as a better candidate for transformation. The ideal transformation narrative, then, may well be one that utilizes gender as a central component of difference.[12]

Both Joseph and Aseneth are described in language that is sometimes significantly gender-specific. Joseph is not only *dunatos* or powerful—an attribute of God in 8.10—he is *anēr dunatos en sophia kai epistēmē,* a man strong (or powerful) in wisdom and knowledge. He is called *sōphrōn* or wise, temperate, reasonable—one of the cardinal virtues of the Greek (male) philosopher. (*Sōphrosynē* is also applied to women, but usually with different connotations, primarily of chastity.) This wisdom and temperance is manifest in, among other things, his ability to remain chaste despite the temptations of seductive Egyptian women and to refuse Pentephres' offer of additional hospitality in order to continue with his task of collecting grain.

In contrast to Joseph's wisdom and self-control, Aseneth is miserable and foolish (*aphrōn kai thraseia*). Her initial failure to perceive the truth about Joseph and her acceptance of false Egyptian gossip about him exemplify her ignorance, a stereotypical trait of women in ancient sources. In other words, not only is Joseph obviously male and Aseneth obviously female, but in her initial state, Aseneth exemplifies the most negative aspects of ancient constructions of the feminine, while Joseph exemplifies virtuous masculinity. The only exception to this concerns Aseneth's sexuality: she, like Joseph, is chaste from beginning to end. But since the outcome of the story must be Aseneth's marriage to Joseph and the conception and birth of their sons, Manasseh and Ephraim, that is probably the one characteristic that the story cannot manipulate.

Aseneth's transformation utilizes gender in yet another central way. At the outset, Aseneth is not only a woman but also, in several respects, the wrong sort of woman. Despite the (reconstructed) reading that Aseneth was in no way like the daughters of the Egyptians but in all ways like the daughters of the Hebrews, Aseneth lacks the virtues of the Israelite matriarchs and is initially arrogant, unsubmissive, and disdainful of men.

Even in small details, the text(s) may draw upon prevailing ancient gender constructions. When Joseph refuses to kiss Aseneth, as Pentephres has instructed, Aseneth breaks into tears and gazes intently at Joseph. Many ancient authors claim that the gaze of a woman was sexual and highly dangerous to men and insisted that proper women should never look directly at a man. Typical is Sirach 26.9: "The licentiousness of a woman is made known by her raised gaze and by her eyelids."[13] Aseneth's action here may thus contribute to her pretransformation portrait as an insolent foreign woman. It may also, however, be intended to intensify the portrait of Aseneth as a woman overcome with sexual desire, although less so in the shorter text, where such a portrait is as false an image of Aseneth as her initial slanders are of Joseph. And of course, the two readings are by no means mutually exclusive.

After her transformation, Aseneth is the epitome of the good woman: she is submissive, willing if necessary to be servile, appropriately affectionate toward men, the ideal wife and, soon, mother. This, by the way, may point not so much toward a conception of the Other as woman as to a characterization of the Other in which "their" women are not properly submissive and do not conform to appropriate gender categories, whereas "our" women are and do.

Such an analysis tempers other readings of the story, such as that by Doty in which Aseneth's transformation is viewed as the ultimate result of a personal quest for self-knowledge and redemption. Doty reads this tale as that of a female protagonist who gains the knowledge and insight that lead to personal transformation, comparable to quest narratives for male heroes.[14] Her analysis is problematic not the least because the final outcome of Aseneth's story is the traditional ending for tales of women—marriage to the hero. But even if *Aseneth* has elements of ancient quest narratives, we must still acknowledge that the catalyst of her transformation is a male authority figure and that Aseneth's initial response to her newly acquired wisdom is to pray to be subservient to that male figure for the rest of eternity:

13.12/**13.15**

Deliver me to [Joseph] as a servant **and slave,** (that) **and** I (may) **will make his bed and** wash his feet and wait on him **and be a slave to him** and serve him for all the rest of my life.

In a hierarchical system at which Joseph stood at the top, Aseneth hopes only to assume a position at the very bottom, the precise antithesis of the social position she held only instants earlier as the virgin daughter of an aristocratic family who aspired to marry the (false) son of (the false) God.

I have argued in several preceding chapters that Aseneth's desire to assume the position of slave or servant may be read as an integral part of narratives that depict the encounter between humans and angelic or other divine beings and the formulas for such encounters. In virtually all of these examples, the human assuming the status of slave or servant is male (perhaps because Aseneth is one of the few nonbiblical depictions of an encounter between a woman and an angel). Certainly, for later Christian readers of the story, the pious person who seeks to be a slave to God was in the company of such exemplars as the apostle Paul himself. This may appear to suggest, then, that Aseneth's desire to subordinate herself to Joseph has no particular significance with regard to gender. On the contrary, however, I wish to suggest that it is precisely the construction of feminine gender as subordinate and submissive that is at work in this imagery. Before the masculine God, or angel, or other powerful divine emanation, petitioners are as women and as slaves, whose status itself incorporates an element of gender differentiation, for in their relation to their owners, slaves, too, assumed the role of women in relation to men. Nowhere is this perhaps more apparent than in the matter of sexual behavior, whereby male slave owners easily availed themselves of the sexual services of both male and female slaves.[15] For a woman, then, the acquisition of wisdom appears to include recognition and acceptance of her subordinate status.

Veiling and Unveiling

While gender thus plays a significant role in the presentation of Aseneth's transformation, it is actually an explicit element once, in both the shorter and longer reconstructions at 15.1. In this scene, Aseneth has just returned to the angel's presence, having followed his instructions in 14.12–13 to take off her mourning clothes, shake off the residue from the mud, wash her face in living water, and dress in pristine garments. Aseneth has, however, done one thing the angel did not specify: she has covered her head with a beautiful veil.

When she stands before the angel, he remarks on this immediately: "Lift off the veil from your head, because today you are a holy virgin, and your head is as a young man's."[16] Aseneth complies, and nothing further is said about the veil. After the angel departs, Aseneth will again change her clothing, this time into a purified version of the garments she wore at the outset, and will again cover her head with a veil.

The very words of the angel himself signal that Aseneth's transformation includes at least a temporary change in her gender identity. One possibility, favored by Philonenko, is that the author intended here to signify Aseneth's androgyny, which characterizes the status of initiates in many religious traditions. If so, this verse presumes a social system in which Aseneth's veil symbolizes her gender (and probably also her place within ancient social hierarchy), whereas the absence of the veil symbolizes her distancing from her gender and her (temporary) removal from that same hierarchy. Here we may also have a more specific allusion to the state of the primordial being in Genesis 1.26–27, understood to have been initially without gender discrimination.[17]

Alternatively, the author may have intended to signify Aseneth's transformation into neutral masculinity. Numerous ancient texts utilize the metaphor of becoming male as a stage in the salvation of the soul, which is, as we have noted before, feminine in Greek. Although most of the examples are demonstrably Christian, Philo utilized this metaphor extensively, particularly in his account of the women among the monastic Jewish Therapeutic society.[18] Interestingly, though, particularly in light of the possible associations of *Aseneth* with Neoplatonic imagery, is the fact that this motif also occurs in Porphyry, in his letter to his wife, Marcella, which exhorts her to continue in the philosophic life during his prolonged absence.

> So then, if we should rise above their witchcraft and guard against their seductive snare, we have enchained what has enchained us. Therefore, do not be overly concerned about whether your body is male or female; do not regard yourself as a woman, Marcella, for I did not devote myself to you as such. Flee from every effeminate element of the soul as if you are clothed in a male body. For the most blessed offspring come from virginal soul and unmated Intelligence.[19]

It is also of interest that Paul's arguments about women's headcoverings are explicitly supported by his exegesis of the creation of human beings in Genesis 1–3. In 1 Corinthians 11.7, he argues: "For a man ought not to have his head veiled/covered, since he is the image and reflection/glory [*doxa*] of God; but woman is the reflection/glory [*doxa*] of man," interpreting Genesis 1.26–27 with Genesis 2.21–25. For Paul, creation establishes a divine hierarchy of God–man–woman, which he believed had to be preserved in human social relationships as well. If the author of this passage in *Aseneth* had similar concepts in mind, we might infer that because Aseneth's head is today like that of a young man, it is inappropriate for her to cover her head. For the moment, at least, Aseneth stands in a human–divine hierarchy as though she were male and as the direct image of the divine, as the primordial *anthrōpos* in Genesis 1.26–27 was the direct image or glory of God and perhaps also androgynous.

Aseneth may thus share with the writings of Philo, many Christian texts, and ancient philosophical traditions, particularly those we now call Neoplatonic, a construction of gender in which one's sex was not unconditionally and irrevocably identical with one's gender. Although usually one and the same, gender and biological sex could be, and sometimes were, separable. Consider, for instance, the saying attributed (in the fifth century C.E.) to the desert mother Sarah, "According to nature I am a woman, but not according to my thoughts," or her reputed remark to some male monks, "It is I who am a man, you who are women."[20] But as Amma Sarah's last remark makes clear, such transference still retains the values accorded to masculine and feminine: when Sarah sees herself as male, it is positive, whereas her designation of the monks as women is almost certainly an insult. Whether this suggests that Amma Sarah (or any other female ascetic) was not the origin of this saying, I cannot say.[21]

In this same vein, we might also consider a narrative in the *Acts of Thomas* concerning a newly married young royal couple.[22] The night of their wedding, Jesus, in the form of his twin brother, the apostle Judas Thomas, appears in their bridal chamber before they can consummate the marriage and dissuades them from doing so, persuading them instead to adopt permanent chastity. The next morning, the bride is found sitting uncovered. Her mother, seeing her this way, asks why she sits with her husband, unashamed, as though long-married, an inquiry seconded by her father.[23] The bride responds: "That I do not veil myself is because the mirror of shame has been taken away from me: I am no longer ashamed or abashed, since the work of shame and bashfulness has been removed from me."[24] Here, as in *Aseneth* 15.1, sexuality and veiling are clearly linked: the unveiled woman is "asexual."

Aseneth as Potential Medium of Exchange between Men

In an important article written over twenty years ago, Gayle Rubin illuminated the centrality of what she called "the traffic in women," systems of exchange in which men give their female kin to other men as wives (and take someone else's kin as their own wives) in complicated interactions whose primary function is the establishment and solidification of bonds between men.[25] This model explicates at least one feature of the *Aseneth* stories, a feature that has, I think, been misread by some earlier interpreters, namely the significance of the sister/wife terminology. It suggests that ancient practices of calling wives "sisters" may be rooted in systems of exchange, where men exchange "sisters" (female relatives) for "wives" and take for their own wives someone else's sister. Seen through the lens of exchange, a wife is also a sister—though with the exception of true sibling marriage in ancient Egypt, rarely one's own.

Beyond this interesting but relatively minor insight, to what extent is the theory of "traffic in women" useful in analyzing *Aseneth*? Although the story may be read as the exchange of Aseneth between her father, Pentephres, and her husband, Joseph, numerous elements in the plot complicate this reading. One would have expected the transfer of Aseneth to involve a transaction either between the fathers of the couple (Jacob and Pentephres) or the groom and the father of the bride—this last, for instance, is the language of many Jewish marriage documents of this period, to the extent that these are extant. Yet both of the biological fathers in the tale, Jacob and Pentephres, are somewhat squeezed out of the transaction, which is, in fact, characterized as one between Joseph and Pharaoh. At the very point where Pentephres offers to make the wedding for Aseneth and Joseph, Joseph refuses, insisting that Pharaoh (whom he calls, in the shorter text, his father) must be a party to the wedding, that it is he who must give Aseneth to Joseph.

I have argued earlier that one way to read this is intertextual—the story now in Genesis asserts that Pharaoh gave Aseneth to Joseph (and does not trouble itself with the social mechanisms by which such a transfer takes place—it assumes, perhaps, that all women are the property of the king). Thus the story struggles to bring the narrative into accord with this preexistent detail. But this is quite interesting, for it suggests that the real exchange of Aseneth involves not Joseph and Pentephres but Joseph and Pharaoh. Further, if Joseph and Pharoah are themselves, as I have argued, earthly representations of God and the son of God, this exchange now has a double layer of meaning. If Aseneth is the earthly representation of Metanoia, the daughter/sister of God, the exchange of Aseneth is also God giving his daughter as wife to his son.

Further, the text plays extensively with the inverse transaction, as it were—the giving of Aseneth to the actual biological son of Pharaoh. In a motif of reversal that appears both at the beginning and at the end, it is the son of Pharaoh (along with every other eligible Egyptian man) who desires to marry Aseneth and who, unsuccessful at contracting a lawful union, plots (also unsuccessfully) to bring about the death of Joseph and thus acquire Aseneth as wife. Initially Aseneth herself, in defiance of her father, asserts that rather than marry Joseph, she will indeed marry the biological son of Pharaoh, a pledge she never actually retracts and that simply disappears from the narrative.

In these same last chapters, Aseneth is much more transparently a medium of male conflict and alliance. The son of Pharaoh, represented as jealous and heartsick over the loss of Aseneth to Joseph, seeks the allegiance of Joseph's own brothers in the plot. Failing to enlist Simeon and Levi (sons of Jacob and Leah), he then attempts an alliance with the men born to Jacob's concubines Bilhah and Zilpah, namely, Dan, Gad, Asher, and Naphtali, having heard that these brothers were already hostile to Joseph.

Rubin's main point is that the exchange of women is intended to bind together men who are not already so bound—to give them descendants in common, forge systems of exchange, and connect them through various means of mutual benefit. But if marriage as an exchange between men generally undergirds ancient constructions of marriage, it is not so easy to see its effects here. Regardless of who might be the true central male parties to the exchange, it is not clear how either is helped or mutually obligated in the process. After the wedding, for instance, Aseneth's father (and mother) disappear from the narrative. Of far more interest to the text, then, is the relationship between Joseph and Pharoah—how, for instance, Pharoah can be called Joseph's father when he obviously isn't. But *Aseneth* seems relatively disinterested in the commonality of their descendents, and neither Pentephres or Pharoah figures in the ancestry of Manasseh and Ephraim. Although I will suggest below that the theory of marriage as a traffic in women is not irrelevant to *Aseneth,* such concerns and constructions may here be subordinated to other issues.

Aseneth, Gender, and the Construction of Marriage

In the last few years, numerous studies have focused particularly on the construction of gender in Hellenistic novels and early Christian apocryphal acts. Although, as I suggested in the introduction to this study, *Aseneth* does not precisely fit the genre of ancient romance, it has enough in common with ancient novels, both polytheist and Christian, that a consideration of this research may be fruitful for an analysis of gender in *Aseneth* itself.

Among the major insights of this literature has been the recognition that the centrality of licit marriage in polytheist romances reflects a revised construction of marriage that begins to emerge particularly in the second century C.E. In this new construction, marriage, at least among elites, was understood as a divinely ordained and sanctioned harmony of two persons, in which concord, fidelity, and friendship played central roles. It would be an overstatement to say that this new representation of marriage envisioned the spouses as absolute equals. But this new understanding of marriage constituted a significant departure from older constructions of marriage, with their expectations of enormous disparities of age, education, and intellect between husbands and wives and their assumption that marriage was primarily concerned with the production of licit heirs, the maintenance of households, and the transmission of property. This reconfiguration of marriage appears particularly suited to the interests of elite society in creating and promoting a harmonious social order. As Judith Perkins writes:

> In the second century the married couple was employed as the image for the type of devotion and harmony holding between all members of a society. The ideal romance, with its narrative focus on the couple, can be read as having a similar subtext—a celebration of the social order as epitomized by the central couple's union preserved through every circumstance.[26]

The polytheist novels that celebrate this image of marriage focus, as many scholars have observed, on the centrality of chastity for both the hero and the heroine. Indeed, much of the plot of the classic Hellenistic romances involves numerous threats to the chastity of each member of a pair of separated lovers, whose eventual reunion is made sweeter by their ability to maintain their fidelity throughout repeated (and sometimes fantastic) challenges. While female chastity may long have been an ancient ideal, what is particularly striking in Hellenistic novels is the equal emphasis on male chastity.

While some scholars have seen in these novels an intensified emphasis on personal desire, Perkins disagrees. Drawing on the symbolic equation of the human body and the social body (elucidated particularly by the work of anthropologist Mary Douglas),[27] Perkins suggests that this interest in mutual chastity demonstrates the degree to which the romances, seemingly concerned with individual attraction, are really concerned with larger social issues.

> The emphasis on chastity in the romance, on maintaining a body free from penetration or mingling with anyone other than that particular person society has sanctioned through marriage, also indicates the social agenda for the genre. The goal of chastity, namely, to restrict the body to those socially approved and designated, is society's most overt manifestation of its power over both nature and its members. Chastity is the manifestation of society's power inserted into the very body of its subjects; it acts as the actual embodiment of social control. By focusing on marriage and chastity (even introducing a concern for male chastity), the romance not only reveals, but emphasizes, its concern for the

social. The romance narrative focused on the social body at the same time that it focused on the body of the beloved.[28]

Narratives of separated lovers who demonstrate their abiding fidelity despite tremendous obstacles and who are eventually reunited in concord and commitment served, she suggests, "to manifest in the early empire the Greek elites' idealizing dream of their society and the social structures supporting and surrounding them."[29] As couples transform and subordinate their individual desires into the harmony of a married couple, approved by society, they become a representation of larger social concord.[30]

In support of her thesis, Perkins points to a number of key elements in polytheist romances. The role of the gods in bringing together the lovers or, indeed, in ordaining the marriage well in advance demonstrated a classic element of elite ideology—that the way things are is the way they are supposed to be. The virtual identification of the well-born protagonists with the gods was apparent most particularly in the remarkable beauty of the lovers, an identification that, Perkins argues, further strengthened the claims of the elite classes to deserve their wealth, position, and prosperity.[31]

Perkins further argues that the central concern for social transformation helps explain the emphasis on death that is common to several of the romances. Not only was there an ancient association between death and marriage but ritualized death plays a central role in ancient initations, particularly those of the various mysteries. One has only to think of Demeter, Persephone, Hades, and the Eleusinian mysteries to see the point. For Perkins, this constellation points further, to the interpretation of the romance "as a story of initiation, a story of the individual's initiation into the social order epitomized in marriage."[32]

Although Perkin's work has still more implications for *Aseneth* that I will consider shortly, much of what she suggests here is tantalizing. Precisely the elements she sees as central—the elite status of the lovers; their mutual chastity; their extraordinary beauty; their virtual identification with the gods; the role of the divine in ordaining the marriage; the relatively egalitarian quality of the marriage; and the linkages of death, initiation, and marriage—all are blatantly apparent in the *Aseneth* narrative. And while there might be any number of ways to account for the presence of these elements in the tale individually, the specific combination does raise the possibility that *Aseneth,* too, may be concerned with similar social concerns within the same general social and cultural contexts.

Drawing on the work of Egger,[33] Perkins also notes that the romance narratives did not focus significantly on the bearing of children (something that is also true of *Aseneth,* despite the fact that the story hinges on the eventual births of Manasseh and Ephraim). With Egger, she sees this as evidence that ancient romances "provided an idealized depiction of the patriarchal system whose inherent purpose as a social institution was the retention and passing on of male power and privilege."[34] This retention and transmission was accomplished particularly through the exchange of women, an exchange whose primary social function, as we have just considered, is the creation, maintenance, and strengthening of bonds between men. As Perkins reads them, the novels focus on the narrative of husbands endlessly replacing fathers, a perpetual cycle that guarantees the perpetual replication of society itself. Discerning this theme in *Aseneth* is quite complex, but it is most apparent in Joseph's succession of Pharaoh and in Pharaoh's giving Aseneth to Joseph, despite the "minor" difficulty that Aseneth is the daughter of Pentephres and Joseph the son of Jacob.

Aseneth as the Object of the Male Gaze

Another significant insight of recent feminist critique of ancient novels is the recognition that implicit in all ancient novels (if not virtually all ancient writing) is the male gaze. That is, the eye that sees the scenes painted by the words of the texts is presumed by the text to be that of a male (and almost always a free, elite male and usually an adult—although the degree to which the gaze may be adolescent is an interesting question).

Once we recognize that even female readers and listeners thus "see" through a male lens, the precise nature of what we see becomes problematic. Much of *Aseneth* shows the male viewer something that in fact the text tells us no man had ever seen: the body of Aseneth.[35] The text opens by emphasizing Aseneth's beauty and the fact that she is the (unseen) object of desire of all the men in Egypt. In 3.9–11, we watch her dress. In 8.4, we watch Joseph put his hand on her chest, allegedly to prevent her from obeying her father's order to kiss him, while in the longer version of this passage (to which I will return below), we are given to visualize her breasts "standing up like apples." In 9.1 we watch her collapse in the presumed privacy of her chambers, on her bed, sweating and weeping. At 10.11, we watch her take off all the garments we saw her put on in 3.9–11; we watch her dress instead in mourning clothes, and we see her abase her body in mud and ashes—we watch her stretched out on the floor for a full week. At 14.15–17, we watch her change her clothes yet again, wash her face, and cover her head; at 15.1, we watch her uncover herself at the angel's command. We watch throughout the intimacy of Aseneth and the angelic visitor in her bedroom, including the scene where he puts honey in her mouth; at 18.3, one more time, we watch Aseneth get dressed.

There is thus the disturbing question of whether there is a pornographic element to this text, not unlike the pornographic gaze of the male eye in the story of the innocent Susanna, falsely accused of adultery by lecherous elders whose advances Susanna had resisted, or even like the gaze of the male eye that watches the scene of Judith in Holofernes's tent. Although the characterization of the gaze as male is not at all a function of the gender of actual readers, the effects of the male gaze may truly be different for different putative readers. Is it pornography when ancient Syrian monks, for example, gaze through the lens of the male eye on the beautiful, secluded Aseneth repeatedly dressing and undressing? Is it any different when we imagine the ancient reader to be a married Jewish woman or a Christian celibate one? Is it any different when we ourselves are gazing?

Female Characters as the "Stand-ins" for Male Readers
Engaged in Debates about Masculine Identity

In a provocative new study, Kate Cooper suggests that in ancient Christian romances (particularly the so-called Apocryphal Acts of the Apostles), women are at the center of contests between men, contests that are themselves about who, ultimately, is the truest exemplar of masculine self-control: the aristocratic male who "owns" the sexuality of the woman or the male apostle to whom she ultimately transfers her allegiance in Apocryphal Act after Apocryphal Act. In contrast to previous scholarship, including some of my own,[36] that sought to see the Apocryphal Acts, like *Aseneth,* as fictionalized narratives of real women's experiences, such romances, Cooper argues, are not about women per se but about gender—and not femininity but masculinity, about who is the truly masculine man.[37]

> The challenge by the apostle to the householder is the urgent message of these narratives, and it is essentially a conflict *between men* [emphasis in original]. The challenge posed here by Christianity is not really about women, or even about sexual continence, but about authority and the social order. In this way, tales of continence uses [*sic*] the narrative momentum of romance and the enticement of the romantic heroine, to make a contest for authority, encoded in the contest between two pretenders to the heroine's allegiance.[38]

In Cooper's reading, these tales in Apocryphal Acts demonstrate and reflect the particular subversive quality of Christianity in the second and third centuries as an antithesis of elite values. The challenge to aristocratic norms is expressed particularly in debates about masculinity. In the Apocryphal Acts, it is ultimately always the itinerant apostle who demonstrates himself, rather than his elite rival, to be the ultimate exemplar of masculine self-control.

Cooper points out that while the Apocryphal Acts appear to be about chastity, in reality

> there is a rhetorical sleight of hand at work in the stories. For these texts precisely do *not* celebrate *sophrosyne*—chastity—the virtue proper to a devoted, and fertile, wife, celebrated by the ancients as the female counterpart to male self-mastery. Instead, they celebrate heroines who substitute for *sophrosyne* the potentially antithetical virtue of *enkrateia,* continence.[39]

While I am not altogether ready, with Cooper, to abandon the Apocryphal Acts as narratives of historical and social verisimilitude, I think her arguments here have much merit and shed some additional light on the potential dynamics of *Aseneth.*

Given the centrality of both male and female virginity and sexual fidelity in *Aseneth,* these issues are worth pursuing further. Perkins argues that in the conceptual world of earlier Greek society, the contribution of (free) women to the social order consisted of their devotion to marriage and their production of legitimate heirs, while men were expected to devote themselves particularly to warfare. But in the Roman period, the majority of free men (particularly elite Greeks) no longer had such obligations, necessitating, Perkins argues, a new symbolic means for men to address their devotion to the social order. Chastity, she proposes, was just the ticket. One significance of this, of course, is that a previously feminine virtue is now extended to men as well, carrying with it the potential for adjusted constructions of gender.

Both Perkins and Brent Shaw,[40] in their recent discussions of early Christian narratives of suffering and martyrdom, point out that something similar undergirds Christian ideologies of martyrdom. While the Roman government intentionally inflicted pain on deviants, Christian and otherwise, for the primary purpose of demonstrating its power, Christians subverted the dominance of the empire, and of polytheist culture, precisely through the embracing of pain and the valoration of physical suffering. By interpreting pain, suffering, and even death as vindication and glorification, Christians stripped the cultural meaning from their experience and "reinscribed" it with a different meaning.

But constructions of gender are deeply implicated in this process. As Shaw demonstrates, endurance of suffering was a central component in ancient constructions of gender, linked closely with ideas about inherent female passivity. To be female was to endure, to suffer, to experience passively, to be acted upon, and, often, to be humiliated. Roman torture, whether of Christians, Jews, or others considered threats to Roman order, inevitably drew upon paradigms of gender: the torturer as male and the tortured as female. Placing a premium on the endurance of suffering thus also extends a paradigmatic feminine virtue to men as well as women.

The implications of this are substantial, and only some are directly relevant to discussions of *Aseneth*.[41] But the extension of a form of chastity previously expected only of women to both men and women in elite circles of the second and third centuries and the extension and revalorization of the previously feminine quality of endurance of pain, suffering, and humiliation to Christian martyrs, male and female alike, may help us to rethink the prominence of women in literature from the late Hellenistic period on, including, as Shaw notes, writers such as Musonius Rufus, Plutarch, and Seneca, not to mention Jewish and Christian narratives of martyrdom and suffering.[42] It becomes easier for women's experience to serve as representative for "human" experience.

Of particular interest, though, is the observation that the extension of these constituent elements of the feminine to men seems to have been accomplished in part by reinscribing these traits as masculine. Although I do not want to rule out the possibility that some "feminizing" of the masculine, or even of men, takes place in the process, I think it far more likely that what we have is both a transference and an inversion of values. Characteristics previously denigrated and associated with the feminine become valued and masculinized, although their ability to function subversively depends on a tension between their femininity and their value. If endurance of suffering loses its association with the feminine altogether, I would suspect that it would also lose its ability to subvert the prevailing social order.

This transference of gendered valuation allows a different interpretation of the meaning of "becoming male" in ancient texts, including, perhaps, *Aseneth* itself. Ironically, by enduring what were once typically female conditions of suffering, pain, and humiliation, women now are seen to "become male," as numerous Christian narratives demonstrate.[43]

What might this tell us about *Aseneth*? I have already suggested that, at the very least, we must position *Aseneth* somewhere within these ancient conversations about marriage and gender identity. The concept of marriage in *Aseneth* seems to me very like the relatively egalitarian union of the harmonious couple, in which fidelity and concord (manifested here particularly in their devotion to the same God and in their attainment of similar mystical status) are of far more interest than the production and raising of legitimate heirs. The repeated emphasis on the chastity of both Joseph and

Aseneth also seems to place the tale squarely within an elite late-antique matrix.[44] In its understanding of chastity, as Cooper's analysis allows us to see clearly, *Aseneth* is much closer to polytheist novels than to Christian Apocryphal Acts. In *Aseneth,* female chastity is precisely the feminine form of *sōphrosynē,* "the virtue proper to a devoted, and fertile, wife,"[45] and Aseneth herself becomes precisely such a spouse. It is not at all that form of Christian chastity that translates to abstinence; on the contrary, with a divinely ordained spouse, marital sexuality is seen to be blessed and fruitful.

Earlier, I considered the significance of Aseneth's depiction as "a young man" following her repentance. Here, I wish to add that the dynamic of becoming male implicit in the analysis of Perkins and Shaw is quite different from at least one other ancient understanding of how women "become male," namely, that found in Philo's treatise on the contemplative Therapeutics. The Therapeutrides (the female members of the community) do not endure suffering, now understood as a masculine virtue, and thereby "become male"; on the contrary, they become male by renouncing the body and sexuality and by adopting more traditional masculine activities of the mind, together with control of the body through ascetic practice (diet, clothing, sexuality, and so forth).

Viewed from this perspective, Aseneth's temporary androgyny is (like much else about the text) precisely neither one nor the other. Aseneth does not reject either sexuality or the body. She does not suffer and endure pain and humiliation at the hands of a hierarchical superior, although it may not be irrelevant that she voluntarily subjects herself to a certain amount of humiliation and abasement and imagines herself to be persecuted and hated (12.7–11). She clearly demonstrates self-control and knowledge, and her acceptance of Joseph's God brings not death and the otherworldly crown of a martyr but glorification and the pleasures of marriage and the reward of children in this life.

What might all this suggest about the religious self-understanding of the author(s) of *Aseneth?* While I examine various possibilities in detail in chapter 9, here I want to consider how this discussion might factor into the question of whether and how we might decide authorial identity.

Would any Christians have been interested in a tale of marriage that seems fundamentally consonant with the ideas of marriage manifest in the Greek romances? At the very least, it seems unlikely that the author(s) of *Aseneth* would have been terribly sympathetic to the narrators of the Apocryphal Acts. My only hesitation on this point is that *Aseneth* is set at a time well before the coming of Christ is understood to license the renunciation of sexuality and marriage in some Christian circles.

As I shall explore in chapter 9, it is nevertheless quite possible that what some Christians do in fact do is tell a story of the marriage of Christ and the church that draws on the analogy of human marriage prevalent in these centuries. Such a story might carry the meaning that the marriage of Christ and the church produces a spiritual concord and harmony that is best for the social order as well.

But another possibility emerges that is prompted in part by Cooper's excavation of the tension between Christian advocacy of celibacy and the realities of married women's lives.[46] As the legitimation of Christianity removed actual martyrdom from the repertoire of Christian suffering and as Christianity's incursion into Roman society went both deeper and wider from the early fourth century on, celibacy as normative behavior became more and more problematic. One possibility, then, is that if it is of Christian composition, *Aseneth* constitutes a voice in support of marital sexuality as a more appropriate form of Christian chastity than celibacy.[47]

Would any Jews have been interested in a tale so consistent with later antique constructions of marriage? The sages of the Mishnah and other early rabbis do not spring immediately to mind. Certainly, however, I can imagine that Jews prospering in Greek cities such as Ephesus or Aphrodisias or Sardis might well have been interested in a tale that offered a "Jewish" marriage as a paradigm of concord. Although one might initially wonder at the choice of this particular biblical example as the marriage par excellence, a brief review of some of the other choices suggests that Joseph and Aseneth might, in fact, be particularly apt. It would be difficult to represent any of the patriarchs as advocates of marital chastity: Abraham and Isaac both allow the Philistine king, Abimelech, to mistake their wives, Sarah and Rebekah, for their sisters, putting their wives' chastity at grave risk (Gen 20 and 26, respectively). Abraham had a concubine while married to Sarah and another wife after Sarah died, which would not have endeared him to Christians advocating one marriage to one spouse. Jacob had two wives and their handmaids as well. Moses, too, appears to have had two wives. Joseph, in short, turns out to be far more of a paragon of virtue than we might have realized before.

Then, too, as I have suggested earlier, it may be that the driving force behind the formulation of this story lies elsewhere, but that once set in motion, this particular culturally powerful paradigm is appropriated by the composer(s) of the story. As I have suggested already in the previous chapter and will pursue further in chapter 9, it may again be tempting to think of a *theosebic* author (or authors), for whom the incorporation of all of these elements might have been easiest, and who, in fact, tells a story that holds all of these culturally diverse elements together.

The Uses of Gender in the Longer Version

Although both versions of *Aseneth* draw upon ancient constructions of the feminine, it is particularly noteworthy that the alterations of the longer text consistently address matters of gender, often introducing themes of gender that are only minimally present or absent altogether from the shorter text.[48]

The first instance of such alteration occurs fairly early in the texts, when Aseneth first meets Joseph. There, we may recall, the longer text graphically depicts Aseneth as sexually aroused by Joseph, associating her with the dangerous Egyptian women overcome by Joseph's beauty, in a manner totally absent in the shorter text:

8.3–4/**8.4–5**
And Pentephres said to Aseneth, "Come forward and kiss your brother." And as she came forward to kiss Joseph, (he) **Joseph** stretched out his right hand, and placed it on her chest [*to stēthos*], **between her two breasts, and her breasts were already standing up like ripe apples.**

The second instance occurs in the final lines of Joseph's initial prayer for Aseneth.

8.10/8.11

And may she drink the cup of your blessing, (she whom you chose before she was conceived) **and number her among your people, that you have chosen before all (things) came into being** and may she enter into your rest,[49] which you have prepared for your chosen ones **and live in your eternal life for ever and ever.**

In chapter 2, I briefly explored some of the ramifications of the language of the shorter text, particularly its association of Aseneth with Wisdom and with a plethora of male biblical figures chosen by God before their birth. Among other things, the alteration of the longer text eradicates these associations, particularly the classification of Aseneth with a list of chosen men.

The two silent soliloquies inserted prior to Aseneth's prayer in chapter 12 afford a more complex example. I have suggested in chapter 3 that the addition of these soliloquies addresses a number of redactive concerns, such as the desire to resolve an apparent tension between Aseneth's statement in 12.7 that she was not worthy to open her mouth before God and the fact she does just that and the wish to expand on the imagery of a passage such as Psalm 29.11–12 (LXX/OG)[50] in addition to being consistent with ancient adjurative practices.[51]

From a feminist perspective, it is quite tempting to see the longer narrative as reflective of ancient ideas about gender and speech. Many ancient sources evince a widely held belief that in women, silence was ideal. "A silent wife is a gift from the Lord" (Sir 26.14). Even more interestingly, many ancient writers also connect women's speech with women's sexuality, drawing a clear analogy between the mouth and the vagina. The chaste woman had a closed mouth and a closed vagina (except, of course, to her licit husband); the unchaste woman opened her mouth to speech and her vagina to illicit intercourse.[52] These mouths were seen to be so closely connected that some writers offer up the public speech of a woman as de facto evidence of her unchastity.[53] Interestingly, the traditions in Proverbs make a somewhat more subtle distinction, by associating Woman Wisdom with speech that leads to righteousness and the Foreign/Strange Woman with speech that leads to sexual immorality.[54]

We might then view the insertions of the longer text as the product of a redactor who is concerned with these issues and who may even intend to connect Aseneth's virginity with her silence here, blurring the fine distinction in Proverbs and stressing the blunter association of women's speech with women's lack of chastity. This Aseneth might be understood to utter her first two prayers silently to counter the possible implication that the seemingly chaste Aseneth was engaged in unchaste, inappropriate speech. Although these insertions clearly have multiple functions in the text, such a reading is consistent with the general pattern of revisions in the longer text.

In at least one other ancient text, the silence of a woman has moral implications that are themselves associated with gendered expectations. In Pseudo-Philo's retelling of the birth of Samson (Judg 13), the husband and wife (Manoah and Eluma, as she is here called) argue over which one of them is infertile (understood to be in either case the action of God). Eluma prays to God, who tells her that it is she (though she will now conceive and bear Samson)—after which she goes to her husband and tells him that henceforth she will be silent because she did not believe him when he said she was to blame.[55]

In *Aseneth* 13, the redactive changes have an effect similar to that in chapter 12. Here, Aseneth recapitulates in hymnic form the prior narrative of her abasement:

13.9
But pardon me, Lord, because I sinned against you in ignorance **being a virgin and erred unwittingly** and spoke blasphemy against my lord Joseph.

The small but remarkable additional words "being a virgin" appear to connect Aseneth's ignorance either with her virginity or with her gender. Since all versions of the text repeatedly emphasize Joseph's virginity as well, I am tempted to conclude that the redactor has in mind the latter—Aseneth's ignorance is associated with her gender.

Both the longer and shorter versions end this scene with Aseneth's fervent prayer that rather than be given to Joseph as an aristocratic wife, she become his servant forever:

3.12/**13.15**
Deliver me to [Joseph] as a servant **and slave,** (that) **and** I (may) **will make his bed and** wash his feet and wait on him **and be a slave to him** and serve him for all the rest of my life.

The longer text differs from the shorter in its inclusion of Aseneth's wish to make Joseph's bed. This certainly does not appear to develop biblical or other traditional imagery nor to relate to adjurative practices, and it is interesting that bed making was typically women's work.

The longer version's revisions of the description of Metanoia in chapter 15 may display similar tendencies, offering a diminished portrait of Metanoia more reliant on ancient constructions of the proper woman. This Metanoia is defined not only as the daughter of God but also as the sister of the angelic being, and she is loved by them not for her role in the salvation of the repentant but for her qualities of beauty, chastity, good disposition, and meekness. Although these are frequently stereotypically feminine characteristics in ancient constructions of gender, we have seen earlier in this chapter that in late antique fiction, these were extended to men as well. Further, since I have already shown that these changes are the result of the addition of traditional details, it is difficult to say whether the redactor's intention was to domesticate the image of Metanoia or whether the effect is accidental. But nevertheless, it appears to be there and is consistent with other changes.[56]

As I have already noted in chapter 3, one of the most fascinating gender-related alterations in the longer text occurs in the scene with the honeycomb. In the shorter version, the angel simply breaks off a piece of the comb, eats it, and puts some honey into Aseneth's mouth with his hand. In the longer version, before he gives her the honey, he instructs her, "Eat," and she does:

16.9/**16.15–16x**
And the figure stretched out his right hand and broke off (a piece) from the comb and ate, and **what was left he** put (a piece) of the comb into Aseneth's mouth with his hand **and said to her, "Eat." And she ate.**

This seemingly modest change nevertheless transforms the text into an inversion of Genesis 2–3. There a woman eats the fruit of mortality and shares it with her husband; here a husband figure eats the food of immortality and then gives some to the woman, explicitly telling her to eat it.

This passage is enormously suggestive and problematic. It appears that the divine couple of Joseph and Aseneth restore the damage done by Adam and Eve, affording human beings a means to return to their original angelic state and, indeed, acquiring precisely the immortality that God feared Adam and Eve might aquire had they remained in Eden (Gen 3.22–24). What does this mean for Aseneth's identity as a woman? What, precisely, is Aseneth's role in the reversal of Eve's actions? Must Eve's deeds be compensated for by those of another woman (as some Christian writers interpreted the perfect obedience of Mary to be the reversal of Eve's disobedience)?[57] And what precisely must that compensation be? Genesis 3.1–5 and following may be read (and, indeed, has been so read) to imply that Eve learned of the forbidden fruit not from God directly but rather from Adam, and therefore, it is Eve's disobedience *to her husband* that leads to their shared mortality. By contrast, it is Aseneth's obedience to the angelic double of her husband, Joseph, that obtains immortality for her. And although the masculine figure also eats, thus formally reversing the actions of Adam and Eve, he is already an angelic being, and it is hardly necessary for him to eat angelic food in order to receive immortality.[58] It is significant that the actions of Aseneth and "Joseph" undo death but not sexuality, as opposed to other ancient interpretations (virtually all Christian) in which angelic identity and/or restoration to the primordial state undid both. But given the inescapable parameter of this story, that Aseneth must marry Joseph and give birth to both Manasseh and Ephraim, we could hardly expect otherwise!

It is fairly obvious that Aseneth here functions as a salvific figure, not only for her reversal of Eve's actions but also for the role she will play as City of Refuge. Female saviors are fairly rare in the religions of the Greco-Roman world, with the important exception of Isis, so that this portrait of Aseneth may be quite significant precisely for its presentation of a salvific female.[59] And it is also obvious that Aseneth is depicted in all versions of this story as the recipient of divine mysteries and wisdom. But if my reading of this section of the longer text is correct, its subliminal message is that Paradise is restored when women are properly obedient to their husbands, a view probably shared by the author of the Pastoral Epistles (and many early rabbis as well!). They then regain the immortality that Eve traded for knowledge. This, too, is consonant with the identification of Aseneth with Wisdom and of Wisdom with the Virtuous Woman, who is similarly obedient, industrious, and fruitful.

The longer text's revisions of Aseneth's prayer in the wake of the angel's departure may intentionally reinforce the gendered imagery of Aseneth's prior ignorance. In the shorter text, Aseneth utters only a brief prayer, asking forgiveness for having spoken evil in ignorance. In the longer text, she is far more self-deprecating. Calling herself audacious and lacking sense (an attribute of the Strange Woman in Prov 9.13), Aseneth berates herself for having said that an *anthrōpos* came into her room from out of heaven and for not having realized that it was [G]od. Her final comment here resembles that in the shorter text, but with two subtle differences. First, she says it "in herself," recalling her earlier silent prayers. Second, whereas the shorter text has her confess to having spoken evil in ignorance, in line with the earlier scenes in which Aseneth slanders Joseph in ignorance, the longer text claims that she has spoken all her words in ignorance, a broader and more devastating claim.

In the shorter text, a servant then announces Joseph's arrival. When Joseph sees Aseneth, he calls her to him, saying that he has received good news about her from heaven. They embrace each other for a long time, after which Aseneth invites Joseph into her house and, taking his hand, leads him inside. This scene thus revisits their initial meeting, but whereas then Joseph refused to touch Aseneth, now he embraces her gladly, signifying her transformation into an acceptable spouse for him.

In the shorter text, the location of the action plays a modest role. From her rooms, which we know are upstairs, Aseneth comes down to meet Joseph. Whether he is still outside the doors of the courtyard or inside them is not specified. After they greet and embrace, Aseneth takes Joseph into "her" house. The longer text displays much more interest in the question of location, repeatedly specifying who is where. In particular, that text clarifies that Joseph and Aseneth meet outside the house but still inside the courtyard, whose gates have been closed behind Joseph, leaving foreigners outside. This detail suggests redaction sensitive to ancient social norms of gendered space. In many ancient sources, there is an integral connection between physical space and women's sexuality. Domestic space was considered the proper physical sphere of women, especially virgins. Virginity and chastity were symbolized by enclosure, including walled cities and walled gardens. Respectably married women could venture into certain public spaces provided they were symbolically "housed," either by being accompanied by a retinue of domestic slaves and/or by wearing clothing that signified their respectability (and concealed their bodies). In the longer text, the still virgin and unmarried Aseneth does not yet leave the confines of the courtyard and remains behind the closed gates.

These differences may suggest several explanations. First, the longer text may be Christian or at least one layer of its revisions may be Christian. This is suggested, among other things, by the revisions to the eating of the honey, if my reading of the longer text is correct. That is, the use of Aseneth to undo the damage of Eve sounds a particularly Christian theme, although this role is typically assigned to Mary, the mother of Jesus.[60]

Second, it may be that those who redacted the shorter text into a longer version understood it to be advocating views of women and of gender relations that they wished to refute or at least minimize. Not inconceivably, they knew that Aseneth was used in ancient debates about women's roles that we know to have been prevalent in some Christian circles, as late as the fourth and fifth centuries—although, unlike Tertullian's report about the story of Thecla,[61] we have no such evidence for the use of Aseneth by anyone.

Gender and Angelic Transformation

One of the most distinctive aspects of *Aseneth* remains its portrayal of a woman's effective drawing down of an angel, which results in her own angelic transformation. As I noted in previous chapters, encounters between women and angels, while hardly routine, are not without precedent either in the Hebrew Bible or in Christian scripture.[62] They are, however, virtually without precedent in the corpus of early Jewish visionary accounts, both those usually classed as pseudepigrapha and those associated with *hekhalot* traditions. There are two possible exceptions, as I also noted earlier—the appearance of an angel to Eve, in the *Life of Adam and Eve,* and the story of the daughters of Job in the *Testament of Job.* In the first case, although an angel does appear to Eve, it is only to show her the burial of Adam's body at the hands of angels and the ascent of Adam's soul to heaven, and the entire sequence functions as a rebuke to Eve. In the second case, the daughters of Job do not explicitly encounter angels, although they are said to acquire the ability to compose hymns in angelic dialects, and they clearly serve as conduits between heaven and earth, enabling humans to participate in angelic liturgies (or perhaps replicate them on earth). Furthermore, the identification of both of these texts as unambiguously Jewish is plagued by many of the same difficulties as the identification of *Aseneth.*[63]

Encounters between women and angels are found occasionally in late antique Christian narratives, but, interestingly, the best examples I have been able to catalogue at present are precisely those stories thought by other scholars to depend directly or indirectly on the story of Aseneth. In particular, the story of Penelope, later named Irene, contains an elaborate encounter between Penelope/Irene and an angel of God that has significant similarities to the Aseneth narratives.[64]

What then, is the significance of the narrative of a woman who draws down an angel and is herself transformed into an angel as well? To some extent, the answer may depend upon the real social, historical, and cultural milieu of the story. If, for example, *Aseneth* was composed in conscious awareness of the *hekhalot* traditions, we might argue that it is an intentional response to those traditions, particularly to their stance that such experiences are limited to men. The story of *Aseneth* reveals that women, too, are capable of angelic adjuration and transformation, although the subtext of both shorter and longer versions may well be that women so transformed still conform to traditional gender expectations during their earthly lives. In this regard, as in several others, the text is quite consonant with the stance of Paul in 1 Corinthians. Even its advocacy of marriage and childbearing might not contradict this, given its fictive historic setting prior to the coming of Christ.[65] But if we set aside its Pauline consonance for the moment, then it also may be that the repeated efforts of the longer text to emphasize and denigrate Aseneth's female gender may be a response to interpretations of the shorter text as minimizing gender difference.

Furthermore, if *Aseneth* is to be located within the same context as the *hekhalot* traditions (a stance I am not necessarily advocating), it might also suggest that the story was used to legitimate women who functioned in roles analogous to those discussed by Morray-Jones, Jack Lightstone, and others: as holy persons who mediated between heaven and earth, linking the liturgies of the heavens above with those of humans on earth.[66] As we have seen, such a role is explicitly assigned to the daughters of Job in the *Testament of Job,* although no ancient sources testify to the presence of Jewish women acting in such capacities.[67] This is highly speculative, but it attempts to take seriously the implications of such stories for men and to apply those implications to women.

Constructions of Gender in Both Versions of *Aseneth*

Within the shorter and the longer versions alike, the portraits of both women and men are highly artificial. As we have seen, virtually everything about the characters, from their physical and moral attributes to their actions and speeches and their clothing and possessions, is constructed from ancient texts and traditions, particularly, although hardly exclusively, Greek Jewish scripture. On the whole, both texts utilize constructions of gender that were fairly conventional in Greco-Roman antiquity. A complex hierarchy, both on earth and in heaven, is the norm. Women, at least proper women, are subordinate (and subservient) to men, as are slaves to their owners and subjects to their rulers, although class is clearly a factor: male slaves and servants are subordinate to free aristocratic women. In the cosmos, human beings are subordinate to angels, who are in turn subordinate before God.

Both versions of *Aseneth* utilize ancient stereotypical associations of gender. It is the female Aseneth who is foolish, ignorant, and lacking self-discipline; and the male Joseph who is wise and self-controlled. It is the woman who is Other, the male who is Self, the woman who is human, the male who is divine. But none of this is absolute. By drawing particularly on the dichotomy of the Wise and Strange Women in numerous Wisdom traditions, the authors are able to portray the transformation of Aseneth from foolish and ignorant to wise and discerning, from Other to Self, from mortal human to angelic immortal, from Egyptian idolater to one who reveres the true God. In this endeavor, they may also be aided by the subtler, less dichotomous constructions of gender in late antique fiction that we have considered in this chapter.

It is not inconceivable that this subtlety intends at least a modest critique of certain ancient constructions of gender. This is even more likely if we imagine the alternatives to be the more overtly hostile writings such as The Wisdom of Jesus ben Sira (Sirach). Alternatively, we might argue that *Aseneth*'s relative lack of hostility to women is nothing more than a byproduct of the author's need to transform her into an acceptable wife for Joseph and that in the desire to accomplish this, Aseneth's negative femaleness becomes subordinated to her positive *theosebeia,* her inclusion in the community of those who revere God.

Such an interpretation becomes less persuasive when we consider the differences between this account of the marriage between Aseneth and Joseph and rabbinic legends, legends that occur in sources whose date, we may now recall, are probably fourth century C.E. and later.[68] As I explore in the appendix, none of those legends is anything like our Aseneth story, and several claim that Aseneth was really the daughter of Joseph's niece, Dinah (who had been raped by a Canaanite named Shechem according to Gen 34), and only the adopted daughter of Pentephres. It is tempting to speculate that these different stories circulate in communities with somewhat different ideas about gender and with somewhat differing social structures consonant with those ideas—although the key differences among the stories seem not to be gender constructs but the identification of Aseneth as really an Israelite and not a Gentile after all. And, of course, if *Aseneth* is Christian, then rabbinic legends are almost beside the point, since each tradition would be oriented to fundamentally different interests in the Joseph narrative.

Interestingly, the texts manifest no explicit tension around issues of gender, although the longer version does consistently demonstrate more discomfort about gender than the shorter version, particularly in places where the shorter version appears to make troubling claims about Aseneth, as in its statement that Aseneth was chosen by God before her birth. As we have seen, many of the differences between the two versions are to be found at precisely such points, with the longer redaction consistently depicting Aseneth as a bit closer to ancient conventions about acceptable women.

Aseneth and Ancient Social Reality

As we have seen, studies on the relationship between Greek novels and social reality caution us about seeking too close a correspondence between the details of the text and the social reality of the author(s) and ancient audience(s). Whether, then, the texts of *Aseneth* say much about the real experiences of women and men is extremely difficult to determine. In a general sense, *Aseneth*'s portrait of ancient social life is consistent with what we know from numerous other sources. Elite, aristocratic families did live in large houses in relative luxury, with retinues of servants and slaves, and did own massive country estates. Daughters of such families were likely to be raised in relative seclusion, with dedicated female companions. Beyond such generalities, some of the more specific details of the story are also consistent with other sources, such as Aseneth's age at marriage (eighteen). Yet other details, such as the fact that Aseneth's parents have only one living child and appear to have had a total of two children, seem unusual, although not impossible, and more consistent with folktales and popular narratives, including not only Greek romances but also late antique Christian narratives and martyrologies (which may themselves be indebted to the genre of Greek novels).

Egger's analysis of the representation of women and marriage in Greek novels affords some additional insight into this question. While she acknowledges that the success of fiction requires a certain degree of plausibility and therefore correspondence with the social reality of its audience,[69] she emphasizes that "Greek novels (like most fiction) certainly do not offer—and do not strive to offer—images directly representational of their contemporary environments."[70]

Focusing specifically on the presentation of private marriage law in ancient romances, Egger concludes that Greek novelists utilized not the realities of marital law and practice as we can reconstruct them from existing legal and historical sources but rather "a combination of old and new legal assumptions, literary allusions and contemporary practice."[71] Furthermore, she demonstrates that although Greek novelists do not always archaize in their representation of the social reality of their characters, when they do archaize, they inevitably "impose upon their women limitations and incapacities that did not exist in their same degree for their approximately contemporary readers."[72] In particular, the construction of marital law in the Greek novels represents a regression from the advances of Hellenistic law, which gave women considerably greater autonomy in comparison to earlier Athenian regulation.[73] "[W]omen's legal conditions in the Greek novels lag behind the reality of their contemporary readers," a lag that Egger finds characteristic of the novels' general presentation of women.[74] "The fabrication of femininity, as endorsed by the texts, is conventional and archaizing as compared to contemporary reality."

Additionally, Egger points out that the resultant "disabling" of women in these texts is accomplished subtly.[75] Modern readers of these novels have been struck by their apparent characterization of women as unusually powerful and predominant in comparison to the representation of women in much other ancient literature. While Egger agrees that women predominate in these narratives, she finds the heroines of Greek romances "immensely emotionally powerful and erotically ravishing" but otherwise "restricted and disempowered. . . . The price paid for women's erotic centrality is their social containment in the realms of law and marriage, among others."[76]

Together with our earlier discussion of gender construction in ancient fiction, Egger's observations suggest that the representation of women in Hellenistic novels is far from straightforward and points to underlying efforts of the authors to construct femininity in ways that hint at social conflict over women's roles. If Egger is correct that Greek fiction constructs women as more constrained than they actually were and marital law as more consonant with those constraints than it actually was, we may surmise that these stories are to some degree polemical, that they simultaneously wish for such a reality and present it as attractive and desirable to its readers.

At the very least, of course, this suggests that it is imprudent to use ancient fiction as unqualified evidence for the social practices of the authors and audiences, particularly ancient fiction such as *Aseneth,* whose authorship, date, and social location cannot be determined independently from the clues in the text itself. But of even greater significance is the recognition that the representation of reality in the text is likely to be ideological: while seeming to "describe" a particular reality, it in fact takes a stance on that reality, although whether that stance is negative or positive may conceivably vary.

Further, we must keep in mind that even in its own time(s), *Aseneth* is a story about a past far distant from, and probably idealized by, its authors and audiences. To the degree that the story depends heavily on biblical and related traditions for its construction of that idealized past, I now think that it says little about the lives and experiences of "real" persons in the author(s)'s own times and places apart from the kinds of general social correspondences I have noted.

This is particularly important not only for questions about women's history and experiences but for other issues as well. For instance, some scholars have grounded their dating of *Aseneth* in their perception of the text's positive portrayal of relations between Jews and Egyptians, a portrayal that they take to reflect historical reality or plausibility and thus date at no later than the early second century C.E., before the revolts of 115–17 C.E. in North Africa would have rendered such a portrait more problematic. The literary convention of setting Greek romances in an idealized past makes it much more likely that *Aseneth,* too, is set in an idealized portrait of ancient Egypt that, like other romances, is sometimes also anachronistic and is, in any case, intended to be taken as such and not as a reliable portrait of the social world of the authors and audiences.

The work of Egger, Perkins, Cooper, Shaw, and others accentuates the probability that the representation of women and the construction of gender in both the shorter and longer texts of *Aseneth* are at best only of modest use for reconstructing the realities of women's lives and the range of constructions of gender prevalent when the texts were initially composed and redacted. Egger's observations about the presentation of both women and marriage in Greek novels are generally true for *Aseneth* as well, although with some important qualifications. Aseneth is presented as both emotional and erotic, although both forms of the text are considerably less detailed in their eroticism than the typical Greek novel. Just as the novels tend to portray women as constrained socially and legally and to minimize the representation of women as autonomous, so, too, when Aseneth attempts to act autonomously (for instance, by refusing her father's suggestion that she marry Joseph), the text's condemnation of that autonomy is readily apparent. Conversely, Aseneth's eventual conformity to appropriate gender roles is praised and affirmed, and her rewards are precisely those of Greek romance, namely, legitimate marriage, legitimate male heirs, and familial acceptance.

Yet there is another subtle level here that may point to a more complex context. Although Aseneth is an erotic figure whose reputation is so powerful that even men who have never seen her desire to marry her—the element of Aseneth's erotic appeal is minimized in this text relative to that in Hellenistic novels. Eroticism is not the means by which Aseneth gains anything, including Joseph; rather it is by her piety, humility, wisdom, and acceptance of God that she receives these rewards. One could in fact argue that in some regards (e.g., obedience to God, honoring of parents), Aseneth is a(n intentional?) critique of Hellenistic novels—although they, too, have strong religious components—so that perhaps it is a matter of degree and not kind, as well as, of course, a matter of claims about the true God.

To the degree, then, that *Aseneth* utilizes the conventions of ancient romance narratives, it offers a complex blend of authorial images of an idealized past interwoven with elements of correspondence to a social reality recognizable to ancient readers. I am now highly dubious about the probability that *Aseneth* reflects actual rituals of conversion to some form of Greco-Roman Judaism, contrary to the opinion of many other scholars. But to the degree that it also draws on adjurative and mystical traditions of Greco-Roman antiquity, *Aseneth* may allude more specifically to the worldviews and maybe even some of the actual practices of "real" people.

The Gender of the Author(s) and Audiences

Although it is difficult for us to know whether the any of the authors or redactors of *Aseneth* may have been women,[77] it seems much more likely that women comprised at least part of the audience that read *Aseneth* directly or heard it read aloud. Egger offers two categories of evidence that women were among the readers of Greek novels in general: (1) some women possessed the necessary literacy and leisure time to read or hear texts read aloud and (2) women are represented as readers and writers within the novels themselves.[78] General evidence for the literacy of women from the first through the fourth centuries C.E. would appear to be relevant to *Aseneth* as well, although obviously more precise evidence for the literacy of Jewish and Christian women would be appropriate as well. It may be interesting that *Aseneth* itself is silent on the question of women as readers and writers within the narrative. Neither Aseneth nor any other female character is depicted as reading or writing, although they are not explicitly portrayed as illiterate. Yet literacy figures relatively little in the text as an activity of male characters either,[79] so if there are conclusions to be drawn about the portrayal of literacy, they may not be gender-specific here.

What is the significance of a female audience for *Aseneth?* Egger suggests that the combination of strong female eroticism and women's social containment in Hellenistic novels constitutes "a hoary patriarchal fantasy" whose appeal to women may seem somewhat paradoxical. Noting, however, the immense popularity of contemporary "Harlequin"-type romantic fiction that appeals to millions of women in America alone, Egger proposes that a similar dynamic may have operated in antiquity as well: "The same kind of comfort that is entailed in traditionally restricted but secure gender roles may have been one of the attractions of the Greek novels, too."[80] In a tantalizing note, Egger raises the possibility that "when strictly circumscribed models of femininity (as well as of masculinity) are relaxed, fantasies about the security of traditional, more limited gender identities tend to increase," and she notes that the sales of paperback romances have increased dramatically since the late 1960s,[81] when the current women's movement began to have substantial impact on gender roles in America. If the flourishing of Greek novels in the early centuries of the Roman empire, particularly in non-Roman circles, suggests discomfort over changing gender roles in much of the Roman empire, we might also consider the degree to which *Aseneth* also represents a response to those same circumstances, modified perhaps by the specific religious concerns of its authors, whether Jewish, Christian, or otherwise.

Finally, on the question of authorship and gender, Egger's observations about the fundamental male character of this particular fantasy might appear to support the thesis that the author or authors of *Aseneth* were male, a thesis that on balance is more likely than not, although on the evidence we have we can never be sure. The fact that modern Harlequin novels are regularly written by women should remind us that ideology is a poor clue to authorial gender. Yet our assumptions about the gender of both author(s) and audience(s) do matter in our readings of texts, and it would be wise both to be explicit about those assumptions and to continue to consider in what ways the text(s) look different when we envision a female author rather than a male or a female reader rather than a male.[82]

NOTES

1. There are, of course, exceptions: the Book of Judith; the story of Susanna and the Elders; the account of the virtuous mother of the seven martyred sons in 4 Macc; the retellings of narratives of exemplary biblical women in Ps. Philo. Nevertheless, the statement as phrased is still quite accurate. Interestingly, however, narratives of exemplary Christian women are far more numerous, particularly from the third century on.

2. This is particularly true of scholars in the last fifty years or so, including Philonenko, Burchard, Sänger, Chesnutt, and Bohak. In the recently published revision of his 1986 dissertation, Chesnutt does recognize the need for additional research into the significance of Aseneth's gender (*From Death to Life,* 268–69). Recent dissertations such as Doty, *From Ivory Tower,* and Humphrey, *Ladies and the Cities,* are more attentive to issues of gender, although Humphrey treats only the use of female imagery—especially the city as feminine. The most significant attempt to deal seriously with issues of gender is the new study by Angela Standhartinger, *Das Frauenbild im Judentum der hellenistischen Zeit: Ein Beitrag anhand von "Joseph und Aseneth,"* Arbeiten zur Geschichte des antiken Judentums und des Urchristentums (Leiden: E. J. Brill, 1995).

3. I cannot exempt myself from such a charge in the past.

4. Esp. Ross S. Kraemer, *Her Share of the Blessings, Women's Religions among Pagans, Jews, and Christians in the Greco-Roman World* (New York: Oxford University Press, 1992), 110–12.

5. Bohak, *"Joseph and Aseneth."*

6. See, e.g., Cooper, *Virgin and the Bride.*

7. A.-J. Levine, "Diaspora as Metaphor: Bodies and Boundaries in the Book of Tobit," in Andrew Overman and R. S. MacLennan, eds., *Diaspora Judaism: Essays in Honor of and in Dialogue with A. Thomas Kraabel,* South Florida Studies in Judaism (Atlanta: Scholars Press, 1992), 105–17.

8. Levine, "Diaspora as Metaphor," 105.

9. Levine, "Diaspora as Metaphor," 117.

10. In the central passage that might be relevant, 8.5–6, Joseph claims that a Θεοσεβὴς ἀνὴρ (whatever the referent) does not kiss or embrace foreign women but only those women of his own family and tribe: "But a Θεοσεβὴς ἀνὴρ (a man who reveres God) will kiss his mother; and his sister **by his mother and his sister** who is of his own tribe and family; and his wife, who shares his bed; those women who with their mouths bless the living God." But note that nothing in this passage defines the group from which a Θεοσεβὴς ἀνὴρ may take a wife, even while it defines the women he may kiss: his mother and his sister. In fact, since the passage then goes on to describe them as women who with their mouths bless the living God rather than the dead gods of Aseneth, the text can be read to mean that the sole qualification for the wife of a Θεοσεβὴς ἀνὴρ is that she, too, bless the living God with her mouth. Endogamy here would appear to be irrelevant.

While one might argue that the marriage of Joseph provides a less convenient forum than the story of Tobit for the expression and resolution of anxiety about diaspora existence, it is interesting to remember that some rabbinic formulations of Aseneth do endeavor to make the marriage of Joseph endogamous by turning Aseneth into the daughter of Joseph's sister, Dinah (see the appendix). Since it seems to me not impossible that the formulators of *Aseneth* are aware of such a claim but do not accept it, the failure to fashion the marriage of Joseph and Aseneth into an endogamous one might be seen as further evidence that *Aseneth* has its origins in social and historical contexts very different from those of a work like Tobit. That is, the fact that Aseneth's repentance and mystical encounter are sufficient to transform her into an appropriate wife for Joseph, regardless of her birth and lineage, may point to authors and initial readers for whom such matters were also irrelevant to their standing before the divine.

11. The primary signifiers of identity in the text are Θεοσεβὴς for Joseph, his brothers, and his community and "Egyptians."

12. It would be interesting to speculate on the connection between this and the perception, itself problematic, that the majority of converts to Judaism in antiquity were women.

13. Translation mine. On ancient understandings of the gaze, see Blake Leyerle, "John Chrysostom on the Gaze," *JECS* 1, no. 2 (1993): 159–74.

14. Doty, *From Ivory Tower.* This interpretation is further challenged, I think, by recent postmodern criticism of ancient novels; see later discussion.

15. If I am right about this, even women slave owners could coerce their male slaves into sexual relations, effectively becoming male with regard to their feminized slaves.

16. νεανίσκος. Interestingly, this is the word used in the Gospel of Mark 16.5 for the being encountered by the women who come to Jesus' now-empty tomb—who in Matthew 28.2 becomes an angel of the Lord (ἄγγελος κυρίου) and in Luke 24.4, two men (ἄνδρες). Whether this suggests that it could here have an angelic connotation seems impossible to determine; its ordinary meaning is as translated.

17. See, e.g., Wayne Meeks, "The Image of the Androgyne: Some Uses of a Symbol in Earliest Christianity," *History of Religions* 13, no. 3 (1974): 185–89.

18. *On the Contemplative Life,* 68. On this see Kraemer, "Monastic Jewish Women in Greco-Roman Egypt: Philo on the Therapeutrides," *Signs: Journal of Women in Culture and Society* 14, no. 1 (1989): 342–70. On the more general question, see Richard Baer, *Philo's Use of the Categories Male and Female* (Leiden: E. J. Brill, 1971).

19. *Letter to Marcella* 33, in O'Brien, *To Marcella.* Wicker's own commentary here is unremarkable, but her paraphrasing of the passage makes me think that Porphyry here shares some of Philo's hierarchical ranking of irrational feminine soul, rational male soul, virginal soul. The last phrase is reminiscent of Philo's statement about the Therapeutrides' preference for spiritual children, in *On the Contemplative Life,* 68–69.

20. *Sayings of the Desert Fathers,* in Kraemer, *Maenads,* no. 66. Other examples include Perpetua, who dreams of herself as a male gladiator (no. 53); Thecla, who disguises herself as a man (no. 114); Pelagia (no. 125), who lives many years as a male monk, undetected by her "brethren."

21. However, it may be that tales of women becoming men are usually narrated by men. The theme also occurs in Hellenistic novels. Although the question may merit further consideration, I would be surprised to find that rabbinic Jewish sources ever utilize such a model; rather, exemplary women are likely there to remain women. This is true in such prerabbinic texts as Esther, Judith, Susanna, and so forth. Apart from Philo, the motif is rare in demonstrably Jewish sources, although 4 Macc makes much of the masculine virtues of the mother of the seven martyrs and it designates her as male.

22. *Acts of Thomas,* 4–16.

23. *Acts of Thomas,* 13.

24. *Acts of Thomas,* 14, translation from J. K. Elliott, *The Apocryphal New Testament* (Oxford: Oxford University Press, 1993).

25. Gayle Rubin, "The Traffic in Women: Notes on the 'Political Economy' of Sex," in Rayna R. Reiter, ed., *Toward an Anthropology of Women* (New York: Monthly Review Press), 157–211.

26. Perkins, *Suffering Self,* 49.

27. See, in particular, *Natural Symbols: Explorations in Cosmology* (London: Barrie and Rockcliffe; New York: Pantheon, 1970; reprint, 1973). Readers of Kraemer, *Her Share of the Blessings,* will be perhaps too familiar with Douglas's work and its implications for women's religions in antiquity.

28. Perkins, *Suffering Self,* 46–47.

29. Perkins, *Suffering Self,* 47.

30. Perkins, *Suffering Self,* 62.

31. Perkins, *Suffering Self,* 52–53.

32. Perkins, *Suffering Self,* 64.

33. Egger, "Women," 260–80.

34. Perkins, *Suffering Self,* 73.

35. *Aseneth* 2.1.

36. See, e.g., Ross S. Kraemer, "The Conversion of Women to Ascetic Forms of Christianity," *Signs: Journal of Women in Culture and Society* 6, no. 2 (1980): 298–307, reprinted in Judith M. Bennet, Elizabeth A. Clark, Jean O'Barr, B. Anne Vilen, and Sarah Westphal-Wihl, eds., *Sisters and Workers in the Middle Ages* (Chicago: University of Chicago Press, 1989), 198–207; Virginia Burrus, *Chastity as Autonomy: Women in the Stories of the Apocryphal Acts,* Studies in Women and Religion (Lewiston, NY: Edwin Mellen Press, 1987); Stevan Davies, *The Revolt of the Widows: The Social World of the Apocryphal Acts of the Apostles* (Champaign-Urbana: University of Illinois Press, 1980); Dennis Ronald MacDonald, *The Legend and the Apostle: The Battle for Paul in Story and Canon* (Philadelphia: Westminster Press, 1983).

I am particularly grateful to Virginia Burrus for sharing her latest work on these issues, work that includes a rethinking of the book cited here.

37. Cooper, *Virgin and the Bride,* 54–55.

38. Cooper, *Virgin and the Bride,* 55.

39. Cooper, *Virgin and the Bride,* 56.

40. Brent Shaw, "Body/Power/Identity: The Passions of the Martyrs," *JECS* 4, no. 3 (1996): 269–312.

41. For instance, it seems likely that paradigms of joint marital chastity and emphasis on concord and friendship contribute to the emergence of Christian paradigms of celibate marriage, since this is already a move away from marriage as centered on childbearing and the transmission of property to a construction of marriage as the perfect union of two like-minded souls—in which case the idea of a celibate marriage is not so far away. *Aseneth,* however, is clearly not a tale of celibate marriage.

42. Shaw writes: "[T]his new talk about the body is actually a discourse on a discourse; it is a way male writers could use the female body as a corporeal means of interpreting their world, including forms of resistance to it" ("Passions of the Martyrs," 295).

43. See n. 20. See also Gillian Cloke, *"This Female Man of God": Women and Spiritual Power in the Patristic Age,* A.D. *350–450* (London: Routledge, 1995).

44. It is true that an emphasis on Joseph's chastity may be found also in early midrashic traditions, although further analysis of those materials might suggest that they, too, have some relation to these same ideas. Further, while early interpretive traditions about Joseph were concerned with whether he resisted Potiphar's wife and how he knew to do so, they can address these concerns without constructing Joseph as totally without sexual experience, something the text of *Aseneth* nevertheless does.

45. Cooper, *Virgin and the Bride,* 56.

46. Cooper, *Virgin and the Bride,* 92–115.

47. In addition to Cooper's discussion and the work of Peter Brown, *The Body and Society: Men, Women, and Sexual Renunciation in Early Christianity* (New York: Columbia University Press, 1988), see also the useful discussion in Robert Markus, *The End of Ancient Christianity* (Cambridge: Cambridge University Press, 1990), 38–43, on Christian conflict over the importance of celibacy. Particularly interesting is the example he adduces (38) from Socrates, *H.E.* 1.11, that at the Council of Nicaea, Paphnutius defended marriage, asserting that "a married man's intercourse with his wife deserved the name of chastity."

48. For another consideration of these differences, see Standhartinger, *Das Frauenbild,* whose acceptance of the thesis that *Aseneth* is the product of early Hellenistic Jewish circles makes it less useful for my purposes.

49. Interestingly, later on the longer text will substitute the notion of rest for that of the bridal chamber in chap. 15 and insert Aseneth's place of rest in the scene with Levi in chap. 22.

50. "You have turned my mourning into dancing; you have taken off my sackcloth and clothed me with joy, so that my soul may praise you and not be silent."

51. See also chapter 6, on the significance of silence in theurgic liturgy.

52. These associations are present in rabbinic sources as well, e.g., *b. Ber* 3a, where marital intercourse is described as a woman "conversing" with her husband; also *b. Ned* 20a–b, on the marital intercourse of R. Eliezer and his wife, Imma Shalom.

53. See esp. Kathleen E. Corley, *Private Women, Public Meals: Social Conflict in the Synoptic Tradition* (Peabody, MA: Hendricksen, 1993), 24–79, esp. 42–44.

54. E.g., Prov 8.1–8, 31.26, on the speech of the Wise Woman; 2.16, 5.3, 6.24, 7.4, 7.21, on the Strange Woman and the adulterous woman.

55. *Ps. Philo* 42, esp. 42.4.

56. Standhartinger (*Frauenbild,* esp. 189–204) suggests that the shorter text presents Aseneth, Metanoia, and Wisdom (all identified with one another) as unequivocally female, while the longer text undercuts these associations and attempts to masculinize Wisdom, for instance, in its arrogation of Aseneth's roles to Joseph. These differences reflect, in her view, debates in hellenistic Jewish circles over the gender of Wisdom/Logos, discernible particularly in Philo. Such debates reverberate also, she thinks, in early Christian circles, discernible beneath Paul's correspondence with the Corinthians. While her thesis is interesting, it is too dependent, in my view, on the unexamined assumptions that *Aseneth* is both early and Jewish.

57. E.g., Irenaeus, *Against Heresies* III.22.4.

58. It is interesting that whether or not angels actually ate is a matter of concern to ancient writers. The angels who appear to Abraham in Gen 18 are said, without nuance, to eat, while the angel who appears in Judg 13 declines the proffered meal. The angel Raphael, who appears to Tobit and his son, Tobias, says pointedly of his apparent consumption of food, "I did not really eat or drink anything—but what you saw was a vision" (12.19).

59. Gail Paterson Corrington, *Her Image of Salvation: Female Saviors and Formative Christianity* (Louisville, KY: Westminster Press, 1992).

60. While the assignment of this role to a figure other than Mary might appear to argue against a Christian connection, it seems somewhat bizarre to assign so fundamental a cosmic reversal to a figure in the early stages of Jewish history, particularly since that history then continues without any indication that Paradise has been restored or the actions of Adam and Eve undone. For Christian readers for whom Aseneth was a symbolic type, as in Ephrem or Aphrahat, though, this association of Aseneth with Eve would have made much more sense and posed much less in the way of problems.

61. *On Baptism,* 17.5. Tertullian claims that the story is used to license women performing baptisms. For recent discussions of precisely what Tertullian has in mind, see Willy Rordorf, "Tertullien et les *ACTES DE PAUL* (à propos de *bapt.* 17, 5)" in *Lex Orandi, Lex Credendi: Paradosis: Beiträge zur Geschichte der altchristlichen Literatur und Theologie XXXVI, Gesammelte Aufsätze zum 60. Geburtstag* (Freiburg: Universitätsverlag, 1993), 475–84.

62. In the Gospel of Luke, an angel appears to Mary, announcing the forthcoming conception and birth of Jesus, although the angelic annunciation of the conception and birth of John the Baptist is made to his father, not his mother, Elizabeth. The annunciation to Mary could then be construed as demonstration or confirmation that Jesus had no earthly father; alternatively, or additionally, it affirms the special nature of Mary. In the synoptic Gospels, as well as the Gospel of Peter, women learn of the resurrection of Jesus from one (Mark, Matthew, Peter) or two (Luke) angels. In the Gospel of John, two angels appear to Mary of Magdala, although the description of their appearance is attenuated and followed immediately by the appearance of Jesus himself. Interestingly, as I noted above, in Mark, the figure is called νεανίσκος, the same term the angel uses with regard to Aseneth's head; in Matthew, it is an angel of the Lord; in Luke, two men (ἄνδρες); in John, two angels; in Peter, a young man (νεανίσκος). Both Matthew and Luke expand the Markan scene to incorporate both traditional description of angelic garments and traditional responses of fear.

63. See chapter 5, nn. 180–81.

64. See chapter 8. We might also note a tale in the *Acts of Thomas,* 51–59. There, a young woman who had refused her lover's offer to adopt a chaste relationship is subsequently murdered by him (a tale of domestic abuse in ancient garb?). When the young man confesses, Thomas resurrects the woman. She then relates a short apocalyptic vision, in which, apparently after death, an ugly, dirty man took her on a tour of hell, populated particularly by persons who have committed various sexual sins, and then returned her to the custody of Thomas.

65. This is certainly a stance taken by later ascetic writers who argued that marriage was

necessary prior to the birth of Christ, in order that he might be born into the Davidic household; only after his birth is marriage no longer necessary.

66. See chapters 6 and 11.

67. Juvenal, *Satire* 6, does caricature a Jewish woman as high priestess (Kraemer, *Maenads,* entry 25).

68. See chapter 1 and the appendix.

69. Egger, "Marriage," 263.

70. Egger, "Marriage," 262; for additional discussion of the general question, see references on p. 275, n. 13.

71. Egger, "Marriage," 271.

72. Egger, "Marriage," 271.

73. Egger, "Marriage," 266–69.

74. Egger, "Marriage," 269.

75. Egger, "Marriage," 271.

76. Egger, "Marriage," 272–73.

77. See chapter 1; see also Kraemer, "Women's Authorship of Jewish and Christian Literature in the Greco-Roman Period," in Amy-Jill Levine, ed., *"Women Like this": New Perspectives on Jewish Women in the Greco-Roman Period,* Early Judaism and Its Literature 1 (Atlanta: Scholars Press, 1991), 221–42.

78. Egger, Marriage," 264.

79. The only character who ever reads is Levi, who sees letters written in the heavens and tells them to Aseneth in 22.9 (Philonenko, *Joseph et Aséneth*). Interestingly, in the Christian narrative of Irene, the heroine is explicitly portrayed as studying with a tutor while imprisoned in her tower.

80. Egger, "Marriage," 273.

81. Egger, "Marriage," 279–80, n. 54.

82. We might also consider the possibility that some form of *Aseneth* was composed for a female patron, a possibility that may be stronger if we consider *Aseneth* to be of Christian origin (though on what it might mean to describe the text[s] in this way, see chapter 9). For an interesting discussion of the role of Christian women as patrons in the later Roman empire, see Elizabeth A. Clark, "Ideology, History, and the Construction of 'Woman' in Late Ancient Christianity," *JECS* 2, no. 2 (1994): 155–84.

Relocating *Aseneth*

CHAPTER EIGHT

The Dating of *Aseneth* Reconsidered

Dull as discussions of dating usually are, even for specialists, much hinges on the dating of the Aseneth stories. *Aseneth* is extant principally in Greek, which was almost certainly the language of its composition, and in Latin, Slavic, Armenian, and Roumanian, all in manuscripts that date no earlier than the tenth century C.E. Two Syriac manuscripts that date to the sixth or seventh centuries C.E. contain a translation of *Aseneth* as part of an anonymous historical compilation of twelve books covering the period from creation through 569 C.E., known as the *Church History* or the *Syriac Chronicle* of Pseudo-Zacharias Rhetor.[1] The same *Chronicle* prefaces the translation of *Aseneth* with two chapters. The first is an anonymous letter to one Moses, reporting the discovery of a little Greek book called the *Book of Asyath* and requesting a translation into Syriac; the second is a response by Moses sending the requested translation. This Moses is apparently one Moses of Inghila, who is known to have translated another Greek work into Syriac in the second half of the sixth century. Taken together, the identification of the translator as Moses of Inghila and the inclusion of the material in the *Syriac Chronicle* suggest that the Aseneth story was composed in Greek prior to 569 C.E.[2] No ancient fragments of *Aseneth* have ever been identified that antedate the Syriac manuscripts, and no ancient author is known to quote it directly.

Apart from the Syriac attestation to a Greek edition, the earliest allusion to the Greek stories appears to be found in a medieval work by Peter the Deacon of Monte Cassino, entitled *On the Holy Places,* written before 1137. There the author describes the Egyptian city of Heliopolis, where stood the Temple of the Sun, the house of Petefres, and the house of Aseneth.[3] Since we know of Aseneth's house only from the tale of *Aseneth,* scholars such as Christoph Burchard consider this a probable allusion to our story. If, furthermore, as some scholars believe, Peter found this description in the now lost beginning of the late fourth- or early fifth-century pilgrimage diary by a woman named Egeria,[4] and if Egeria got it from our *Aseneth* tradition, the original *Aseneth* cannot be later than the fourth century C.E. This logic is a little optimistic, since even if Egeria knew of a place called Aseneth's house, and even if we only know of her house from our texts, the passage as we have it in Peter the Deacon is not necessarily proof of the existence of our Aseneth story. Rather, it testifies only to the existence of a legend about Aseneth's house that would not be difficult to generate out of the biblical texts themselves. And Burchard himself expresses some doubt about whether the Heliopolis tradition (purportedly) in Egeria in fact reflects knowledge of our *Aseneth*.[5]

Neither the tradition in Peter the Deacon nor the Syriac *Aseneth* in Pseudo-Zacharias compels us to argue for a date earlier than the late fourth or early fifth century C.E. Despite this, *Aseneth* is generally assigned a date of somewhere between the first century B.C.E. and the early second century C.E. for a variety of reasons that, as we shall see, are extraordinarily problematic.

To a significant degree, arguments about the dating of *Aseneth* are tied to assumptions about the Jewishness of the text. Partly because we have no Greek literary texts known with absolute certainty to have been authored by Jews after the end of the first or perhaps the beginning of the second century C.E., many scholars tend to assume that any Jewish text authored in Greek is likely to have been written before that terminus. This identification of (presumably) Jewish Greek texts as relatively early continues, then, to reinforce the idea that all such texts are early and appears to strengthen the belief that no Jewish literary texts survive from the period after, say, the Bar Kokhba rebellion (132–35 C.E.). Conversely, any undated Greek text thought to be Jewish is assigned a relatively early date, and any ambiguous Greek text of demonstrably late date is considered unlikely to be Jewish.

The problems with these assumptions are manifold. Josephus is the last known Jewish author to have written in Greek, although texts whose authors are essentially unknown, such as 4 Ezra, may postdate Josephus by some years. Yet ample evidence, both literary and archeological, demonstrates that a large number of Jews, if not the numerical majority in the Greco-Roman world, continued to use Greek in their daily lives, their worship, their reading of Jewish scripture, and the affairs of their synagogues to the end of late antiquity. It is simply incredible to think that these Jews stopped writing literary works after the first century C.E.

As Goodenough suggests in his monumental *Jewish Symbols in the Greco-Roman Period,* some of the answer may lie in the fact that all Greek Jewish literature has been transmitted not by Jews but by Christians, although their respective motives in this regard were quite different. Goodenough's observations on these matters are worth reproducing at length:

> The earliest Christians, however, and this is of the greatest importance, preserved and even alluded to hellenized Jewish literature only if it was pre-Christian, or written in the first or second century after Christ. Christian traditions of the first centuries as taken from the Christian writers refer to the contemporary writings of not a single Jew. . . . [T]he . . . writings of pre-Christian hellenized Jews seem to have been preserved as part of what Eusebius called the "preparation" for Christianity. . . . Writings produced by Jews who denounced Christianity, and continued to live the life of the Law (whatever that may have

meant to them), to build synagogues, and put menorahs on their graves, would not have commended themselves to Christian study and copying.

So if hellenized Jews did exist and write books in the early Christian centuries, neither Christians nor the rabbinic Jews who ultimately dominated Judaism would have cared to preserve their writings. . . . That we have no writings from these Jews simply indicates that if they did write, as we must presume some of them did, they wrote books of a kind unpleasing to the rabbis, and of course, to the Christians.[6]

While there is much wisdom in Goodenough's interpretation of the motives of both Christians and rabbinic Jews, it is also the case that modern scholars (some of whom may have inherited these assumptions of ancient Christians and/or rabbinic Jews) have too quickly accepted the claim that no Jewish works survive that were composed in Greek after the early second century C.E. In the specific case of *Aseneth,* this has meant that evidence in favor of a relatively late date has received short shrift once the text has been judged to be Jewish. Interestingly, Batiffol, the first scholar to publish the Greek text a little over a century ago, initially dated *Aseneth* to the fourth or the fifth century C.E., a stance from which, as we shall see, he quickly retreated when challenged.[7] The modern French scholar of *Aseneth,* Philonenko, attributes Batiffol's initial dating to his assessment that the text was Christian.[8] While Philonenko may have been correct that these two elements were linked in Batiffol's mind, it is equally true that the judgments of Philonenko and others have been linked to their identification of the text as Jewish. The fact remains that no hard evidence compels a date prior to the fourth century C.E.[9]

Arguments for dating *Aseneth* no later than the beginning of the second century C.E. have further depended on assumptions about the location of the author. Philonenko's judgment that the text was written in Egypt and his insistence on the significance of this fact for the dating of the text are representative of the views of many scholars. "Any proposition for the dating [of *Aseneth*] which does not take into account the Egyptian origin of the novel must be rejected."[10] Burchard has exercised more caution on this point, as on many, noting that alternative geographic locations have never been explored in any detail, but in the end, he, too, considers Egypt "the most likely birthplace" of our tale.[11]

Scholars who accept an Egyptian provenance for *Aseneth* have further reasoned that it must have been written prior to the years 115–117 C.E., when a major Jewish uprising in Egypt and North Africa seems to have resulted in the decimation of most of the Jewish communities in those regions.[12] Not only would this have decreased the number of potential authors, but also it would have rendered implausible a text that envisions such amicable relations between "Hebrews" and "Egyptians."

In a curiously circular manner, the argument that *Aseneth* was composed by an Egyptian Jew is sometimes undergirded by the assumption that it dates to approximately the first century C.E. Since much Greek Jewish literature whose provenance is known with some certainty seems to have come from Egypt, scholars tend, probably too easily, to assign an Egyptian provenance to anything that has some potential association with Egypt and exhibits no obvious indications to the contrary. As I will pursue further in chapter 10, arguments for Egyptian provenance are not nearly as persuasive as they might initially appear and cannot be used as independent evidence for dating the text(s).

Yet another interlocking argument for an early date for *Aseneth* has been the belief that its central concern was Jewish missionizing and the place of proselytes within Jewish life.[13] Because the story is perceived to be about "conversion," many scholars, influenced enormously by Christian paradigms, have believed that the story is about proselytism, that is, about efforts on the part of Jews to persuade non-Jews to abandon polytheism, adopt Jewish practices and beliefs, and enter into communal Jewish life. They have further assumed that such concerns must have driven *Aseneth*'s composition.[14] From the fact that the Roman emperor Hadrian outlawed the circumcision of non-Jews about the time of the Bar Kokhba revolt (c. 132–35 C.E.),[15] some scholars have further concluded that both active Jewish and Jewish acceptance of converts would largely have ceased at this time, establishing the early second century C.E. as the latest possible date for *Aseneth*.[16]

Although these arguments acquire validity through repetition, they have by no means the force of certainty or even strong probability. As we have seen, the formulation and composition of the *Aseneth* narratives could have been and probably were grounded in a number of concerns whose relationship to actual social circumstances is uncertain at best, including concerns about anomalies in the biblical story of Genesis. Some of the most recent studies of *Aseneth* have argued that its heavy dependence on biblical allusions and imagery belies the pagan audience that the missionary hypothesis requires.[17] Even if *Aseneth* is primarily concerned with Jewish proselytism and conversion to Judaism, it is simply untrue that no historical and social context for such concerns exists in Greco-Roman antiquity after the second century C.E. Inscriptional evidence from Rome to Asia Minor points to pagans adopting Jewish practices and beliefs and designating themselves as proselytes in the second, third, and fourth centuries C.E.[18] It may be the case that such activity is less likely to have flourished in Egypt after the second century. But as I have pointed out and will expand further later, the evidence for an Egyptian provenance itself depends on some of the very same assumptions it is then used to prove. *Pace* Philonenko, it is simply not the case that any efforts to situate the composition of *Aseneth* must take into account its Egyptian origins.

Several other factors are relevant to a discussion of probable date. One is the apparent absence of any knowledge of this Aseneth story in early Jewish sources. Virtually no trace of it appears in ancient Jewish exegetical traditions preserved in Greek. Fragments of early Greek Jewish writers such as Demetrius the Chronographer or Artapanus that retell the biblical narratives include references to Joseph's marriage to Aseneth but show no trace of the story.[19] Neither Philo nor Josephus appears to know the story or any elements of it.[20] The *Testament of Joseph* in the *Testament of the Twelve Patriarchs* focuses at length on the episode of Joseph and the wife of Potiphar (whom, consonant with the Septuagint translation, it calls Petephres) but mentions his marriage to Aseneth only twice. In 18.3 Joseph recalls that "on account of my humility and patient endurance I took to myself a wife, the daughter of the priest of Heliopolis; a hundred talents of gold were given to me along with her, and my Lord caused them [the Egyptians] to be my servants."[21] In 20.3, Joseph instructs his children to take not only his bones back to the land of Israel for burial but also those of Aseneth, which he instructs them to bury "by the hippodrome, near Rachel."

Jubilees similarly seems unacquainted with our story, merely identifying Aseneth as the wife of Joseph (34.20) and the mother of Manasseh and Ephraim (44.24). *Jubilees* 40.10 explicitly equates Joseph's master, Potiphar (Hebrew: Potiphar), with Aseneth's father (Hebrew: Potiphera) so that Aseneth becomes Potiphar's daughter:[22] "And [Pharaoh] gave the daughter of Potiphar, the daughter of the priest of Heliopolis, the chief of the guard, to Joseph (as) a wife." This claim is, in fact, in direct opposition to our Aseneth stories, which assume that her father, Pentephres, and Joseph's former master are two different people.[23] Interestingly, although *Aseneth* focuses on Levi as a prophet and as a mystagogue who defends Aseneth from attack in the second portion of the story, the *Testament of Levi* contains no mention of Aseneth.

Pseudo-Philo's *Biblical Antiquities,* which is otherwise distinctive for its extensive materials about biblical women,[24] has nothing to say about Aseneth, omitting any mention of her in the genealogy of Jacob and Joseph. Yet it also contains a curious passage about Joseph that may suggest that the author is unacquainted with our *Aseneth* story. In retelling the story of Samson, the author has God rebuke him for his marriage to the Philistine Delilah, contrasting Samson unfavorably with, of all persons, "Joseph, my servant, who was in a foreign land and became a crown for his brothers because he was not willing to afflict his own seed" (43.5).[25] Apparently, what the author has in mind here is Genesis 39, where Joseph resists the advances of an Egyptian woman: the wife of his master, Potiphar. According to Genesis itself, Joseph appears to resist her overtures because she is Potiphar's wife, not because she is a foreigner (Gen 39.9), and the story is generally read that way in later Jewish interpretation.[26] The contrast of Samson with Joseph in the *Biblical Antiquities* is then somewhat intriguing, since Samson's flaw is clearly intermarriage (and sexual contact with a foreigner, which leads to procreation?) and not adultery. But in this regard it is a particularly peculiar choice of contrasts since only two chapters later Genesis records the marriage of Joseph to the daughter of an Egyptian priest! Joseph in this regard would seem to be a less than ideal choice with which to upbraid Samson. Since it seems unlikely that Pseudo-Philo has simply forgotten this crucial detail of Joseph's biography, what if anything may we conclude is relevant to our Aseneth story?

One possibility is that while Pseudo-Philo is not ignorant of Joseph's marriage to Aseneth, it recedes here from the author's consciousness in favor of the strong traditions about Joseph's great virtue in the face of sexual temptation by a foreigner. Furthermore, the author's failure to adduce our Aseneth story at this point might constitute evidence that he does not know it, since such an account of Aseneth's renunciation of idolatry and transformation into an acceptable bride for Joseph would serve the author's purposes quite well.[27]

The author's apparent lack of embarassment about the inconsistency of his portrait of Joseph as one who resists foreign women might also suggest that he both knows a tradition about Aseneth that resolves this difficulty and assumes that his readers do, too.[28] While this is not inconceivable, it strikes me as highly implausible. Given the author's strong convictions about intermarriage, it seems unlikely that he would pass up an opportunity to absolve the biblical Joseph of any such apparent hypocrisy. Further, his silence on the marriage of Joseph in his detailed retelling of the life of Joseph strengthens the probability that Aseneth is an embarassment for Pseudo-Philo rather than a nonissue. Finally, in order for the author to consider the marriage of Joseph in need of no discussion, such explanatory tales (whether the rabbinic Dinah legend, our

Aseneth stories, or anything else) would need to have been exceedingly well known, in which case it seems odd that we have no evidence for them in sources contemporaneous with or antecedent to Pseudo-Philo (c. mid–first century C.E.).[29] I am thus tempted to conclude that Pseudo-Philo is unaware of any such stories.

An intriguing tidbit about Aseneth occurs in the Genesis commentary of the third-century Christian writer, Origen, according to which Aseneth's father and Joseph's master were one and the same.[30] After Aseneth informed her father of her mother's deceit about Joseph, her father gave Aseneth to Joseph to show the Egyptians he held no grudge against Joseph. It may be significant that Origen doesn't adduce our *Aseneth,* since Origen's concern here is whether Potiphar and Potiphera were one and the same.

In his *Commentary on the Gospel of John,* though, Origen cites a passage from an otherwise essentially unknown work that he describes as apocrypha circulating among the Hebrews, called the *Prayer of Joseph,* which may relate more closely to at least some versions of the Greek *Aseneth.*[31]

> I, Jacob, who is speaking to you, am also Israel, an angel of God and a ruling spirit. Abraham and Isaac were created before any work. But I, Jacob, who men call Jacob but whose name is Israel am he who God called Israel which means, a man seeing God, because I am the firstborn of every living thing to whom God gives life.
>
> And when I was coming up from Syrian Mesopotamia, Uriel, the angel of God, came forth and said that "I [Jacob-Israel] had descended to earth and I had tabernacled among men and that I had been called by the name of Jacob." He envied me and fought with me and wrestled with me saying that his name and the name that is before every angel was to be above mine. I told him his name and what rank he held among the sons of God. "Are you not Uriel, the eighth after me: and I, Israel, the archangel of the power of the Lord and the chief captain among the sons of God? Am I not Israel, the first minister before the face of God?" And I called upon my God by the inextinguishable name.

Philonenko proposes that the angelic view of Jacob in the *Prayer* influenced the portrait of Jacob in the longer version at **22.7–8** (although not the shorter), which reads:

> Jacob was exceedingly beautiful to look at, and his old age (was) like the youth of a handsome (young) man, . . . and his sinews and his shoulders and his arms were like (those) of an angel, and his thighs and his calves and his feet like (those) of a giant. And Jacob was like a man who had wrestled with God.

Philonenko writes: "It seems reasonable to admit that the redactor of the first long recension was inspired for this addition by the *Prayer of Joseph.* This recension would have been later, then, than the *Prayer of Joseph,*" whose date, he admits, is difficult to determine, although obviously it must predate Origen.[32]

Although the testimony of Origen allows us only to date the *Prayer of Joseph* no later than the early third century C.E., Jonathan Z. Smith suggests a date from the first century C.E., citing only "various parallels to hellenistic and Aramaic materials."[33] Regardless of its date, the story about Aseneth that Origen transmits is antithetical to our *Aseneth* and tells us nothing directly about the date of the Greek stories. The connection between the portrait of Jacob as an angel in the *Prayer of Joseph* and in the longer reconstruction of *Aseneth* is more suggestive, although not definitive. Even if the redactor of the longer reconstruction utilized the *Prayer of Joseph,* our inability to date the latter with much more precision than the third-century terminus makes any relationship between the two of minimal use in securing a date for *Aseneth.*

At the very least, this survey of early Jewish exegetical traditions preserved in Greek and/or Latin suggests that neither our Aseneth story nor any of its distinctive elements were known to the authors of these sources. Further, it suggests that the biblical Aseneth story was of little interest to these retellers of Genesis and that it was a source of little if any controversy or speculation, although Pseudo-Philo's silence on the marriage may conceivably derive from a self-conscious discomfort. In part because all of these texts are usually dated before the second century C.E., this certainly does not *preclude* a relatively early date for *Aseneth* (particularly a date at the end of the first or the very beginning of the second century C.E.). However, it does suggest that if *Aseneth* was composed prior to 100 C.E., it had a very limited circulation and either drew on Aseneth traditions that have somehow eluded all other ancient sources or represents the work of a highly individual exegete. While none of this is impossible, there is no particular reason to argue for such a scenario and, as we shall see, considerable reason to argue against it.

The Import of Rabbinic Traditions for the Dating of *Aseneth*

As I sketched above, when Batiffol first published a Greek text of *Aseneth* a little more than a century ago, he identified it as a Christian text composed in the fifth century C.E., in the vicinity of Phrygian Hierapolis, a city in central Asia Minor now known as Pammukkale. Its primary source, he proposed, was a Jewish haggadic legend, no longer extant, which he titled "The Legend of Dina and Aseneth." This legend, according to which Aseneth was in reality the daughter of Joseph's niece Dinah, was, he argued, also the basis for stories we now have in numerous late rabbinic sources and was itself finalized in the fourth century C.E.[34]

Reviewers of Batiffol took him to task immediately on many points, among them his contention that the story of Dinah underlay *Aseneth.*[35] In response, Batiffol modified his views, conceding the possibility that Aseneth was Jewish and early.[36] Nevertheless, subsequent scholars were divided in their opinions, as Chesnutt conveniently chronicles.[37] E. W. Brooks, who published a revised edition of the text, concurred with Batiffol's initial judgment that the text was Christian, while K. Kohler argued for its Jewish missionary character in an entry in the *Jewish Encyclopedia.*[38] Interestingly, Jewish scholars seem to have leaned in favor of a Jewish identification, while Christian scholars generally favored a Christian author.[39]

Despite Batiffol's own reconsideration, an eminent rabbinics scholar still found it necessary thirty-five years later to challenge Batiffol with regard to both the dating and the provenance of the story, while defending Batiffol's thesis that an haggadic legend of Aseneth as the daughter of Dinah undergirded the Greek text(s). Victor Aptowitzer argued that the Greek was not a Christian composition but was, on the contrary, a thinly Christianized translation of a thoroughly rabbinic text originally composed in Hebrew in the first century C.E. by a Jew living in Palestine, whom he took for granted was a man. While subsequent scholars generally have rejected

Aptowitzer's contention that the text was written in Palestine in Hebrew,[40] all now essentially concur with the broad outlines of his thesis that the Greek *Aseneth* was authored by a Jew around the first century C.E.[41]

Apart from his contention that *Aseneth* was composed in Greek, the arguments and judgments of Batiffol were largely jettisoned. While the arguments for dating *Aseneth* are hardly derived solely from Aptowitzer's theses, his claims about *Aseneth*'s dependence on an early rabbinic Dinah legend play an important part in arguments about the date and religious identification of *Aseneth* in the work of Philonenko, who remains to this date editor of the only published critical edition. In his introduction to Cook's English translation of Philonenko's text, H. F. D. Sparks accepts the early dating of the Dinah traditions but asserts that "these legends have no direct contact with *Joseph and Aseneth* in the form in which we know it."[42] Burchard dismissed the significance of the Dinah legend as a source for *Aseneth,* at least in the Syriac form that Oppenheim published in the nineteenth century,[43] arguing that if anything, the Syriac legend was dependent on our *Aseneth* story and not vice versa.[44] Although I concur with this judgment, the Dinah traditions require more detailed consideration before we may confidently set them aside as a possible factor in the dating of *Aseneth.*

Batiffol, and Aptowitzer after him, grounded their discussions in similar observations. Both agreed that the earliest clear testimony to the existence of *Aseneth* was the Syriac translation of Moses of Inghila in the mid–sixth century C.E. For Batiffol, this gave him license only to place the Greek about a century earlier, based on the description of the Greek as "very old." For Aptowitzer, though, this proved merely the jumping-off point for what ultimately became a leap of approximately 500 years.

Batiffol also took seriously the complaint of the anonymous writer who commissioned Moses' translation that he could understand the story (*historia*) of Aseneth but not the allegory (*theōria*). For Batiffol, it was precisely the allegorical interpretation of *Aseneth* that demonstrated the Christian character of the text.[45] He concluded that the Greek *Aseneth* represented a Christian transformation of an earlier Jewish legend about Aseneth, whose trace was reflected in the designation "*historia*" by the anonymous Syrian.[46]

Batiffol was led to this conclusion at least in part by a peculiarity in the text that Aptowitzer also found odd. Near the beginning of the story, when Joseph sees Aseneth at her window (7.2), he asks Pentephres to send her away, fearing that the sight of him will trigger desire in her. But Pentephres replies that Aseneth is no foreign woman but his daughter, a virgin who detests men. He then actually calls her Joseph's sister (7.8), whereupon Joseph rejoices and tells Pentephres to send for Aseneth, whom he loves henceforth as his sister (7.11). Finding this characterization of Aseneth perplexing, Batiffol proposed two different but related explanations.

The first he drew from rabbinic traditions that claimed that Aseneth was the daughter of Joseph's niece, Dinah, who had been raped, according to Genesis 34, by a Canaanite named Shechem. Batiffol was careful to note that the rabbinic collections from which he cited this story date, in their present forms, no earlier than the seventh century C.E. Acknowledging that later rabbinic sources often preserve earlier materials, he located the origins of the Dinah legend in the fourth century C.E. He then proposed that such a legend, preserved now only in bits and pieces in various rabbinic sources and in the very late Syriac fragment published by Oppenheim,[47] was the basis both for those rabbinic tellings and for the Greek "Christian" *Aseneth.*

Batiffol was aware, though, that his "Christian" *Aseneth* contains no explicit mention of the Dinah story and offers, at least in Batiffol's reading, a completely different explanation for the sibling relationship of Joseph and Aseneth. Focusing on Pentephres' description of Aseneth as a virgin, Batiffol proposed that the Christian author accounted for the tie between Joseph and Aseneth as a spiritual tie, over against the blood tie demonstrated in the Dinah legend.[48] In Batiffol's view, the Christian author knew the Dinah story yet offered an alternative and, by Christian standards, superior explanation for the designation of Aseneth and Joseph as sister and brother.

Aptowitzer, too, began his analysis of the date of *Aseneth* with the testimony transmitted with the Syriac translation of *Aseneth* contained in the *Syriac Chronicle.* He, too, agreed that since the accompanying letter calls the *Book of Aseneth* "very old," the translated Greek must have been at least 100 years earlier.[49] He also concurred with Batiffol's assessment that the Greek *Aseneth* presumes the existence of the Dinah legend, from which it nevertheless diverged. But at this point, Aptowitzer parted company with Batiffol's original analysis on three major points: the original language of composition, the date, and the religious identification of the author.[50] Where Batiffol had seen distinctive Christian symbolism, Aptowitzer saw a profusion of rabbinic parallels. Partly on linguistic grounds, Aptowitzer was persuaded that Batiffol's Greek text was itself a translation from the Hebrew, which, he argued, had to be at least a century older than the Greek that Moses of Inghila translated into Syriac.[51] (Ironically, though, the preface offers somewhat contrary testimony: no sooner does the anonymous writer to Moses discover and read the little *Book of Asyath* than he commissions its translation, suggesting that the process could transpire in considerably less than one century.) This reasoning took him back to the fourth century C.E., the date Batiffol initially offered for the crystallization of the Dinah legend. Aptowitzer's lengthy analysis of rabbinic traditions in *Aseneth* led him ultimately to argue for a date around the first century C.E.

Aptowitzer endeavored to demonstrate that *Aseneth* drew heavily on traditions and associations that occur in a melange of Jewish sources. Although many of those materials occur only in relatively late Jewish compilations, Aptowitzer's confidence that late Jewish sources transmit much older traditions[52] enabled him to dispense with any critical analysis of the dating of specific traditions. For Aptowitzer, any similarities between *Aseneth* and midrashic sources was testimony both to the Jewish origins of the stories contained in the Greek *Aseneth* and to the dependence of the latter upon the former.

Most compelling for Aptowitzer, though, was his analysis of the Dinah traditions. He shared Batiffol's judgment that the Dinah story underlay both the scene discussed above and the description of Aseneth as "in all ways like the daughters of the Hebrews" (1.8) and therefore that *Aseneth* had to have been composed after the formulation of the Dinah traditions.[53]

But whereas Batiffol, cognizant that the earliest explicit occurrences of the Dinah legend were relatively late, was content to assign the Dinah story a date in the fourth century, with *Aseneth* itself composed half a century to a century later, Aptowitzer argued differently. He was further convinced that the story of Dinah as Aseneth's mother underlay a tradition about Aseneth being partially blind, which occurs in some manuscripts of *Genesis Rabbah*.[54] There, when Joseph brings his sons to be blessed by the dying Jacob, the elder patriarch asks of the children, "Who are these?" (Gen 48.8). Joseph replies, "They are my sons, whom God gave me בזה" and he brings forth Asenath, whom the text describes as blind in one eye. Although the text says nothing about the significance of this handicap, Aptowitzer linked it to other traditions about Dinah's child being blind, which unfortunately he does not document.[55] Since the passage also contains a comment attributed to Rabbi Ammi, who is traditionally dated to the late third century C.E., Aptowitzer viewed this as the "oldest *literary* trace" of the legend, which, he said, "must *naturally* be much older."[56] Aptowitzer now thought he had evidence to place the Dinah tradition significantly earlier than the third century. On the basis of such strained reasoning, together with the imaginative suggestion that the composition of Aseneth was related to the conversion of Queen Helena of Adiabene detailed by Josephus,[57] he confidently assigned a first-century C.E. date to what he believed to be the Hebrew original.

Although Aptowitzer's claims about Rabbi Ammi and the Dinah tradition were crucial to his argument about the date of *Aseneth*,[58] and thus played a not insignificant role in the history of scholarship, they turn out to be highly problematic. In the first place, it is not at all clear that Aptowitzer's interpretation of the passage as an allusion to the Dinah tradition is correct.[59] Aptowitzer himself was troubled by the fact that other passages in *Genesis Rabbah* explicitly identify Aseneth as the biological daughter of Pentephres and therefore contradict traditions in which her parents were Dinah and Shechem.[60] The passage on which Aptowitzer relied does not occur in most manuscripts of *Genesis Rabbah* and is found in a section of the work that appears to have been particularly prone to much later accretions.[61] Whether it is thus reliable testimony to early forms of *Genesis Rabbah,* let alone to the circulation of the Dinah legend in the third century, seems seriously problematic.

While Aptowitzer focused on the legend of Dinah as the mother of Aseneth, rabbinic sources in fact transmit three different views about Aseneth's identity, which are presented in detail in the appendix. Taken as a whole, these views testify to discomfort about Joseph's marriage to Aseneth, but they are rooted in the peculiar complexities of ancient biblical exegesis and midrash. Some sources unambiguously designate Aseneth a proselyte, while others deny that she was truly the daughter of Potiphera and make her the daughter of Dinah and Shechem instead. Still other traditions assert that her father was something other than an Egyptian priest. These varying interpretations about Aseneth are obviously facilitated by the rather terse and somewhat ambiguous nature of the biblical verses, which simply state that Pharaoh gave Joseph Aseneth, the daughter of Potiphera, priest of On, as his wife (Gen 41.45). But the majority of midrashic Jewish traditions about Aseneth are clearly affected by ancient identifications of Joseph's father-in-law, Potiphera, with his master, Potiphar (Gen 37.36, 39). The intersection of these two stories assimilates Potiphar's titles and traits to Potiphera, and vice versa, with significant results.

Interestingly enough, no demonstrably early rabbinic sources, such as the Mishnah or Tosefta, contain traditions about Aseneth, whether as proselyte or as daughter of Dinah. Such traditions are also absent from the two Talmudim.[62] Probably the earliest rabbinic reference to Aseneth occurs in *Genesis Rabbah,* if that compilation should properly be assigned a date of fourth or fifth century C.E.[63] Later midrashic compositions and anthologies of rabbinic traditions contain numerous interesting materials about Aseneth, discussed in the appendix.

One tradition about Joseph known from rabbinic sources does occur in *Aseneth* 7.6: "Joseph had before his eyes at all times the face of Jacob his father, and he remembered the commandments of his father," who had warned him to stay away from foreign women and therefore enabled him to resist the gifts of the Egyptian women. Its earliest appearance in rabbinic sources appears to be in the Babylonian Talmud.[64] Interestingly, it is precisely its presence in *Aseneth* (which he takes to be first century C.E.) that Kugel sees as evidence of the early date of this particular Joseph tradition.[65] But, of course, if *Aseneth* is not demonstrably early, Kugel's argument here loses some of its force, and the significance of this common tradition, itself not clear under any circumstances, becomes even weaker.[66]

Hence it seems reasonable to conclude that rabbinic traditions about Aseneth provide us no useful evidence for dating the story extant in our Greek texts[67] nor contradict the possibility that *Aseneth* was composed toward the latter portion of the Greco-Roman period.

Aseneth in Early Christian Traditions, Including Early Byzantine Hagiography

In the search to secure a date for the Greek *Aseneth* stories, it is crucial to consider the evidence from Christian sources, particularly when we remember that not only are the texts preserved and transmitted only by Christians but also that it is only among Christians that we are *certain* the texts had an audience.

It may be significant that no Christian sources testify to the presence of Aseneth traditions prior to the third century C.E.[68] In the mid–third century, as we have already seen, Origen reports a story about Aseneth[69] and quotes a passage from the otherwise lost *Prayer of Joseph,* in which Jacob is described as an angelic figure in imagery reminiscent of the description of Jacob in the longer reconstruction of *Aseneth.*[70] Despite Philonenko's analysis, the links between these stories are thin and do not materially advance the discussion of dating. The angelic portrait of Jacob common to the *Prayer of Joseph* and to a longer recension of *Aseneth* could easily have come from a common source. Not inconceivably, it could have been generated spontaneously in at least one case. Further, Origen's mention of the Jewish identification of Potiphar and Pentephres is clearly not a reference to our *Aseneth,* and, in fact, his failure to mention an Aseneth story that distinguishes between the two suggests that he does not know such a story or, at the very least, doesn't know it as Jewish.

The most compelling Christian evidence that bears on the date of the Greek stories of Aseneth may be found in three Christian hagiographies that both Burchard and Philonenko and, more recently, Schwartz believe to be dependent on *Aseneth:* the "martyrdoms" of saints Barbara, Christine, and Irene. The *Passion of Saint Christine* is known from a Greek papyrus fragment found at Oxyrhynchus, dated to the fifth or sixth centuries C.E.,[71] while Syriac texts of Barbara and Irene occur in a manuscript

discovered in 1892 in the convent of St. Catherine on Mt. Sinai, transcribed and published with English translations by Agnes Smith Lewis in 1900.[72] The manuscript,
which contains the stories of fourteen holy women, was written by John the Stylite
(or Recluse) of Beth-Mari-Kaddisha, in Qanun, "a monastery near to the town of
Kaukub of Antioch" in the late eighth century. Interestingly, while Lewis subsequently discovered that a number of these stories occur in Syriac manuscripts in the
British Museum, some of them dating to the fifth century C.E.,[73] she found no Syriac
manuscript of Barbara or Irene in the British Museum.

Several scholars have argued that a version of our Aseneth story was known to the
author of *Irene,* which, in turn, they believe was utilized by the author of *Christine.*[74]
Without resolving the precise nature of the relationship between the three martyrologies, it is still the case that if one or more of these stories draws on our *Aseneth,* it
might allow us to establish a more precise upper limit for its composition.

Regrettably, none of the evidence concerning these dates produces a meaningfully
better dating than that available from the Syriac translation of *Aseneth* in Pseudo-
Zacharias and its apparent history. If *Irene* is assumed to be the earliest of the three
tales and to have utilized *Aseneth,* it might allow us to argue for the existence of the
latter already in the fourth century C.E., given *Irene*'s own setting in the mid–fourth
century[75] and given the intriguing arguments of Michel van Esbroeck that the story of
Irene, whose name means "peace," reflects historical circumstances of the mid–fourth
century.[76] The existence of a fifth- or sixth-century C.E. papyrus fragment of *Christine*
is also helpful, if consistent with our other evidence.

Still, the relationship between these tales of martyred Christian women and our
Aseneth is far from clear. Philonenko points out that none of the three is absolutely
identical to *Aseneth* and that each contains some but not all of the details of the story.
Although he thought it possible that all three drew on *Aseneth,* he also poses the possibility that there was an intermediate text between *Aseneth* and the martyrologies and
that none knew *Aseneth* directly.[77] Because both Philonenko and Burchard (as well as
van Esbroeck and Schwartz to a more limited degree) assume *Aseneth* to be earlier
by several centuries than any of these Christian tales, they are compelled to argue that
Aseneth must in some way have influenced *Barbara, Irene,* and *Christine,* and not
vice versa, although they may easily differ on their precise understandings of the relationships between the other three. But once we surrender the assumption that *Aseneth*
is early and reopen the possibility that it, too, was composed late, the possible explanations for the relationships among these stories become more complex. The tales of
Barbara, Irene, and Christine further testify to the appeal of the elements common to
all four stories in the fifth, sixth, and seventh centuries C.E., particularly in Syriac circles, but they do not afford us a secure base for dating *Aseneth.* Nevertheless, I would
argue that they provide further contextualization for it, as I will discuss again in the
next chapter.

One other piece of evidence from Christian sources might be mentioned here. In
the early part of the nineteenth century, the British Museum acquired several papyrus
fragments written in Sahidic Coptic that mention both Aseneth and Dinah by name.[78]
The origins of these papyri are now totally obscured. One fragment reads, "He gave
her the name Aseneth, which means 'she who was saved from death'"; the second

reads, "at that place where Dinah her/his daughter by him/from him went out."[79] For the moment, I have deliberately left the second unpunctuated.

Philonenko acknowledged the similarity of the first fragment to *Aseneth* 27.8 (where Aseneth calls herself the one whom God has saved from death) but made no mention of the fragment regarding Dinah, despite his belief that the Dinah legend underlay *Aseneth*. Van Esbroeck, who seems to have missed Philonenko's observations here, construed the second fragment as evidence that Christians knew "without doubt" Aseneth as the daughter of Dinah.[80]

Were van Esbroeck to be correct and were the papyrus to be early (fourth century C.E.), we might have found the earliest corroboration of the Dinah story, in close proximity to a tradition about Aseneth known in the Greek materials. Unfortunately, in his publication of the fragment, W. Crum offers no observations on the date of the papyrus. More important, though, I believe van Esbroeck has misconstrued the text. I think that *tefsheere,* which literally means "his daughter," applies not to Dinah's daughter by Shechem, here presumed to be Aseneth, but to Dinah herself, the daughter of Jacob, and that the fragment is in fact a paraphrase and perhaps commentary on Genesis 34.1: "And Dinah, the daughter of Leah, whom she bore to Jacob, went out. . . ." Crum suggests that all the related fragments here appear to be part of a commentary or homily on Genesis. What they appear to have in common is their interest in Jacob, so that the supposed proximity of Aseneth and Dinah may then easily be explained by their common association with Jacob—one his daughter, the other his daughter-in-law—and not by any presumed relationship between them.

Since in any case, these papyri are highly unlikely to antedate the fourth century,[81] they are, at best, testimony to an Aseneth tradition consonant with one in the Greek stories, from a chronological period consistent with the preponderance of our evidence: the fourth century C.E. or later.

Conclusion: Dating

The cumulative evidence overwhelmingly places our *Aseneth* no earlier than the third or fourth century C.E., on both negative and positive criteria. No ancient author quotes it or clearly alludes to it before the sixth century C.E., when the "prologue" to a Syriac translation acknowledges the existence of a "very old" Greek text. The travelogue of a Christian woman who probably lived in the late fourth or early fifth century might have contained a tradition about Aseneth's house, but as we have seen, this is far from an unambiguous reference to our Greek texts; even if it were, it would still locate the texts no earlier than the fourth century C.E. Aseneth traditions in authors and sources dating prior to the fourth century C.E. show no knowledge of our story, and on the contrary, testify to Aseneth traditions that presume the identity of Aseneth's father and Joseph's master, in direct contradiction of the Greek stories. Rabbinic traditions in which Aseneth was the daughter of Joseph's niece Dinah and the Canaanite Shechem occur only in sources that appear to be no earlier than the Islamic period,[82] and there is no compelling evidence that these traditions should be dated to the early centuries of our era. In any case, though, the Dinah traditions appear either independent of our Aseneth stories or, not inconceivably, responsive to it[83] and offer no useful evidence for dating the Greek texts. A Coptic papyrus fragment of uncertain date and provenance, but almost certainly no earlier than the fourth century C.E. and probably later, offers an etymology of Aseneth's name that echoes a description of Aseneth in the Greek stories. Finally, the *Passion of St. Christine,* known from a Greek papyrus fragment dating to the fifth or sixth century C.E. may have drawn, directly or indirectly, on some form of our *Aseneth* story and therefore provide additional testimony to its existence by the fifth century C.E. If, further, *Christine* utilized *Irene,* we might be able to push back the date of *Aseneth* to the fourth century C.E., assuming a late fourth-century date for *Irene.*

In the face of significant evidence to the contrary, it seems to me at least minorly perverse to argue that a Greek *Aseneth* was composed prior to the early second century C.E. and yet has no discernible life until three centuries later, when it suddenly seems to burst onto the scene, cropping up perhaps in Egeria, definitely in Syria, as the possible basis of fifth-century Christian martyrologies, and echoed perhaps in a Coptic commentary or homily on Genesis no earlier than the fourth century C.E. and more likely several centuries later. That the vast majority of contemporary scholars has taken just such a stance seems to me in the end to be less about the nature of the evidence and more about other, rarely articulated concerns. Here, I still find pertinent Goodenough's observations about scholarly reluctance to envision Jews composing in Greek well into late antiquity, a reluctance shared alike by self-consciously Christian and Jewish scholars, as well as by those who believe themselves to approach the ancient sources without regard to their own cultural identifications. For some scholars, this reluctance may be grounded in implicit theological concerns; for others, it may be the result of an unself-conscious acceptance of what comes, perhaps understandably, to pass for conventional scholarly wisdom.

For others, even more subtle concerns may be relevant. As I have indicated, the arguments for dating *Aseneth* early are very much linked to the belief that, at least in some initial form, it was composed by a Jewish author and not by a Christian, while, conversely, the arguments for a late date have been closely linked with the theory that the author was Christian. The tendency to assume that texts known to be transmitted by Christians are of Christian (as opposed to Jewish) composition, in the absence of clear evidence for Jewish composition, could easily be construed as a form of Christian hegemony and as Christian expropriation of Jewish traditions. As more and more scholars have become sensitive to the potential for anti-Judaism that lurks in the methodological morass of distinguishing Jewish from Christian in the Greco-Roman world, it may also be the case that the classification of ambiguous texts as Christian carries with it potentially disturbing implications, with the ironic result that we may be far too quick to catalogue as Jewish texts those whose origins are far less apparent.

The very nature of the evidence for dating *Aseneth* makes it impossible for us to do more than delineate reasonable parameters. Since there seems to be no debate that some form of our tale was originally composed in Greek, that composition can be no later than the sixth century C.E., when some version of the Greek is translated into Syriac. And, at the other extreme, one may reasonably argue that it cannot have been composed any earlier than the third century B.C.E., an approximate date for the beginning of the translation of Jewish scriptures into Greek.[84]

The evidence and arguments I have amassed here seem to me sufficient to support a date for *Aseneth* no earlier than the third century C.E. and to place the composition of the Greek texts, both the shorter and the longer versions, in the late third to late fourth centuries C.E. But given the serious implications of such dating, which I will explore a little more in the last chapter, I will not be surprised if other scholars continue to resist the rethinking that this conclusion requires.

NOTES

1. On Ps. Zacharias, see *EEC* 2:884. The real Zacharias lived in the late fifth/early sixth century C.E. The text is apparently a Syriac translation of a Greek original. An English translation (which unfortunately omits the Aseneth material) is available as *The Syriac Chronicle Known as That of Zachariah of Mitylene,* trans. F. J. Hamilton and E. W. Brooks (London: Methuen, 1899; reprint, New York: AMS Press, 1979). In the introduction, Brooks notes that only chaps. 3–6 are actually derived from the earlier work by Zachariah: the Aseneth material comes in bk. 1, chap. 6. For discussion of the manuscripts, see Hamilton and Brooks, *Syriac Chronicle,* 1–2; for dates, see Philonenko, *Joseph et Aséneth,* 12.

2. Hypothetically, the Aseneth material could have been inserted later and the accompanying letters could be fictitious support for an earlier date, but this seems excessively skeptical.

3. Burchard, "Joseph and Aseneth," 187.

4. See Burchard, "The Present State of Research," for details and references. For arguments that Egeria's pilgrimage took place c. 380–84, see P. Devos, "La date du voyage d'Egerie," *Analecta Bollandiana* 85 (1967): 105–43.

5. Burchard, "Joseph and Aseneth," 196; see also Burchard, "The Present State of Research," 44, where he is cautious in his mention of Egeria.

6. Goodenough, *Jewish Symbols,* 1:9–10.

7. Batiffol, "Livre," 37.

8. Philonenko, *Joseph et Aséneth,* 108. Batiffol subsequently conceded the possibility of first-century Jewish authorship in the face of a critique by Massebieau and Duchesne in his own review of M. R. James, *Apocrypha Anecdota II, Revue Biblique* 7 (1898): 302–4. See Chesnutt, *From Death to Life,* 24.

9. Alone at the time among recent scholars, Sparks took a similarly agnostic stance in his introduction to Cook's translation in *AOT,* 468. Even more recently, Martin Goodman, *Mission and Conversion: Proselytizing in the Religious History of the Roman Empire* (Oxford: Clarendon Press, 1994), 128, remarks in passing that *Aseneth* must obviously be later than the Septuagint translation and earlier than its sixth-century Syriac translation. Nevertheless, his discussion presumes a conventional dating.

10. Philonenko, *Joseph et Aséneth,* 108.

11. Burchard, "The Present State of Research," 39.

12. Burchard, "The Present State of Research," 39.

13. See Philonenko, *Joseph et Aséneth,* 102, with references to various other scholars who have underscored this point, from Massebieau and Duchesne in the nineteenth century on. Chesnutt's survey of the history of scholarship on *Aseneth* provides additional details (26–30). More recently, others have adhered to this position, including Eugene V. Gallagher, "Conversion and Community in Late Antiquity," *Journal of Religion* 73, no. 1 (1993): 1–15, and Chesnutt.

14. In his earlier writing, Burchard characterized *Aseneth* as "eine jüdische-hellenistiche Missionschrift" (*Untersuchungen,* 142). But in his most recent work, Burchard has expressed reservations about this, writing, "I have been more inclined to think that [it] was meant to

explain to Jews, proselytes and maybe Godfearer [*sic*], what privileges they possessed as compared with their pagan environment" ("The Present State of Research," 46). Chesnutt, too, while analyzing *Aseneth* as a representation of conversion, ultimately finds it doubtful that *Aseneth* was written as a missionary tract (*From Death to Life,* 81). Sänger attempted to place *Aseneth* within a precise historical and social context of conflicts between Jews and Egyptians in Alexandria in the fourth decade of the first century C.E. ("Erwagungen zur historiche Einordnung und zur Datierung von 'Joseph und Aseneth,'" *ZNTW* 76 [1985]: 86–106 = *Colloque de Strasbourg* 1983 [Paris, 1985], 181–202).

15. There has been considerable discussion about whether Hadrian's proscription was a causal factor or a response to the revolt, but the problem is irrelevant for our purposes.

16. Chesnutt, *From Death to Life,* 81. Philonenko, *Joseph et Aséneth,* 108–9, argues for the revolts of 115–17 C.E. as a more likely terminus, and Burchard, "The Recent State of Research," 39, agrees on this point.

17. Sänger, "Bekehrung und Exodus: Zum jüdischen Traditionshintergrund von 'Joseph und Aseneth,'" *JSJ* 10 (1979): 33–36; see also the summary and discussion in Chesnutt, *From Death to Life,* 50–51. As noted earlier, Burchard, "The Present State of Research," now argues for an audience of Jews, proselytes, and perhaps "God-fearers." And see also Martin Goodman, who argues that *Aseneth* "was not a plausible missionary tract, since the text assumed the reader's familiarity with the biblical story of Joseph" (*Mission and Conversion,* 79).

18. Inscriptions of proselytes from Rome: *CIJ* 21, 68, 202, 222, 256, 462, 523, also perhaps *CIJ* 576 from Venosa (fifth century C.E.). Additionally, a number of Latin inscriptions from Rome and elsewhere use the designation "metuens" or "metuentes" that may also signify "proselytism:" *CIJ* 5, 285, 524, 529, 642. *CIL* 8:4321, from North Africa, may also read "metuens." A. Schalit thought that a very important mosaic from a North African synagogue (*CIL* 8:12457a) was the gift of a woman proselyte, but the designation is based solely on the assumption that a single abbreviated "P" stands for proselyte, a highly dubious assumption (Schalit, "A Clash of Ideologies," in A. Toynbee, ed., *The Crucible of Christianity,* [New York: World Publishing Co., 1969], 63). Three men are designated as proselytes in the Aphrodisias inscription (Reynolds and Tannenbaum, *Jews and Godfearers.*) Here I have not included the numerous references to θεοσεβής, which many scholars believe often designates pagan adoption of Jewish beliefs and practices; see chapter 9.

19. Demetrius, frags. 2, 12, from Eusebius, *Preparation for the Gospel,* 9.21; Artapanus, frags. 2, 3, from Eusebius, *Preparation,* 9.27. Texts and translations in Carl R. Holladay, *Fragments from Hellenistic Jewish Authors,* vol. 1: *Historians,* Text and Translations 20, Pseudepigrapha Series 10 (Chico, CA: Scholars Press, 1983); translations also in *OTP* 2:850 (Demetrius); *OTP* 2:897 (Artapanus).

20. Perhaps on the contrary, Philo's identification (*LA* 3:236) of Aseneth's father with Joseph's owner suggests that he doesn't know this story, which contradicts that identification. In his work *On Joseph,* Philo says only that Pharaoh betrothed to Joseph "the most distinguished of Egyptian women, the daughter of the priest of the Sun," without specifying Aseneth's name (121).

21. Translation by Kee in *OTP* 1:823. There are some noteworthy features to this: in Genesis, Pharaoh gives Aseneth to Joseph; here, Pharaoh's agency appears to be muted. The tradition of the 100 talents of gold is not in Genesis (nor in *Aseneth*).

22. See also Philo, above, n. 19.

23. These conflicting identifications are particularly relevant for the question of the relationship between our stories and the rabbinic traditions; see the appendix.

24. See the discussions in Frederick J. Murphy, *Pseudo-Philo: Rewriting the Bible* (New York: Oxford University Press, 1993); Cheryl Anne Brown, *No Longer Be Silent: First Cen-*

tury Jewish Portraits of Biblical Women, Gender and the Biblical Tradition (Louisville, KY: Westminster Press, 1992); Pieter W. van der Horst, "Portraits of Biblical Women in Pseudo-Philo's Liber Antiquitatum Biblicarum," in *Essays on the Jewish World of Early Christianity* (Göttingen: Vandenhoeck and Ruprecht, 1990), 111–22; Betsy Halpern Amaru, "Portraits of Women in Pseudo-Philo's Biblical Antiquities," in Amy-Jill Levine, ed., *"Women Like This": New Perspectives on Jewish Women in the Greco-Roman Period,* Septuagint and Cognate Studies (Atlanta: Scholars Press, 1991), 83–106.

25. Translation from Harrington, *OTP* 2:357.

26. Kugel, *In Potiphar's House,* 99.

27. Both intermarriage and idolatry (often equated) are of serious concern to Ps. Philo (see Murphy, *Pseudo-Philo,* 252–54). Elsewhere, the author portrays the battle between David and Goliath as the battle between two kinsmen: Goliath as the descendant of Orphah and David as the descendant of Ruth. David defeats Goliath because Orphah chose the gods of the Philistines, while Ruth chose "the ways of the most Powerful" (61.6).

28. This was pointed out to me by Robert Kraft, who also thinks that the phrase, "would not afflict his seed," is peculiar language for adultery and therefore might rather apply to the marriage of Joseph and Aseneth, relying on an element in our Aseneth stories, namely, the insistence that Joseph did not sleep with Aseneth until she "converted." Although not inconceivable, this seems unlikely to me, particularly since Ps. Philo routinely associates sex with foreigners with the conception of tainted children. For example, in his retelling of the Exodus events, the Egyptians planned not only to kill all male Hebrew babies but to marry all female babies to Egyptians (9.1). The Israelites then consider whether to avoid having any further children in order to prevent their offspring from serving idols. The concern seems to be not just for their immediate daughters but for their descendants as well. Thus, Ps. Philo seems to be particularly concerned that if Joseph had sex with Potiphar's wife, he might father an idolater. It may also be the case that while opposed to adultery, mingling with Gentiles is, for Ps. Philo, the far greater ill, which would also explain his omission of Aseneth but wouldn't explain why he brought up Joseph's sexuality at all. Interestingly, Ps. Philo also conveniently omits any discussion of Moses' marriages to non-Israelite women.

29. On the dating of Ps. Philo, see Harrington's discussion in *OTP* 2:299 and Murphy, *Pseudo-Philo,* 6. My work on redating *Aseneth* has made me hypercautious about arguments for dating in general, particularly in the absence of highly reliable indicators such as external attestation, explicit internal references, ancient manuscript evidence, and the like, although the discussions of Harrington and Murphy seem reasonable enough on the surface.

30. Origen, *Commentary on Genesis* 46–47, *PG* 12:136. Aptowitzer ("Asenath," 257) quotes part of the Greek; Philonenko (*Joseph et Aséneth,* 39) reproduces Batiffol's translation ("Livre," 17–18).

31. Origen, *Commentary on John* 2.31 (25); critical edition, E. Preuschen, GCS 10, p. 189f. Also in C. Blanc, *Origene: Commentary sur Saint Jean,* SC 120 (1966), 188–90 (pp. 334–37). English translation in R. Heine, *Origen, Commentary on the Gospel According to John Books 1–10,* FC (1989), 145–46. For details and discussion of other ancient references to such a work, as well as another English translation, see Smith, *OTP* 2:699–714.

32. Philonenko, *Joseph et Aséneth,* 39.

33. *OTP* 2:700.

34. Batiffol, "Livre," conveniently summarizes his own argument on 36–37.

35. L. Massebieau, "Comte-rendu de l'édition de Batiffol," *Annales de Bibliographie Théologique* 11 (1889): 161–72; L. Duchesne, Review of "Le Livre de la Prière d'Asenath," by P. Batiffol, *Bulletin Critique* 10 (1889): 461–66.

36. See n. 8.

37. Chesnutt, *From Death to Life,* 23–30.

38. K. Kohler, "Asenath, Life and Confession or Prayer Of," *Jewish Encyclopedia* (1902), 2:172–76.

39. Kraft points to a similar phenomenon generally in the assessment of pseudepigraphic works in "The Pseudepigrapha in Christianity," in John Reeves, ed., *Tracing the Threads: Studies in the Vitality of Jewish Pseudepigrapha,* Early Judaism and Its Literature 6 (Atlanta: Scholars Press, 1994), 55–86, also available electronically at http://ccat.sas.upenn.edu/rs/rak/kraft.html.

40. Riessler also argued for a Hebrew original (see Burchard, "Joseph and Aseneth," 181).

41. A recent exception is Bohak, *Joseph and Aseneth,* who argues for an earlier date in the early second century B.C.E..

42. *AOT,* 468–69.

43. G. Oppenheim, *Fabuli Josephi et Asenathae apocrypha e libro Syriaco Latine versa* (Berlin, 1886).

44. Burchard, "Joseph et Aseneth," 183.

45. Batiffol, "Livre," 19.

46. However, whether these are the best translations for ἱστορία and θεωρία might be debated; ἱστορία can certainly mean a narrative or story, but allegory is not a usual translation for θεωρία, which normally connotes a public spectacle but which might here connote something perceived or observed (s.v. *BAG(D)*; Liddell-Scott). In Neoplatonic circles, θεωρία designates a philosophical contemplation that is contrasted with theurgy (Wallis, *Neoplatonism,* 107); see chapter 6.

47. See n. 43.

48. Batiffol, "Livre," 11.

49. Aptowitzer, "Asenath," 254, n. 40.

50. Aptowitzer does not appear to have known that Batiffol had recanted.

51. Aptowitzer, "Asenath," 255.

52. Aptowitzer, "Asenath," 257, n. 44.

53. Ironically, had Aptowitzer been truly critical in his dating of those traditions, he might have ended up dating *Aseneth* closer to the fourth century, because as I explain in the appendix, the Dinah traditions do not occur in early collations and need not be early themselves.

54. *Gen. R.* 97, see below, note 61.

55. Aptowitzer, "Asenath," 253. Aptowitzer's translation reads as follows: "When, however, Israel perceived the sons of Joseph, he asked 'who are these.' Said Rabbi Ammi, 'who is that one who is destined one day to lead Israel astray to idol-worship, and will cause fifty myriads on them to fall on one day.' And Joseph answered his father and said, 'They are my sons, whom God hath given me בזה.' *He brought Asenath, who was blind in one eye, near to him* [emphasis in original]," (252, with a portion of the Hebrew text in n. 35). For additional discussion of this passage and its attendant problems, see the appendix.

56. Aptowitzer, "Asenath," 255; emphasis in the first quotation is original, in the second it is added.

57. *AJ* 20.17–53, 92–93.

58. Philonenko, *Joseph et Aséneth,* 37, accepts the argument that the author of *Aseneth* knew the Dinah legend, and he acknowledges without dispute Aptowitzer's claim that it dates to Ammi in the third century.

59. Freedman, *Genesis Rabbah,* for instance, appears to read Aseneth's appearance as Joseph's proof that they are indeed his sons, since she is his wife, although this interpretation does not explain the significance of Aseneth's partial blindness (2:935, n. 3). Freedman would appear to take her eyesight as irrelevant to the larger issues of this text.

60. Aptowitzer, "Asenath," 255. For details, see the appendix.

61. It does occur in an important manuscript, Vat. Ebr. 30, from Egypt (dated to the tenth or eleventh century). On the problem of continuing accretions to the manuscripts, see Freedman, *Genesis Rabbah,* who writes that "even then [after its redaction, perhaps as late as the sixth century C.E.] the text was still subject to accretions, and from Vayyishlach we find extensive passages bearing marks of the later Haggadah. In Vayyigash the commentary is no longer verse by verse, while much of Vayechi was probably drawn from the Tanhuma homiles" (xxxix). The portion under consideration comes from Vayechi.

62. The so-called minor tractate *Soferim,* transmitted with the Babylonian Talmud, includes a tradition that Dinah was six years old when she gave birth to Aseneth (*Soferim* 21 = 43b). Like all rabbinic literature, *Soferim* is assumed to contain older material, but in its current form, it apparently dates to the mid–eighth century C.E.; Strack and Stemberger, *Introduction to the Talmud and Midrash,* 248, state: "[I]n its present form [it] cannot be dated prior to the middle of the eighth century, even if earlier forms must be assumed."

63. On the dating of *Genesis Rabbah,* see Strack and Stemberger, *Introduction to the Talmud and Midrash,* 303–4, whose arguments for a date of post–400 C.E. seem reasonable.

64. *B. Sot.* 36b. For additional rabbinic references and extensive discussion of the development of this material, see Kugel, *In Potiphar's House,* 106–12.

65. Kugel, *In Potiphar's House,* 109.

66. A similar, but not identical, tradition occurs in *Jub* 39.7–8, where Joseph resists the temptations of Potiphar's wife by remembering the commandments of Abraham that Jacob, his father, used to read. There is an interesting consistency in the differences between the two traditions: in *Jubilees,* a commandment to stay away from the wives of other men is said to dissuade Joseph from having sex with the wife of another man (Potiphar), whereas in *Aseneth,* a commandment to stay away from foreign women (not other men's wives) is used to account for Joseph's ability to resist the gifts of smitten Egyptian women, only some of whom may be construed as the wives of other men, while others, including Aseneth herself, are clearly not.

67. It may be of some interest, however, that according to *m. Sot.* 9.14 and *t. Sot.* 8, brides ceased wearing crowns on their heads after the destruction of the Temple in 70 C.E. (I owe this reference to Tal Ilan, *Jewish Women in Greco-Roman Palestine: An Inquiry into Image and Status,* Texte und Studien zum Antiken Judentum 44 [Tübingen: J. C. B. Mohr (Paul Siebeck), 1995], 95). One might thus wonder whether the description of the crowned Aseneth as a bride provides some clue as to date. On the surface, this rabbinic observation could conceivably point to a fairly early date. However, we would have to make a series of assumptions that I am unwilling to concede; among them that *Aseneth* is both definitively Jewish and consistent with rabbinic forms of Judaism. Even if both of these were to be true, we must remember that *Aseneth* is fictively pre–70 C.E., and as I have shown earlier, many elements of Aseneth's appearance and accoutrements may be drawn from traditional components and not contemporaneous social practice.

68. See *Biblia Patristica, Index des Citations et Allusions Bibliques dans la littérature Patristique* (Paris: Editions du Centre National de la Recherche Scientifique, 1975–); also *Clavis Patrum Graecorum.*

69. See earlier discussion; see also Philonenko, *Joseph et Aséneth,* 38–40; Origen, *Commentary on Genesis* 46–47.

70. Origen, *Commentary on John* 2:188–90. See also earlier discussion, this chapter, and chapter 3.

71. Published in *Papyri greci i latini,* 1, Florence, 1912, 57–62; for the text of the Messina manuscript, see M. Norsa, "Martirio di Santa Cristina nel cod. Messin. 29," *Studi Italiani e Filologia Classica* 19 (1912): 316–27; see also P. Paschini, "Richerche agiografiche. S. Cristina di Bolsena," *RAC* 2 (1925): 3–4, 167–94; and the entries in *BHG* 301y.

72. Lewis, *Select Narratives.* For a cataloguing of the Greek manuscripts of *Irene,* see *BHG*

952y–954c. Greek texts of both *Barbara* and *Irene* were published by A. Wirth, *Danae in christlichen Legenden* (Vienna, 1892), 102–12, 116–48, respectively.

73. I.e., the story of Mary the slave of Tertullian, Sophia, and Cyprian and Justa (fifth-century manuscripts); also those of Eugenia, Marina, Euphrosyne, Onesima (also earlier; Lewis, *Select Narratives,* doesn't give dates). In all, the St. Catherine's manuscript included Thecla, Eugenia, Pelagia, Marina, Euphrosyne, Onesima, Drusis, Barbara, Mary, Irene, Euphemia, Sophia, Theodosia, Theodota.

74. Schwartz, "Recherches," esp. 281–84; Burchard, "Joseph and Aseneth," 196, Burchard, *Untersuchungen,* 134–37; see also Philonenko's discussion of the possible relationships, *Joseph et Aséneth,* 110–17. Esbroeck, "Review," does seem to concur that the three martyrologies reflect the existence of our Aseneth story, although with less confidence about their precise relationships. Burchard also notes here, n. 97, that K. Berger, *Auferstehung des Propheten und die Erhöhung des Menschensohnes: Traditionsgeschichtliche Untersuchungen zur Deutung des Geschickes Jesu in frühchristlichen Texten,* Studien zur Umwelt des Neuen Testaments 13 (Gottingen, 1976), 564–65, n. 403, expressed doubt on this point.

75. Irene is said to have been born in 621, according to Seleucid reckoning (= 310 C.E.).

76. Van Esbroeck, "Review," 408–9.

77. Philonenko, *Joseph et Aséneth,* 115–16.

78. Published by W. Crum in *Catalogue of Coptic Manuscripts in the British Museum,* 1905 no. 1013c (Crum's no. 271). The numbering in Philonenko (and in Esbroeck's review of Philonenko) is incorrect. Philonenko may only have known O. von Lemm, *Koptische Miscellen* (Leipzig, 1914), 3–4; the volume is given as 1, but the volume and date do not match with OCLC listings.

79. Translated from van Esbroeck's French translation.

80. He writes that neither Burchard nor Philonenko "had recourse to the Coptic papyrus" ("Review," 407).

81. It may more likely date four or five centuries later.

82. See the appendix.

83. See later discussion in chapter 9.

84. As noted earlier, n. 9, these broad parameters are both acknowledged and then largely disregarded by Goodman, *Mission and Conversion.*

CHAPTER NINE

The Authorial Identity of
Aseneth Reconsidered

As was true in the debate over date, the current consensus that *Aseneth* was authored by a Jew was not reached quickly. Early scholars of the Greek texts took varying stances on this question, which to some degree seem to correlate with their own religious identification.

Yet just as the belief that *Aseneth* was Jewish bolstered the claim that it was early, the belief that it was early bolstered the claim that it was Jewish. And just as the claim that *Aseneth* is early is subject to critique, so too is the assertion that the texts are Jewish, although in the end, it is in my view more likely that the author(s) of *Aseneth* were Jewish than that they wrote before the early second century C.E.

Before we can profitably assess whether *Aseneth* is Jewish or Christian, it is important to clarify what it means to classify texts as Jewish or Christian. After all, in some ways, all versions of *Aseneth* are Christian, that is, they are transmitted, so far as we know, only by Christians and were almost certainly understood to have symbolic Christian referents.[1] If these texts were used and transmitted by Jews in antiquity, they have left no trace in traditions known to have been transmitted by Jews, rabbinic or otherwise, although this is true enough of other, self-consciously Jewish works.[2]

When scholars discuss the "origins" of a work such as *Aseneth,* they are generally talking not about the life of texts but about the imputed self-understanding of the author and/or redactors. To make such determinations implies among other things that individual texts have individual authors, whose self-understanding is, at least in theory, accessible. Further, in the case of texts that, like *Aseneth,* currently exist in multiple and significantly different versions, it implies that an earliest, if not original, version of the text can be detected and reconstructed and that when we seek information about the origins of a text, we are seeking information about the author and context of that earliest or original work.

In the case of *Aseneth,* these assumptions turn out to be particularly vexing. As Philonenko observes in his own discussion of the subject, the older views of scholars were significantly affected by the particular version of the text they read or considered earliest. Much energy has subsequently been devoted to the debate between Philonenko and Burchard over which of the existing versions is closest to the original and over which reconstruction of that original is most plausible, since all scholars concede that none of the extant manuscripts is likely to preserve any such original in its entirety. In this study, I have taken the position that at least one reconstruction of the longer text, that is, Burchard's, represents, generally, an intentional redaction of the shorter text approximated in Philonenko's reconstruction, and to that extent, I am not prepared to insist that the shorter text we have represents some ideal "original" text. I do think, though, that this shorter text had at least one author and that the longer text represents the work of one or more individuals, whose precise designation of "author" or "editor" or "redactor" depends in part on how we view such revision. Philonenko conceded that several of his "second" and "third" longer recensions of *Aseneth* are Christian but insisted that the shorter version, for whose priority he argued, was unambiguously Jewish.[3] By this I assume he means that the author of the shorter text was self-consciously Jewish, while those who were responsible for the longer recensions were self-consciously Christian.

Philonenko may well be right that differing authors of the differing versions of *Aseneth* had differing self-understandings, which may in part account for the diverse views of scholars about the Jewish or Christian identity of the text, and in the discussion that follows, I will address the question of whether and how we might assess the imputed identity of the author of the shorter recension, in particular, where many of the arguments I will raise for one recension are applicable as well to the other. Nevertheless, the problem is not simply one of differing stances of differing authors or redactors.

Part of the difficulty also lies in a contemporary scholarly tendency to attempt to distinguish between "Jewish" and "Christian"—ancient texts and persons alike—despite the fact that most of us know how complex these issues really are. Thus we debate whether a given text is Jewish or Christian, as though those categories are both clear-cut and mutually exclusive. I do believe that persons in antiquity would generally have had fairly clear senses of their own cultural, ethnic, and religious identity, but I am less certain that we would find their categories easy to map onto our own, even our own understandings of ancient categories as distinguished from modern ones. How, for instance, should we classify one of John Chrysostom's parishioners, who, while ostensibly Christian, were drawn to the practices and teachings of the synagogue in Antioch in the late fourth century C.E.?[4] Supposing such a person heard the story of Joseph one day in synagogue and chose to tell the tale of how his marriage to Aseneth came about? Would the resulting tale be Jewish? Christian? Supposing that same person subsequently renounced the church or the synagogue or vacillated back and forth. What would the tale be then? Although many other similarly complicated scenarios are possible, this one example should be sufficient to demonstrate the dilemma we face.

Is *Aseneth* Jewish?

With this in mind, what is the probability that *Aseneth* was composed by a person whose religious self-identification was (exclusively) Jewish? Apart from the circular linkage of the dating of the text(s) and its religious origins, there are several arguments for Jewish authorship. These include the subject of the story itself, the presence of certain interpretive techniques and concerns, knowledge of the Septuagint, consonance with adjuration traditions and techniques known from other Jewish sources, and absence of explicit Christian language.

Before taking up each of these in detail, I want to comment briefly on one phrase in *Aseneth* that some scholars have taken as clear indication of "Jewish interests" if not of Jewish authorship outright,[5] namely, the claim at 1.7–8 that Aseneth "was in no way like the daughters of the Egyptians, but was in all ways like the daughters of the Hebrews. For she was tall like Sarah, and in the bloom of youth like Rebecca and beautiful like Rachel." Apart from the textual difficulties of reconstructing this line,[6] those who read the line in this way fail, I think, to take seriously that denying Aseneth's resemblance to the Egyptians, and even asserting her total resemblance to the daughters of the Hebrews, is only a statement about Jews if we already knew that the authors made that identification. Certainly in many Christian circles, the linkages between biblical figures and contemporaneous Jews were by no means presumed. On the contrary, Christian self-understanding as the new Israel and the true inheritors of God's promises to the Hebrews or Israelites could easily facilitate a reading of this passage not as a statement that Aseneth (and therefore her author) was Jewish but simply as a statement that she wasn't "really" a Gentile. I have already discussed some of the possible implications of this passage,[7] but here I simply want to reiterate that I see no inherent reason why this line reveals the exclusive Jewishness of the author.

The Subject of the Story Itself

Scholars who have considered this issue at all, rather than take it for granted, have argued that a story designed to explain the marriage of Joseph to the daughter of an Egyptian priest is much more likely to have been of interest to Jews than to Christians.[8] This presumes that Jews would have found the marriage troubling, while Christians would not have. But in actuality, the very popularity of the text among Christians demonstrates that Christians found the tale quite compelling and presumably had considerable interest in the themes it presented, including the marriage of an Israelite to a Gentile.[9] Further, the evidence from demonstrably Jewish sources suggests that what some Jews found problematic about Joseph and Aseneth was not Aseneth's identity as a Gentile but other issues: the equation of her father with Joseph's eunuch master and the description of Aseneth's father as a priest.[10] It is, of course, the case that these traditions reflect the concerns of rabbinic Jews that may not have been of much interest to the extensive communities of Greek-speaking Jews in the fourth and fifth centuries C.E., or even earlier, for whom questions of intermarriage and proselytism may have been of much more concern. My major points here are only that the issues to which the texts address themselves do not really allow us to identify the religion of the author and are, in fact, obviously consonant with Christian concerns and different from those of known Jewish sources. Whether they were consistent with the concerns of Jews who have left us no (other) identifiable literature by which to gauge their interests is virtually impossible to say.

Interpretive Techniques

As I have explored particularly in chapters 2 and 3, the Greek stories of Aseneth display an interest in material and motifs that we now know particularly through Jewish biblical texts, although whether and to what degree the authors of *Aseneth* were self-consciously engaging actual biblical texts remain difficult questions. Further, in some ways, the exegetical and compositional techniques utilized by these authors are in some ways analogous to rabbinic midrashim. Aptowitzer's entire study was intended to demonstrate that a plethora of elements in the Greek stories had rabbinic parallels of one sort or another and that the work as a whole displayed typically Jewish materials and methods of interpretation. Although the specific elements Aptowitzer construed as parallels are usually unconvincing, a case can be made that the author(s) and redactor(s) of *Aseneth* were intimately familiar with Jewish scripture (in Greek), whose language and imagery they drew on extensively in the construction of the *Aseneth* stories. While I should emphasize here again that the degree of self-conscious use of materials acknowledged as "scriptural" (whatever that might have meant to ancient authors and readers) remains an open question, some may find it tempting to argue, as did Aptowitzer, that such interests and techniques are more typically Jewish than Christian.

Yet even if the composition of *Aseneth* demonstrates the use of interpretive techniques known to us in midrashic Jewish sources, this does not preclude Christian authorship. Without entering into too extensive a discussion of Christian composition of what may be termed "parabiblical" materials, we should keep in mind that Christians certainly had an interest in such materials and compositions, as is obvious by their transmission of such works.

Interestingly, one of the best examples of a Christian parabiblical composition relevant to the discussion of *Aseneth* is a work known as *The Life of Joseph*.[11] Regardless of the textual family to which they belong, more than half of the Greek manuscripts of *Aseneth* also contain this text.[12] *The Life of Joseph* appears to be part of the corpus of works known as Ephrem Graecus—works in Greek associated with the fourth-century Syrian Christian hymnist. Ephrem's great popularity apparently led to the composition of a large number of works in Greek, "some of which are literal translations, some mosaics of authentic and inauthentic works, and some distinct creations only remotely inspired by Ephraem Syrus,"[13] composed from the fourth through the sixth century C.E. Gary Vikan argues that *The Life of Joseph* itself is either a literal translation of a lost Syriac work by Ephrem, a translation made in the fifth or sixth century C.E., or a "distinct Greek creation," of the same period, perhaps indirectly inspired by Ephrem.[14] *The Life of Joseph* appears to be an extensive Christian retelling and expansion of the life of Joseph, which is interesting not the least because it demonstrates that Christians apparently did compose such stories about figures from the Hebrew Bible and thus that the composition of *Aseneth* by a Christian is inherently plausible. Significantly, though, it contains no mention of the marriage of Joseph and Aseneth, which may in part account for their long history of joint transmission.

A significant number of Christian authors are known to have been well acquainted with Jewish sources and to have read Hebrew as well as Greek and Latin, such as Origen himself, Jerome, and others. Although the Syrian Ephrem does not appear to have read Greek or Hebrew, his writings reveal a thorough conversance with many aspects of Jewish parabiblical traditions, and his own hymns manifest an intense interest in these themes. Some Christians clearly knew biblical phrases well enough to integrate them easily into a literary composition: Jerome claims that Paula knew scripture by heart and represents her speech as studded with biblical quotations.[15] (He also praises her fluency in Hebrew and her accentless pronunciation.)[16] The letter of Moses of Inghila accompanying the translation of *Aseneth* into Syriac is also studded with biblical phrases.

Knowledge of the Septuagint

Numerous scholars have observed that the author(s) of *Aseneth* seems well acquainted with the Greek translation of the Hebrew Bible commonly, if imprecisely, known as the Septuagint.[17] Much of *Aseneth*'s vocabulary can be found in the Septuagint/Old Greek,[18] and as we have seen, certain scenes seem constructed upon the language of an Old Greek translation, such as the expansion of Judges 13 in *Aseneth* **15.6,** the deployment of Song of Songs in **18.7–9,** and numerous others.[19] Here, too, it is important to keep in mind that this observation is predicated upon the assumption that the author(s) of *Aseneth* is self-consciously familiar with a biblical text, an assumption itself probably linked to scholarly beliefs about Jewish use of actual biblical texts and manuscripts. Even if the author(s) and redactor(s) of *Aseneth* were self-consciously utilizing biblical writings, the assertion that they drew primarily if not entirely on the Septuagint/Old Greek is difficult to demonstrate, given the absence of alternate readings for relevant passages in other translations such as Aquila, Theodotion, or Symmachus.[20]

Regrettably, in any case, such observation contributes little to the discussion of the religious identification of the author or authors. If previous scholars were correct in their dating of *Aseneth* sometime before the second century C.E., use of the Septuagint/Old Greek becomes unremarkable for Jewish or Christian authors. If the text is late, the situation becomes a little more complex but ultimately offers us no assistance.

Some if not many scholars have argued that Jews ceased to use the Septuagint translation by about the third century C.E., if not even earlier, in favor of translations such as Aquila and Theodotion that, among other things, offered alternative readings for passages such as Isaiah 7.14 that had become central to disputes between Jews and Christians.[21] Were this to be demonstrably the case, the clear use of Septuagint in a late writing might rule out Jewish authorship. However, it is by no means clear that Jews uniformly abandoned the Septuagint.[22] Roman legislation under Justinian in 533 C.E.

that claims to adjudicate a dispute among Jews over the appropriate language in which to read Scripture in synagogues includes a ruling that Jews may read in whatever language they choose but that Jews who choose to read in Greek must read either the Septuagint or Aquila.[23] While it seems possible to argue that Justinian seized this opportunity to impose on Jews a translation that they had ceased to read precisely for its perceived facilitation of Christian theological interests, Justinian's acceptance of Aquila and his insistence that Jews themselves had sought intervention in this dispute might suggest that both translations had continued to be read in at least some Jewish circles.

Ironically, if we could demonstrate that *Aseneth* (1) is the product of a Jewish author or authors, (2) was composed later than the third century C.E., and (3) makes self-conscious use of particular biblical texts, we might be able to argue that *Aseneth* itself is testimony to late Jewish usage of the Septuagint. The ease with which such arguments lapse into unbreakable circularity suggests that it would be better to exclude this criterion from consideration in either the dating or the religious identification of *Aseneth*.

Consonance with Adjuration Traditions and Techniques

As I have demonstrated in detail in chapter 4, all versions of *Aseneth* display considerable familiarity with ancient traditions and techniques for adjuring divine beings and compelling them to do the will of the petitioner. Known to us particularly from the collection of papyri found in Egypt, and dating mostly from the fourth century C.E., many of the so-called Greek magical papyri utilize Hebrew phrases and names for God, biblical figures such as Moses and Abraham, and other elements known from Jewish sources. Although scholars continue to debate the precise nature of the relationship between these traditions and Jewish praxis and beliefs, it is clear that Jews were associated with powerful and effective techniques for summoning divine beings and forces and compelling them to do the bidding of the summoner.

Although many Jewish sources from classical rabbinic texts to esoteric mystical writings demonstrate that such associations were shared by many Jews themselves, particularly compelling testimony to such practices and beliefs emerges from the Hebrew manual reconstructed from writings found in the Cairo Geniza known as *Sepher ha-Razim* (Book of the mysteries). We have seen that there are significant affinities between Aseneth's behavior and prescriptions for the adjuration of the Greek sun god Helios set forth in *Sepher ha-Razim,* which is variously dated by scholars to sometime between the fourth and the sixth centuries C.E.[24] and thus roughly contemporaneous with the chronological parameters I have proposed for *Aseneth.*

While these similarities may well point to a Jewish author or authors for *Aseneth,* it is important to remember that virtually everyone in antiquity engaged in adjurative practices, binding spells, protective countermeasures, and myriad related behaviors that seem to show little concern for the kinds of neat boundaries between Jews, Christians, and pagans that modern scholars often seem to desire.[25] While many of the adjurative elements in *Aseneth* are paralleled in materials with Jewish associations, others occur in formulas with no particularly Jewish connections.

Absence of Explicitly Christian Language, Imagery, and Allusions

The absence of any explicit and undeniable Christian language, such as direct references to Christ, the gospels, the blessed Virgin Mary, and/or Christian scriptural quotations, is sometimes offered as evidence that *Aseneth* must not be Christian.[26]

In attempting to assess the religious self-identification of the author(s) and redactor(s) of *Aseneth,* it may be instructive to compare *Aseneth* with the explicitly Christian legends of *Barbara, Irene,* and *Christine,* with which, as I noted in the preceding chapter, it appears to have some literary relationship. All three stories are distinct from *Aseneth* in their explicitly Christian symbols; the appearance of Jesus; their concern with Christian theological issues; their references to the Virgin Mary; and, most significantly, their rejection of marriage and sexuality. If the linchpin of the Aseneth tale is her marriage to Joseph, the linchpin of these martyrologies is the renunciation of marriage and the wrath such renunciation brings on women, together with its ultimate rewards. In this regard, they are typical of the interests of Syrian Christianity, with its heavy emphasis on asceticism as the sine qua non of the Christian life, initially for all Christians and eventually as the ideal Christian life, possible for many but not for all.[27]

Yet we should not be too quick to see these differences between *Aseneth* and related Christian martyrologies as stemming from the religious self-identification of their authors. The manifestly Christian coloring of the martyrologies does show us what Christian novels might look like, but these are also about explicitly Christian women who live after the time of Jesus and whose fate is inextricably linked to their acceptance of Christ and their devotion to him. As I shall explore in greater detail, the lack of blatantly overt Christian concerns in *Aseneth* might still only evidence a careful and self-conscious pseudepigrapher, who nevertheless saw in the story of the conversion of Aseneth a paradigm that later Christians could emulate. *Aseneth*'s emphasis on marriage and childbearing could be taken to represent Jewish values rather than Christian ones, but it could also constitute a Christian critique or repudiation of asceticism and the denial of marriage, while continuing to value virginity and chastity in their proper places.

There is, in fact, a major methodological issue here that becomes, by definition, almost impossible to broach. Unquestionably, Christian writers wrote any number of works on figures from the Hebrew Bible, particularly the prophets and persons in Genesis, about whom they preached sermons and composed hymns. Some, like Origen, wrote whole commentaries on biblical books such as Genesis. It does appear to be the case that those works attributable to known Christian authors inevitably display some explicit Christian attributes, as in the case of Ephrem's identification of Ephraim as a type or symbol of Christ or his intepretation of the marriage of Joseph and Aseneth as a model of the marriage of Christ and the church of the Gentiles. In attempting to consider whether *Aseneth* might have been composed by a Christian author, it would certainly help to be able to point to other Christian parabiblical narratives that contain, as does *Aseneth,* no explicit and undeniable references to Christ or other unequivocably Christian figures, symbols, and imagery.[28]

Yet the catch lies precisely here. A significant number of ancient texts preserved by Christians (and not by Jews), in Greek, Latin, Syriac, Armenian, Coptic, Ethiopic,

Slavonic, and so forth, are just like *Aseneth* in their absence of explicitly Christian language and symbols, in their anonymity or pseudonymity, and in their resistance to firm dating. Precisely because these texts lack any explicit Christian identifiers, they are now uniformly classified as Jewish; because they are classed as Jewish, they are generally dated early. When such texts exhibit "minor" Christian features, such features are generally considered the results of Christian interpolation and transmission of previously pristine Jewish compositions.[29] The result, ironically, is that any anonymous or pseudonymous parabiblical text that does not scream Christian at us is almost certain to be labeled Jewish (and relatively early), thus greatly reducing the chances that we will ever identify a Christian parabiblical composition that lacks explicit Christian features.[30]

Certainly, it would help if known Christian authors composed such works with no explicit Christian markers; regrettably, to the best of my knowledge, they do not. However, the problem here may be partly one of genre: while known Christian authors do indeed compose works about figures and themes in the Hebrew Bible, I cannot think of a single parabiblical narrative like *Aseneth* with a known author, Christian or otherwise. This may suggest that the anonymous or pseudonymous character of such works is structural. Stories that purport to tell the truth about persons and events living in the biblical past weaken their own claim to legitimacy if they have known human authors. It is by precisely such an attack that Tertullian attempted to discredit the otherwise anonymous *Acts of (Paul and) Thecla.*[31] Such stories' claim to truthfulness rests in their seeming antiquity—a claim that can only be subverted if the author is known and his (her?) sources of information are subjected to (ancient) critical inquiry.[32] For our purposes, the significance of this may well be that careful pseudepigraphers, whether Jewish or Christian, would not easily tip their hands by the blatant use of knowledge of the "future," that is, their own present. We know that they sometimes handled this through the device of retrojected prophecy (as in the Book of Daniel), but I can think of no pseudepigraphon that clearly and explicitly identifies the social, historical, and religious context of its authors,[33] although this is not to say that pseudepigraphers do not sometimes give themselves away through obvious devices such as retrojected prophecy as well as anachronistic slips of one sort or another. In brief, then, despite the absence of demonstrably Christian analogous works, the argument that *Aseneth* draws heavily on biblical traditions and particular modes of interpretation does not either demonstrate Jewish authorship or rule out Christian authorship, even apart from the vexing possibility of an author who was both Jewish and Christian.

Despite, then, the repeated assertions of numerous scholars that Aseneth is unequivocally Jewish in composition, the actual evidence for the Jewish identity of the author(s) of *Aseneth* is ambiguous at best. Nothing mitigates compellingly in favor of Jewish authorship, but nothing mitigates absolutely against it, either. Such allegedly Jewish elements as the use of traditional materials and compositional techniques known from Jewish sources were known to others, including Samaritans, Christian Jews (or "Jewish-Christians"), non-Jewish Christians, and probably many others. The adjurative and mystical traditions associated with Jewish circles are also associated with Christian and pagan practices and practitioners. The text has no known Jewish life of any kind.

Is *Aseneth* Christian?

If it is by no means certain that *Aseneth* was composed by a person whose (exclusive) self-understanding was Jewish, is it possible that it was composed by a person whose self-understanding, exclusive or perhaps otherwise, was at least in some form Christian? Because Batiffol, the editor of the first modern edition, argued, at least initially, for the Christian character of *Aseneth,* we may begin with a reconsideration of his arguments. His judgment that the Greek *Aseneth* was a Christian composition "after the manner of post-Constantinian hagiographic legends"[34] rested particularly on the claim that the text grafted a symbolic interpretation of Joseph and Aseneth onto older Jewish stories about the marriage[35] and that such symbolic interpretation could only have been Christian. In Batiffol's view, Joseph was an obvious type of Christ. The figure of Aseneth gave him a little more pause. Conceding that Aseneth might represent the feminized Church, he was nevertheless intrigued by a reading of Aseneth as the soul passing from paganism to Christianity, whose story was a symbolic commentary on the initiation of a catechumen into the Christian sacramental life.[36] Despite numerous Christian sources that utilize marital imagery for conversion, Batiffol found this interpretation strained as well since *Aseneth* contains insufficient mention of the ritual baptism that played such a crucial part in (other) Christian sources. Ultimately, he settled on a view of Aseneth as Virginity, focusing particularly on her designation within the texts as *parthenos hagnē,* a term rampant in Christian sources.[37]

Other scholars found Batiffol's specific arguments deeply flawed. Philonenko, for example, points out that while many Christian writers from Origen to Augustine saw Joseph as a type of Christ, nothing in the texts of *Aseneth* associates the two, and the life of Joseph bears no resemblance to the life of Jesus. Philonenko seized on Batiffol's own uncertainty about Aseneth's symbolic value as proof of the inaccuracy of his thesis.[38] Yet Batiffol's arguments may not have been as far off the mark as his critics would have them. As we have already observed and will shortly explore further, Christian writers, particularly in the Syriac tradition, did perceive significant resemblances between the life of Joseph and the life of Jesus and did see Aseneth as a type of the church.[39] Even if some of Batiffol's arguments may themselves be faulty, it is not inconceivable to me that his initial assessment of the text was more accurate than not.

The current scholarly consensus notwithstanding,[40] the arguments in support of Christian authorship for the earliest form of *Aseneth* are considerable. First is the incontrovertible fact, as I have emphasized both in the introduction and in the previous section, that all forms of *Aseneth* as we know them are demonstrably Christian and that we have absolutely no evidence that these texts were ever transmitted by Jews. The force of this observation should not be underestimated. Although no scholar who has written on *Aseneth* is unaware of its Christian history of transmission, few if any have found this a deterrent to the claim that the text is nevertheless Jewish. Nor am I overly impressed with arguments that *Aseneth* is not unique among Jewish texts preserved only by Christians. Although it is true that virtually all Jewish literature composed in Greek has been transmitted only by Christians, the converse is obviously not the case, namely, that all Greek literature transmitted by Christians was originally composed by Jews. The dilemma, then, is to determine reliable criteria of classification, a task that continues to prove far more vexing than most scholars have been willing to concede.[41] In the absence of any hard evidence that *Aseneth* is Jewish and given the clear evidence of its Christian history, the burden of proof seems to me to lie with whose who insist that at least some initial form of the story is Jewish, a burden that, as I have endeavored to demonstrate in the previous discussion, scholars have thus far failed to meet with any degree of certainty.

Second, contrary to the view that the very concerns of *Aseneth* point to its Jewish milieu, the converse may be true. If *Aseneth* is indeed about paradigmatic proselytes, it is relatively easy to argue that such a theme, developed and expanded as in our stories, would have been more suited to purposes of Christian propaganda and interest in proselytism from idolatry, in the third, fourth, and fifth centuries C.E., than to Jewish concerns in that same period. That is, although proselytism was of great concern to Christians virtually from the inception of the Jesus movement,[42] the greatest period of pagan conversion to Christianity actually occurs in the period from the early fourth century C.E., when Christianity becomes licit with the support of Constantine, through the end of the fifth century, when the vast majority of inhabitants of the ancient Mediterranean are at least nominally Christian.[43] Although both Christian writers and late Roman legislation suggest that Judaism continued to attract both pagans and Christians as late as the end of the fourth century, if not after, the degree to which Jews themselves may have actively sought proselytes is difficult to know. Legislation enacted after the Christianization of Rome was clearly intended to discourage and penalize any such activity; how much that legislation is itself evidence for Jewish proselytism remains a subject of unresolved debate among scholars.[44]

Further supporting a Christian origin for *Aseneth* may be the known Christian predilection for composing, copying, and circulating stories about holy women, particularly in some circles. As noted in the previous chapter, the stories of Barbara and Irene were found in a Syriac palimpsest whose introit describes the contents as "[s]elect narratives about the holy women."[45] The manuscript itself was written out by a Syrian monk who tore apart a valuable gospels manuscript to do so and who expressed his desire that others would profit from the spiritual lessons of such stories.[46]

This collection points to a tradition of stories told about women in male Syrian monasteries, which comports with the testimony about the book of *Aseneth* in the *Syrian Chronicle*. If such monks collected and preserved such stories, is it also possible that such monks composed at least some of these texts, including perhaps our Aseneth tale?[47]

Although no Christian writers through the end of late antiquity demonstrate knowledge of the *Aseneth* stories,[48] several Syrian writers evince some interest in the marriage and, perhaps more important, interpret it within an explicitly Christian context. In the fourth century, both Aphrahat and Ephrem drew on the figure of Joseph as a type of Christ and on Aseneth as a type of the church of the Gentiles. Aphrahat wrote: "Joseph married the daughter of an unclean priest and Jesus brought to himself the church from the unclean Gentiles."[49] Ephrem composed a hymn to the city of Ephrem, a portion of which is addressed specifically to the biblical figure whose name he shared, Ephraim, the son of Aseneth and Joseph:

> You are the son of Asenath, the daughter of a pagan priest
> she is a symbol of the church of the Gentiles.

She loved Joseph, and Joseph's son
in truth the holy church loved.
She had many children by the Crucified,
and on every member the cross is engraved.
By the symbol of Ephrem crosses are crowded into her,
by the birth from water.[50]

I will return to the significance of Ephrem and Aphrahat for the historical context of *Aseneth* shortly.

Aseneth also displays some significant affinities with known Christian texts and traditions that have been virtually ignored, largely because of the assumption that the story is Jewish and antedates these Christian sources. Significantly, the great majority of the sources I shall discuss are connected with Syrian Christian communities, either quite directly (the *Odes of Solomon,* the writings of Ephrem, Aphrahat, and one or two others) or indirectly, particularly the apocryphal *Acts of Thomas.*

The *Odes of Solomon* are intriguing for a variety of reasons. Extant now primarily in Syriac, which may have been the language of their original composition,[51] in their current form they are clearly Christian. Ironically, whether they are a case of Jewish psalms/odes reworked by Christian author(s), composed by a "Jewish" Christian, or simply within a particular tradition is impossible to say—a dilemma analogous, perhaps, to that posed by *Aseneth.* While there is some debate about their precise date,[52] if they are a unified composition they must antedate the third-century Greek papyrus of Ode 11.[53]

Numerous odes employ language highly reminiscent of *Aseneth.*[54] Consider the following selection:

Ode 7.8–9 (cf. *Aseneth* 8.11, **8.9**)
He who created Wisdom
is wiser than his works;
And he who created me before I came into being
knew what I should do when I came into being.
Therefore he had great pity on me when I came into being,
and granted me to ask of him, and to receive of his sacrifice.

Ode 11.10–19 (cf. *Aseneth* 8.11, **8.9, 15.5, 16.16,** 8.10)[55]
I let go the folly lying on the earth,
I stripped it off and cast it from me;
The Lord renewed me by his garment,
[*ho kurios* **enekainisen** *me en tō evdumati autou*]
and revived me with his light,
[*kai anekthēsato me tō phōti autou*]
and recalled me to life by his incorruption
[*kai* **anazōopoiēsen** *me tē aphtharsia autou*]

It is particularly instructive to compare these lines with *Aseneth* 8.11:[56]

kai **anakainison** *ta pneumati sou*
kai anaplason autēn tē cheiri sou (tē kruphaia)
kai **anaizōopoiēson** *tē zōē sou*

Ode 11.12b–19
I became like the earth that sprouts and rejoices [*gelōsa*] in its fruits
And the Lord became/was to me as/like the sun
Upon the face of the earth;
My eyes shone
And my face was sprinkled with dew
And my breath took pleasure
In the pleasant fragrance of the Lord:
And he brought me to his paradise,
Where are the riches of the delight of the Lord
[*hopou ho ploutos tēs truphēs kupiou*]
I saw mature [*hōraia*] and fruitbearing [*karpophora*] trees
[cf. *Aseneth* 2.19: *dendra hōraia pantodapa kai karpophora*]
And I worshipped [*prosekunēsa*] the Lord because of his glory:
And I said, Blessed, O Lord, are those who have been planted upon the earth
those who have a place in your paradise,
and grow up in the growth of your trees
[cf. *Aseneth* **16.16**: *idou dē apo tēs sēmeron hai sarkes sou bruousin hōs anthē zōēs apo*
    tēs gēs tou hypsistai[57] *kai ta osta sou pianthēsontai hōs hai kedroi tou paradeisou tēs*
    truphēs tou theou]
and have moved from darkness to light.
[cf. *Aseneth* 8.10].

Ode 11.22–23
The place of your paradise is great [*polus*],
And nothing is idle;
But rather bears fruit.

Consider next Ode 13[58]

Behold, the Lord is our mirror;
Open the[59] eyes and see them in him;
And learn how your faces are,[60]
And declare hymns[61] to his Spirit;
And wipe the huntress[62] from your faces,
And love his holiness, and put it on
And you will be spotless always with him.

    This hymn corresponds quite nicely to Aseneth's use of the water basin as a mirror in chapter 18. In the longer version, Aseneth is explicitly said to see her face and to rejoice at her image. In neither text does the sight of her reflection prompt her to wash her face, but she has already done so in an earlier scene. The longer text is explicit that she does not wash, for fear of washing off her beauty. Looking in the reflective water, she sees how her face is.

    Ode 15[63] shares *Aseneth*'s penchant for solar imagery:

As the sun is a joy to those who seek its day,
So my joy is the Lord;
Because he is my sun,
And his rays roused me,

And his light dispelled all the darkness from my face.
I obtained eyes by him,
And saw his holy day;
Ears became mine,
And I heard his truth.
The thought of knowledge became mine,
And I delighted myself through him.
I forsook the way of error,
And I went to him and received from him deliverance without grudging.
And according to his gift he gave to me,
And according to his great beauty he made me.
I put on incorruption through his name,
And I put off corruption by his grace.
Death was destroyed from before my face,
And Sheol was brought to nothing at my word.
And immortal life rose up in the land of the Lord,
And it became known to his faithful ones,
And was given unsparingly to all those who trust in him.
Hallelujah.

This ode is particularly intriguing for its images are especially close to Aseneth's encounter with Joseph. As Christ here is the sun, whose light dispels darkness from before the soul's face, so Joseph is Helios, whose light dispels darkness before Aseneth. She hears the truth Joseph/Helios speaks; she forsakes error; she puts off corruption (her clothing and her idolatry; see also the language of Joseph's prayers) and puts on incorruption. As Christ is here greatly beautiful, so is Joseph.

Verses 7–8 may be fruitfully juxtaposed with *Aseneth* **21.21**:

Joseph the Powerful One of God . . .
he pulled me down from my sovereignty
and humbled me from my arrogance[64]
and by his beauty he caught me,
and by his wisdom he grasped me like a fish on a hook,
and by his spirit, as by bait of life, he enshared me,
and by his power he confirmed me,
and brought me to the God of the ages
and to the chief of the house of the Most High,
and gave me to eat bread of life,
and to drink a cup of wisdom,
and I became his bride for ever and ever.

Verses 9–10 may be read as a reasonable paraphrase of *Aseneth* 16.13–17, the scene with the bees: "Death was destroyed before my face, and Sheol was brought to nothing at my word [or the word of Joseph]; and immortal life [the bees] rose up in the land of the Lord [the courtyard garden]."

Themes similar to those of *Aseneth* occur also in Ode 21, with its emphasis on the transition from darkness to light. Ode 23 contains an intriguing reference to the tablet and the finger of God. In this ode, God's thought is like a letter. Note the final stanza (vv. 21–22):

[T]he letter became a great tablet
written entirely by the finger of God
And the name of the Father was upon it,
and of the Son, and of the Holy Spirit,
to reign for ever and ever.

The imagery of the finger of God occurs only in the longer reconstruction of *Aseneth* at **15.4** and **15.12x.** In addition, the last phrase of the ode also occurs in the longer text of *Aseneth* at **19.5** but not in the shorter.[65]

Particularly intriguing is Ode 36, if this may be read as the experience of the soul, or an individual soul, and not only as a representation of the unique experience of Christ:

I was at rest upon the Spirit of the Lord,
And she lifted me up to the height;
and made me stand on my feet
in the height of the Lord
before his perfection and glory.
While I gave glory by the composition of his odes,
she bore me forth before the face of the Lord
and while[66] I was a (son of) man,[67]
I was called light,[68]
the Son of God,
While I gave glory among those giving glory,
And the greatest (was) I of the great.
For according to the greatness of the Most High,
so she made me;
and according to his renewal,
he renewed me.

And he anointed me from his fullness,
and I was one of those near him.
And my mouth was opened
like a cloud of dew,
and my heart belched up
like a belching of righteousness.
And my nearness was in peace,
and I was solidly set by the Spirit of rule.
Alleluia.

Among the many provocative similarities with the imagery of *Aseneth* (the description of the speaker as light and as Son of God; the centrality of renewal; and anointing), we might note especially Aseneth's rest, which occurs only in the longer reconstruction at **8.9, 15.7,** and **22.13.**[69] The theme of rest occurs elsewhere in the *Odes,* including Odes 37 and 38. It may also be worth remarking that only in the longer reconstruction is the exhalation of the angel's mouth likened to dew (indirectly), at **16.8–11,** where the honeycomb is explicitly likened to dew from heaven (**16.8**) and the exhalation of the angel's mouth is likened to the exhalation of the honeycomb (**16.9**). In the longer reconstruction at **16.14,** the honey itself is said to have come from the "dew of the roses of life that are in the paradise of God."

Yet another example of themes prevalent in *Aseneth* may be seen in Ode 40:[70]

Like honey dripping from the honeycomb of bees,
and milk flowing from the woman who loves her sons,
so also is my hope upon you, my God.

Like a spring belching up its waters,
so my heart belches up the Lord's hymn,
and my lips bring forth a hymn to him.
And my tongue is sweet by his antiphons,
and my members are anointed by his odes,
and my face greatly rejoices in his exultation,
and my spirit exults in his love,
and my soul shines in him.

And fear will trust in him,
and salvation will be solidly set in him.
And his gain is immortal life,
and the incorrupted will receive it.

[A]nd his gain is immortal life,
and those who receive it are incorruptible.

As these instances suggest, numerous themes in the *Odes* may be significant for assessing the cultural context and self-understanding of the author(s) and redactor(s) of *Aseneth*. The view of immortal life in the *Odes,* as synthesized by James Charlesworth, seems highly consistent with the view in *Aseneth:*

> The Odist . . . exults in his salvation and experience of immortality because he has taken off a corrupt garment and put on a garment of incorruption (15:8), a garment of light (21:3) and the Lord's garment. . . . Another way of expressing his experience of immortality is the pictorial metaphor that he is one of the fruit-bearing trees that has been planted by the Lord in Paradise (cf 11:16a–24; 20:7). All of this language is used to state emphatically that his immortality is geographically here and chronologically now. The most significant quality of immortality for the Odist is the incorruption that it entails; he who is joined to the Beloved "shall be found incorrupted in all ages" (8:22). In Ode 3, immediately after stating that the lover has been united to the Beloved, the Odist states, "Indeed he who is joined to him who is immortal, / truly will be immortal" (3:8). The Lord's purpose and will for the believer is eternal life and a perfection that is incorruptible (cf 9:4). The one who trusts in the Lord has the assurance of redemption (40:5) and possesses immortal life and incorruptibility.[71]

Except for the absence of any explicit mention of Christ, this description could easily stand for *Aseneth* as well.

Furthermore, like *Aseneth,* the *Odes,* at least according to Charlesworth, do not explicitly quote scripture but do seem to draw on a few passages, particularly those in Ezekiel 47 and 37.4–6, Proverbs 8.22, Isaiah 58.8, Genesis 2.2., and Psalm 22. It is thought-provoking that some of these same verses (Prov 8.22 as the creation of Wisdom before creation, and Is 58.8) may play a role in the construction of *Aseneth*. Psalm 22 is not inconsistent with the representation of Aseneth's repentance, and various other verses known to us now from precisely these books have figured significantly in my own analysis in chapters 2 and 3.

Interestingly, although Charlesworth considers the relationship of the *Odes* to "apocrypha"—a category that he appears to construe broadly—he never mentions *Aseneth*.[72] This may be a function of his acceptance of the consensus view that *Aseneth* is Jewish and probably earlier than (or barely contemporaneous with) his dating of the *Odes*. But he does emphasize the possible relationship of the *Odes* to two texts relevant for *Aseneth* as well, namely, *1 Enoch* and the *Psalms of Solomon*. Here he is considering the image of the holy ones as trees of life in paradise, an image that may be present in *Aseneth* as well, especially in the longer version. Charlesworth points out, for instance, that in the *Odes* and in the *Psalms of Solomon* 14, the righteous are described as trees planted in Paradise. Similar imagery occurs at *Aseneth* **16.16,** where Aseneth's bones will grow as "the cedars in the paradise of delight of God."

Although it may be impossible to demonstrate precise connections between *Aseneth* and the *Odes,* it is clear that the same themes and images are present in both. It is true, of course, that these themes themselves are present in earlier Jewish Wisdom traditions, but the specific constellations in which they are expressed in the *Odes* are remarkably consonant with *Aseneth,* particularly in the longer reconstruction. Further, it is difficult to point to a demonstrably early Jewish work that bears the same degree of similarity to *Aseneth.* At the very least, both *Aseneth* and the *Odes* could easily be at home in the same community. Nor is it at all impossible that *Aseneth* has its origins in a Syrian Christian community that also produced the *Odes.*

Another work with strong Syrian connections that may be significant for locating the origins of *Aseneth* is the *Acts of Thomas.* Often assigned a third-century C.E. date, the *Acts* appear to have been composed initially in Syriac, although the extant Syriac texts seem to derive from Greek translations of earlier Syriac versions.[73] Given the fact that our earliest manuscripts of *Aseneth* are also Syriac and locate a Greek *Aseneth* in Syria in the mid–sixth century C.E., this may be of particular significance.

On the surface, *Aseneth* and the *Acts of Thomas* are very different tales. The former recounts how two biblical characters met, married, engaged in licit sexual intercourse, and produced two sons, while the latter contains numerous tales in which the apostle Thomas dissuades women and men from participating even in licit marital intercourse. But once we keep in mind that some Christians understood the story of Joseph and Aseneth to be a tale of Christ and the church, this distinction becomes less significant and their similarities become more apparent. They share certain significant imagery and themes, ranging from the prominence of garments as metaphors for identity to the use of angelic doubles.

In the *Acts of Thomas,* I (chaps. 1–16), Thomas, the twin brother of Jesus and, not surprisingly, also a carpenter, goes to India as a slave, where he is straightway compelled (along with all the inhabitants of the city of Andrapolis) to attend the wedding of the king's only daughter. Once at the festivities, Thomas sings a rather strange hymn in his native tongue, which is overheard and understood by a flute girl, also a Hebrew, hired to play at the wedding.

The extant Greek and Syriac versions of this hymn are somewhat different, but both are interesting. On its face, the hymn is a wedding song, with clear allusions to Song of Songs. The obviously metaphorical bride is described in imagery comparable, although not identical, to that of Song of Songs 4, 6, and 7, focusing on her garments, her head, her feet, her tongue, her neck, her fingers, her bridal chamber, her gates, and her bridesmaids. Here it may be noteworthy that the longer version of *Aseneth,* but not the shorter, describes the transformed Aseneth at **18.9** in imagery obviously drawn from Song of Songs.[74] Although clearly the texts of *Thomas* intend a subversive reading of his "wedding" hymn, the language of the Greek remains ambiguous, while the extant Syriac is much more explicit in its Christian allusions and its interpretation of the marriage. The opening line of the Greek reads, "The maiden [*korē*] is the daughter of the light," while the Syriac reads, "My church is the daughter of light."

The response of the flute girl to Thomas's hymn is particularly interesting in its resemblance to Aseneth's response to Joseph and to Joseph's angelic double. As Aseneth gazes unflinchingly at Joseph in response to his prayer for her, an act whose complex implications I have previously considered,[75] so the flute girl gazes steadily at Thomas in response to his recitation of the hymn.[76] As Aseneth is struck by Joseph's great beauty and consumed by emotion for him, so the flute girl "loved him as one belonging to her race, and he was also beautiful in appearance above all who were there."[77] When Thomas then demonstrates his prophetic powers, the flute girl responds much as Aseneth responds to Joseph: this man, she says, is either God or the Apostle of God.[78] Given the strong emphasis on sexual continence in *Thomas,* the encounter between the apostle and the flute girl has a different resolution than that between Joseph and Aseneth, but the flute girl clearly attains joy and "repose."[79]

Having revealed himself as a man of unusual power, Thomas is immediately coerced by the king into offering a highly ambiguous prayer for the bride and groom. Subsequently, Jesus appears in the bridal chamber in the bodily form of Thomas and dissuades the bride and groom from consummating the marriage. He does so in part by persuading them of the dire consequences of (ordinary) children, promising them the delights of spiritual children instead. In *Aseneth,* of course, a heavenly figure appears in Aseneth's bedchamber in the bodily form of Joseph and announces not only her forgiveness but also her forthcoming marriage to Joseph (that will yield "ordinary" but important children).

Particularly striking is the dialogue in *Thomas* when the bridal couple are greeted the next morning. The bride is found sitting uncovered; her mother, seeing her this way, asks why she sits with her husband, unashamed, as though long-married. The father, too, inquires about this.[80] The bride responds as follows: "That I do not veil[81] myself is because the mirror of shame has been taken away from me: I am no longer ashamed or abashed, since the work of shame and bashfulness has been removed from me."[82] Here, as in *Aseneth* 15.1,[83] where the angelic figure instructs Aseneth to remove her headcovering, sexuality and covering are clearly linked; the unveiled woman is "asexual": "[A]nd seeing her, he said to her, 'Lift off the veil from your head, for today you are a holy virgin, and your head is as a young man's.'"

Further, the formal conversion and baptism of Mygdonia in the Tenth Act[84] have some interesting similarities with *Aseneth,* in their usage of water, bread, and oil. Mygdonia begs her nurse Marcia (whom she calls "mother and nurse") to bring her a loaf, a small amount of water, and oil.[85] After Marcia procures all this, Mygdonia stands before Thomas with uncovered head. He pours the oil on her head and prays over her; he then has Marcia undress Mygdonia and redress her in a linen dress. He baptizes Mygdonia in a spring (after which she gets dressed again). Then he gives her the bread and water (not wine) as body of Christ and cup of the Son of God (*AThom* 121). So, too, when the angelic figure appears in Aseneth's chamber, he announces that she will "eat the bread of life and drink the cup of immortality and be anointed with the ointment of incorruptibility" (*Aseneth* 15.4). As Mygdonia stands before Thomas with uncovered head, so, too, does the angel instruct Aseneth to remove her veil, standing before him uncovered. Aseneth, too, changes her garments. Although there is no explicit Christian baptism (consonant with the fictitious setting of the story in biblical Egypt), Aseneth does wash in living water at the instruction of the angel (14.12 and 14.17); and in 18.7, after the departure of the angel, she calls for pure spring water, in which she sees the image of her transfigured face.

The so-called *Hymn of the Pearl,*[86] within *Thomas,* also recalls the imagery of *Aseneth,* with its extended emphasis on the royal garment.[87] As Aseneth's identity is repeatedly symbolized in her garments, from her initial royal but idolatrous clothing, to the mourning garments of her symbolic death, to the new garments that mark her new existence, to the primordial wedding garment that may point to her true identity as the pristine human, so does the *Hymn* employ the image of the royal garment in the journey of the protagonist (usually assumed by scholars to represent the Soul).[88] As Aseneth first appears clothed in royal garments embroidered in gold and encrusted with gems, so, too, the protagonist first has a "garment set with gems and spangled with gold" (108.9) that his royal parents take from him, as they send him on his appointed journey in search of the Pearl in Egypt. Instead, the protagonist clothes himself in ordinary, dirty clothing that he removes as he journeys home, having finally found the Pearl. Only then does he see the image of his garment before him, in which he recognizes his true self, in a scene reminiscent of Aseneth's moment of recognition when she looks in the bowl of spring water and sees her transformed self.

> But when suddenly I saw my garment reflected as in a mirror,
> I perceived in it my whole self as well
> And through it I knew and saw myself. . . .
> The fine garment of glorious colours,
> Which was embroidered with gold, precious stones, and pearls. . . .
> The image of the King of Kings was all over it.[89]

Numerous other elements in the *Hymn* recall *Aseneth,* from the general theme of the aristocratic or royal child to the more specific feature of alienation from the parents, followed by reconciliation. As I have noted earlier, this is a particular feature of the longer, but not the shorter, version of *Aseneth.* In the extended speech in chapter 12, Aseneth proclaims her desolate state as an orphan abandoned by her parents and prays instead to God as Father to protect her. In the end of the longer version, Aseneth is reconciled to her parents, who themselves praise God (20.6–8). Both tales are set in Egypt, although perhaps for differing reasons, and feature a ferocious animal enemy: the savage lion in *Aseneth,* the devouring serpent in the *Hymn.* Both Aseneth and the unnamed protagonist of the *Hymn* are named in the Book of Life.[90]

Additionally, stories in other Apocryphal Acts show signs of similiarity with our *Aseneth.* I have argued in chapters 3 and 7 that the longer version of *Aseneth* represents Aseneth's transformation as a reversal of Eve's transgression.[91] In the *Acts of Andrew,* Maximilla's conversion is clearly linked with Eve's sin, as is implicit in

Aseneth; furthermore, it is precisely obedience by a woman that undoes Eve's disobedience. Andrew says to Maximilla:

> I rightly see in you Eve repenting and in me Adam converting. For what she suffered through ignorance, you—whose soul I seek—must now redress through conversion. . . . You healed her deficiency by not experiencing the same passions, and I have perfected Adam's imperfection by fleeing to God for refuge.[92] Where Eve disobeyed, you obeyed; what Adam agreed to, I flee from; the things that tripped them up, we have recognized. For it is ordained that each person should correct his or her own fall.[93]

It is interesting that Maximilla's actions are construed as obedience to God, since she is clearly here disobedient to her husband. The motif of Adam and Eve continues: "Just as Adam died in Eve through his complicity with her, so also I now live in you through your observing the commandment of the Lord and through your transporting yourself to a state worth of your being."[94]

Intriguing though these similarities are, there are significant differences between these tales of Christian proselytes whose devotion to Jesus is defined by sexual abstinence and that of Aseneth, whose devotion to Joseph is expressed through sexual love, fidelity, and childbearing. Where Jesus/Thomas denounces marriage, the angelic Joseph double endorses marriage and its consequences, children. In the *Acts of Andrew,* it is Maximilla's disavowal of Eve's sexuality and her disobedience to her husband that effect her salvation, whereas in *Aseneth,* it is the acceptance of sexuality and submission to her husband that wins Aseneth divine favor. *Aseneth*'s message is clearly that sexuality and marriage are good and divinely ordained.

While these observations suggest that *Aseneth* may not have been composed within exactly the same circles as the *Acts of Thomas* or within the same precise ascetic worldview as the *Acts of Andrew* and other related apocrypha, we should not see the differences between them as indicative of mutually exclusive worldviews. It would not be too difficult to read *Aseneth* as another tale of the salvation of the quintessential or perhaps even primordial Soul, just as most scholars read the *Hymn of the Pearl* as a tale of the Soul, equated with primordial Adam, in search of its true identity and union with God the Father and constructed upon the base of the parables of the Prodigal Son (Luke 15.11–32) and the Pearl (Matt 13.45–46).[95] Particularly within Syriac circles, where bridal imagery (perhaps itself drawn from the tale of Adam and Eve) was a central metaphor of the union of God and the Soul, and Christ and the Church, the marriage of Joseph and Aseneth could easily have afforded the opportunity to tell yet another version of this paradigmatic myth, made even easier by the feminine identity of the protagonist. Viewed from such a perspective, the fact that *Aseneth* culminates in marriage does not make it any less appropriate for those Syrian circles that rejected ordinary marriage and preached sexual abstinence as the sine qua non of Christian identity, as does the *Acts of Thomas.* Rather, the marriage of Joseph and Aseneth provides a paradigm for spiritual marriage of various sorts. Further, Syrian Christians seem to have believed that the prohibition against sexuality and marriage only came into effect with the coming of Christ, so that even if their union were construed to have had an ordinary dimension of sexuality resulting in the birth of Manasseh and Ephraim, it could easily have been incorporated into an ascetic Christian theology by virtue of its historical chronology.[96]

Although these affinities are highly intriguing, they are by themselves insufficient demonstration of the Christian composition of *Aseneth,* let alone a Syrian context for that composition. The works of several Syrian Christian writers, most notably Ephrem and Aphrahat, both of whom lived in the fourth century C.E., not only contain explicit Christian interpretations of the marriage of Joseph and Aseneth, as I have already noted, but also employ much of the specific imagery of *Aseneth.* This appears, as we shall see, particularly true of the imagery of the longer version, at least in some cases. At a minimum, then, a detailed comparison allows us to understand why the text flourished in Syrian Christian circles and may even suggest to some, as it does to me, that our *Aseneth* could easily have had a Christian author.

As numerous scholars of Syrian Christianity have remarked, the cultural amalgam that flourished in Syrian cities such as Edessa and Nisibis in the fourth century was extraordinary, if not unique, in the ancient world. Sebastian Brock observes that "three very different cultural traditions, Ancient Mesopotamian, Jewish and Greek, find a meeting point in Ephrem to an extent that cannot be paralleled in any other early Christian writer."[97] Although Ephrem himself appears to have known no Greek, he was apparently aware of Greek Jewish scripture, and his works display a familiarity with many Jewish traditions found only outside the Bible, including some from Targumim, midrashim, and other parabiblical sources. Just how Ephrem knew this is unclear, since as Brock points out "there is absolutely no evidence that he drew directly on Jewish literary sources in either Aramaic or Hebrew."[98] Brock also notes that some of these traditions are found among Christian writers only in Ephrem and some other early Syriac writers. The melange of materials in Ephrem demonstrates that, at the very least, ancient biblical and parabiblical traditions could be known indirectly, rather than directly—an important observation for the hypothesis that *Aseneth* is a Christian composition.

Although apparently all known Syrian Christian authors wrote in Syriac, it is virtually certain that some Syrian Christians not only knew but also wrote in Greek.[99] For our purposes, this is particularly significant, since it demonstrates that *Aseneth* could have been composed in Greek by a Christian in a Syrian Christian community such as Edessa or Nisibis.

Of further interest is the probability that the Syrian churches of Aphrahat and Ephrem had their historical roots in the Jewish community of Adiabene,[100] a community whose conversion to Judaism centuries earlier is chronicled by Josephus.[101] What is particularly interesting here is the fact that the first Adiabenene converts were Queen Helena and her son Izates. According to Josephus, Helena subsequently came to Jerusalem on pilgrimage and spent a considerable personal fortune providing food to the inhabitants during a famine.[102] If this is in fact the case, one might argue that a community that traced its roots to the conversion of a woman might be very interested in the tale of another woman "convert," particularly one whose religious quest could be portrayed as paradigmatic and whose biblical past might even legitimate their own origins.[103]

Whatever the relation of Ephrem and Aphrahat to Syrian Jewish communities, their writings exhibit considerable interest in some of the themes and imagery of *Aseneth.* Although the imagery of Christ as Bridegroom and the church as Bride is already an established one before fourth-century Syriac writers, Ephrem's penchant for bridal imagery is particularly evident.

While Christ was obviously the paradigmatic Bridegroom, there appear to have been several candidates for the paradigmatic Bride, including the individual soul and the Church collective. Early Christian Syriac writers debated how to reconcile biblical images of the Bride of God as Israel with their interpretation of the Church as Bride of Christ. According to one view, the Church is in fact composed of two elements: the People (the Jews) and the Peoples (the Gentiles), thus incorporating Israel as Bride within the larger metaphor of the Church as Bride. According to the more predominant view, held by Ephrem and others, the Bride of Christ was solely the Church gathered from the Peoples, that is, the Gentiles.[104]

In his hymn entitled *Resurrection,* Ephrem portrays the events at Sinai as paradigmatic: Moses goes up to the bridal chamber, while Israel the Bride rejects the King and falls in love with the Calf, thus committing adultery. But God gives Israel a second chance—in the entry into Jerusalem. While the first part of this sequence doesn't pertain particularly to our Aseneth story,[105] the next stanza is strikingly reminiscent of that portion of the plot of *Aseneth* where she and Joseph first meet.

> The daughter of Sarah beheld the King's Son,
> she saw He was chaste, and she became downcast;
> she saw He was pure, and so she played sick,
> for she was used to adulterers;
> she accused Him so that she might not herself be accused.[106]

In our texts, Aseneth is in all ways like the daughters of the Hebrews and is identified by her resemblance to Sarah, Rebecca, and Rachel. By the time she sees Joseph, she has refused to marry him, preferring the son of Pharaoh. Joseph is indeed, in the shorter text at least, the King's son, and he is chaste. When Aseneth sees him and perceives his chastity (which she has impugned), she becomes downcast and plays sick—in fact, in the scene with her *suntrophē,* she literally lies about having a headache. Since there is no particular reason to argue that these specific details of *Aseneth* have their origins in any of the concerns discussed in previous chapters (exegetical anomalies, consonance with adjurative paradigms, and so forth), the consonance here is noteworthy. The consonance, of course, is not perfect: our Aseneth is not used to adulterers, although her expressed intention to marry the son of Pharaoh might be construed in this manner.

Ephrem's hymn continues with the Bridegroom rejecting the daughter of Sarah and going elsewhere—to the Nations. Yet again, Aseneth in this respect is quite interesting—for she is, in fact, the Bride who combines Israel and the Nations in her person: the daughter of the Egyptian priest Pentephres, she is nevertheless in all ways like the daughters of the Hebrews.

Syriac writers elaborate on the marital metaphor for Christ and the church though precise language and imagery. Robert Murray points out, for instance, that the phrase "'Bride Adorned'[107] seems to have been a consecrated phrase at least from the time of the very early Syriac version of the Didascalia, where it appears." In both versions of *Aseneth* she is described as *"kekosmēmenēn hos numphēn theou"*[108] (adorned as a divine bride or as a bride of God), although in this scene, she wears garments embroidered with emblems of pagan gods. At the conclusion of her transformation, Aseneth again clothes herself in bridal garments, this time devoid of any such emblems, and is seen by her parents "dressed in bridal garments" (20.4).

In Syriac writers, bridal garments (as well as royal garments) appear to have had complex theological associations. According to Brock, Ephrem and others seem to have subscribed to a tradition that Adam and Eve were originally clothed not in garments of skin but in garments of light or a robe of glory.[109] In Ephrem, the purpose of Christ's incarnation is to restore this lost robe of glory to Adam, returning Adam (and Eve) to Eden in the garment of light.[110] Brock argues that Ephrem associated this garment with baptism and identified it with a wedding garment, relying on an exegesis of Matthew 22.1–14.

> When the newly baptized are told to "preserve" their recently acquired "robe of glory," there lies behind this an allusion to the parable of the wedding in Matthew 22:1–14, where the guest who turns up at the wedding feast without his wedding garment is thrown out. From later writers we learn explicitly that the wedding garment is none other than "the robe of glory," acquired at baptism, which must be kept unspotted for the eschatological wedding feast: it is *not* the case that the wedding guest never had a wedding garment; rather, he had been given one—at baptism—but he had lost or soiled it.[111]

As a result of her encounter with the angelic double of Joseph, Aseneth changes her clothing twice. In the first instance, at the angel's command, she removes the filthy garments of mourning she has worn during her week of penance and replaces them with a *"stolēn kainēn athikton"* (a new, immaculate robe [14.13]).[112] The remainder of her encounter with the angel takes place while she wears this garment. But in 15.10, the angel instructs her to change into a wedding garment, which she only does after the angel departs back up to the heavens. It is this garment that has associations strikingly similar to those of the bridal garment in Ephrem, for it is not just a bridal robe (*stolēn gamou*) but ancient and primordial (*tēn archaian, tēn protēn*).[113] Although no version of the text is explicit on this point, these adjectives do suggest that this robe is not just very old but does indeed have some mystical primordial characteristic.[114] The crucial element here may be the association with marriage. This is particularly true in the longer reconstructions of the text, where I have argued that Aseneth and the angelic double of Joseph reverse the primordial sin of Eve and Adam.

In his *Hymns on Virginity,* Ephrem draws on images that recall additional motifs in *Aseneth,* weaving together the images of John the Baptist as friend of the Bridegroom and as lamp (John 5.35) with the lamps of the virgins in Matthew 25. For Ephrem, John the Baptist and the lamp are friends of the two bridegrooms, who are themselves Christ and the Sun. "The eye sees with the help of a lamp, which resembles the sun, its true bridegroom."[115] This image and others in the same passage suggest that the true Bridegroom enables the Bride to see truly. In *Aseneth,* it is the angelic figure who has the human form of Joseph but the divine attributes of Helios, the Sun, who enables Aseneth to truly see the mystery of the bees.

Ephrem's imagery of Mary as Bride is also provocative. For Ephrem, Mary is not only the Mother of Christ but also the Bride and Sister of Christ, along with all chaste souls.[116] This constellation of attributes recalls the enigmatic figure of Metanoia. In the shorter version, Metanoia is the daughter of the Most High and the mother of virgins, who is herself *parthenos* (virgin) and who prepares a bridal chamber for those who love God. In the longer version, she is daughter of the Most High, guardian of virgins, who prepares a place of rest, and sister of the equally enigmatic angelic figure. Further, as Aseneth's double she may be considered a bride, and she has explicit bridal associations in the shorter version.

The passage that particularly intrigues me here is from Ephrem's Armenian hymns:

> In the mirror of the commandments
> I will behold my interior face
> so that I may wash off the dirt on my soul
> and clean away the filth of my mind,
> lest the Holy One to whom I am betrothed sees me
> and stands back from me in abhorrence.[117]

This passage is obviously reminiscent of the scene in the longer reconstruction in which Aseneth sees her reflection (**18.7–11**). There, although not in the shorter version, Aseneth seeks to wash her face lest Joseph see her and reject her. Only when she looks into the mirror does she see her own glorious face.

Although the personified figure of Metanoia in *Aseneth* appears virtually unique in ancient sources, it is precisely in Syriac that the Holy Spirit is grammatically feminine and in Syrian Christian sources that we find considerable interest in the utility of that association.[118] Although I do not wish to argue that Metanoia should necessarily be construed as a form of the Holy Spirit, there are certain elements in Syriac representations of both the Holy Spirit and Mary that resemble key features of Metanoia. For instance, in the shorter version, Metanoia is the daughter of God and the mother of virgins; in her unceasing intervention for the repentant, she is remarkably comparable to the intercessory Mary and perhaps also a reformed and repentant Eve. In the longer version, she loses the attribute of motherhood but gains the role of sister of the heavenly double of Joseph (who in a Christian context is clearly a type of Christ, if not Christ himself).

Numerous Syrian sources explore the image of the Holy Spirit as Mother, offering various scenarios for how the parents of Jesus could be the feminine Spirit and the female Mary.[119] Some of the debate about the relationship between God and the Spirit may underlie our Metanoia material. Particularly noteworthy is a passage from Ephrem extant only in Armenian, articulating the relationship between God and the Holy Spirit, utilizing the analogy of Eve and Adam: "It is not said of Eve that she was Adam's sister or his daughter, but that she came from him; likewise it is not to be said that the Spirit is a daughter or a sister, but that (she) is *from* God and consubstantial with him."[120]

If Metanoia represents the Holy Spirit, this passage may reflect disagreement with her portrait in *Aseneth,* where she is daughter of God (and in the longer version, whose Syriac translation we have, sister of the Son of God); or alternatively, it may suggest that Metanoia is not the Holy Spirit but a different female figure who may better be identified with Eve and so with Mary (herself the female figure who undoes the sin of Eve).

Yet another intriguing similarity between *Aseneth* and Syriac traditions pertains to the symbolism of olives. In *Aseneth* 5.7, Joseph first appears in Pentephres' courtyard bearing an olive branch laden with fruit, an association that cannot be derived from the biblical narrative. I have argued earlier that Joseph's presentation here relies heavily on late antique depictions of Helios, particularly Helios as an icon of the Emperor, but the olive branch is the least obvious component of that representation.[121]

In both Ephrem and Aphrahat, the olive is a particularly apt symbol for Christ.[122] Ephrem, for example, interprets the olive leaf of the dove of Noah with reference to Christ. In his *Hymns on Virginity,* he writes:

> Let oil in all its forms acknowledge You in Your entirety
> for oil gives rest to all.
> The olive served Christ, who gives life to all,
> depicting Him in its abundance, its branches and leaves . . .
> with its branches it depicted the symbol of His victory.[123]

Oil is also a mirror for the many facets of Christ.[124] In both Ephrem and Aphrahat, the image of Christ as light-giving olive is often used in conjunction with the image of Christ as Tree of Life.[125] While other explanations for Joseph bearing an olive branch may be plausible, the plethora of images common to *Aseneth* and fourth-century Syrian sources may also suggest that a strong candidate is the olive's association with Christ, here represented as Joseph.[126]

Still another significant similarity concerns the transformation of Aseneth into a divine being. In prior chapters, I have offered a multiplicity of contexts in which that transformation would have made sense in antiquity; here I would like to propose yet another. According to Brock,[127] Ephrem had a particularly interesting understanding of the doctrine of theosis—that is, of humans become divinized. He appears to have believed that Adam and Eve were created neither mortal nor immortal—and that their actions in the Garden determined which they would become. Because they followed the Serpent, they became mortal—had they done otherwise, they would have become immortal.

> Had the serpent been rejected, along with sin, they would have eaten of the Tree of Life,
> and the Tree of Knowledge would no longer have been withheld from them. From the latter they would have acquired infallible knowledge, while from the former they would have received immortal life. They would have acquired divinity in humanity. And had they thus acquired infallible knowledge and immortal life, they would have done so in this body.[128]

According to Brock, theosis is part of the "exchange of names." Although it preserves a gap between God and his creation, God creates Adam with the potential to become a "created god." "What characterizes the divinity that has been made available for humanity is, according to Ephrem, the possession of immortality and infallible knowledge."[129] Furthermore, Brock claims that theosis "is just a way of making explicit what it means to become 'children of God,' seeing that in the Semitic languages the term *bar,* 'son of,' may have the sense of 'sharing in the attributes of' or 'belonging to the category of.'"[130]

This is extremely close to what transpires in *Aseneth*. While Joseph is already divinized and repeatedly called Son of God (e.g., 21.3/**21.4**), so, too, Aseneth becomes divinized and daughter of God (21.3/**21.4**). What Aseneth acquires from the double of Joseph is precisely both immortality and infallible knowledge. Brock considers Ephrem's doctrine of theosis firmly rooted in his exegesis of Genesis, although it seems to me highly likely that it was influenced by late antique religious developments more broadly, including beliefs in the apotheosis of emperors.[131]

It is also noteworthy that Ephrem claims that Eve desired to become divine in order "that she might become head over her head and that she might be giving orders to him from whom she received orders, seeing that she would have become senior in divinity to Adam to whom she was junior in humanity."[132]

If I am correct in my thesis that in the longer version the angel's verbal order to Aseneth to eat the honey together with Aseneth's compliant obedience constitute an intentional reversal of Genesis, we may have here another instance of resonance with the longer version of *Aseneth*. But in any case, Ephrem's beliefs here are consonant with those of *Aseneth,* which depicts Aseneth's own theosis, in this life, in the body.

Still another intriguing similarity between Syrian Christianity and *Aseneth* is the title "City of Refuge."[133] But unlike some of the other common imagery explored in this discussion, the phrase "City of Refuge" poses an interesting problem of method. Among Syriac sources, it occurs in the *Acts of Judas Thomas* as both a title of Christ and a reference to the church. In his discussion of this title, Murray saw both its usage in Philo[134] and its occurrence in *Aseneth* as suggestive of a Jewish background to a symbolic interpretation of the biblical cities of refuge. Murray was admittedly affected by his acceptance of Philonenko's judgment that *Aseneth* is a relatively early Jewish work and by the fact that it was clearly available to Syriac writers in the sixth century and might, he suggests, even have been known in the fourth, although he gives no argument for this.[135]

Although his own analysis rested on the belief that *Aseneth* antedates the *Acts of Judas Thomas* by at least a century or more, his final comments are not without interest. In Syriac, the initial name of Aseneth as City of Refuge is paraphrased as "metropolis" (*emmâ da-mdînâtâ*), but later the angel blesses the maids and calls them the seven pillars in the City of Refuge (*mdînat gawsâ*) and "all of them 'daughters of the city of the *bêt gawsâ*) [*sic*] of the elect.'"[136] He concludes:

> The original author evidently sees Aseneth not only as an ideal proselyte but also as a symbol of the Jewish community which receives proselytes. If the witness of the later Syriac version is not equally clear, we must remember how for both Aphrahat and Ephrem Aseneth is the type of the Church from the Gentiles; when we add to this the use of *bet gawsa* as a title of Christ and Church, we may consider it likely, though not probable, that both the Jewish story and these Syriac Christian usages reflect, once again, a common midrashic background.[137]

Yet if *Aseneth* is composed contemporaneously with the *Acts of Thomas,* or even later, and if it is not necessarily Jewish, the interpretative possibilities become more complex. *Aseneth* might draw on the *Acts of Thomas*. Both might still draw on a common tradition but one that was uniquely Christian. In fact, the absence of the City of

Refuge tradition in other known Jewish midrashic materials about Aseneth might be taken as further evidence of the Christian character of this identification. While Philo does constitute proof that a hellenistic Jewish author could interpret the biblical cities of refuge symbolically, the known Christian use of Aseneth as the Church of the Gentiles and use of the City of Refuge as a title of the Church does strengthen the possibility that we have here a subtle indicator of Christian authorship (particularly since, by the fourth century, Philo was clearly being read by Christians as something approaching a Christian author).[138] Further, if we exclude Philo, the presence of this tradition only in *Aseneth* and in the *Acts of Thomas* could point to a localized tradition, although this is, of course, something of an argument from silence.

Next, we may consider another unusual tradition common to the longer text of *Aseneth* and Ephrem, namely, the use of the Coal of Fire in Isaiah 6.6. In chapter 4, I argued that it is precisely this passage on which the redactor of the longer text relies to construct a portion of the scene with the angelic being. Ephrem identifies the Coal of Fire with Christ and gives the following description of the encounter of Christ with Anna in the temple:

> The prophetess Anna embraced Him
> and put her mouth to His lips.
> The Spirit rested on her lips, as on Isaiah's
> his mouth was silent, but the Coal of Fire
> opened up his mouth by touching his lips.[139]

In response, Anna then sings a hymn to Christ. Furthermore, in Ephrem, Christians are able to consume the Coal of Fire, whereas even the seraph in Isaiah, let alone Isaiah himself, could not.[140]

Although I have not exhausted the similarities and possible points of contact between Syriac Christian writers and *Aseneth,* one other relatively minor element in Ephrem is also worth noting. In Ephrem, as in *Aseneth,* bees appear as a symbol of the raising of the dead, at least in his interpretation of the bees and the honey in Judges 14, the story of Samson, a symbolic reading not apparent in the original biblical text.[141]

What, then, is the significance of this mass of similar imagery and associations in our *Aseneth* and in Syrian Christian writings from the third and fourth centuries? Clearly, none of these parallels is so unique and so striking as to demonstrate some clear and unambiguous relationship between the two. And clearly, the thrust of chapters 4, 5, and 6 in this study has been to illuminate the degree to which many elements of *Aseneth* are consonant with the wide range of religious imagery prevalent in the later antique Greco-Roman world. Still, I would suggest that particularly when contrasted with what we do know of extant Jewish traditions about Aseneth and given the fact that our earliest sure evidence for the existence of *Aseneth* comes from Syria, this constellation of commonality constitutes a considerable argument for the Christian composition of the text(s).

Further, while a striking number of images from Ephrem in particular have counterparts in *Aseneth,* some elements particular to the longer reconstruction show the most affinity with specific elements and imagery in Ephrem. These include the scene with the reflecting water (18.7/**18.9–11**); Christ the Sun who enables the Bride to see; Eve and theosis; the Coal of Fire in Aseneth's encounter with the angelic being; and perhaps others as well. To me, this strengthens the possibility that at the very least, the longer version, if not also the shorter version, may indeed be Christian,[142] and Syrian to boot, a point I will pursue in chapter 10.

One other element in the longer reconstruction of *Aseneth* may also support the plausibility of the text(s) as Christian in composition, namely, the inserted silent prayers of chapter 11. Van der Horst surveys the evidence for silent prayer in early Jewish sources, concluding that while occasional references in both rabbinic and nonrabbinic Jewish texts condone silent prayer (influenced particularly by the silent prayer of Hannah in 1 Sam 1), they are few and far between in comparison with those passages that presume vocalized prayer as the norm.[143]

That silent prayer was not de rigueur in at least some ancient Jewish circles is evident in Pseudo-Philo's retelling of Hannah's prayer. Explaining why Hannah prays in silence, the author writes:

> And Hannah did not want to pray out loud *as all people do* [emphasis added]. For then she thought, saying, "Perhaps I am not worthy to be heard, and Peninnah will then be even more eager to taunt me as she does daily when she says, "Where is your God in whom you trust?" And I know that neither she who has many sons is rich nor she who has few is poor, but whoever abounds in the will of God is rich. For who may know what I have prayed for? If they know that I am not heard in my prayer, they will blaspheme. And I will not have any witness except in my own soul, because my tears are the servant of my prayers.[144]

Van der Horst also documents a growing Christian advocacy of silent prayer, beginning with Clement of Alexandria in the second century and becoming more apparent in third- and fourth-century writings, a development he attributes in part to the influence of Neoplatonic philosophy[145] and in part to the ideal of monastic silence from the fourth century on.[146] Yet, as he observes, even in the third century, major Christian writings still envision vocalized prayer as the norm and silent prayer as more or less unheard of.[147] Of particular interest for our purposes are his examples of fourth-century Christian writers, such as Cyril of Jerusalem, who read 1 Samuel 1 together with 1 Corinthians 14 to argue that women should pray silently in church.[148] Thus, the insertion of silent prayers into Aseneth's soliloquy appears consistent with my hypothesis that the texts date to the third or fourth century and may even point, if tentatively, to a Christian redactor, although as van der Horst demonstrates, it is not absolutely incompatible with Jewish ideas about prayer.

There is one final piece of evidence that may lend support to the suggestion that *Aseneth* is a work of self-conscious Christian composition, the Coptic text on the installation of the archangel Michael.[149] In chapter 5, I noted the similarities between the description of Michael in this text and that of both Joseph's angelic double and Aseneth's double, Metanoia, in *Aseneth:* Michael is associated with the sun; he is greatest of the angels in heaven; he is called great and mighty, good and gentle. He has no other role than continual intercession, and he prostrates himself before God and prays and weeps on behalf of sinning human beings. Since this comes closer than any other source we can identify to combining the attributes of the divine Son and Daughter in *Aseneth,* it seems not insignificant that the text in which this constellation occurs is explicitly Christian.

Despite, then, the contemporary affirmation of older scholars' rejection of Batiffol's initial identification of the text as Christian, there are few if any hard arguments against Christian authorship, apart from the absence of irrefutably explicit and obvious Christian concerns and the insistence that the text is early and therefore Jewish, all of which I have addressed.[150] Although the arguments of scholars who argued in the past for Christian composition of *Aseneth* may often have been flawed, their proponents may have been right for the wrong reasons. In support of Christian composition, the text has a well-known Christian life, beginning no later than the sixth century C.E. and possibly earlier. As we have seen in some detail, both the shorter and longer versions display significant and sometimes highly unusual similarities with many known Christian traditions, such as those found in the *Odes of Solomon*, in the Apocryphal Acts, particularly those of Thomas, and the writings of Syrian Christians such as Ephrem, revealing the manner in which various Christians must have read *Aseneth* and strengthening the possibility of primary Christian composition.

A Third Alternative: That *Aseneth* Was Composed by a "God-Fearer" (*Theosebēs*)

Before we attempt to formulate any conclusion about the religious self-identification of the author(s) of *Aseneth,* we should consider the possibility that the author of the text was neither, in our terms, a Jew or a Christian but of a differing self-understanding. It is within the realm of possibility that the author of *Aseneth* was, by self-definition, a *theosebēs* (literally meaning, "one who reveres or fears God"), here employed as a technical term for a devotee of the God of Israel, who was neither born into a Jewish or Christian family nor a formal convert to either. The evidence for such a possibility derives from several observations.

First, the language of the text itself never uses the term *Ioudaios* (the Greek word conventionally translated as "Jew")[151] or even *ethnē* (nations or Gentiles). Rather, its terms for the categories of "we" and "they" are, in both shorter and longer reconstructions, *theosebēs* and Egyptians. In the first portion of the story, at 4.9, Joseph is described as a *theosebēs anēr* (a man who reveres or fears God), and his initial speech before Aseneth at 8.5–7 describes the attributes of both the *theosebēs anēr* and the *theosebēs gunē*. In the second portion of the story, Levi, Jacob, and other of Joseph's brothers are described as *theosebeis andres* (at 22.8, 23.9, 23.10, 28.4, 29.3). Although the term occurs a dozen times in Philonenko's reconstruction and fourteen times in Burchard's version, it occurs only two other times in the entire corpus of "pseudepigrapha"[152] and occurs rarely in demonstrably early Greek Jewish writings.[153]

However, the term *theosebēs* occurs in a number of inscriptions associated with Jews, particularly those dating from the third through the fifth centuries, from numerous diaspora communities, especially those of Sardis, Miletus, Aphrodisias, and other cities in ancient Asia Minor.[154] That there were Greco-Roman pagans who became enamored of the God worshiped by Jews and who participated in varying degrees of Jewish ritual life and observance is uncontestable.[155] That such persons were also sometimes designated as *theosebēs* or equivalent Latin terms meaning "God-fearers" seems highly likely, although this continues to be the source of scholarly debate,[156] and it seems equally clear, at least to me, that not every usage of the term, whether in literary sources or on inscriptions, carries this meaning.[157] An inscription found in Aphrodisias has been construed by many scholars to constitute proof that *theosebēs* was used as a technical term for pagan adherents or sympathizers with Judaism,[158] although I am not altogether convinced this is the case, either at Aphrodisias or elsewhere.

Because all twentieth-century scholarship has placed *Aseneth* no later than the early second century C.E., the possible connections between the text's relatively frequent usage of *theosebēs* and the evidence for persons so designated in Greco-Roman inscriptions associated with Jews and/or Judaism have remained unexplored. But if, in fact, *Aseneth* was composed in close chronological proximity to these inscriptions, their common usage of the term *theosebēs* requires additional consideration. Without engaging in what has become a complex and highly technical debate in more detail than necessary, if even some persons in late antiquity used the term *theosebēs* of themselves and of others to designate affinity with Judaism, we must consider the possibility that such a person could have been responsible for the composition of a text such as *Aseneth*.[159] Certainly it seems feasible that at least some persons so designated would have had the necessary education and resources to write a book and even the detailed familiarity with the traditions present in Greek Jewish scripture that *Aseneth* appears to presuppose. If, as some scholars propose, there were significant numbers of such persons at various times and places in late antiquity, why not assume that at least a few of them might have composed literary works appropriate to their interests and concerns? One or more ancient converts to Judaism are reputed to have translated the Hebrew Bible into Greek, including Aquila and perhaps also Theodotion.[160] If proselytes were either sufficiently well educated to begin with or acquired the necessary literacy and facility with language and texts subsequent to their conversion, why not also the so-called *theosebeis?*

This theory has the advantage of accounting for *Aseneth*'s affinities with numerous ancient traditions and for some of its peculiar, almost chameleonlike, qualities. Admittedly, such explanations do tend to reinforce the notion that ancient religious categories were strongly fixed and incapable of accommodating the kinds of ambiguity we see in *Aseneth.* Nevertheless, it is also true that the major motifs and concerns of *Aseneth* are likely to have been of compelling interest to such persons, particularly if we keep in mind that Aseneth's transformation does not obligate her to much in the way of specific ritual obligation, precisely the kinds of things that may have been of concern to Greco-Roman pagan devotees of Judaism.

Conclusion

Although I would dearly love to be able to determine with even reasonable certainty the religious self-understanding of the author of the earliest form of *Aseneth* to which we might have access, in the end, I do not think the evidence allows us to do so. While at times it seems quite possible to me that the author was a Jew with no other religious affiliations, I also see no compelling reasons to rule out the possibility that the author was a Christian, and sometimes I think the evidence tips slightly in that direction. Not inconceivably, a Christian author might also have understood himself to be

Jewish as well, but such a combination is not necessary to account for *Aseneth* in any of its forms. With Philonenko and others, I do think it likely that some of the forms of *Aseneth* we presently have do reflect intentional Christian revision, regardless of the identity of the earliest author.

While I think a "theosebic" author less likely, I cannot rule such an author out either. Further, I think it remotely possible that *Aseneth* could have been composed by a Samaritan, or perhaps, to put it differently, I cannot argue with certainty that *Aseneth* could not have been composed by a Samaritan, an option we tend to forget in the determination of authorial identity of anonymous and pseudonymous texts from later antiquity.[161]

If, then, I am certain of anything about *Aseneth*'s author or authors, it is that we cannot be at all certain of the specifics of their own religious and cultural self-understanding, and no amount of "consensual" assertion to the contrary changes this. Difficult though it may be for scholars to concede such uncertainty, I do not see that the evidence allows us to say anything more definitive. The consequences of this agnosticism, as I shall develop in the final chapter, are considerable and may well contribute to scholarly resistance to such conclusions.

NOTES

1. That Joseph was elsewhere taken as a type for Jesus is clear from numerous Christian writers such as Tertullian (*Against Marcion* 3.18); Origen, Jerome, Chrysostom, and Augustine (for references, see Batiffol, "Livre," 24); Ambrose (*On Joseph the Patriarch,* PL 14, 641); and Cyril of Alexandra (*Glaphyra on Gen.* 6). See also *On Passover,* 59: "If you wish to see the mystery of the Lord . . . look at Joseph who was sold." This work is conventionally attributed to Melito of Sardis, but see now the Ph.D. dissertation (University of Pennsylvania, 1996) of Lynn Cohick, "Reassessing the Use of Scriptural Material and Interpretations of the *Peri Pascha* Attributed to Melito of Sardis." See further the discussion of Aphrahat and Ephrem on Christian interpretation of Aseneth in this chapter.

Although Batiffol, "Livre," initially argued for the association of Joseph with Christ, Philonenko, *Joseph et Aséneth,* countered that none of the details of *Aseneth* link Joseph to Jesus (99); consequently he thought it unlikely that the author(s) of *Aseneth* intended such associations when they composed it.

2. The most obvious example of this would be the works of Philo. Other candidates might include writings attributed to Ps. Philo, Ps. Hecateus, and *Test. Moses,* assuming, of course, that these *are* originally the work of self-consciously Jewish authors. Obviously, the most problematic are texts that are not "blatantly" Christian. Works thought to have been composed in Hebrew, such as Ps. Philo, can for these purposes also be assumed to have been Jewish, although if one were really to push the edges of the methodological envelope, one might even insist that the use of Hebrew by itself is not definitive evidence of non-Christian authorship either. Since, surely, there were Christians, in some places and periods, who spoke and wrote Hebrew, the question is whether they would ever have composed works like this. For a particularly helpful exploration of some of the preliminary issues here, see Kraft, "Pseudepigrapha," 55–86.

3. Philonenko, *Joseph et Aséneth,* 101.

4. Chrysostom, *Against Judaizing Christians.*

5. Sparks, *AOT,* 469, sees this as evidence of Jewish interests, although he then points to

other evidence of Christian concerns; several colleagues have mentioned to me their sense that this line is dispositive during conversations in the course of writing this book.

6. See the apparatus in Philonenko, *Joseph et Aséneth,* 130; see also the discussion in chapter 2.

7. See chapter 2.

8. "Le mariage de Joseph et Aséneth posait une question à la conscience juive" (Philonenko, *Joseph et Aséneth,* 101).

9. However, it may be true that Christians were particularly interested in the symbolic value of the story as a metaphor for the conversion of Gentiles to Christianity, as in Aphrahat or Ephrem; see the discussion later in this chapter.

10. See chapter 2.

11. There appears to be no modern edition of *LJ*. There is an old Latin translation by Giuseppe Simone Assemani: *Sancti patri nostri Ephraem Syri: Opera omnia quae exstant: graece, syriacque, latine,* vol. 1 (Rome, 1737).

12. Gary Vikan, "Illuminated Manuscripts of Pseudo-Ephraem's Life of Joseph and the Romance of Joseph and Aseneth" (Ph.D. dissertation, Princeton University, 1976). In most cases, however, the text transmitted is that of Batiffol (A), which both Burchard and Philonenko consider to show signs of Christian redaction. Ps. Zacharias Rhetor does not, however, contain the *Life of Joseph,* which may or may not be suggestive of a later date for the composition of the latter. The same linkage of the two texts occurs in Armenian manuscript traditions.

13. Vikan, "Illuminated Manuscripts," 23.

14. Vikan, "Illuminated Manuscripts," 23.

15. Jerome, *Letter to Eustochium,* 18–19.

16. Jerome, *Letter to Eustochium,* 26.

17. Philonenko, *Joseph et Aséneth,* 101. See also G. Delling, "Einwirkungen der Sprache der Septuaginta in 'Joseph und Aseneth,'" *JSJ* 9 (1978): 29–56.

18. Philonenko, *Joseph et Aséneth,* 28–30.

19. See chapter 3.

20. We do not have, for instance, alternate readings for Judg 13.

21. See, e.g., Emanuel Tov, "The Septuagint," in Martin Jan Mulder, ed., *Mikra: Text, Translation, Reading, and Interpretation of the Hebrew Bible in Ancient Judaism and Early Christianity,* CRINT (Assen/Mastricht: Van Gorcum; Philadelphia: Fortress Press, 1988), 163, who suggests that Jews relegated this translation to Christians as early as the late first century C.E. See also Henry Barclay Swete, *An Introduction to the Old Testament in Greek* (Cambridge: Cambridge University Press, 1902; reprint, New York: KTAV, 1968), 30, and Emil Schürer, *The History of the Jewish People in the Age of Jesus Christ (175 B.C.–A.D. 135),* ed. Geza Vermes, Fergus Millar, Matthew Black, and Pamela Vermes (London: T. & T. Clark, 1973–87), 3:493. It has also been suggested that the availability of different Hebrew texts, sanctioned by an emergent rabbinic orthodoxy, contributed to Jewish abandonment of the Septuagint.

22. See, e.g., Trebilco's discussion of inscriptions from Asia Minor that appear to quote from the Septuagint Deuteronomy (*Jewish Communities in Asia Minor,* 60–78). But this can cut both ways: third-century inscriptions that clearly use the LXX may testify to Jewish usage of that translation if they can be identified as Jewish on other grounds, but if their use of the LXX is the only proof of their Jewishness, the argument fails since then they might be Christian or conceivably neither.

23. Amnon Linder, *The Jews in Imperial Roman Legislation* (Detroit: Wayne State University Press; Jerusalem: Israel Academy of Sciences and Humanities, 1987), no. 66.

24. See chapter 4.

25. Gager, *Curse Tablets,* 243–45.

26. E.g., Philonenko, *Joseph et Aséneth,* 101: *Aseneth* ignores the entire New Testament.

27. Sebastian P. Brock and Susan Ashbrook Harvey, *Holy Women of the Syrian Orient* (Berkeley: University of California Press, 1987), 7–12.

28. See Kraft, "Pseudepigrapha in Christianity," esp. 61–63, 74–76.

29. For a brief but sensible critical discussion of this, see Sparks, *AOT,* xiv–xv. Kraft ("Pseudepigrapha") surveys older scholars who assumed that Christian work would be explicitly so and that such works were presumed then to be Jewish. Interestingly, F. C. Burkitt (*Jewish and Christian Apocalypses* [London: Milford, 1914], 76, cited in Kraft, "Pseudepigrapha," 62) argued that the burden of proof lay precisely there.

30. The discussion of date and "origin" of the *Lives of the Prophets* in *OTP* 2:379–82 is a good case in point of a text whose earliest manuscript dates from the sixth century, is extant only in Christian manuscripts, is not known from any quotations or citations in Jewish sources or even early Christian sources, and, like *Aseneth,* is there argued to be both early (first century C.E.) and Jewish. *The Ascension of Isaiah* in *OTP* 2:143–76 provides another excellent example of comparable methodological problems. In its current form, it is explicitly Christian and has interesting problems of date, transmission, translation, and so forth. For a recent treatment, see R. G. Hall, "Isaiah's Ascent to See the Beloved: An Ancient Jewish Source for the *Ascension of Isaiah,*" *JBL* 113, no. 3 (1994): 463–84, which contains some very astute remarks about the difficulty of differentiating Jewish from Christian from gnostic and other categorizations and about texts that display simultaneously characteristics of what we consider multiple identity.

31. *On Baptism* 17.5. See Rordorf, "Tertullien et les Actes de Paul," 475–84.

32. Without entering into consideration of the dynamic by which such works were composed, it may be worth pointing out that some persons probably did perceive themselves to be the conduits of such stories rather than their authors—although this may be charitable.

33. The author of 4 Ezra 3.1 may come close to this, with a carefully couched claim to be written thirty years after the destruction of the Temple, allegedly the first but almost certainly the second and so apparently c. 100 C.E. Michael Stone suggests that this reference is likely to be derived from Ezek 1.1 yet a date of c. 100 C.E. falls within the parameters for date (during the reign of Domitian, 81–96 C.E.) that he reaches on other grounds (*Fourth Ezra: Hermeneia— a Critical and Historical Commentary on the Bible* [Minneapolis: Fortress Press, 1990], 9–10, 53–55). Although we think we have decoded the events and chronology of Daniel, it can in no way be said to offer "clear and explicit identification" of its context.

34. Batiffol, "Livre," 37.

35. Batiffol ("Livre," 18) thought that a Jewish legend of Dinah and Aseneth that achieved fixed form in the fourth century C.E. underlay not only *Aseneth,* which he took to be a Christian composition, but also Dinah traditions in *Targum Ps. Jonathan*, *Pirke de Rabbi Eliezer,* and a Syriac version published by Oppenheim (*Fabula Josephi et Asenethae Apocrypha E Libro Syriaco Latine Versa;* see chapter 8 and the appendix.

36. Batiffol, "Livre," 25.

37. Batiffol, "Livre," 26–29. In the shorter version, the phrase is twice applied to Aseneth at 15.1 and 19.1; it is once applied to Metanoia at 15.8. In the longer version, it occurs additionally at **15.2, 15.4,** and **15.6** (see chapter 3).

38. Critique of Batiffol, in Philonenko, *Joseph et Aséneth,* 99–100. As a term for the church, it appears in some interesting early sources, including the epitaph of Abercius from Hierapolis in Asia Minor (published in William Ramsay, *Cities and Bishoprics of Phrygia,* vol. 1, pt. 2 (Oxford: Clarendon Press, 1895–97; reprint, New York: Arno Press, 1975), #657; English translation in J. Stevenson, ed., *A New Eusebius: Documents Illustrative of the History of the Church to A.D. 337* (London: SPCK, 1968); Justin, *Dial. Try.* 38.4. In Clement, *Paed.* 1.42.1, the church is called "mother" and "parthenos"; see A. F. J. Klijn, *The Acts of Thomas: Introduction, Text, Commentary,* Supplement 5 to Novum Testamentum (Leiden: E. J. Brill, 1962), for additional references and discussion (168–69).

39. See n. 1 and later discussion, this chapter. I am indebted to Prof. Gordon Lathrop of the Lutheran Theological Seminary in Philadelphia for first calling the references to Aphrahat and Ephrem to my attention. Further, the prologue to the McKells manuscript of the *Life of Joseph,* which also contains a recension of our *Aseneth,* enumerates at length the similarities between the life of Joseph and that of Christ.

40. For a recent restatement and defense of this consensus, see Chesnutt, *From Death to Life,* 71–76, esp. 74, where he writes, "The cumulative effect of numerous terms, motifs and ideas in Joseph and Aseneth which have strong affinities in Hellenistic Judaism and which are devoid of any exclusively Christian traits, is telling." Part of his argument rests on an early date for *Aseneth,* part on his belief that concern for conversion is central to the work: "It is difficult to imagine that a Christian author would have represented conversion to Christianity in such general religious terms that its specifically Christian profile is lost." He then offers a laundry list of typical Christian elements lacking in *Aseneth:* baptism, faith, love, justification, salvation, and church. While I agree with some of Chesnutt's critique of previous attempts to identify Aseneth as Christian, based for instance on a perceived affinity between the Eucharist and the bread, cup, and ointment, it is my contention that when one casts the net of Christianity a little wider, the possibility of a Christian context becomes much greater.

41. See again Kraft, "Pseudepigrapha."

42. Or at least from the period immediately following the death of Jesus.

43. See, e.g., Ramsay MacMullen, *Christianizing the Roman Empire, AD 100–400* (New Haven: Yale University Press, 1984).

44. For legislation, see Linder, *The Jews in Roman Imperial Legislation,* 80–82, for discussion and references. Scot McKnight, *A Light to the Nations: Jewish Missionary Activity in the Second Temple Period* (Minneapolis: Fortress Press, 1991), finds little evidence for active Jewish missionizing in the period before 70 C.E.; Martin Goodman, *Mission and Conversion,* reaches a similar conclusion, relying particularly on an analysis of rabbinic references. Louis Feldman, *Jew and Gentile in the Ancient World* (Princeton, NJ: Princeton University Press, 1993), offers a lengthy refutation of both Goodman (in advance of publication) and McKnight that is not without serious difficulties of its own. Chapter 8 treats evidence for the earlier period, chapter 9 evidence for outreach to "sympathizers," and chapter 10 evidence for conversion to Judaism in the third, fourth, and fifth centuries. Although I often do not share Feldman's conclusions, his collation of the later evidence is particularly detailed and useful.

Interestingly, *Aseneth* figures significantly in some of Goodman's evidence for conversion to Judaism, particularly in support of his argument that "it is *a priori* probable that in antiquity, as now, at least some conversions to Judaism took place to facilitate a marriage" (*Mission and Conversion,* p. 78). Interestingly, Feldman attributes to Goodman a much less nuanced view than what appears in print: "Goodman assumes that the majority of conversions to Judaism in antiquity, as today, took place to facilitate a marriage" (*Jew and Gentile,* 291). Feldman goes on to claim that Goodman's support for this position is particularly *Aseneth* and counters with the argument that those Roman writers who fulminate against Jewish proselytism never mention intermarriage as an issue. In fact, I tend to sympathize with Feldman's position here, but the more salient point is that if *Aseneth* is not the text Goodman (and Feldman) takes it to be, his argument about the correlations between conversion and marriage are much weakened.

45. Lewis, *Select Narratives,* 1.

46. From the colophon, Lewis, *Select Narratives,* 206.

47. It may be of some significance that among the tales collected here, one is the biblical Susannah, but otherwise, the rest are stories of nonbiblical women. Of even further interest may be the fact that the manuscript concludes with acknowledged excerpts from Ephrem's *Hymns on Paradise.* The actual hymn is not identified but it is, in fact, Hymn 6: 6.8, 6.12, 6.18, and 6.23.

48. Excepting the putative lost beginning of the Travels of Egeria; see chapter 8.

49. *Demonstrations* 21:957:3–5. For Aphrahat, Aseneth was the first of several types of the church as Bride of Christ. See Murray, *Symbols,* 136.

50. Hymns on Virginity 21.9, in Kathleen McVey, ed. and trans., *Ephrem the Syrian, Hymns,* The Classics of Western Spirituality (Mahwah, NJ: Paulist Press, 1989), 353.

51. The earliest extant text is a third-century C.E. Greek papyrus. On this question, see Marcella Franzmann, *"The Odes of Solomon": An Analysis of the Poetical Structure and Form,* Novum Testamentum et Orbis Antiquus 20, Universitätsverlag Freiburg Schweiz (Göttingen: Vandenhoeck and Ruprecht, 1991), 3.

52. Charlesworth (*OTP* 2:726–27) dates them about 100 C.E.; Sparks (*AOT,* 686) sets slightly later parameters (100–200 C.E.). According to Franzmann, *Odes of Solomon,* 2, Drijvers argues for a late third-century C.E. date.

53. However, true caution might prompt one to say only that Ode 11 must be no later than the third-century papyrus.

54. Interestingly, though, Chesnutt confines his discussion of these similarities to a single sentence and footnote, despite the fact that his dissertation director had previously published an edition of the Syriac Odes (James H. Charlesworth, *The Odes of Solomon* [Oxford: Oxford University Press, 1973; reprint, Text and Translations, Pseudepigrapha Series 7, Missoula, MT: Scholars Press, 1978]). Writing about the possible connections between *Aseneth* and *hekhalot* traditions, Chesnutt says, "Similar imagery is to be found in the Odes of Solomon" (*From Death to Life,* 211), and lists (in n. 78) Odes 1.1–4, 5.12, 9.8, 9.11, 11.11, 15.2, 17.1, 17.4, 20.7–8, 21.3, and 28.7. In his discussion of "new creation imagery" in *Aseneth,* he pays no attention at all to the language of Ode 11, instead searching for analogies in rabbinic traditions, citing Philonenko, *Joseph et Aséneth,* 173, on the same point.

55. This one ode is extant in Greek: M. Testuz, *Papyrus Bodmer,* 10–12, 47–69; text and English translation also in Franzmann, *Odes of Solomon,* 86–89, Syriac and English translation, 83–86. I have here generally followed the translation in Franzmann, with some minor modifications to clarify the consonance with *Aseneth,* as also indicated by the reproduction of the Greek.

56. Chesnutt, *From Death to Life,* gives this amazingly short shrift, confining it, as noted above, to a footnote.

57. The phrase "Most High" is pervasive in the *Odes* as in *Aseneth.*

58. Translation of the Syriac from Franzmann, *Odes of Solomon;* divergences from Charlesworth, *Odes,* are given in the notes.

59. Charlesworth, *Odes*: "your."

60. Charlesworth, *Odes*: "how your face is."

61. Charlesworth, *Odes*: "utter praises."

62. Charlesworth, *Odes*: "filth." He notes that this term is otherwise unknown in Syriac. Franzmann discusses the difficulty of this reading (*Odes of Solomon,* 109). For her own argument that the text should be amended to "harlotry," see M. Franzmann, "'Wipe the Harlotry from Your Faces': A Brief Note on Ode of Solomon 13.3," *ZNW* 77 (1986): 282–83. Given the imagery in *Aseneth* 18, it might be interesting to speculate that what is wiped off in both *Aseneth* and the ode is idolatry, an association both of illicit sexuality and of the huntress, if what is meant by this is an allusion to a goddess like Artemis/Diana.

63. Translation here is from Charlesworth, *Odes;* Franzmann's (*Odes of Solomon*) translation differs little.

64. I have altered Burchard's translation in these two lines but otherwise followed it here.

65. Burchard, "Joseph and Aseneth," notes parallels, inter alia, to Wis Sol 3.8; Ps 10.16 (LXX 9.37), 146.10; Rev 11.15.

66. Charlesworth, *Odes*: "although."

67. Charlesworth, *Odes:* "Son of Man." For Franzmann's critique, see *Odes of Solomon,* 249, note to 3b.

68. Charlesworth, *Odes:* "named the Shining One."

69. Neither ἀνάπαυσις nor ἀναπαύω occur in the shorter reconstruction.

70. Translation from Franzmann, *Odes of Solomon.*

71. *OTP* 2:731.

72. Chesnutt does, briefly, but dismisses any meaningful connection.

73. For discussion, see Elliott, *Apocryphal New Testament,* 439–42, who locates the composition in Edessa; see also Klijn, *Acts of Thomas,* 13–14, and Drijvers, in *NTA* II 323.

74. In fact, were it not so fraught with methodological difficulties, a subtle clue to the Christian composition might be found in *Aseneth*'s extensive use of imagery drawn from the Song of Songs. In the prologue to his own allegorical commentary on the Song of Songs, Origen claimed that Jewish teachers restricted access to the Song of Songs to persons of considerable maturity, although he doesn't specify the age. (Jerome apparently thought that meant thirty; Gregory of Nazianzus thought it meant twenty-five; for references, see Halperin, *Faces of the Chariot,* 26, n. 17). Yet, obviously, Origen himself is testimony to early Christian allegorical exegesis of the text, whereas the evidence for relatively early Jewish allegorical interpretation of Song of Songs is more problematic (see Jay Treat, "Lost Keys: Text and Interpretation in Old Greek Song of Songs and Its Earliest Manuscript Witnesses" (Ph.D. dissertation, University of Pennsylvania, 1996). Even in the absence of allegorical imagery, it may be that few relatively early Jewish compositions would intentionally and/or explicitly draw on Song of Songs imagery, lessening the probability that *Aseneth* is Jewish and strengthening the odds of Christian composition. However, the date would become a factor here—if Origen was correct, the earlier the date of composition, the less likely that a Jewish author would draw on Song of Songs. But the arguments are really more complex: Origen does not say that Jews don't read Song of Songs, he only says that Jewish teachers restrict access to it, and certainly enough people would have had such access to make this argument of limited utility. Nevertheless, it is interesting that the longer reconstruction, which has other affinities with Christian themes, is much more explicit in its use of Song of Songs.

75. See chapter 6.

76. *AThom* 8; *Aseneth* 8.8.

77. *AThom* 8. The Syriac and Greek are quite close here.

78. Compare this to Aseneth's response in 6.2 and 6.6, where, on first seeing Joseph, she realizes that he is Son of God, or her response to the departure of the angelic double, whom she now knows to have been "God."

79. *AThom* 16.

80. *AThom* 13.

81. Greek σκεπάζω, "to cover" or "to shelter." At *Aseneth* 15.6/**15.7,** the same verb is used with the connotation of shelter or protection (Aseneth will shelter many peoples under her wings as City of Refuge), but in the shorter text at 18.6, it is used as in *Thomas:* Aseneth "covers" her head with a veil (θέριστρον). In the longer text at **18.6,** the verb is κατεκάλυψε.

82. *AThom* 14, translation from Elliott, *Apocryphal New Testament.*

83. See chapter 7.

84. *AThom* 119–21.

85. *AThom* 120.

86. *AThom* 108–13; for recent commentary, see Paul-Hubert Poirer, *L'hymne de la perle des "Actes de Thomas": Introduction, texte-traduction, commentaire,* (Louvain-la-Neuve: [Centre d'histoire des religions], 1981), cited in Klijn, in *NTA* II 330.

87. Discussion and some interesting references from Klijn, in *NTA* II 332.

88. See Elliott, *Apocryphal New Testament,* 441, for a brief summary of this issue.

89. *AThom* 112.

90. Hymn 47.

91. See chapter 6.

92. Eve's actions are the verbal form of *Metanoia;* Adam's are ἐπιστρέφω. Andrew/Adam "flees for refuge to God" (προσφυγὼν τῷ θεῷ). This language is particularly familiar from *Aseneth.* There, the verb is usually καταφεύγω (the shorter reconstruction at 12.7, 13.1, and 15.7; the longer reconstruction at **11.11, 12.3,** and **13.2**). προσφεύγω occurs in the longer reconstruction at **12.6** but is absent from the shorter text.

93. *AAndrew* 37(5), trans. Elliot, *Apocryphal New Testament;* virtually identical to that of Dennis Ronald MacDonald, *The Passion of Andrew, the Acts of Andrew, and the Acts of Andrew and Matthias in the City of the Cannibals,* Texts and Translations 33, Christian Apocrypha Series 1 (Atlanta: Scholars Press, 1990).

94. 39(7). One might also pursue some of the similarities between Andrew's speech to Maximilla in 38(6), where he repeatedly addresses her as male (or perhaps as the androgynous human of Gen 1; the Greek is ἄνθρωπος, which Elliot translates as "man" but MacDonald translates as "human"). This section as well as 40(8) employs metaphors of sight and seeing that call to mind the angel's final words to Aseneth after he has shown her the mystery of the bees, "[H]ave you seen this?" (ἑώρακας τὸ ῥῆμα τοῦτο), and she replies "[Y]es, I have seen all this."

95. It might also be interesting to consider the possibility of intertextual relations between *Aseneth* and the story of the Prodigal Son.

96. It may even be plausible to read *Aseneth* as a critique of the models of conversion offered in these circles. See chapter 7.

97. Brock, *Luminous Eye,* 21.

98. Brock, *Luminous Eye,* 20.

99. Both the *Ps. Clementines* and the *Didascalia* appear to be works written in Greek that nevertheless come from a Syriac milieu (Murray, *Symbols,* 26). The corpus of Ephrem Graecus probably also counts here, and elsewhere Murray makes an aside that presumes both Syriac- and Greek-speaking Syrian Christians.

100. "Whatever is the truth about Christian origins elsewhere in the Syriac-speaking area, the Christianity of Aphrahat and Ephrem is best accountable for as a breakaway movement among the Jewish community in Adiabene" (Murray, *Symbols,* 8). Murray cites approvingly, on this model of Adiabene Judaism as the root of Aphrahat's Christianity, an early study by Jacob Neusner, *Aphrahat and Judaism: The Christian–Jewish Argument in Fourth-Century Iran* (Leiden: E. J. Brill, 1971), 144–49. For Murray this also explains Syriac fathers' knowledge of Jewish traditions that by the fourth century he believes they could not have received directly. Since, however, he takes Ephrem himself as evidence that Christians were "in danger of" converting "back" to Judaism (19), it would not be difficult to argue that the traffic in traditions could have continued to flow both ways in this area.

101. *Ant.* 20.17–53, 92–96.

102. *Ant.* 20.49.

103. Interestingly, this argument has been made, in a different way, by Aptowitzer ("Asenath") who saw a connection between Aseneth and the conversion of Helena, although he thought the composition considerably closer to the historical Helena.

104. Brock, *Luminous Eye,* 117.

105. The stanza concludes with an interesting line that certainly could be taken to describe our Aseneth: "Blessed is He who made chaste the infatuated one."

106. 3.4–5, cited in Brock, *Luminous Eye,* 119.

107. *Kallṭâ mṣabbattâ;* Murray, *Symbols,* 132.

108. Philonenko, *Joseph et Asèneth,* 4:2; Burchard, "Joseph and Aseneth," 4:1.

109. According to *Gen R.* 20:12, R. Meir had a Torah manuscript that read Gen 3.21 this way: "In R. Meir's Torah it was found written, 'Garments of light'; this refers to Adam's garments, which were like a torch [shedding radiance], broad at the bottom and narrow at the top" (trans. Freedman). That is, it read עור (skin) instead of אור (light).

110. Brock, *Luminous Eye,* 87–88, citing *Nativity* 1:43.

111. Brock, *Luminous Eye,* 94–95.

112. At 14.15 the same robe is again called καινή, as well as ἐπίσημον (distinctive, fine, perhaps elegant) and λαμπρά (brilliant, radiant, perhaps luminous). Interestingly, in the parable of the Prodigal Son (Luke 15.11–24), the returning son is also dressed in a πρώτη στολή by his rejoicing father (Luke 15.22).

113. Manuscripts B and H characterize the στολή as γάμου, ἀρχαία, and πρώτη, while ironically, several manuscripts of the "longer" text have only some of this language. The phrase τὴν ἀρχαίαν, τὴν πρώτην may be somewhat redundant, since ἀρχαία can easily connote "original" or "primordial," as well as "ancient."

114. See chapters 2.

115. Virginity 5.9, from Brock, *Luminous Eye,* 123.

116. Brock, *Luminous Eye,* 127.

117. 6.42–47, in Brock, *Luminous Eye,* 129.

118. Discussed extensively by Murray, *Symbols,* 312–20; see also ibid., chap. 4, "The Church, Bride and Mother."

119. See Murray, *Symbols,* 312–20, where he also considers that the prominence of this image may account for the diminished metaphor of the Church as Mother in Syrian Christianity.

120. *EC Arm.* 19, 15 (CSCO 137, Arm. I, p. 277.11–15), cited and translated in Murray, *Symbols.* There are several difficulties with this passage, discussed in ibid., 318–19.

121. However, see chapter 6 for the possible depiction of Sol Imperator with olives.

122. See esp. Murray, *Symbols,* 115–29, for detailed discussion.

123. 7.13–14.

124. Brock, *Luminous Eye,* 58–59.

125. E.g., Aphrahat, *Demonstration* 23; see also Murray, *Symbols,* 125, where he cites a passage from Ephrem (*EC* 21.11) where he explicitly says, "The olive is the symbol of Christ, for from him sprang milk, water and oil"; see also Murray, *Symbols,* 320–23. From Murray's citation (323) of Cyril of Alexandria, it is obvious that the association of Christ with the olive could be derived from Romans 9–11.

126. However, to play the devil's advocate, nothing in *Aseneth* explicitly identifies the trees in the garden with olives, which we might expect if the symbolism were more explicit, since in Syriac writers, Christ is identified with the Tree of Life in the garden and with olives. In 2 Enoch [B], the garden is said to contain an olive tree alongside the Tree of Life. For other Christian sources that associate the tree of life with olives, see Ginsberg, *Legends,* 5:119 (his list includes 5 Ezra; the *Recognitions*; Hippolytus; and Origen, *Against Celsus*). Ginsberg notes that rabbinic literature does not specifically identify the Tree of Life or know the tradition of the life-giving oil found in the *Life of Adam and Eve,* inter alia. I have (thus far) not located any traditions associating Joseph and olives, in Ginsberg or elsewhere.

127. Brock, *Luminous Eye,* 148–54.

128. *Commentary on Genesis,* 2:23, trans. Brock, *Luminous Eye.*

129. Brock, *Luminous Eye,* 154.

130. Brock, *Luminous Eye,* 154.

131. Brock, *Luminous Eye,* 148, points out that this idea is already present in fourth-century Greek writers (I presume here he means Christian) and will become particularly important in (Ps.) Dionysius the Areopagite.

132. *CG* 2:20.

133. See Murray, *Symbols,* 297–98.

134. See chapter 2.

135. Murray, *Symbols,* 298. Philonenko's *Joseph et Aséneth* was published in 1968, Murray's *Symbols* in 1975.

136. Murray, *Symbols,* 298, from the Syriac edition of Brooks, *Zacharias Rhetor,* 38.16.

137. Murray, *Symbols,* 298.

138. Eusebius, for instance, although he knew that Philo was "Hebrew by race" (*H.E.* 2.4.2), read Philo's description of the Therapeutics as an admiring portrait of early Christian ascetics and supposed that the works by ancient authors read by the Therapeutics were probably gospels and other early Christian writings (*H.E.* 2.17.12). His lavish praise of Philo suggests that for Eusebius, Philo was a virtual Christian. Particularly striking is Eusebius's conviction that the presence of women as aged virgins among the Therapeutics constitutes definitive proof that they were Christians (*H.E.* 2.17.19).

139. *Nativity* 6.13–14, in Brock, *Luminous Eye,* 103.

140. *Faith* 10.10, in Brock, *Luminous Eye,* 104.

141. See Murray, *Symbols,* 292.

142. Philonenko thinks that his second and third long recensions (manuscripts H and A, respectively) were clearly Christian (*Joseph et Aséneth,* 101), although he isn't so sure about family b, represented best by manuscript F. Interestingly, Sparks remains agnostic on the subject, seeing the statement that Aseneth was in all ways like the daughters of the Hebrews as indicative of Jewish interests (although see my discussion at the beginning of this chapter), whereas he considers the formula of bread, drink, and ointment as well as the scene with the angel and the honeycomb to be strongly suggestive of Christian interest (in *AOT* 469). Burchard, of course, considers the longer reconstruction to be Jewish, and I don't think he ever considers that the shorter could be anything but Jewish either; he may well concede the Christian revision of A (Batiffol's text).

143. Van der Horst, "Silent Prayer," 12–16. Of the texts he considers, particularly interesting is *The Life of Adam and Eve,* where Adam's injunction to Eve that they pray silently to God appears connected to the defilement of their lips through the eating of the forbidden fruit. Aseneth's lips are similarly defiled through her worship of idols, from her prayers to her consumption of idolatrous food and drink (*Aseneth* 8), and such an interpretation could be offered here, although the fact that Aseneth follows her silent prayers with vocalized prayer weakens this.

144. Ps. Philo 50:5, trans. from *OTP* 2:364; see also van der Horst, "Silent Prayer," 13–14.

145. Van der Horst, "Silent Prayer," 17–18.

146. Van der Horst, "Silent Prayer," 19–20.

147. Van der Horst, "Silent Prayer," 20, citing both Origen, *On Prayer* and the *Apostolic Constitutions* 7:33.2.

148. That this was clearly not the stance of the author of 1 Cor 11 seems clear.

149. Hall, "Installation of the Archangel Michael. For details, see chapter 5.

150. In his refutation of Batiffol, Aptowitzer, "Asenath," had an interesting argument against Christian authorship that rested on the association with Dinah. If Aseneth was the daughter of Dinah, a marriage between Aseneth and Joseph was an uncle–niece marriage (bride marries her mother's brother), which Christians forbade, and therefore Christians could not have written the story. But since *Aseneth* does not in fact presume that Aseneth is Dinah's daughter, this line of reasoning is irrelevant.

151. As A. Thomas Kraabel has pointed out, *Ioudaios* can, on occasion, carry a geographic meaning of Judean ("The Roman Diaspora: Six Questionable Assumptions," *JJS* 33, no. 1/2 [1982]: 445–64) and, as I have argued, may sometimes further connote pagan adherence to

Judaism (Ross S. Kraemer, "On the Meaning of the Term 'Jew' in Greco-Roman Inscriptions," *HTR* 82, no. 1 [1989]: 35–53).

152. *Letter of Aristeas* 179.3 and *T. Naph.* 1.10.

153. Josephus calls Poppaea, wife of Nero, θεοσεβὴς (*AJ* 20.195); Philo does not seem to use this language to designate persons, although he does use τὸ θεοσεβὲς to designate piety (*On the Change of Names* 197). It also occurs in John 9.31: "We know that God does not hear sinners, but does hear one who reveres God [τις θεοσεβὴς] and does the will of God" (translation mine; cf. the NRSV "[God] does listen to one who worships him and obeys his will"). Reynolds and Tannenbaum claim that "of θεοσεβεῖς as a class literary and religious texts after the Septuagint say nothing" (*Jews and Godfearers,* 53).

154. Most significant of which is an inscription found at Aphrodisias in the 1970s, published with extensive commentary by Reynolds and Tannenbaum in *Jews and Godfearers.* Other inscriptions include *CIJ* 202, 228 (both from Rome), 500 (original provenance unknown), 619a (from Venosa); *IG* 12.1.593, Lifshitz, *Donateurs* 17, 18, 28, 30, and *CIJ* 748 (all from various places in Asia Minor); *CIRB* 71 (from Panticapaeum on the Black Sea). For further discussion and bibliography, see Reynolds and Tannenbaum, *Jews and Godfearers,* 48–67.

155. For recent discussion of Greco-Roman pagan interest in Judaism, see John G. Gager, *The Origins of Anti-Semitism: Attitudes toward Judaism in Pagan and Christian Antiquity* (New York: Oxford University Press, 1983); Feldman, *Jew and Gentile;* Goodman, *Mission and Conversion;* McKnight, *A Light to the Nations.*

156. There is an extensive literature on the question. Transcriptions of the Aphrodisias inscription circulated informally among scholars in advance of its actual publication by Reynolds and Tannenbaum, so that a few studies published prior to 1987 take that discovery into acount, but most of the following were unaware of this evidence: H. Bellen, "Συναγωγὴ τῶν Ἰουδαίων καὶ Θεοσεβῶν. Die Aussage einer bosporanischen Freilassungsinschrift (CIRB 71) zum Problem der 'Gottesfürchtigen,'" *JAC* 8/9 (1965–66): 171–76; J. Bernays, "Die Gottesfürchtigen bei Juvenal," in *Commentationes philologae in honorem Theodori Mommseni* (Berlin: Weidmann, 1877), 563–69, reprinted in *Gesammelte Abhandlungen von Jacob Bernays,* vol. 2, ed. H. K. Usener (Berlin: Hertz, 1885; reprint, Hildesheim: Georg Olms, 1971), 71–80; Feldman, "Jewish Sympathisers"; Feldman, "Omnipresence of the God-fearers"; Finn, "The Godfearers Reconsidered"; Kraabel, "Disappearance of the 'God-fearers'"; Baruch Lifshitz, "Du nouveau sur les 'sympathisants,'" *JSJ* 1 (1970): 77–84; R. S. MacLennan and A. T. Kraabel, "The God-fearers: A Literary and Theological Invention," *BAR* 12, no. 5 (Sept./Oct. 1986): 17–26, 46–53; Seigert, "Gottesfürchtige und Sympathisanten"; Smallwood, "Alleged Jewish Tendencies." The following studies for the most part take the evidence from Aphrodisias into account: Cohen, "Crossing the Boundary," Feldman, "Proselytes and Sympathizers"; Goodman, "Review"; Jerome Murphy-O'Connor, "Lots of God-fearers? Theosebeis in the Aphrodisias Inscription," *Revue Biblique* 99 (1992): 418–24; Overman, "Godfearers"; R. Tannenbaum, "Jews and God-fearers in the Holy City of Aphrodite," *BAR* 12, no. 5 (1986): 55–57; Trebilco, "'God-worshippers' in Asia Minor," chap. 7 of *Jewish Communities in Asia Minor,* Society for New Testament Studies Monograph Series 69 (Cambridge: Cambridge University Press, 1991), 147–66; van der Horst, "Jews and Christians in Aphrodisias"; Williams, θεοσεβὴς γάρ ἦν: The Jewish Tendencies of Poppaea Sabina," *JTS* 39 (1988): 97–111.

157. That this is patently false for literary usages is clear. Herodotus uses the term to designate the piety of the Egyptians (2.37, 1.86). Trebilco (*Jewish Communities in Asia Minor,* 146–47, with notes on 246–47) catalogues occurrences of θεοσεβὴς in classical Greek authors and in a number of other inscriptions. In addition to those instances, Strabo (*Geography* 7.3.3) reports that according to Poseidonius, the Mysians are called θεοσεβεῖς on account of their religiously movitated vegetarianism. (The Mysians were associated with Thrace, and, interestingly,

Strabo continues, some Thracian men were known for their abstinence from sexual relations with women.) Θεοσεβής further occurs in the Greek magical papyri (*PGM* 4:685), where the petitioner describes (him)self as εὐσεβής καὶ θεοσεβής (literally, εὐσεβεῖ καὶ θεοσεβεῖ: "you send to me, who am pious and God-revering, health and soundness of body").

Additionally, θεοσεβής and closely related forms are prevalent in numerous Christian authors and sources, as a search of the TLG CD-ROM demonstrates, with some of particular interest for *Aseneth*. The phrase ἀνὴρ θεοσεβέστατος (most God-revering man) occurs in the *Acts of Andrew* (the *Passion of Andrew* 2, in MacDonald's edition, 326), where it is a description of Andrew himself; at 60.7, Andrew is again described as ἀνηρ θεοσεβής. Θεοσεβής occurs as a term for Thecla in the *Acts of (Paul and) Thecla* 38; in the *Acts of John* 63 to refer to Andronicus, "who formerly was not the god-fearing [θεοσεβής] man he is now"; and in the *Acts of John* 76 to refer to the converted Callimachus. It also appears in Eusebius's quotation from Melito's book to Antoninus Verus (Marcus Aurelius): "It has never before happened . . . that the race of the religious [τὸ τῶν θεοσεβῶν γένος] should be persecuted" (*H.E.* 4.26.5, trans. K. Lake in the *LCL*). Here, although Melito obviously intends a reference to the persecution of Christians, the term itself may be construed broadly. However we classify the Emperor Julian, he uses this language in a letter to Atarbius (Letter 37) to designate pious pagans with no Jewish associations whatsoever and as a designation for Alexander (Letter 111.21) and Diogenes (*Against Heraclius the Cynic* 8.26). The abbreviation θεοσεβ also describes a bishop named Gerontius in a Christian dedicatory inscription from the Syrian town of Fîq in the Golan Heights (Robert C. Gregg and Dan Urman, *Jews, Pagans, and Christians in the Golan Heights: Greek and Other Inscriptions of the Roman and Byzantine Eras,* University of South Florida Studies in the History of Judaism 140 [Atlanta: Scholars Press, 1996], no. 22 [pp. 31–32]).

158. See nn. 152, 155.

159. Although, interestingly, the prevalence of θεοσεβής in those Christian sources where it appears to apply to Christians, particularly those works known or thought to date from the second, third, and fourth centuries (such as Apocryphal Acts, Origen, and Melito apud Eusebius) might also be considered evidence in support of self-conscious Christian authorship of *Aseneth.*

160. Schürer, *History of the Jews* 3:493–99, including references to ancient sources that identify Aquila and Theodotion as proselytes. The author of this particular section, Martin Goodman, accepts the traditional identification for both, particularly on the basis of the early testimony of Irenaeus (in Eusebius).

161. I had hoped to include a second appendix to this study, examining the possibility that *Aseneth* could be of Samaritan composition. Ultimately, though, space considerations mandated that I reserve such a study for publication elsewhere. Here I can only briefly summarize the factors that make such a possibility worth examination.

The story of Joseph's marriage to Aseneth would have been of particular interest to ancient Samaritans, who traced their descent to Joseph and his sons, Manasseh and Ephraim, and who might have been particularly concerned to legitimate the marriage and elaborate on its circumstances. Much of the distinctive language of *Aseneth* (including use of Ἑβραῖος but not Ἰουδαῖος to designate Joseph and his community, the designation of Joseph as ὁ δυνατός τοῦ θεοῦ and other examples) as well as the interest in angelology would be consistent with a Samaritan context.

Particularly intriguing is the existence of an eighteenth-century Samaritan commentary on Genesis (*The Joseph Cycle [Genesis 37–45] in the Samaritan-Arabic commentary of Meshalma ibn Murjan,* ed. and trans. Gladys Levine Rosen [Ph.D. dissertation, Columbia University, 1951]). This work not only is generally consonant with the Greek *Aseneth* stories but also explicitly rejects earlier Aseneth traditions that are themselves incompatible with the

Greek narratives: the identification of Potiphar and Potiphera and the claim that Aseneth was Dinah's daughter (on which, see the appendix). To the best of my knowledge, no other traditional source, whether Jewish, Christian, or Muslim, takes the stance of this text.

Further, though the composition of our Aseneth narratives in Greek might seem unusual for a Samaritan composition, there is ample epigraphic evidence for Samaritan use of Greek in the later Roman empire (see, e.g., P. Bruneau, "Les Israelites de Delos et la juiverie delienne," *BCH* 106 [1982]: 465–504; A. T. Kraabel, "New Evidence on the Samaritan Diaspora Has Been Found on Delos," *BA* 47 [March 1984]: 44–46, reprinted in Andrew Overman and R. S. MacLennan, eds., *Diaspora Judaism: Essays in Honor of and in Dialogue with A. Thomas Kraabel,* South Florida Studies in Judaism [Atlanta: Scholars Press, 1992], 331–34; Reinhard Pummer, "Inscriptions," in Alan D. Crown, ed., *The Samaritans* [Tübingen: J. C. B. Mohr (Paul Siebeck), 1989], 190–94).

Finally, the size of the Samaritan population in late antiquity may have been approximately a quarter the size of the Jewish population. This suggests that we ought not to neglect consideration of Samaritans as possible authors of anonymous and pseudonymous literature that stands in a biblical trajectory. For discussion of the Samaritans in late antiquity, see A. Crown, "The Samaritans in the Byzantine Orbit," *Bulletin of the John Rylands University Library of Manchester* 69, no. 1 (1989): 96–138, and "Samaritan Religion in the Fourth Century," *Nederlands Theologisch Tijdschrift* 41, no. 1 (1986): 29–47.

CHAPTER TEN

The Provenance of *Aseneth* Reconsidered

Despite Burchard's recognition that the possibilitity of alternative provenance had never been properly explored, Philonenko's insistence that *Aseneth* was composed in Egypt has garnered general acceptance. Not surprisingly, the assumption that *Aseneth* was composed in Egypt is particularly susceptible to critique, linked as it is to the highly questionable assumptions that the text is both Jewish and relatively early. In this brief chapter, I will propose that while it is certainly possible that Egypt was the site where *Aseneth* was composed, it is no more likely than several other locations and is perhaps less likely than at least one, namely, Syria.

Egypt

The evidence for an Egyptian provenance for *Aseneth* is derived in part from the location of the story itself. Because it takes place in Egypt, some would reason, it is likely to have been written in Egypt, as though persons living in Egypt were the only ones interested in stories set in Egypt. Yet the Egyptian setting is dictated by the Joseph tradition itself, which, in the biblical narrative of Genesis, places Joseph in Egypt at the time of his marriage to Aseneth. By itself, this tradition constitutes no clue to the location and the identity of the author(s).

Philonenko's insistence that the text was composed in Egypt was partially related to his interlocking claims about its Jewish composition and its relatively early date, as I have explained previously. But his conclusion that the text was written in Egypt (or perhaps, more precisely, by an Egyptian Jew) depended on more. Underneath the structure of the story, he saw evidence of ancient Egyptian tales such as that of the Predestined Prince, while beneath the figure of Aseneth herself, Philonenko saw strong reminiscences of the Egyptian goddess Neith, whose name, in fact, Aseneth appears to bear. For Philonenko, such reminiscences were the result of authorial intention, constituting strong evidence for an Egyptian Jewish author. But Philonenko's analysis of the centrality of Neith, while interesting, is not compelling, particularly because the name of Neith is already an attribute of the biblical character and because many of the elements he saw as unique to Neith, such as the association with bees, are in fact much more widely attested.[1]

Philonenko and others have also adduced similarities between *Aseneth* and the writings of Philo of Alexandria as further support for their thesis. Because they assume *Aseneth* to be early, many scholars, including Philonenko, have limited their search for similar materials to authors and texts they thought earlier or contemporaneous, and thus they missed much of the fascinating material this study has sought to explore.[2] While the similarities between Philo and *Aseneth* are sometimes quite interesting, as in the case of his interpretation of the cities of refuge and his concern with solar imagery or with the number seven, they do no more than suggest either an author who knew Philo or similar writings or even just broad common cultural or intellectual traditions. Certainly we know that the writings of Philo were of great interest to subsequent Christian allegoricists, and Philo, like *Aseneth,* was ultimately transmitted and copied only by Christians.

The thesis of Egyptian provenance has been supported by a few other arguments, including the claim that concerns about proselytism and relations with Egyptians would have been of particular interest to Jews living in Greco-Roman Egypt. In general, this argument is advocated in tandem with the claim that such concerns were rendered moot by the aftermath of the uprisings of 115–17 C.E. and the second Jewish revolt under Bar Kokhba in 132–35 C.E.[3] and is closely linked with the assumption that the text is early.

Since I have demonstrated in chapter 8 that there is considerable evidence to date *Aseneth* a century or more after these events, any claim that the text was composed in Egypt needs to make sense for late Roman Egypt. The significant similarities between Aseneth's encounter with the angelic being and various ancient adjurative materials, including the Greek magical papyri and *Sepher ha-Razim* (the composite text whose components were discovered in the Cairo Genizah, although they are thought to have been authored in Palestine), might support a later Egyptian provenance. Yet such practices were widespread in antiquity, and the consonance with the Greek magical papyri may be attributed to the historical happenstance that papyrus is native to Egypt and survives only in climates similar to that of southern Egypt, making it unlikely that similar sources will be preserved in climatically different regions.

It is, of course, not impossible for the text to have been composed in late Roman Egypt by a Jew, a Christian, or someone else. That there were Greek-speaking Jews living in Egypt in the third and fourth centuries is adequately attested by papyri and by references in Christian writers.[4] Scholars from Victor Tcherikover to Roger Bagnall believe that Egyptian Jewry was largely decimated in the early second century and tend to characterize Jews living in Roman Egypt in subsequent centuries as relatively marginalized. While they may be correct in this assessment, this still does not rule out a Jewish author living in Egypt, but it may well make it considerably less likely. On the other hand, a Christian author in late Roman Egypt is possible, although by no means necessary. Despite the insistence of previous scholars that the text was composed in Egypt, there is surprisingly little evidence that it circulated in Egypt. No papyrus fragments of the text in any language have been identified, and the Coptic fragments discussed in chapter 9 cannot be taken as even indirect proof of the circulation of *Aseneth,* regardless of the date of those fragments. If, in fact, *Aseneth* was composed in Egypt, we might expect it to be reflected in Coptic or Ethiopic translations, but so far this is not the case.

Some scholars have suggested that an Egyptian origin for *Aseneth* is supported by the use of details from ordinary Egyptian life in the Roman period.[5] But as we have seen, virtually all of the "realia" in *Aseneth,* such as Aseneth's food, clothing, household possessions, or relations with parents and servants, can be accounted for either as a construct formulated out of exegetical concerns or as derivative of pervasive Greco-Roman social patterns. They are thus without value for the question of authorial location and geographic community.[6]

Asia Minor

Once the arguments for an Egyptian provenance are seen to be less than impeccable, other places of origins deserve consideration. In his initial publication of *Aseneth,* Batiffol proposed that the text was composed in Asia Minor. Part of his hypothesis rested on a convoluted connection between Aseneth's veiling and evidence for Christian disputes about women's headcoverings, particularly in the North African writer Tertullian, whose claims about veiling Batiffol traced to Tertullian's own associations with the New Prophecy (often known as Montanism), a charismatic prophetic movement that originated in a region in Asia Minor known as Phrygia.[7]

More interesting are Batiffol's attempts to locate *Aseneth* in Asia Minor on the basis of his belief that the unnamed angelic *archistratēgos* was in fact the archangel Michael, whose popularity is attested in ancient Asia Minor, particularly in Christian sources. Battifol adduces several interesting texts as evidence to support the association of Michael and Asia Minor, including "The Miracle of St. Michael in Chonos."[8] This text, which he dates no earlier than the seventh century but which he claimed seemed to be the remains of a much older story, from the Hieropolitan legends of Philip and Bartholomew,[9] tells the story of one Archippos of Hierapolis, a hermit who consecrated himself to safeguard a shrine (*euktērion*) of St. Michael. One day, a flood threatened the shrine. Archippos threw himself down on the ground and prayed to God and the archangel Michael to protect the shrine. For ten days, he neither ate nor drank nor rose up from the ground. He prayed to God: "Blessed be God, I will never leave the shrine, for I have faith that God, by the intermediary of the archistrategos Michael, will protect this corner of earth." On the tenth day, the archangel Michael appeared, told Archippos not to fear, and restrained the flood. In memory of this event, "all illness will be cured in that *euktērion,* and all who seek refuge [*katafygei*] in faith and fear, and invoke the Father and the Son and the Holy Spirit and Michael, his archistrategos, he who remembers the name of God and mine, . . . will be guarded [*episkiazousa*] in that place (by) my power and the grace of God."[10]

The similarities of this language with *Aseneth* are intriguing. In any case, this legend becomes associated with the basilica of St. Conon. Batiffol also adduces the *Life of Saint Cononis,* about a pagan living on a village outside Isaura whose parents planned to marry him to a young woman named Anne. On the day of the wedding, the archangel Michael appears in a white robe and reveals to Conon the mysteries of truth and the excellence of chastity. Mistaking the angel for a man, Conon asks Michael to baptize him, whereupon Michael takes him to a source of water and baptizes him in the name of the Father, the Son, and the Holy Spirit. He then gives him a precious stone, blesses him, and anoints him, after which the angel disappears. Conon then lives in a chaste marriage with his wife, near a shrine (*euktērion*), and becomes the apostle to Isaura. The similarities of this tale, too, to our *Aseneth* are not without some interest.

Since, however, Batiffol's thesis was integrally related to his initial claim that *Aseneth* was a late Christian composition, it was largely ignored once scholars classified the text as Jewish and early. Yet beyond the intriguing parallels of these tales with our *Aseneth,* there are some significant affinities between *Aseneth* and the cultural world of late antique Asia Minor that may make such a locale worth reconsidering, regardless of the religious affiliation of the writers.

Whether or not Joseph's angelic double should be identified with the archangel Michael, there is no question that the texts, both longer and shorter, display angelic interests.[11] A significant number of inscriptions, primarily from ancient Asia Minor, point to extensive pagan interest in angels,[12] an interest shared with Jews and Christians alike. Among the many dedications such as those "to Zeus the Highest and to the Divine Angel" or to "Zeus the Highest and the Divine Heavenly Angel"[13] is an altar dedicated to "The Highest God and [to] Holy Refuge,"[14] this last phrase startlingly reminiscent of *Aseneth,* although, as we have seen and as Mitchell points out, the idea of God as refuge occurs in numerous places in Jewish scripture, particularly in the Psalms.[15]

Mitchell maintains that these dedications, and many others like them, point to a basic theological idea of a supreme being and his heavenly messenger that constituted the pervasive religious outlook of the entire later Roman empire, held in common, for the most part, by pagans, Jews, and Christians alike.[16] Furthermore, in many such circles, the figure of Helios, central to our *Aseneth* texts, is particularly prominent. Mitchell cites, for instance, a Christian epitaph from Phrygia with a bust of Helios and the so-called Eumenian formula (warning would-be grave violators that they would be accountable "before God").[17]

Several other factors may support the feasibility of Asia Minor as the provenance of *Aseneth.* On the one hand, thriving communities of Greek-speaking Jews are documented for the cities, towns, and villages of the region from the first century on, if not earlier, while Paul's letters and other early Christian writings demonstrate the existence of Christian churches from the mid–first century on. Further, a considerable proportion of the so-called *theosebēs* inscriptions come from Aphrodisias, Sardis, and other cities in Asia Minor.

Given the text's focus on a female protagonist, it is also noteworthy that epigraphic evidence from Asia Minor documents a long and complex tradition of women involved in the public life of pagan, Jewish, and Christian communities alike.[18] Christian sources in particular demonstrate the activity of women prophets and charismatic religious leaders.[19] Particularly provocative is an inscription mentioned by Mitchell of a Christian prophet named Nanas, whom he surmises to be Montanist, "who claimed to have gazed in awe on the face of the Lord," prayed and praised God with hymns night and day, and is said to become an inspired intermediary with the title *episkopē angelikos.*[20]

Also noteworthy is the fact that one of *Aseneth*'s most common epithets for God, "the Most High,"[21] is particularly frequent in inscriptions from Asia Minor. Given the popularity of the Greek term *hypsistos* as the standard (Septuagint/Old Greek) translation for the Hebrew *('el)'elyon,* its usage in *Aseneth* may not be all that surprising. But it also occurs not only in inscriptions known to be Jewish (or Christian) but in other inscriptions as well. Some of these appear to originate among devotees of a deity called Theos Hypsistos, whose ties to Judaism and Jewish practices remain the subject of scholarly debate.[22]

Finally, written sources and archeological finds suggest that a particularly rich mix of religious beliefs and practices flourished in Roman-period Asia Minor, at least through the fourth century and probably to the end of late antiquity. Jewish and Gentile contributors to the same charitable enterprise,[23] cemeteries of Jews, Christians, and pagans alike, and a range of other evidence points to porous communal boundaries in many areas. Mitchell's characterization of the religious climate there is particularly relevant:

> Outwardly, at least, there was much in common between the paganism of late Roman Asia Minor and contemporary Judaism and Christianity. God was an awesome, remote and abstract figure to be reached through the agency of divine intermediaries, such as angels, or human ones, such as prophets. The language which men chose to describe the supreme god of both pagans and Christians was sometimes indistinguishable, and had close affinities with language that was taken over and elaborated in the philosophy of the age. Fourth-century Christian doctrine and thought is shot through with philosophical, sometimes specifically Neo-platonic ideas. . . .
>
> In Phrygia, pagan, Christian and Jew, living together in the same communities, in harmony more often than in conflict, found ways and devices to accommodate one another's beliefs.[24]

In other words, Roman Asia Minor produced precisely the kind of complex religious and cultural climate in which a multivalent text like *Aseneth* might have been both composed and well received.

Syria

Although the earliest certain testimony to the existence of *Aseneth,* as well as the earliest known manuscripts, comes from eastern Syria, little consideration has been given to the region as the provenance of any original composition. Several factors are responsible for this, I suspect. First, the consensus (with which, for once, I concur) that *Aseneth* was composed in Greek may have obscured at least eastern Syria as a possibility on the assumption that the vast majority of the inhabitants of the eastern portion of the region spoke and wrote primarily in Semitic languages, including Aramaic and Syriac. Greek-speaking Jews and Christians are, of course, well attested for the western portions of Syria through late antiquity, including Antioch, Sidon, Tyre, and so forth.[25] Second, most scholars tend to associate at least eastern Syria with Christian communities, rather than with Jews, so that the assumption that *Aseneth* was composed by a Jew in Greek tended to further rule out Syrian provenance as a reasonable probability.

Yet, again, none of these arguments is compelling. The anonymous testimony transmitted with the Syriac *Aseneth* claims that a Greek form of the story could be found in a church library in eastern Syria (in Resaina) in the fifth century, and we know that some Syrian Christians did read and compose Greek. Whether Jewish communities in places such as Edessa or Nisibis would have utilized Greek to any degree is difficult to know, but we do have evidence for Greek-speaking Jews in various parts of eastern Syria and adjacent regions[26] and, of course, in the form of Greek inscriptions from the synagogue at Dura Europos on the Euphrates River in the third century C.E.

The arguments in support of Syrian provenance, particularly eastern Syria, whether Edessa, Nisibis, or elsewhere, should by now be obvious, beginning with the manuscript evidence and the many similarities between *Aseneth* and the themes and imagery of Syrian Christian sources from the third and fourth centuries C.E., explored particularly in chapter 9. Obviously, then, a Syrian locale for the composition of *Aseneth* seems somewhat more likely if the text was initially composed by a Christian, but it seems not at all impossible that a Jewish author in the same region could also have been responsible.

The Land of Israel

To the best of my knowledge, only Aptowitzer argued that *Aseneth* was composed in Palestine, and he did so based on his belief that it was composed in Hebrew. While his logic is thus irrelevant, even the land of Israel itself is not an impossible choice for authorship of the text, particularly when we recall that it is precisely the synagogues of Hammath Tiberias, Beth Alpha, Na'aran, and now Sepphoris that contain late antique Jewish Helios mosaics and numerous Greek inscriptions.[27] The probable composition of the components of *Sepher ha-Razim* in the land of Israel could also be adduced in support of such provenance.

Conclusion

In truth, *Aseneth* could have been composed virtually anywhere in the Greek-speaking world in the late Roman period, from Egypt to the land of Israel, to Syria, to Asia Minor, and perhaps even, although I have not argued this specifically here, to Rome itself. The earliest references to the text and the oldest manuscripts come from eastern Syria, and *Aseneth* displays many affinities with Syrian Christian traditions. The imagery of Helios is consonant with that of mosaics found in Jewish synagogues in the land of Israel, but Helios is also prominent in the inscriptions of Asia Minor, where angelic motifs flourish among Jews, Christians, and pagans alike. The text's unusual fondness for the self-designation *theosebēs* would clearly have made it at home in Asia Minor in the third century in particular, though *theosebēs* inscriptions have been found elsewhere.[28] The strong similarities with adjurative traditions might point to Egypt, the origin of the many papyri with adjurative formulas and instructions, although given the widespread use of such materials in antiquity, other locales could also account for such interest.

Finally, then, although once again certainty would be more satisfying, the fact remains that we do not know where any version of *Aseneth* was composed. From my perspective, the probability of provenance is linked to the religious self-understanding of the author, itself no longer accessible. If the text was initially written by a Christian, I would probably personally favor Syria, followed perhaps by Asia Minor, while if the initial composer was a non-Christian Jew, I might vote for somewhere in the land of Israel itself. Since, unfortunately, nothing in the text itself argues definitively for any of these, provenance is of no help in arguments for authorial identification.

In the absence of better evidence, then, on the question of provenance as well as on the question of authorial self-understanding, agnosticism, frustrating though it may be, remains the most reasonable stance.

NOTES

1. Sänger, "Bekehrung und Exodus," takes Philonenko to task on the significance of Neith.

2. But, here again, it is important to acknowledge Kee's recognition of the possible significance of *hekhalot* traditions ("Socio-Cultural Setting of 'Joseph and Asenath'" and "Socio-Religious Setting and Aims of 'Joseph and Asenath'"), as well as Chesnutt's (*From Death to Life*) consideration and rejection of possible connections between *Aseneth* and a range of late antique religious materials, partly due to his assumptions about date but also to his assumptions about the Jewish identity of the author(s), both discussed in chapter 5.

3. See also chapter 8.

4. Papryi collected in *CPJ* 3. For discussion of the history of Jews in late Roman Egypt, see *CPJ* 1:94–111 (which is not without its methodological problems); see also E. Mary Small-wood, *The Jews under Roman Rule, from Pompey to Diocletan: A Study in Political Relations* (Leiden: E. J. Brill, 1976; reprint, 1981), 516–19. Bagnall, *Egypt in Late Antiquity,* 275–78, gives a brief survey of the evidence for Jews in Egypt after 115–17 C.E., where he agrees with the general portrait of a decimated community and further disagrees with the identification as Jews of persons in papyri with biblical names. Doing so further decreases the evidence for Jews in the second and third centuries. W. Horbury and D. Noy, *Jewish Inscriptions from Graeco-Roman Egypt* (Cambridge: Cambridge University Press, 1992), 256, index a number of inscriptions from the second century C.E. through the fifth century C.E., but in most cases, the identification of these as Jewish is not definitive. Of particular interest, though, is one inscription thought to be evidence for the (re)building of a synagogue in late Roman Alexandria: no. 15 = *CIJ* 1438.

5. See, e.g., Chesnutt, *From Death to Life,* 265–67.

6. There may be one significant exception to this—the calendrical references in 1.1–2 and the agricultural reference in 4.4; see chap. 4, n. 35.

7. Batiffol, "Livre," 30–31; Tertullian, *On the Veiling of Virgins*. The New Prophecy was characterized, among other things, by women leaders and prophets; see Kraemer, *Her Share of the Blessings,* 157–73.

8. Batiffol, "Livre," 31–34. Mitchell also argues for the popularity of Michael in Asia

Minor, but unfortunately, the reference he gives to his own discussion is incorrect. See also the references for Michael in *BHG* 2:118–23.

9. Batiffol, "Livre," 32–33.

10. Vat Gr. 807, 73–77, excerpt on p. 33, n. 1.

11. However, the term "angel" occurs less frequently in the text than one might imagine. Aseneth's heavenly visitor is actually called ἄνθρωπος, not ἄγγελος, which occurs in the shorter text only at 14.2, where it describes the morning star; at 15.8, as a reference to the angels in heaven who love Metanoia; at 16.8, referring to the angels in heaven who eat the honeycomb; at 23.2 and 24.3, where it designates the messengers of Pharaoh's son; and at 25.7, where it again refers to heavenly angels.

12. See the detailed discussion, with extensive references, in Mitchell, *Anatolia,* 43–51. See also Sheppard, "Pagan Cults of Angels"; Kearsley, "Angels in Asia Minor"; Sokolowski, "Sur le culte d'angelos."

13. Mitchell, *Anatolia,* 45, n. 262; texts from Robert, *Opera Minora Selecta* 1:414; also E. Varınhoğlu, *Epigraphica Anatolia* 12 (1988): 79, n. 6, 85, n. 7, 86, nn. 8–9, 87, nn. 10–11.

14. Mitchell, *Anatolia,* 34, fig. 16, with references. See also chapter 6.

15. Mitchell, *Anatolia,* 49.

16. Mitchell, *Anatolia,* 45–46.

17. Mitchell, *Anatolia,* 47. The formula is documented for Jewish and Christian epitaphs alike and sometimes occurs on inscriptions whose religious identity is otherwise ambiguous.

18. See, e.g., Kraemer, *Her Share of the Blessings,* 80–92; Ramsay MacMullen, "Women in Public in the Roman Empire," *Historia* 29 (1980): 208–18; R. A. Kearsley, "Asiarchs, Ἀρχιερεῖς, and the Ἀρχιερείαι of Asia," *Greek, Roman, and Byzantine Studies* 27 (1986): 183–92, and "Asiarchs, Archiereis, and Archiereiai of Asia: New Evidence from Amorium in Phrygia," *Epigraphica Anatolia* 16 (1990) 69-80; Riet van Bremen, "Women and Wealth," in Averil Cameron and Amelie Kuhrt, eds., *Images of Women in Antiquity* (Detroit: Wayne State University Press, 1983), 223–42, and *The Limits of Participation: Women and Civic Life in the Greek East in the Hellenistic and Roman Periods,* Dutch Monographs on Ancient History and Archaeology 15 (Amsterdam: J. C. Gieben, 1996).

19. Kraemer, *Her Share of the Blessings,* 80–92.

20. Text in Carolyn Henriette Emilie Haspels, *The Highlands of Phrygia: Sites and Monuments* (Princeton, NJ: Princeton University Press, 1971), 338, n. 106.

21. Forms of ὕψιστος occur twelve times in the shorter text and thirty-seven times in the longer, perhaps a significant and interesting difference. In the LXX/OG, it is the usual translation for עליון and occurs frequently in the Psalms and in Sirach, inter alia.

22. On the question of the *hypsistoi,* see Trebilco, *Jewish Communities in Asia Minor,* 127–44. See esp. Mitchell's discussion (*Anatolia,* 50–51) of the Hypsistiani (from Gregory of Nyssa, *In Eunomium*); see also Epiphanius, *Panarion* 80, on the Massaliani or Euphemitai, who worship only one God they call *Pantokrator;* they pray, without sacrifice, at dawn and sunset in open places known as *euktēria* or *proseuchē,* with lamps and torches. The title *Pantokrator,* although known from some Jewish inscriptions, does not occur in *Aseneth.*

23. I.e., the inscription from Aphrodisias published by Reynolds and Tannenbaum, *Jews and Godfearers at Aphrodisias* (see chapter 9).

24. Mitchell, *Anatolia,* 48–49.

25. For references, see Schürer 3:14–15.

26. Schürer 3:8–17.

27. See chapter 6.

28. E.g., *CIJ* 202, 228 (both from Rome); 500 (original provenance unknown but perhaps from Rome or environs); 619a (from Venosa). See chapter 9.

CHAPTER ELEVEN

Aseneth Reconsidered

When Robert Kraft first introduced me, in the early 1970s, to the study of the assortment of texts conveniently but inaccurately labeled pseudepigrapha, I found myself extraordinarily discomfited. Works like *Aseneth* struck me as frustratingly free-floating, lacking any obvious historical and social context by which to ground my study of them. Years of reading at least some of these texts has muted my sense of alienation and deepened my appreciation for these texts, but as I contemplate the conclusion of this study, I am acutely aware that, despite all our scrupulous and meticulous analysis, *Aseneth* continues to resist our attempts to see through its forms to the ancient worlds and authors behind it. Like the ancient image of the chameleon, its texts tend to resemble whatever we lay them against, leaving me more and more resigned to our inability to pin the texts down to a particular interpretation and a particular context.

Nevertheless, in this final chapter, I want to recapitulate, briefly, the arguments of this study and to pursue a little further what it might mean to view *Aseneth* as the product of the later Roman empire.

Review

I began this study by arguing that the basic narrative framework of *Aseneth* was probably generated out of a desire to account for the marriage of the Egyptian Aseneth to the patriarch Joseph, within the constraints of a narrative now found in Genesis itself. So, for instance, Joseph meets Aseneth while collecting grain against the forthcoming seven years of famine and refuses to have contact with a Gentile woman. Before the marriage can transpire, then, Aseneth must somehow be transformed into an acceptable wife. She accomplishes this transformation through repentance, including a confession of her sins, prayer, fasting, mourning, and placing herself in God's hands. That this repentance is deemed acceptable by God is signaled by the appearance of an angelic double of Joseph, and Aseneth is appropriately transformed. No longer a foreign woman but now a *theosebēs gunē,* a woman who reveres God, she is now an acceptable bride, and the human Joseph returns to marry her and father Manasseh and Ephraim.

For each of these elements, and many others, the composer(s) of the shorter text drew freely, but not slavishly or precisely, on materials familiar to us from biblical and parabiblical traditions. Aseneth herself is described in language found in Song of Songs, from the figure of Wisdom and of the Foreign Woman. The initial episode between Aseneth and her father demonstrates her insolence and ignorance and answers the question: in what ways was Aseneth ignorant, insolent, and arrogant (all characteristics of the Foreign Woman)? Both her repentance and the demonstration of her acceptance by God draw on material now present particularly in Esther, Psalms, Proverbs, and Judges.

In the author, or perhaps authors, of the shorter version, we have someone clearly familiar with Jewish scriptural traditions and apparently with the language of the Septuagint/Old Greek.[1] This author does not ever quote Jewish scripture directly and does utilize one tradition known to us from rabbinic sources and from *Jubilees,* namely, that Joseph managed to resist the sexual temptations of Egyptian women because he remembered the commandments of his father, Jacob, to avoid foreign women.[2]

Yet, as we have seen, the specific details of *Aseneth* cannot be accounted for solely by the kind of process that James Kugel illuminates so effectively in his study of the midrashic traditions of Joseph in Potiphar's house. Many specific elements of the narrative appear instead to be drawn from paradigms of the adjuration of divine beings and the transformation of the soul, often into an angelic being, paradigms widespread in the later Greco-Roman world among Jews, Christians, and polytheists alike. These elements display particular consonance with images, practices, politics, and cosmologies characteristic of the late third and fourth centuries C.E. The explicit use of Helios imagery in the shorter text has intriguing if puzzling political ramifications.

The author of the shorter text seems intimately familiar not only with adjurative practices and patterns but also with a cosmology and a mystery of the bees that has its closest identifiable analogue in third-century Neoplatonic sources, namely, Porphyry's *On the Cave of the Nymphs,* in which bees represent souls. In *Aseneth,* the drama of the bees is thus the drama of the fate of souls. For the author of the shorter text, that Aseneth is a woman seems generally unproblematic. The general representation of gender construction is fairly conventional and consistent with late antique notions both of gender and of marriage that themselves appear modified from earlier constructions.

By comparison, in the longer text, biblical imagery and associations are typically made more explicit, for example, in the use of Song of Songs 4.1–5 to expand the description of the transformed Aseneth, the introduction and elaboration of the language of Exodus 34.6 in the formulation and expansion of Aseneth's prayers, the closer conformity with Judges 13 in the narrative of Aseneth's encounter with the angel, and numerous other examples set forth in chapter 3. The longer text often clarifies ambiguities in the shorter, indicating which window, which hand, which bees, and so forth. Perceived errors are corrected—Pharaoh is not Joseph's father; he is "like" Joseph's father.

Most crucially, though, the longer text displays strong concerns about angels, angel worship, angelic transformation, and a figure bearing strong resemblance to traditions about the Name-Bearing Angel in ancient Jewish (and Christian) sources, pointing to a redactor and perhaps also a community for which these issues are of particular concern. The affinities of these traditions with texts such as *2* and *3 Enoch* point perhaps to the fourth century, if not a little later, for the time of redaction.

Further, a significant number of revisions in the longer text appear focused on issues of gender, suggesting an author or authors concerned to address the ways in which the shorter text may have been construed by prior readers. The subtle differences in the use of Helios imagery may also suggest an altered political context or perspective. Some of the revisions of the longer text may point to some level of Christian redaction, including an implicit reversal of the Adam and Eve story in the scene where Aseneth eats the honey and possible allusions to Mary in the recasting of the figure of Metanoia.

Contrary to the prevailing scholarly consensus, I have argued in this book in favor of the relative priority of a shorter version of the story, represented by Philonenko's reconstruction, and for the thesis that the longer text, represented by Burchard's reconstruction, constitutes an intentional redaction and elaboration on a shorter text. Still contrary to that same consensus, I have also argued that the evidence for classifying *Aseneth* as a work of self-conscious Jewish composition, for dating it no later than the early second century C.E., and for locating its author in Hellenistic Egypt is extremely weak and based on a series of interlocking assumptions that do not hold up under careful scrutiny. Rather, I suggest that there are considerable reasons to date the shorter text to the third century C.E. (or perhaps the early fourth century) and the longer revision to sometime thereafter, although obviously no later than the sixth-century C.E. Syriac translation of a version of the longer story. Against the insistence that the author was self-consciously and exclusively Jewish, I have pointed out that while I consider the matter unresolvable, there are strong reasons to consider all versions of the story the product of Christian authorship, and other alternatives, ranging from a "theosebic" authorship to Samaritan composition, are not outside the realm of possibility. Likewise, on the question of geographic provenance, depending in part on the religious self-identification of the author(s), I think a number of locations are equally feasible, including Syria, Asia Minor, and the land of Israel itself. And where I once was willing to entertain the possibility of a female author, I am now less persuaded that this is likely, although I concede that again, here, too, we do not (and probably cannot) really know.

Implications

This study has implications that are both particular to the text(s) of *Aseneth* itself and more broadly pertinent to the study of late antiquity. In the case of *Aseneth,* it seems clear to me that it can no longer be presumed early, Jewish, or composed in Egypt.

Arguments that have relied on these presumptions about the text to make certain points, about, for example, the nature of first-century Greek-speaking Jewish concerns or communities or the conversion of non-Jews to Judaism in this period, need to be reexamined, all the more so if *Aseneth* is the only or the primary evidence on which they rely. To the extent that some of this critique is self-directed, it may facilitate its acceptance; at the very least, it means that I need to revise my own use of *Aseneth* as evidence for Jewish women and women's Judaisms in the Greco-Roman period.

Freeing *Aseneth* from its previous anchor in hellenistic Judaism of the first century C.E. or thereabouts allows me to pursue a little further the implications of its possible associations with the multiplicity of religious issues and practices in the later Roman empire. For instance, setting Aseneth's encounter with the angelic double of Joseph within the context of ancient adjurations of angels and other suprahuman beings enables us to explore further the implications of the association of Aseneth and adjuration for ancient author(s) and readers.

One obvious implication is that modern distinctions between religion and magic, a term I have reluctantly but studiously avoided in this discussion, are both inadequate and inappropriate here.[3] The author(s) of the Greek Aseneth stories clearly could and did interweave several paradigms in the telling of the story that they obviously expected their readers to comprehend. No hard-and-fast lines were drawn by the author(s) between the depictions of human encounters with angels in the texts they almost certainly considered Scripture, on the one hand, and widespread popular ideas about how human beings could obtain the services of divine beings, on the other. If I am correct that at least the earlier versions of *Aseneth* were composed in the third or fourth century C.E. by author(s) conversant with the kinds of materials and practices reflected in collections such as *Sepher ha-Razim* and the so-called Greek magical papyri, then we may ask some questions about the cosmology and social location of the author(s) and their putative audiences.

In his recent anthology of ancient curse tablets and binding spells, John Gager briefly addresses a question that confronts many modern interpreters of these materials. Did such spells, curses, and adjurations actually bring about the desired results, and if not, why did people engage in them or practice them? Gager argues that questions about whether such rituals work are the wrong questions; clearly they were perceived or believed to work or to have the potential to work. The right questions are about what they do for the practitioners, giving them a sense that they can control an otherwise arbitrary and capricious world. Spells compelling the divine to do the petitioner's will constitute a response of empowerment by those who might otherwise see themselves as without any power or control. Counterspells (spells to prevent other spells from taking effect) function in an analogous way, and the two taken together provide excellent explanations for why the consequences of spells do or do not transpire. If evil befalls your opponent or your desired love object swoons in your arms, it is because your performance has been powerful and successful; if not, it is because counterspells prevented it.[4] Further, these spells are so complex, time-consuming, and precise that they may contain the explanations for their own failure within just such complexity. Should the desired results not transpire, one can always look not just to counterspells but to minute flaws in one's own performance: failure to perform the rites at just the right time, in just the right manner, and so forth. And, presumably, one can always try again.

Implicit in these practices, then, is a cosmology of an arbitrary and capricious universe and/or, simultaneously, a highly competitive environment in which the rules are not apparent and wealth and prestige cannot be obtained by predictable paths. Neither righteousness nor hard work reaps rewards reliably.

Although Gager contends that virtually everyone in the ancient world believed in the efficacy of spells and counterspells, including protective amulets, such a cosmology is clearly the worldview of the disenfranchised. On the theory that one does not need a *daimon* to procure what one can easily obtain by ordinary means, the language of many of the adjurative papyri points poignantly to a primary clientele of relatively powerless persons. In the spell of Pnouthis for acquiring an assistant (portions of which I have discussed numerous times in chapter 4),[5] some of the social dynamics are particularly transparent.

This assistant does an astonishing variety of things, reflecting the desires of those who do not otherwise have access to such goods, services, and control over others.

> If you give him a command, straightway he performs the task: he sends dreams, he brings women, men without the use of magical material, he kills, he destroys, he stirs up winds from the earth, he carries gold, silver, bronze, and he gives them to you whenever the need arises. And he frees from bonds a person chained in prison, he opens doors.[6]

This same assistant provides you with abundant foods, including those prestigious ones in otherwise limited supply: fine wine, olive oil, plenty of vegetables. Only pork and fish are excepted! He prepares fabulous banquets on command, complete with ornate rooms with gold ceilings and even snazzily dressed *daimones* to serve.[7] When you journey abroad, he will accompany you and give you money whenever you need it, as your own ancient private banker. When you die, he will give your body an elaborate funeral, while taking your soul into the air with him.[8]

Within such a cosmology, where does *Aseneth* stand? Although it is difficult to be certain, it seems to me that while walking the walk and talking the talk of adjuration, *Aseneth* to some degree subverts the implications of adjurative practices. I am confident that ancient readers and listeners would have recognized in Aseneth's behavior precisely the paradigms of adjuration and would have fully expected the angel's appearance in her bedroom and the promises of life and prosperity that he brings. But at the same time, it may be that subtle distinctions matter here and that *Aseneth* insists that righteousness and worship of the one true God of Joseph will result in the power, riches, and success in love and politics that others attempt to acquire through the careful adjuration of powerful beings.

Yet like so much else, this matter is complex. I have also argued in this study that the drama of the bees draws heavily on Neoplatonic symbolism and imagery and that *Aseneth* has much in common with Neoplatonic theurgy, even while it is not wholly that either. It may be particularly significant, then, to recall that ancient Neoplatonists themselves worried about the implications of their belief that the proper rites could compel the appearance of the gods and solved the problem with their insistence that it was precisely the gods themselves who had taught these rites to humans. Nothing in *Aseneth* is explicit on any of these points, but it may well be that in its ability to straddle these categories, *Aseneth* has much in common with Neoplatonic interpretation of theurgy.

Comparison with the *hekhalot* materials discussed particularly in chapter 5 has related implications. Numerous scholars have seen a tension in the *hekhalot* materials with rabbinic cosmology, in which merit accrues to men through the study of Torah, a lifelong process that requires memorization (and is perhaps always in danger of being lost). In this system, the merit accorded the study of Torah is, by definition, limited to certain persons and is not available to non-Jews, Jewish women, or uneducated Jewish men, thus establishing a hierarchy quite analogous to that represented by the ancient system of priests and temple. In such a system, while good persons may suffer, righteousness is ultimately rewarded and the universe, created and ruled by a righteous God, is fundamentally just. By contrast, the results envisioned by actualization of the rituals in *hekhalot* traditions are significantly different: access to the divine, indeed transformation into the divine, is available to far broader classes of persons:

> "Akiba, my son," [God] said, "[I swear] by this throne of glory that I sit on, this precious object that my two hands established, that I will attend even to someone who has just this moment converted to Judaism, as long as his body is pure of idol-worship, and bloodshed and illicit sex."[9]

> "[A]nyone" who is free from idolatry, lewdness, bloodshed, slander, false oath, profanation of the (divine) name, impudence and baseless animosity, and who observes all the command and prohibitions, can erect a ladder in his house and "descend" to the Merkavah.[10]

Both the *hekhalot* materials and the adjurative formulas they resemble in significant ways share an underlying cosmology, one in which access to the divine and its concomitant rewards is essentially an arbitrary process. One suspects that those who wrote, read, and recommended such processes thought the universe itself fairly arbitrary. Certainly, their understanding of how to achieve angelic status centers on precise performance of ritual and the knowledge of powerful language that, properly utilized, guarantees attainment of the desired end. I do not mean to suggest here that they gave no consideration to the importance of righteous behavior, indeed, I cannot imagine that they thought that sinners could become angels. But it would not surprise me to learn (if we could know such things) that they did not believe that merely being free from sin afforded one access to the divine.

Other insights into the dynamic and context of *hekhalot* traditions may be of further interest. Swartz points out that the origins of the idea that visionary experience is the product of human instigation, rather than divine initiation, lie in responses to the loss of the second Temple in Jerusalem as a "locus for the approach of the localized, potent Presence of God."[11] Those whom Swartz dubs "the architects of rabbinic Judaism" saw good deeds and the study and practice of Torah as sufficient substitutes for Temple rites of atonement and were unconcerned about the presence (or absence) of God. In contrast, the traditions preserved in early Jewish mystical sources emanate from Jews who were concerned with the potential loss of the Divine Presence, with its dire implications for human welfare. Whether offering ways for humans to ascend to the heavens and obtain heavenly power or offering ways for humans to compel the divine to descend to earth and bring down those powers, mystical traditions assured their adherents of human ability to guarantee the continued presence and benefits of the divine. Further, as Swartz subsequently suggests, in the *hekhalot* texts authority resides not in a chain of elite transmission of knowledge but in an object, a ritual, or name itself and is, therefore, at least in theory, available to anyone (perhaps even repentant Gentile women).[12]

The work of Morray-Jones on transformational mysticism and of Jack Lightstone on "the commerce of the sacred" in diaspora Jewish communities allows us to identify yet another dimension. Morray-Jones proposes that the *hekhalot* traditions presuppose the idea that certain persons were able to achieve a transformation into the likeness of divine Glory that conferred upon them supernatural powers and mediatory functions. Such persons served as intercessors between the earthly community and the realm of God. Lightstone suggests that in diaspora Jewish communities, distanced from the Temple even before its destruction, it was not only certain persons who could function in such intermediary roles. The dead in their tombs could also serve in this role, while the physical presence of Torah scrolls in synagogues could have the effect of transforming mundane space into a conduit to the heavens.[13]

In her work on the dynamics of theurgy, Sarah Johnston suggests that charismatic, theurgic leaders "obviated the need for any geographic center of sacred power." Theurgy, like ascent in general, is portable and not dependent on any particular sacred space. She also suggests that lack of geographic affiliation might have been particularly effective for a religious system that understood itself as "anti-material, as was the case with theurgy: in refusing to plant itself in any place within the physical world, theurgy reiterated its message that spiritual fulfillment lay outside of this world altogether."[14]

Johnston is particularly concerned here to elucidate the dynamics of Neoplatonic theurgy, and she argues that the absence of a specific cultic location for theurgic practice could even be understood as a deliberate critique in "a late antique world that offered, perhaps, too many potential loci of spiritual power." But her observations are more broadly applicable, for whether the question is the destruction (or remoteness) of the locus of power or simply too many such loci, the end result is the same, namely, the formulation of traditions through which contact with the divine is in the hands of humans and not dependent on particulars of place[15] or on divine whim. Thus, it may well be that the paramount religious concerns of at least some Jews and non-Jews overlapped materially in the late antique world.

The material considered so far locates the *hekhalot* materials firmly in a rabbinic matrix. If Swartz (and others) see the origins of the *hekhalot* worldview as a response to separation from the Temple, one might then argue for the relatively early dating of these traditions, not too far in time from the destruction of the Temple in 70 C.E. And in fact, both Morray-Jones and Alan Segal argue quite effectively that major components of transformational mysticism are already visible in Paul, who writes well before 70 C.E. (although it is also true that distance from the Temple was already a potential issue for Jews living far from its precincts).[16] Nevertheless, the precise adjurative practices of *hekhalot,* with their emphasis on the arbitrary possession of Torah and their power over divine beings, are not at all typical of Paul's experience.

But without becoming mired in questions of "origins," it does seem that the specifics of the *hekhalot* traditions, with their interest in access to Torah and their control over angels, do presuppose opposition to a well-developed rabbinic system, which, in turn, suggests a relatively late date. Halperin actually suggests that Jewish speculation about palaces of heaven represents a Jewish response to a specific historical impetus: "the splendid religious edifices built by Constantine and his successors, which both advertised the church's victory on earth and symbolized its great unseen glories."[17] If he is correct about this and if the similarities between *Aseneth* and the *hekhalot* traditions point to a common cultural context, this may further support the dating I have suggested for *Aseneth.*

Yet another set of events in the late fourth century may be relevant to the general discussion of texts that may be seen to compensate for the loss of the Temple in Jerusalem as the locus of human access to the divine. As part of his program of the restoration of temples and his assault on Christianity, the polytheist emperor Julian authorized the rebuilding of the Temple in Jerusalem. His premature death in 363 C.E. brought these plans to an effective halt. For Christians, the hand of God was clearly discernible in Julian's death and his concomitant failure to restore polytheism and temple sacrifices in Jerusalem. One imagines that for at least some Jews, the promised restoration is likely to have had profound religious significance, while its failure is likely to have elicited responses typical for such profound disappointment. In particular, it seems possible that one consequence might have been renewed and/or increased interest in precisely the sorts of traditions that address the absence of the Temple and all the more so in those geographic regions where the restoration would have had the greatest effect.

Much of this speculation hinges, of course, on the assessment of *Aseneth* as the product of self-consciously Jewish composition, a point on which I remain steadfastly agnostic. But should that be the case, we may suggest the following.

If there is thus a tension between the *hekhalot* traditions and those of rabbinic sources, a tension that accurately reflects the differing historical realities, social locations, and experiences of their proponents, *Aseneth* may represent yet another voice in the ancient conversation. In *Aseneth,* the techniques of adjuration are utilized, with predictable results: a human being renounces idolatry; performs appropriate prefatory rites; spends seven days in mourning, fasting, and bodily mortification; and thus receives a visitation by a glorious manifestation of the divine. Yet I have no doubt that for the authors of all versions of *Aseneth,* the underlying cosmology here is a moral and just one: all of Aseneth's rituals may be requisite for transformation but so is initial confession of sin and rejection of idolatry. I do not think this is very far from the cosmology of the *hekhalot* materials, but there are some significant differences. The combination of active repentance with adjurative techniques may represent a somewhat different stance from a somewhat different social location. But in addition, Aseneth is not just a human being but a woman, and an Egyptian idolater to boot. No *hekhalot* traditions envision a woman capable of undergoing angelic transformation. Further, if Morray-Jones and Lightstone are correct that persons who have undergone such transformation were then understood to be capable of serving as conduits for their communities, Aseneth is again extraordinary, at least if the text is Jewish. There are, of course, ample instances of women serving as conduits in Christian sources, including figures like Perpetua and other martyrs, not to mention Mary, the mother of Jesus.

One of the most fascinating yet difficult aspects of *Aseneth* remains its use of Helios imagery. Here I want to return to some of Staerman's arguments, initially presented in chapter 6. In addition to noting that traditional Roman religion was inadequate to the task of unifying the empire in the third century, Staerman illuminates just how much was riding on the acceptance of the imperial cult in that century, particularly in comparison with earlier periods. It was, she notes, scarcely by chance that Christians were persecuted in the third century precisely for their resistance to the imperial cult. Although Christian refusal to worship the emperor had never been well received and had always been construed as a threat to the welfare of the entire empire, in the third century, Christian challenges to imperial worship took on greatly heightened political and symbolic significance.[18]

In light of these observations, any interpretation of the Helios imagery in *Aseneth* must explore the political and theological implications for any putative community. If *Aseneth* is the product of a Jewish author, we must consider whether Jewish acceptance of solar ideology, regardless of the reinterpretation employed, should be construed as a form of acquiescence to Roman ideology and perhaps even as a statement of solidarity and participation in Roman culture. The presence of imperial Helios imagery in at least one fourth-century Jewish synagogue (Hammath Tiberias, discussed at length in chapter 6) points strongly either to such a reading or to an extraordinarily subtle critique. Similar questions must be asked about any putative Samaritan author, while an author who would have been most comfortable with the label "God-revering" might have had the least difficulty assimilating imperial solar imagery to the figure of Joseph and God.

The question of how veneration of Helios functions in an avowedly monotheistic context is complex. Helios could have been viewed as a manifestation of an otherwise invisible Deity or as a divine being subordinate to God analogous to the many divine beings believed by Jews to have such an identity, angels among them. Goodenough proposed an interesting solution: "[B]oth Helios and the menorah . . . suggest cosmic worship; not that Jews worshipped the cosmos, but, as we have seen, they worshipped with the cosmos the God who had created and now directs the cosmos and humanity."[19]

In his analysis of the Helios mosaic at Hammath Tiberias, Dothan disavowed Goodenough's interpretation, asserting that "Helios representation had no more religious significance for the fourth century Jews of Tiberias than the theophoric names of contemporary Roman Jews . . . had for their bearers."[20] I find this startling on both points.

Given the prominence of Helios in the center-floor mosaics of Hammath Tiberias and other late antique synagogues, it seems hard to imagine that it had no religious significance. On the basis of the connections I have explored elsewhere, it seems worth speculating that the representation of Helios had, on the contrary, great religious significance and might, in fact, constitute depiction of precisely the Name-Bearing Angel documented in such a wide range of sources.

In any case, Garth Fowden's discussion of late antique monotheism suggests more. On the one hand, Fowden points to the evidence for an emerging "consciously universal . . . henotheist or monotheist religion."[21] "This is certainly the case at holy places where the worship of a primary god or goddess attracts other divinities, generates a multiplicity of cults, and, eventually, stimulates speculation about their interrelationship."[22] Focusing in this study on the relationship between the emergence of a universalist monotheism and political consolidation into one "cosmos," earthly and heavenly, Fowden is particularly interested in the consonance between the two and in the understanding of temples as symbolic of the cosmos, with "the stability of the universe dependent on the correct performance of temple cults."[23]

If I am correct that *Aseneth* is written (if not also revised) in the third or even fourth century, then regardless of the religious self-understanding of its author(s), it is composed amid precisely these cultural contexts and conditions. What might that mean? In Aseneth's rejection of her Egyptian gods, the story denies the feasibility of any crass syncretism; it does not accommodate the gods of the Egyptians in the worship of the One God of Joseph. Yet it draws heavily on the kinds of accommodations to monotheism (or perhaps henotheism) that Fowden identifies, including the presence of angelic beings and, of course, the strong Helios imagery so prevalent in precisely these centuries. And *Aseneth* has some rather interestingly political overtones in its favorable portrait of Pharaoh and in the power of Pharaoh that ultimately accrues to Joseph. While some of this could easily be derived from the narrative found now in Genesis, the presentation of Pharaoh as virtually God is a particularly intense reading that might point to the authorial political commentary.

If the text is Christian, much of this might read differently. Christian rejection of the imperial cult, whether in its solar manifestation or otherwise, is well documented, despite the numbers of Christians who lapsed on this point, temporarily or otherwise. Staerman herself makes the fascinating argument that in the end, even the imperial solar ideology was insufficient to address the crisis of the third century and that only Christianity was able to do this by promising ordinary people a kingdom on earth that replaced the power of eternal Rome. Christianity, she claims, provided a form of protection against the power of the elite: the image of Jesus Christ, close to people and merciful, whom all could follow, together with the image of a Father God vastly more powerful than earthly rulers.[24] But interestingly, at this point, even Christianity adopts the iconography of Sol Invictus, although now only for Christ, not for the emperor. This may suggest that if *Aseneth* is wholly the product of Christian composition, it is unlikely to have been written before the late fourth century, when Christians were more likely to be comfortable appropriating the imagery of Helios for Joseph, here understood as a type of Christ. Indeed, one might wonder whether it is precisely the association of Christ with Helios and of Joseph with Christ that could ground the representation of Joseph as Helios.

In the end, our ability to resolve these issues is greatly constrained by the interlocking nature of the arguments. As with so many other aspects of *Aseneth,* how one interprets all of this imagery depends a great deal on what one thinks the text might be, and yet, what one thinks the text might be is partly determined by its very engagement with this imagery. Nevertheless, it is my hope that future scholarship will take these possibilities seriously and pursue them further.

To move beyond questions of late antique religion, the issues I have explored in rethinking the date, authorship, and provenance of *Aseneth* have broader implications for the whole question of dating and identification of anonymous and pseudonymous works in Greek and Latin, preserved only by Christians (or at least, insofar as we know, not by Jews), particularly those with little if any "explicit" Christian content. I have had occasion to point to some examples in the discussion of *Aseneth,* including works such as the *Testament of Job,* the *Life of Adam and Eve,* and *The History of the Rechabites,* but I think there are probably many texts whose identity and context need to be revisited.

In particular, the range of options for the origins and use of such texts also needs reconsideration. Most discussions of these texts are framed primarily in terms of Jews and Christians, with occasional reference to "Jewish-Christians," often as a strategy when a text proves resistant to neat categorization along these lines or when explicitly Christian elements cannot be neatly excised from a text that otherwise seems somehow particularly Jewish. To the best of my knowledge, no one ever considers Samaritan composition an option. Further, although numerous recent scholars postulate the existence of communities of "God-fearers," and occasionally even "pagan" monotheists, Andersen's suggestion that *2 Enoch* might emanate from a community of "God-fearers," is extremely rare.[25] If the difficulty identifying *Aseneth* has taught me anything, it is that the problem may lie as much with our contemporary categories as with anything about the text, its authors, or its ancient audiences.

Still, by their very nature, pseudepigraphic texts are notoriously resistant to dating and classification. Although I am personally comfortable with the conclusion that *Aseneth* is much more likely to have been composed no earlier than the third century C.E., I also recognize that many, if not most, of my colleagues may find it difficult to assent to this conclusion. To them, I can only suggest that they reflect again on the nature of the available evidence, for to the extent that there is meaningful evidence, it all weighs on the late side of the scale. In the end, there is no evidence per se and only a few arguments that *Aseneth* is earlier than this, let alone as early as the first century C.E. One argument colleagues have raised, particularly in conversation, is that since some texts known only in later forms do turn out to be early (one might think here of the *Damascus Document,* initially discovered in the medieval Cairo genizah and eventually also found at Qumran), *Aseneth,* too, might be early. Surely, by itself, this is barely an argument. Because something might be the case does not remotely make it so; it is at best a necessary but insufficient element in the attempt to date *Aseneth* (or any pseudepigraphon) early. More persuasive to scholars in the past has been the linkage of claims of *Aseneth*'s Jewishness, its Egyptian provenance, and its relatively early dating, as I have discussed at length above. I believe I have effectively dismantled those links, revealing their circular character. I have demonstrated that (1) while *Aseneth* might be Jewish, the evidence is simply not dispositive and it could easily be the product of Christian composition, theosebic composition, and perhaps even other alternatives; (2) that the arguments for Egyptian provenance are similarly not dispositive; and (3) that even if *Aseneth* is Jewish, it is at least equally likely, and in my view far more likely, to have originated in Greek-speaking Jewish circles of the late third century C.E. or later. Scholars who persist in the belief that *Aseneth* is early, in the face of the evidence and arguments I have amassed here, will have to do more than assert that belief and need, I think, to reflect carefully on what is at stake in assigning the text(s) an early date, given the tenuous nature of the evidence.

In the end, *Aseneth* remains an enigma in many ways—we do not and at present cannot know for certain the self-understanding of its author, authors or redactors, nor can we be certain when or where it was first composed and then revised, in whatever direction. Nevertheless, I find the text less of an enigma when I read it as the product of an author of whose religious self-understanding I am uncertain, steeped in the particular cultural confluences of late antiquity (the third to the fifth or even sixth centuries), than when I read it as the product of a Jewish author no later than the revolts of 115–17 C.E. It is true that, individually, many of the elements of late antiquity may have existed earlier, although they are attested better (and sometimes only) in later sources. But my point here, in part, is that even if *Aseneth* is a Jewish composition, some specific elements are difficult to demonstrate for the earlier period, while if the text is a Christian composition, a stance I think almost equally likely, it is much more likely to be late, and in either case, the totality of images seems, at least to me, much more comprehensible in the late Roman empire than in its beginning. In the absence of better evidence, caution seems to me to be the best alternative, and that caution requires us not to assume that the text or texts are early and not to hinge any other arguments—particularly arguments about the "nature" of Roman-period Judaism, about the existence of specific exegetical traditions, or about women and the feminine[26]—on the presumed early date and presumed Jewish authorship of *Aseneth.*

Reassessing the relationship of the shorter and longer reconstructions of *Aseneth* also has implications beyond these texts. With some of my colleagues, I have begun to think that efforts to decipher the history of redaction of texts now extant in multiple forms are of limited utility. Rather than the often frustrating pursuit of elusive "original" texts, I think there is much to be said for taking the various forms of texts as testimony to their authors and readers, wherever that leads. While my self-understanding as a historian makes the pursuit of origins often appealing, I am nevertheless concerned that in the study of religion in the ancient world, the search for "original" texts is itself inextricably linked with theological pursuits, including the search for the "original" (read "true" if not also "divinely revealed") text. As one who still endeavors to be a historian of religion in antiquity, and of women's religions in particular, I am more and more attracted to the multiplicity of texts as testimony to the multiplicity of people's lives, experiences, and self-understanding in antiquity.

In the case of *Aseneth,* I am really arguing several things: I believe that a close comparison of the divergent readings of the shorter and longer reconstructions reveals patterns of difference that point to the differing concerns and perspectives of the "authors." In this sense, I strongly disagree with those scholars who have accepted Burchard's earlier arguments that the longer reconstruction antedates the shorter, which is then seen as an intentional abridgment.

But more important, I take issue with those scholars who, in accepting Burchard's judgment, find it sufficient to consider the longer text the "true" text and to base their arguments and interpretations solely on that text, considering the differences between the two reconstructions insignificant and unimportant. At the very least, it is clear to me that those differences, often a matter of a few words here and there, nevertheless alter the story, the plot, and the characters themselves in ways that are not trivial and that point beyond the texts to the visions of the storytellers themselves and perhaps to their social worlds. I would hope that those who read this book will no longer be content to accept the consensus of handbooks but will consider the evidence carefully and will, in any case, consider the range of *Aseneth* readings in their efforts to make sense of the stories.

NOTES

1. I don't see any hard evidence that we can be certain that the author(s) used the LXX/OG rather than alternate Greek Jewish translations, such as Aquila, Theodotion, or Symmachus. It would be particularly difficult to show this for the shorter version, which draws on paradigms found in biblical texts but never adheres closely to those texts (if, indeed, it knows them directly). But it is clear, particularly in the longer version, that the author is familiar with Jewish scriptural traditions in Greek.

2. It would be interesting to consider whether this tradition itself drives the formulation of the story—that is, how could Joseph have married a foreign woman if he knew that such contact was forbidden? The implicit answer of the text is that Aseneth must be transformed into a woman who is no longer foreign.

3. See chapter 3; see also Gager, *Curse Tablets,* 24–25.

4. Gager, *Curse Tablets,* 21–24, 218–22.

5. *PGM* 1:42–195.

6. *PGM* 1:97–101.

7. *PGM* 1:98–132, excerpts.

8. *PGM* 1:172–80.

9. Schäfer, *Synopse,* §686, translated in Halperin, *Faces of the Chariot,* 382.

10. Schäfer, *Synopse,* §199, translated in Schäfer, *Hidden and Manifest God,* 146.

11. Swartz, *Mystical Prayer,* 28.

12. Swartz, "Book and Tradition."

13. Morray-Jones, "Transformational Mysticism"; Jack Lightstone, *The Commerce of the Sacred: Mediation of the Divine among Jews in the Graeco-Roman Diaspora,* Brown Judaic Studies 59 (Chico, CA: Scholars Press, 1984).

14. Johnston, "Theurgic Ascent," 174.

15. This argument may seem contradicted by my earlier suggestions that Aseneth's transformation and adjuration of the heavenly Joseph take place within a temple. But (*pace* Bohak) I do not think that the text thereby insists that contact with the divine can only take place in a specific temple, although it might be read to mean that any space can be transformed into a temple, if necessary, even the private apartments of a woman.

16. Christopher Morray-Jones, "Paradise Revisited (2 Cor 12:1–12); The Jewish Mystical Background of Paul's Apostolate, part 1, *HTR* 86, no. 2 (1993): 177–217; Segal, *Paul.*

17. Halperin, *Faces of the Chariot,* 353, noting in particular Eusebius's panegyric on the building of the churches (*H. E.* 10.4.2–72).

18. Staerman, "Le culte impérial," 378.

19. Goodenough, *Jewish Symbols,* 12:187.

20. Dothan, *Hammath Tiberias,* 87–88. For a similar stance, see also Rachel Hachlili, "The Zodiac in Ancient Jewish Art: Representation and Significance," *BASOR* 28 (1977): 61–77.

21. Fowden, *Empire to Commonwealth,* 41.

22. Fowden, *Empire to Commonwealth,* 41, citing the examples of Eleusis and the Isis aretology from Maroneia in Thrace.

23. Fowden, *Empire to Commonwealth,* 42.

24. Staerman, "Le culte impérial," 379.

25. Andersen, in *OTP* 1:96, discussed in chapters 5 and 9.

26. In this vein, I consider unfortunate Angela Standhartinger's recent conclusion that the differing versions of *Aseneth* are a useful background for analyzing divergent stances toward women in early Christian communities (*Das Frauenbild*).

Appendix

Aseneth in Rabbinic Traditions

The precise connections between the tale(s) of *Aseneth* in Greek and rabbinic traditions about Aseneth are difficult to discern. Numerous earlier scholars, including Batiffol, Aptowitzer, Philonenko, and others, assumed that rabbinic legends about Dinah as the mother of Aseneth antedate and underlie the Greek *Aseneth*. At various points in this book, I have argued that such an assumption is highly problematic for a variety of reasons. In his study of Joseph traditions, Kugel relies on an early dating of *Aseneth* to support his thesis that rabbinic traditions whereby Joseph knows to refuse the offer of Potiphar's wife because he remembers the teachings of his father Jacob are also early.[1] In this appendix, I wish to survey rabbinic traditions about Aseneth and to make some suggestions about their probable relationships, if any, to the Greek *Aseneth*.

Traditions about Aseneth in late antique and medieval rabbinic sources may be sorted into four major categories: (1) that Aseneth was the biological daughter of Potiphera and/or his wife; (2) that Aseneth was a proselyte; (3) that Aseneth's father was not an Egyptian priest; (4) that Aseneth was the daughter of Dinah. The first and fourth categories encompass traditions that contain a variety of other elements as well. In some cases, traditions in category 1 probably assume that Aseneth was a proselyte but are not explicit in this regard, while traditions in category 4 would seem to assume that Aseneth was not a proselyte or counter assumptions that she was.

The Individual Traditions

That Aseneth Was the Biological Daughter of Potiphar/Potiphera and/or His Wife

GENESIS RABBAH (Early Fifth Century C.E.?)

The tradition that Aseneth was the biological child of Potiphera and/or his wife occurs twice in *Genesis Rabbah*.[2] Commenting on the proximity of the stories of Tamar and

Potiphar's wife, *Genesis Rabbah* 85.2 offers the interpretation that both women had pure motives for their apparently inappropriate sexual behavior. In the name of R. Joshua b. Levi, we read the claim that "[Potiphar's wife] saw by her astrological arts that she was to produce a child by [Joseph], but she did not know whether it was to be from her or from her daughter." Thus she mistakenly attempted to seduce Joseph, not realizing that it was her daughter (Aseneth) whom he would marry and by whom he would father sons.

Aseneth is obliquely mentioned again in *Genesis Rabbah* 86.3, which contains a saying by R. Joshua of Siknin in the name of R. Levi that while normally masters cause their slaves to eat priestly food, Joseph caused his master to eat priestly food. This surprising claim is based on a tradition that a priest named Eleazar married a daughter (or female descendant) of Joseph. Since Eleazar's descendants would have been eligible to eat priestly food and since he and Potiphar would have had common descendants subsequent to Eleazar's marriage into Joseph's family, Joseph would have been the instrument whereby Potiphar's descendants, understood as Potiphar himself, ate priestly food. The complex logic of this argument aside, this tradition only makes sense if Aseneth was herself the daughter of Potiphar.

THE PRAYER OF JOSEPH, apud Origen, *Commentary on Genesis* 46–47

While not strictly rabbinic, the tradition recounted by Origen, attributed to the *Prayer of Joseph,* might also be noted again here.[3] In that work, Aseneth was the ordinary daughter of Potiphar and his wife, who informed her father of her mother's treachery about Joseph and whom Potiphar ultimately married to Joseph in order to show that he held no grudge against him.

We should note several things about these passages. First, they equate Potiphar, Joseph's master, and Potiphera, the priest of On. Second, taken together, they assume that Aseneth was the biological child of Potiphar and/or his wife.[4] Third, if such stories were formulated and transmitted by people who adhered to a matrilineal principle of Jewish identity, they must presume that Aseneth was a proselyte, although they are not explicit on this point. Fourth, the rabbinic stories are transmitted in the name of rabbis thought to have lived in the third century C.E., R. Joshua and R. Levi.[5] Origen, too, writes in the third century.

That Aseneth Was a Proselyte

NUMBERS RABBAH (Compiled c. Twelfth Century C.E.?)

In a discussion in defense of proselyte ancestors, *Numbers Rabbah* 1:8.4 reads:

> The Holy One, blessed be He, however, said to [Joshua], 'Go, mark the plant from which you yourself have sprung! Is it not from proselytes," as it says, *"And unto Joseph in the land of Egypt were born Manasseh and Ephraim whom Asenath the daughter of Potiphera priest of On bore"* (Gen 46.20).[6]

The problems associated with the dating of *Numbers Rabbah* and its component traditions are considerable. The current scholarly consensus is that *Numbers Rabbah* is a medieval compilation whose underlying framework is a much earlier lost Midrash known as *Tanḥuma,* itself no earlier than the fifth century C.E.[7]

Numbers Rabbah actually has two parts. While the second is thought to follow the text of *Tanḥuma* closely, the first, where the Aseneth tradition is found, is thought to have "revised, amplified, interpolated and modified the groundwork to such an extent as to obliterate almost entirely all traces of the underlying source."[8] Thus it appears particularly difficult to date its designation of Aseneth as a proselyte.

MIDRASH TADSHE (Eleventh Century C.E.?)

The late compilation in *Midrash Tadshe*[9] also contains unambiguous description of Aseneth as a proselyte.[10] As with *Numbers Rabbah,* its late date and uncertain origins make it difficult to place its understanding of Aseneth within a secure trajectory.

Aseneth's Father Was Not an Egyptian Priest

TARGUM ONQELOS (Third Century C.E.) and *TARGUM NEOFITI 1* (Fourth Century C.E.?)

Two Aramaic paraphrastic translations of the Hebrew Bible, *Targum Onqelos*[11] and *Targum Neofiti 1*[12] contain phrasings of the Aseneth verses in Genesis that identify her father not as a priest (*kohen*) but as a great man or master of his city. According to *Targum Onqelos* to Genesis 41.45, Aseneth was the daughter of Potiphera, "chief" (*rabba'*) of On. The same phrasing occurs in Genesis 41.50, and 46.20. In his critical notes, Bernard Grossfeld comments that this substitution of *rabba'* for *kohen* addresses two concerns of the Aramaic translators: how the patriarch Joseph could marry the daughter of a non-Israelite priest, which he detects also in the treatment of Moses' marriage to the daughter of a Midianite priest, and how a non-Aaronide could be called *kohen.*[13] The central discomfort here appears to be about priesthood and not about Aseneth's Egyptian birth.

Targum Neofiti 1 appears to exhibit similar discomfort, also identifying Aseneth in Genesis 41.45 as the daughter of Potiphera, "*rabba'* of Tanis." While *Targum Neofiti* to 41.50 repeats this, the targum to 46.20 replaces Tanis with the biblical Hebrew "*On.*"

Aseneth Was the Daughter of Dinah (and Shechem)

A central part of Aptowitzer's thesis that *Aseneth* was both early and Jewish rested on his belief that rabbinic traditions making Aseneth the daughter of Dinah and Shechem were both relatively early and known to the author of *Aseneth.* Numerous rabbinic traditions do explicitly identify Aseneth as the offspring of Dinah and Shechem (as does the late Syriac manuscript published by G. Oppenheim),[14] but as we shall shortly see, all of these occur in late compilations, although, as I noted in chapter 8, the tradition is never found in demonstrably earlier rabbinic sources, such as Mishnah and Tosefta, or even the Talmudim. Aptowitzer's argument thus relied chiefly on his analysis of an opaque passage in *Genesis Rabbah* 97 with a particularly problematic textual history. Although I have discussed this passage previously in chapter 8, I will return to it here in more detail.

GENESIS RABBAH 97

Based on a publication of the passage in an article of J. Theodor,[15] Aptowitzer translated the relevant passage as follows:

> When, however, Israel perceived the sons of Joseph, he asked "who are these." Said Rabbi Ammi, "who is that one who is destined one day to lead Israel astray to idol-worship, and will cause fifty myriads of them to fall on one day." And Joseph answered his father and said, "They are my sons, whom God hath given me בזה." *He brought Asenath, who was blind in one eye, near to him* [emphasis in original].

This scene is, as Aptowitzer characterizes it, quite puzzling. Both Jacob's query to Joseph and Joseph's reply are direct quotations of Genesis 48.8. The commentary seems particularly concerned with two issues: why Jacob asks who the children are and why the text reads בזה. In the text of Genesis, both questions appear to have straightforward answers. Since Genesis 48.10 describes Jacob as having the poor eyesight of old age, it seems reasonable that he asks who the children are because he cannot see them well enough to recognize them. Similarly, ancient readers of Genesis probably understood בזה as "here"; this, at least, is consistent with the Septuagint translation ἐνταῦθα. But בזה could also clearly mean "by this one [fem.]," that is, "by her," and Joseph's introduction of Aseneth to demonstrate "by her" seems to suggest just this. Of more interest to Aptowitzer was how the rabbis explained Jacob's question; he argues that the scene can only make sense here if "Jacob perceived unworthy descendants of the sons of Joseph in the spirit and believed that this had its basis in the unworthiness of Joseph's wife, since, as he thought, she was one of the daughters of Egypt."[16] When, then, Joseph brings forth the visually impaired Aseneth, Jacob recognizes that she is kin, because of the tradition, Aptowitzer argues, that the child born to Dinah was either born partially blind or became blind in one eye as a result of her exposure (for which Jacob was himself responsible). Aptowitzer provides no references here to support such a tradition, although his language suggests he has some passages in mind.[17]

Since traditions of Aseneth as Dinah's daughter are demonstrably present elsewhere, the significance of this passage for Aptowitzer was primarily its presumably trustworthy quotation of a (late) third-century sage, R. Ammi: "The oldest trace of this legend [of Dinah and Aseneth] is to be found in the statement of Rabbi Ammi at the *end* of the third century—the oldest *literary* trace of the narration, for the legend itself must naturally be much older." And if the legend itself must be much older, and *Aseneth* knows the legend, *Aseneth* itself can easily be much older, as well. For Aptowitzer, "could have been" easily became "was."

But apart from the flaws in Aptowitzer's reasoning as they affect questions about the date of *Aseneth* (which I have also noted previously in chapter 8), there are other significant difficulties with this passage. In the first place, it is by no means clear that the story refers to Dinah. As I noted in chapter 8, and have detailed here, other passages in *Genesis Rabbah* present Aseneth unambiguously as the biological daughter of Pentephres (and/or his wife, who obviously cannot have been Dinah). Aptowitzer's response to this was simply to suggest that "at that time the legend was not very widespread and that it had not as yet been recognized and accepted by all."[18]

But other alternatives exist. The simplest might be that Aptowitzer is wrong that this tale implies a biological tie to Dinah. But even if he is correct that such an association accounts for the reference to Aseneth's eyesight, it is by no means clear that this passage is reliable proof of an early date for that tradition.

It is even difficult to phrase the problem properly. In part, the question is what we mean when we speak of something called *Genesis Rabbah.*[19] Like all rabbinic compilations, *Genesis. Rabbah* contains an assortment of materials likely to have been formulated at different times. If we use the phrase *"Genesis Rabbah"* to designate a work that at some point in time (say, between the late fourth and the early sixth centuries C.E.) acquired a relatively fixed form, then the initial question I wish to raise is whether the passage adduced by Aptowitzer should, in fact, be included in that designation.

The question arises from the manuscript evidence.[20] Aptowitzer relied on an article by J. Theodor, one of the editors of the critical edition of *Genesis Rabbah,* for the text of this passage, which does not occur in most manuscripts of *Genesis Rabbah.*[21] It does occur, though, in one of the most important witnesses to *Genesis Rabbah,* Vat. Ebr. 30, which contains an additional commentary attributed to R. Hanina.

AND ISRAEL BEHELD JOSEPH'S SONS, AND SAID: WHO (MI) ARE THESE ([Gen] XLVIII, 8)? Who is this, said R. Ami, who will one day turn Israel to idolatry and cause fifty myriads to fall in one day [see 2 Chron 13.17]? R. Hanina son of R. Adda commented: This is the numerical value of *mi.*
AND JOSEPH SAID UNTO HIS FATHER: THEY ARE MY SONS, etc. ([Gen] XLVIII, 9). He produced Asenath, who was blind in one eye.[22]

In fact, the textual situation for the chapters of *Genesis Rabbah* that cover the portion Vayechi (Gen 47.28ff.) is particularly problematic. H. Freedman actually provides three different translations here. He gives first a translation of J. Theodor and Ch. Albeck, *Midrash Bereshit Rabba,* chapter 96, that begins with commentary on Genesis 47.28 and gets only a few verses further before digressing at length on the subject of burial in the land of Israel. Then he gives a translation of a midrash found, he notes, in most manuscripts.[23] Also designated chapter 96, it comments only on Genesis 49.1, while the next chapter, 97, comments on Genesis 49.3–50.10.

Having done so, Freedman then notes that "Chapters XCV–XCVI of cur. edd. [current editions] do not really belong to Genesis Rabbah, and in MSV [Vat. Ebr. 30] the following three chapters, XCV–XCVII replace them." Freedman then prints a translation of Vat. Ebr. 30, covering Genesis 46.29–48.9. Finally, for the remainder of *Genesis Rabbah,* he returns to the text of "current editions" for chapters 97–100, covering Genesis 48.15–50.26, the last verse of Genesis.

In his brief introduction to his translation, Freedman also notes that even after an initial redaction later than the redaction of the Palestinian Talmud, "the text [of *Genesis Rabbah*] was still subject to accretions, and from Vayyishlach we find extensive passages bearing marks of the later Haggadah. In Vayyigash the commentary is no longer verse by verse, while much of Vayechi was probably drawn from the Tanḥuma homiles."[24] Since the passage at issue falls into Vayechi, it would appear that whether it would have been found in early versions of *Genesis Rabbah* or whether it is the result of continuing redactive activity is unclear. If the latter, then even if the story of a partially blind Aseneth alludes to the Dinah tradition, it cannot easily be adduced as evidence for an early dating.

It is probably worth remarking that for Aptowitzer, it was the attribution of a part of the passage to the third-century R. Ammi that offered crucial evidence for the antiquity of the tradition and not just its location in a compilation redacted perhaps as early as the fourth century C.E. For Aptowitzer, that attribution was not subject to critique. But a more critical treatment of rabbinic traditions suggests that the mere attribution of a commentary by Ammi is insufficient guarantor of its antiquity, all the more so if the source in which the commentary occurs is itself subject to serious questions. Aptowitzer's belief that the Dinah story underlies *Genesis Rabbah* 97 notwithstanding, then, we shall now see that in rabbinic traditions, accounts of Dinah as the mother of Aseneth occur only in relatively late anthologies that in their current forms date approximately from the eighth century C.E. or later.

SOFERIM 21 = 43b (Eighth Century C.E.)

The so-called minor tractate *Soferim,* now transmitted with the (Babylonian) Talmud, contains the problematic claim that Dinah was six years old when she gave birth to Aseneth as a result of the rape by Shechem.[25] It also recounts that Michael (the angel) then descended and took the baby Aseneth to the house of Potiphar. *Soferim* also claims that Rebekah was three years old when she left her father's house. That both ages are correct readings is evident from the passage itself, which revolves around a claim that Aramean fathers had sex with their virgin daughters after the daughters were three years old, prior to marrying them off![26]

PIRḲÊ DE RABBI ELIEZER (Eighth or Ninth Century C.E.)

The fullest traditions about Aseneth and Dinah may be found in *Pirḳê de Rabbi Eliezer* (*PRE*), or the *Chapters of Rabbi Eliezer the Great*.[27] According to *PRE* 38, which deals with Joseph and his brothers, Shechem seduced Dinah by sending out dancing girls who played pipes in the streets, and he enticed Dinah out of her house, where he was able to seize and rape her. Consequently, Dinah conceived and gave birth to Aseneth.

What happened next is slightly ambiguous, but the essential story line is clear. Dinah's brothers wished to kill "her," probably the child, to preserve the family reputation. Jacob, however,

> wrote the Holy Name upon a golden plate, and suspended it about her neck[28] and sent her away.[29] She went her way.[30] . . . Michael the angel descended and took her, and brought her down to Egypt to the house of Potiphera; because Asenath was destined to become the wife of Joseph. Now the wife of Potiphera was barren, and (Asenath) grew up with her as a daughter. When Joseph came down to Egypt he married her.[31]

A previous passage in *PRE* 36 (Jacob and Laban) contains a tradition in the name of Eliezer that when the sons of Jacob were born, their future wives were all born with them, except for Joseph, since his predestined spouse was Asenath, the daughter of Dinah.

Gerald Friedlander notes that this story is also found in Midrash Aggadah, Yalkut, and elsewhere.[32]

TARGUM PSEUDO-JONATHAN (Seventh or Eighth Century C.E.?)

Targum Pseudo-Jonathan's[33] treatment of Aseneth differs significantly from the intepretations offered both in *Onqelos* and *Neofiti*. Whereas both of those, as we saw, concerned themselves only with the identity of Aseneth's Egyptian father, denying his "priesthood," *Pseudo-Jonathan* to *Genesis* 41.45 combines the language of *Neofiti* and *Onqelos* with the claim that Aseneth was the daughter of Dinah: "[Pharaoh] gave [Joseph] as wife Asenath, whom Dinah had borne to Shechem, and whom the wife of Potiphera, chief of Tanis, had reared."

At Genesis 41.50, *Pseudo-Jonathan* reads: "Two sons were born to Joseph, whom Asenath, who had grown up in the house of Potiphera, the chief of Tanis, had born to him." More consistent than *Neofiti, Pseudo-Jonathan* to Genesis 45.20 retains the name of Tanis: "To Joseph were born sons in the land of Egypt, Manasseh and Ephraim, whom Asenath, daughter of Dinah, who had grown up in the house of Potiphera, chief of Tanis, bore him."

Alone among these three targumic traditions,[34] then, *Pseudo-Jonathan* resolves discomfort over Joseph's marriage to Aseneth not merely by denying the priesthood of Potiphera but by denying that Potiphera was her father at all. In fact, the juxtaposition of these two elements suggests that for the "author" of *Pseudo-Jonathan,* the priesthood of Potiphera was not the only concern: Aseneth's Egyptian birth (and implicit conversion?) were also disturbing.

Pseudo-Jonathan evinces similar concerns in its treatment of another problematic passage close to the biblical verses about Joseph and Aseneth, namely, the statement in Genesis 38.2 that Judah married the daughter of a Canaanite. Where both *Neofiti* and *Onqelos* translate this without alteration from the Hebrew,[35] *Pseudo-Jonathan* substitutes "merchant" for Canaanite and adds in addition that Judah "proselytized her" before he had intercourse with her. Michael Maher points out that these two revisions of the biblical text are essentially contradictory: if the force of designating the father as a merchant was to deny his Canaanite identity, converting the daughter prior to marriage reasserts it[36] or at least reasserts his foreign identity. The treatment of Judah's wife suggests that the "author" of *Pseudo-Jonathan* was concerned about marriages between Israelite men and foreign women to a degree lacking in other targumic traditions.

Aseneth in Midrashic Traditions: A Tentative Trajectory

Dating all of these texts and analyzing the relationships of the traditions within them, together with the relationships between them, is, by the very nature of the texts themselves, extraordinarily difficult.[37] The tendencies of traditional Jewish scholarship not to concern itself much with critical discussion of these relationships or of the chronological development of haggadic traditions also hampers critical analysis. Fortunately, though, recent scholarship has begun to address some of these questions.

For example, numerous theories have been proffered for the relationships between *Targum Pseudo-Jonathan* and *Targum Onqelos,* in particular. In the introduction to his 1992 English translation of *Pseudo-Jonathan* (with critical notes), Maher favors *Pseudo-Jonathan*'s reliance on *Onqelos* and characterizes *Pseudo-Jonathan* as, at the very least, "a Palestinian targum modified under the influence of Onqelos."[38] The treatment of Aseneth in those two targumim accords with such a model. Maher cites with apparent approval the conclusions of several scholars that *Pseudo-Jonathan* knew and utilized *Pirke de Rebbe Eliezer,* a model that has the ability to account for the specific traditions about Aseneth present in *Pseudo-Jonathan* yet lacking in *Onqelos* and *Neofiti 1.* These studies assist us in the formulation of a tentative trajectory of the Aseneth traditions in midrashic sources, as follows.

All the extant Aseneth traditions appear dependent on and knowledgeable of the biblical narrative, which as I noted at the outset, contains no additional discussion or commentary on the marriage of Joseph and Aseneth. The beginning of our trajectory is thus Genesis 41.45, 41.50, and 46.20.

The earliest commentary on the marriage continues to find the story unremarkable and raises no questions of "conversion." Rather, it focuses on a series of questions that depend on the identification of Potiphar in Genesis 37.36 and Genesis 39 with Potiphera in Genesis 41 and 46.

Despite the similarity of their names in Hebrew, nothing in the Hebrew narrative explicitly suggests such an identification, and the simplest reading of the Hebrew is that these are two different characters. In the Greek translation of the Hebrew Genesis, though, the names of the two men are no longer similar but essentially identical.[39] It seems possible that the process of translation triggers speculation about Aseneth that the original Hebrew did not, although it might also reflect an interpretive tradition in which the identification had already been made. The earliest association of the two appears to occur in *Jubilees* (34.11, 40.10), thought to have been composed in Hebrew in the first half of the second century B.C.E..[40] The identification of Joseph's master with Joseph's father-in-law poses a series of exegetical problems to which subsequent traditions appear to be addressed and has a major impact on the formation of Aseneth traditions as well. To see the full dimensions of the problem, we must consider the relevant biblical verses and the questions they were likely to generate in antiquity.

According to Genesis 37.36, "the Midianites sold him [Joseph] to Potiphar" (לפוטיפר סריס פרעה שר הטבחים). Genesis 39.1 contains the same description, adding only that Potiphar was איש מצרי—an Egyptian (man). The Hebrew phrase סריס פרעה posed significant interpretive dilemmas in antiquity. Newer English translations reflect a recent consensus that סריס means an officer, but ancient translators of the Hebrew clearly took it to mean a eunuch, a castrated male. This is apparent in the LXX for Genesis 39.2 Πετεφρης ὁ εὐνοῦχος Φαραω, ἀρχιμάγειρος, ἀνὴρ Αἰγύπτιος. Interestingly, the LXX for Genesis 37.36 offers a slightly different translation: τῷ Πετεφρη τῷ σπάδοντι Φαραω, ἀρχιμαγείρῳ. While σπάδων seems also to carry the meaning of castrated, the use of two different terms to translate the same Hebrew word may point to some concern about the identication of Potiphar as a eunuch.[41] This is the only place in the LXX/OG that translates סריס as σπάδων.

The description of Joseph's master as eunuch (understood to mean castrated) had the potential to create a major exegetical difficulty, in that he is also said to have a wife, the very wife who, in Genesis 39, attempts to seduce Joseph and then accuses Joseph of attempted rape. By itself, this is not unsolvable: Potiphar could have been a married eunuch. In fact, precisely such a tradition occurs in the Babylonian Talmud, which relates that Potiphar bought Joseph for himself (meaning, for sexual purposes) and that, as a result, the angel Gabriel castrated him (presumably so that he could not consummate his desires on the hapless Joseph).[42] The story continues with an etymology of the name Potiphera as derived from *pera* (mutilated). *Genesis Rabbah* 86.3 contains a similar, anonymous, tradition that God himself castrated Potiphar when the latter purchased Joseph in order to commit sodomy with him. In the verses immediately preceding, after explicitly equating the two men, *Genesis Rabbah* offers a different etymology for the name: "He was called . . . Potiphera because he uncovered himself (po'er) in honour of idols."[43]

One Islamic tradition, in *The History of al-Tabari,* appears to address the dilemma of a married eunuch with a curious twist. Rather than attribute Potiphar's state to divine punishment for improper sexual desires, al-Tabari accepts Potiphar's castration on its face and accounts for the behavior of his wife as the actions of a desperate virgin whose husband could not have intercourse with her. Motivated by frustration and Joseph's extraordinary beauty, Potiphar's wife attempted to seduce Joseph. In this retelling, Joseph ultimately marries the wife, whom he finds to be a virgin and with whom he then has Manasseh and Ephraim. The story in al-Tabari is of particular interest because it demonstrates the existence of a tradition that saw a difficulty with a married eunuch yet made no apparent link between Potiphar and Potiphera, who appear in this story not to be the same person, since the wife of one is (probably) the daughter of the other.[44]

Nevertheless, the identification of Potiphar as a eunuch is likely to have become particularly problematic once Potiphar and Potiphera are identified, for then we have not only a eunuch with a wife but a eunuch with a daughter. Genesis 41.45, 41.50, and 46.20 unambiguously called Aseneth אן כהן פרע בתדפוטי (the daughter of Potiphera, priest of On). So, too, the LXX/OG, which calls Aseneth θυγάτηρ Πετεφρη.

We may summarize so far as follows. The traditions about Joseph in the house of Potiphar the eunuch generate one set of exegetical questions, including the potential oddity of a married eunuch. But as James Kugel has demonstrated eloquently, the story of Joseph in Potiphar's house generated far more concern about Joseph and Potiphar's wife than about Potiphar himself.[45] The story about Joseph's marriage to Aseneth (Hebrew: Asnath), the daughter of Potiphera, the priest of On, generated even less exegesis, particularly in the Jewish sources we have already reviewed. Although we might expect considerable discomfort over Joseph's marriage to the daughter of an Egyptian priest, exegetical traditions that are demonstrably early and Jewish evidence only minor interest in the topic, regardless of the language in which those traditions survive.

The identification of Joseph's master with his father-in-law produces a magnified set of problems. Not only might one wonder how Aseneth could be Potiphar's child if he was a eunuch, but also one might worry how Joseph could have married the daughter of a man he stood accused (if falsely) of trying to cuckold.

It is interesting that the earliest witness to the identification of Joseph's master and father-in-law—namely, *Jubilees*—does not appear troubled by its own apparent claim that Pharaoh married Joseph to the daughter of a eunuch (although in the actual verse where the marriage is mentioned, Potiphar is simply [and conveniently?] called only "priest of Heliopolis, the chief cook").[46] *Jubilees* seems fairly straightforwardly to understand Potiphar as the natural father of Aseneth.

Particularly interesting for our purposes are the targumim, which translate סריס not as eunuch but as officer. In his English translation of *Targum Neofiti 1,* Martin McNamara observes: "Apart from Tg. Isa 56:3f (where the literal translation is inevitable), the Tgs. never render this term of the HT literally." Neofiti translates סריס as *slyt,* "officer," "ruler," while other targumim use *rb,* "magnate," and so forth.[47] This appears consistent with the probability, as we have seen, that both *Onqelos* and *Neofiti 1* understood Aseneth to be the natural daughter of Potiphera and a proselyte; it is also consistent with their silence on the Dinah story.

It is thus interesting to propose that the equation of Potiphar and Potiphera led some ancient exegetes (although obviously not all) to worry about how a eunuch could have had a biological daughter (to use our terminology). The stories in *b. Sotah* and *Genesis Rabbah* offer one solution, although it is only implicit in those passages, namely, that Potiphar became a eunuch after he purchased Joseph and therefore could have had both a wife and a child prior to his castration. Tellingly, it is precisely *Genesis Rabbah* that elsewhere understands Aseneth as the biological child of her mother, Potiphar's wife, and that, *pace* Aptowitzer, contains no demonstrable mention of the Dinah tradition.[48] Not inconceivably, even that tradition may reflect concern for Potiphar's state, in that it does not explicitly portray Aseneth as Potiphar's daughter! Interestingly, the understanding of the biblical סריס as something other than castrated occurs also in *Numbers Rabbah* 11, in the same part that, as we saw earlier, contains the tradition of Aseneth as unambiguously a proselyte.[49]

Perhaps, then, we should see the Dinah story as an alternate answer to the same concerns, for according to all those traditions in which Aseneth's mother was really Dinah, Potiphar (the eunuch) was not her real father, nor his wife her real mother. The various versions of how Dinah's daughter got to Potiphar's house in Egypt may be seen to arise from the need to explain why Aseneth did not live with her mother in Israel.

I have no doubt that there is more to the development of the Dinah traditions than this. Since the problem of the eunuch father could be, and was, addressed in other ways, the Dinah traditions must have other (or additional) concerns, and I suspect that their function points to their origins. Because they have the effect of making Aseneth an Israelite, they may have been prompted by concerns over Aseneth's foreign birth. Aptowitzer thought, against Batiffol, that Aseneth's foreign birth was not the central problem, given the extensive evidence that rabbinic law permitted intermarriage provided only that the non-Jewish spouse convert prior to the marriage (as does our Aseneth).[50] Rather, he thought it was her Egyptian birth, that made her a descendant of the cursed Ham. Not inconceivably, the spinners of the Dinah story were motivated by numerous concerns, including Aseneth's seemingly foreign birth and traditions of her conversion, which, not withstanding Aptowitzer's arguments, may have troubled exegetes in some quarters. While (implicit) denials of Potiphar's actual castration and the Dinah tradition seem to be generally mutually exclusive, they are found combined in the *Targum Pseudo-Jonathan.* But, as Maher notes and as we have seen earlier, the author of *Pseudo-Jonathan* was not beyond combining mutually exclusive explanations of Judah's marriage to a foreign woman (e.g., her father wasn't a Canaanite, but Judah converted her anyway prior to the marriage!) and may have done essentially the same thing here by retaining the earlier targumic denial of Potiphar's castration with the Dinah tradition.[51]

Finally, on the subject of the Potiphar traditions, it is worth remarking that the second problem raised by the equation of Potiphar and Potiphera, namely, how Joseph could marry the daughter of a man he stood accused of trying to cuckold, is addressed in the tradition Origen cites from the lost *Prayer of Joseph*. As we have noted earlier, there Potiphar gave his daughter to Joseph because Aseneth herself had revealed her mother's impropriety, thus divorcing Aseneth from any blame by association, and because he wished to show publicly that he held no grudge against Joseph.

Reconstructing the Probable Development of Aseneth Traditions, Rabbinic and Otherwise

Early exegetes, then, took Genesis 41 and 46 at face value. Aseneth, the daughter of Potiphera, married Joseph, and their sons are the eponymous ancestors of the half-tribes Manasseh and Ephraim. Demonstrably early Greek Jewish authors such as Philo and Josephus and the authors of "rewritten" Bible such as Pseudo-Philo show no interest whatsoever in Joseph's marriage to Aseneth.

The trigger for the relatively modest early traditions about Aseneth that we find in *Jubilees* and the early targumim of *Onqelos* and *Neofiti 1* seems to have been the identification of Joseph's owner, Potiphar, with Joseph's father-in-law, Potiphera. Ultimately, although it is hard to say precisely when, the transfer of Potiphar's characterization as a eunuch to Potiphera creates exegetical difficulties that various rabbinic Aseneth stories appear to address and resolve in differing ways. Yet, as we have seen, the earlier traditions consistently identify Aseneth as the biological daughter at least of her mother, Potiphar/Potiphera's wife, and usually of Potiphar/Potiphera himself.

Of particular interest for our study of the Greek Aseneth stories is that the traditions generated by the identification of Potiphar and Potiphera do not explicitly identify Aseneth as a proselyte. That they assumed it seems reasonable,[52] but it is curious that they do not state it outright, and the only rabbinic sources that do unambiguously state this are of uncertain date (*Numbers Rabbah*) or quite late (*Midrash Tadshe*).

The Dinah traditions that played such a central role in Aptowitzer's analysis and thus, ultimately, in subsequent arguments for the dating of *Aseneth* appear likely themselves to be late responses to the exegetical dilemmas posed by the identification of Potiphar and Potiphera. As I have pointed out, their origins lie not only in that association but also in other or additional concerns. Not inconceivably, precisely one of those is the very claim that Aseneth was a proselyte, to which they offer an alternative and antithetical interpretation.

Regrettably, despite Aptowitzer's lengthy analysis, it is difficult to place the Greek Aseneth stories within this trajectory of traditions. I do not think the tradition of Aseneth as proselyte is likely to have developed before the articulation of the matrilineal principle, but even this is not certain and, in any case, does not assist in locating the stories in any constructive way. What is significant, though, is that our stories do not equate Pentephres with Joseph's former master, despite their apparent acquaintance with the LXX/OG, and they are matter of fact in claiming that Aseneth's mother and father are Pentephres and his unnamed wife. In this regard, they are either intentional rejections of those traditions or ignorant of them and of their implications. It is not inconceivable that they are motivated by differing exegetical concerns that were troubled by the marriage, but not for the reasons that undergird rabbinic traditions.

While their relationship to the Dinah stories remains uncertain, our investigation here has yielded some significant results. *Pace* Aptowitzer, and Philonenko who followed him on this point, the Greek Aseneth stories contain no hint of the tradition that Aseneth's mother was the raped Dinah. There is no evidence that the Dinah tradition circulated prior to the seventh or eight century C.E., and the assumption that it must be earlier has no foundation apart from the general belief that later midrashic sources contain earlier materials.

This is significant for two major reasons. First, it demolishes Aptowitzer's arguments, which became the foundation on which *Aseneth* has been dated to the first century C.E. Second, since the collections in which the Dinah legends occur are all later than our earliest secure evidence for *Aseneth,* namely, the Syriac manuscripts of the *Syrian Chronicle,* it seems not impossible that the Dinah traditions themselves are a response if not to our *Aseneth* directly then to similar traditions. It may be quite significant that the earliest attestation of the Dinah legend appears to be the Syriac tale printed by Oppenheim, which Aptowitzer assumed to reflect earlier rabbinic traditions but which could quite conceivably itself be formulated in response to the Syriac *Aseneth* and form the basis of material found in later midrashic sources.

In conclusion, then, our analysis of Aseneth in rabbinic traditions has shown that the Dinah traditions are unlikely to antedate the composition of the Greek *Aseneth* and that rabbinic and midrashic sources provide no assistance in dating *Aseneth* prior to the fourth or fifth century C.E. Contrary to the arguments of Aptowitzer and those who relied on his work, the evidence from rabbinic traditions is actually consistent with my arguments for dating the Greek *Aseneth* relatively late.

NOTES

1. Kugel, *In Potiphar's House,* 109. The problem addressed by these traditions is how Joseph could have known that this was wrong (that is, a violation of the law) if the law forbidding such behavior had not yet been revealed to Moses.

2. Stemberger, in *Introduction to Talmud and Midrash,* argues that because the final editor/redactor of *Genesis Rabbah* knows Mishnah, the Babylonian Talmud, various halachic midrashim and targumim, and the translation of Aquila; quotes Palestinian rabbis thought to have lived as late as c. 400 C.E.; and refers to Diocletan and perhaps alludes to Julian, *Gen. R.* cannot have been redacted before the early fifth century C.E. (301–304). There are some serious difficulties concerning the redaction and transmission of *Gen. R.* that I treat below, in the section on traditions that Aseneth was the daughter of Dinah and Shechem.

3. Also in Philonenko, *Joseph et Aséneth,* 39; Batiffol, "Livre," 17–18; Aptowitzer, "Asenath," which also reproduces the Greek, 257, n. 44. On the date of the *Prayer,* Jonathan Z. Smith, in *OTP* 2:700, argues for first century C.E., but the evidence is hardly definitive.

4. *Gen. R.* 86.3 also contains a tradition that Potiphar was a eunuch. This tradition functions elsewhere to bolster the claim that Potiphar was not Aseneth's real father (see Ginsberg, *Legends,* 5:337–38). But here this cannot be. Commenting on the phrase "Eunuch סריס of Pharaoh," *Gen. R.* says (anonymously), "This intimates that he was castrated, thus teaching that he [Potiphar] purchased him for the purpose of sodomy, whereupon the Holy One, blessed be He, emasculated him." Juxtaposed with the immediately preceding verses, this story can only mean that Potiphar was castrated after he fathered Aseneth and not before. It thus contradicts not only those sources that deny Potiphar's paternity of Aseneth but also the story in *al-Tabari* (William M. Brinner, *The History of al-Tabari,* vol. 2: *Prophets and Patriarchs* [Albany: SUNY Press, 1987], where Joseph marries not Potiphar's daughter but his wife, who turns out to have been a virgin since her husband was a eunuch and incapable of intercourse! In addition to several other places in *Gen. R.* where Aseneth is clearly Potiphar's biological child (85.2, 87.4), *Midrash ha-Gadol* also considers Aseneth Potiphar's biological daughter.

5. S.v. *EJ* 10:282–84, 11:100–102. For my purposes, the historical veracity of such ascription is irrelevant here.

6. Translation, J. Slotki, *Midrash Rabbah: Numbers,* 3d ed. (New York: Soncino Press, 1983), 1:213.

7. *Tanhuma* subsequently existed in a version known as *Yelammedenu,* which is also lost but which is quoted extensively in *Yalkut* and elsewhere. The extant editions of *Midrash Tanhuma* draw from these earlier versions but have been substantially amended and supplemented. For discussion, see Slotki, *Midrash Rabbah,* 1:vii–viii, and Strack and Stemberger, *Introduction to Talmud and Midrash,* 337–39.

8. Slotki, *Numbers Rabbah,* 1:viii.

9. This is thought perhaps to have been the work of Mosheh ha-Darshan of Narbonne in the eleventh century C.E.; see Strack and Stemberger, *Introduction to Talmud and Midrash,* 376.

10. *Midrash Tadshe* 21 (ed. A. Epstein, *Qadmoniot* 43).

11. Grossfeld, *Targum Onqelos,* 33–35, dates the current form of *T. Onqelos* to the third century C.E., with a "proto" *Onqelos* in the second C.E.

12. McNamara, *Targum Neofiti 1, 43–45.*

13. Grossfeld, *Targum Onqelos,* 139, n. 22.

14. Oppenheim, *Fabuli Josephi.*

15. *Gen. R.* 97 (to Gen 48.8–9), according to Theodor, in the Festschrift for Jacob Guttman, special edition, p. 23. The standard edition of *Gen. R.* is J. Theodor and Ch. Albeck, *Midrash Bereshit Rabba: Critical Edition with Notes and Commentary* (in Hebrew), 3 vols. (Berlin and Jerusalem, 1893–1936); English translations in Freedman, *Genesis Rabbah,* and in Neusner, *Genesis Rabbah.*

16. Aptowitzer, "Asenath," 252–53.

17. "The sign of [Jacob's] recognition [of Aseneth's lineage] was the fact that she was half-blind, as we are told in the following. V. Dinah gave birth to her child in the house of her parents. However, the child either was born partially blind or lost one eye subsequently as a result of her exposure, for which Jacob himself was responsible" (Aptowitzer, "Asenath," 253). If the references for this tradition are elsewhere in the article, I have managed to miss them altogether, and I have been otherwise unable to locate this tradition.

18. Aptowizer, "Asenath," 255.

19. I don't here intend to explore questions about whether *Genesis Rabbah* was actually the title of a compilation, which is itself a problem; see Strack and Stemberger, *Introduction to Talmud and Midrash,* 300–301.

20. For additional details, see Strack and Stemberger, *Introduction to Talmud and Midrash,* 305.

21. Including, I think, the primary manuscript on which Theodor and Albeck relied, MS British Museum, Add. 27169.

22. Translation of Vat. Ebr. 30, from Freedman, *Genesis Rabbah,* 935.

23. But not Vat. Ebr. 30 and not the Temanite manuscript; see Freedman, *Genesis Rabbah,* 892, n. 1. The midrash is taken from a text first printed as *New Version of Bereshith Rabbah on the Blessings of the Patriarch Jacob* in the work Mishpatai Shavuot of Hai Gaon, printed in Venice, 1601, and in Hamburg, 1781.

24. Freedman, *Genesis Rabbah,* xxix.

25. Dated in its current form to the eighth century C.E., although Strack and Stemberger, *Introduction to Talmud and Midrash,* 248, note that earlier forms may have existed.

26. Rebekah here is said to have avoided such a fate. Similar ideas about Gentile men defiling young girls occur in *m. Ket.* 1.2: "A convert, a woman taken captive, and a slave girl who were redeemed or who converted of who were freed at an age of less than three years and one day—their marriage contract is two hundred [*zuz*] [the ketubah of a virgin]." Translation from Jacob Neusner, *The Mishnah: A New Translation* (New Haven: Yale University Press, 1988).

27. English translation in Friedlander, *Pirk̂e de Rabbi Eliezer.* Subsequent references to Friedlander are to this volume. According to Strack and Stemberger, *Pirk̂e de Rabbi Eliezer* dates to the eighth or ninth century C.E. Stemberger, *Introduction to Talmud and Midrash,* 357, offers the following assessment: "[D]espite its use of a wealth of older tradition [and] its knowledge of pseudepigrapha . . . the work must be regarded . . . as the creative achievement of a personal author."

28. Apparently Aseneth's.

29. The tradition that foundlings discovered with identifying amulets may be counted as Israelite occurs in *b. Kidd.* 73b, but with no mention of Aseneth as an example.

30. However, I don't understand how the baby Aseneth could go her way.

31. *PRE* 38, trans. Friedlander.

32. Friedlander attributes its presence in Midrash Aggadah to direct borrowing from *PRE.* He also notes that traditions about the sterility of Potiphar's wife occur in the Koran, Joseph Sura; *Midrash Haggadol, Lekach Tob,* and *Yalkut* to Pss., 732; and he observes that *Gen. R.* 86.3 and *b. Sot.* 13b presume the opposite (288 n. 6).

33. Maher, *Targum Pseudo-Jonathan,* 12–13. Maher points out that Ps. Jonathan is repeatedly distinctive in its traditions and atypical of other targumim. He characterizes it as more like "rewritten Bible." He favors the view that Ps. Jonathan used *Onqelos* (1, n. 5) and also *Pirk̂e de Rabbi Eliezer,* and he makes the interesting suggestion that Ps. Jonathan was not the work of a *meturgeman,* nor intended as a synagogue text. The arguments for a post-Islamic date for the final redaction or composition of Ps. Jonathan have been challenged recently by Robert Hayward, "The Date of Targum Pseudo-Jonathan: Some Comments," *JJS* 40 (1989): 7–30, and rebutted by A. Shinan, on whose work Maher particularly relied: "Dating Targum Pseudo-Jonathan: Some More Comments," *JJS* 41 (1990): 57–61. But for our purposes, this discussion is not crucial since the primary thrust of Hayward's critique is whether Ps. Jonathan is post-Islamic.

34. The extant fragments of other Palestinian targumim do not contain sections on these verses, as far as I can tell.

35. However, some manuscripts of *Onqelos* read, "merchant." Maher acknowledges this in his notes to Ps. Jonathan, but the edition of Ps. Jonathan gives no explanation for preferring the reading of Canaanite.

36. Maher, *Targum Ps. Jonathan,* 12, n. 4.

37. The nonspecialist is particularly disadvantaged, hence I am forced to rely here on the discussions of others, although not without critique.

38. Maher, *Targum Ps. Jonathan,* 1, n. 6; see also generally 9–12.

39. Both are called Πετεφρης. Numerous variants to all relevant verses include Πεντεφρη and others.

40. See Wintermute's discussion of dating in *OTP* 2:43–44, where he relies heavily on the arguments of J. VanderKam, who proposes an actual date of 161–40 B.C.E., based on the dates of the latest historical events to which *Jubilees* alludes.

41. It is also intriguing that Aquila and Symmachus for Gen 37.36 read not "Petephres" but "Fourtoufar." If this reading were consistent in Gen 39, it would suggest that Aquila and Symmachus sought to stress the difference between the two men, but at Gen 39, they apparently revert to Petephres. Conceivably, one reading or the other is evidence of discomfort over this, and Gen 39 could point to harmonization.

42. *B. Sot.* 13b.

43. Trans. Freedman, *Genesis Rabbah.* Neusner's, *Genesis Rabbah,* 3:222, translation is a little more graphic: "He was called Potiphera because he exposed himself before idols."

44. Joseph, 392, English translation in Brinner, *History of al-Tabari.*

45. Kugel, *In Potiphar's House.*

46. *Jub* 39.2, and 34.11 conflate Potiphar and Potiphera; the marriage is mentioned in 40.10.

47. McNamara, *Targum Neofiti 1,* 171, n. 21.

48. Interestingly, Freedman, *Genesis Rabbah,* does suggest that *Gen. R.* 90.4 might contain an allusion to the Dinah tradition. Here, commenting on the meaning of Joseph's new name, we read, "R. Aha said: The name connotes: The one that was hidden here, thou hast come to reveal her." Freedman seems to suggest that perhaps this alludes that part of the Dinah legend where Jacob tied a "disc" (amulet) around the baby to facilitate her later identification. Freedman writes: "She was the Asenath whom Joseph married, but he saw the disc and hid it, so that her identity might not be known" (829, n. 4). But he doesn't take a strong stand.

49. See M. Jastrow, *Dictionary of Talmud Bavli, Yerushalmi, Midrashic Literature, and Targumim* (1903; reprint, New York: Pardes, 1950), 2:1027, where it is understood to mean "mediator" or "manager."

50. Aptowitzer, "Asenath," 241.

51. Maher, *Targum Ps. Jonathan: Genesis,* 127, n. 4.

52. It is interesting to speculate why it seems reasonable to think the tradents of these stories envisioned Aseneth as a proselyte. Ancient readers who adhered to patrilineal principles in the determination of Israelite (and/or Jewish) identity, such as the authors and editors of Genesis, would have perceived certain problems in the identification of the two men, such as those we have just examined, but they would still not have been troubled about the consequences of Aseneth's marriage to Joseph for the status of Manasseh and Ephraim as founders of Israelite tribes. Such readers are likely to have assumed that the children of a male Israelite take the identity of their fathers, so that Joseph's sons are unquestionably members of his tribe and community. Nevertheless, no rabbinic traditions do this. On the origins of the matrilineal principle, see Cohen, "Origins of the Matrilineal Principle in Rabbinic Law."

Bibliography

Alexander, P. S. "Incantations and Books of Magic." In Emil Schürer, *The History of the Jews in the Age of Jesus Christ*, ed., G. Vermes, F. Millar, and M. Goodman. Edinburgh: T & T Clark, 1986, 3, pt. 1:342–79.

Allenbach, J., et al. *Biblia Patristica: Index des citations et allusions bibliques dans la littérature patristique*. 6 vols. Paris: Editions du Centre Nationale de la Recherche Scientifique, 1975–82.

Amaru, Betsy Halpern. "Portraits of Women in Pseudo-Philo's Biblical Antiquities." In Amy-Jill Levine, ed., *"Women Like This": New Perspectives on Jewish Women in the Greco-Roman Period*. Septuagint and Cognate Studies. Atlanta: Scholars Press, 1991, 83–106.

Amidon, Philip R. *The Panarion of St. Epiphanius, Bishop of Salamis: Selected Passages*. New York: Oxford University Press, 1990.

Aptowitzer, V. "Asenath, the Wife of Joseph: A Haggadic Literary-Historical Study." *Hebrew Union College Annual* 1 (1924): 239–306.

Armstrong, A. H. *Cambridge History of Later Greek and Early Medieval Philosophy*. Cambridge: Cambridge University Press, 1970.

————. "Man in the Cosmos: A Study of Some Differences between Pagan Neoplatonism and Christianity." In W. den Boer et al., eds., *Romanitas et Christianitas: Studia Iano Henrico Waszink*. Amsterdam: North Holland Publishing Co., 1973, 5–14. Reprinted in A. H. Armstrong, *Plotinian and Christian Studies*. London: Variorum, 1979, chap. 22.

Assemani, Giuseppe Simone. *Sancti patris nostri Ephraem Syri: Opera omnia quae exstant: graece, syriacque, latine*. Vol. 1. Rome, 1737.

Athanassakis, Apostolos N. *The Orphic Hymns: Text, Translation, and Notes*. Texts and Translations 12, Graeco-Roman Religion Series 4. Missoula, MT: Scholars Press, 1977.

Avi-Yonah, M., and N. Makhouly. "A Sixth-Century Synagogue at Isfiya." *Quarterly of the Department of Antiquities in Palestine* 3 (1933): 118–31.

Baer, Richard. *Philo's Use of the Categories Male and Female*. Leiden: E. J. Brill, 1971.

Barker, Margaret. *The Great Angel: A Study of Israel's Second God*. Louisville, KY: Westminster/John Knox Press, 1992.

Bartsch, Shadi. *Decoding the Ancient Novel: The Reader and the Role of Description in Heliodorus and Achilles Tatius.* Princeton, NJ: Princeton University Press, 1989.

Batiffol, P. "Le Livre de la Prière d'Aseneth." In *Studia patristica: Etudes d'ancienne littérature chrétienne.* Vol. 1/2. Paris: Leroux, 1889–90, 1–115.

———. "Revue de M. R. James, *Apocrypha Anecdota.*" *Revue Biblique* 7 (1898): 302–4.

Bean, G. E. "Notes and Inscriptions from Pisidia, II." *Anatolian Studies* 10 (1960): 43–82.

Beckwith, R. "The Solar Calendar of 'Joseph and Aseneth': A Suggestion." *JSJ* 15 (1984): 90–111.

Bellen, H. "Συναγωγὴ τῶν Ἰουδαίων καὶ Θεοσεβῶν. Die Aussage einer bosporanischen Freilassungsinschrift (CIRB 71) zum Problem der 'Gottesfürchtigen.'" *JAC* 8/9 (1965–66): 171–76.

Berchman, Robert M. *From Philo to Origen: Middle Platonism in Transition.* Chico, CA: Scholars Press, 1984.

Berger, Klaus. *Auferstehung des Propheten und die Erhöhung des Menschensohnes: Traditionsgeschichtliche Untersuchungen zur Deutung des Geschickes Jesu in frühchristlichen Texten.* Studien zur Umwelt des Neuen Testaments 13. Gottingen: Vandenhoeck und Ruprecht, 1976.

Bernays, J. "Die Gottesfürchtigen bei Juvenal." In *Commentationes philologae in honorem Theodori Mommseni.* Berlin: Weidmann, 1877, 563–69. Reprinted in *Gesammelte Abhandlungen von Jacob Bernays,* vol. 2, ed. H. K. Usener. Berlin: Hertz, 1885; reprint, Hildesheim: Georg Olms, 1971, 71–80.

Bertrand, Daniel A. *La vie grecque d'Adam et d'Eve: Introduction, texte, traduction, et commentaire.* Recherches Intertestamentaires 1. Paris: Librairie Adrien Maisonneuve, 1987.

Bettini, Maurizio. "The Bee, the Moth, and the Bat: Natural Symbols and Representations of the Soul." Pt. 3 of *Anthropology and Roman Culture: Kinship, Time, Images of the Soul,* trans. John van Sickle. Ancient Society and History. Baltimore: Johns Hopkins University Press, 1991.

Betz, Hans Dieter. "Magic and Mystery in the Greek Magical Papyri." In Christopher A. Faraone and Dirk Obbink, eds., *Magika Hiera: Ancient Greek Magic and Religion.* New York: Oxford University Press, 1991, 244–59.

———, ed. *The Greek Magical Papyri in Translation, Including the Demotic Spells.* Chicago: University of Chicago Press, 1986.

Black, M. "The Origin of the Name Metatron." *Vetus Testamentum* 1, no. 3 (1951): 217–19.

Bohak, Gideon. *"Joseph and Aseneth" and the Jewish Temple in Heliopolis.* Early Judaism and Its Literature 10. Atlanta: Scholars Press, 1996.

———. Review of Randall D. Chesnutt, *From Death to Life: Conversion in "Joseph and Aseneth." Ioudaios Review* 5.008, May 1995.

Boswell, John. *Same-Sex Unions in Pre-modern Europe.* New York: Villard Books, 1994.

Bréhier, E. *Les idées philosophes et religieuses de Philo d'Alexandrie.* Paris: Librairie philosophique J. Vrin, 1925. 3d ed., 1950.

Brilliant, Richard. *Gesture and Rank in Roman Art: The Use of Gesture to Denote Status in Roman Sculpture and Coinage.* Memoirs of the Connecticut Academy of Arts and Sciences 14 (February 1963).

Brock, Sebastian P. *The Luminous Eye: The Spiritual World Vision of Saint Ephrem.* Cistercian Studies Series 124. Kalamazoo: Cistercian Publications, 1992.

Brock, Sebastian P., and Susan Ashbrook Harvey. *Holy Women of the Syrian Orient.* Translated, with an introduction. Berkeley: University of California Press, 1987.

Brooks, E. W. *"Joseph and Asenath": The Confession and Prayer of Asenath, Daughter of Pentephres the Priest.* London: Society for Promoting Christian Knowledge; New York: Macmillan, 1918.

Brown, Cheryl Anne. *No Longer Be Silent: First Century Jewish Portraits of Biblical Women.* Gender and the Biblical Tradition. Louisville, KY: Westminster Press, 1992.

Brown, Peter. *The Body and Society: Men, Women, and Sexual Renunciation in Early Christianity.* New York: Columbia University Press, 1988.

Bruneau, P. "Les Israelites de Delos et la juiverie délienne." *BCH* 106 (1982): 465–504.

Budge, E. A. Wallis. *The Book of the Dead.* 2d ed. London: K. Paul, Trench, Trubner; New York: E. P. Dutton, 1923.

Burchard, Christoph. "Der jüdische Asenethroman und seine Nachwirkung: Von Egeria zu Anna Katharina Emmerick oder von Moses aus Aggel zu Karl Kerénye." *ANRW* II.20. 543–648.

_____. *Gesammelte Studien zu Joseph und Asenath.* Studia in Veteris Testamenti Pseudepigrapha 13. Leiden: E. J. Brill, 1996.

_____. "Joseph and Aseneth: A New Translation and Introduction." In James H. Charlesworth, ed., *The Old Testament Pseudepigrapha,* vol. 2. Garden City, NY: Doubleday, 1985, 177–247.

_____. "Joseph und Aseneth." *JSHRZ* 2, no. 4 (1983).

_____. "The Present State of Research on Joseph and Aseneth." In J. Neusner, Peder Borgen, Esnest S. Frerichs, and Richard Horsley, eds., *New Perspectives on Judaism,* vol. 2: *Religion, Literature, and Society in Ancient Israel, Formative Christianity and Judaism: Ancient Israel and Christianity.* Lanham, MD: University Press of America, 1987, 31–52.

_____. *Untersuchungen zu "Joseph und Aseneth," Uberlieferung—Urtsbestimmung.* WUNT 8. Tübingen: Gutersloh, 1965.

_____. "Zum Text von 'Joseph und Aseneth.'" *JSJ* 1, no. 3 (1970): 3–34.

Burrus, Virginia. *Chastity as Autonomy: Women in the Stories of the Apocryphal Act.* Studies in Women and Religion. Lewiston, NY: Edwin Mellen Press, 1987.

Cameron, Averil. *The Later Roman Empire.* Cambridge, MA: Harvard University Press, 1993.

Camp, Claudia. *Wisdom and the Feminine in the Book of Proverbs.* Bible and Literature 11. Sheffield: Almond Press, 1985.

Caquot, A. "L'abeille et le miel dans l'Israel antique." In Remy Chauvin, ed., *Traité de biologie de l'abeille,* vol. 5: *Histoire, ethnographie, et folklore.* Paris: Masson, 1968, 43–49.

Charlesworth, James H. *The Odes of Solomon.* Oxford: Oxford University Press, 1973. Reprint, Text and Translations, Pseudepigrapha Series 7. Missoula, MT: Scholars Press, 1978.

_____. "The Portrayal of the Righteous as an Angel." In J. Collins and G. W. E. Nickelsburg, eds., *Ideal Figures in Ancient Judaism: Profiles and Paradigms.* Chico, CA: Scholars Press, 1980, 135–51.

Chesnutt, Randall D. "Conversion in 'Joseph and Aseneth': Its Nature, Function, and Relation to Contemporaneous Paradigms of Conversion and Initiation." Ph.D. dissertation, Duke University, 1986.

_____. *From Death to Life: Conversion in "Joseph and Aseneth".* Journal for the Study of the Pseudepigrapha Supplement Series 16. Sheffield: Sheffield Academic Press, 1995.

_____. "The Social Setting and Purpose of Joseph and Aseneth." *JSP* 2 (1988): 21–48.

Chiat, Marilyn Joyce Segal. *Handbook of Synagogue Architecture.* Brown Judaic Studies 29. Chico, CA: Scholars Press, 1982.

Chouliara-Raios, Hélène. *L'abeille et le miel en Egypte d'après les Papyrus Grecs.* Ioannina, Greece: Universite de Jannina, 1989.

Clark, Elizabeth A. "Ideology, History, and the Construction of 'Woman' in Christian Antiquity." *JECS* 2, no. 2 (1994): 155–84.

Clark, Mary T. "The Neoplatonism of Marius Victorinus the Christian." In H. J. Blumenthal and R. A. Markus, eds., *Neoplatonism and Early Christian Thought: Esssays in Honour of A. H. Amstrong.* London: Variorum, 1981, 153–59.

Cloke, Gillian. *"This Female Man of God": Women and Spiritual Power in the Patristic Age,* A.D. *350–450.* London: Routledge, 1995.

Cohen, Shaye J. D. "Crossing the Boundary and Becoming a Jew." *HTR* 82 (1989): 13–33.

_____. "The Origins of the Matrilineal Principle in Rabbinic Law." *Association of Jewish Studies Review* 10 (1985): 19–53.

_____. "The Prohibition of Intermarriage from the Bible to the Talmud." *Hebrew Annual Review* 7 (1983): 23–29.

Collins, Adela Yarbro. "The Seven Heavens in Jewish and Christian Apocalypses." In John J. Collins and Michael Fishbane, eds., *Death, Ecstasy, and Other Worldly Journeys: Essays in Memory of Ioan P. Culianu.* Saratoga Springs: SUNY Press, 1995, 57–92.

Collins, John J. "A Throne in the Heavens: Apotheosis in Pre-Christian Judaism." In John J. Collins and Michael Fishbane, eds., *Death, Ecstasy, and Other Worldly Journeys: Essays in Memory of Ioan P. Culianu.* Saratoga Springs: SUNY Press, 1995, 43–58.

Cook, A. B. "The Bee in Greek Mythology." *Journal of Hellenic Studies* 15 (1895): 1–24.

Cooper, Kate. *The Virgin and the Bride: Idealized Womanhood in Late Antiquity.* Cambridge: Harvard University Press, 1996.

Corley, Kathleen E. *Private Women, Public Meals: Social Conflict in the Synoptic Tradition.* Peabody, MA: Hendricksen, 1993.

Corrington, Gail Paterson. *Her Image of Salvation: Female Saviors and Formative Christianity.* Louisville, KY: Westminster Press, 1992.

Crown, Alan D. "Samaritan Religion in the Fourth Century." *NedTTs* 41, no. 1 (1986): 29–47.

_____. "The Samaritans in the Byzantine Orbit." *Bulletin of the John Rylands University Library of Manchester* 69, no. 1 (1989): 96–138.

Cumont, Franz. *Astrology and Religion among the Greeks and Romans.* New York: G. P. Putnam's Sons, 1912. Reprint, New York: Dover Publications, 1960.

_____. *The Mysteries of Mithra.* Trans. Thomas J. McCormack. New York: Dover Publications, 1956.

_____. *Textes et monuments figurés relatifs aux mystères de Mithra.* Brussels: H. Lamertin, 1899.

Davies, Percival Vaughan. *Macrobius: The Saturnalia.* Translated, with an introduction and notes. New York: Columbia University Press, 1969.

Davies, Stevan. *The Revolt of the Widows: The Social World of the Apocryphal Acts of the Apostles.* Champaign-Urbana: University of Illinois Press, 1980.

De Jonge, Marinus. "Patriarchs, Testaments of the Twelve." *ABD* 5:181–86.

_____. *The Testaments of the Twelve Patriarchs: A Study of Their Text, Composition, and Origin.* Leiden: E. J. Brill, 1953.

Delling, G. "Einwirkungen der Sprache der Septuaginta in 'Joseph und Aseneth.'" *JSJ* 9 (1978): 29–56.

Denis, Albert-Marie. *Concordance grecque des pseudépigraphes d'ancien testament: Concordance, corpus des textes, indices.* Avec la collaboration d'Yvonne Janssens et le concours du CETEDOC. Louvain-la-Neuve: Université Catholique de Louvain, 1987.

Des Places, Edouard, ed. *Oracles Chaldaiques: Avec un choix de commentaires anciens.* Paris: Les Belles Lettres, 1971.

Devos, P. "La date du voyage d'Egerie." *Analecta Bollandiana* 85 (1967): 105–43.

Dodds, E. R. *Pagan and Christian in an Age of Anxiety: Some Aspects of Religious Experience from Marcus Aurelius to Constantine.* Cambridge: Cambridge University Press, 1965. Reprint, New York: W. W. Norton, 1970.

Doody, Margaret Anne. *The True Story of the Novel.* New Brunswick, NJ: Rutgers University Press, 1996.

Dothan, Moshe. *Hammath Tiberias: Early Synagogues and the Hellenistic and Roman Remains.* Jerusalem: Israel Exploration Society, 1983.

Doty, Susan Elizabeth Hog. "From Ivory Tower to City of Refuge: The Role and Function of the Protagonist in 'Joseph and Aseneth' and Related Narratives." Ph.D. Dissertation, Iliff School of Theology and University of Denver, 1989.

Douglas, Mary. *Natural Symbols: Explorations in Cosmology.* London: Barrie and Rockcliffe; New York: Pantheon, 1970. Reprint, 1973.

Drijvers, Hans J. W. "Marcionism in Syria: Principles, Problems, Polemics." *The Second Century* 6 (1987/88): 153–72.

_____. "Odes of Solomon and Psalms of Mani: Christians and Manichaeans in Third-Century Syria." In R. van den Broek and M. J. Vermaseren, eds., *Studies in Gnosticism and Hellenistic Religions Presented to G. Quispel on the Occasion of His 65th Birthday.* EPRO 91. Leiden: E. J. Brill, 1981, 117–30.

Duchesne, L. Review of "Le Livre de la Prière d'Aseneth," by P. Batiffol. *Bulletin Critique* 10 (1889): 461–66.

Egger, Brigitte. "Women and Marriage in the Greek Novels: The Boundaries of Romance." In James Tatum, ed., *The Search for the Ancient Novel.* Baltimore: Johns Hopkins University Press, 1994, 260–80.

Elderkin, G. "The Bee of Artemis." *American Journal of Philology* 60 (1939): 203–13.

Elior, Rachel. "Mysticism, Magic and Angelology: The Perception of Angels in Hekhalot Literature." *Jewish Studies Quarterly* 1, no. 1 (1993): 3–53.

_____. Review of *Faces of the Chariot,* by David Halperin. *Numen* 37 (1990): 241–47.

Elliott, J. K. *The Apocryphal New Testament: A Collection of Apocryphal Christian Literature in an English Translation.* Oxford: Clarendon Press; New York: Oxford University Press, 1993.

Fauth, W. "Tatrosjah-Totrosjah und Metatron in der jüdischen Merkabah-Mystik." *JSJ* 22, no. 1 (1991): 40–87.

Feldman, Louis. *Jew and Gentile in the Ancient World.* Princeton, NJ: Princeton University Press, 1993.

_____. "'Jewish Sympathisers' in Classical Literature and Inscriptions." *TAPA* 81 (1950): 200–208.

_____. "The Omnipresence of the God-fearers." *BAR* 12, no. 5 (Sept./Oct. 1986): 58–63.

_____. "Proselytes and Sympathizers in the Light of the New Inscriptions from Aphrodisias." *REJ* 148 (1989): 265–305.

Finn, T. M. "The Godfearers Reconsidered." *CBQ* 47 (1985): 75–84.

Fossum, Jarl E. *The Name of God and the Angel of the Lord: Samaritan and Jewish Concepts of Intermediation and the Origin of Gnosticism.* Tübingen: J. C. B. Mohr (Paul Siebeck), 1985.

Fowden, Garth. *Empire to Commonwealth: Consequences of Monotheism in Late Antiquity.* Princeton, NJ: Princeton University Press, 1993.

Franzman, Majella. *"The Odes of Solomon": An Analysis of the Poetical Structure and Form.* Novum Testamentum et Orbis Antiquus 20, Freiburg: Universitätsverlag; Göttingen: Vandenhoeck and Ruprecht, 1991.

_____. "'Wipe the Harlotry from Your Faces': A Brief Note on Ode of Solomon 13.3." *ZNW* 77 (1986): 282–83.

Freedman, H. *Midrash Rabbah: Genesis.* 3d ed. London: Soncino Press, 1983.

Friberg, Jöran. "Numbers and Counting." *ABD* 4:1139–46.

Friedlander, Gerald. *Pirḳê de Rabbi Eliezer: The Chapters of Rabbi Eliezer the Great.* London, 1916. Reprint, New York: Sepher-Hermon Press, 1981.

Gager, John G. *Curse Tablets and Binding Spells from the Ancient World.* New York: Oxford University Press, 1992.

———. *The Origins of Anti-Semitism: Attitudes toward Judaism in Pagan and Christian Antiquity.* New York: Oxford University Press, 1983.

Gallagher, Eugene V. "Conversion and Community in Late Antiquity." *Journal of Religion* 73, no. 1 (1993): 1–15.

Geerard, Maurice. *Clavis Patrum Graecorum.* Turnhout: Brepols, 1974–83.

Ginsberg, Louis. *Legends of the Jews.* Trans. Henrietta Szold. Vol. 3, trans. Paul Radin. 7 vols. Philadelphia: Jewish Publication Society, 1909–38.

Goodenough, Erwin Ramsdell. *Jewish Symbols in the Greco-Roman Period.* Bollingen Series 37. 13 volumes. New York: Pantheon, 1953–68. Vol. 13, Princeton, NJ: Princeton University Press, 1968.

Goodman, Martin. *Mission and Conversion: Proselytizing in the Religious History of the Roman Empire.* Oxford: Clarendon Press, 1994.

———. Review of Joyce Reynolds and Robert Tannenbaum, *Jews and Godfearers at Aphrodisias: Greek Inscriptions with Commentary. JRS* 78 (1988): 261–62.

Graf, Fritz. "Prayer in Magical and Religious Ritual." In Christopher A. Faraone and Dirk Obbink, eds., *Magika Hiera: Ancient Greek Magic and Religion.* New York: Oxford University Press, 1991, 188–97.

Greenberg, Moshe. *Biblical Prose Prayer as a Window to the Popular Religion of Ancient Israel.* Berkeley: University of California Press, 1983.

Grossfeld, Bernard. *The Targum Onqelos to Genesis.* Translated, with a critical introduction, apparatus, and notes. Aramaic Bible, vol. 6. Wilmington, DE: Michael Glazier, 1988.

Gruenwald, Ithamar. "Sefer Ha-Razim." In *Apocalyptic and Merkavah Mysticism.* Leiden: E. J. Brill, 1980, 225–34.

———."ראיית יחזקאל" (The visions of Ezekiel; in Hebrew). In Israel Weinstock, ed., *Temirin: Texts and Studies in Kabbala and Hasidim,* vol. 1. Jerusalem: Mossad Harav Kook, 1972.

Gurtler, Gary M. *Plotinus: The Experience of Unity.* New York: Peter Lang, 1989.

Hachlili, Rachel. "The Zodiac in Ancient Jewish Art: Representation and Significance." *BASOR* 28 (Dec. 1977): 61–77.

Hall, R. G. "Installation of the Archangel Michael." *Coptic Church Review* 5 (1984): 108–11.

———. "Isaiah's Ascent to See the Beloved: An Ancient Jewish Source for the Ascension of Isaiah." *JBL* 113, no. 3 (1994): 463–84.

Halperin, David J. *The Faces of the Chariot: Early Jewish Responses to Ezekiel's Vision.* Tübingen: J. C. B. Mohr (Paul Siebeck), 1988.

Halsberghe, G. H. *The Cult of Sol Invictus.* EPRO 23. Leiden: E. J. Brill, 1972.

Hamilton, F. J., and E. W. Brooks. *The Syriac Chronicle Known as That of Zachariah of Mitylene.* London: Methuen, 1899. Reprint, New York: AMS Press, 1979.

Hamilton, Victor P. "Marriage (OT and ANE)." *ABD* 4:559–69.

Hanfman, G. F. *The Seasons Sarcophagus in Dumbarton Oaks.* Cambridge, MA: Harvard University Press, 1951.

Haspels, Carolyn Henriette Emilie. *The Highlands of Phrygia: Sites and Monuments.* Princeton, NJ: Princeton Unversity Press, 1971.

Hatch, Edwin, and Henry A. Redpath. *A Concordance to the Septuagint and the Other Greek Versions of the Old Testament (Including the Apocryphal Books).* 2 vols. Oxford, 1897; supplements, 1900–1906. Reprint, Graz: Akademische Druck-Verlagsanstalt, 1954.

Hayward, Robert. "The Date of Targum Pseudo-Jonathan: Some Comments." *JJS* 40 (1989): 7–30.

Himmelfarb, Martha. *Ascent to Heaven in Jewish and Christian Apocalypses.* New York: Oxford University Press, 1992.

_____. "Heavenly Ascent and the Relationship of the Apocalypses and the *Hekhalot* Literature." *HUCA* 59 (1988): 73–100.

_____. "The Practice of Ascent in the Ancient Mediterranean World." In John J. Collins and Michael Fishbane, eds., *Death, Ecstasy, and Other Worldly Journeys: Essays in Memory of Ioan P. Culianu.* Saratoga Springs: SUNY Press, 1995, 123–37.

_____. Review of *Faces of the Chariot* by David Halperin. *Critical Review of Books in Religion* 3 (1990): 340–42.

_____. *Tours of Hell.* Philadelphia: University of Pennsylvania Press, 1983.

Holladay, Carl R. *Fragments from Hellenistic Jewish Authors.* vol. 1: *Historians.* Text and Translations 20, Pseudepigraphia Series 10. Chico, CA: Scholars Press, 1983.

Hopkins, Keith M. "Brother-Sister Marriage in Roman Egypt." *Comparative Studies in Society and History* 22 (1980): 303–54.

Horbury, William, and David Noy. *Jewish Inscriptions of Graeco-Roman Egypt.* Cambridge: Cambridge University Press, 1992.

Humphrey, Edith M. *The Ladies and the Cities: Transformation and Apocalyptic Identity in "Joseph and Aseneth," 4 Ezra, The Apocalypse, and "The Shepherd."* Sheffield: Sheffield Academic Press, 1995.

Hurtado, Larry. *One God, One Lord: Early Christian Devotion and Ancient Jewish Monotheism.* Philadelphia: Fortress Press, 1988.

Ilan, Tal. *Jewish Women in Greco-Roman Palestine: An Inquiry into Image and Status.* Texte und Studien zum Antiken Judentum 44. Tübingen: J. C. B. Mohr (Paul Siebeck), 1995.

Israelstam, J. and Judah J. Slotki. *Midrash Rabbah: Leviticus.* 3d ed. London: Soncino Press, 1983.

Jastrow, M. *Dictionary of Talmud Bavli, Yerushalmi, Midrashic Literature, and Targumim.* 2 vols. 1903. Reprint, New York: Pardes, 1950.

Jellinek, A. *Bet ha-Midrash.* Vienna, 1853–57. Reprint, Jerusalem, 1967.

Johnston, Sarah Iles. "Rising to the Occasion: Theurgic Ascent in Its Cultural Milieu." In Peter Schäfer and Hans G. Kippenberg, eds., *Envisioning Magic: A Princeton Seminar and Symposium.* Leiden: E. J. Brill, 1997, 165–94.

Kantorowicz, Ernst H. "Oriens Augusti—Lever du Roi." *Dumbarton Oaks Papers* 17 (1963): 119–77.

Kearsley, Rosalinde A. "Angels in Asia Minor: The Cult of Hosios and Dikaios." *NewDocs* 6 (1992): 206–9.

_____. "Asiarchs, Ἀρχιερεῖς, and the Ἀρχιερεῖαι of Asia." *Greek, Roman, and Byzantine Studies* 27 (1986): 183–92.

_____. "Asiarchs, Archiereis, and Archiereiai of Asia: New Evidence from Amorium in Phrygia." *Epigraphica Anatolia* 16 (1990): 69–80.

Kee, Howard C. "The Socio-Cultural Setting of 'Joseph and Aseneth.'" *New Testament Studies* 29 (1983): 394–413.

_____. "The Socio-Religious Setting and Aims of 'Joseph and Asenath.'" In *SBL Seminar Papers.* Missoula, MT: Scholars Press, 1976, 183–92.

Kenny, John Peter. *Mystical Monotheism: A Study in Ancient Platonic Theology.* Hanover, NH: University Press of New England (for Brown University Press), 1991.

King, Karen, ed. *Images of the Feminine in Gnosticism.* Philadelphia: Fortress Press, 1988.

Klijn, A. F. J. *The Acts of Thomas: Introduction, Text, Commentary.* Supplement 5 to *Novum Testamentum.* Leiden: E. J. Brill, 1962.

Knight, Chris H., "Towards a Critical Introduction to 'The History of the Rechabites.'" *JSJ* 26, no. 3 (1995): 324–42.

Kohler, K. "Asenath, Life and Confession or Prayer Of." *Jewish Encyclopedia.* Vol. 2. 1902, 172–76.

Konstan, David. *Sexual Symmetry: Love in the Ancient Novel and Related Genres.* Princeton, NJ: Princeton University Press, 1994.

Kraabel, A. Thomas. "The Disappearance of the 'God-fearers.'" *Numen* 28 (1981): 113–26. Reprinted in Andrew Overman and R. S. MacLennan, eds., *Diaspora Judaism: Essays in Honor of and in Dialogue with A. Thomas Kraabel.* South Florida Studies in Judaism. Atlanta: Scholars Press, 1992, 119–30.

_____. "New Evidence on the Samaritan Diaspora Has Been Found on Delos." *BA* 47 (March 1984): 44–46. Reprinted in Andrew Overman and R. S. MacLennan, eds., *Diaspora Judaism: Essays in Honor of and in Dialogue with A. Thomas Kraabel.* South Florida Studies in Judaism. Atlanta: Scholars Press, 1992, 331–34.

_____. "The Roman Diaspora: Six Questionable Assumptions." *JJS* 33, no. 1/2 (1982): 445–64. Reprinted in Andrew Overman and R. S. MacLennan, eds., *Diaspora Judaism: Essays in Honor of and in Dialogue with A. Thomas Kraabel.* South Florida Studies in Judaism. Atlanta: Scholars Press, 1992, 1–20.

Kraemer, Ross S. "The Conversion of Women to Ascetic Forms of Christianity." *Signs: Journal of Women in Culture and Society* 6, no. 2 (1980): 298–307. Reprinted in Judith M. Bennet, Elizabeth A. Clark, Jean O'Barr, B. Anne Vilen, and Sarah Westphal-Wihl, eds., *Sisters and Workers in the Middle Ages.* Chicago: University of Chicago Press, 1989, 198–207.

_____. *Her Share of the Blessings: Women's Religions among Pagans, Jews, and Christians in the Greco-Roman World.* New York: Oxford University Press, 1992.

_____. "Jewish Mothers and Daughters in the Greco-Roman World." In Shaye J. D. Cohen, ed., *The Jewish Family in Antiquity.* Brown Judaic Studies 289. Atlanta: Scholars Press, 1993, 89–112.

_____. "Jewish Tuna and Christian Fish: Identifying Religious Affiliation in Epigraphic Sources." *HTR* 84, no. 2 (1991): 141–62.

_____. *Maenads, Martyrs, Matrons, Monastics: A Sourcebook of Women's Religions in the Greco-Roman World.* Philadelphia: Fortress Press, 1988.

_____. "Monastic Jewish Women in Greco-Roman Egypt: Philo on the Therapeutrides." *Signs: Journal of Women in Culture and Society* 14, no. 1 (1989): 342–70.

_____. "On the Meaning of the Term 'Jew' in Greco-Roman Inscriptions." *HTR* 82, no. 1 (1989): 35–53. Reprinted in Andrew Overman and R. S. MacLennan, eds., *Diaspora Judaism: Essays in Honor of and in Dialogue with A. Thomas Kraabel.* South Florida Studies in Judaism. Atlanta: Scholars Press, 1992, 311–29.

_____. "Women's Authorship of Jewish and Christian Literature in the Greco-Roman Period." In Amy-Jill Levine, ed., *"Women Like This": New Perspectives on Jewish Women in the Greco-Roman Period.* Early Judaism and Its Literature 1. Atlanta: Scholars Press, 1991, 221–42.

Kraft, Robert A. "The Pseudepigrapha in Christianity." In John Reeves, ed., *Tracing the Threads: Studies in the Vitality of Jewish Pseudepigrapha.* Early Judaism and Its Literature 6. Atlanta: Scholars Press, 1994, 55–86. Also available electronically at http://ccat.sas.upenn.edu/rs/rak/kraft.html.

Kugel, James. *In Potiphar's House: The Interpretive Life of Biblical Texts.* San Francisco: Harper Collins, 1990. Reprint, Cambridge, MA: Harvard University Press, 1994.

_____. "Levi's Elevation to the Priesthood in Second Temple Writings." *HTR* 86 (1993): 1–64.

_____. "The Story of Dinah in the *Testament of Levi.*" *HTR* 85 (1992): 1–34.

Kugel, James, and Rowan A. Greer. *Early Biblical Interpretation.* Philadelphia: Westminster Press, 1986.

Lamberton, Robert. *Homer the Theologian: Neoplatonic Allegorical Reading.* Berkeley: University of California Press, 1986.

Lampe, G. W. H. *A Patristic Greek Lexicon.* Oxford: Clarendon Press, 1961–68.

Layton, Bentley. *The Gnostic Scriptures: A New Translation.* London: SCM; Garden City, NY: Doubleday, 1987.

Lefebure, E. "L'abeille en Egypte." *Sphinx* 11 (1908): 1–25.

Leibovici, M. "L'abeille et le miel dans l'histoire des religions." In Remy Chauvin, ed., *Traité de biologie de l'abeille.* Vol. 5: *Histoire, ethnographie, et folklore.* Paris: Masson, 1968, 35–40.

Lesses, Rebecca. "The Adjuration of the Prince of the Presence: Performative Utterance in a Jewish Ritual." In Marvin Meyer and Paul Mirecki, eds., *Ancient Magic and Ritual Power,* Religions in the Greco-Roman World 129. Leiden: E. J. Brill, 1995, 185–206.

Levine, A.-J. "Diaspora as Metaphor: Bodies and Boundaries in the Book of Tobit." In Andrew Overman and R. S. MacLennan, eds., *Diaspora Judaism: Essays in Honor of and in Dialogue with A. Thomas Kraabel,* South Florida Studies in Judaism. Atlanta: Scholars Press, 1992, 105–17.

Levison, John R. "The Exoneration of Eve in the 'Apocalypse of Moses' 15–30." *JSJ* 20, no. 2 (1989): 135–50.

Lewis, Agnes Smith. *Select Narratives of Holy Women from the Syro-Antiochene or Sinar Palimpsest, as Written above the Old Syriac Gospels by John the Stylite, of Beth-Mari-Qanun in A.D. 778.* London: C. J. Clay and Sons, 1900.

Leyerle, Blake. "John Chrysostom on the Gaze." *JECS* 1, no. 2 (1993): 159–74.

Lieberman, Saul. *Greek in Jewish Palestine: Studies in the Life and Manners of Jewish Palestine in the II–IV Centuries C.E.* Philadelphia: Jewish Publication Society, 1942. Reprinted in *Greek in Jewish Palestine/Hellenism in Jewish Palestine,* with an introduction by Dov Zlotnick. New York: The Jewish Theological Seminary of America, 1994.

———. *Hellenism in Jewish Palestine: Studies in the Literary Transmission, Beliefs, and Manners of Palestine in the I Century B.C.E.—IV Century C.E.* New York: Jewish Theological Seminary of America, 1950. Reprinted in *Greek in Jewish Palestine/Hellenism Jewish Palestine,* with an introduction by Dov Zlotnick. New York: Jewish Theological Seminary of America, 1994.

———. "Metatron: The Meaning of His Name and His Functions." In Itamar Gruenwald, ed., *Apocalyptic and Merkavah Mysticism.* Leiden: E. J. Brill, 1980, 235–41.

Lifshitz, Baruch. "Du nouveau sur les 'sympathisants'." *JSJ* 1 (1970): 77–84.

———. "Prolegomenon" to Jean-Baptiste Frey, ed., *Corpus Inscriptionum Judaicarum: Jewish Inscriptions from the Third Century B.C. to the Seventh Century A.D.* Vol. 1: *Europe.* Rome: Pontifico Istituto di Archaeologia Cristiana, 1936. Reprint, New York: KTAV Publishing House, 1975, 21–104.

Lightstone, Jack. *The Commerce of the Sacred: Mediation of the Divine among Jews in the Graeco-Roman Diaspora.* Brown Judaic Studies 59. Chico, CA: Scholars Press, 1984.

Linder, Amnon. *The Jews in Imperial Roman Legislation.* Edited, with introductions, translation, and commentary. Detroit: Wayne State University Press; Jerusalem: Israel Academy of Sciences and Humanities, 1987.

Lloyd, A. C. *The Anatomy of Neoplatonism.* Oxford: Clarendon Press, 1990.

L'Orange, H. P. "Sol Invictus Imperator. Ein Beitrag zur Apotheose." *Symbolae Osloenses* 14 (1935): 86–114.

———. *Studies on the Iconography of Cosmic Kingship in the Ancient World.* Instituttet for Sammenlignende Kulturforskning. Serie A: Forelesninger 23. Oslo: H. Aschehoug (W. Nygaard), 1953.

Louw, Johannes P., and Eugene A. Nida. *A Greek-English Lexicon of the New Testament Based on Semantic Domains.* New York: United Bible Societies, 1988.

Luck, Georg. "Theurgy and Forms of Worship in Neoplatonism." In Jacob Neusner, Ernst

Frerichs, and Paul Virgil McCracken Flesher, eds., *Religion, Science, and Magic: In Concert and in Conflict*. New York: Oxford University Press, 1989, 185–225.

MacDonald, Dennis Ronald. *The Acts of Andrew and the Acts of Andrew and Matthias in the City of the Cannibals*. Texts and Translations 33. Christian Apocrypha Series 1. Atlanta: Scholars Press, 1990.

_____. *The Legend and the Apostle: The Battle for Paul in Story and Canon*. Philadelphia: Westminster Press, 1983.

MacLennan, R. S., and A. T. Kraabel. "The God-fearers: A Literary and Theological Invention." *BAR* 12, no. 5 (Sept./Oct. 1986): 46–53.

MacMullen, Ramsay. *Christianizing the Roman Empire, A.D. 100–400*. New Haven: Yale University Press, 1984.

_____. "Women in Public in the Roman Empire." *Historia* 29 (1980): 208–18.

Maher, Michael. *Targum Pseudo-Jonathan: Genesis*. Translated, with introduction and notes. Aramaic Bible, vol. 1B. Collegeville, MN: Liturgical Press, 1992.

Majercik, Ruth. *The Chaldean Oracles: Text, Translation, and Commentary*. Studies in Greek and Roman Religion 5. Leiden: E. J. Brill, 1989.

Margolioth, Mordecai. *Sepher ha-Razim: A Newly Discovered Book of Magic from the Talmudic Period*. Jerusalem, 1966 (Hebrew).

Markus, Robert. *The End of Ancient Christianity*. Cambridge: Cambridge University Press, 1990.

Massebieau, L. "Comte-rendu de l'édition de Batiffol," *Annales de Bibliographie Théologique* 11 (1889): 161–72.

Mattingly, Harold. *Coins of the Roman Empire in the British Museum*. London: Trustees of the British Museum, 1950.

McKnight, Scot. *A Light to the Nations: Jewish Missionary Activity in the Second Temple Period*. Minneapolis: Fortress Press, 1991.

McNamara, Martin. *Targum Neofiti 1: Genesis*. Translated, with apparatus and notes. Aramaic Bible, vol. 1A. Collegeville, MN: Liturgical Press, 1992.

McVey, Kathleen, ed. and trans. *Ephrem the Syrian, Hymns*. The Classics of Western Spirituality. Mahwah, NJ: Paulist Press, 1989.

Meeks, Wayne. "The Image of the Androgyne: Some Uses of a Symbol in Earliest Christianity." *History of Religions* 13, no. 3 (1974): 165–208.

Merkur, Daniel. "The Visionary Practices of Jewish Apocalyptists." In L. Bryce Boyer and Simon A. Grolnick, eds., *The Psychoanalytic Study of Society*, vol. 14. Hillsdale, NJ: Analytic Press, 1989.

Meredith, Anthony. "Porphyry and Julian against the Christians." *ANRW* II.23.2: 1119–49.

Meyers, Carol. "Temple, Jerusalem." *ABD* 6:350–69.

Millar, Fergus. *The Roman Near East, 31 BC–AD 337*. Cambridge, MA: Harvard University Press, 1993.

Mitchell, Stephen. *Anatolia: Land, Men, and Gods in Asia Minor*. Vol. 2: *The Rise of the Church*. Oxford: Clarendon Press, 1993.

Morgan, Michael. *Sepher ha-Razim: The Book of the Mysteries*. Texts and Translations 25, Pseudepigrapha Series 11. Chico, CA: Scholars Press, 1983.

Morray-Jones, Christopher. "Paradise Revisited (2 Cor 12:1–12) The Jewish Mystical Background of Paul's Apostolate, part 1." 177–217.

_____. "Transformational Mysticism in the Apocalyptic-Merkabah Tradition." *JJS* 43, no. 1 (1992): 1–31.

Murphy, Frederick J. *Pseudo-Philo: Rewriting the Bible*. New York: Oxford University Press, 1993.

Murphy-O'Connor, Jerome. "Lots of God-fearers? Theosebeis in the Aphrodisias Inscription." *Revue Biblique* 99 (1992): 418–24.

Neusner, Jacob. *Aphrahat and Judaism: The Christian–Jewish Argument in Fourth-Century Iran.* Leiden: E. J. Brill, 1971.

_____. *Genesis Rabbah: The Judaic Commentary to the Book of Genesis: A New American Translation.* 3 vols. Brown Judaic Studies 106. Atlanta: Scholars Press, 1985.

_____. *The Mishnah: A New Translation.* New Haven: Yale University Press, 1988.

Newman, Carey. *Paul's Glory-Christology: Tradition and Rhetoric.* Leiden: E. J. Brill, 1992.

Newsom, Carol. *Songs of the Sabbath Sacrifice: A critical edition.* Harvard Semitic Studies 27. Atlanta: Scholars Press, 1985.

Nickelsburg, G. W. E. *Resurrection, Immortality, and Eternal Life in Intertestamental Judaism.* Cambridge: Harvard University Press, 1972.

Niehoff, Maren. "The Figure of Joseph in the Targums," *JJS* 28 (1988): 234–50.

North, Helen. *Sophrosyne: Self-Knowledge and Self-Restraint in Greek Literature.* Ithaca: Cornell University Press, 1966.

Noy, David. *Jewish Inscriptions from Western Europe,* Vol. 2: *The City of Rome.* Cambridge: Cambridge University Press, 1995.

Odeberg, H. *3 Enoch.* Cambridge: Cambridge University Press, 1928. Reprint, New York: KTAV, 1973.

Oppenheim, G. *Fabuli Josephi et Asenathae apocrypha e libro Syriaco Latine versa.* Berlin, 1886.

Overman, J. A. "The Godfearers: Some Neglected Features," *JSNT* 32 (1988): 17–26.

Parry, Donald W., Stephen D. Ricks, and John W. Welch. *A Bibliography of Temples of the Ancient Near East and Mediterranean World.* Lewiston, NY: Edwin Mellen Press, 1991.

Perkins, Judith. *The Suffering Self: Pain and Narrative Representation in the Early Christian Era.* London: Routledge, 1995.

Pervo, Richard I. "The Ancient Novel Becomes Christian." In Gareth Schmeling, ed., *The Novel in the Ancient World.* Mnemosyne, Bibliotheca Classica Batava Supplement 159. Leiden: E. J. Brill, 1996, 685–712.

_____. "Joseph and Asenath and the Greek Novel." In SBL *Seminar Papers.* Missoula, MT: Scholars Press, 1976, 171–81.

Phillips, C. R., III. *"Nullum Crimen Sine Lege:* Socioreligious Sanctions on Magic." In Chris Faraone and Dirk Obbink, eds., *Magika Hiera: Ancient Greek Magic and Religion.* New York: Oxford University Press, 1991, 260–76.

Philonenko, Marc. "Initiation et mystère dans 'Joseph et Aséneth.'" In C. J. Bleeker, ed., *Initiation.* Supplements to *Numen,* Studies in the History of Religions 10. Leiden: E. J. Brill, 1965, 147–53.

_____. "Joseph and Asenath." *Encyclopedia Judaica.* Vol. 10. Jerusalem: Macmillan, 1971–72, cols. 223–24.

_____. *"Joseph et Aséneth": Introduction, texte critique, traduction, et notes.* Studia Postbiblica. Leiden: E. J. Brill, 1968.

_____. "'Joseph et Aséneth': Questions actuelles." In W. C. van Unnik, ed., *La littérature entre Tenach et Mischna: Quelques problems.* Leiden: E. J. Brill, 1974, 73–76.

_____. "Joseph und Asenath." In B. Reicke and L. Rost, eds., *Biblisch-historisches Handwörterbuch: Landeskunde, Geschichte, Religion, Kultur, Literatur.* Vol. 2. Göttingen: Vandenhoeck and Ruprecht, 1962–66, cols. 889–90.

_____. "Le 'Testament de Job' et les Thérapeutes." *Semitica* 8 (1958): 41–53.

_____. "Un mystère juif?" In *Mystères et syncrétismes.* Etudes d'histoire des religions 2. Paris: Guethner, 1975, 65–70.

Poirier, Paul-Hubert. *L'hymne de la perle des "Actes de Thomas": Introduction, texte, traduction, commentaire.* Louvain-la-Neuve: [Centre d'histoire des religions], 1981.

Pomeroy, Sarah B. "The Persian King and the Queen Bee." *AJAH* 9 (1984): 98–108.

Porton, Gary. "Defining Midrash." In Jacob Neusner, ed., *Study of Ancient Judaism.* Vol. 1. New York: KTAV, 1981.

Preisendanz, Karl. ed. *Papyri Graecae Magicae. Die Griechischen Zauberpapyri.* 2d ed. 2 vols. Stuttgart: Teubner, 1973–74.

Puech, Emile. *La croyance des Esséniens en la vie future: Immortalité, resurrection, vie éternelle? Histoire d'une croyance dans le judaïsme ancien.* Etudes Bibliques N.s. 21–22. Paris: Librairie Lecoffre, 1993.

Pummer, Reinhard. "Inscriptions." In Alan D. Crown, ed., *The Samaritans.* Tübingen: J. C. B. Mohr (Paul Siebeck), 1989, 190–94.

Ramsay, William Mitchell. *Cities and Bishoprics of Phrygia.* Vol. 1, pt. 2. Oxford: Clarendon Press, 1895–97. Reprint, New York: Arno Press, 1975.

Ransome, Hilda. *The Sacred Bee in Ancient Times and Folklore.* London: Allen and Unwin, 1937; reprint, Bridgwater, Eng., 1986.

Reardon, B. P., ed. *Collected Ancient Greek Novels.* Berkeley: University of California Press, 1989.

Reissler, P. "Joseph und Asenath. Eine altjüdische Erzählung." *TQ* 103 (1922): 1–22, 145–83.

Reynolds, Joyce, and Robert Tannanbaum. *Jews and Godfearers at Aphrodisias: Greek Inscriptions with Commentary.* Suppl. vol. 12. Cambridge: Cambridge Philological Society, 1987.

Rist, J. M. *Plotinus: The Road to Reality.* Cambridge: Cambridge University Press, 1977.

Robert, Louis. *Opera Minora Selecta: Epigraphie et antiquités grecques.* 7 vols. Amsterdam: A. M. Hakkert, 1969–90.

_____. "Reliefs, votifs, et cultes d'Anatolie." *Anatolia: Revue Annuelle d'Archéologie* 3 (1958): 137–44.

Rordorf, Willy. "Tertullien et les Actes de Paul (à propos de *Bapt.* 17, 5)." In *Lex Orandi, Lex Credendi: Paradosis: Beiträge zur Geschichte der altchristlichen Literatur und Theologie XXXVI.* Gesammelte Aufsätze zum 60. Geburtstag. Freiburg: Universitätsverlag, 1993, 475–84.

Rosen, Gladys Levine, ed. and trans. "The Joseph Cycle (Genesis 37–45) in the Samaritan-Arabic Commentary of Meshalma ibn Murjan." Ph.D. dissertation, Columbia University, 1951.

Rousselle, Aline. *Porneia: On Desire and the Body in Antiquity.* Trans. Felicia Pheasant. London: Basil Blackwell, 1987.

Rubin, Gayle. "The Traffic in Women: Notes on the 'Political Economy' of Sex." In Rayna R. Reiter, ed., *Toward an Anthropology of Women.* New York: Monthly Review Press, 1975, 157–211.

Sandelin, Karl-Gustav. "A Wisdom Meal in the Romance 'Joseph and Aseneth.'" In *Wisdom as Nourisher: A Study of the Old Testament Theme, Its Development within Early Judaism, and Its Impact on Early Christianity.* Abo, Sweden: Abo Akademi, 1986, 151–57.

Sänger, Dietrich. *Antikes Judentum und die Mysterien: Religionsgechichtliche Untersuchungen zu "Joseph und Aseneth."* WUNT 2.5. Tübingen: J. C. B. Mohr (Paul Siebeck), 1980.

_____. "Bekehrung und Exodus: Zum jüdischen Traditionshintergrund von 'Joseph und Aseneth.'" *JSJ* 10 (1979): 11–36.

_____. "Erwagungen zur historiche Einordnung und zur Datierung von 'Joseph und Aseneth.'" *ZNTW* 76 (1985): 86–106 = Colloque de Strasbourg 1983 (Paris, 1985), 181–202.

_____. "Jüdisch-hellenistiche missionsliteratur und die Weisheit." *Kairos* 23 (1981): 231–42.

Sappington, Thomas J. *Revelation and Redemption at Colossae.* JSNT Supplement Series 53. Sheffield: JSOT Press, 1991.

Schäfer, Peter. "The Aim and Purpose of Early Jewish Mysticism." In *Hekhalot-Studien*. Texte und Studien zum Antiken Judentum 19. Tübingen, J. C. B. Mohr (Paul Siebeck), 1988, 277–95.

_____. *The Hidden and Manifest God: Some Major Themes in Early Jewish Mysticism*. Trans. Aubrey Pomerance. Albany: SUNY Press, 1992. Originally published as *Der verborgene und offenbare Gott: Haupthemen der frühen jüdischen Mystik*. Tübingen: J. C. B. Mohr (Paul Siebeck), 1991.

_____. "Jewish Magic Literature in Late Antiquity and Early Middle Ages." *JJS* 41 (1990): 75–91.

_____. *Synopse zur Hekhalot-Literatur in Zusammenarbeit mit Margarete Schlüter und Hans Georg von Mutius: Herausgegeben von Peter Schäfer*. Texte und Studien zum Antiken Judentum 2. Tübingen: J. C. B. Mohr (Paul Siebeck), 1981.

_____. "Tradition and Redaction in Hekhalot Literature." In *Hekhalot-Studien*. Texte und Studien zum Antiken Judentum 19. Tübingen: J. C. B. Mohr (Paul Siebeck), 1988, 8–16.

Schalit, A. "A Clash of Ideologies." In A. Toynbee, ed., *The Crucible of Christianity: Judaism, Hellenism, and the Historical Background to the Christian Faith*. New York: World Publishing Co., 1969, 47–76.

Schmeling, Gareth, ed. *The Novel in the Ancient World*. Mnemosyne, Bibliotheca Classica Batava Supplement 159. Leiden: E. J. Brill, 1996.

Scholem, Gershom. *Major Trends in Jewish Mysticism*. 3d ed. New York: Schocken Books, 1954. Reprint, 1960.

Schürer, Emil. *The History of the Jewish People in the Age of Jesus Christ (175 B.C.–A.D. 135)*. Ed. Geza Vermes, Fergus Millar, Matthew Black, and Pamela Vermes. 3 vols. London: T. & T. Clark, 1973–87.

Schwartz, Jacques. "Recherches sur l'évolution du roman de 'Joseph et Aseneth.'" *REJ* 143 (1984): 273–85.

Scott, Alan. *Origen and the Life of the Stars: A History of an Idea*. Oxford: Clarendon Press, 1991.

Seigert, F. "Gottesfürchtige und Sympathisanten." *JSJ* 4 (1973): 109–64.

Segal, Alan. "Heavenly Ascent." *ANRW* II.23.2, 1333–94.

_____. "Paul and the Beginning of Jewish Mysticism." In John J. Collins and Michael Fishbane, eds., *Death, Ecstasy, and Other Worldly Journeys: Essays in Memory of Ioan P. Culianu*. Saratoga Springs: SUNY Press, 1995, 95–122.

_____. *Paul the Convert: The Apostolate and Apostasy of Saul the Pharisee*. New Haven: Yale University Press, 1990.

Seyrig, H. "Le culte du Soleil en Syrie à l'époque romaine." *Syria* 48 (1971): 337–73.

Shaw, Brent. "Body/Power/Identity: The Passions of the Martyrs." *JECS* 4, no. 3 (1996): 269–312.

Shaw, Gregory. *Theurgy and the Soul: The Neoplatonism of Iamblichus*. State College: Pennsylvania State University Press, 1995.

Sheppard, A. R.R. "Pagan Cults of Angels in Roman Asia Minor." *Talanta* 12–13 (1980–81): 77–101.

Shinan, A. "Dating Targum Pseudo-Jonathan: Some More Comments." *JJS* 41 (1990): 57–61.

Slotki, J. *Midrash Rabbah: Numbers*. 3d ed. 2 vols. New York: Soncino Press, 1983.

Sly, Dorothy. *Philo's Perception of Women*. Brown Judaic Studies 209. Atlanta: Scholars Press, 1990.

Smallwood, E. Mary. "The Alleged Jewish Tendencies of Poppaea Sabina." *JTS* 10 (1959): 329–35.

_____. *The Jews under Roman Rule, From Pompey to Diocletan: A Study in Political Relations*. Leiden: E. J. Brill, 1976. Reprint, 1981.

Smith, A. "Porphyrian Studies since 1913." *ANRW* II.36.2: 717–73.

Smith, Edgar W. "'Joseph and Asenath' and Early Christian Literature: A Contribution to the Corpus Hellenisticum Novi Testamenti." Ph.D. dissertation, Claremont Graduate School, 1974.

Smith, Morton. "Ascent to the Heavens and the Beginning of Christianity." *Eranos-Jahrbuch* 50 (1981): 403–29.

_____. "Ascent to the Heavens and Deification in 4QM^a." In Lawrence Schiffman, ed., *Archaeology and History: The New York University Conference in Memory of Yigael Yadin.* JSP Series 8; JSOT/ASOR Monographs 2. Sheffield: JSOT Press, 1990.

_____. "Helios in Palestine." *Eretz Israel* 16 (1982): 199–214.

Smith, Robert, and John Lounibos, eds. *Pagan and Christian Anxiety: A Response to E. R. Dodds.* Lanham, MD: University of America Press, 1984.

Smith, Rowland. *Julian's Gods: Religion and Philosophy in the Thought and Action of Julian the Apostate.* London: Routledge, 1995.

Sokolowski, F. "Sur le culte d'angelos dans le paganisme grec et romain." *HTR* 53 (1960): 225–9.

Sparks, H. F. D., ed. *Apocryphal Old Testament.* Oxford: Clarendon Press, 1984.

Speiser, E. A. *Genesis: A New Translation with Introduction and Commentary.* Anchor Bible. Garden City, NY: Doubleday, 1964.

Spittler, Russell. "Job, Testament of." *ABD* 3:869–71.

Staerman, E. M. "Le culte impérial, le culte du Soleil, et celui du Temps." In Marie-Madeleine Mactoux and Evelyne Geny, eds., *Mélanges Pierre Leveque,* vol. 4. Paris: Les Belles Lettres, 1990, 361–79.

Standhartinger, Angela. *Das Frauenbild im Judentum der hellenistischen Zeit: Ein Beitrag anhand von "Joseph und Aseneth."* Arbeiten zur Geschichte des antiken Judentums und des urchristentums 26. Leiden: E. J. Brill, 1995.

Stevenson, J., ed. *A New Eusebius: Documents Illustrative of the History of the Church to A.D. 337.* London: SPCK, 1968.

Stiernon, D. "Zacharias Scholasticus or the Rhetor." *EEC* 2:884.

Strack, H. L., and G. Stemberger. *Introduction to the Talmud and Midrash.* Trans. Markus Bockmuehl. Minneapolis: Fortress Press, 1992. (English translation of *Einleitung in Talmud und Midrash,* Munich: Oscar Beck, 1982.)

Stroumsa, Gedaliahu. "Form(s) of God: Some Notes on Metatron and Christ." *HTR* 76, no. 3 (1983): 269–88.

Sukenik, E. L. *The Ancient Synagogue of Beth Alpha.* Jerusalem: University Press; London: Oxford University Press, 1932.

_____. *Ancient Synagogues in Palestine and Greece.* Schweich Lectures of the British Academy, 1930. Published for the British Academy by H. Milford. London: Oxford University Press, 1934.

Swartz, Michael. "Book and Tradition in Hekhalot and Magical Literatures." *Jewish Thought and Philosophy* 3 (1994): 189–229.

_____. "Magical Piety in Ancient and Medieval Judaism." In Marvin Meyer and Paul Mirecki, eds., *Ancient Magic and Ritual Power.* Religions in the Greco-Roman World 129. Leiden: E. J. Brill, 1995, 167–83.

_____. *Mystical Prayer in Ancient Judaism.* Tübingen: J. C. B. Mohr (Paul Siebeck), 1992.

Swete, Henry Barclay. *An Introduction to the Old Testament in Greek.* Cambridge: Cambridge University Press, 1902; reprint, New York: KTAV, 1968.

Tannenbaum, R. "Jews and God-fearers in the Holy City of Aphrodite." *BAR* 12, no. 5 (1986): 55–57.

Tatum, James, ed. *The Search for the Ancient Novel.* Baltimore: Johns Hopkins University Press, 1994.

Taylor, J. Glen. *Yahweh and the Sun: Biblical and Archaeological Evidence for Sun Worship in Ancient Israel.* JSOT Supplement Series 111. Sheffield: JSOT Press, 1993.

Testuz, M. *Papyrus Bodmer, X–XII, X. Correspondance apocryphe des Corinthiens et de l'apôtre Paul. XI. Onzième Ode de Salomon. XII. Fragment d'un hymne liturgique: Manuscrit du IIIe siècle.* Cologny-Genève: Bibliothèque Bodmer, 1959.

Theodor, J. and Ch. Albeck. *Midrash Bereshit Rabba: Critical Edition with Notes and Commentary* (in Hebrew). 3 vols. Berlin, 1893–1936.

Tov, Emanuel. "The Septuagint." In Martin Jan Mulder, ed., *Mikra: Text, Translation, Reading, and Interpretation of the Hebrew Bible in Ancient Judaism and Early Christianity.* CRINT. Assen/Mastricht: Van Gorcum; Philadelphia, Fortress Press, 1988, 161–88.

Trebilco, Paul R. *Jewish Communities in Asia Minor.* Society for New Testament Studies Monograph Series 69. Cambridge: Cambridge University Press, 1991.

Trible, Phyllis. *God and the Rhetoric of Sexuality.* Overtures to Biblical Theology. Philadelphia: Fortress Press, 1978.

Turcan, R. *Héliogabale et le sacre du soleil.* Paris: Editions Albin Michel, 1985.

_____. "Le culte impérial au III siècle." *ANRW* II.16.2:996–1084.

Turner, Victor. *The Ritual Process: Structure and Anti-Structure.* New York: Cornell University Press, 1969. Reprint, 1977.

Van Bremen, Riet. *The Limits of Participation: Women and Civic Life in the Greek East in the Hellenistic and Roman Periods.* Dutch Monographs on Ancient History and Archaeology 15. Amsterdam: J. C. Gieben, 1996.

_____. "Women and Wealth." In Averil Cameron and Amelie Kuhrt, eds., *Images of Women in Antiquity.* Detroit: Wayne State University Press, 1983, 223–42.

Van der Horst, Pieter W. *Ancient Jewish Epitaphs: An Introductory Survey of a Millennium of Jewish Funeral Epigraphy (300 B.C.E.–700 C.E.).* Kampen: Kok Pharos, 1991.

_____. "Jews and Christians in Aphrodisias in the Light of Their Relations in Other Cities of Asia Minor." *NedTTs* 43 (1989): 106–21.

_____. "Portraits of Biblical Women in Pseudo-Philo's Liber Antiquitatum Biblicarum." In *Essays on the Jewish World of Early Christianity.* Göttingen: Vandenhoeck and Ruprecht, 1990, 111–22.

_____. "Silent Prayer in Antiquity." *Numen* 41 (1994): 1–25.

Van Esbroeck, Michel. Untitled review of Philonenko and Burchard. *Analecta Bollandiana* 86 (1968): 404–10.

Vermes, Geza. "Bible and Midrash: Early Old Testament Exegesis." In *Post-Biblical Jewish Studies.* Studies in Judaism in Late Antiquity 8. Leiden: E. J. Brill, 1975, 59–91.

Vikan, Gary. "Illustrated Manuscripts of Pseudo-Ephraem's Life of Joseph and the Romance of Joseph and Aseneth." Ph.D. dissertation, Princeton University, 1976.

Wallace, Howard N. "Eden, Garden of." *ABD* 2:281–83.

_____. "Garden of God." *ABD* 2:906–907.

Wallis, R. T. *Neoplatonism.* London: Duckworth, 1972.

_____, ed. *Neoplatonism and Gnosticism.* Albany: State University of New York Press, 1992.

Walsh, P. G. *Apuleius: The Golden Ass.* Oxford: Clarendon Press, 1994.

Weavers, John William. *Genesis, Septuaginta: Vetus Testamentum Graecum,* vol. 1. Gottingen: Vandenhoeck und Ruprecht, 1974.

Weiss, Ze'ev, and Ehud Netzer. *Promise and Redemption: A Synagogue Mosaic from Sepphoris* (English and Hebrew). Jerusalem: Israel Museum, 1996.

Whitfield, B. G. "Virgil and the Bees." *Greece and Rome,* ser. 3 (1956): 99–117.

Wicker, Kathleen. *Porphyry the Philosopher to Marcella: Text and Translation with Introduc-tion and Notes.* Atlanta: Scholars Press, 1987.

Williams, Frank. *The Panarion of Epiphanius of Salamis.* Bk. 1, Sects. 1–46. Leiden: E. J. Brill, 1987.

Williams, M. H. "θεοσεβὴς γαρ ἦν The Jewish Tendencies of Poppaea Sabina." *JTS* 39 (1988): 97–111.

Wills, Lawrence M. *The Jewish Novel in the Ancient World.* Ithaca: Cornell University Press, 1995.

———. "The Jewish Novellas." In John Morgan and Richard Stoneman, eds., *Greek Fiction: The Greek Novel in Context.* London: Routledge, 1994, 223–38.

Index of Ancient Sources

Ancient Texts

(Alphabetically by author or title. The symbol § designates notation from Peter Schäfer, ed., Synopse. Biblical citations follow the NRSV except as noted.)

Papyri

Inscriptions

Index of Modern Authors

Index of Subjects